THE
WORLD BOOK
ENCYCLOPEDIA

D
Volume 5

FIELD ENTERPRISES EDUCATIONAL CORPORATION
CHICAGO · LONDON · ROME · SYDNEY · TORONTO

THE WORLD BOOK ENCYCLOPEDIA

COPYRIGHT © 1964, U.S.A.

by FIELD ENTERPRISES EDUCATIONAL CORPORATION

All rights reserved. This volume may not be reproduced in whole or in part in any form without written permission from the publishers.

Copyright © 1963, 1962, 1961, 1960, 1959, 1958, 1957 by Field Enterprises Educational Corporation. Copyright © 1957, 1956, 1955, 1954, 1953, 1952, 1951, 1950, 1949, 1948 by Field Enterprises, Inc. Copyright 1948, 1947, 1946, 1945, 1944, 1943, 1942, 1941, 1940, 1939, 1938 by The Quarrie Corporation. Copyright 1937, 1936, 1935, 1934, 1933, 1931, 1930, 1929 by W. F. Quarrie & Company. THE WORLD BOOK, Copyright 1928, 1927, 1926, 1925, 1923, 1922, 1921, 1919, 1918, 1917 by W. F. Quarrie & Company. Copyrights renewed 1964, 1963, 1962, 1961, 1960, 1958 by Field Enterprises Educational Corporation. Copyrights renewed 1957, 1956, 1955, 1954, 1953, 1952, 1950 by Field Enterprises, Inc.

International Copyright © 1964, 1963, 1962, 1961, 1960, 1959, 1958, 1957 by Field Enterprises Educational Corporation. International Copyright © 1957, 1956, 1955, 1954, 1953, 1952, 1951, 1950, 1949, 1948 by Field Enterprises, Inc. International Copyright 1948, 1947 by The Quarrie Corporation.

Printed in the United States of America
FDA

LIBRARY OF CONGRESS CATALOG NUMBER 64-7000

THE WORLD BOOK

Dd is the fourth letter of our alphabet. It was also the fourth letter in the alphabet used by the Semites, who once lived in Syria and Palestine. They named it *daleth*, a word that meant *door*. It is believed that this word came from one of the *hieroglyphs*, or picture writings, the ancient Egyptians used. They drew a picture of a door with panels. See ALPHABET.

Uses. *D* or *d* ranks as about the tenth most frequently used letter in books, newspapers, and other printed material in English. When used on a report card, *D* usually means poor work or near failure in a school subject. In music, it names one note of the scale. As an abbreviation, *D* stands for the isotope *deuterium* in chemistry, for *electric displacement* in electronics, and for *500* in the Roman numeral system. The symbol *d* represents the *penny* in the British money system. It also denotes *drag* in aeronautics, and the fourth known quantity in algebra. The symbol *D* or *d* stands for *diameter* in mathematics and physics, or a wider than average shoe.

Pronunciation. In English, a person pronounces *d* with his tongue touching the roof of his mouth just back of his teeth. In French, Dutch, and Italian, the tongue touches the upper front teeth. In German, a *d* at the beginning of a word, followed by a vowel, resembles the English *d* sound. Otherwise, it usually has a *t* sound. The Spanish *d* is expressed more softly than in English when it is at the beginning of a word. Elsewhere, it has a *th* sound, similar to *the* in English, not the *th* of *thin*. See PRONUNCIATION.

I. J. GELB and J. M. WELLS

The fourth letter took its shape from an ancient Egyptian symbol used to show a door. Its sound came from the Semitic word *daleth*, which means *door*.

The Romans rounded the capital D to its present form about A.D. 114.

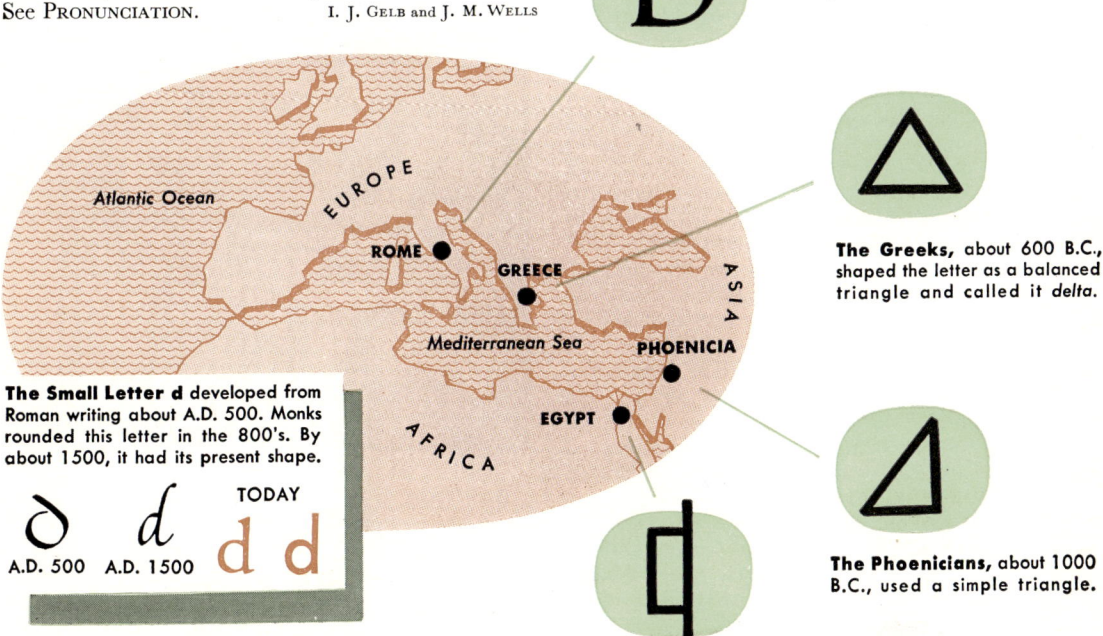

The Greeks, about 600 B.C., shaped the letter as a balanced triangle and called it *delta*.

The Small Letter d developed from Roman writing about A.D. 500. Monks rounded this letter in the 800's. By about 1500, it had its present shape.

A.D. 500   A.D. 1500   TODAY

The Phoenicians, about 1000 B.C., used a simple triangle.

The Egyptians, about 3000 B.C., wrote with a symbol that represented a door with panels.

DABCHICK

DABCHICK. See GREBE.

DACCA, *DAK uh* (pop. 350,000; met. area 720,000; alt. 26 ft.), is the capital of East Pakistan (see PAKISTAN [color map]). It is the trade and industrial center of the country. Many of Dacca's buildings and monuments date back to the 1600's. ROBERT I. CRANE

DACE, HORNED. See CHUB.

DACHAU, *DAH kow*, was one of the first concentration camps set up in Germany by the Nazis. Established in 1933, it stood near the town of Dachau, 10 miles from Munich. Dachau was built as an extermination camp for Jews and political prisoners. After 1943, many prisoners worked in arms factories that were built there. The Nazis performed brutal medical experiments on more than 3,500 persons at Dachau. Almost all of these prisoners died. Thousands more were executed or died of starvation and epidemics. United States forces liberated about 32,000 prisoners at Dachau on April 29, 1945. WILLIAM A. JENKS

DACHSHUND, *DAHKS hoont*, is a dog known for its long body and short legs. It is considered the national dog of Germany, where the breed originated. The dachshund has a cone-shaped head, a slim tapering muzzle, and long drooping ears. Its front legs are slightly curved. It has a large chest and a long pointed tail. Its glossy coat is usually black or tan, but it may be red, yellow, gray, spotted, or striped. Most dachshunds have short smooth hair. But many are wirehaired. Others have long, silky hair.

The dachshund is a strong, hardy, alert dog with a good sense of smell. In central Europe, it was once used to hunt badgers. Dachshund means *badger dog* in German. A dachshund makes a good pet. See also DOG (color picture, Hounds). HENRY P. DAVIS

DACRON is the DuPont Company's trademark for a synthetic fiber used in clothing, home furnishings, and industry. It can be readily cleaned because stains do not soak easily into the material. It resists fading and wrinkling. Dacron is also used to make curtains, drapes, and pillow fillings. Industry uses Dacron for fire hoses, filters, and other products.

Dacron is manufactured from a combination of coal, air, water, petroleum, limestone, and natural gases that results in *ethylene glycol* and *terephthalic acid*. These compounds are in turn combined to make a fluid *polymer*, or composition of large molecules (see POLYMERIZATION). The polymer is forced through tiny holes in a spraylike device called a *spinneret* (see RAYON, diagram). Heat and a vacuum cause the material to emerge as a filament. Dacron can be made as a long, continuous yarn, without the usual spinning needed to make wool and cotton yarns. To give Dacron a cotton or wool appearance, it can also be made into short lengths called *staple*. The staple can be spun or twisted into yarn on the same machines used for spinning wool yarns.

British and DuPont chemists developed Dacron in the early 1940's. The British called it *Terylene*. DuPont bought the exclusive right to United States production from the British. Dacron appeared on the U.S. market in 1951. CHARLES H. RUTLEDGE

DACTYLIC METER. See METER (poetry).

DADDY LONGLEGS is a popular name in America for a harmless, long-legged creature related to the spider. Its legs are bent and its body hangs close to the ground. It is not an insect, but an *arachnid* (see ARACHNID). Another name for it is *harvestman*. In England, the *crane fly* is called *daddy longlegs*. The crane fly is an insect which has wings and looks much like a large mosquito.

Scientific Classification. The harvestman belongs to the class *Arachnida*. It makes up the order *Phalangida*. The crane fly belongs to the class *Insecta*, order *Diptera*, and family *Tipulidae*. EDWARD A. CHAPIN

DADE, FRANCIS L. See FLORIDA (Territorial Days).

DAEDALUS, *DED ah lus*, was an architect and sculptor in Greek mythology. According to the myth, he was jealous of one of his pupils named Talos, and killed him. Because of this he had to escape from Athens to Crete. There he built the labyrinth of the Minotaur.

Daedalus and his son Icarus offended the king of Crete and were imprisoned. In order to escape, Daedalus made two pairs of large wings out of feathers and wax. He and Icarus flew away with these fastened on their shoulders, but Icarus fell into the sea. Daedalus is Greek for *the cunning worker*. PADRAIC COLUM

See also LABYRINTH; MINOTAUR.

Daedalus and his son Icarus, *right*, shown in this bas-relief on a Roman villa, escaped from Crete with waxen wings. The sun melted the wax on Icarus' wings and he fell into the sea.
Villa Albani, Rome (Alinari)

DAFFODIL, *DAF oh dil*, is a yellow flower that blooms in the early spring. It is a kind of *narcissus*, and comes from Europe, where it grows wild in the woods. It is also grown in gardens in America and other regions.

There are many kinds of daffodils. The best known daffodil is also called the *trumpet narcissus*. It has a single blossom at the end of each stalk. The daffodil has a very large flower and five or six bluish-green leaves about 15 inches long on each stalk.

The Daffodil has a yellow, tube-shaped flower with a fluted edge. Delicate petals that are of varying shades of yellow grow at the base of these spring flowers.
Ferry-Morse Seed Co.

Daffodil bulbs should be planted in autumn. They should be planted in free, open soil, about four inches deep and about five inches apart. Blossoms usually first appear in April.

Scientific Classification. Daffodils belong to the family *Amaryllidaceae*. They are classified as genus *Narcissus*, species *pseudonarcissus*. DONALD WYMAN

See also BULB; FLOWER (color picture, Spring Garden Flowers); NARCISSUS.

DAFNE, *DAF nee*, the first opera written, was produced in Italy in 1597. See OPERA (Development).

DAFOE, JOHN W. See MANITOBA (Famous Manitobans).

DA GAMA, *duh GA muh*, **VASCO,** *VAS koh* (1469?-1524), a Portuguese explorer, was the first man to sail around the Cape of Good Hope to India. King John II of Portugal originally chose Da Gama's father to command the expedition. But both the king and the elder Da Gama died before their plans were completed. The new king, Manuel I, gave the command to Vasco. His four-ship expedition left Portugal on July 8, 1497. The fleet rounded the Cape of Good Hope in November, and arrived at Calicut (now Kozhikode), India, in May, 1498.

The Indian ruler received Da Gama coolly. Arab traders, resenting Da Gama's presence, set the Hindus against him, and the Portuguese were in constant danger. When he returned to Portugal with a cargo of spice, the king rewarded him with the title of Admiral of the Sea of the Indies. Later, the king made Da Gama Count of Vidigueira and helped him become wealthy.

Da Gama made another voyage to India in 1502 and 1503, to avenge Indian violence against Portuguese sailors and to establish colonies. He retired after that voyage, but during the

Vasco Da Gama
Newberry Library

DAGUERREOTYPE

next 20 years he acted as adviser to King Manuel and his successor, King John III.

In 1524, because his representatives had ruled badly in India, the king sent Da Gama there as viceroy. Da Gama died at Cochin, India, on Christmas Eve, 1524. He was born in the town of Sines. CHARLES E. NOWELL

DAGGER is a short-bladed sword. It is divided into three parts. These are the *blade*, which may be from six to eighteen inches long, the *guard*, and the *handle*, or *hilt*. Daggers are ordinarily worn at the belt and placed in a sheath or a scabbard.

In Scotland, a dagger is called a *dirk;* in France, a *poniard;* and in Italy, a *stiletto*. Pioneers in America carried a dagger called the *bowie knife*. The earliest form of bayonet was a dagger with a tapered handle which would fit into the muzzle of a musket. Stone Age men used daggers made of flint or horn from animals such as reindeer. JACK O'CONNOR

See also BAYONET; BOWIE KNIFE.

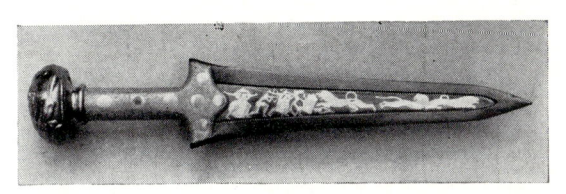

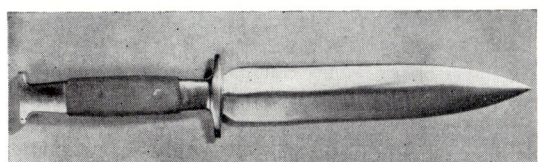

The Metropolitan Mus. of Art, New York; Press Syndicate
Different Types of Daggers have been used as weapons since ancient times. The blade of the Mycenaean dagger, 1600 B.C., *top*, was decorated with gold figures. Commandos used a razor-sharp knife, *bottom*, during World War II.

DAGHESTAN, *DAG us TAN*, or **DAGESTAN,** is a state, or autonomous republic, in the Russian Soviet Federated Socialist Republic. It is located on the west shore of the Caspian Sea. Daghestan has a population of about 1,165,000, and covers an area of 18,700 square miles. The capital is Makhachkala.

DAGON was a god of the Philistines. See SAMSON.

DAGUERRE, *DAH GAIR*, **LOUIS JACQUES MANDÉ** (1787-1851), was a French inventor and painter. He perfected the daguerreotype process of making permanent pictures. He opened the "Diorama," a theater without actors, in 1822, in Paris. In it he produced effects of moonlight and other lights by illuminating transparent canvas scenery painted on both sides. In 1829, he began working with Joseph Nicéphore Niépce (1765-1833), a French physicist. Daguerre perfected the daguerreotype process after Niépce's death. See also DAGUERREOTYPE. BEAUMONT NEWHALL

DAGUERREOTYPE, *duh GAIR oh tipe*, is one of the first forms of photographic print. It was named for its inventor Louis J. M. Daguerre. Daguerre first described the technique of making daguerreotypes in 1839. He made a polished, silvered copper plate light-sensitive by subjecting it to iodine fumes. He then exposed it from

3

A Daguerreotype Picture was printed on a thin copper plate. These pictures look much like later tintypes.

Eastman Historical Photographic Collection

Petals of the Azura Dahlia Curve Inward at the Tips.
J. Horace McFarland

The Fairy Dahlia Is Also Called the Pompon.
J. Horace McFarland

3 to 30 minutes in a camera. He developed the image with mercury vapor, and "fixed" it with sodium thiosulfate (*hypo*). Improvements made in 1840 increased the sensitivity of the plate by bromine fuming, and enriched the image by toning it with gold chloride. The highlights of a daguerreotype are whitish. The shadows are bare, mirrorlike areas which appear dark when the plate is held to reflect a dark field. The permanency of the process and its ability to record minute details are its outstanding characteristics. After 1851, the wet collodion process gradually took the place of the daguerreotype. In the 1800's, Americans used daguerreotypes a great deal, especially for portraits. BEAUMONT NEWHALL

See also DAGUERRE, LOUIS J. M.; TALBOTYPE.

DAHLGREN, *DAL gruhn*, **JOHN ADOLPHUS BERNARD** (1809-1870), an American naval officer and inventor, developed the Dahlgren gun that became famous during the Civil War. He served as chief of the U.S. Navy Bureau of Ordnance, and built a gun factory, where he made and tested his naval cannon.

He became commandant of the Washington Navy Yard and unofficial aide to President Lincoln in 1861, and directed the defense of Washington. Later he served as commander of the Union Navy's South Atlantic Blockading Squadron. Dahlgren was born in Philadelphia. RICHARD S. WEST, JR.

DAHLIA, *DAHL yuh*, is the name of a popular group of flowers cultivated from the original dahlia of Mexico. Some are shaped like balls; others have long, flat petals. *Cactus dahlias* have double blossoms with long, twisted petals. Dahlias are now grown throughout the United States, in southern Canada, and in Europe. They are named for the Swedish botanist, Anders Dahl.

Dahlias grow from *tuberous*, or thick, fleshy roots that look somewhat like bulbs. They should be planted in rich, well-drained soil, and in full sun after all danger of frost has passed. Dahlia stalks are brittle; the taller kinds should be tied to strong stakes. After the first frost, the roots should be dug up and stored for the winter in a dry place, at a temperature between 40° F. and 55° F. Storing the entire root clump, with soil attached, will stop shriveling. At planting time, the roots should be separated carefully and planted about 6 inches deep. Dahlias flower in the late summer.

Scientific Classification. Dahlias belong to the family *Compositae*. Most of them are genus *Dahlia*, species *variabilis*. The cactus dahlia is *D. juarezi*. GEORGE A. BEACH

See also FLOWER (color picture, Fall Garden Flowers).

4

The Palace of Justice in Cotonou provides a modern background for a woman peddling food. Many government offices are located in Cotonou, although Porto Novo is the capital of Dahomey.

Marc and Evelyne Bernheim, Rapho-Guillumette

DAHOMEY, *duh HO mih*, is a country on the west coast of Africa. It was formerly a territory in French West Africa and gained its independence as the REPUBLIC OF DAHOMEY in 1960. The country's name in French, the official language, is RÉPUBLIQUE DU DAHOMEY.

The Land. Dahomey is one of the smallest countries in Africa. It covers 44,696 square miles, about the area of Pennsylvania. Long and narrow, it stretches 415 miles north from the Gulf of Guinea. It widens from 77 miles along the coast to 180 miles in the north. Togo borders Dahomey on the west, Upper Volta and Niger on the north, and Nigeria on the east.

The coast of Dahomey is flat and sandy. It has no natural harbors and heavy surf makes landing difficult. Small boats load and unload ships anchored off shore except at the man-made port of Cotonou. Large lagoons lie behind the coastal strip. Beyond the lagoons, the land is flat and forested. A great marsh lies 50 miles inland. Farther north, Dahomey rises to a low plateau. The country's greatest elevation, about 2,500 feet, is in the Atakora Mountains in the northwest.

The rivers in lower Dahomey flow south into the Gulf of Guinea. Those in upper Dahomey drain north into the Niger and Volta rivers. The Ouémé, the country's longest river, flows 280 miles into the Gulf of Guinea.

Southern Dahomey has a hot and humid climate. Temperatures range between 72° and 93°F. A great rainy season occurs in the south from April to July, and a shorter one from September to November. Northern Dahomey has more variations in daily temperatures and less humidity. A rainy season occurs in the north from April to October, and a dry season from October to April. Average annual rainfall is 20 inches in the southeast, 50 inches in central Dahomey, and 35 inches in the north.

The People. Dahomey has a population of 2,150,000, about as many people as Mississippi. It has an average of 48 persons to the square mile. But two-thirds of the people live in the southern third of the country. Almost all of the people belong to one of Dahomey's many tribes. The largest tribes are the Fon and the Adja in the south and the Bariba in the northwest. Only about 3,000 white persons live in Dahomey.

Porto Novo (pop. 30,000) is the capital of Dahomey. Cotonou (40,000) is the commercial center and the chief port. Other large towns include Abomey (20,000),

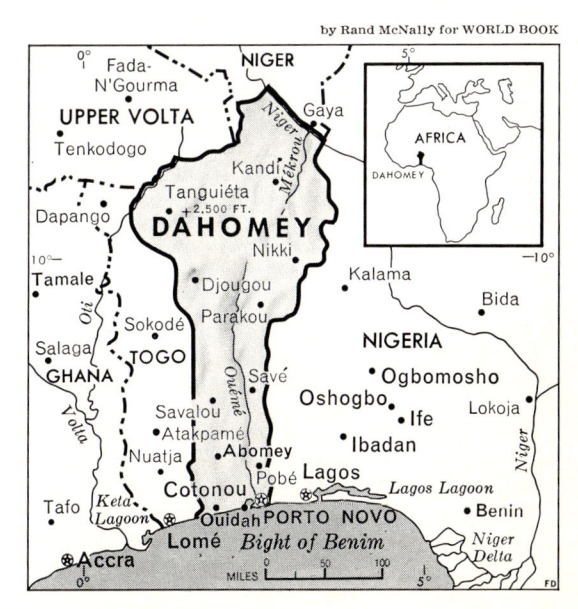

FACTS IN BRIEF

Type of Government: Republic.
Capital: Porto Novo.
Official Language: French.
Head of Government: President.
Legislature: National Assembly (70 members).
Area: 44,696 square miles. *Greatest distance:* (north-south) 415 miles; (east-west) 180 miles. *Coastline,* 77 miles.
Population: 2,150,000. *Density,* 48 persons per sq. mi.
Chief Products: *Agriculture,* cassava, coffee, corn, cotton, palm oil and kernels, peanuts, shea nuts, yams. *Manufacturing and Processing,* coconut fiber, cotton, palm oil, peanuts, soap.
Flag: The flag has a green vertical stripe and two horizontal stripes, the top one yellow and the bottom one red. See FLAG (color picture, Flags of Africa).
Money: *Basic unit,* franc. See MONEY (table, Values).

---

by Rand McNally for WORLD BOOK

4a

DAHOMEY

Ouidah (15,000), Djougou (7,000), and Parakou (5,000).

Economic Conditions. Dahomey is primarily an agricultural country. Palm trees are its chief source of wealth. The leading exports are palm oil and kernels used in making soap and margarine. Other exports include coffee, cotton, peanuts, shea nuts used in making butter, and tobacco. The chief food crops include beans, cassava, corn, millet, rice, sorghum, sweet potatoes, and yams. The people also raise cattle, goats, hogs, and sheep. Dahomey has some chromite, gold, iron ore, lignite, and phosphates, but there is little mining. The only industries are agricultural processing plants.

Dahomey has 360 miles of railroad. Lines run from Cotonou along the coast and inland. There are 3,700 miles of roads, but many are passable only in the dry season. Dahomey has five airports, the chief one at Cotonou.

Education. About 95 of every 100 adults in Dahomey cannot read or write. But 30 of every 100 school-age children are enrolled in schools. The public school system has 37,000 students and includes 230 elementary schools and 5 secondary schools. More than half of the school children attend private mission schools. The country has no universities.

Government. Dahomey has a president and a vice-president. Both are elected for five-year terms. A single-house legislature, the National Assembly, has 70 members elected for five-year terms.

History. Dahomey traces its history back to the 1100's and 1200's. Several African kingdoms developed in this region. By the 1600's, the kingdom of Dahomey, with its capital at Abomey, dominated the area. The king of Dahomey used *Amazons* (women soldiers) in his army. By the 1600's, European nations had established slave trading posts along the coast. During the 1800's, palm-oil trade replaced the slave trade. In 1851, France signed a trade agreement with the kingdom of Dahomey. When the king of Dahomey attacked French trading posts in a trade dispute in 1892, the French defeated him and annexed Dahomey.

In 1904, Dahomey became a territory in French West Africa. The French built railroads and roads and encouraged coffee growing. Under the 1946 French constitution, Dahomey became an overseas territory in the French Union. Dahomey voted to become an autonomous republic within the French Community in 1958, then declared itself an independent republic outside the French Community on Aug. 1, 1960. In September, 1960, Dahomey became a member of the United Nations. IMMANUEL WALLERSTEIN

See also NIGER RIVER; PALM OIL; PORTO NOVO.

DAIKON. See RADISH.

DÁIL ÉIREANN. See IRELAND (Government).

DAIMIO. See JAPAN (Restoration of the Emperor); SAMURAI.

DAIMLER, *DIME ler,* **GOTTLIEB** (1834-1900), a German engineer, developed an internal-combustion engine light enough to power an automobile. He and Wilhelm Maybach worked with motors for years, and produced a motor-bicycle in 1885. They made a four-wheeled car in 1886. The Daimler Company was founded in 1890, and produced the Mercedes car. The Daimler and Benz companies merged to make the Mercedes-Benz car in 1926. SMITH HEMPSTONE OLIVER

See also BENZ, KARL; MAYBACH, WILHELM.

DAIREN. See TALIEN.

DAIRY BELT. See DAIRYING (Dairy Farms).

Off to School! Children in Ganvié, a lagoon village in Dahomey, ride to school in dugout canoes instead of in buses. They live in thatch-roofed huts built on piles.

Marc and Evelyne Bernheim, Rapho-Guillumette

Shoppers in Cotonou, the commercial center of Dahomey, balance their purchases on their heads. Many residents use bicycles for transportation.

DAIRYING is that branch of agriculture which is concerned with producing milk, butter, evaporated milk, ice cream, cheese, and dried milk products. It includes the care and feeding of the cattle which give the milk. Dairy farming is one of the leading farm activities in the United States, with a cash return in some years as high as $5,300,000,000. More than 2,000,000 farm families earn all or part of their living from dairying.

Each person in the United States consumes an average of about 700 pounds of dairy products every year. In the United States, dairy goods account for 20 cents of each dollar most families spend for food. These items make up their second largest food expense, ranking behind only the combined expenses for meat, fish, poultry, and eggs. Liquid milk and cream make up about half of the dairy goods used in the country, and butter accounts for about a fourth. The remainder includes cheese, ice cream, evaporated and condensed milk, and dry whole milk.

There are about 20,000,000 dairy cows on farms in the United States today. These cows produce about 126,000,000,000 pounds of milk each year, and 4,800,000,000 pounds of butterfat. The average yearly milk production per cow is about 6,300 pounds, an increase of more than 2,000 pounds per cow in the past thirty years. Butterfat production per cow during this period has increased from 163.2 to 235 pounds. About 59,000,000,000 pounds of milk a year are used for manufactured dairy products. Of this amount, fat from about 28,700,000,000 pounds of milk is used to make creamery butter; about 12,754,000,000 pounds of milk are used to make cheese; up to 6,300,000,000 pounds are used for evaporated and condensed milk products, and 7,400,000,000 pounds are used for ice cream and other frozen dairy products. Less than 20 per cent of the yearly total milk production is used on farms for making butter, feeding calves, and other purposes.

Dairy Farms

Many farmers raise a few cattle to provide milk for their families, and sell the surplus. Other farms may have herds of several hundred purebred cattle which provide milk. The average herd will have 15 to 20 cows. A broad belt of states stretching from New England west to Wisconsin, Iowa, and Minnesota is often considered the dairy belt. But dairying is carried on in many other places in the United States, especially near large cities. Some dairying is done far from cities, since modern processing equipment and transportation make it possible to ship milk long distances. Climate is important because most dairy cattle do not thrive in very cold or very hot climates. Rainfall is needed to grow the hay and pasture crops on which the cattle feed.

Dairy Cattle. The six most important breeds of dairy cattle in the United States are the Holstein-Friesian, Jersey, Guernsey, Ayrshire, Brown Swiss, and the Milking Shorthorn. The various breeds of dairy cattle differ in their size and appearance. The composition of their milk and the amount of milk they produce also vary somewhat.

Holstein-Friesian cattle, often called merely Holsteins, produce the most milk. Their milk, however, does not contain as high a percentage of the natural fat called *butterfat* as does the milk of the other breeds. Butterfat gives milk its richness. It is the part of milk used in mak-

Hoard's Dairyman

Prize Dairy Cattle, such as these Ayrshire cows, can produce more than 2 gallons of fresh milk each in a single day.

ing butter. The Brown Swiss is second in the amount of milk produced, while the Ayrshire is third and the Guernsey fourth. The milk of Jersey and Guernsey cows is yellower in color than the milk of the Holstein and contains a higher percentage of butterfat. The Holstein milk contains about 3.7 per cent butterfat while the milk of Jersey and Guernsey cows contains around 5 per cent butterfat. Its rich butterfat content gives this milk a rather yellow color. Brown Swiss and Ayrshire cows produce milk with a butterfat content between that of Holstein and Jersey cows. Many dairy cows are not a pure breed but a mixture of two or more breeds. These are called "grade" cows.

The breed of cattle kept on a dairy farm will depend upon the farmer's breed preference and the market for milk. Sometimes it will be more advantageous to keep Holsteins because of the quantity of milk they produce. In other regions, it may be more profitable to raise Guernseys and Jerseys because they are efficient in the production of butterfat.

5

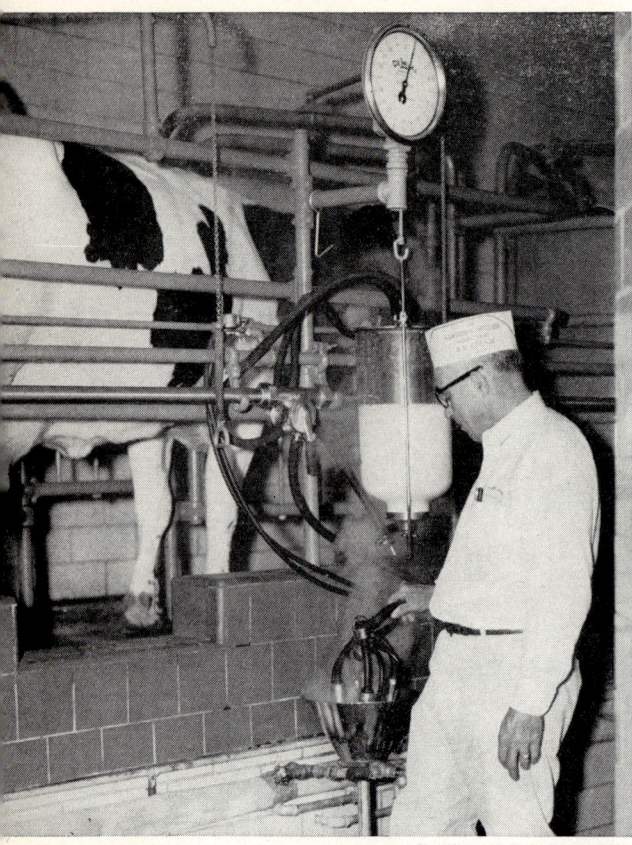

Hawthorn-Mellody Farms Dairy

The Milking Parlor of a Dairy Farm is a special room kept spotlessly clean. After machines milk the cows, the milk is weighed and piped to tanks for storage until it can be pasteurized.

Improvement of Milk Production. Throughout modern times the production of milk from individual cows has increased steadily. This is largely because of improved methods of breeding, feeding, and caring for dairy cattle. Many dairymen keep records of milk and butterfat production of each cow in the herd. The offspring of the best producers are mated, and in this way the breed is constantly improved. The best purebred dairy cattle may cost several thousand dollars and are valued for the qualities they can give their offspring.

Farmers in many localities have organized dairy herd improvement associations. Each association employs a supervisor who keeps milk and butterfat production records of the cows belonging to the members of the association. This supervisor also advises the members on the best ways of feeding and caring for their cattle. In cooperative breeding associations, the farmers put their money together and buy bulls of better quality than any of the individual members of the association could afford. It is often said that a dairy herd is no better than its bull, but the best bulls are very expensive. There are two ways in which the services of bulls are shared in a cooperative breeding association. In the *bull ring* the bulls are rotated, each one being used by one or more herds for a period of two years and then passed on to another group. Rotating the bulls every two years prevents inbreeding, which is not considered good practice.

The second method is *artificial insemination*, which is conducted by trained technicians, usually veterinarians. This practice permits one bull to serve many more cows than would be possible if he were kept with one herd. It also helps to control certain diseases.

In the United States, the average yearly production per cow is about 7,000 pounds of milk and about 260 pounds of butterfat. In the best herds, each cow may produce as much as 12,000 pounds of milk and 400 pounds of butterfat per year. One cow is known to have produced more than 42,000 pounds of milk in a single year.

Milking the cows is usually done twice a day, once at five in the morning and again at five at night. On a good dairy farm, the cows are carefully brushed and washed before being milked, to keep the milk clean. An average dairy cow gives about twelve quarts of milk a day. Many farmers with only a few cows still milk their cows by hand. A good milker can milk eight to ten cows in an hour. On larger dairy farms a milking machine is used. The machine pumps the milk from the cow's udder and empties it into a covered pail. The milking machine is taken apart after every milking and each part is washed. In this way the milk is always kept pure and sweet.

In the summer, the cows may go out to the pasture between milkings, but in the winter they are kept in the barn for nearly the entire day. A modern dairy barn is kept very clean. Each cow has a separate stall, and metal pipes called *stanchions* are placed around her neck to see that she keeps her place in the stall. A well-trained cow entering the barn will go to her own stall and put her head through the open stanchions. When all the cows have taken their places, the stanchions are closed by pulling a lever at the end of the row of stalls. Each stanchion may be opened or closed separately. The cows have separate feeding troughs and drinking cups. A trough runs behind the cattle stalls. The manure from the cattle falls into the trough, and then is shoveled into containers and removed. The barn must also be well ventilated to protect the health of the cows and the flavor of the milk. On many farms the barns are washed from time to time with a disinfectant to kill germs and thus protect the health of the herd. In some barns, workers step into a pan of disinfectant before entering the milking barn.

Hay is usually stored in the barn loft. Silage, which is the chopped-up stalks of corn or other crops which cattle eat, is stored in a silo. Most dairy farms also have a milkhouse where the milk is kept cool until it can be shipped. The milking machines, pails, and other equipment are usually washed and sterilized in the milkhouse. The dairy laws of many communities require that milkhouses be maintained on farms selling milk to their market.

Feeding. A good dairy cow may weigh up to 1,700 pounds and produce 8,000 pounds or more of milk during a year. In order to do this, the cow will eat the pasture grass from two acres of ground during five summer months. During the winter, she will eat about 6,300 pounds of silage and about 2,700 pounds of alfalfa or clover hay. Throughout the entire year the cow will eat almost two thousand pounds of grain. She will drink about eleven and one-half tons of water during a year, or about eight gallons per day.

DAIRYING

The dairy farmer tries to balance the cow's diet to make sure that it includes all the essential food elements. The cows are usually fed grain mixtures at the rate of one pound for every three to five pounds of milk that are produced. Such mixtures may contain ground corn, ground oats, soybean meal, salt, bone meal, and various minerals. When the cow is feeding on high-grade hay made up of leguminous plants such as alfalfa, clover, or lespedeza, the amount of oats and corn in the mixture is high. When the cow is eating poorer hay made up of timothy, the amount of soybean or cottonseed meal, which is rich in protein, is greatly increased, and bone meal and minerals are added to provide other necessary food elements.

Laws Regulating Dairy Farming

Many states and local governments have laws regulating the conditions under which milk can be produced and sold. This is essential because of the many ways in which milk can become contaminated. Many diseases of cattle can be given to human beings through impure milk. Tuberculosis was often spread in this way, until tubercular cows were removed from dairy herds. Most cities require a certificate from a dairy showing that all its cows have successfully passed the tuberculin test. The barns housing the cattle must be kept clean. All the various vessels to which the milk is transferred as it passes from the cow to the consumer must be clean, sterilized, and dry.

Laws regulating dairies usually require that the operator of a dairy must have a license. From time to time the dairy barns are inspected to make sure that no sanitary regulations are being violated. Workers in both dairies and milk plants are given periodic physical examinations to make sure that they are not spreaders of disease. The milk itself is tested, to make sure that its composition meets the legal standard and it contains no impurities or disease-causing bacteria.

Some producers of milk have joined together to produce what is known as *certified milk*. This term can only be used by dairies which produce milk under the most sanitary conditions possible, specified by the American Association of Medical Milk Commissions. These dairies are regularly and strictly inspected by local medical milk commissions. Most communities have laws dealing with *Grade A* milk. These laws cover the health of cows and workers, and sanitary conditions.

Leading Dairy Companies

Five dairy companies rank among the 25 largest food-processing firms in the United States. These companies are the National Dairy Products Corporation, New York, N.Y.; Borden Company, New York, N.Y.; Beatrice Foods Company, Chicago, Ill.; Carnation Company, Los Angeles, Cal.; and Foremost Dairies, Incorporated, San Francisco, Cal. The table *25 Largest Food-Processing Companies* with the FOOD article shows the assets, number of employees, year of founding, and amount of sales a year for each of these leading dairying companies.

Dairying Around the World

Dairying is carried on in many countries of the world. Denmark and Switzerland are famed for their dairy products. In Norway and Switzerland the cattle are taken up to meadows in the mountains where they are pastured all summer. In the fall they are brought down to the lowlands and kept in barns during the winter.

In many countries, goats are an important dairy animal. In the United States, however, only a very small proportion of the milk produced comes from goats. In some countries the milk of other animals is used. Sheep milk is used in making certain kinds of cheese. In Arabia, camel's milk is drunk, and in other places the milk of mares. The Laplanders drink reindeer milk, and in Egypt the milk of the water buffalo is used by those who cannot afford a cow.

History of Dairying

Years ago cows gave milk only during the spring, summer, and fall when they could be fed in open pastures. What little milk the cows gave was used by the farmer and his family as milk or butter. Only small amounts of it could be sold.

Columbus brought the first cattle to the Americas in 1493. The English brought cows into the Jamestown settlement in the early 1600's, and, later, cows were also brought to Plymouth and other New England settlements. Cattle raising spread quickly. An important step forward in the care of dairy cattle came from colonial Massachusetts. In 1655 William Pynchon began feeding his cattle grain and hay during the wintertime. They gave milk all winter. This method of Pynchon's is called stall-feeding and made possible the year-round production of milk.

After the pioneers began to move westward, it was discovered that cattle manure helped keep the soil productive. More cattle were kept, and the surplus milk was sold.

The biggest development in the growth of dairying in the United States came after 1840, when the large cities began to develop. Before that time it had not been difficult to supply the cities, because farm and city were close together. After the cities grew, came the problem of shipping milk to the consumer. Milk was first shipped into New York City by train in 1841. In a few years the large cities in the United States were receiving milk from farms fifty and more miles away.

For many years, dairy products were manufactured on the farm. In 1850 almost 315,000,000 pounds of butter were made on farms in the United States. But as city markets increased it became necessary to produce and process milk on a larger scale. The first butter factory, or creamery, was set up in New York about 1856. Soon there were many butter factories scattered throughout the Eastern and Midwestern states. The manufacture of milk products has become highly industrialized, and creameries are found throughout the country. The amount of butter produced on farms is small compared to that made in creameries.   MILTON FAIRMAN

Related Articles in WORLD BOOK include:

Agriculture	Farm Life (color picture, Milking the Cows)
Barn	
Bran	Hay
Butter	Milk
Cattle	Milking Machine
Cheese	Pasture
Cooperative	Silo
Disease (Diseases of Animals)	

DAISY

The Large Shasta Daisy has four-inch blossoms and saw-toothed leaves. It was named by Luther Burbank, the botanist.
Ferry-Morse Seed Co.

DAISY, *DAY zih,* is a name given to many flowers. It means *day's eye,* because the daisy looks somewhat like an eye, with its round yellow center. Its petals grow around the center like rays of the sun. The daisy opens its blossoms in the morning and closes them at night.

The American daisy is actually a wild chrysanthemum, and has several other names. Some people call it the *oxeye daisy* because of its yellow center. Farmers are troubled by daisies that grow in their fields. They call that flower the *whiteweed.* Some people give it the name of *marguerite,* because of its slender beauty. The American daisy has been improved by breeders, and there are many varieties. The daisy is one of the flowers for the month of April.

Scientific Classification. Daisies belong to the family *Compositae.* The English daisy is genus *Bellis,* species *perennis.* The common white American daisy is *Chrysanthemum leucanthemum.* Most of the new, larger daisies are *C. maximum.*   GEORGE A. BEACH

See also BLACK-EYED SUSAN; BURBANK, LUTHER; COMPOSITE FAMILY; FLOWER (color picture, Fall Garden Flowers).

DAKAR, *dah KAHR* (pop. 230,887; alt. 25 ft.), is the capital of Senegal and the westernmost city on the continent of Africa. Dakar is an important transportation and commercial center. For location, see AFRICA (color map). The city has a hot climate, with a rainy season from the middle of June until late September. The docks of Dakar usually are piled high with peanuts awaiting export. The city's industries include food processing, printing, and the manufacture of bricks, soap, and cigarettes. In 1941, an airline established a route between Dakar and Natal, Brazil. This is the shortest route across the South Atlantic. About 16,000 Europeans live in Dakar.   ALAN P. MERRIAM

DAKOTA. See NORTH DAKOTA; SOUTH DAKOTA.

DAKOTA INDIANS. See SIOUX INDIANS.

DAKOTA WESLEYAN UNIVERSITY is a coeducational liberal arts school at Mitchell, S. Dak. It is controlled by the Methodist Church. Emphasis is given to music, art, forensics, teacher training, business administration, prelaw, premedical, and pre-engineering courses. Dakota Wesleyan University was founded in 1885. For enrollment, see UNIVERSITIES AND COLLEGES (table).

DALADIER, *DAH LAH DYAY,* ÉDOUARD (1884-   ), served as French Premier in 1933, 1934, and from 1938 to 1940. He agreed at Munich in 1938 to let Hitler partition Czechoslovakia (see MUNICH AGREEMENT). He served as a Radical Socialist deputy from 1919 to 1940. After France fell to Germany, he was imprisoned from 1941 until 1945. He testified against Marshal Henri Philippe Pétain in 1945, accusing him of collaborating with Germany. Daladier was born at Carpentras, in Vaucluse, France.   E. J. KNAPTON

DALAI LAMA, *dah LIE LAH muh,* was the supreme ruler of Tibet until the Chinese Communists invaded his country in 1950. The Communists now actually rule the nation. They brought back the Panchen Lama, who had been exiled for years in China, to share nominal political power and spiritual rule with the Dalai Lama. Tibetans revolted unsuccessfully against Chinese rule in 1959, and the Dalai Lama fled to India. The Panchen Lama then became the nominal ruler.

Lamaists believe that the Dalai Lama is the *reincarnation,* or reborn soul, of the man who ruled the people before him, and that he was born at exactly the moment the former Dalai Lama died. The wise men of the country watch a holy lake for the appearance of the face of the new Dalai Lama. They then search among children born at the right moment for a face to match the one seen in the lake.   THEODORE H. E. CHEN

See also LAMAISTS; PANCHEN LAMA; TIBET.

The Dalai Lama, dressed in embroidered robes, burned incense at an altar in the Kwang Chi Temple during a visit to Peking.
Eastfoto

DALÉN, NILS GUSTAF. See ACETYLENE.

DALHOUSIE UNIVERSITY, *dal HOW zih,* is a coeducational school in Halifax, Nova Scotia, Canada. A board of governors controls it. Dalhousie accepts students of all denominations. It has faculties of arts and science (including commerce, music, and pharmacy), law, medicine, dentistry, graduate studies, and nursing. The arts and science school offers a three-year course in engineering.

The university was founded in 1818 upon the suggestion of George Ramsay, Earl of Dalhousie, then lieutenant-governor of Nova Scotia. The original funds came from customs collected at Castine, a town now in Maine which the British occupied during the War of

1812. In 1923, the University of King's College, which is associated with Dalhousie, was removed from Windsor, Nova Scotia, to Halifax. King's College grants degrees in divinity, but not in the arts. For enrollment, see CANADA (Education [table]). A. E. KERR

DALI, *DAH lee,* **SALVADOR FELIPE JACINTO** (1904-   ), a famous surrealist painter, is best known for his dreamlike paintings. In them, he showed people and objects transformed into fantastic images that were often set in deserted landscapes. He painted his subjects with a careful, almost photographic realism (see SURREALISM). Dali was born in Figueras, Spain. He studied art in Madrid. GEORGE D. CULLER

Salvador Dali's *The Persistence of Memory* with its limp watches is typical of his attention to detail.
The Museum of Modern Art, New York

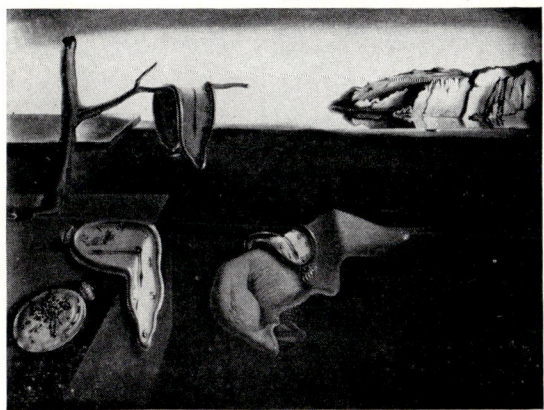

DALLAPICCOLA, *dahl lah PEEK koh lah,* **LUIGI** (1904-   ), is an Italian composer. In much of his music, he uses a 12-tone system derived from that of Schönberg. His important works include an opera, *The Prisoner,* and the *Songs of Imprisonment,* based upon texts by Boethius, Savonarola, and Mary, Queen of Scots. Dallapiccola was born in Pazin, Istria (now in Yugoslavia). HALSEY STEVENS

DALLAS, *DAL uhs,* Tex. (pop. 679,684; met. area, 1,083,601; alt. 435 ft.), is a leading southwestern city. It is the chief inland spot-cotton market of the world,

Dallas Chamber of Commerce

DALLAS, GEORGE MIFFLIN

and leads in cotton-gin production. Dallas lies on the Trinity River in northeast Texas, about 30 miles east of Fort Worth (see TEXAS [map]).

Industry. A Federal Reserve Bank and 29 other banks help make Dallas the financial center of the Southwest. It is also a leading convention city and insurance headquarters. The Dallas Cotton Exchange is the world's largest building devoted to cotton commerce. Dallas ranks with New York and Los Angeles as a top U.S. fashion center. More than 200 apparel and textile manufacturers are located there. The Nieman-Marcus Company in Dallas is one of the world's most famous department stores. Dallas is also the center for more than a thousand firms engaged in the oil industry and allied fields. Other industries include cement plants, electronics works, grain elevators, iron and steel plants, flour mills, and publishing firms.

Transportation. Nine main-line railway systems and four federal highways supply transportation. The city is one of the country's leading air traffic centers.

Cultural Life and Recreation. Dallas supports a symphony orchestra, a civic opera company, and a repertory theater. Baylor Dental School, Southern Methodist University, the University of Dallas, Southwestern Medical College of the University of Texas, and the Graduate Research Center of the Southwest are there. Dallas has more than 100 elementary and high schools. It is diocesan headquarters for the Episcopal and Roman Catholic churches. The State Fair of Texas, held there each October, is the largest of its kind in the world. The Texas Hall of State stands on the fairgrounds.

History. The first settler, John Neely Bryan, arrived in the area in 1841. The city has a council-manager form of government. H. BAILEY CARROLL

See also CITY (color picture, City Flags); RADAR (picture, A Radar Map of Dallas).

DALLAS, GEORGE MIFFLIN (1792-1864), served as Vice-President of the United States from 1845 to 1849 under President James K. Polk. He was a loyal supporter of Polk's policies. His tie-breaking vote in favor of a low tariff bill Polk favored in 1846 destroyed him politically in Pennsylvania, his home state.

Brown Bros.
George Mifflin Dallas

The Cotton Bowl in Dallas is the largest stadium in the Southwest. It holds more than 75,000 persons. It is named to emphasize Dallas' importance as a major cotton market.

DALLES

He served as a Democratic U.S. Senator from Pennsylvania from 1831 to 1833, as minister to Russia from 1837 to 1839, and as minister to England from 1856 to 1861. While in England, he helped settle disputes over the Clayton-Bulwer Treaty (see CLAYTON-BULWER TREATY). Dallas also held office as mayor of Philadelphia, U.S. district attorney, and attorney general of Pennsylvania. During the War of 1812, he was secretary to Albert Gallatin, the minister to Russia. Dallas was born in Philadelphia.   IRVING G. WILLIAMS

DALLES, *dalz,* are deep gorges in which rivers flow rapidly over basaltic rocks or slabs. The name comes from the French *dalle,* meaning *slab* or *tile.* The singular form of dalles in English is *dell,* and in many parts of the country these gorges are called *dells* instead of *dalles.* French explorers gave the name *dalles* to scenic gorges of North American rivers, especially those located in the northern part of the United States.

Notable dalles in the United States include the *Wisconsin Dells* on the Wisconsin River, near Wisconsin Dells, Wis.; the *Saint Louis River Dalles* near Duluth, Minn.; and the *Saint Croix River Dalles* between Wisconsin and Minnesota.   F. G. WALTON SMITH

See also WISCONSIN (color picture, The Wisconsin Dells); WISCONSIN RIVER.

DALLIN, *DAL in,* **CYRUS EDWIN** (1861-1944), an American sculptor, used American Indian life as the theme for many of his greatest works. *Appeal to the Great Spirit*, at the entrance to the Boston Museum of Fine Arts, is typical of his realistic and dramatic style. His other works include *Signal of Peace* in Lincoln Park, Chicago; *Pioneer Monument* in Salt Lake City; and *Sir Isaac Newton* in the Library of Congress in Washington, D.C. Dallin was born in Springville, Utah. He studied at the École des Beaux-Arts and Julian Academy in Paris. He taught in Boston.   JEAN LIPMAN

See also KANSAS CITY (picture, *The Scout*); MASSASOIT (picture).

Museum of Fine Arts, Boston
Appeal to the Great Spirit is a Cyrus Dallin statue.

DALMATIA, *dal MAY shih uh,* a district of Yugoslavia, is a long, narrow strip of land which extends for more than 200 miles along the eastern shore of the Adriatic Sea. The Dalmatian coast is deeply indented and fringed with many islands.

Dalmatia lies in the Dinaric Alps. The chief rivers are the Neretva and the Krka. They flow into the Adriatic Sea. The most important cities are Split, Dubrovnik, Šibenik, and Zadar.

Most of the people are Croatians, but a few Italians also live there. The most important industry is fishing. Olives, grapes, cherries, and other fruits are grown in the valleys near the coast. Dalmatia was part of ancient Illyria. The Romans conquered both Illyria and Dalmatia in

Dalmatia Lies on the Coast of Yugoslavia.

the 200's B.C. Later, between the A.D. 600's and 1400's, the Slavs invaded Dalmatia. After the defeat of Napoleon in 1815, the Great Powers gave Dalmatia to Austria. The province declared its independence of Austria in 1918 and became part of Yugoslavia after World War I. During World War II, Italian forces occupied most of Dalmatia. In 1949, Dalmatia became an *oblast* (region) of Croatia, one of the Yugoslav republics. Its capital is Split.   JOSEPH S. ROUCEK

See also CLOTHING (color picture, Europe); YUGOSLAVIA (color map).

DALMATIAN is a medium-sized dog that looks like a pointer. It is usually white, covered with many black or liver-colored spots. The spots vary in size from a dime to a half dollar. Dalmatian puppies are pure white when they are born. The spots appear after about three or four weeks. Dalmatians make good watchdogs. They are alert, curious, clean, and useful. They also can be taught to hunt. Another name for the Dalmatian is the *coach dog.* These dogs used to run along between the wheels of coaches or carriages, and were companions to the horses. The breed was named for Dalmatia, an area on the Adriatic Sea, but experts are not sure where the dogs were first raised. See also DOG (color picture, Nonsporting Dogs).   JOSEPHINE Z. RINE

DALTON, JOHN (1766-1844), an English schoolmaster and chemist, proposed his atomic theory of matter about 1803. It became one of the foundations of chemistry. He deduced from his theory: (1) the Law of Multiple Proportions, (2) chemical formulas showing the atomic composition of molecules, and (3) the first table of atomic weights, though this proved to be inaccurate. He also investigated color blindness, sometimes called *Daltonism,* which he had. He was born in Eaglesfield. See also ATOM (Dalton's Theory).   SIDNEY ROSEN

DALTON'S LAW OF PARTIAL PRESSURES applies to a mixture of several chemically inactive gases in a container. Within limits, the total pressure of this mixture equals the sum of the pressures each gas exerts by itself. John Dalton, an English chemist, formulated the law in 1802.

DALY, ARNOLD (1875-1927), was an American actor and producer. He introduced George Bernard Shaw's plays to American audiences, beginning in 1903 with *Candida,* in which he was an actor as well as the producer. He was born in Brooklyn, and first appeared as an actor in small stock companies. Daly gained a reputation in both England and the United States while he was still in his 20's.   WILLIAM VAN LENNEP

DALY, MARCUS. See MONTANA (Famous Montanans).

10

Storage Dams have been built across rivers to form water reservoirs for thousands of years. Beavers use logs, stones, and mud in their dams, *above*. Bantu tribesmen in South Africa use hand-operated dams, *left*, to store water for irrigation.

DAM is a barrier placed across a river to stop the flow of water. Dams may vary in size from a small earth or rock barrier to a massive concrete structure hundreds of feet high. The idea of building dams to form reservoirs for storing water seems to be as old as civilization. Since the beginning of recorded history, man has found it necessary to accumulate water during wet seasons so that he can water his cattle and crops during dry spells. The ruins of ancient dams exist in the Tigris and Nile river valleys. The Romans built many dams in Italy, Spain, and North Africa. Some of them are still used.

Throughout man's history, wherever people settled, an important first concern was to locate an adequate water supply. In many regions, streams full of water during certain seasons of the year become dry at other times, perhaps when water is most needed. At first, men built small dams of brush, earth, and rock that would store enough water for immediate needs. But floods frequently washed these small dams away. As communities grew and populations increased, men learned to construct larger dams that would provide a more permanent and abundant water supply. These dams could store enough water to meet man's needs not only during seasonal drops in the water supply, but also during drought periods covering several years. Later, men learned how to harness the energy of surging waters and use it to produce electric power for homes and industries.

What Does a Dam Do?

As a barrier across a river or stream, a dam stops the flow of water. It then stores the water, creating a lake or reservoir, and raises the level of the water as high as the dam itself. The stored water is available for many uses. The dam also raises the water surface from the level of the original river bed to a higher level. This permits water to be diverted by the natural flow of gravity to adjacent lands. The stored water also flows through hydraulic turbines, producing electric power that is used in homes and industries. Water released from the dam in uniform quantities assures water for fish and other wildlife in the stream below the dam. Otherwise, the stream would go dry there. Water released in larger quantities permits river navigation throughout the year. Where dams create large reservoirs, floodwaters can be held back and released gradually over longer periods of time without overflowing riverbanks.

Reservoirs or lakes created by dams provide recreational areas for boating and swimming. They give refuge to fish and wildlife. They help preserve farm lands by reducing soil erosion. Much soil erosion occurs

Hydroelectric Dams harness the currents of many rivers, and provide power for homes and industries. La Tuque Dam, about 75 miles northwest of the city of Quebec, is one of ten large hydroelectric dams on Canada's swift-flowing St. Maurice River.

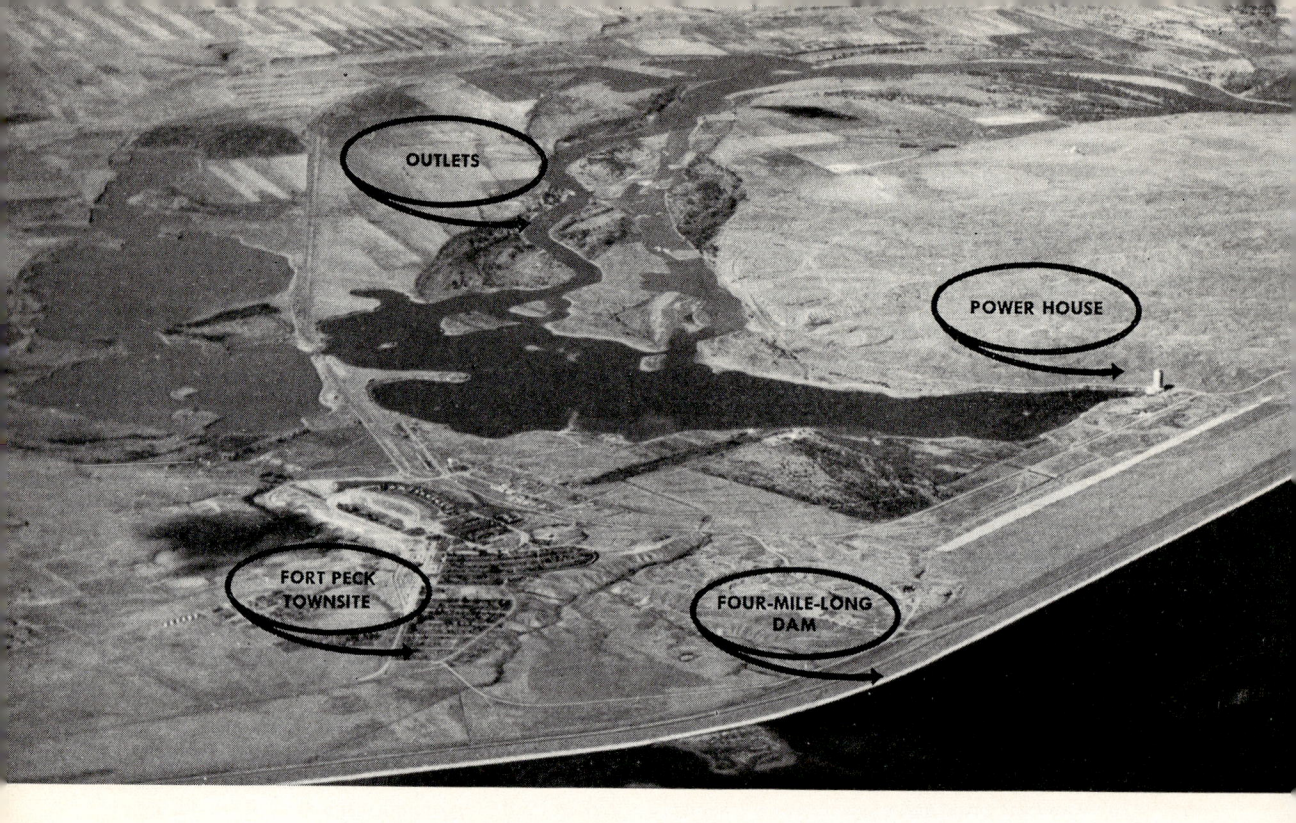

World's Highest and Largest Dams

Ten Highest Dams

Dam	Location	Type	Height (Feet)
Nourek	Russia	Earthfill	990†
Grand Dixence	Switzerland	Gravity	932
Vajont	Italy	Arch	873
Mauvoisin	Switzerland	Arch	778
Bhakra	India	Straight Gravity	740
Oroville	United States	Earthfill	735†
Hoover	United States	Arch	726
Glen Canyon	United States	Arch	710†
Manicouagan	Canada	Multiple Arch	650†
Kurobe No. 4	Japan	Arch	636†

† Under Construction

Ten Largest Dams*

Dam	Location	Type	Volume (Cubic Yards)
Fort Peck	United States	Earth	125,628,000
Oahe	United States	Earth	91,800,000
San Luis	United States	Earth	78,000,000†
Oroville	United States	Earth	77,000,000†
Mangla	Pakistan	Earth	75,000,000†
Garrison	United States	Earth	66,500,000
Nourek	Russia	Earth	65,500,000†
Fort Randall	United States	Earth	53,000,000
Aswân High	Egypt	Earth	53,000,000†
Kuibyshev	Russia	Earth	48,500,000

* Largest in volume content   † Under Construction

---

when rivers flood their valleys, and swift floodwaters carry off the rich topsoils.

Kinds of Dams

Man builds many kinds of dams. Each dam is built to suit the character of the damsite and the materials available for its construction. *Rock-fill* or *stone masonry dams* may be most economical where rock is abundant. *Timber dams* are built where lumber is plentiful. Concrete is a common construction material for dams, but cement and gravel are not always available without heavy transportation costs. *Earth dams* prove most economical in many locations. In some locations, building *hollow dams* saves materials. In narrow canyons, thin *arch dams* may prove most suitable. But in wide river valleys, where the area to be covered by the dam would be very large, flat-slab dams, and dams built of earth, steel, or timber may be less costly.

Masonry Dams. Several types of dams qualify as masonry dams. But, in general, these are dams built of solid, substantial materials. Structures made of stone cut in shapes, or of concrete poured into interlocking blocks or segments to form a solid mass, are called *masonry dams*. A *gravity dam* is generally made of concrete or of cut-stone blocks. It depends for stability primarily on the weight of materials that are used in its construction.

In order to conserve materials, and where the weight required for the stability of the dam can be reduced, men have designed modifications of the gravity dam. A *hollow dam* has a hollow portion inside its main body. If the face of the dam is held up by supporting walls or buttresses, the dam is called a *buttress dam*. A *flat-slab dam* is a dam which has a flat slab placed across buttress supports at a 45° angle. The weight of the water holds down the slab. In some cases, the slab can be formed into an arch which is supported by the buttresses. The arch is located between each pair of buttresses. This type of dam is called a *multiple-arch dam*.

But many variations in these types of dams occur.

FORT PECK DAM

Largest Dam in the World is the Fort Peck Dam. It stretches almost four miles across the Missouri River in northeastern Montana. Completed in 1940, the dam contains more than 125,000,000 cubic yards of earth, stone, and steel.

U.S. Army Corps of Engineers

Powerhouse of the dam generates electricity for farms and cities in Montana and North and South Dakota.

Mile-Long Spillway of the dam carries excess water from the reservoir to the Missouri River. It drops 215 feet.

Fort Peck Reservoir, created by the dam, is 189 miles long and 16 miles wide. The lake has been stocked with many fish.

Dams constructed in narrow canyons to form an arch are called *arch dams*. Some dams use a very thin arch. The arches of some dams almost form a dome. The arches in others are thickened to include the principles of the gravity dam, where the weight adds to the dam's stability. In the latter case, the principles of the arch dam and the gravity dam are combined in the design, and the structure is called an *arch-gravity dam*.

Embankment Dams. The *earth-fill dam* is the most common type of embankment dam. This dam is constructed by hauling selected earth materials into place, and compacting layer upon layer with heavy rollers to form a watertight mass. Materials placed in the dam are graded according to density, with the fine materials located in the center. Coarser materials are placed in outside zones, blanketed with a cover of rock, called *riprap*. This serves as an outside protection against the wave action of the reservoir and against wind, rain, and ice. Walls made of reinforced concrete to cut off water passage are frequently used in the center section. These cut-off walls may be made of sheet-metal piling driven deep below the excavated foundation level. Frequently, thinned-out cement, called *grout*, is pumped under great pressure into the foundation. It fills cracks and fissures, thus supplementing the cut-off walls and making the foundation watertight.

Semihydraulic-fill and *hydraulic-fill dams* are other modifications of the embankment dam. These dams are constructed by pumping wet, fine materials into their central sections, and allowing the water to drain off. Where rock is available, it may prove most economical to build a *rock-fill dam*. Most dams of this type are constructed of coarse, heavy rock and boulders. These are graded in size to permit them to fit together more compactly. Such dams, however, must have other means of preventing water from passing through them. Many of

13

A WORLD BOOK SCIENCE PROJECT
BUILDING A MODEL DAM

The purpose of this project is to show how a dam can turn a nearly useless river into a valuable asset. One part of the model represents a shallow, almost useless, stream. The other part shows how a dam can make the stream a source of power, irrigation, and recreation.

Three plastic soda straws
Large cork
Thin, stiff plastic
Wire coat hanger
Green sponge
Two toy boats
Pail
Two catch pans
Two flexible tubes

Front Piece — 6 in., 2 in., 6 in., 2 in., 6 in., 9 in., 9 in., 9 in., 9 in.
Back Piece — 12 in., 8 in., 12 in., 8 in., 12 in., 36 in.
Dam — 18 in., 4 in.
Side Pieces — 12 in., 30 in., 6 in.
Top Pieces — 10 in., 33 in.

Assembling the Base. Cut pieces of ¼-inch plywood according to the pattern and dimensions given, *above*. Nail the front, back, and sides together as shown, *left*. Then nail on the four top pieces as shown. Be sure to let the top pieces overhang the front of the base by 1 inch.

Waterproofing the Model. After assembling the base, smooth off all rough edges with sandpaper. Use caulking compound to seal the joints in the two troughs. Prepare the dam as shown in the detailed illustration on the opposite page, and nail it in place in the trough. Caulk these joints, also. Then paint the whole model with a waterproof paint.

14

Making the Dam. Drill three holes in the triangular wooden piece as shown, *below*. Use a drill the same size as the diameter of the plastic straws. Push the straws through the holes, and put caulking compound around each to make a watertight seal.

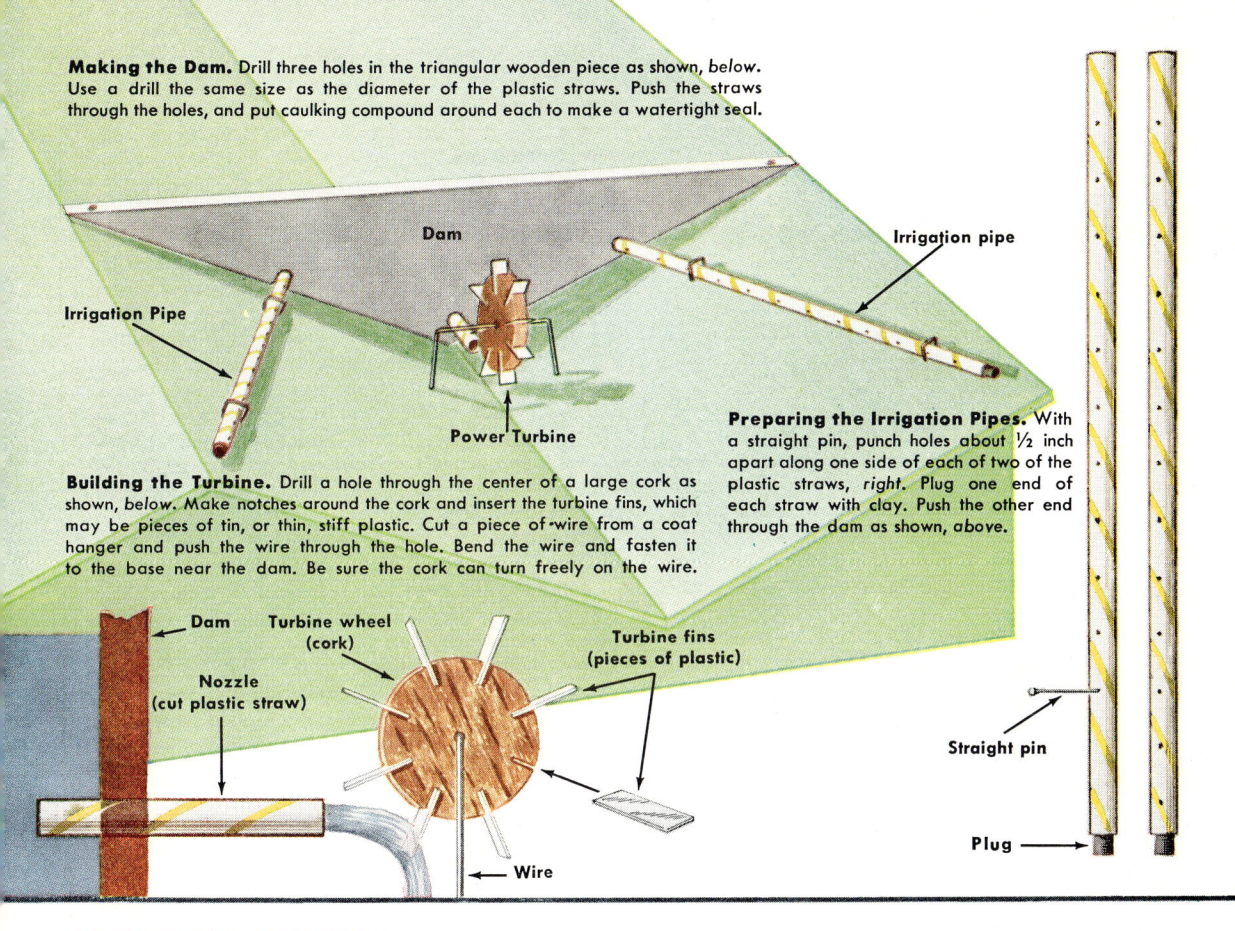

Dam

Irrigation pipe

Irrigation Pipe

Power Turbine

Building the Turbine. Drill a hole through the center of a large cork as shown, *below*. Make notches around the cork and insert the turbine fins, which may be pieces of tin, or thin, stiff plastic. Cut a piece of wire from a coat hanger and push the wire through the hole. Bend the wire and fasten it to the base near the dam. Be sure the cork can turn freely on the wire.

Preparing the Irrigation Pipes. With a straight pin, punch holes about ½ inch apart along one side of each of two of the plastic straws, *right*. Plug one end of each straw with clay. Push the other end through the dam as shown, *above*.

Dam
Turbine wheel (cork)
Nozzle (cut plastic straw)
Turbine fins (pieces of plastic)
Wire

Straight pin

Plug

HOW THE MODEL WORKS

Demonstrating the Project. Glue small pieces of green sponge to represent trees in each of the troughs as shown, *below*. Place catch pans under the overhang at the front of each trough. Set a pail of water on a platform behind the model. Put two flexible tubes in the pail, and let water run slowly into the troughs. The water will flow right out of the trough without a dam. But in the other trough, a lake will form behind the dam. The "irrigation pipes" will take water to areas away from the dam. The jet of water coming through the tube at the base of the dam will cause the turbine to turn.

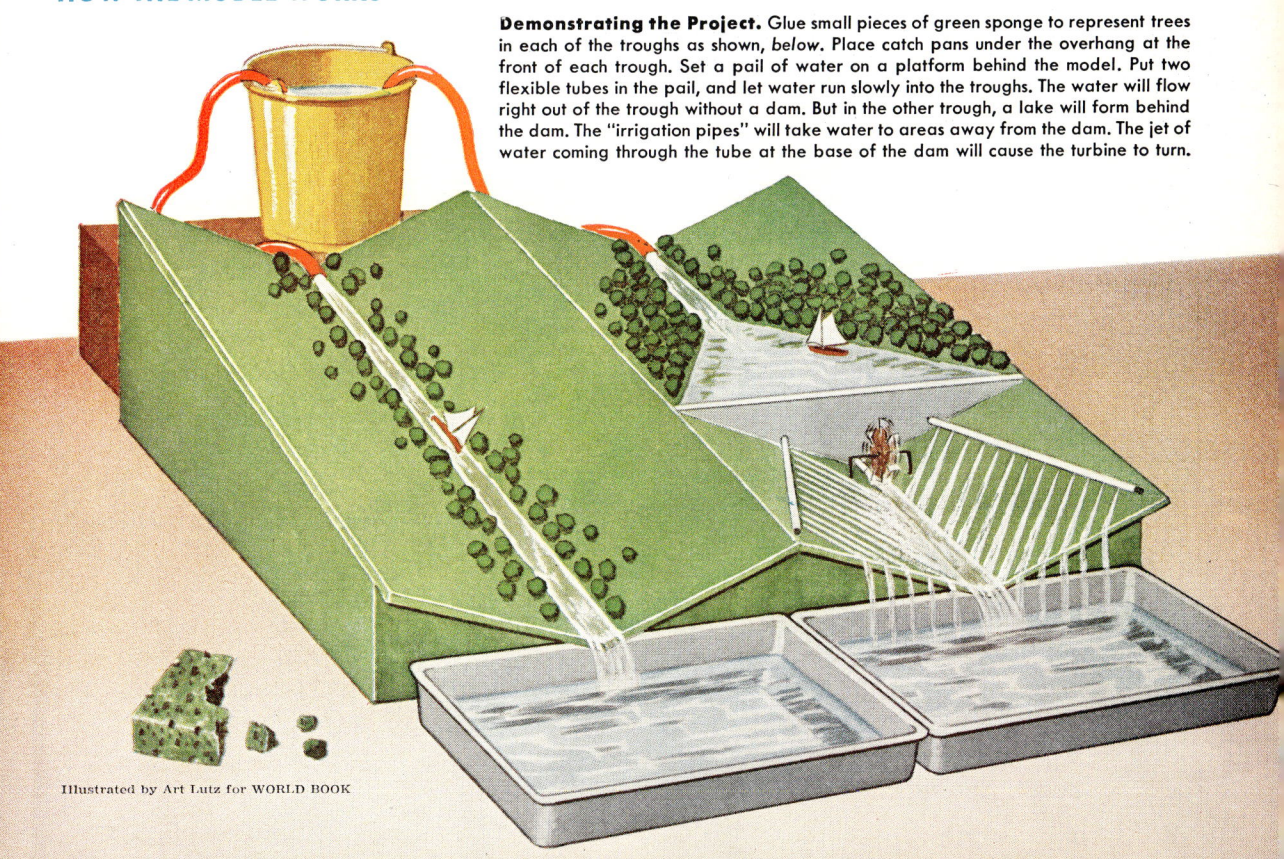

Illustrated by Art Lutz for WORLD BOOK

DAM

them have a blanket of concrete, steel, clay, or asphalt on the side facing the water. This blanket makes the dam watertight. Combinations of rock and earth result in a type of dam called an *earth-and-rock-fill dam*.

Other Types of Dams. *Timber dams* are built where lumber is available and the dam is relatively small. The timber is weighted down with rock. Planking or other watertight material forms the facing. *Metal dams* have watertight facings and supports of steel.

Dams with movable gates are built where it is necessary to let large quantities of water, ice, or driftwood pass by the dam. A *roller dam* has a large roller located horizontally between piers. It can be raised and lowered. When the roller is raised, ice and other materials pass through the dam without much loss of reservoir water level. Many kinds of gates or wickets are used in these dams. Common types include the *taintor-gate dam*, *beartrap dam*, and *wicket-gate dam*.

In 1963, France began building a dam on the Rance River at St. Malo for the world's first tidal power plant. St. Malo has some of the world's highest tides. They rise to a maximum of 44 feet and an annual average of 28 feet. Water will fill the dam during high tide and flow through turbines during low tide.

How Men Build Dams

In order to construct a dam, the builders must first gather and study much information. The site where the dam is to be erected must be examined for its formation, quality of foundation, and the availability of suitable construction materials. A careful analysis must be made of the stream-flow characteristics. The area to be covered by the reservoir that the dam creates must be outlined when determining the height of the dam at any given site. This requires detailed topographic mapping and geologic studies. Subsurface drillings are necessary to determine the condition, quality, and location of the rock formation under the damsite.

All property in the reservoir area must be bought or relocated. This occasionally requires the relocation of entire towns, highways, railroads, and utilities. Engineers must also determine the amount of mud, silt,

Bhakra Dam on India's Sutlej River is one of the world's highest dams. The 740-foot high concrete dam was completed in 1961.
Wide World

and debris which the dam will stop. This will determine the useful life of the reservoir, because when the reservoir becomes filled with this material it can no longer store water. If the dam is to be used for generating power, outlets must be provided which will connect to generating equipment. If the water is to be used for irrigation or municipal supply, outlets to control its release to canals or aqueducts must be built.

When the damsite has been selected, means must be found to remove or bypass the flow of the stream from the river bed so that the foundation can be excavated and the concrete, earth, or rock placed. To divert the flow of the river from the area, frequently half of the river bed is excavated at one time. The other half is used for the flow of the river. In some cases, it is more economical to bore a tunnel through an adjacent canyon wall, permitting the entire flow of the river to pass around the damsite. To accomplish this, *cofferdams* (small dams placed temporarily across a stream) are built upstream to divert the river into the tunnel. After the dam has been built high enough, the diversion tunnel is closed with gates, and permanently plugged.

In designing the dam, provision must be made to bypass water when the reservoir is full, without overtopping the dam. For this purpose, a *spillway* is built.

In order to release water from behind the dam when the reservoir is not full, dams are equipped with reservoir outlets. These outlets consist of specially designed valves which can be opened and closed under high water pressure. Some of the many kinds of valves used for this purpose are called *needle valves*, *gate valves*, *slide valves*, and *cylinder gates*.   T. W. MERMEL

Related Articles. See also the Electric Power sections of certain state, province, and country articles, such as ALABAMA (Electric Power), and the following articles.

DAMS OF THE UNITED STATES

Alder	Fort Supply	Parker
American Falls	Friant	Pensacola
Anderson Ranch	Garrison	Pine Flat
Arrowrock	Grand Coulee	Reagan
Bagnell	Hansen	Roosevelt
Bartlett	Hoover	Ross
Belle Fourche	Hungry Horse	Safe Harbor
Bonneville	John Martin	Salt Springs
Buffalo Bill	Kanopolis	Saluda
Cherry Creek	Kensico	San Gabriel
Clearwater	Kentucky	Santa Fe
Coolidge	Keokuk	Santee-Cooper
Detroit	Kingsley	Project
Diablo	Marshall Ford	Sardis
Elephant Butte	Merwin	Shadow
Exchequer	Mud Mountain	Mountain
Falcón	New Croton	Shasta
Fontana	O'Shaughnessy	Watauga
Fort Peck	Owyhee	Winsor
Fort Randall	Pardee	Wolf Creek

FOREIGN DAMS

Aswân	Chambon	Génissiat
Cárdenas	Dneproges	Grand Dixence
Castillon	Gatún Lake	Hume

UNCLASSIFIED

Austria (picture, Limberg Dam)	Irrigation
	Missouri River Basin Project
Central Valley Project	Reservoir
Electric Power	Rio Grande Project
Floods and Flood Control	Saint Lawrence Seaway
India (picture, Water and Power Shortages)	Tennessee Valley Authority
	Water Power

DAMAGES is a general term in law for the amount one person can recover from another in a lawsuit. A person who has suffered loss or injury through someone else's fault or carelessness may sue for a sum of money. The money repays him for his loss or compensates him for his injury. In order to collect damages from the other person, it is usually necessary to show that he acted wrongly or carelessly.

In the United States, but not in Great Britain or Canada, a person who sues for damages usually must also show that no carelessness or wrongdoing of his own had anything to do with causing the injury. If a suit for damages is tried before a jury, the jury usually decides on the damages.

As a rule, a person can recover only *actual damages*. This is particularly true if the wrongdoer is only *negligent* (careless), and not *malicious* (meaning to do harm). If a man's car has been wrecked negligently, he can recover only what the car was worth.

If the court finds that a man has been injured, but has suffered no significant loss, it may award *nominal damages*, perhaps of only a few cents. Suits brought as a matter of principle are often settled in this way.

If the court thinks that the conduct of the person responsible for the injury or loss deserves punishment, it may award *punitive damages*. The person who has brought the suit may then collect much more than his actual loss. In order to encourage people to bring certain kinds of suits, the law may require the payment of more than actual losses. THOMAS A. COWAN

See also MALICE; NEGLIGENCE; TORT.

DAMÃO. See GOA.

DAMASCUS, *duh MAS kus* (pop. 408,774), the capital of Syria, is one of the oldest and most important caravan cities in the Middle East. For hundreds of years, Damascus has been famous for its craftsmen, who have made excellent inlaid metalwork, silk brocades, steel sword blades, and wooden mosaics.

Location and Appearance. Damascus lies in a beautiful oasis, or fertile area in the desert. The Barada River and several canals supply it with water. The oasis spreads eastward from the foothills of the Anti-Lebanon Mountains into the Syrian Desert. It lies at an altitude of about 2,250 feet. Damascus enjoys a pleasant climate most of the year, but the *Khamsin*, a desert wind, sometimes makes the city hot and dusty.

Damascus combines the old and the new. The new sections of the city are spacious, and contain many modern buildings. But some ancient streets are narrow and crowded. The *bazaars* (open shops and markets) are usually roofed with tin. Some old stone houses look like prisons from the outside. But they are beautifully decorated inside, and often have enclosed gardens.

Damascus contains many *mosques* (Moslem houses of worship). The Great Mosque of the Omayyad *caliphs* (rulers) is the most famous in the city. It was originally a Byzantine church. Artists covered the inside walls with beautiful *mosaics* (see MOSAIC). Pilgrims still visit the tomb of Saladin, one of the city's most famous rulers.

History. Damascus was probably founded before 2000 B.C. Aramaeans from the Syrian Desert first lived there. The city grew in importance until it became the caravan center of Syria after about 1000 B.C. Since the A.D. 600's, many Moslems who make the *Hadj* (pilgrimage to Mecca) have begun their long journey from Damascus. Suleiman I, the Turkish ruler of Damascus in the 1500's, built a beautiful mosque and inn called the *Tekkiya*. Turkish pilgrims lived there while they waited for the Hadj. Today it is used as a college mosque.

For a brief time after World War I, Damascus was the

N.E.N.A., Black Star

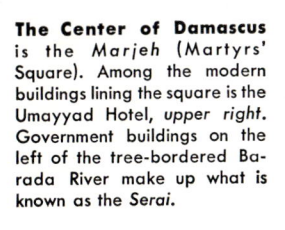

The Center of Damascus is the *Marjeh* (Martyrs' Square). Among the modern buildings lining the square is the Umayyad Hotel, *upper right*. Government buildings on the left of the tree-bordered Barada River make up what is known as the *Serai*.

DAMASK

capital of an Arab kingdom. When Syria became a French mandate of the League of Nations in 1920, French troops occupied Damascus. The Syrians clashed violently with the French for many years. In 1925 and 1926, French forces shelled the city. At the end of World War II, Damascus became the capital of the Republic of Syria. Damascus became the provincial capital of Syria in 1958, when Syria became a province of the United Arab Republic. In 1961, Syria withdrew from the United Arab Republic in a bloodless rebellion. Damascus became the capital of the Republic of Syria once again. CHRISTINA PHELPS HARRIS

See also SYRIA (pictures).

DAMASK is a firm, lustrous fabric that may be woven from any fiber. Its flat, woven design appears on both sides of the fabric.

In table damask, the design may be sateen weave with *floats* (longer, raised threads) in the *filling* (crosswise) threads. The background may be a satin weave with floats in the *warp* (lengthwise) threads. Single table damask has a four-float construction, and double damask has a seven-float construction. The double damask has more yarn, and the floats may pass over 18 to 20 yarns in an elaborate design. Damask's luster depends on length of floats, length of fibers used, closeness of weave, and uniformity of yarns. HAZEL B. STRAHAN

DAMASUS is the name of two popes of the Roman Catholic Church.

Saint Damasus I served as pope from 366 to 384. He became famous for building churches and repairing the catacombs in Rome (see CATACOMBS). He also ornamented the tombs of martyrs. Damasus was deeply interested in the Bible and decided which books should make it up. He and Saint Jerome corrected the Latin translations, and the result was the Latin Vulgate, the standard version of the Bible in the Roman Catholic Church. Damasus was born in Rome.

Damasus II, a Bavarian, was elected pope on July 17, 1048. He had held office for less than a month when he died. GUSTAVE WEIGEL and FULTON J. SHEEN

DAME SCHOOL. See COLONIAL LIFE IN AMERICA (Education; picture, At Dame Schools).

DAMIEN DE VEUSTER, DAH MYAN duh vus TAR, JOSEPH (1840-1888), was a Roman Catholic priest who gave his life to the care of lepers in a colony at Molokai, Hawaii. Father Damien was born in Belgium and became a member of the Fathers of the Sacred Hearts of Jesus and Mary. He was sent to Molokai as resident priest (see HAWAII [The Islands]). But because of the difficulty in getting doctors, Father Damien was obliged to serve as a doctor as well. He was stricken with leprosy himself in 1885. FULTON J. SHEEN

DAMOCLES, DAM oh kleez, was a courtier of the Greek tyrant Dionysius of Syracuse. Damocles talked so much about the happiness of Dionysius that the tyrant decided to teach him a lesson. He invited Damocles to sit at his own place at a banquet. Damocles was horrified to find a sword suspended by a single hair above his head. Dionysius thus showed the uncertainty of his life, even when he seemed to be secure. "The sword of Damocles" came to be used for a dreaded tragedy that may happen at any moment. The Roman orator, Cicero, told this story. C. BRADFORD WELLES

DAMON AND PYTHIAS, DAY mun, PITH ih us, were two noble Greek youths of Syracuse. Their friendship and loyalty to each other made them famous. According to a popular legend, Pythias, or Phintias, had been condemned to death by Dionysius of Syracuse. He was allowed to leave the city to put his affairs in order when Damon promised to die in place of Pythias if Pythias failed to keep his promise. Pythias was delayed, and arrived just in time to save Damon from death. Dionysius so admired this display of friendship that he pardoned Pythias and asked the two to become his friends. C. BRADFORD WELLES

DAMP is a name for poisonous gases found in mines. They are often found in coal mines, where they are a hazard to miners. The most common one, *firedamp*, is chiefly methane, a tasteless, odorless gas. It forms when decaying plant matter produces coal, and gets trapped in coal seams. When miners cut into these seams, the gas is released. It burns readily and can explode when mixed with air. When firedamp explodes, it leaves a deadly gas called *afterdamp*, which contains carbon dioxide, carbon monoxide, and nitrogen.

Chokedamp and *blackdamp* are common names for carbon dioxide, CO_2, a gas that is denser than air. It gathers at the bottom of pits and valleys in mines, where it shuts off the oxygen supply.

Miners once carried canaries into the mines to test for gases. If the birds collapsed, it meant that gas was present. Today, various mechanical, chemical, and electrical devices are used to test for the presence of these gases. LEWIS F. HATCH

See also COAL (Mine Safety Measures); DAVY, SIR HUMPHRY; METHANE; MINING; SAFETY LAMP.

DAMPING OFF is a plant disease caused by fungi that live near the surface of the soil (see FUNGI). It affects all kinds of plants. Damping off may rot seeds before they begin to sprout, kill *seedlings* (young plants) before they grow above the ground, or destroy the stems of seedlings just above the surface of the soil. Damping off cannot be cured. But farmers can prevent it by planting seeds in soil free from fungi, or by treating seeds with a protective dust. WILLIAM F. HANNA

DAMROSCH, DAM rahsh, was the family name of a father and son who spent their lives educating Americans to serious music. They came from a family of German musicians, but carried on their musical careers in the United States.

Leopold Damrosch (1832-1885), violinist and conductor, founded the New York Symphony Society in 1878, and conducted its orchestra until his death. Damrosch was born in Posen, Prussia. After receiving his degree in medicine from the University of Berlin in 1854, he turned to a career in music. He joined the Weimar court orchestra as violinist under Franz Liszt. Damrosch came to the United States in 1871 to become conductor of the German Male Choral Society. He introduced German opera at the Metropolitan Opera House.

Walter Johannes Damrosch (1862-1950), son of Leopold, conducted the New York Symphony Orchestra in 1925 in the first symphonic program ever broadcast on radio. From 1928 to 1947, Damrosch served as musical counsel for the National Broadcasting Company. Children throughout the nation learned about great music by listening to the Music Appreciation Hour he directed. The music of such composers as Wagner,

Stravinsky, Gershwin, Ravel, and Elgar became popular, in part, through Damrosch's efforts.

Walter Damrosch was born in Breslau, Silesia, and came to the United States with his father in 1871. He succeeded his father as director of the Oratorio and Symphony societies of New York City in 1885. Later he founded the Damrosch Opera Company to present Wagnerian operas. Damrosch reorganized the New York Symphony Society in 1903, and served as its conductor until 1927.

Walter Damrosch — NBC

Charles Anderson Dana — Brown Bros.

Richard Henry Dana, Jr. — Brown Bros.

In addition to his conducting and educational work, Damrosch composed such operas as *The Scarlet Letter*, *Cyrano de Bergerac*, *The Man Without a Country*, and *Manila Te Deum*, celebrating Admiral George Dewey's victory. He wrote several songs, including "Danny Deever" and "Mandalay." IRVING KOLODIN

DAMSEL FLY. See DRAGONFLY.

DANA, *DAY nuh,* **CHARLES ANDERSON** (1819-1897), editor and part owner of the New York *Sun*, built it into one of the most important newspapers of its time. Dana and his associates paid $175,000 for the *Sun* in 1868. Under his management its value rose to an estimated $5,000,000. He made the *Sun* a witty, terse, and outspoken newspaper.

Dana was born on Aug. 8, 1819, at Hinsdale, N.H. He studied at Harvard University. In 1842, he became a member of the Brook Farm Association, an experimental social community at West Roxbury, Mass., and wrote for its publications, *The Harbinger* and *The Dial* (see BROOK FARM). He joined the staff of the New York *Tribune* in 1847, and later became its managing editor. He resigned in 1862 because he disagreed with *Tribune* owner Horace Greeley about the newspaper's stand on the Civil War. Dana served as an assistant secretary of war from 1863 to 1865. JOHN E. DREWRY

DANA, JAMES DWIGHT (1813-1895), was an American geologist, mineralogist, and zoologist. He was mineralogist and geologist of a government exploring expedition in the Pacific Ocean under Captain Charles Wilkes from 1838 to 1842. He also collected and studied corals and *crustaceans* (hard-shelled water creatures). He served as a professor at Yale from 1856 to 1890.

Later, he became editor in chief of the *American Journal of Science*. His most important books were *System of Mineralogy*, *Manual of Geology*, and *On Corals and Coral Islands*. He was born in Utica, N.Y., and was graduated from Yale University. CARROLL LANE FENTON

DANA, JOHN COTTON (1856-1929), was an American librarian. After he became head of the Denver Public Library in 1889, he started the first children's library and was the first to open all bookshelves to readers. He later worked in the Springfield (Mass.) Public Library, then became director of the Newark (N.J.) Public Library from 1902 to 1929. He made the Newark library famous by extending its services to everyone. Dana was born in Woodstock, Vt., and spent his early life as a surveyor, engineer, and lawyer. R. B. DOWNS

DANA, RICHARD HENRY, JR. (1815-1882), a maritime lawyer and author, wrote *Two Years Before the Mast* (1840). The book was a best seller that was widely imitated. He also wrote *A Seaman's Friend* (1841) to help seamen know their rights and secure justice.

An attack of measles damaged his eyesight after his sophomore year at Harvard College. He became an ordinary seaman in 1834 to cure his health, and sailed around Cape Horn to California on the brig *Pilgrim*. He returned in 1836 aboard the *Alert*, and was graduated from Harvard Law School in 1840.

Dana wanted to serve his country in a high office, but he was defeated, because he put honor and justice above self-interest. Congress failed to confirm Dana's appointment as ambassador to England in 1876 when Dana refused to defend himself against false testimony. He worked for the Free Soil party and fought for freedom for fugitive slaves (see FREE SOIL PARTY). He was born in Cambridge, Mass. WILLIAM H. GILMAN

DANA COLLEGE is an Evangelical Lutheran coeducational college at Blair, Nebr., founded in 1884. It offers liberal arts and teacher preparatory courses leading to B.S. and B.A. degrees. For enrollment, see UNIVERSITIES AND COLLEGES (table).

DANAË was a Greek goddess. See PERSEUS.

DANBURY, Conn. (pop. 22,928; alt. 370 ft.), the *Hat City*, makes more hats than any other American city. Over 35 Danbury factories make hats and related products such as hat boxes. The Danbury Fair held each fall is one of the largest annual fairs in Connecticut. The Still River runs through Danbury, which lies in southwestern Connecticut (see CONNECTICUT [map]).

Other products of the city include surgical, electrical, and metal products; bearings; clothing; boxes; furniture; insulating materials; plastics; helicopters; and airplane and air-conditioner parts.

Eight Norwalk families founded Danbury in 1685. It was incorporated as a town in 1687. In 1777, during the Revolutionary War, the British raided and burned Danbury because it was an army supply center. Zadoc Benedict established the nation's first beaver-hat factory there in 1780. Danbury has a mayor-council form of government. ALBERT E. VAN DUSEN

DANBURY STATE COLLEGE is a coeducational state-controlled school at Danbury, Conn. Courses lead to B.S. and M.S. degrees. Danbury State College was founded in 1904. For enrollment, see UNIVERSITIES AND COLLEGES (table).

DANCE MUSIC. See POPULAR MUSIC.

DANCING

From Kate Seredy's The Good Master, *courtesy The Viking Press*

DANCING is the oldest and liveliest of the arts. Men in all countries and in all times have expressed their feelings in rhythm and body movement. Our ancestors left pictures or writings which told of their dances. Men who study these records have found out why these people of ancient times danced, and how they danced.

The dance is the language of the body. It draws people together in their thoughts and feelings. A dancer can communicate any subject and any idea to his audience. His movements may interpret religious history or beliefs, or they may interpret things in our everyday life.

A dance may be social, so that everyone may take part in it. Or it may be entirely personal to the dancer. And, as in poetry and song, the dance may be in any style or form. It may be funny or sad. It may tell a story or merely describe an idea.

There are many reasons for dancing. Children dance because of the joy they feel. Their healthy little bodies will not remain quiet. Some primitive peoples believe dances will bring them magic powers. They dance to bring victory, health, or life. Much of our social dancing today is for the sake of companionship. And there are persons who dance to find relief from the sameness of everyday life. The dance reaches its most beautiful form with those who treat it as an art. These artists dance to give beauty and inspiration to others.

Dancing has been called the mother of the other arts. Throughout the ages, the dancing body has inspired the musician, the sculptor, and the painter. The drama of most countries started in their dances. The beginnings of music have been traced to the dance. The first music was merely a rhythm for the early dances. Perhaps it was only a chanting voice, the beat of a drum, the sound of two sticks struck together, or the clapping of hands. The dance has given richly to the other arts, and has in turn received much from the other arts.

Primitive Dance

The earliest records of people dancing are cave paintings in northern Spain. Scientists believe that these pictures were drawn about 50,000 years ago. The cave men could not write. The only records they left were such pictures. We can tell a great deal about their way of life from studying these pictures.

Probably the most important activity in the life of primitive peoples and ancient civilizations is the dance. From the dim past until today, primitive man has danced when his children were born, when they were old enough to be accepted as adult members of the tribe, when they were married, and when they died. He has danced to gain courage for battle. When the enemy was beaten, he has danced to celebrate the victory and to pray to his gods. Primitive medicine men have danced to drive away evil spirits which were thought to bring disease and misfortune. Primitive farmers had special ceremonial dances to bring rain and make crops grow. The primitive hunter and fisherman imitated in their dances the movements of the animals and fish they hoped to bring home.

Even among primitive dancers, there were special artists. All young men had to learn their own tribal dances. Some were better dancers than the others. These were sent away to be trained by tribes that were especially famous for dancing. After the training, the young men returned to their own tribes to teach others.

Primitive tribes held dance festivals. For weeks, months, and even years they practiced the dance steps. When festival time came, the dancers did not miss a step. They felt the whole purpose of the dance was lost if a single dancer moved out of turn. In some tribes in the New Hebrides, the older men stood by with bow and arrow and shot any dancer who made a mistake.

Primitive tribes today are just as serious about the dance as they were hundreds of years ago. Expeditions have brought back motion pictures of the primitive dances among the peoples of Africa, Australia, and the Pacific islands. Anyone who sees these movies will realize that the dance is a ruling part of primitive life.

Development of the Dance

Egypt got its dances from the peasant, or working, class. This is shown from records made as long ago as 2200 B.C. The Egyptians believed that their gods danced. Thus, magic and religion inspired the early dances. Often the priests performed them. One interesting dance which the priests did was an astronomical dance. In this the priests expressed symbolically the harmony of the universe, with every star and planet in its place and moving in rhythm with the others.

Egyptian kings must have danced. Ancient writings (hieroglyphics) and carvings on tombs show kings dancing before their gods. But the proud Egyptians had no social dance, and they did not dance for joy.

Some of the religious dances had acrobatic movements. In time these dances lost their meaning and were performed only for exhibition. The Egyptians brought dancers in from other countries and put them on exhibition. The dwarfs from Ethiopia were especially famous. The Egyptian dance was changed after 1500 B.C., when Egypt conquered the Near East. Lovely Asiatic girl dancers were brought into Egypt. The old dance had been masculine and severe, with open movements. But the Asiatic dancers were light and feminine, and the dance became gentler under their influence.

Greek Dancing also came from religion. Most of the Greek writings about dancing have been lost. We have

FOLK DANCES OF MANY COUNTRIES

The Hoop Dance is one of the several dances performed as religious ceremonies by the Pueblo Indians of Taos, New Mexico.

Folk Dances such as this are a gay and important feature at the midsummer festival of the Norwegians.

The Sword Dance is a feature of the Highland games of Scotland.

Bolivian Indians take part in one of their lively traditional dances at the mountain village of Sorata. The women wear derby hats as a part of their everyday costumes.

Maori Men of New Zealand perform an age-old ceremonial dance. Such dances are among the customs the Maoris have retained for thousands of years.

A Brisk Russian Folk Dance is made colorful by red Russian boots and embroidered costumes.

U.S. Indian Service; Sawders; Black Star; Chicago Board of Ed.

DANCING

learned about their ancient dances from sculpture and vase-paintings. There were special dances for each god.

Dances in honor of the god Dionysus were the beginning of the drama in Greece. The earliest drama was performed by principal actors and a chorus. The principal actors were speaker-actors. They wore heavy costumes, masks, and thick-soled shoes. The chorus was made up of dancer-actors. They wore light, flowing garments. The chorus danced, spoke, and sang, using their hands chiefly for expression. Among the stage dances were the slow and worshipful *Emmeleia* of the tragedy; the frolicsome *Kordax* of the comedy; and the vivid jumping and turning *Sikinnis* of the satirical drama.

The Greeks had other forms of dancing. Specially trained performers gave educational and acrobatic dances. Public festivals featured ball games in dance form. A thrilling weapon dance, the *Pyrrhic*, was performed by warriors. In this dance, the warriors prepared for battle by practicing movements of attack and defense. It was popular in Sparta. All strong Spartan lads from the age of five had to learn it. There was a Greek saying that the best dancer was the best fighter.

Even the philosophers danced in ancient Greece. Great men such as Plato and Socrates admired the dance. It is said that Socrates himself danced to celebrate the siege of Crete.

Romans added little new material to the dance. Like the Greeks, they had religious ceremonial dances. But even these came from the Etruscans, who held power in Italy before the Romans. The Romans in time spread their power throughout the Mediterranean world. Thus, Rome became important as a place where the dances of other nations were combined. The Romans were the first to appreciate the beauty of the Spanish dances.

The Roman theater was copied from the Greek theater. The Romans had wild dances for the god Bacchus, much like the dances the Greeks performed for Dionysus. But Romans themselves did little dancing. They brought in dancers from all the lands they conquered.

In Asia Minor and Egypt the Romans founded the art of *pantomime*. Pantomime is acting without speech. Rome developed the pantomime dance to a high degree. The dancers acted out stories through movements of their bodies. The most famous dancers of pantomime were Pylades and Bathyllus.

The Middle Ages saw the growth of social dancing and the rise of the dancing master, or teacher. There was little stage dancing. The Church controlled the theater, and only religious plays were presented. But the common people had a wonderful time in their folk dances. On holidays they danced for fun alone. Then they forgot the religious meanings of their dances, and out of these dances developed the so-called *social dances*.

In time the nobles also began to dance. They changed the simple dances of the common people into elaborate affairs. They wore brilliant and expensive costumes, and danced at court before the king and queen. The country folk had twirled happily in the *carol*, a circular dance. At court the noblemen danced a slow and stately carol with much stiff and elegant posturing. The nobles also started new creations, called *danza*. These were danced in couples or by men or ladies alone.

The growth of cities brought a new class of rich merchants and tradesmen. They wished to show off their wealth and social position, so they took up the stately dancing of the nobles. Social dances became more intricate and difficult. Soon dancing masters were needed to teach the new difficult steps.

The Renaissance (about 1500) brought again the refreshing influence of the common people. A new liveliness took the place of the stately dances of the Middle Ages. This influence was felt in all the countries of Europe. Italy danced the *pavan*, a stately ceremonial dance, and the *galliard*, a vivacious leaping dance. France presented the *courante*, with its quick running steps. Germany had the sprightly *allemande*, and Spain the passionate *saraband* and the *chaconne*. The most lively dance of all was the *volte* of southern France. The volte was the favorite dance of England's Queen Elizabeth I, and was popular throughout Great Britain.

During the 1600's, dancing lost much of its grace and charm. Gone was the gay mood of the Renaissance dances. The once light and hurried courante became stately and formal. The passionate saraband changed into a stiff and heavy dance. After 1650 the style changed again. Elegance and gracefulness became the new tone. Gentlemen bowed and ladies curtsied politely. Toes were pointed "just so," and steps were small and light. Lully, the French composer, arranged dances at the French court. He introduced the *minuet*, the *bourrée*, and the *passepied*. Another newcomer to the ballroom was the *gavotte*. All showed great elegance.

Late in the 1600's England's country dances came into style. Of these, the *contredanse* and the *square dances* are still popular. In the contredanse, partners arranged themselves in lines facing each other. For square dances, the dancers formed a square. The minuet was also very popular in England from 1650 to 1750.

The 1700's brought the new German *waltz*. This is still today one of the most popular of all dance steps. People had become tired of the difficult steps of older dances. The waltz has only one simple step. The dancers may move anywhere they wish on the floor. The waltz brought democracy, simplicity, and naturalness to ballroom dancing. And because it was so simple to learn, dancing masters lost their popularity.

The 1800's featured new dances which were taken from the common people. The *galop* and the *polka* were of Czech origin, and the *mazurka* was Polish. Early in the 1800's, there developed dances for couples. One of these was the *quadrille*. It was like the old English square dances and was popular for over a hundred years.

The 1900's have seen a great change in ballroom dancing. The young people found the waltz tiresome. They turned to the group dances, to the dances of the North American Creole or Negro, or to the dances of the South American countries.

The Brazilian *maxixe* in 1890 broke up the waltz pattern of turns and glides. The Negro influence showed in new rhythms which took the world by storm. In 1900 people danced the *one-step* and the *turkey trot*. The *cakewalk* (ancestor of *swing* music) was followed by the *fox trot*, the *shimmy*, the *Charleston*, and the *black bottom*.

Latin America contributed the Cuban *habanera*. The Argentines turned the habanera into a new dance, the *tango*. This gained wide popularity before World War I. After it came the *paso doble*, the *rhumba*, and the *conga*. These gave way to the *mambo, cha cha,* and *merengue*.

DANCING

High School Students Enjoyed Dancing the "Big Apple," a dance which was very popular in America in the 1930's.

The ballroom dance reached its highest point of violence and frenzy as the *jitterbugs* danced to *swing* music. Some jitterbug boys would even swing their girl partners over their heads. *Rock 'n' roll* dancing replaced jitterbugging during the 1950's and 1960's. The "Twist" became a big favorite of the rock 'n' rollers.

In the United States, clubs have sprung up which teach the folk dances of all nations. People from other lands try to keep alive the traditions of their homelands. One of the first traditions is the dance. The airplane and international education have brought us closer to other countries. Learning the dances of other peoples is one way of learning more about them.

Stage Dancing

The dance became clearly divided into two types. In the 1600's, one type was the dance as a social enjoyment. The other was the dance as a show, with performers dancing for an audience.

Ballet reached its first artistic peak under Louis XIV of France. Ballets were given as early as the late Middle Ages, and this kind of dancing flourished in Italy in the 1500's. Louis XIV, who ruled from 1643 to 1715, was the leading dancer of the realm. He was seriously interested in the dance as an art, and spent a great deal of money on elaborate ballets. Besides this, he started the Royal Academy of Dance and Music. During Louis' reign, ballet became more alive and expressive. It borrowed many steps from the ballroom dances.

Women came onto the stage in the early 1700's. Mlle. Camargo was the first to use a short skirt for the ballet. This was to show her footwork better. She was also the first woman dancer to use certain jumps— among them the *entrechat*. Another ballerina, Mlle. Sallé, invented her own movements.

One of the greatest names of the period in ballet is Jean-Georges Noverre (1727-1810). He put new life in the dance. His first dramatic ballet was produced in 1761. Another great ballet dancer was Gaetano Vestris. He was called the king of dancers because of his skill.

In the 1800's, Salvatore Vigano originated the romantic ballet. Another new idea was toe dancing. Marie Taglioni was one of the first to perform on her toes. Fanny Elssler made popular the folk dances of Spain and other countries.

Russia has taken a great place in the ballet. Anna Pavlova and Vaslav Nijinsky, who performed in the early 1900's, represent ballet at its best. Pavlova will always be remembered for her dance *The Swan*, and Nijinsky for his *Spectre de la Rose*, *The Afternoon of a Faun*, and *Petrouchka*. See BALLET.

Exhibition Dancing is another kind of theater dance. There are many types of exhibition dances. Among them are the *acrobatic* and *adagio* dances, and the dances taken from the Orient and Spain. The Negro minstrel made America's greatest contribution to the exhibition dance. In the middle of the 1800's, "Jim Crow" Rice started the rage for a song and dance number called *Jim Crow*. Other early American dances were the *essence*, performed in soft shoes, and the *clog*, danced in wooden shoes. *Hand dancing*, introduced by Eddie Foy, was a great novelty. And the expert tapping of the *cane dance* began with Eddie Horan.

All these types of dancing, including the *soft shoe*, *buck and wing*, *sand*, *stair*, and *pedestal* dancing, were the beginning of a great tradition, from Ed Christy to George M. Cohan and such masters of tap dancing as Bill Robinson, Paul Draper, Fred Astaire, and Gene Kelly. Tap dancers wear metal taps on their shoes to make the unusual rhythms clearly heard. Astaire and Kelly put ballet steps into their tap dancing.

Exhibition ballroom dancing became famous with

The Jitterbug Dance Was Popular in the 1940's.

21

DANCING

Ballet Dancers Perform in *Princess Aurora*. *Hurok*

Irene and Vernon Castle, who originated the *Castle walk*. The Castles danced all over the United States and in Europe in the *cakewalk*, *one-step*, *fox trot*, and *tango*.

Some colorful dances of other countries have been used on the stage. The Russian *Cossack* dances, the Hawaiian *hula*, and the Spanish *flamenco* are popular.

Modern Dance

The 1900's brought new life and new forms to the dance. This new life started with the ideas of Isadora Duncan. She was tired of artificial forms, and fought for a simple and natural dance. She was inspired by the art of ancient Greece, and she preached the natural use of the body clothed in easy flowing garments. Her feet were bare as she danced. There was no scenery on the stage to draw attention from the dancing body. The entire Western world felt Isadora Duncan's influence on the dance.

Much has been done with the modern dance since the time of Isadora Duncan. Now the entire body is used to express anything that can be danced. The dance comes from within the performer. He follows no set patterns, but creates his own movements and style according to the idea for the dance. The themes of the modern dance are taken from the ups and downs of real life in its tragic as well as its humorous aspects.

The first great "modern dancer" was Mary Wigman. She used the new and different ideas of Rudolf von Laban of Germany, and founded her own school. Soon dancers from the Von Laban and Wigman schools were performing throughout Europe.

At the time of Isadora Duncan, there was also a famous new dancer in America. This was Ruth St. Denis, who turned to the Oriental countries for her inspiration. She, too, looked to the deeper realities of life. In her case these deeper realities were of a religious nature. She won fame during a two-year tour in Germany. Afterward, she and her husband, Ted Shawn, opened the Denishawn school of dancing in America.

But Denishawn students struck out on their own lines after leaving the school. This happened almost ten years later than the European movement which changed Isadora Duncan's dance. The three leaders of the revolt were Martha Graham, Doris Humphrey, and Charles Weidman. They dropped the elaborate staging and developed the dance as a personal and simple art.

Hanya Holm brought the ideas of Mary Wigman to America. She opened a school in New York in 1931, thus bringing together the American and German dance.

The modern dance reached its peak in America toward the end of the 1930's. Martha Graham, Doris Humphrey, Charles Weidman, and Hanya Holm danced, composed, taught, and traveled. In a very short time they spread the new dance across the country.

The modern dance has influenced other kinds of dancing too. Michel Fokine was greatly impressed after seeing Isadora Duncan in Russia. As a result, he brought many fresh ideas into ballet. Musical comedy, also, has borrowed much from the modern dance. The modern dance has also become a favorite with persons from all walks of life who dance for their own pleasure.

Oriental Dance

The Middle East gave full importance to song and dance. But there the dance was usually concerned with religion or ceremony. Ancient Semitic shepherds had their shepherd dances. Semitic farmers had special dances for the wheat harvest and for the grape harvest.

The Bible often mentions dancing. The Hebrew of the Old Testament danced at festivals. During the fall

George Gatts

Exhibition Ballroom Dancing and Ballet. Veloz and Yolanda, a team of exhibition ballroom dancers, were especially noted for their performances of Latin-American dance forms.

festival, men in Jerusalem tossed burning torches into the air and caught them while dancing. David in the Bible whirled and skipped before the Ark of the Covenant. The women danced when he returned after slaying Goliath. After the Jews passed through the Red Sea, Miriam and the maidens danced in chorus, with singing and beating of the timbrel. Hebrew dancing expressed happiness, for we read in the Bible of "a time to mourn and a time to dance."

The Arabs had a great many dances. Some are closely related to Hebrew dances. One of the early Arab dances is like the sword dance of the bride described in the Hebrew "Song of Songs." In the Arab world we find the religious sect of the whirling dervish. The dervishes twisted and turned to imitate the movements of the planets. Their movements called for aid from the good stars and appeased the evil stars.

The Persians had a classic dance which had seven basic steps which were supposed to be related to the planets. In Persia as in Arabia we find the religious cult of the whirling dervishes. But Persia was best known for its muscle dances. In these the dancer showed perfect control of muscles which many people hardly used at all. Ancient Persian records show that dancers traveled with the armies in 300 B.C.

Arabia and Persia both enjoyed acrobatic dancing. The juggler, the contortionist, and rope and acrobatic dancers amazed the crowds at bazaars and private par-

DANCING

Dance Magazine
Fred Astaire, a world-famous tap dancer, added ballet movements to his dance steps.

Hanya Holm Co.
The Dance May Be a Personal and Simple Art.

ties. Most of the dances were done by young men, sometimes in women's costumes. They clacked castanets and jingled tambourines to add sparkle to the dance.

The Far East is best known for its gesture dances, which were perfected thousands of years ago in India. In these dances, every gesture, every movement, has a meaning. The dancer can tell a wonderful story merely by placing certain parts of his body in certain positions. Only by hard work could a student learn the language of gesture. Dancing in India is not for entertainment. It has a higher purpose. Dance is supposed to be a gift of the god Siva. Every dance contains a prayer. The dance may be dramatic or it may be humorous. But its movements tell the legends of the Hindu gods and heroes. Every audience understands the complicated language of the dance. The *Nautch* dance, a survival of old Indian culture, is part of all festivities.

As the Hindu religion spread, so did the mythical legends and dances of the Hindus. From India the dances traveled to Thailand, Indonesia, Cambodia, and Burma. In each country they took on the special characteristics of the people.

Tibet is a part of China, but its dances came from India, rather than China. We know that some dances of the Tibetan monasteries have not changed since about A.D. 900. The best known of these is the Tibetan Black Hat Devil Dance. Another dance is like a play. Monks act the parts (see MASK [picture, Monks of Tibet]).

China's ceremonial dances are as old as the country's history. The Chinese dances of today can be traced directly back to six ancient dances of the Chou dynasty (1027-256 B.C.). These were the *split-feather* dance, to drive away evil spirits; the *whole-feather*, used in worship; the *regulating* dance, to drive away ill winds; the *tail* dance, featuring an ox's tail, the symbol of agriculture; the *shield* dance, showing a defensive battle attitude; and the *battle-ax* dance, showing preparedness to strike if necessary. To these was added a seventh, the *humanity* dance. Here battle-axes, whole feathers, and oxtails were used merely as ornaments. The purpose of the dance was acted out by gestures. Chinese dancing takes place at funerals, sacrifices, and big festivals.

The Chinese theater was well begun in the 700's. Performances combined dancing, singing, and acting. There was no scenery or special lighting. The only attempt at realism was in the elaborate costumes. The audience was not the people, but the emperor and the priests. Performances, then as now, lasted for hours. The greatest name from this art is that of Mei Lan-fang.

DANCING

Among the Chinese, acrobatic dancing holds a high place. One of the reasons military plays are so popular is that they feature very fine acrobatic dancing.

Japan's people built their first dances around religion. They were greatly influenced by China. The stern but popular *Nō* plays were based on dancelike movements and gestures. The first Nō plays were written in the 1300's by a father and son, Kan-ami and Zeami. The dramas followed definite forms. A chorus would chant the story while the actors, wearing masks, danced and used pantomime. Simple gestures often were used to convey complicated meanings. Most Nō plays were short, and several were given on the same program. Often a brief dance-drama called a *kyogen* was presented between the Nō plays. These types of dramas have been passed down from father to son for many generations. In the last 600 years, the actors have been descendants of the original actors.

In the 1600's a new and livelier form of dance-drama arose in Japan. This was the *Kabuki*. The Kabuki took many movements and gestures from the older Nō dramas. Kabuki plays often lasted from morning to night, in contrast to the shorter Nō dramas.

Another old dance still appears on very special occasions. This is the *Bugaku*, an ancient court dance.

Japan has its popular dances, too. Among the favorite folk dances are the *Bon and Catfish*, the religious *Kagura*, and the lion-mask dances. The people also have country dances, such as the beautiful cherry blossom dances. Much of the dancing is done by lovely geisha girls.

Careers in Dancing

Dancing is a highly competitive field with limited opportunities. There are many more dancers seeking positions than there are positions available for them. Only the most capable reach the top.

Requirements. A person who wishes to be a dancer must be physically strong. In addition to great talent, he must have charm, grace, and physical attractiveness. He must love to dance so much that he will be able to continue his career in spite of many obstacles.

Training for a career in dancing begins at an early age. Some children start dancing lessons when they are as young as seven or eight. Almost all dancing, except ballroom, requires a knowledge of ballet. Students spend many hours practicing basic ballet movements and exercises. After years of technical training, a student is ready to enter a professional dance school or to study professionally with a private teacher. A dancer never really finishes his training. He must continue to take lessons and practice throughout his career. Dancers who wish to teach in a high school or college must have a bachelor's or master's degree.

Working Conditions. Successful dancers may achieve great fame and wealth. They travel throughout the world and meet famous and interesting people. But anyone entering the field must be prepared to spend long hours looking for openings, to accept part-time positions in related fields, and to face many hardships. Many dancers must support themselves by teaching in dance studios or offering private lessons.

Several organizations serve dancers in various fields. Ballet dancers belong to the American Guild of Musical Artists; dancers in Broadway plays belong to Chorus Equity; and television performers belong to the American Federation of Television and Radio Artists. These organizations assure minimum wages and notify members of job openings.

Dancers find the most opportunities in the entertainment centers of New York City and Los Angeles, and in other large cities such as Chicago, Detroit, Boston, Philadelphia, and San Francisco. HANYA HOLM

Related Articles. See BALLET with its list of Related Articles. Other related articles in WORLD BOOK include:

BIOGRAPHIES

Astaire, Fred	Graham, Martha	Saint Denis, Ruth
Castle (family)	Greco, José	Shawn, "Ted,"
Duncan, Isadora	Robinson, Bill	Edwin M.

KINDS OF DANCES

Allemande	Folk Dancing	Schottische
Bolero	Fox Trot	Square Dance
Charleston	Gigue	Tango
Conga	Hornpipe	Tarantella
Cotillion	Minuet	Two-Step
Flamenco	Rhumba	Waltz

PICTURES OF DANCERS

The following articles have pictures of dancers.

Australia	Oklahoma
Bolivia	Pacific Islands
India	Philippines
Indian, American	Pygmy
Ireland	Spain
Jews	Thailand
Lithuania	Zapotec Indians
North Carolina	

UNCLASSIFIED

Buffalo Ceremonials	Mask
Castanets	Pantomime
Choreographer	Rain Dance
Japanese Literature (Drama)	Rhythm

Outline

I. **Primitive Dance**
II. **Development of the Dance**
   A. Egypt
   B. Greek Dancing
   C. Romans
   D. The Middle Ages
   E. The Renaissance
   F. During the 1600's
   G. The 1700's
   H. The 1800's
   I. The 1900's
III. **Stage Dancing**
   A. Ballet
   B. Exhibition Dancing
IV. **Modern Dance**
V. **Oriental Dance**
   A. The Middle East
   B. The Bible
   C. The Arabs
   D. The Persians
   E. The Far East
VI. **Careers in Dancing**

Questions

Why were dancers in the New Hebrides sometimes shot?

What dances are the ancestors of the modern *jitterbugging* or *swing*?

What character in the Bible danced before the Ark of the Covenant?

What new ideas and forms did Isadora Duncan introduce to the dance?

What people imitated the movements of the planets in their dances?

What people dance at funerals?

In what country do monks still dance?

What people danced while flinging burning torches into the air?

What is the name of the famous ballet dance for which Pavlova is remembered?

DANDELION, *DAN dee LY un,* is a bright-yellow wild flower that grows in lawns and meadows. Throughout the temperate regions of the world, gardeners usually consider it a troublesome weed, difficult to control.

The early colonists brought the dandelion to America from Europe. Its name comes from the French words *dent de lion,* meaning lion's tooth. It has smooth leaves with coarse notches, which look like teeth. The golden-yellow head is really a cluster of flowers. The dandelion has a smooth, straight, and hollow stem, and the entire plant contains a white, milky juice. The root is long, thick, and pointed, with hairlike root branches growing from it. The dandelion differs from most other plants in the manner in which it reproduces. Its ovaries form fertile seeds without having to be pollinated (see POLLEN AND POLLINATION).

Young dandelion leaves can be used in salads or they can be cooked. They taste best when they are young, before the plant has blossomed. Wine sometimes is made from the flowers.

John H. Gerard
The Long Dandelion Root is called a *taproot.* Small *branch* roots grow out from its sides.

In order to keep dandelion plants from growing on lawns, gardeners must cut deep into their roots. The roots often grow more than three feet long in soft, rich earth. Slicing close under the surface only encourages the plants to grow. Gardeners sometimes spray dandelions with a chemical called 2,4-D (dichlorophenoxyacetic acid). This chemical destroys the dandelions, but it does not harm grass.

Scientific Classification. The dandelion is a member of the family *Compositae.* The common dandelion is genus *Taraxacum,* species *officinale.* ARTHUR CRONQUIST

See also FLOWER (color picture, Bright Yellow Dandelions).

DANDIE DINMONT TERRIER is a dog that got its name from a book. In Sir Walter Scott's novel, *Guy Mannering,* a farmer named Dandie Dinmont raised an unusual pack of terriers that were all the color of either pepper or mustard. In the book, the dogs were famous as hunters of foxes, badgers, and otters. A new breed was later called Dandie Dinmont for the farmer in the book. This terrier has a big head and large, soft brown eyes. Its forehead is covered by a topknot, and its ears hang low. It has a crisp, shaggy coat. The Dandie has a long slim body, and weighs about 20 pounds. Because its hind legs are longer than its front legs, it seems tipped up from behind. JOSEPHINE Z. RINE

See also DOG (color picture, Terriers).

DANDRUFF is made up of flakes of skin thrown off by the scalp. The flakes are mixed with grease from the oil glands. Some scaling of the skin of the scalp is normal. But when the scalp loses many scales, the product is called *dandruff.* Some dandruff can be prevented by proper washing, brushing, and occasional oiling of the hair and scalp. Dandruff does not cause baldness.

Some cases of dandruff result from a disease called *seborrhea,* which many authorities consider a bacterial disease. In seborrhea, the scalp itches and is red, and the dandruff is more greasy than usual. Keeping the hair and scalp clean helps to prevent seborrhea, but it is wise to see a doctor for treatment. LEON H. WARREN

See also HAIR.

DANE. See DENMARK; ENGLAND (History).

DANEGELD, meaning *Dane money,* was a land tax levied in England in the 900's and 1000's. Danish raiders often attacked England, and the king raised the first danegeld in 991 to buy them off. Later kings also used the tax to hire soldiers and improve the fleet.

DANELAW. See ALFRED THE GREAT.

DANFORTH FOUNDATION offers graduate fellowships for college chaplains, college teachers, and college senior men preparing for college teaching. The foundation, set up by Mr. and Mrs. William H. Danforth, was incorporated in Missouri in 1927. Its offices are at 835 S. Eighth Street, St. Louis 2, Mo. For assets, see FOUNDATIONS (table).

DANIEL is a well-known Biblical character. The Book of Daniel, chapter I, dramatically tells the story of his rise from the position of captive slave in the royal palace to that of a trusted adviser to the king.

Some scholars believe that the book was written about 165 B.C. Others believe that it was written earlier. Its purpose was to encourage persecuted Jews in their desperate struggle against the oppression of Antiochus IV, King of Syria from 176 to 164 B.C.

Nebuchadnezzar, King of Babylon, captured a group of people from Jerusalem in about the year 600 B.C., among them several young people of royal descent. Daniel was one of these. The captives were well fed, but Daniel refused to eat the food, which by Jewish law

The Dandelion Blossoms open in the morning and close in the evening. The flowers, when they ripen, form feathered, cottony seeds which the wind carries far and wide.
J. Horace McFarland

25

Daniel Was Thrown into the Lions' Den for Breaking a Babylonian Law, but the Lions Did Not Harm Him. *Culver*

was impure. Instead he ate a simple diet of cereal. This attracted the king's attention. Daniel won favor when he interpreted a dream that had puzzled the wise men. The king made him ruler of Babylon.

The Bible also tells how Daniel foretold the madness of Nebuchadnezzar, how he remained safe when thrown into a den of lions, and how he told Belshazzar the meaning of the mysterious handwriting on the wall (see HANDWRITING ON THE WALL).

The last part of the Book of Daniel tells of the eventual triumph of right and of truth, and predicts the destruction of evil. WALTER G. WILLIAMS

See also BELSHAZZAR; NEBUCHADNEZZAR.

DANIEL, PRICE. See TEXAS (Famous Texans).

DANIELL CELL. See BATTERY (Closed-Circuit Cells).

DANIELS is the family name of two American editors and statesmen, father and son.

Josephus Daniels (1862-1948), the father, served as Secretary of the Navy from 1913 to 1921, and as ambassador to Mexico from 1933 to 1942. Daniels was born at Washington, N.C., and was educated at the University of North Carolina. He entered newspaper work in Wilson, N.C. Daniels consolidated the *State Chronicle* and the *North Carolinian* in 1894 to form the Raleigh *News and Observer*, which he edited until his death. ALVIN E. AUSTIN

Jonathan Worth Daniels (1902-   ), the son, first became known for *A Southerner Discovers the South* (1938). He later wrote *The Man of Independence* (1950), a biography of Harry S. Truman. *The End of Innocence* (1954) tells of Washington, D.C., during World War I. Daniels was born in Raleigh, N.C. He became editor of the Raleigh *News and Observer* in 1948. CARL NIEMEYER

DANILOVA, *dahn EE loh vuh,* **ALEXANDRA** (1904-   ), a Russian-born ballet dancer, was prima ballerina of the Ballet Russe de Monte Carlo from 1938 to 1952. She danced with Sergei Diaghilev's Ballets Russes from 1925 to 1929. Danilova was born in Peterhof (now Petrodvorets), Russia. DORATHI BOCK PIERRE

DANISH WEST INDIES was the name of the Virgin Islands in the Caribbean Sea when they were ruled by Denmark. See VIRGIN ISLANDS (History).

D'ANNUNZIO, *duh NOON tsih oh,* **GABRIELE** (1863-1938), PRINCE OF MONTE NEVOSO, was an Italian novelist, dramatist, and poet. He was also a political leader who promoted Italian patriotism. D'Annunzio led an Italian force that seized the Austrian seaport of Fiume (now Rijeka) for Italy in 1919 (see RIJEKA).

D'Annunzio was born in the province of Pescara, in southern Italy. His love affair with actress Eleonora Duse created a scandal when he wrote about it in a frank novel, *The Flame*, published in 1900 (see DUSE, ELEONORA). He also wrote many romantic plays, including *La Gioconda* and *The Dead City*. JOHN W. GASSNER

DANTE ALIGHIERI, *DAN tee,* or *DAHN tay, AH lee GYAY ree* (1265-1321), was perhaps the greatest poet of the Middle Ages. His love for the beautiful girl, Beatrice Portinari, inspired his best writings (see BEATRICE PORTINARI). His outstanding works are his *New Life* and the *Divine Comedy* (see DIVINE COMEDY).

The *New Life*, in poetry and prose, tells of Dante's spiritual attachment to Beatrice. A saintly conception of Beatrice again inspired his greatest work, the *Divine Comedy*, a magnificent allegorical poem.

Dante Alighieri
Brown Bros.

26

This poem tells of man's struggle through hell and purgatory, where the Roman poet Virgil is his guide, and of his search for God in Paradise, where Beatrice is his guide.

Dante is often called the father of Italian literature, because of his clear, simple style of writing, and polished, poetic use of the Italian language. Chaucer and Milton imitated him, but he has been regarded as one of the world's greatest poets only since the 1800's. At that time the Romantic writers Schlegel, Shelley, Carlyle, Hugo, and Longfellow recognized his importance and praised his fine poetic imagination, his perfect style, and his sincere poetic character. Dante also wrote books in Latin, one of which is *On Monarchy*, a book that advocates a separation of the church and state.

Dante was born in Florence, Italy. His parents died when he was young, and a statesman, Brunetto Latini, supervised his education. Many scholars think that Dante studied philosophy at Bologna and Padua, and theology at Paris. As a young man he served in the Florentine army. After Beatrice's death in 1292, he married Gemma Donati. Shortly after his marriage, he entered politics and became a Guelph (see GUELPHS AND GHIBELLINES). He held high office in Florence, but a hostile faction exiled him in 1302. WERNER P. FRIEDERICH

Dante Visited Hell, Purgatory, and Heaven in his poem, *The Divine Comedy*. This etching by Gustave Doré shows Dante being led by Virgil, the Roman poet.

DANTON, *DAHN TAWN*, **GEORGES JACQUES** (1759-1794), was a great leader of the French Revolution. His policy was "boldness, and more boldness, and ever more boldness, and France is saved!" He perhaps did more to create and defend the French Republic than any other person. Danton was partly responsible for the massacres of the Reign of Terror, which he considered necessary for the safety of his country. When he believed that safety was assured, he advocated more humane policies. He wished to restore, rather than to destroy,

DANUBE RIVER

the normal life of France.

Danton was born at Arcis-sur-Aube, of middle-class parents. At the beginning of the revolution he was a successful lawyer in Paris, and a leader of the Cordeliers Club, one of the militant factions of the extreme Republicans. This group favored ridding France of the monarchy. They achieved their purpose on Aug. 10, 1792, when they forced the legislative assembly to imprison Louis XVI. Danton, who is referred to as "the Man of August 10th" because of his leadership in this movement, became minister of justice.

Georges J. Danton

Danton and his associates, Camille Desmoulins, Maximilien Robespierre, and Jean Paul Marat, established the national convention of revolutionary leaders and the revolutionary tribunal. These two bodies ruled France for the next three years. Almost anyone could be brought before the jury of the tribunal. Their victims were not only traitors, but also persons suspected of being too mild in their political views. Danton and Desmoulins soon recognized the need for stamping out this violence. They felt that the convention should relax its policy and prepare a workable republican constitution for an orderly government. Danton suggested halting the violence.

Robespierre was jealous of Danton's success. He ordered Danton arrested for disloyalty, and brought before the tribunal. Danton's fiery and eloquent denunciation alarmed the members, who feared loss of their power. He was condemned and executed. His execution climaxed the Reign of Terror. ANDRÉ MAUROIS

See also FRENCH REVOLUTION; MARAT, JEAN PAUL; ROBESPIERRE.

DANUBE RIVER is one of the great waterways of Europe. The Danube drains nearly one-tenth the area of the whole of Europe. The river basin covers 315,000 square miles, and includes southern Germany, Austria, Hungary, Yugoslavia, Bulgaria, Romania, and part of Czechoslovakia.

The Danube is formed by two small mountain streams which join in the Black Forest near Donaueschingen, Germany. The river runs east and south, winding for 1,725 miles to its mouth in the Black Sea. In length, the Danube is second only to the Volga among the rivers of Europe. See EUROPE (color map).

The Danube has been deepened by canals and channels to make it the chief water route for the commerce of central Europe. A canal makes it possible for boats to travel through the Iron Gate, a gorge with rapids where the Danube breaks through the Transylvanian Alps in Romania. At Ulm, the head of navigation in Bavaria, the Danube is connected to the Rhine River by the Ludwig Canal. Large cities located on the Danube River include Vienna, Budapest, and Belgrade.

The "beautiful blue Danube" is famous in song and history. Roman colonies were established in the valley

27

The Danube River flows through fertile valleys, dotted with ancient castles and terraced vineyards. The Huns, Magyars, and Turks led their armies into Europe through the picturesque, winding valley of this historic river.

Leon, Pix

of the Danube. The Huns, Magyars, and Turks made their conquests through this valley, and the river is sometimes called *a highway of races*. JAMES K. POLLOCK

See also RIVER (picture, Longest Rivers).

DANZIG, *DAN sig*, or, in Polish, GDANSK, *g'DAHN y'sk* (pop. 286,000; met. area, 500,000; alt. 49 ft.), is a port four miles from the Baltic Sea. It lies on the Vistula River, Poland's most important waterway. Its location has made the city one of the leading ports of central Europe. For location, see POLAND (color map).

Description. Danzig is rich in historical buildings of many styles. One of the best known is the Church of Saint Mary's, or *Marienkirche*, originally built in the 1300's. Another noted building is the town hall.

Industry and Trade. Airlines, railroads, and waterways connect Danzig with the beet-sugar, grain, and timber districts of Germany, Poland, and Russia. Coal is an important export. The city has large distilleries, flour mills, shipyards, steel mills, and sugar refineries. After World War I, the Poles built a port called *Gdynia* eight miles west of Danzig. It took much of Danzig's shipping and trade.

History. The Slavs founded Danzig in the 900's. It became a rich trading center of the German Hanseatic League during the Middle Ages (see HANSEATIC LEAGUE). It became a vassal city of the Polish king in 1466, but had complete self-government. When Russia and Prussia divided Poland late in the 1700's, Danzig fell into Prussian hands.

The Free City of Danzig was set up after World War I. It covered 754 square miles and had a population of 415,000. Poland controlled the railroads and the collection of customs duties. Danzig had its own assembly, and was supervised by a commissioner representing the League of Nations (see POLISH CORRIDOR). In 1939, the Germans demanded that Danzig be united with Germany, but Poland refused. Germany invaded Po-

Eastfoto

The Danzig Shipyard is the site of many ship launchings. The 10,700-ton *Marceli Nowotko* slides into the water at a launching in 1955. It was the first ship of its size to be built in a Polish shipyard.

land in 1939, and Danzig fell into German hands. Bombs seriously damaged Danzig during World War II. The Germans held Danzig until the end of the war, when the city became part of Poland. Most of the city has been rebuilt. M. KAMIL DZIEWANOWSKI

DAPHNE, *DAF nee*, was the daughter of the river-god Peneus in Greek mythology. She wanted to be a huntress and to remain unmarried like her patron, Artemis (see DIANA). Eros (Cupid) shot her with a leaden arrow to keep her from loving anyone. But at the same time he wounded Apollo with a golden arrow to make him love Daphne (see APOLLO). Apollo pursued Daphne everywhere. One day, when he was about to catch her, Daphne called on her father to protect her from her handsome lover. He changed her into a laurel tree. Apollo then made the laurel his sacred tree, and wore a wreath of laurel leaves for his crown. The laurel wreath has been a symbol of honor since that time. PADRAIC COLUM

Alinari

Daphne and Apollo, a statue by Giovanni Bernini, is in the Villa Borghese, Rome.

DAPHNIA. See WATER FLEA.

DAR. See DAUGHTERS OF THE AMERICAN REVOLUTION, NATIONAL SOCIETY OF.

DAR ES SALAAM, *DAHR ehs suh LAHM* (pop. 128,742; alt. 25 ft.), is the capital of Tanganyika and one of the most important ports in eastern Africa. The city lies on a long, landlocked harbor about 40 miles southwest of Zanzibar. A railroad connects it with the interior. British forces captured Dar es Salaam during World War I. See also TANGANYIKA. HIBBERD V. B. KLINE, JR.

DARAZI. See DRUSES.

DARDANELLES, *DAHR d'n ELZ*, is a strait which joins the Aegean Sea with the Sea of Marmara. The strait is part of a waterway which leads from the landlocked Black Sea to the Mediterranean. Also part of this waterway is the Bosporus, a second strait which joins the Black Sea and the Sea of Marmara.

The word *Dardanelles* comes from the ancient Greek city of Dardanus, on Asia's side of the strait. The ancient Greeks called this strait the *Hellespont*.

At its narrowest point, the Dardanelles is about one mile wide from the European shore to the Asiatic. The average width of the strait is 3 to 4 miles. It is about 37 miles long, and the average depth is 200 feet. The Dardanelles usually has a strong surface current in the direction of the Aegean Sea, but a powerful undercurrent flows east and carries salty water through the Sea of Marmara and the Bosporus into the Black Sea. This undercurrent keeps the Black Sea from becoming a fresh-water body.

As early as 481 B.C., Xerxes led an army across the Dardanelles near Abydos and invaded Europe. In 334 B.C., Alexander led his army over a bridge of boats across the Dardanelles into Asia. Hundreds of years later, the strait was important to the defense of the Byzantine Empire. After that empire fell, the Ottoman Turks ruled the Dardanelles. See BYZANTINE EMPIRE.

The Dardanelles Lies Between Europe and Asia.

In 1841, the great powers of Europe—Great Britain, France, Prussia, and Austria—agreed to give Turkey control of the passage of ships through the Dardanelles. This agreement was renewed in 1856 and again in 1871 and 1878. The Treaty of Lausanne in 1923 opened the Dardanelles to all nations. In 1936, the Montreux convention gave Turkey permission to remilitarize the strait. Early in World War II, the strait was closed to all ships except those with special permission from Turkey. Although the possession of the Dardanelles was threatened during the war, Turkey kept control of this important waterway. After World War II, Russia unsuccessfully attempted to gain control of the Dardanelles. The Western Powers supported Turkey's rights to the strategic strait. ROBERT O. REID

Related Articles in WORLD BOOK include:
Aegean Sea	Hellespont	Marmara, Sea of
Black Sea	Lausanne,	Turkey
Bosporus	Treaty of	

DARE, VIRGINIA (1587- ?), was the first English child born in America. Her parents were members of a band of 150 colonists sent by Sir Walter Raleigh in 1587 to establish a colony on Chesapeake Bay. They settled on Roanoke Island (now in North Carolina). Virginia Dare was the daughter of Ananias Dare and Ellinor White. She was born on August 18, and was named Virginia in what is believed to have been the first English christening ceremony in America. See also LOST COLONY. J. CARLYLE SITTERSON

The Baptism of Virginia Dare, in 1587, is believed to have been the first English christening in America.

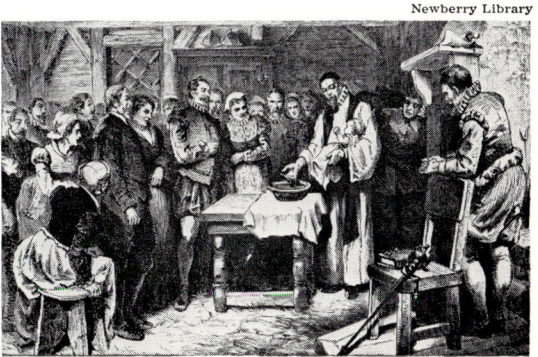

Newberry Library

DARIEN

DARIEN, *DAIR ih EHN,* is the name of a gulf of the Caribbean Sea on the north coast of South America, between Colombia and Panama. A small inlet at the southern end of the gulf is called the *Gulf of Urabá.* The province of Panama that lies along the border of Colombia is also called *Darien.* The name formerly was given to the area now known as the Isthmus of Panama. See also PANAMA, ISTHMUS OF. BOSTWICK H. KETCHUM

DARÍO, *dah REE oh,* **RUBÉN** (1867-1916), was the pen name of Félix Rubén García-Sarmiento. He was one of the greatest Latin-American poets.

Blue (1888), a collection of stories and poems, earned him a high reputation in Latin America and Spain. Its new developments in prose and poetry are due mostly to French influence. *Profane Prose* (1896) established him as one of the most skillful Spanish-language poets, and as leader of the literary movement known as *Modernism. Songs of Life and Hope* (1905) showed a new vigor, a pride in race and in Latin America. *Song to Argentina* (1910), his longest single poem, pictures that country's past achievements and promising future. Darío was born in Metapa, Nicaragua. He served as Nicaraguan consul in Paris, and as Nicaraguan minister to Brazil and Spain. HARVEY L. JOHNSON

DARIUS, *duh RI us,* was the name of three kings of ancient Persia (now Iran).

Darius I (558?-486 B.C.) was one of the most distinguished of eastern rulers. A record of his early achievements is carved in cuneiform writing on a high cliff known as Behistun Rock, in western Persia (see CUNEIFORM). Darius became king in 521 B.C. He put down widespread revolts, and, later, conducted military campaigns in Armenia, east of the Caspian Sea, and in northwestern India. He is credited with organizing the Persian Empire into efficient administrative units called *satrapies.* He also reorganized the tax system, and encouraged trade with other countries. His army invaded Greece after conflicts with Greeks in Asia Minor and a campaign against the Scythians in Europe. It was defeated at Marathon in 490 B.C. (see MARATHON). Darius I died while preparing for a new attack on Greece. His son, Xerxes, succeeded him to the throne.

Darius II ruled the Persian Empire from 424 to 404 B.C. Chaos and revolt struck the empire during his weak reign.

Darius III, the last king of Persia, ruled from 336 to 330 B.C. He inherited a corrupt empire that was about to collapse. Alexander became king of Macedon in 336, and swept through western Asia in a great attack on Persia. Darius III was defeated at Issus in 333 B.C., and was crushed two years later at Gaugemela, near Arbela. He fled to his eastern provinces, and was murdered by his own men. E. A. SPEISER

See also ALEXANDER THE GREAT; IRAN (History).

DARIUS GREEN AND HIS FLYING MACHINE. See TROWBRIDGE, JOHN T.

DARJEELING, *dahr JEE ling* (pop. 33,605), is the summer capital of the state of West Bengal in eastern India. It lies on the lower slopes of the Himalayas, north of Calcutta. The city stands about 7,100 feet above sea level. The high altitude makes the city cool and pleasant the year round. Persons who live in the Indian lowlands seek relief from the heat by going up to Darjeeling in September and October. The peaks of Kanchenjunga and Mount Everest can be seen from the city. The well-known Darjeeling tea grows on hillsides around the city. A railroad climbs to the city through tea plantations and forests of teakwood. Darjeeling's wide square serves as an open-air bazaar where tribesmen do their trading. ROBERT I. CRANE

DARK AGES is a term once used to mean the same thing as Middle Ages. We now know that much of the Dark Ages was dark only to historians writing in the

The Court of King Darius is shown on a carved stone panel that stands in the entrance of the Treasury building in Persepolis, Iran. The monarch is seated on the throne and his son Xerxes stands behind him, with members of his court.

Oriental Institute, University of Chicago

Renaissance. We can rightly apply the term only to the period from the 400's to the 1000's. Even then we cannot apply it to the Byzantine Empire (see BYZANTINE EMPIRE), which preserved the important features of Greek and Roman life. Nor can the term *Dark Ages* be applied to the splendid Arab culture which spread over northern Africa and into Spain. But civilization almost completely disappeared in much of western Europe during this period. Only a few places, such as monasteries, preserved Latin learning. Greek learning almost disappeared. Few persons received any schooling.

Authors of the period had little sense of style, and showed great ignorance by accepting popular stories as true. People completely forgot many of the arts and crafts of the ancient world. See MIDDLE AGES.

The desperate poverty which ruined the western provinces of the Roman Empire may well have caused the Dark Ages. When economic conditions improved and trade revived, the flourishing Age of the Crusades followed the Dark Ages. WILLIAM F. McDONALD

DARK AND BLOODY GROUND, a name given to Kentucky because of Indian wars. See KENTUCKY.

DARK CONTINENT. See AFRICA.

DARK STAR is a star which can be seen only by means of scientific instruments. Most of its light is given off by infrared rays (see INFRARED RAYS). Dark stars have surface temperatures of about 1,000° C., which is cooler than the surfaces of the stars we see. Dark stars can be photographed with infrared-sensitive photographic plates. Astronomers also know of a dark star's presence when it is a member of a double star, or *binary,* system. Then they determine the effect of the dark star's gravitational pull on its visible companion. Dark stars were discovered in the 1700's. CHARLES ANTHONY FEDERER, JR.

DARLING, "DING," JAY NORWOOD (1876-1962), was an American cartoonist whose drawings portray national events and human weaknesses. At the height of his career, probably more than a million persons enjoyed his cartoons daily. He won the Pulitzer prize for editorial cartooning in 1924 and in 1943.

Darling became a cartoonist for the *Sioux City Journal* in 1901, and joined the staff of *The Des Moines Register* in 1906. After 1917, his cartoons were syndicated through *The New York Tribune.* He wrote and illustrated *Ding Goes to Russia* (1932). He was interested in wildlife, and served as director of the United States Biological Survey in 1934 and 1935. He also was honorary president of the National Wildlife Federation. Darling was born in Norwood, Mich. DICK SPENCER III

See also GAME (picture).

DARLING, GRACE HORSLEY (1815-1842), became a famous English heroine by helping save nine survivors of a shipwreck. She lived at Longstone Lighthouse on one of the Farne Islands, off the English coast. Her father was keeper of the lighthouse. The steamer *Forfarshire* was wrecked on Sept. 7, 1838. Through a telescope, she saw several persons clinging to a rock. During a storm, she rowed to the rescue with her father. The Humane Society awarded them gold medals. She was born in Bamborough, Northumberland. HELEN E. MARSHALL

DARLING RIVER. See MURRAY RIVER.

DARMSTADT. See HESSE.

DARNEL grows as a weed in grain fields. It is thought to be the *tares* mentioned in the Bible (Matt. 13: 24-30).

DARNLEY, LORD. See MARY, QUEEN OF SCOTS (Her Reign).

DARROW, CLARENCE SEWARD (1857-1938), was a famous American criminal lawyer. He also was one of the first to be called a "labor lawyer." This was because of his enthusiasm in fighting legal battles for organized labor. He became known as the legal champion of the unfortunate and oppressed. Darrow defended Eugene V. Debs in an 1894 labor strike case. One of his best-known trials was the 1925 John T. Scopes case, in which he defended the right to teach evolution in Tennessee schools. Darrow also defended Loeb and Leopold in their 1924 trial for the murder of Bobby Franks. In later years, Darrow toured the country debating social issues with noted opponents. He was born in Kinsman, Ohio, and lived in Chicago where he practiced after 1888. He retired in 1927. Darrow's books include *Crime, Its Cause and Treatment; Resist Not Evil; Eye for an Eye;* and *Farmington.* H. G. REUSCHLEIN

N.Y. Herald Tribune and Des Moines Register
"Why Call Them Sportsmen?" Through his cartoons, "Ding" Darling fought for the conservation of wildlife in America.

Clarence Darrow, *left,* opposed William Jennings Bryan, *right,* during the famous John Scopes trial at Dayton, Tenn., in 1925.
Wide World

DART

DART. See BLOWGUN; DARTS.

DARTER is a name for several kinds of dwarf freshwater fishes of the perch family found in eastern North America. The smallest is the *least darter*, scarcely more than an inch long. The largest, the *log perch*, may reach 8 inches. The breeding males of most darters have brilliant colors. Some are as gaily colored as coral-reef fishes.

The Johnny Darter, like other darter fish, has no air bladder. It has to flap its chest fins to keep afloat in the water.

Their markings are generally metallic green and bright red. The *rainbow darter* is the best known of the species with bright colors. The *Johnny darter* is plainer, but more common. Almost all darters live under and around stones in rapids. Here they catch insects and other small animals. They swim in spurts from one resting place to another.

Scientific Classification. The darter belongs to the family *Percidae*. The least darter is genus *Microperca*, species *microperca*. The log perch is *Percina caprodes*. The rainbow darter is *Poecilichthys caeruleus*. The Johnny darter is *Boleosoma nigrum*. CARL L. HUBBS

DARTER, a large tropical bird, lives in swamps, ponds, and rivers in nearly all the warm regions of the world. The American darter is about 3 feet long, with a long thin neck, small head, and pointed bill. It has glossy black plumage, silvery markings on the back of the neck and wings, and a broad brown-tipped tail. The bill is olive above and yellow below. The feet are olive with yellow webs. The darter feeds on fish and other water life. It is an excellent swimmer and a strong flier. It is sometimes called the *snakebird* because it occasionally swims half submerged, with only its long, snakelike neck visible above the water. The American darter is also called the *water turkey*.

Arthur H. Fisher
The Darter, or Snakebird

Scientific Classification. Darters are members of the family *Anhingidae*. The American darter is classified as genus *Anhinga*, species *anhinga*. ALEXANDER WETMORE

DARTMOOR is a rocky plateau in south Devonshire, England. It covers a wooded area of about 350 square miles. High Willhays (2,039 feet) is the highest point. Dartmoor Prison, scene of the Dartmoor Massacre of 1815, is at Prince Town. In the massacre, the British killed 7 American prisoners of the War of 1812, and wounded 60, as they tried to escape. FRANCIS H. HERRICK

DARTMOUTH, N.S. (pop. 46,966; alt. 13 ft.), lies on the eastern shore of Halifax harbor, opposite Halifax. Its chief industries are oil refining, electronics, wire manufacture, and ship maintenance and repair. A naval arms depot and the Shearwater naval air station are located there. Dartmouth's population increased 50 per cent during the period from 1941 to 1961. The city was founded in 1750, and it was incorporated as a city in 1961. For location, see NOVA SCOTIA (color map). THOMAS H. RADDALL

DARTMOUTH COLLEGE is a privately endowed liberal arts school for men in Hanover, N.H. Associated with it are three professional graduate schools, Dartmouth Medical School, Thayer School of Engineering, and the Amos Tuck School of Business Administration. Courses lead to A.B., B.S., M.A., M.S., and M.B.A. degrees. The college also awards Ph.D. degrees in mathematics and in molecular biology. Baker Library is one of the largest undergraduate college libraries in the United States. It is noted for its Stefansson Arctic collection (see STEFANSSON, VILHJALMUR).

Eleazar Wheelock founded the college as Moor's Indian Charity School about 1750, at Lebanon, Conn. He later expanded the school and moved it to Hanover. In 1819, Daniel Webster, a Dartmouth alumnus, won the Dartmouth College Case before the Supreme Court (see DARTMOUTH COLLEGE CASE). For enrollment, see UNIVERSITIES AND COLLEGES (table). GEORGE O'CONNELL

DARTMOUTH COLLEGE CASE, or DARTMOUTH COLLEGE v. WOODWARD, upheld the constitutional freedom from unreasonable government interference with contracts. The Supreme Court of the United States decided this case in 1819. The decision helped protect the rights of private property and encouraged the development of the free-enterprise system.

In 1769, King George III of Great Britain granted Dartmouth College a charter as a private school. This charter was to last "forever." The various states succeeded to the rights and obligations of such charters when they became independent. But in 1816, New Hampshire tried to make Dartmouth College the state university by canceling the charter. Former trustees of the college claimed that the royal charter was still valid. They brought suit to recover the school seal and records from William H. Woodward, the college secretary. Daniel Webster, a graduate of Dartmouth, presented the trustees' case before the Supreme Court in one of his greatest arguments. The court held for the trustees. It ruled that the state had "impaired the obligation" of the charter in violation of Article I, Section 10 of the Constitution. Because of this case, legislatures today put time limitations in charters or include provisions allowing cancellation by the government under proper circumstances. JERRE S. WILLIAMS

DARTS is a game of skill in which players try to hit the *bull's-eye* (center of a target) by throwing darts. A *dart* is a small arrowlike object with stiff guiding feathers at one end and a sharp metal point at the other. Darts for children are made with rubber suction cups instead of points. The target is usually made of cork or Beaverboard.

Players throw from a line 10 to 20 feet from the target. If a player hits the bull's-eye, he scores the highest number of points possible for one throw. If he hits the first circle outside the bull's-eye, he scores the next highest

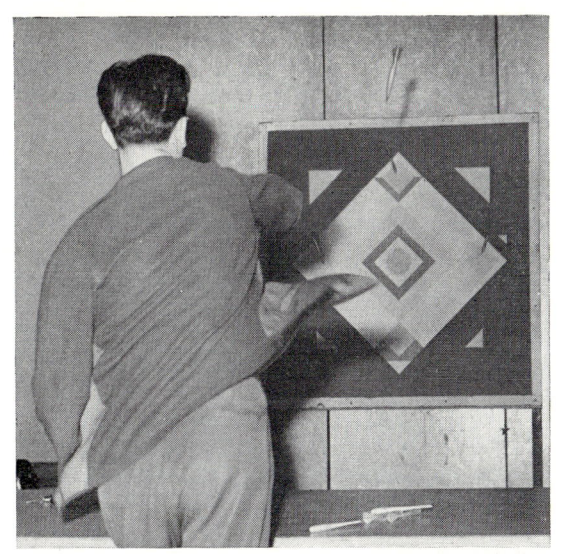

Baseball Darts is played on a board marked like a baseball diamond. "Hits" are made by landing on the bases or the home-run circle in the middle. Dark sections are "outs."

number, and so on. The players decide on the number of points for each circle.

Each player in turn throws his darts at the target. The players then add up the points for their throws, and the one who has the highest number of points wins. Before starting the game, players sometimes choose a certain number as a winning score. ELMER D. MITCHELL

DARWIN (pop. 12,335; alt. 50 ft.) is the capital and largest city of the Northern Territory of Australia. It is an air gateway to Australia and the chief port in the Northern Territory. For location, see AUSTRALIA (color map). It served as Australia's northernmost defense post in World War II. The discovery of uranium south of Darwin in 1949 stimulated its growth.

Darwin was planned in 1869 as the first station in Australia on a telegraph line connecting Australia with Europe. It was named for Charles Darwin. The Australian Commonwealth governs Darwin. C. M. H. CLARK

DARWIN is the name of two noted biologists, father and son.

Charles Robert Darwin (1809-1882) was a British naturalist whose theory of evolution through natural selection caused a revolution in biological science. His book, *On the Origin of Species by Means of Natural Selection, or the Preservation of Favoured Races in the Struggle for Life* (1859), presented the facts on which he based his concept of the gradual changes of plants and animals.

His Books. Before *The Origin of Species* was published, several scientists, including Darwin's grandfather, Erasmus Darwin, had proposed evolutionary theories. Charles Darwin is famous for the theory because he was the first to collect factual evidence for it, through experimentation and observation. Alfred Russel Wallace, an English naturalist, worked out a statement of evolution similar to Darwin's shortly before Darwin's book was published (see WALLACE, ALFRED RUSSEL).

Wallace's paper and an abstract of Darwin's book were presented together at a meeting of the Linnean Society in London in 1858. The next year, Darwin published *The Origin of Species.* Such noted scientists as Thomas Henry Huxley, Sir Charles Lyell, and Asa Gray supported Darwin's disputed work. Its principles and facts, with some modifications, have since been accepted by many groups as a part of biological science.

The storm of debate following the publication of *The Origin of Species* increased in 1871 when Darwin published *The Descent of Man.* This book outlines his theory that man came from the same group of animals as the chimpanzee and other apes. He also wrote *The Variation of Animals and Plants under Domestication* (1868), *Insectivorous Plants* (1875), and *The Power of Movement in Plants* (1880).

His Life. Darwin was born on Feb. 12, 1809, at Shrewsbury, and was educated at the universities of Edinburgh and Cambridge. His father wanted him to become a clergyman, but Darwin was more interested in natural science. Soon after he was graduated, he sailed as a naturalist with a British expedition aboard the H.M.S. *Beagle* in December, 1831.

During this five-year exploratory voyage along the coast of South America and to the Galápagos and other islands in the Pacific Ocean, Darwin searched

Charles R. Darwin

for fossils, and studied plants, animals, and geology.

Darwin returned from the voyage in poor health, and illness hampered him during the remainder of his life. He settled in London in 1836, and began writing the first of his books. In 1839, Darwin married his cousin, Emma Wedgwood. They had five sons. In 1842, Darwin moved from London to Down. He was buried in Westminster Abbey. ROGERS McVAUGH

See also EVOLUTION; NATURAL SELECTION.

Sir Francis Darwin (1848-1925) was an English botanist, the son of Charles R. Darwin. He assisted his father, and later became a reader in botany at Trinity College, Cambridge. His major works included *Life and Letters of Charles Darwin* (1887), *Power of Movement in Plants,* which he wrote with his father (1880), and *Foundations of the Origin of Species* (1913). Darwin was born in Down and studied at Cambridge. He was knighted in 1913. LORUS J. and MARGERY MILNE

DARWIN, ERASMUS. See EVOLUTION (History).

DASHEEN is another name for taro. See TARO.

DASHT-I-KAVIR. See IRAN (Land Regions).

DASHT-I-LUT. See IRAN (Land Regions).

DAS KAPITAL. See MARX, KARL; COMMUNISM (Modern Communism).

DASYURE, *DASS ih yoor*, is a small, catlike animal that lives in Australia. It has short legs, a long bushy tail, and a pouch in which it carries its young (see MARSUPIAL). Dasyures climb trees and eat meat.

Scientific Classification. Dasyures belong to the family *Dasyuridae.* The common dasyure is genus *Dasyurus,* species *viverrinus.* HAROLD E. ANTHONY

DATA PROCESSING. See COMPUTER.

Cultivating a Date Orchard in southern California helps prepare the ground for irrigation. To conserve space, date palms and grapefruit trees are planted alternately.

Clusters of Dates that have as many as 200 dates each and weigh up to 25 pounds grow on palm trees. The dates have a rich golden color while they are hanging on the tree.

DATE AND DATE PALM are the fruit and tree that supply one of the chief articles of food in north Africa and the Middle East. The Bible speaks of the date palm as the palm tree, and the poetry and proverbs of the East often mention it. Men probably cultivated the date palm before any other tree known to history. Sun-baked bricks, made more than 5,000 years ago in Mesopotamia, record directions for growing the tree.

Egypt and Iraq rank as the world's leading producers of dates. Other important date-growing regions include Saudi Arabia, Iran, Algeria, Pakistan, and Morocco. Growers in California and Arizona cultivate most of the date palm trees in the United States. In California, the date palm grows in the Salton Basin and some hot valleys in the interior. Arizona has good date-growing areas in the lower Salt River Valley and in the Colorado River Valley near Yuma. It has other date palm groves, scattered mostly in the Gila Valley and the upper Colorado River Valley. Texas grows date palms in the lower Rio Grande Valley and certain areas between Laredo and San Antonio.

The Tree. Next to the coconut palm, the date palm is the most interesting and useful of the palm family. The stem stands tall and straight, about the same thickness all the way up. A magnificent crown of large leaves shaped like feathers grows on the top. From earliest times, pagans, Jews, and Christians have used these palm leaves in their religious services. The flowers growing among the leaves attract little attention. Male and female flowers grow on separate trees. When cultivators raise date palms in orchards, they carry the pollen by hand to the female flowers. The fruit grows and ripens after the flowers have received the pollen.

Date palms begin to bear fruit six to ten years after planting. They require a hot dry climate. They grow best in a temperature that stays around 90° F. for three months of the year. The trees grow well in a sandy, alkaline soil. Growers often rely on irrigation to supply the water needed by the roots. During the ripening season, rain harms the fruits, and growers protect them by covering them with paper bags. Algerian date trees grow in deep pits dug in the soil of an oasis. The roots of the trees reach moisture far below the surface.

Date palms grow 40 to 100 feet high. Growers consider a yearly yield of 100 to 200 pounds of dates for a tree as very good, but some trees produce more.

The Fruit. On the trees, dates have a rich golden color. Most people know them best when they are dried. Then they are sweet, fleshy, oblong fruit, a deep russet or brown, over an inch long. The long tough seed has a furrow along one side. People eat dates either fresh or dried, and use them in cooking. The Arabs pound and mix them together to make cakes.

Other Uses. The date palm supplies us with other things besides fruit. The tree trunk and other parts provide fuel and building materials for fences. The large leaves can be used to weave matting, baskets, and bags. Rope is made from the fiber. The buds can be eaten as a vegetable. A liquor, called *arrack*, may be made from dates. The fruit seeds can be roasted as a substitute for coffee, or ground to yield oil. After removing the oil, farmers may use the rest of the seeds to feed cattle.

Scientific Classification. The date palm belongs to the family *Palmaceae*, or the palm family. It is genus *Phoenix*, species *dactylifera*.   IVAN MURRAY JOHNSTON

See also PALM.

DATE LINE. See NEWSPAPER (Newspaper Terms).

DATE LINE, INTERNATIONAL. See INTERNATIONAL DATE LINE.

DATURA, *duh TYOO ruh*, is a group of poisonous shrubs and trees, including the Jimson weed and horn of plenty. These large bushy plants, also called *thorn apple*, have toothed, ill-smelling leaves, prickly fruit, and white to lavender trumpet-shaped flowers. Daturas

Workers Harvest the Date Crop from a heavily laden tree in Libya. A single tree produces from 100 to 600 pounds of fruit a year, and may bear for a hundred years.

are native to the tropics, but now grow in eastern North America as well.

Scientific Classification. Daturas make up a genus in the potato family, *Solanaceae*. The Jimson weed is genus *Datura*, species *stramonium*.   J. J. LEVISON

See also JIMSON WEED; NIGHTSHADE.

DAUDET, DOH DAY, **ALPHONSE** (1840-1897), a French novelist and short-story writer, became popular with young readers for his easy, readable style. His *Monday Tales* and *Letters From My Mill*, inspired by provincial folklore, rank among the most popular books of tales. One of his boastful and cowardly characters, Tartarin in *Tartarin of Tarascon*, enjoyed widespread fame.

He published his best-known novels, *Jack*, *Sapho*, and *The Nabob*, between 1875 and 1890. His drama, *L'Arlésienne*, was set to music by Georges Bizet, the French composer. *Le Petit Chose*, a sentimental story, told of the hardships and poverty Daudet experienced in his early life.

Daudet was born in Nîmes and lived in Provence. After an unhappy childhood, he went to Paris where he received the job of secretary to the half brother of Napoleon III.   HENRI PEYRE

DAUGHERTY, JAMES HENRY (1889-   ), is an American artist and author of children's books. He won the 1940 Newbery medal for *Daniel Boone*, which he wrote and illustrated. He also wrote and illustrated *Andy and the Lion* (1938), *Poor Richard* (1941), *Abraham Lincoln* (1943), *Of Courage Undaunted* (1951), and *Magna Charta* (1956). He also painted murals.

Daugherty was born in Asheville, N.C., and lived most of his boyhood life in Indiana and Ohio. He studied at the Corcoran School of Art in Washington, D.C., and at the Pennsylvania Academy of Fine Arts in Philadelphia.   GEORGE E. BUTLER

See also LITERATURE FOR CHILDREN (picture, Daniel Boone Escapes from the Indians).

DAUGHTERS OF THE CONFEDERACY

DAUGHTER OF THE REGIMENT. See OPERA (Some of the Famous Operas).

DAUGHTERS OF THE AMERICAN REVOLUTION (D.A.R.) is an organization of women directly descended from persons who aided in establishing American independence. Women over 18 years of age who can prove such descent are eligible for membership. D.A.R. programs promote appreciation of the past, patriotic service in the present, and educational training for the future. The D.A.R. aids in preserving historic shrines that keep alive the memory of men and women who won American independence. It encourages the study of American history, and maintains relics and records of early America.

The organization owns and operates two schools in remote mountain areas of Alabama and South Carolina that are cut off from regular school systems. It also aids six other schools and colleges. It publishes a *Manual for Citizenship* to help foreign-born residents of the United States in becoming citizens. The D.A.R. sponsors Junior American Citizens Clubs for schoolchildren, provides

Memorial Continental Hall in Washington, D.C., is headquarters of the Daughters of the American Revolution. The building was designed by Edward Pierce Casey and was built in 1910 at a cost said to be more than $500,000.

scholarships for American Indians, and runs an annual Good Citizenship contest in U.S. high schools. The organization's official publication is *The D.A.R. Magazine*.

The D.A.R., officially the NATIONAL SOCIETY OF THE DAUGHTERS OF THE AMERICAN REVOLUTION, was founded in Washington, D.C., in 1890. It was chartered by Congress in 1896. The organization has over 187,000 members in more than 2,850 chapters in the United States and other countries. National headquarters are located at 1776 D St. NW, Washington 6, D.C. They consist of three adjoining buildings.

Memorial Continental Hall houses one of the largest genealogical libraries in the United States. The building also contains 28 State Rooms that are furnished in historic American styles. The Administration Building houses the society's business offices and a museum. Constitution Hall is an auditorium where the society holds its annual Continental Congress, and where many concerts and lectures are given.   MARGUERITE SCHONDAU

DAUGHTERS OF THE CONFEDERACY, UNITED, is an organization of women directly descended from members of the army and navy of the Confederacy. The organization was founded in 1894 at Nashville, Tenn.,

DAUGHTERS OF THE NILE

by the widows, wives, mothers, and sisters of Confederate fighting men. The original purposes of the group were to honor the memory of the Confederacy and to help needy Confederate soldiers and sailors and their families. The organization now has 36,000 members. There are 1,000 chapters in the United States, and one chapter in Paris, France. The group engages in educational and philanthropic activities, and preserves records and data of the Confederacy. The national office is in Memorial Building, 328 North Blvd., Richmond 20, Va. LOUISIANNA JACO

DAUGHTERS OF THE NILE. See MASONRY (Organization).

DAUGHTERS OF UNION VETERANS OF THE CIVIL WAR. See SONS OF UNION VETERANS OF THE CIVIL WAR.

D'AULAIRE, *doh LAIR,* is the family name of a husband and wife who are writers and illustrators of children's books.

Edgar Parin d'Aulaire (1898-   ) and his wife, **Ingri Mortenson d'Aulaire** (1904-   ), won the Caldecott medal in 1940 for their picture-book biography, *Abraham Lincoln.* They draw directly on lithographic stone in making their illustrations. Their career as book collaborators began in 1931 with *The Magic Rug.*

Their books include *Ola, Ola and Blakken, Children of the North Lights, Conquest of the Atlantic, George Washington, Benjamin Franklin,* and *Pocahontas.* They also illustrated *The Lord's Prayer, East of the Sun and West of the Moon,* and *Johnny Blossom.*

Edgar was born in Campoblenio, Switzerland, and Ingri in Kongsberg, Norway. They met in Munich, Germany, and were married in 1925. They have lived in the United States since 1929. RUTH HILL VIGUERS

See also LITERATURE FOR CHILDREN (picture, Ola).

DAUMIER, *DOH MYAY,* **HONORÉ,** *oh noh RAY,* (1808-1879), was a French lithographer, caricaturist, and painter. He made lithographic caricatures of legal and political leaders for newspapers. He was imprisoned for six months in 1832 for a caricature he drew of King Louis Philippe, which was entitled *Gargantua.*

Daumier's lithographs won fame for their biting satire. Many of his paintings are of traditional subjects. He painted people and places as he saw them. He pioneered realism in his paintings, but they did not gain recognition until after his death. He produced about 3,950 lithographs and some 200 paintings.

His painting, *Don Quixote,* and his series of satirical lithographs are perhaps the best known of his works. One of his paintings, *The Third Class Carriage,* appears in color in the PAINTING article.

Daumier was born in Marseille, the son of a glazier. He was reared in Paris, and became a bookseller's clerk and a process server to a lawyer. He studied painting with Alexandre Lenoir, but his real training as an artist came from what he observed on the streets and in the courts. His father tried to discourage him from becoming an artist. In 1877, Daumier became blind. He died at Valmondois, near Paris. S. W. HAYTER

DAUPHIN, *DAW fin,* was the official title of the oldest son of the king of France from 1349 to 1830. The title was similar to that of "Prince of Wales" in England. The lords of Viennois and Auvergne, whose lands were known as Dauphiné, first used the title. The last lord of Viennois had no heir. He gave his lands to Philip VI, on condition that either the king or the heir to the throne should be lord of Dauphiné and should have the title "Dauphin of France."

At first the dauphin had many privileges as ruler of his lands. But the title became merely honorary after Dauphiné was put under the same rule as all the other provinces of France. J. SALWYN SCHAPIRO

D.A.V. See DISABLED AMERICAN VETERANS.

DAVAINE, CASIMIR. See ANTHRAX.

DAVAO, *DAH vow* (pop. 47,486; alt. 76 ft.), is the chief port of southern Mindanao Island in the Philippines. For location, see PHILIPPINES (color map). Davao overlooks Davao Gulf on the southeastern shore of the island. The highest Philippine mountain, 9,690-foot Mount Apo, is 25 miles west of Davao.

Most of the people of Davao live in bamboo and wooden houses. This prosperous city has a busy, modern business district. Davao serves as the center of the abacá industry of the southern Philippine Islands. Factories in Davao process the fibers of the abacá plant, also known as Manila hemp. The fibers are used to make rope. Davao also ships lumber and copra, the dried meat of the coconut. RUSSELL H. FIFIELD and CARLOS P. ROMULO

DAVENPORT, Iowa (pop. 88,981; alt. 590 ft.), is the largest city in a metropolitan area that includes three Illinois cities—Rock Island, Moline, and East Moline. These four cities, having a total population of 200,281, are called the *Quad-Cities.* Davenport is located on the west bank of the Mississippi River. For location, see IOWA (inset on color map).

The principal industries of Davenport include the manufacture of aluminum, cement, flour, locomotives, electronic equipment, men's clothing, and iron and steel products. The Aluminum Company of America opened a plant in Davenport in the late 1940's.

The first railroad from the East reached the Mississippi opposite Davenport in 1854. At this point, the first bridge across the river was erected in 1856. The city now has excellent rail, motor, river, and air trans-

Daumier ridiculed "realists" in his lithograph *The Rejected Painter* (1859). His caption said, "They refused my work... The idiots."
Bibliothèque Nationale

David

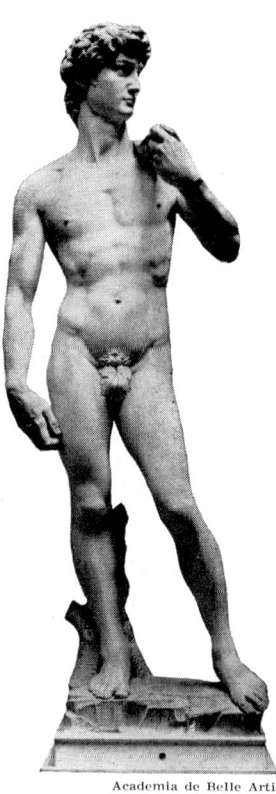

port services. Davenport is the home of St. Ambrose College, the Palmer College of Chiropractic, and the Annie Wittenmeyer Orphans' Home.

George Davenport, a fur trader, and Antoine LeClaire, a half-breed interpreter, helped to found Davenport in 1836. LeClaire received the land from the Indians in 1832. The town was incorporated in 1839, and a city charter was issued in 1851. Davenport has a mayor-council form of government. WILLIAM J. PETERSEN

DAVID (1000?B.C.) was the second king of Israel and the successor of Saul. A humble shepherd lad of Bethlehem, he became the best-loved national figure in Israel's political life. He was a great warrior. As a boy, armed only with a slingshot, he killed Goliath, the giant Philistine warrior. He built an empire for his son, Solomon, and founded a famous line of kings. They ruled the Southern Kingdom of Israel for more than 400 years, until Jerusalem was destroyed in 586 B.C.

The Bible tells of David's skill as a performer on the harp and as a poet. He wrote one of his most famous poems (II Sam. 1:19-27) as a tribute to King Saul and his son, Jonathan, after they lost their lives in battle against the Philistines. Tradition says David wrote many of the Psalms (see PSALMS). He moved the tabernacle to Jerusalem and made his capital the religious as well as political center of the Hebrew state.

His Youth. David was the youngest of eight brothers. He was handsome, and had a ruddy complexion. As a boy, he distinguished himself for bravery by slaying a lion and a bear that attacked his flock. The prophet Samuel anointed him for the kingship after it became apparent that Saul was not proving himself worthy of the crown. As a member of Saul's court, David played his harp and sang in Saul's palace at Gibeah. His friendship with Saul's son, Jonathan, is one of the most touching tales in the Old Testament. But David became a victim of Saul's jealous rage. He had to flee for his life and was hunted like an outlaw until Saul's death (see SAUL). David had a remarkable personality. He was exceptionally gentle and charming, and showed an unusual gift for attracting friends. In his dealings with Saul, he displayed great character that contrasted sharply with Saul's weakness. His tact, patience, and moderation in his youth fitted him for the high office he held later.

His Early Rule. He ruled as king of the tribe of Judah at Hebron for $7\frac{1}{2}$ years until he was elected king of all the tribes. Then he conquered the Jebusite stronghold of Jerusalem and made it his capital. This was important, because Jerusalem's central location made possible his complete control of the 12 tribes. David's capital was called the City of David when he made it his royal residence. It offered a fortification that could hardly be taken by an enemy.

His Conquests. The Philistines tried to crush David when he became king of united Israel (see PHILISTINE). He beat back their attacks, and conquered them. This was the greatest victory of his career. David also defeated the Moabites, Aramaeans, Ammonites, Edomites, and Amalekites. He carved out an empire that extended from the region of Hums, bordering Hamath, on the north, to Ezion-geber on the Gulf of Akabah (now Aqaba), in the south.

His Administration of the kingdom was effective. This is clearly shown by the strong kingdom he left behind him. He was much more efficient than Saul. David patterned his administration in part after Egyptian models. His important officers included the recorder and scribe, or secretary, and the Council of Thirty. His army became an efficiently organized fighting machine. It included a select personal bodyguard called Cherethites and Pelethites.

His Later Life. David's successes had a weakening effect on his character. He left the fighting of his wars to his generals, and remained in Jerusalem. Prosperity and luxury robbed him of his early self-control. He was a true worshiper and lover of the God of Israel, but he sinned seriously because of his infatuation for Bathsheba (see BATHSHEBA). He repented, but was punished for the rest of his life. His son, Absalom, rebelled against him and was killed (see ABSALOM). The revolt brought trouble between North and South Israel. Many people feel that David's sufferings were designed by God to purify David's character. After David's death, his son Solomon became king (see SOLOMON). Trouble between the regions of Israel increased during his reign. The regions split into the kingdoms of Israel and Judah during the reign of David's grandson, Rehoboam. MERRILL F. UNGER

David Killed Goliath with a single stone fired from his slingshot, and the Philistine army fled in terror.

DAVID

DAVID was the name of two kings of Scotland.

David I (1084-1153), the youngest son of Malcolm III Canmore, became king of Scotland in 1124. He invaded England twice, once to support his niece Matilda's claim to the English throne, and again to gain the earldom of Northumbria for his son, Henry. David won the support of the many Anglo-Norman barons in Scotland.

David II (1324-1371), the son of Robert Bruce, was married to Joanna, daughter of King Edward II of England, at the age of 4. He became king in 1329. David fled to France when England invaded Scotland. He later fought with France against England in 1349. The English captured him. They released him 11 years later, and he returned to Scotland. ROBERT S. HOYT

DAVID, HOUSE OF. See HOUSE OF DAVID.

DAVID, *dah VEED*, **JACQUES LOUIS** (1748-1825), was the leading French painter during the French Revolution and Napoleonic era. His painting, *The Oath of the Horatii*, became a great success in 1785. It greatly aroused revolutionary feelings in France. This and the paintings, *The Tennis Court Oath* and *The Death of Marat*, became important symbols of the French Revolution. David's style is sculptural and severe. It shows fine color and design, and is realistic.

David was born in Paris. He mastered the classical style of history painting in Rome (for an explanation of *Neo-Classicism*, see PAINTING [In the 1800's]). David was a member of the Jacobin political party during the French Revolution, and voted for the death of King Louis XVI. Under Napoleon he painted the great events of the Emperor's life. JOSEPH C. SLOANE

See also FRENCH REVOLUTION (picture, The Death of Marat); LAVOISIER, ANTOINE (picture); NAPOLEON I (picture).

DAVID, SAINT (520?-589?), is the patron saint of Wales and one of the most popular British saints. He was born into a royal family, and studied under the Welsh monk, Saint Paulinus. Later, David founded monasteries, including St. David's at Mynyw, or Menevia, in southwest Wales. When he was elected primate of the Welsh Church, he moved its see to St. David's. In art David is shown standing on a mound with a dove on one shoulder. JAMES A. CORBETT and FULTON J. SHEEN

DAVID, STAR OF or **SHIELD OF,** is the universal symbol of Judaism. It appears on the flag of the State of Israel, in synagogues, on Jewish ritual objects and on emblems of organizations. It is made up of two triangles that interlace to form a six-pointed star. The figure itself is an ancient one. Scholars do not know when it became widespread as a Jewish symbol. As far as is known, it first appeared

The Star of David

on a Jewish holy seal in Sidon in the 600's B.C. (?). The name *shield of David* is found in a Hebrew manuscript of the 1500's. LEONARD C. MISHKIN

DAVID COPPERFIELD, a novel by Charles Dickens, vividly portrays the life of an orphan. David's stepfather, Mr. Murdstone, tries to harm him. So does the "humble" Uriah Heep. But his aunt, Miss Betsey Trotwood, and the cheerful ne'er-do-well, Mr. Micawber, befriend him. He finally becomes a famous author and marries Agnes Wickfield. The novel first appeared in serial form in 1849 and 1850. See also DICKENS, CHARLES.

DAVID LIPSCOMB COLLEGE is a coeducational liberal arts school in Nashville, Tenn. In addition to a standard curriculum, the college requires Bible study each school day. David Lipscomb was founded in 1891. For enrollment, see UNIVERSITIES AND COLLEGES (table).

DAVIDSON, JO (1883-1952), an American portrait sculptor, created heads of many famous people. His work is direct and lifelike, solid yet crisp. He has been called a "biographer in bronze." He worked chiefly in terra cotta and bronze. His best-known works include portraits of General Pershing and Franklin D. Roosevelt.

Davidson was born in New York City. He studied for three years at the Art Students' League there, but then decided on a medical career. While at Yale Medical School, he saw work done by art students in a modeling class, and chose to become a sculptor. He went to Paris in 1907 to work and study. Davidson served as a war correspondent in World War I. WILLIAM MACDONALD

Jo Davidson, a noted American sculptor, carved a famous bust of Charles de Gaulle, the President of France.
United Press Int.

DAVIDSON COLLEGE is a liberal arts school for men at Davidson, N.C. It is controlled by the Presbyterian Church. Davidson grants A.B. and B.S. degrees and has an ROTC unit. The school was founded in 1836. Woodrow Wilson was once a student in the school. For enrollment, see UNIVERSITIES AND COLLEGES (table).

DAVIES, ARTHUR BOWEN (1862-1928), was an American painter and art historian. His paintings were dreamlike visions of poetry. *Unicorns*, his best-known work, is in The Metropolitan Museum of Art in New York City. The painter was a leader in "The Eight," a group of American painters who revolted against the National Academy of Design in 1908. He was born in Utica, N.Y., on Sept. 26, 1862. EDWIN L. FULWIDER

DAVIES, SIR LOUIS HENRY (1845-1924), served as Chief Justice of the Supreme Court of Canada from 1918 until his death. Born at Charlottetown, Prince Edward Island, he was the first "Islander" to hold this post. He had been prime minister and attorney-general of his home province from 1876 to 1879. He served in the Canadian parliament as a Liberal from 1882 to 1901, when he was appointed a *puisne*, or associate, justice of the Supreme Court. J. E. HODGETTS

Leonardo da Vinci was fascinated by natural forms, and his notebooks are filled with sketches of men and animals. He drew a famous self-portrait, *left*.

DA VINCI, *duh VEEN chee*, **LEONARDO** (1452-1519), was one of the greatest artists of the Italian Renaissance, and the greatest experimental scientist of his age. He displayed genius in almost all the arts and sciences. Leonardo was a painter, sculptor, architect, musician, and art critic. He studied the sciences as an inventor, a civil and military engineer, a botanist, an astronomer, and a geologist. He became the leading student of anatomy of his time. Da Vinci also pioneered studies of flying. He sketched flying machines based on the way birds fly. Leonardo's many designs show that he had a knowledge of aviation far beyond his own time. See AVIATION (Men Send Objects into the Air).

Early Life. Leonardo was born in the little village of Vinci. His father, Piero da Vinci, may have served as the village notary and lawyer. His mother was a peasant girl named Caterina. Piero's parents took Leonardo into their home and raised him. The boy showed one side of his genius by working out difficult problems in mathematics and engineering. But he showed greatest promise in drawing and painting. As a result, his father took him to Florence to study with Andrea del Verrocchio.

Da Vinci studied painting, sculpture, and engineering under Verrocchio. He painted the figure of an angel in Verrocchio's *Baptism of Christ* while he was still a student. Many people thought that the angel was the best part of the painting. The angel was Leonardo's first completed work, as far as art historians know. Da Vinci soon painted better than his teacher, and the painters' guild in Florence admitted him in 1472. He went on working with Verrocchio until about 1476, but he developed a different style. In his *Adoration of the Magi*, an unfinished panel, he showed that he preferred more idealistic painting than did Verrocchio.

Work in Milan. In the early 1480's, Leonardo entered the service of Lodovico Sforza, who later became Duke of Milan. Leonardo may have gone to Milan to design and cast an immense bronze statue in memory of Francesco Sforza. Leonardo never finished this work, but he did complete a painting, *The Madonna of the Rocks*, in his early years in Milan. This painting was the first to show completely the style for which Leonardo is best known. He arranged his figures formally, making a triangular composition, and filled the foreground with

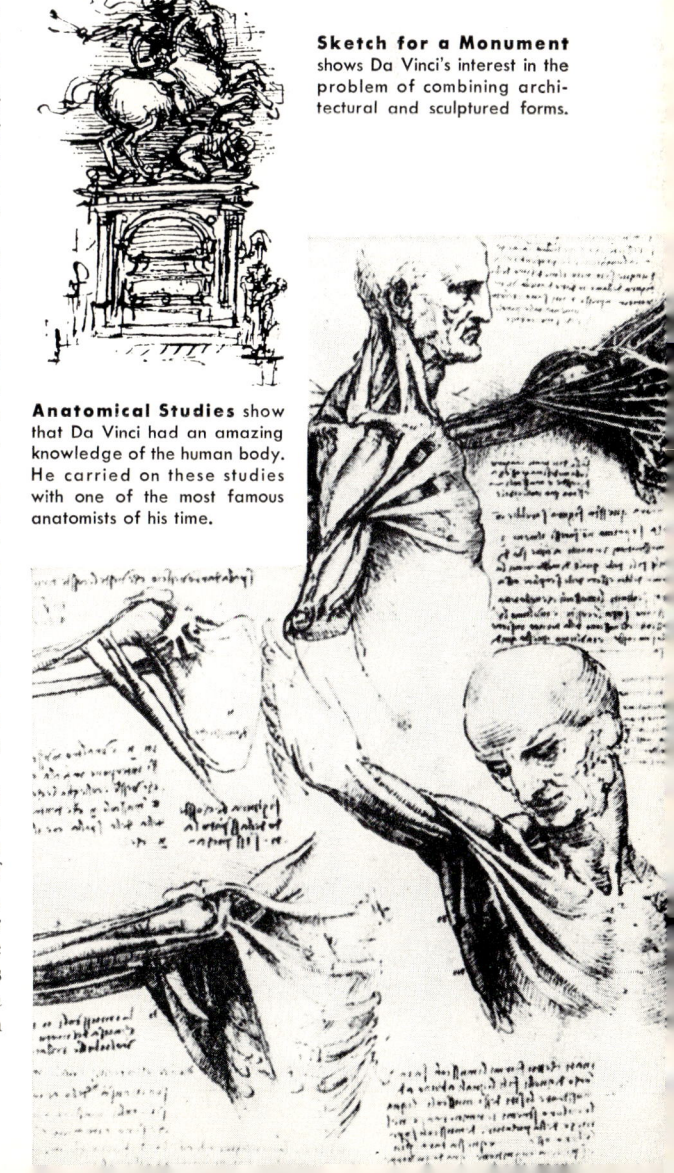

Sketch for a Monument shows Da Vinci's interest in the problem of combining architectural and sculptured forms.

Anatomical Studies show that Da Vinci had an amazing knowledge of the human body. He carried on these studies with one of the most famous anatomists of his time.

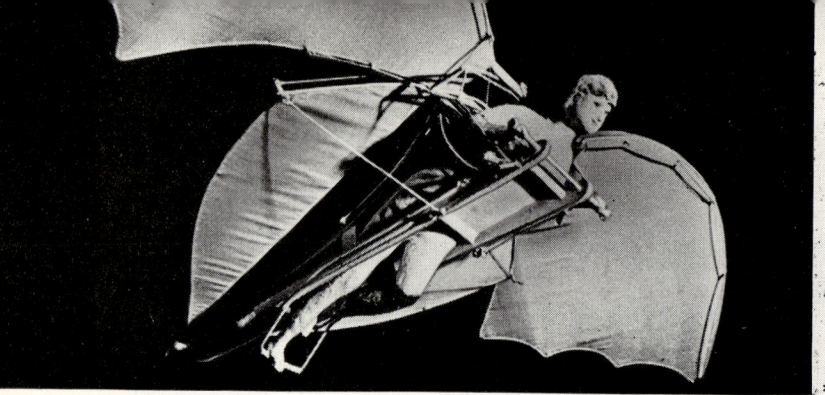

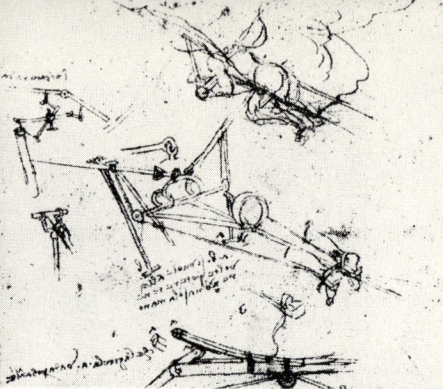

detailed studies of plants. During this period, Leonardo also painted a mural, *The Last Supper*, in the dining hall of the monastery of Santa Maria delle Grazie. Many persons consider this mural one of the greatest paintings in the world, even though its colors have faded badly. It still shows Leonardo's amazing knowledge of anatomy and perspective. Most noteworthy is the masterful way in which he shows the complex emotions in the hearts of Christ's disciples. The painting is reproduced in color in the JESUS CHRIST article.

Leonardo worked on projects for the diversion of rivers while he served the duke, and developed a canal system with locks that are still in operation. He designed court pageants and new fortifications for Milan. He delighted the duke with his great ability as a musician and singer. He performed on his lute and on many mechanical instruments he had invented, making up both words and music as he went along.

Work in Florence. French troops seized Milan in 1499 and forced the duke to flee. Leonardo returned to Florence, where he painted a portrait of the wife of a merchant named Giocondo. The mysterious smile Leonardo painted in *The Mona Lisa* or *La Gioconda* has been the subject of endless discussion. People especially like the simplicity and dignity of this painting, which appears in color in the PAINTING article. The mountain landscape in the background is in perfect atmospheric perspective, and seems to lead the viewer into infinity. Da Vinci resumed his studies of theoretical mathematics while in Florence. He also made many drawings of the anatomy of the human body. He began work on *The Virgin and Child with Saint Anne* at this time, but did not complete the painting for several years, possibly in France.

In 1502 and 1503, Leonardo took some time from his studies in Florence to work for the general Cesare

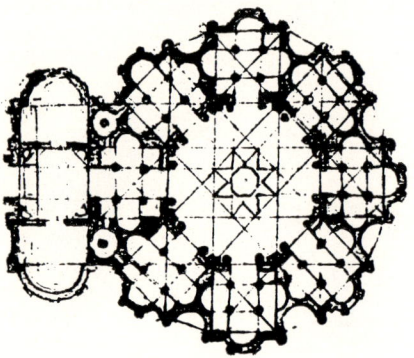

DA VINCI... DESIGNER

As a Designer and Inventor, Da Vinci understood principles about machines and processes that were not put to use until long after his death. The International Business Machines Corp. built many models from his drawings. He sketched a flying machine, *above*, and a "machine gun," *opposite page*. He worked on metal projectiles, *right*, that could be aimed more accurately than heavy stone balls. His ideas for an aerial screw, *far right*, forecast the development of the propeller and the helicopter.

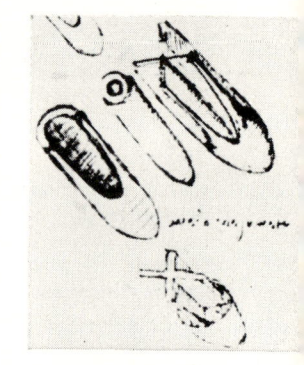

...ARCHITECT

As an Architect, Da Vinci used the principles of geometry in his sketches for buildings. One of the problems he studied involved supporting a dome above a round building, as sketched *above*. He later spent several years in Rome, working on plans for Saint Peter's Church and other buildings in the Vatican.

...INVENTOR

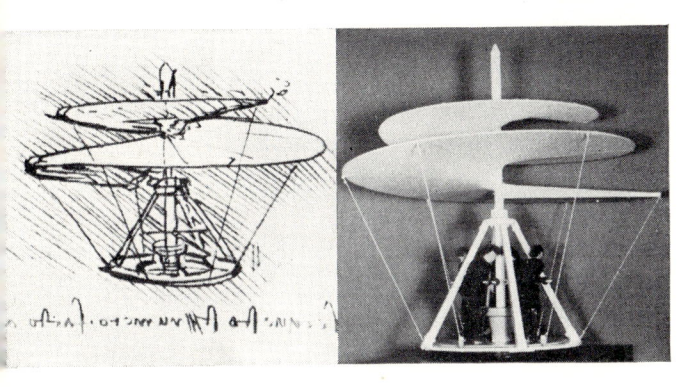

Sketches from Da Vinci's *Notebooks* and other models courtesy International Business Machines Corp.

Borgia. Da Vinci studied provincial fortifications in Italy for him, and drew some excellent maps of important military areas. Later, the maps were used to plan a peacetime system of canals for his own city of Florence. He also designed a breech-loading cannon and an armored vehicle like a tank. Back in Florence, Leonardo started a series of frescoes of the Battle of Anghiari in the Palazzo Vecchio. He never finished the frescoes, and they have since been completely destroyed. His clay models, sketches, and parts of the finished cartoon, as well as copies of the finished central panel by other artists, enable us to reconstruct the painting.

Later Years. Leonardo returned to Milan in 1506, this time in the service of Louis XII of France. He went on studying anatomy, and concentrated his engineering on research on hydraulics and aeronautics. Six years later, he joined Bramante, Raphael, and Michelangelo in Rome to work for Pope Leo X. The four great artists worked on designs and construction of the new Church of St. Peter. Some of them also worked on other new or enlarged buildings and rooms in the Vatican.

Several French kings admired Leonardo's work and invited him to live in France. Da Vinci finally accepted Francis I's invitation in 1516, and settled in the small castle of Cloux, near Amboise. He lived there in a princely fashion until he died, on May 2, 1519.

Leonardo's Genius. Historians regard Leonardo as one of the most original and capable men of the Renaissance. He dealt with all kinds of problems. His paintings reveal a sensitive approach to color and a keen sense of detail. Unfortunately, his many other activities prevented him from completing many paintings. Scholars often read Leonardo's *Treatise on Painting* to see what he thought about his own compositions and about the works of others. People interested in the many sides of Leonardo's genius study other pages of his many notebooks. Leonardo was ambidextrous, and he wrote his notes backwards with his left hand. He then read them with a mirror. Nearly 7,000 pages from his notebooks exist today. He sketched ideas and inventions on them, along with his notes. His comments ranged over such fields as painting, anatomy, and the philosophy of living.

RAYMOND S. STITES

...GEOLOGIST

As a Geologist, Da Vinci studied landscapes, rock formations, and the movement of water. In a famous drawing, *above*, he tried to show the action of water in a whirlpool, indicating currents below the surface as well as the surface pattern he could see. He wrote his notes backwards, and read them with a mirror.

See also AVIATION; HELICOPTER; JET PROPULSION (table, Red-Letter Dates); PAINTING; PARACHUTE.

DAVIS, BENJAMIN O.

DAVIS, BENJAMIN O. See NEGRO (Through the World Wars; pictures, Famous Negro Firsts).

DAVIS, DAVID (1815-1886), an American judge and statesman, helped his close friend Abraham Lincoln obtain the nomination for President in 1860. Lincoln appointed Davis to the Supreme Court of the United States in 1862. Davis was nominated for President by the National Labor Reform party in 1872. He resigned from the Supreme Court in 1877, and was elected to the United States Senate from Illinois as an independent. His election prevented him from serving on the Electoral Commission in the disputed presidential election of 1876. This was important because Davis' vote as a member of the Commission might have elected Democrat Samuel J. Tilden (see ELECTORAL COMMISSION). Davis was born in Cecil County, Maryland, and was graduated from Kenyon College. ARTHUR A. EKIRCH, JR.

DAVIS, DWIGHT FILLEY (1879-1945), an American statesman, established the Davis Cup in 1900. This is an annual award for the world champion tennis team (see DAVIS CUP). Davis served as Secretary of War from 1925 to 1929 in the Cabinet of President Calvin Coolidge. He was governor general of the Philippine Islands from 1929 to 1932. He became director of the Specialist Corps in the United States Army in 1942. Davis was born in St. Louis, Mo., and was graduated from Harvard University. He became a lieutenant colonel in World War I, and received the Distinguished Service Cross "for extraordinary heroism in action." F. JAY TAYLOR

DAVIS, EDWARD WILSON (1888-   ), an American mining engineer, is known as the "father of taconite" because he discovered how to get iron ore from a rock called taconite (see TACONITE). The rock is found mainly in Minnesota. Davis was born in Cambridge City, Ind., and was graduated from Purdue University. He taught mining engineering at the University of Minnesota for many years. IRA M. FREEMAN

DAVIS, JEFFERSON (1808-1889), served as President of the Confederate States of America during the Civil War. He has been called the man who "symbolized the solemn convictions and tragic fortunes of millions of men." He was not popular with the people of the South during the war, but he won their respect and affection after the war through his suffering in prison and his life-long defense of the Southern cause.

Davis was a statesman with wide experience. He served in the United States House of Representatives and the Senate, and as a Cabinet member. He also won distinction as a soldier. He was a thoughtful student of the Constitution and of political philosophy.

Early Life. Davis was born on June 3, 1808, in Christian (later Todd) County, Kentucky. His father, Sam Davis, was a veteran of the Revolutionary War. His older brother, Joseph, moved to Mississippi and became a successful planter. The Davis family moved there while Jefferson was still an infant, and he grew up in Wilkinson County. He attended the county academy, then entered Transylvania College in Kentucky. At the age of 16, he entered the United States Military Academy, and was graduated with comparatively low grades in 1828.

Davis' army career took him to Forts Howard and Crawford on the Wisconsin frontier. He fought in campaigns against the Indians, and took charge of Indian prisoner removal after the Black Hawk War. After he resigned from the Army in 1835, he married the daughter of his commander, Colonel Zachary Taylor, who later became a general and President of the United States. He took his bride to Mississippi, and settled down to live as a cotton planter. But within three months, both he and his wife became ill with fever, and Mrs. Davis died. Davis traveled for a year, while he regained his strength. For several years after his return to his plantation "Brierfield," on the Mississippi River, he studied history, economics, political philosophy, and the Constitution of the United States. He managed his plantation successfully, and became wealthy.

His Political Career. Davis became interested in politics in 1843, and won a seat as a Democrat in the U.S. House of Representatives in 1845. He resigned from Congress in June, 1846, to become a colonel in a regiment of Mississippi volunteers in the Mexican War. He served under General Zachary Taylor in northern Mexico, and distinguished himself for bravery in the battles of Monterrey and Buena Vista. His deployment of his men in a V shape gave him credit for winning the battle of Buena Vista (see MEXICAN WAR). During the battle, Davis fought all day with a bullet in his foot, and returned home from the war on crutches.

The governor of Mississippi appointed Davis in 1847 to fill out the term of a United States Senator who had died. The next year the state legislature elected him for the rest of the term, and in 1850 for a full term. Henry Clay's famous compromise measures came before the Senate in 1850, and Davis took an active part in opposing them in debate (see COMPROMISE OF 1850). He believed in a strict interpretation of the Constitution, and loyally supported Senator John C. Calhoun, a Southern "states-rights" leader (see CALHOUN, JOHN C.).

Davis believed that Mississippi should not accept the Compromise of 1850, and resigned from the Senate to become the candidate of the States-Rights Democrats for governor. He lost the election, and retired to his plantation in Wilkinson County.

Secretary of War. President Franklin Pierce appointed Davis Secretary of War in 1853. Davis improved the army during his term. He introduced an improved system of infantry tactics, and brought in new and better weapons. During his term the army was enlarged. He organized engineer companies to explore routes for railroads from the Mississippi River to the Pacific Coast. He even tried the experiment of importing camels for army use in the western deserts. At the close of the Pierce Administration in 1857, Davis was re-elected to the Senate from Mississippi. In the Senate, Davis no longer advocated secession, but he defended the rights of the South and slavery. He opposed Stephen A. Douglas' "Freeport Doctrine," which held that the people of a territory could exclude slavery by refusing to protect it. Davis also opposed Douglas' ambition to be the Democratic presidential candidate in 1860 (see DOUGLAS, STEPHEN ARNOLD).

Spokesman for the South. Davis became the champion of the constitutional right of a state to choose and maintain its own institutions. He demanded that Congress protect slavery in the territories. In the positions he took, he considered himself the heir of Calhoun.

After Abraham Lincoln was elected President of the

United States, Mississippi passed an Ordinance of Secession, and Davis resigned from the Senate. Davis hoped to become head of the Army of the Confederate States. But shortly after his return to Mississippi, the convention at Montgomery, Ala., named him provisional President of the Confederacy. He took the oath of office on Feb. 18, 1861. He was inaugurated as regular President of the Confederacy on Feb. 22, 1862.

Leader of the Confederacy. Davis was probably not the wisest choice for president. His health was poor. Although he was a good administrator, he proved to be a poor planner. He had difficulties with his Congress, and bitter critics condemned his management of the war. Yet he acted with dignity, sincerity, and strict devotion to constitutional principle.

Soon after General Robert E. Lee surrendered, Davis was taken prisoner, and imprisoned at Fort Monroe. A grand jury indicted him for treason, and he was held in prison two years awaiting trial. Horace Greeley and other Northern men became his bondsmen in 1867, and he was released on bail. He was never tried.

His Last Years. Davis spent his last years writing and studying at "Beauvoir," his home at Biloxi, Miss., near the Gulf of Mexico. He published *The Rise and Fall of the Confederate Government* in 1881 as a defense against his critics. He appeared often at Confederate reunions, and eventually won the admiration of his fellow Southerners. He died on Dec. 6, 1889, and was buried in New Orleans. His body was moved to Richmond, Va., in 1893, and a monument was built there to his memory. The state of Mississippi presented a statue of Davis to Statuary Hall in 1931. There is also a monument in Richmond for his daughter, Winnie, who was known as "The Daughter of the Confederacy." Davis' birthday, June 3, is a legal holiday in 11 Southern States. Four of them, Kentucky, Louisiana, Tennessee, and Virginia, celebrate it as Confederate Decoration Day.

Varina Howell Davis (1826-1906) became the second wife of Jefferson Davis in 1845. She came from a well-to-do Mississippi plantation family. Mrs. Davis became known as a brilliant and witty hostess, and is credited with helping advance her husband's political career. After the war, she assisted her husband in writing *The Rise and Fall of the Confederate Government*. After his death, she wrote a biography of Davis.   W. B. HESSELTINE

See also MISSISSIPPI (color picture, Beauvoir); CIVIL WAR; CONFEDERATE STATES OF AMERICA; RICHMOND (pictures).

Jefferson Davis with Confederate Military Leaders. This composite picture was made in 1885 from earlier pictures. The group includes, *left to right*, Admiral Raphael Semmes, General John B. Hood, Confederate President Davis, and Generals James Ewell Brown "Jeb" Stuart, Thomas J. "Stonewall" Jackson, Robert E. Lee, Nathan B. Forrest, Joseph E. Johnston, and Pierre Gustave Toutant Beauregard. Semmes, the only naval officer of the group, commanded the Confederate warship *Alabama*.
Culver

DAVIS, JOHN WILLIAM

John W. Davis (U&U)

DAVIS, JOHN WILLIAM (1873-1955), a famous American constitutional lawyer, was the unsuccessful Democratic candidate for the presidency of the United States in 1924, losing to Calvin Coolidge.

Davis represented a wide range of clients as a constitutional lawyer. He argued 140 cases before the Supreme Court of the United States, more than any other lawyer had argued up to that time. Many considered him the most distinguished constitutional lawyer in the United States. But he lost his last and most famous case, his Supreme Court defense of South Carolina's public-school segregation laws, in 1954.

Davis was born in Clarksburg, W.Va., and was graduated from Washington and Lee University. He served as a West Virginia member of the House of Representatives from 1911 to 1913, and was Solicitor General of the United States from 1913 to 1918. He served as ambassador to Great Britain from 1918 to 1921. Queen Elizabeth II of England made him an honorary knight in 1953. ERIC F. GOLDMAN

DAVIS, OWEN (1874-1956), an American playwright, won the 1923 Pulitzer prize for his tragedy, *Icebound*. His other plays include the serious drama *The Detour*, and *The Nervous Wreck*, a farce that later became the musical stage production *Whoopee*. He also wrote several hundred melodramas, such as *Nellie, The Beautiful Cloak Model*. Davis believed that "a play really is a character driven by an emotion along a definite line to a definite end." He was born in Portland, Me. GEORGE FREEDLEY

DAVIS, RICHARD HARDING (1864-1916), romantic adventurer, war correspondent, and writer, became the best-known reporter of his time. He covered six wars for New York and London newspapers. They included the revolution in Cuba and the Spanish-American War that followed it; the Greco-Turkish, Boer, and Russo-Japanese wars; and the early years of World War I. He toured and wrote for magazines about the western United States, the Mediterranean, Central America, and the Congo. He was sensational and dramatic, both in his personality and his writing for publication.

Richard Harding Davis (Brown Bros.)

Davis was born on April 18, 1864, in Philadelphia, the son of novelist Rebecca Harding Davis and L. Clark Davis, editor of the Philadelphia *Public Ledger*. He attended Lehigh and Johns Hopkins universities, and began newspaper work in 1886. He wrote 25 plays, including *The Dictator;* 7 novels, including *Ranson's Folly;* and more than 80 short stories. JOHN TEBBEL

DAVIS, SAMUEL. See TENNESSEE (Famous Tennesseans).

DAVIS, STUART (1894-   ), is an American painter and illustrator. His bright abstract paintings deal with everyday life. Bold areas of intense, pure color and rugged written lines characterize his work. He has taken his inspiration from such things as jazz, motion pictures, gas stations, billboards, and store fronts. He has put words and slogans from street signs and billboards into many of his paintings. The artist's abstract style serves to emphasize the distinctly American flavor of his paintings.

Davis was born in Philadelphia. He studied at the Robert Henri School of Art in New York City, and in Paris. At 19, he exhibited in the famous Armory Show of 1913. The works of Vincent van Gogh, Paul Gauguin, and Henri Matisse deeply impressed him at this exhibition. He painted murals for Radio City Music Hall, Rockefeller Center, and radio station WNYC in New York City. GEORGE D. CULLER

Stuart Davis used bold areas of bright colors in such paintings as *Summer Landscape*. He completed this painting in 1930.
The Museum of Modern Art

DAVIS, WILLIAM MORRIS (1850-1934), an American geographer and geologist, has often been called the founder of physiography. His books and articles are noted for description and geographical analysis. His most notable technical articles dealt with such subjects as the cycle of erosion which wears down high lands. His most important articles were brought together in his *Geographical Essays*.

Davis led the transcontinental excursion sponsored by the American Geographical Society in 1912, in which the leading geographers of the day took part. He was also a division chairman of the National Research Council during World War I.

He was born in Philadelphia and was graduated from Harvard University. He held many teaching positions before being appointed professor of geology there in 1879. He retired in 1912 to travel, do research, write, and lecture. CARROLL LANE FENTON

DAVIS AND ELKINS COLLEGE is a coeducational liberal arts school at Elkins, W.Va. Founded in 1904, it is affiliated with the Presbyterian Church. The college offers bachelor's degrees in arts and sciences. It has a cooperative program in nursing with the University of Pittsburgh and one in forestry with Duke University. For enrollment, see UNIVERSITIES AND COLLEGES (table).

DAVIS CUP is a silver bowl trophy awarded each year to the nation that wins the world's men's tennis championship. Dwight F. Davis, an American statesman and tennis enthusiast, donated the cup in 1900, and competition began in that year (see DAVIS, DWIGHT F.). The Davis Cup tournament features a series of dual meets between nations. Each dual meet consists of one doubles and four singles matches. Competition is organized by geographical zones. Teams from various nations play in European and American zone tournaments. The zone winners then play each other. The winner of this round plays the champion of the previous year in a challenge round for the title. FRED RUSSELL

DAVIS STRAIT. See BAFFIN BAY.

DAVY, SIR HUMPHRY (1778-1829), an English chemist, rose to fame as inventor of the miner's safety lamp. The Davy lamp, perfected in 1815, greatly reduced the risks of coal mine explosions. At the age of 20, Davy experimented with the use of *nitrous oxide*, or "laughing gas," as an anesthetic. When he was 29, he became the first person to isolate the chemical elements *sodium* and *potassium*. He did this by passing an electric current through the fused hydroxides of these elements. He was also first to isolate *barium*, *calcium*, *magnesium*, and *strontium*.

Brown Bros.
Sir Humphry Davy

Davy, son of a poor woodcarver, was born in Penzance, England, on Dec. 17, 1778. In 1802, he became assistant lecturer at the Royal Institution in London. The next year, he became professor of chemistry there. Michael Faraday, the man he had once hired as a laboratory bottle washer, succeeded him in 1813 (see FARADAY, MICHAEL). Davy's experiments and lectures made him famous. During the Napoleonic wars between England and France, he received safe passage to Paris to accept an award from Napoleon. He was knighted in 1812. SIDNEY ROSEN

See also ALUMINUM (History); MAGNESIUM (History); SAFETY LAMP.

DAVY JONES is a humorous name for the spirit of the ocean deep, in sailors' folklore. He is known chiefly through the proverbial term for the bottom of the sea, "Davy Jones' locker." "Davy Jones" is also a common Welsh name. Some have attempted to trace "Jones" to Jonah, the Hebrew prophet who lived three days in the belly of a whale. While the bodies of drowned sailors and those buried at sea and in wrecked ships go to "Davy Jones' locker," the souls of good sailors go to "Fiddler's Green." In some respects, Davy Jones is the present-day equivalent of the mythical Roman sea-god, Neptune. B. A. BOTKIN

DAVY LAMP. See DAVY, SIR HUMPHRY.

DAWES, CHARLES GATES (1865-1951), served as Vice-President of the United States from 1925 to 1929 under President Calvin Coolidge. He won the 1925 Nobel peace prize for arranging a plan for German reparations after World War I (see DAWES PLAN). Dawes entered national politics when he handled Republican party finances in the 1896 campaign.

Harris & Ewing
Charles G. Dawes

DAWSON

He served on the Allied General Purchasing Board during World War I, and became the first director of the federal budget in 1921. He served as ambassador to Great Britain from 1929 to 1932, and as the first chairman of the Reconstruction Finance Corporation in 1932. Dawes was chairman of the board of the City National Bank & Trust Company of Chicago from 1932 until his death in 1951. He was born in Marietta, Ohio, on Aug. 27, 1865. IRVING G. WILLIAMS

DAWES ACT. See INDIAN, AMERICAN (The Coming of the White Man [North America]).

DAWES PLAN was a program for stabilizing German business conditions after World War I. It also provided ways and means by which Germany could pay its reparations to the Allies. The plan was named after Charles G. Dawes, later Vice-President of the United States, who headed the committee that drew it up. The committee had two members each from Belgium, France, Great Britain, Italy, and the United States. The German Reichstag accepted the Dawes Plan in 1924. The plan helped to restore German business and industry. See also RUHR (History); WAR DEBT. NORMAN D. PALMER

DAWSON, Yukon Territory (pop. 881; alt. 1,050 ft.), is the chief trading center of the Klondike region in northwest Canada. It stands at the junction of the Klondike and Yukon rivers, about 50 miles east of Alaska. Thousands of miners flocked to Dawson after prospectors found gold in the region on Aug. 17, 1896. About 45,000 persons lived in the Dawson area in 1898, 1899, and 1900. The city was the capital of the Yukon Territory from 1898 to 1951. W. D. MACBRIDE

See also KLONDIKE; YUKON.

DAWSON was the family name of a father and son who were early Canadian geologists.

Sir John William Dawson (1820-1899), the father, worked in eastern Canada, especially Nova Scotia. He and Sir Charles Lyell discovered bones of amphibians in Coal Age trees. *Acadian Geology* was his most important book. His *Relics of Primeval Life* described ancient fossils called *Eozoon*, some of which now seem to be sea plants. Dawson was born at Pictou, Nova Scotia, and was graduated from the University of Edinburgh in Scotland. He became professor of geology and principal of McGill University in Montreal in 1855.

George Mercer Dawson (1849-1901), the son, became a geologist and naturalist for the North American Boundary Commission in 1873. He joined the Geological Survey of Canada in 1875, and became its director in 1895. He helped settle disputes between the United States and Great Britain over Bering Sea seal fisheries in 1893 (see BERING SEA CONTROVERSY). Dawson was born at Pictou. He attended McGill University, and the Royal School of Mines in London, England. He became president of the Royal Society of Canada in Ottawa in 1893. CARROLL LANE FENTON

45

DAY

DAY. While the earth travels through space around the sun, it also spins on its own axis. A *solar day* is the length of time it takes the earth to turn around once with respect to the sun. We usually say *day* for the time the sun is shining on our part of the earth, and *night* for the time when our part of the earth is dark, or turned away from the sun. But the night is really a part of the whole day. We also say *business day* sometimes to mean the hours of business in any one day.

Each day begins at midnight. In most countries, the day is divided into two parts of 12 hours each. The hours from midnight to noon are the A.M., or *before noon*, hours. The hours from noon to midnight are the P.M., or *after noon*, hours. The military services in the United States, Canada, and other countries often designate the time of day on a 24-hour basis, such as 0100 for one o'clock in the morning, 1200 for noon, and 2400 for midnight.

The Babylonians began their day at sunrise. The ancient Jews began the day at sunset. The Egyptians and the Romans were the first to begin the day at midnight.

The length of daylight changes during the year in all parts of the world because the earth tips first one pole toward the sun and then the other while it travels on its orbit. The longest day in the Northern Hemisphere usually is June 21. It has 13 hours and 13 minutes of daylight at 20° latitude. The same day has 14 hours and 30 minutes at 40° latitude. At 60°, June 21 has 18 hours and 30 minutes of daylight. The shortest day usually is December 21, which has only 10 hours and 47 minutes of daylight at 20° latitude, and 9 hours, 9 minutes at 40°. At 60°, there is only 5 hours and 30 minutes of daylight on December 21. The length of daylight changes very little during the year at the equator.

When the earth tips so that the North Pole faces the sun, the South Pole is continuously dark and the North Pole is always in daylight. Then the earth tips the North Pole away from the sun, and it is dark, while the South Pole has constant daylight. These long periods of darkness and daylight last about six months.

Astronomers use a day called a *sidereal day*. It is based on the period of the earth's rotation as measured by fixed stars. This day equals 23 hours, 56 minutes, and 4.091 seconds of mean solar time.   DONALD H. MENZEL

See also articles on the days of the week; DAYLIGHT SAVING; SIDEREAL TIME; TIME; TWILIGHT.

DAY, BENJAMIN HENRY (1810-1889), founded the first successful "penny paper," the *New York Sun*, in 1833. Day priced his little newspaper at one cent a copy, and sent newsboys onto the streets to sell it. This made the *Sun* a novelty in American journalism. Day also attracted readers by emphasizing the human and dramatic element in the news. By 1836, the *Sun* claimed a circulation of 30,000, the largest in the world. He sold the paper in 1837. Day was born in West Springfield, Mass.   JOHN E. DREWRY

DAY, CLARENCE SHEPARD, JR. (1874-1935), an American author, wrote the ironic and humorous books, *Life with Father* (1935) and *Life with Mother* (1937). Both were produced as plays, and *Life with Father* became one of the most popular plays in the 1940's. He also wrote *This Simian World* (1920), *God and My Father* (1932), and verses called *Scenes from the Mesozoic* (1935).

Alfred A. Knopf
Clarence Day

Day was born in New York City. He was the son of Clarence S. Day, member of the New York Stock Exchange, and grandson of Benjamin Henry Day (1810-1889), who founded the *New York Sun*. An uncle, Benjamin Day, invented the printing process known as *Ben Day*, or *benday*.

Day attended St. Paul's School and Yale University. He worked in his father's brokerage firm, but joined the navy in the Spanish-American War. After the war, he suffered from arthritis and had to stay in bed for the rest of his life. But he did not let illness interfere with his writing.   BERNARD DUFFEY

DAY, JAMES EDWARD (1914-   ), was appointed Postmaster General of the United States by President John F. Kennedy in 1961. From 1950 to 1953, Day served as state insurance commissioner of Illinois. He was born in Jacksonville, Ill., and was graduated cum laude from the Harvard Law School. During World War II, Day served as a naval officer. He served as legal and legislative assistant to Governor Adlai E. Stevenson of Illinois in 1949.   ERIC SEVAREID

DAY LETTER. See TELEGRAPH (Kinds of Telegrams).

DAY LILY is a lily plant whose beautiful blossoms, usually yellow or orange, live only from sunrise to sunset. The flowers grow in loose clusters at the top of a leafless stalk 3 to 5 feet high. Six to twelve flowers make up a cluster, and two or three open each day. The plant's long smooth leaves, 1 to 2 feet long, spring from the fleshy, fibrous root. Because of their hardiness, day lilies can be cultivated easily in rich soil and a moist, shady area. They make excellent border plants, giving a wealth of blossoms from June to September. People sometimes mistake the related *plantain lily* for the day lily. Plantain lilies have white and blue flowers and wide leaves.

Scientific Classification. Day lilies belong to the lily family *Liliaceae*. The tawny-orange day lily is genus *Hemerocallis*, species *H. fulva*. The fragrant, or lemon, day lily is *H. flava*.   ALFRED C. HOTTES

DAY NURSERY. See NURSERY SCHOOL.
DAY OF ATONEMENT. See YOM KIPPUR.

Flower and Buds of the Orange Day Lily. The blooms have six petals, six stamens, and anthers heavy with pollen.
Hugh Spencer

DAYDREAM. See IMAGINATION.

DAYE or **DAY, STEPHEN** (1594?-1668), with his son Matthew, set up and operated the first printing office in what is now the United States. The Dayes arrived at Cambridge, Mass., in 1638. The Rev. Jose Glover financed their passage from England and supplied them with a press, type, and paper. Glover died on the voyage, but his widow carried on with the plan. The first book that came from the press was *The Bay Psalm Book* in 1640. Eleven copies of it survive.

Stephen Daye was born in Cambridge, England, and first worked as a locksmith. He prospected for iron ore in New England. Matthew was evidently in charge of the press. The young printer began his career by issuing a sheet containing *The Freeman's Oath* (1638). RAY NASH

See also VERMONT (Communication).

DAYFLY. See MAY FLY.

DAYLIGHT. See DAY.

DAYLIGHT SAVING is a plan in which clocks are set one hour ahead of standard time for a certain period. As a result, darkness comes one hour later than on standard time. The advantages of this plan include an additional daylight hour available for recreation in the evening. Great Britain adopted daylight time as an economy measure during World War I. The United States adopted it in 1918. Congress repealed the law in 1919, but many cities continued to use daylight saving.

During World War II, daylight saving was again used throughout the United States. Since that time, the use of daylight saving time has depended on the wishes of individual states or cities. Daylight time is not suited for farm work schedules, and is not widely used in rural areas. Areas that use daylight saving time generally put it into effect about the end of April, and return to standard time late in October. WILLIAM MARKOWITZ

DAYR AZ ZAWR (pop. 73,805; alt. 820 ft.) is the communications center of eastern Syria. The city is on the west side of the Euphrates River, about 180 miles southeast of Aleppo (see SYRIA [color map]). Dayr az Zawr is the capital of Dayr az Zawr province.

DAYTON, Ohio (pop. 262,332; alt. 745 ft.), was the home of the Wright brothers, inventors of the first successful airplane. As a result, the city is known throughout the world as the *Home of Aviation.* The Air Force Logistics Command at Wright-Patterson Air Force Base is the U.S. Air Force materiel and procurement center.

Location and Size. Dayton lies in the Miami Valley, in the southwestern part of Ohio (see OHIO [color map]). Dayton is the sixth largest city in Ohio.

The main business section of Dayton lies in a low flood plain. The Miami River flows through the city. Three of its tributaries join it in Dayton. They are the Mad River, the Stillwater River, and Wolf Creek. Towns just outside the city limits of Dayton include Oakwood, Moraine City, Kettering, and Vandalia.

Cultural Life. The University of Dayton is the leading educational institution of the city. The United Theological Seminary also is in Dayton. Other cultural institutions in Dayton include the art institute, the natural history museum, and the U.S. Air Force Museum. Notable structures are the old county courthouse, the Deeds Carillon, and the Wright Memorial.

Industry and Commerce. Dayton has more than 800 manufacturing plants. The city has earned world-wide recognition as a production center for automotive parts and equipment, electrical refrigerators and air conditioners, cash registers, computing machines, and accounting machines. It is the home of the National Cash Register Company, the world's leading manufacturer of cash registers. Other important industries include the manufacture of pumps and compressors, electric motors, machine tools and dies, electric fans and blowers, tires and tubes, and aircraft parts.

Transportation. Dayton's location has helped it to become an important commercial center. It lies on or near the main traffic routes between Pittsburgh and St. Louis, and on the natural route from Cincinnati to Toledo and Detroit by way of the Miami-Maumee valleys. Four large railroads serve Dayton. The city airport is one of the largest in the United States.

Government and History. Settlers from Cincinnati established the village of Dayton in the spring of 1796. It was incorporated in 1805 and named for Jonathan Dayton, who owned land there (see DAYTON, JONATHAN). The city received its charter in 1841. It has a council-manager form of government, and is the seat of Montgomery County.

Floods have damaged the city from time to time. In March, 1913, a flood caused $50,000,000 damage and killed over 100 people. Today, Dayton and the Miami Valley have one of the most effective flood-protection projects in the world. In 1922, the Miami Conservancy District completed the last of five large dams to collect floodwaters in reservoirs. JAMES H. RODABAUGH

DAYTON, JONATHAN (1760-1824), at the age of 26 was the youngest signer of the United States Constitution. He served in the Revolutionary War and in the New Jersey Assembly. Dayton was a member of the

Fairchild Aerial Surveys, Inc.

Dayton is a manufacturing and aviation center in Ohio. The Miami River flows past the downtown district.

DAYTON, UNIVERSITY OF

U.S. Congress from 1791 to 1799 and was the Speaker of the House of Representatives from 1795 to 1799. He served as a U.S. Senator from New Jersey from 1799 to 1805. Dayton was born in Elizabethtown, N.J. He speculated in lands near Dayton, Ohio, which was named for him. ROBERT J. TAYLOR

DAYTON, UNIVERSITY OF, is a Roman Catholic coeducational school at Dayton, Ohio. It admits students of all faiths. The school has divisions of science, arts, business administration, and teacher training, and a college of engineering. In 1951, it opened a two-year technical institute. The university was founded in 1850. For enrollment, see UNIVERSITIES (table).

DAYTONA BEACH, Fla. (pop. 37,395; alt. 7 ft.), a year-round resort city, lies on the Atlantic Ocean and the Halifax River. Its famous hard-packed sand beach extends for 23 miles. The beach is 500 feet wide at low tide. Automobiles may drive on it at all times, and speed records have been set there. For location, see FLORIDA (color map).

Docks, harbors for yachts and other small boats, and shipping piers lie in the Halifax River. Bridges connect the two sections of the city, one built on the mainland and the other on the peninsula. Hotels, motels, and apartment houses line its ocean front and river banks. The city offers many outdoor recreational facilities. Points of interest include Riverfront Park, with many tropical trees and plants; Oceanfront Park, with a large bandshell and an oceanside walk; an auto racing speedway; and City Island Park, an amusement center.

Daytona Beach's industrial activities include citrus-fruit packing and shipping, fishing, and the manufacture of clothing, electronics components, cement, furniture, and boats.

The city was founded in 1870, and incorporated as Daytona in 1876. In 1926, it consolidated with the peninsula towns of Daytona Beach and Seabreeze, and was chartered as Daytona Beach. It has a council-manager form of government. KATHRYN ABBEY HANNA

D.C. See DISTRICT OF COLUMBIA.

D-C. See ELECTRIC CURRENT (Direct).

D-DAY is the term for a secret date on which a military operation is to begin. Peacetime planning of military operations is also based on hypothetical D-Days. Terms such as *D-plus-3* (three days after initial attack) are used to plan the sequence of operations. The expression *D-Day* became current in World War II when it defined the dates set for Allied landings on enemy-held coasts. The most famous D-Day is June 6th, 1944, when the Allies invaded Normandy. STEFAN T. POSSONY

See also WORLD WAR II (The Invasion of Europe).

DDT is the popular name for a powerful insecticide. The three letters come from its chemical name, *dichloro-diphenyl-trichloroethane*. DDT is manufactured from the sedative, chloral hydrate, monochlorbenzene, and sulfuric acid. It can be prepared as a dusting powder, or as an oil or water solution for spraying. It can also be used as an aerosol (see AEROSOL).

DDT first became well known in February, 1944, when the United States Army used it to halt an epidemic of typhus fever in Naples. The powder was dusted over all the inhabitants to destroy body lice, which carry the disease. When used as a solution, DDT will keep clothing free from lice for as long as two months. It remains effective even after the clothes are laundered. DDT will kill a large variety of insects. The United States Department of Agriculture says it is successful against 40 to 50 different kinds, including Japanese beetles, bedbugs, livestock lice, and termites. Some insects, such as flies and mosquitoes, have developed a strong resistance to DDT. Mutation has enabled flies to produce an enzyme which acts as an antidote, giving them an immunity to DDT (see ANTIDOTE; MUTATION).

Airplanes have been used to spread DDT over large areas, and it has been effective in destroying many malaria mosquitoes. However, large-scale spraying may be dangerous because the chemical kills useful insects, such as honeybees. DDT may also destroy other animal life such as fishes, dogs, and livestock. DDT is not recommended for spraying crops that will be used as food for livestock. In large doses, it has a poisonous effect on humans, and should be used with care. DDT was first prepared by a Swiss chemist, Paul Mueller, and patented by the Swiss chemical company, J. R. Geigy, Inc., in 1939 (see MUELLER, PAUL). ANTHONY STANDEN

DEACON, *DEE kun*, is a church official. His duties vary in different churches, but usually he is an assistant to the minister.

DEAD HORSE POINT. See UTAH (Interesting Places to Visit).

DEAD-MAIL OFFICE is a division of the United States Post Office. Letters and parcels that cannot be delivered, or are unclaimed, are sent to this office and its branches. There are two kinds of branches. Most large post offices in the United States have *dead-letter* branches to handle letters. Railroad mail division headquarters maintain *dead parcel post* branches in many cities.

Over 23,000,000 letters and 1,000,000 packages end up at dead-mail offices every year. This dead mail includes: (1) mail that has no return address; (2) letters and parcels containing materials which are not allowed in the mails; (3) mail that is wrongly addressed, or poorly wrapped; and (4) mail addressed to persons who have moved away and cannot be located.

Clerks in the offices open all letters and parcels which cannot be delivered, and, if there is a return address inside, return them to the senders. Most "dead" letters are destroyed immediately. Money contained in letters which cannot be delivered or returned within one year is claimed by the Post Office. The Post Office receives over $100,000 from "dead letters" every year. A sale of the contents of unclaimed parcels is held every three months, adding about $300,000 to Post Office receipts each year. "Dead" magazines go to hospitals.

The Dead-Mail Office is part of the responsibility of an Assistant Postmaster General of the United States. Branch offices were set up in 1917. Before then, all dead mail was sent to the main post office in Washington, D.C. CHARLES R. HOOK, JR.

See also FRANKLIN, BENJAMIN (Civic Leader).

DEAD RECKONING is a way of finding a ship's location on the seas without using the position of the stars. The officers keep a record of the direction in which the ship sails, and how fast it travels. They multiply the speed by the length of time to get the miles. They then trace the ship's course on a map. Dead reckoning has been useful when clouds hide the stars, but ships now usually receive positions by radio. See also NAVIGATION.

The Dead Sea Lies Between Jordan and Israel.

DEAD SEA, the saltiest body of water in the world, is located at the mouth of the River Jordan and forms part of the border between Israel and Jordan. The Dead Sea is about six times as salty as the ocean. It lies at the bottom of the deepest *fault* (break) in the earth's crust, 1,286 feet below the level of the Mediterranean Sea. In the Middle Ages, travelers reported that no birds flew over the Dead Sea because the air in the region was poisonous. But today we know that birds avoid the sea because it contains no fish, and that little plant life can grow because of the saltiness of the water.

The greatest depth of the Dead Sea is 1,310 feet. It is about 48 miles long and 10 miles wide, and covers 405 square miles. The River Jordan flows into the sea from the north through a rapidly descending valley. Smaller streams also empty into the sea. These rivers pour about 6,500,000 tons of fresh water into the Dead Sea every day. This fresh water evaporates in the extreme heat in the Dead Sea basin. Thus the level of the water changes very little and the sea never grows less salty. The water contains about 24 per cent solid matter, mostly common salt. Because of the high salt content, a person can easily float on the surface.

The Dead Sea contains large quantities of minerals. Besides common salt (sodium chloride), the sea contains magnesium chloride, potassium chloride, calcium chloride, and magnesium bromide. These minerals are sources for potash, bromine, table salt, gypsum, and other chemical products. The shores around the Dead Sea are covered with lava, sulfur, and rock salt, because the sea lies near a volcanic zone stretching from Syria through Jordan to northwestern Arabia. Gases escape from the surface of the water and give it an unpleasant odor. The waters of the sea are believed to be valuable in the treatment of certain diseases. A health resort is located at Kallia. On the east side of the sea, the white limestone walls of the Plain of Moab rise sharply as high as 4,400 feet above the water. The plateau of Judea towers 3,000 feet on the west.

Although the waters are thick and gassy, the Dead Sea presents an attractive appearance. The water is sparkling and smooth. Spring-fed lagoons lie around the shores. Water and wind have worn away the mountainsides and caused them to be brightly colored.

The Dead Sea was first mentioned as the *Salt Sea* in the Bible (Gen. 19: 24-26). It tells how the cities of Sodom and Gomorrah were destroyed and then covered by the Salt Sea. CHRISTINA PHELPS HARRIS

DEAD SEA SCROLLS are ancient manuscripts from Palestine. The scrolls were found in caves near the northwestern shore of the Dead Sea (see DEAD SEA [map]). The scrolls have been called the "greatest manuscript discovery of modern times." They include all of the books of the Old Testament except Esther. A few of the books are in nearly complete form. They are the oldest known manuscripts of any books of the Bible.

The first group of scrolls was discovered about 1945. A Bedouin shepherd boy found them in a cave in the *Wadi Qumran* (Qumran Valley). During the late 1940's and early 1950's, archaeologists and Bedouins found 10 additional caves containing ancient writings.

The discoveries consist of separate scrolls and fragments of hundreds of documents. Most of the manuscripts are made of leather and papyrus. These were part of an ancient library which many scholars believe belonged to the Essenes. The Essenes were a Jewish religious sect, many of whom may have lived in the Qumran area from about 100 B.C. to about A.D. 70 (see ESSENES). In 1951, archaeologists began excavating the ruins of a building called Khirbet Qumran. There they found a room containing a table and materials used to write the manuscripts.

In addition to the Old Testament books, the Dead Sea Scrolls include some fragments of the *Septuagint* (the earliest Greek translation of the Old Testament), and parts of the book of Job written in Aramaic. They also include parts of some books of the Apocrypha, such as Tobit and the Wisdom of Solomon, written in Hebrew, Aramaic, and Greek. Scholars also found theological writings and some commentaries to the Bible. Caves in the Wadi Murabb'at, a valley south of the Wadi Qumran, contained fragments of Biblical and other documents, including some written in the Nabataean dialect. These texts date largely from a later historical period preceding and including the Jewish revolt against the Romans in A.D. 132-135. NELSON GLUECK

DEADLINE. See NEWSPAPER (Newspaper Terms).
DEADLY NIGHTSHADE. See BELLADONNA.
DEADWOOD. See BLACK HILLS.
DEADWOOD DICK was a popular dime novel hero of the 1880's. He was created by Edward L. Wheeler, of Titusville, Pa. The original man who inspired the character is said to have been Richard W. Clark, a colorful prospector and gambler of Deadwood, S. Dak., who became an Indian fighter, Pony Express rider, and one of General George Custer's scouts. B. A. BOTKIN

DEAF-MUTE is a person who can neither hear nor speak. Those who are born deaf, or become so in infancy, suffer from dumbness because they cannot hear others speak, and so do not learn to form words. Some deaf-mutes cannot speak because of injuries to their brains. When persons who have already learned to talk become deaf, they retain the power of speech, but their voices often become harsh and unnatural. Deaf-mutes

49

DEAFNESS

often learn a means of speech by using their hands to make the letters of the alphabet. Recently, many methods have been devised to aid deaf-mutes to talk.

Patients watch their teachers, watch photographs of the vocal organs in operation, and motion pictures of the pattern of sound waves produced by their voices.

See also DEAFNESS; HANDICAPPED (The Deaf); LIP READING. G.W. BEADLE

DEAFNESS is the partial or complete inability to hear. About 7 out of 100 children in the public schools cannot hear as well as they should. Ability to hear grows less with age. It has been said that one person out of every four in the United States cannot hear normally.

If a person hears normally, the ear receives sound waves through a tube in the head called the *ear canal*. They strike on a thin membrane, the *eardrum*, which is stretched across a chamber in the ear called the *middle ear*. The eardrum vibrates very sensitively and is delicately connected with the hearing nerve, called the *auditory nerve*, by a very special apparatus in the *inner ear*. The sound sensation travels over this nerve to the brain. The middle ear is connected with the throat by a canal, the *Eustachian tube*, near the inner opening of the nose. Anything which interferes with any one of these parts may cause deafness of varying degrees.

Ordinarily the human ear can hear — or at least the human brain recognizes — sounds which have vibrations of from 20 to 20,000 cycles a second. The ordinary tones in conversation range from 200 to 3,000 vibrations per second in pitch. Some animals seem to hear vibrations of higher pitch. Sound is measured in decibels, a technical unit. A whisper is about 20 decibels in intensity; ordinary conversation, about 50 or 60 decibels (see SOUND [Hearing Sound]).

Hearing is considered good if all the sounds between 64 and 8,192 vibrations at 20 decibels are heard. Deafness which handicaps the person begins when the tones in ordinary speech cannot be heard at a whisper. Sometimes only part of the tone range is interfered with. Deafness can increase until it is almost impossible to hear any sound, but it has been found that most deaf-mutes can hear at least one sound.

Some people are *congenitally deaf* (born deaf) because of some defect in the hearing mechanism. Others become deaf from disease or other causes. When *total deafness* occurs to a child before it has learned to talk, it cannot learn to form words without very special education. It is a deaf-mute.

Causes of Deafness. Injury to the auditory nerve by accident or disease will cause deafness. Meningitis may destroy the nerve, and syphilis is responsible for some cases of deafness in newborn infants. Deafness may be caused by epilepsy or other diseases affecting the parts of the brain which register sound.

Sudden tremendous noise or prolonged loud noise may cause permanent injury to the hearing. Workers in very noisy industries, such as steel mills or foundries, may eventually be affected.

Unequal air pressure on the sensitive eardrum may be a cause of deafness. This deafness is usually temporary unless the pressure on one side is so great as to burst the drum. Sometimes, when a person is going up in a very fast elevator in a very tall building, the hearing will be temporarily lessened and the ears "pop." Passengers in airplanes experience this difficulty, but it soon wears off. A hard blow on the side of the head may cause such unequal pressure that the eardrum is ruptured. A heavy explosion may also rupture the eardrum.

When the eardrum has a hole in it, it does not vibrate properly. The hole may heal over but the scar tissue thus formed is thicker and stiffer than the normal drum. As a result the eardrum vibrates less.

A Hand Alphabet for Deaf and Deaf-Mute Persons allows them to carry on conversations. Special positions of the fingers and hands stand for certain letters of the alphabet. A person uses this alphabet to spell out the words in his conversation. This may be a very slow process at first, but soon the person can develop great facility and speed.

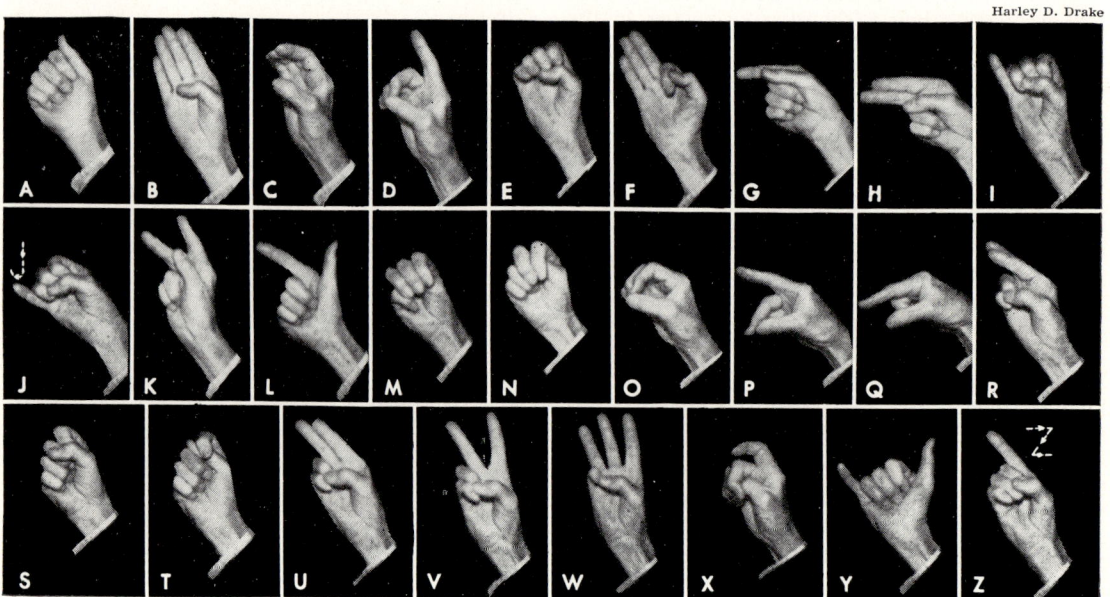

Harley D. Drake

Deaf Pupils in a Special Classroom at a Public School Receive Instruction with Microphone and Hearing Aids.

Most hearing troubles are caused by disease. This disease does not start within the ear but reaches the ear from other parts of the body, usually the nose and throat. Such diseases are particularly important during childhood, when hearing may be injured permanently. The common cold, tonsillitis, scarlet fever, measles, and some other diseases are often causes of such deafness.

Infection in the throat and nose may move up the Eustachian tube to the middle ear and cause inflammation and thickening of the eardrum. Often an abscess is formed in the inner ear and presses inside on the eardrum. Earache is the symptom of this pressure by an abscess. If the drum bursts, the pressure is relieved and the pain is gone, but the eardrum is damaged. If the drum can be pierced by a physician before it bursts, the hole will be small and sharply cut, and will heal sooner with less scar tissue than if it ruptures.

Often contaminated or infected fluids are forced up the Eustachian tube. This results in infection of the middle ear. Pressure of deep swimming and diving may force impure water into the middle ear. Severe nose blowing during throat and nose infections may result in a similar condition.

Infected adenoids may spread infection through the Eustachian tube to the middle ear. Occasionally adenoidal tissue will completely close the Eustachian tube. Then it causes lowered air pressure on the inside of the drum. This interferes with the proper vibration of the drum. Sometimes the swelling of the throat in "sore throat" or tonsillitis will produce a similar result.

Rarely does infection enter the middle ear from outside to affect the eardrum. But anything closing the ear canal will cut off the sound vibrations. Boils in the outer ear or in the canal may cause enough swelling to affect hearing. Excess wax, dirt, or foreign objects in the canal may cut off sound. Scar tissue caused by burns or scalds, or by other accidents, may do so also.

Occasionally the delicate mechanism in the middle and inner ears becomes bony, so that the parts cannot vibrate. This is called *otosclerosis*, and usually appears to be hereditary.

Sometimes "deafness" is not due to any physical change in the ear, but to faulty mental processes. Some patients may be able to hear sounds but do not understand words. Sudden or severe shock may produce this condition. In modern war, concussions from exploding shells sometimes puncture soldiers' eardrums. The eardrums usually heal in a few days, but the soldier may continue to think he is deaf. This is not true deafness, and must be treated as a mental problem.

Treatment. It is essential that any deafness or condition tending to cause deafness should be remedied at once. Infectious diseases should be treated by a competent physician. Middle ear infections can usually be prevented and possible deafness avoided if the causes are treated in time. Some drugs, such as penicillin and sulfa compounds, may be used in curing such infections. Proper lancing of abscesses of the middle ear by a physician does much to relieve the pain and prevent excessive formation of scar tissue. Accumulation of wax or anything else in the ear canal should be removed by a physician. Injury to the eardrum as well as to the canal is often the result of home treatment. Ear surgeons may treat otosclerosis by an operation called *fenestration*, in which they cut a tiny window in the inner ear.

Detection and *prevention* of deafness is particularly important in the public schools. Pupils have their hearing tested at regular intervals with an *audiometer*, an instrument which gives out sounds of known controlled intensity. Pupils not able to hear the normal range of sounds are sent to ear specialists for further examination. Removing the adenoids or tonsils may be advised. Cleaning of the ear canal will sometimes help. Advice may be given to use care in swimming and diving to avoid forcing infection into the middle ear.

Not much can be done to prevent congenital deafness from hereditary causes, but proper care of the mother during pregnancy will do much to prevent some such cases. In cases where the hearing has already been affected, little can be done to bring it back to normal. Various methods of helping the deaf to understand conversation have been used. Lip reading is often very successful. Recent development and improvement of hearing aids has been very encouraging.   G. W. BEADLE

Related Articles in WORLD BOOK include:

Adenoids	Handicapped
Bell, Alexander G.	Hearing Aids
Deaf-Mute	Keller, Helen A.
Ear	Lip Reading
Gallaudet	Mastoid
Gallaudet College	Sign Language

DEAN, WILLIAM FRISCHE

DEAN, WILLIAM FRISCHE (1899-   ), is an American major general who won fame in the early days of the Korean War (1950-1953). North Korean soldiers captured him while he was fighting in the front lines. They held him for more than three years as a prisoner of war. He refused to reveal military secrets despite torture. Dean retired from the army in 1955. He was born in Carlyle, Ill., and was graduated from the University of California in 1922. H. A. DeWeerd

See also KOREAN WAR (The Early Days of the War).

DEANE, SILAS (1737-1789), was an American patriot and diplomat. He was prominent in movements leading to the Revolutionary War. In March, 1776, the Continental Congress sent him to France to buy war supplies. After the Declaration of Independence, Benjamin Franklin and Arthur Lee were sent to join Deane in arranging treaties with France. Deane was recalled in 1788 to account for his financial transactions, but no evidence of dishonesty was found. He was born at Groton, Conn. KENNETH R. ROSSMAN

DE ANGELI, *dee AN juh lih*, **MARGUERITE LOFFT** (1889-   ), is an American author and illustrator of children's books. She became best known for her stories about American minority groups, particularly people born in Europe, Quakers, and Negroes. She won the 1950 Newbery medal for *The Door in the Wall*, a story of England in the 1300's at the time of King Edward III. She wrote and illustrated *Henner's Lydia* (1936), *Thee, Hannah!* (1940), *Elin's Amerika* (1941), *Yonie Wondernose* (1944), and *Black Fox of Lorne* (1956). She was born in Lapeer, Mich., and lived most of her life in Pennsylvania and New Jersey. GEORGE E. BUTLER

DEARBORN, Mich. (pop. 112,007; alt. 605 ft.), the state's fourth largest city, is the home of the main plant of the Ford Motor Company. The city lies along the River Rouge on the western outskirts of Detroit. For location, see MICHIGAN (color map).

Ford industries employ more than one of every three workers in Dearborn. The city's chief products include automobiles, steel, and heating and air-conditioning equipment. The Detroit Metropolitan Airport and Willow Run Airport serve Dearborn.

The city maintains Camp Dearborn, a 626-acre recreational area, 35 miles to the northeast. Greenfield Village and the Edison Institute attract about 700,000 visitors each year (see GREENFIELD VILLAGE). Within Dearborn lies Fairlane, Henry Ford's estate, which was presented to the University of Michigan in 1956. Dearborn has a junior college, the McFadden-Ross Museum, and the Dearborn Historical Museum.

Dearborn was incorporated as a city in 1927. In the following year it united with Fordson, where Henry Ford had built his Rouge plant in 1919. Dearborn has a council-manager government. WILLIS F. DUNBAR

See also FORD (Henry Ford); FORD MOTOR COMPANY; MICHIGAN (color picture, A 1903 Ford).

DEARBORN, HENRY (1751-1829), was an American soldier and political leader. Fort Dearborn at Chicago was named for him (see FORT DEARBORN). He was born at North Hampton, N.H., and served as a captain in the Revolutionary War. He fought at Bunker Hill, went with Benedict Arnold to Quebec, and was serving as a major with General Horatio Gates when the British general, John Burgoyne, surrendered. Dearborn served twice in the U.S. Congress, and was Secretary of War in President Thomas Jefferson's Cabinet from 1801 to 1809. He fought as a major general during the War of 1812, and served as minister to Portugal from 1822 to 1824. RICHARD N. CURRENT

Henry Dearborn, pioneer American soldier, posed for this painting by Gilbert Stuart.

DEATH means the ending of life. Men usually die because the heart stops, and blood no longer circulates and brings nourishment to the cells of the body. But all the cells of the human body do not die at the same time. The hair may continue to grow for several hours after death. The cells of the cortex of the brain are very susceptible to lack of oxygen. They usually die first when the blood ceases to circulate. If the cells of the brain are completely deprived of oxygen for 5 or 10 minutes they can no longer completely regain their ability to function. The cells of the part of the brain called the *medulla oblongata* usually die next. Then the cells of the body's glands and the cells in the muscles which move the bones of the skeleton die. The cells in the skin and in the bones may live for several hours. The smooth muscles in the intestines may be stimulated and contract 12 hours after the heart has stopped beating. In some animals, certain cells have been kept alive for years in the laboratory by means of solutions which contain nourishment.

Scientists have reported experiments in which they apparently have restored life to dead human beings.

An Ancient Paddlewheel River Steamer, the *Suwanee,* gives rides to visitors at Greenfield Village in Dearborn, Mich.
Henry Ford Museum

Restoration would not be possible if death had affected the tissues of the brain. In any case, the person's heart could not have stopped beating for more than a few minutes.

The death of some cells and structures in the body begins even before birth. Certain structures grow during life and then decay and are replaced by new structures. The thymus gland is an example of an organ in the body that tends to disappear after an individual reaches adulthood. Death is also part of the processes of nature. When too many animals or plants live in a certain environment, many of them must die for lack of food, from disease, or because of poisons produced by their own bodies. Nature provides a cycle of experiences including birth, growth, and reproduction. Death is the way in which nature concludes the cycle.

Death, while feared by many, may be relatively calm and peaceful. The famous surgeon, Sir William Osler, found that many of his patients were unaware that they were dying, and that few died in the midst of mental torment. Several years before he died, Heywood Broun, American newspaperman, wrote: "He who dies a thousand deaths meets the final hour with the calmness of one who approaches a well-remembered door."

Death, in literature and myth, has often been portrayed as one of the great enemies of mankind. Many legends tell of man's desire to annihilate death. Death has been the subject for many poems. William Cullen Bryant's poem "Thanatopsis" (meaning *contemplation of death*), Alfred Tennyson's "Crossing the Bar," and Robert Louis Stevenson's "Requiem" show a calm acceptance of death.   ANDREW CONWAY IVY

Related Articles in WORLD BOOK include:

Autopsy	Funeral Customs	Transmigration
Embalming	Immortality	of the Soul
Euthanasia	Life	

DEATH, CIVIL, is the legal term used when a person may still be alive but has not been heard from over a period of time, usually seven years. The law then recognizes that the person may reasonably be assumed to be dead. Then his wife may remarry or his estate may be divided among his heirs. However, if the person returns, he does not lose any of his legal rights. The law will make every attempt to restore what is his, as far as this is possible.   THOMAS A. COWAN

DEATH PENALTY. See CAPITAL PUNISHMENT.

DEATH RATE. See VITAL STATISTICS.

DEATH VALLEY lies in east-central California, near the Nevada border. A group of pioneers named the valley after they crossed it in 1849. They called it *Death Valley* because of the desolate desert environment. It became part of the Death Valley National Monument, set up in 1933. For location, see CALIFORNIA (color map).

Death Valley is a deep trough, about 130 miles long and from 6 to 14 miles wide. The lowest elevation in the Western Hemisphere is near Badwater in Death Valley.

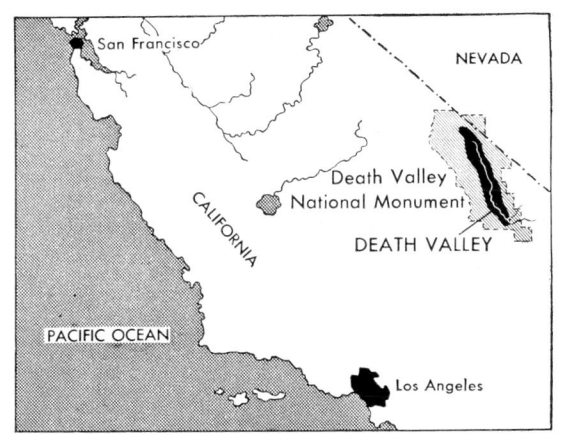

Shifting Sand Dunes, below, cover a small part of Death Valley, which lies in Death Valley National Monument, above.

National Park Service

DEATH VALLEY NATIONAL MONUMENT

It lies 282 feet below sea level. The Panamint Mountains stand west of the valley. Telescope Peak in the Panamint range is 11,045 feet high. The Amargosa Range, composed of the Grapevine, Funeral, and Black mountains, rises to the east.

The valley is a block in the earth's surface, dropped down by faults which form its east and west walls. *Faults* occur when the earth's crust breaks and slips into various positions. Erosion of the steep cliffs has formed beautiful canyons. In the northern part of the Valley is Ubehebe Crater, a small volcano on the west side fault. Flows of lava issue from the faults in the southern part of Death Valley.

During glacial times, the climate was moister, and a large lake occupied Death Valley. Today, rainfall averages less than 1½ inches a year. The highest temperature ever recorded in the United States (134°F.) was reported there on July 10, 1913. Summer temperatures of 125°F. are common. The valley's geological attractions and warm winter sunshine have made it a popular winter-resort area. Plants include the creosote bush, desert holly, and mesquite. Wild life includes bobcats, coyotes, foxes, rats, rabbits, reptiles, and squirrels.

Borax deposits were discovered in Death Valley in 1873. Actual mining began in the early 1880's, and famous 20-mule teams hauled the borax out of the valley. Prospectors also discovered copper, gold, lead, and silver in the nearby mountains. Mining towns sprang up around Death Valley, with such colorful names as Bullfrog, Greenwater, Rhyolite, and Skidoo. The towns died when the ores were exhausted. Today only cluttered debris remains. JOHN W. REITH

DEATH VALLEY NATIONAL MONUMENT is in California and Nevada. It is a desert of scenic, scientific, and historical interest. The valley contains the lowest point in the Western Hemisphere (282 feet below sea level) near Badwater. The 1,907,760-acre monument was established in 1933. See also DEATH VALLEY (map).

DEATH'S-HEAD MOTH is a large *hawk*, or *sphinx*, moth with a thick, hairy body. Many superstitions arose because of the skull-like pattern on its body. The moth lives in Africa and southern Europe, and adults often migrate to northern Europe. They enter beehives to eat honey and may squeak loudly when disturbed. The caterpillar is bright yellow with violet stripes and blue spots. It feeds on the leaves of potato plants.

Scientific Classification. The death's-head moth belongs to the family *Sphingidae*. It is genus *Acherontia*, species *atropos*. ALEXANDER B. KLOTS

See also HAWK MOTH.

DEATHWATCH is a name given to several kinds of small brownish beetles that have the odd habit of knocking their heads against wood. This action produces a peculiar ticking or rapping sound. Superstitious people sometimes believe that the rapping, heard in the quiet of the night, foretells death in the house. The beetles burrow into furniture and woodwork and are often very destructive. The "drugstore beetle," which feasts on drugs stored in shops, is also called deathwatch.

Scientific Classification. The deathwatch is in the order *Coleoptera*. It belongs to the family *Anobiidae*. It is genus *Xestobium*, species *rufovillosum*. H. H. ROSS

DEBATE is a series of formal spoken arguments for and against a definite proposal.

A debate is different from a discussion, although both are fundamental activities in a democracy. *Discussion* is the process by which a problem is recognized and investigated and solutions explored (see FORUM). *Debate* is the process by which the best solution (in propositions of policy) or appraisal (in propositions of fact) is approved and adopted. Discussion begins with a problem, while debate begins with a proposed solution to a problem. A typical discussion might be, "What is wrong with student activities at Main High School?" If this discussion were held and the decision reached was that student activities were not properly guided, then a debate could be held. To select the best solution to the problem of guidance, a logical subject for the debate might be, "Resolved, that a combined student-faculty board should be established to control all student activities of Main High School."

The Formal Debate. In formal debating, the same number of persons speak for each side. They have the opportunity to reply directly to opposing speakers. Affirmative and negative speakers usually alternate, and all the speeches are limited in time. In informal (as in conversation) and in legislative debating, although there is the same opportunity to reply to opposing speakers, the speeches are not necessarily limited in time. There may be no attempt to alternate opposing speakers, and also there may not be the same number of speakers on each side.

Propositions. Subjects for debates are expressed in the form of propositions. A proposition is a carefully worded statement which makes clear the positions of both the affirmative and negative sides.

Propositions should be:

(1) Appropriate to the knowledge, experience, and interests of both speakers and audience.

(2) Debatable, that is, not obviously false or true. The statements should involve an honest difference of opinion, with good arguments and evidence on both sides.

(3) Phrased in the affirmative. Positive statements prevent confusion by making the issue clear-cut.

(4) Restricted to contain only one idea. This keeps the debate within narrow limits.

(5) Worded clearly. The words should be ones that can be defined exactly. This prevents the debate from becoming a mere quibble over the meaning of words.

(6) Worded in such a way that they do not assume to be true, that which must be proved. The following would be a proposition to avoid, "Resolved, that the inefficient committee system of Congress should be reorganized." The word *inefficient* would bring on a flood of arguments which could confuse the real debate issue.

Propositions are of two kinds, those involving fact and those involving policy.

Propositions of fact try to answer the question, "Is this true?" Examples are:

"Resolved, that the expenditures of the advertising department of the XYZ Manufacturing Company during the last year were wasteful."

"Resolved, that radio soap operas have beneficial effects on listeners."

"Resolved, that John Jones did a good job as president of the student council."

Propositions of policy attempt to answer the question,

DEBATE

"Should we change?" Examples are:

"Resolved, that treaties should be ratified by a majority vote in both houses of Congress."

"Resolved, that uniform marriage and divorce laws should be adopted by the federal government."

"Resolved, that the legal voting age should be lowered to eighteen years."

Other Good Debate Subjects might be:

(1) The President of the United States should be elected for one term of six years, and should be ineligible for re-election.

(2) The President of the United States should have the power to veto items in appropriation bills.

(3) Juries should be abolished in criminal trials.

(4) The city of -------- should adopt the city-manager form of government.

(5) States should adopt single-house legislatures.

(6) The President should be elected by direct vote.

(7) Women should receive the same pay as men for the same jobs.

(8) The United Nations should be granted more power to settle international problems.

(9) Chain stores are harmful to public welfare.

(10) Labor unions should be required to incorporate.

(11) Social fraternities in high school should be abolished.

(12) The federal government should own and operate all radio broadcasting stations.

(13) The city of -------- should own and operate its electric light and power plant.

(14) The state of -------- should provide one thousand college and university scholarships each year for promising high school graduates.

(15) Capital punishment should be abolished.

(16) The railroads should be owned and operated by the federal government.

(17) The United States and the British Commonwealth should establish joint citizenship for their citizens.

(18) The members of the cabinet should be required to defend their departments on the floors of the houses of Congress.

(19) The granting of credit for extracurricular school activities is beneficial.

(20) National governments should be replaced by membership in a world government.

(21) "Spectator sports" in high school and college should be abolished.

(22) All high schools should require a four-year course in the basic sciences.

Analysis. After a subject has been selected, and the proposition carefully worded, the next step is analysis of the proposition by both debating teams. Analysis of the proposition begins with a broad understanding of

Chicago Board of Education

Youthful Debaters in a School History Class. Through debates students learn not only to present their ideas clearly, but also what is much more important, to think seriously of the problems facing adults who live in a democracy.

Debating the Cause of American Slavery. This old picture shows one of the seven famous Lincoln-Douglas debates. These took place in various Illinois towns in 1858 and helped to elect Abraham Lincoln to the presidency in 1860.

Chicago Historical Society, © The Torch Press

DEBATE

it. Each member of a team should know as much about the opponents' case as he knows about his own side. Good debaters study the origin and history of a proposition, define its terms, and survey carefully all the arguments and evidence for and against it. After a broad understanding is gained, the debaters have to decide which arguments are *pertinent* (closely related and worthy of being included), and which are *irrelevant* (not closely related, and should be excluded). The areas of agreement and disagreement in the proposition are located by this process. The arguments are narrowed down to points on which the affirmative says "yes" and the negative says "no." This argumentative process is called *finding the issues*.

The Issues. The chief points of difference between the affirmative and the negative are the *main issues*. These may have divisions called *subordinate issues*. There must be a clash of opinion on both the main and the subordinate issues. A good way to help find the issues is to list the opposing arguments in parallel columns. In the subject, "Resolved, that the legal voting age should be lowered to eighteen years," this process might lead to the selection of the following main and subordinate issues:

I. Are young people between the ages of 18 and 21 qualified to vote?
   A. Do they want to vote?
   B. Do they have enough knowledge and judgment to vote intelligently?
   C. Do they have enough interest in the problems of government to vote intelligently?
II. Would lowering the voting age to 18 be beneficial to the country?
   A. Would it raise the quality of the people voting?
   B. Would it lead to better decisions on candidates and public questions?

The Evidence. After the issues have been determined, the next step for the debaters is to find the evidence which will prove the issue true or false. Evidence can be in the form of either facts or opinions. *Facts* are actual occurrences or things that can be proved to exist. They may be made plain by means of description, narration, examples, comparisons, statistics, visual aids, and testimony of fact. *Opinions* are interpretations of facts, and appraisals of the views of others. Only the opinions of persons who are experts on the particular subject should be given in a debate.

Rebuttal. After the issues have been determined, and the evidence selected, the next step is to prepare to answer the arguments and evidence of the other team. The debaters on each team must select the arguments and evidence of their opponents which they believe can be successfully attacked. Then they must prepare their own arguments and their own evidence which will make up the attack.

Several Types of Debates are in use in the high schools and colleges. In the *traditional* form, there are two or three speakers on each side, each of whom makes a *constructive* speech and a *rebuttal* speech. With two speakers on each side, the order of speaking is:

Constructive Speeches (eight minutes each)
  1. First affirmative
  2. First negative
  3. Second affirmative
  4. Second negative

Rebuttal Speeches (four minutes each)
  1. First negative
  2. First affirmative
  3. Second negative
  4. Second affirmative

Another type of debate is the *cross-examination* form, which was developed at the University of Oregon. In this, each of the constructive speakers is cross-examined by an opposing speaker. Then each side presents a rebuttal and a *summary*. A team is usually made up of two speakers. A third speaker is sometimes used on each team to present the rebuttal and summary. With three speakers on each side, the order of speaking is:

Constructive Speeches (eight minutes) and **Cross-Examinations** (four minutes)
  1. First affirmative
  2. Cross-examination by second negative
  3. First negative
  4. Cross-examination by first affirmative
  5. Second affirmative
  6. Cross-examination by first negative
  7. Second negative
  8. Cross-examination by second affirmative

Rebuttal and Summary Speeches (eight minutes)
  1. Third negative
  2. Third affirmative

The Decision. If a decision is to be given in a debate, one or more judges listen to the speakers on both sides. Then each judge decides which team has presented the most convincing argument, and votes for that team. The team that has the most votes is declared the winner of the debate.
                                                           W. HAYES YEAGER

See also ORATORS AND ORATORY; PARLIAMENTARY PROCEDURE; PUBLIC SPEAKING.

DEBENTURE BOND. See BOND.

DEBORAH, *DEHB oh ruh*, was a Biblical prophetess of Israel in the period of the Judges, the 1100's B.C. She was the wife of Lapidoth. Deborah acted as an adviser to her people, and as a judge in their disputes. The Israelite tribes greatly admired her for her wisdom, and she rose to a position of leadership among the people of Israel.

When she heard of the cruel treatment her people had received from the Canaanites, Deborah summoned Barak, the Israelite leader. Together they worked out a plan of action for the army of Israel. They hoped to defeat the Canaanite army under Sisera. They fought near Mount Tabor, on the plain of Esdraelon. A rainstorm aided Israel, turning the plain into mud and trapping the enemy chariots. Sisera fled on foot, and was later murdered in his sleep. The victory was important in Israel's struggle with the Canaanites. One of the most notable victory odes of the Bible is the *Song of Deborah* in Judges 5.   WALTER G. WILLIAMS

DEBRECEN, *DEH breh tsen* (pop. 129,671; alt. 400 ft.), is a city in Hungary. It lies about 137 miles east of Budapest. It is an important railroad junction, and serves as a market center for the eastern Great Plain area. The Reformed Church was so powerful in Debrecen in the 1500's that the city was sometimes called the *Calvinist Rome*. Lajos Kossuth proclaimed Hungarian independence in Debrecen in 1849.   R. JOHN RATH

DEBS, EUGENE VICTOR (1855-1926), was a colorful and eloquent spokesman for the American labor movement and for socialism. He formed the American Railway Union (A.R.U.) in 1893 as an industrial union for all railroad workers regardless of their craft. The A.R.U. ordered its members not to move Pullman cars in 1894, in support of a strike by the workers making Pullman cars. President Grover Cleveland used federal troops to break the strike, charging that it interfered with the mails. Debs went to prison for six months when he refused to comply with a federal court injunction. He came out of jail a confirmed socialist.

Eugene V. Debs
U&U

Debs made a speech condemning war during World War I. He was convicted under the Espionage Law and went to prison in 1918, on a 10-year sentence. President Warren G. Harding commuted his sentence on Christmas Day in 1921.

Debs ran for the presidency on the Socialist ticket in 1904, 1908, 1912, and 1920. He ran his 1920 campaign while still in prison, and received nearly 1,000,000 votes. He wrote *Walls and Bars*, a book dealing with prison conditions and problems.

Debs was born in Terre Haute, Ind., and went to work in the railroad shops at the age of 15. Later he became a locomotive fireman, and was active in the Brotherhood of Locomotive Firemen. He served as national secretary and treasurer of the Brotherhood from 1880 to 1893. Debs served in the Indiana legislature from 1885 to 1892.   JACK BARBASH

DEBT, *det,* is anything owed, especially a sum of money which one person owes to another. The law states that a debt is *all that is due a man under any form of obligation or promise.* A person who owes a debt is called a *debtor,* and the one to whom it is owed is the *creditor.* If the debtor is unwilling or unable to pay the debt, the creditor may bring suit to recover his money. Such a suit brought by one citizen against another is a *civil suit.* If the court finds that the debt is owed, the creditor obtains a *judgment* against the debtor. Then if the debtor fails to pay, the creditor may appeal to the sheriff for an *execution* of judgment. This gives the creditor the right to seize enough property of the debtor to pay the debt and the costs of the process. But there are exceptions as to what property or money may be seized. This law varies in different states, provinces, and territories.

Time Limits on Collection of Debts. The courts ordinarily state that a debtor should pay his debts, even though the creditor does not demand payment. But if the creditor makes no effort to collect the money within a certain number of years, the debt becomes *outlawed* by a *statute of limitations.*

Penalties for Debts. In ancient times, a debtor was handed over to the mercy of his creditors to become a slave. This was true in Greece and Rome, among the Hebrews, and among the Saxons in England. During feudal times, however, every man was first of all a soldier, and armies would have broken up if overlords jailed their men for the debts they owed.

As feudalism declined, and trade and industry rose, harsh treatment of debtors was revived. Prison terms were the usual punishment, and thus no money was recovered. Early American settlers included many fugitives from debtors' prisons.   ROBERT W. MERRY

Related Articles in WORLD BOOK include:
Attachment   Encumbrance   Guaranty   Moratorium
Bankrupt   Garnishment   I.O.U.   National Debt
Bond

DEBT, NATIONAL. See NATIONAL DEBT.

DEBUSSY, *duh BYOO sih,* or, in French, *duh BYOO SEE,* **CLAUDE** (1862-1918), was one of the greatest French composers of the late 1800's. He founded the impressionistic style in music. The symbolist poets and impressionist painters of Paris influenced him early in life. He set out to develop a similar style in music. His full name was ACHILLE CLAUDE DEBUSSY.

His deft orchestration is strewn with flecks of instrumental color in such works as *Prélude à l'Après-midi d'un Faune* (Prelude to the Afternoon of a Faun) (1894), *La Mer* (The Sea) (1905), *Images* (1909), and *Jeux* (Games) (1912). His technique resembles the way impressionist painters stipple their canvases with small dots of separate colors. His orchestral *Nocturnes* (1899) were intended, he tells us, to describe "the variety of impressions and the special effects of light that the word suggests." One of them, "Festivals," he said, portrays "the atmosphere vibrating with sudden flashes of light."

In his songs, and in such piano pieces as *Suite Bergamasque* (1905), Debussy used new harmonic effects that he once described as his "latest experiments in musical chemistry." The suite contains his beautiful "Clair de Lune" (Moonlight). In his operatic masterpiece, *Pelléas and Mélisande* (1902), and in his two books of *Preludes* for piano (1910 and 1913), he explored the psychology of blending the sensations of taste, touch, sight, and sound. He used such titles as "Sounds and Perfumes on

Metropolitan Opera Assn.

Claude Debussy, *below,* composed sensitive works that led to the impressionistic style in music. He based his opera *Pelléas and Mélisande* on a play by Maurice Maeterlinck. In the scene, *right,* Pelléas declares his love for Mélisande.

Culver

DEBYE, PETER

the Evening Air" to describe his works. In part of one book of *Preludes* for piano, called "The Engulfed Cathedral," he described a scene as being "in a sweetly sonorous mist." But all his works are not impressionistic. *The Children's Corner*, written for his little daughter in 1908, includes the well-known "Golliwog's Cake Walk." This and *Minstrels* (1910) show the influence of American Negro entertainers.

Debussy was born at Saint Germain-en-Laye. He began to study the piano at the age of 7, and later entered the Paris Conservatory. In 1884, he won a prize for his cantata, *L'Enfant Prodigue* (The Prodigal Child). The prize included 3 years of study in Rome. Back in Paris, he wrote another cantata, *La Demoiselle Élue* (The Blessed Damozel), in 1888. He proved his genius in 1893 with his *Quartet in G minor*.   WILLIAM FLEMING

DEBYE, *duh BY,* **PETER JOSEPH WILLIAM** (1884-   ), a Dutch physicist and chemist, won the 1936 Nobel prize in chemistry for his studies of molecular structure. He was born in Maastricht, The Netherlands, and attended engineering school at Aachen, Germany. He served as chairman of the Cornell University chemistry department from 1940 to 1950.   CARL T. CHASE

DECAL, or **DECALCOMANIA,** *dee KAL koh MAY nih uh*, is the process of transferring pictures and designs from specially prepared paper to glass, wood, metal, or other surfaces. Decal designs are printed in inks, lacquers, varnishes, or plastics, on special paper coated with an adhesive that loosens in water. When dipped in water, they slide from the paper onto the desired surface. The adhesive will dry and make them stick.

Decals were developed in Germany in the 1800's, and first used on dinnerware. With them, an artist could draw his design and have a printing press produce copies, instead of painting it by hand on every dish.

Today, decals have many uses. People buy them to decorate their homes. Manufacturers of toys and dishes put them on their products. Decals are used as tax stamps and for automobile-licensing stickers, because they are difficult to remove and use again. Many products have decal signs and trademarks. Thousands of decals are used to mark instrument dials in airplanes. Pattern decals cover furniture.   JOHN B. CALKIN

DECALITER. See METRIC SYSTEM.

DECALOGUE is the Ten Commandments. These make up the moral law set forth in the Old Testament. According to the Bible, they were "written with the finger of God" on two tablets of stone, and given to Moses on Mt. Sinai. The Hebrews called these laws the *ten words*. The name *decalogue* comes from the Greek language, and means *ten words*. See also TEN COMMANDMENTS.

DECAMERON. See BOCCACCIO, GIOVANNI.

DECAMETER. See METRIC SYSTEM.

DECATHLON, *dee KATH lahn,* is a two-day contest in 10 events to determine an all-around track and field champion. Athletes compete in the 100-meter dash, broad jump, 16-pound shot-put, high jump, and 400-meter run in that order on the first day. They try the 110-meter hurdles, discus throw, pole vault, javelin throw, and 1,500-meter run on the second day.

The athletes compete against established time and distance standards, instead of against each other. Points are scored on the basis of 1,000 for each event, and the athlete obtaining the most points in all 10 events wins the decathlon. Rafer Johnson of the United States has held the world decathlon record since 1955. He set the present record, 8,392 points, in winning the decathlon in the 1960 Olympic Games.

The Amateur Athletic Union (AAU) holds an annual decathlon event. The decathlon became a part of the Olympic Games in 1912.

Six United States athletes have won the Olympic decathlon title. Harold Osborn won in 1924; James Bausch in 1932; Glenn Morris in 1936; Robert Mathias in 1948 and 1952; Milton Campbell in 1956; and Rafer Johnson in 1960.   FRED RUSSELL

See also TRACK AND FIELD (pictures).

HOW TO APPLY DECALS

1 Cut out the decal and soak it in water for about 10 seconds.

2 Slide part of the decal off the backing, hold it in place, then pull the backing away.

3 Press out all wrinkles and air bubbles with a soft cloth. The decal will remain in place.

Meyercord Co.

DECATUR, Ill. (pop. 78,004; alt. 682 ft.), is an industrial city located in one of the richest farming regions of the United States. It is about 40 miles east of Springfield and about 170 miles southwest of Chicago (see ILLINOIS [color map]). Its major industries process soybeans, make corn products, and build tractors and motor graders. It also has the repair shops of the Wabash Railroad, and iron and brass foundries. Other factories make carburetors, compressors, kites, pharmaceuticals, pumps, store and restaurant fixtures, and water and gas systems. Decatur was settled about 1830. The first post of the Grand Army of the Republic was established there in 1866. The city is the home of Millikin University. Decatur has a council-manager government.   PAUL M. ANGLE

DECATUR, STEPHEN (1779-1820), was one of the most daring officers in the United States Navy during its early years. He is remembered for his toast: "Our country: In her intercourse with foreign nations may she always be right; but our country, right or wrong." Handsome, brave, and honorable, Decatur enjoyed great popularity with his men and with the public. He was one of a group of men who established the naval traditions of the United States. Others were John Barry, John Paul Jones, David Porter, Oliver Hazard Perry, Thomas Macdonough, and Isaac Hull.

Decatur was born in a log cabin at Sinepuxent, Md., on Jan. 5, 1779. He made his first long voyage at the age of eight, when he went to France on a ship commanded by his father, a merchant captain. He became

Stephen Decatur stands victoriously on the deck of a man-of-war after successfully forcing Algiers to sign a peace treaty.
Chicago Historical Society

a midshipman in 1798 during the naval war with France, and rose to lieutenant in 1799. Given command of the *Enterprise* during the war with Tripoli, he captured an enemy vessel that was renamed the *Intrepid*. In this ship he led a picked band into Tripoli Harbor on the night of Feb. 16, 1804, and set fire to the frigate *Philadelphia*, once commanded by his father, which the Tripoli pirates had captured. Not a man was killed and only one was wounded. The English Admiral Horatio Nelson called this exploit, "the most bold and daring act of the age." Because of it, Decatur won a sword from Congress and a captaincy when he was only 25.

Commanding a squadron of three ships in the War of 1812, he captured the British frigate *Macedonian* after a desperate struggle. He became a commodore in 1813, and took command of a squadron in New York Harbor. He attempted to run the British blockade early in 1815, but his flagship, the *President*, struck the bar at Sandy Hook and was damaged. He was forced into a fight against heavy odds. Wounded, he had to surrender. The British sent him to Bermuda as a prisoner of war, but he was soon released.

He next sailed against Algiers, Tunis, and Tripoli, where he forced the rulers to release United States ships and prisoners and to stop molesting U.S. vessels. On his return he became a navy commissioner. Suspended Commodore James Barron, at whose court-martial Decatur had presided, challenged him to a duel in 1820. Decatur was killed by the commodore near Bladensburg, Md. Barron had accused certain officers, headed by Decatur, of persecuting him.   BRADFORD SMITH

See also BARRON, JAMES; BARBARY STATES.

DECAY may be understood by what happens to a piece of raw meat left on a dish in a warm room for a week or more. Bacteria, molds, and yeasts grow in and on the meat and *decompose*, or digest, it. The waste products of their growth remain as "decayed meat." Fruits and vegetables may also decay in the same manner.

When the decomposing substances are proteins, such as meat, fish, eggs, and cheese, bad-smelling gases are produced. *Hydrogen sulfide*, for example, is a bad-smelling gas of rotten eggs. Decay is aided by warmth and moisture, because bacteria grow well under these conditions. Decay sometimes is called *putrefaction*.

The bacteria causing decay are found in soil, air, water, manure, milk, and many other places. They are usually harmless and do a great deal of good by decomposing manure and dead animals and plants. The waste products (products of decay) are of great value as fertilizers.

If bacteria in foods are killed, as by baking or stewing, decay is prevented. Refrigeration retards the growth of bacteria. Decay and food spoilage by bacteria does not take place rapidly in refrigerators. Disinfectants such as carbolic acid stop the progress of decay because they destroy bacteria.   MARTIN FROBISHER, JR.

Related Articles in WORLD BOOK include:
Antiseptic   Fermentation   Ptomaine Poisoning
Bacteria   Food Preservation   Teeth (How Teeth
Biochemistry   Pasteur, Louis   Decay)
Decomposition

DECCAN. See INDIA (Location and Surface Features).
DECELERATION. See ACCELERATION.

DECEMBER

DECEMBER is the twelfth and last month of the year. It was the tenth month in the ancient Roman calendar. The first part of its name, *decem*, means *ten* in Latin. December once had 29 days, but Julius Caesar added two more, making it one of the longest months.

Winter begins in December in the northern half of the world. Some people call it "the frosty month." But winter does not begin until December 21 or 22, and most of December is usually warmer than other winter months. On the first day of winter, the sun reaches the solstice, when it appears to have gone farthest south. In the Northern Hemisphere, it is the shortest day of the year. But it is the longest day in the southern half of the world. The latter part of December has long been a holiday season. The Romans honored Saturn, the god of harvest, with a festival called *Saturnalia*. Today, Christmas is the chief holiday of the month in many countries. Christians celebrate it as the birthday of Jesus Christ, and its color and good feeling shed a glow of good will over the rest of the month. The Druids of northern Europe used mistletoe in a December festival. We still use mistletoe at Christmas.

Activities. In the Northern Hemisphere, most birds have gone to warmer climates. But many animals are active. Mink, ermine, beavers, and foxes grow beautiful coats of fur. Muskrats make their domed homes of ice in frozen streams and ponds. Nature finishes preparing for the long winter ahead. Many people make feeding places for birds and squirrels.

Special Days. People celebrate many holidays in December. They prepare for New Year's Eve parties on the last day of December. Some people in New England observe December 21 as Forefathers' Day in honor of the landing of the Pilgrims at Plymouth on Dec. 21, 1620. People in several European countries celebrate December 6 as the Feast of Saint Nicholas. Many of them exchange gifts on that day. Saint Nicholas is also a patron saint in Greece, Russia, and some other countries.

After Christmas day on December 25, some Christian

IMPORTANT DECEMBER EVENTS

2 Battle of Austerlitz fought between France and the combined forces of Austria and Russia, 1805.
— President Monroe proclaimed the Monroe Doctrine in his message to Congress, 1823.
— Georges Seurat, French painter, born 1859.
— John Brown, American abolitionist, hanged at Charles Town, Va. (now W.Va.), 1859.
— Scientists achieved the first controlled atomic chain reaction, in Chicago, 1942.

VAN BUREN    **JOHNSON**    **WILSON**

3 Gilbert Stuart, American painter, born 1755.
— Illinois admitted to the Union, 1818.
— George B. McClellan, Union general, born 1826.
— Novelist Joseph Conrad born 1857.
4 George Washington retired as Commander in Chief of the Continental Army, 1783.
— Thomas Carlyle, Scottish author, born 1795.
5 Phi Beta Kappa, honorary scholastic fraternity, founded at the College of William and Mary, 1776.
— Martin Van Buren, eighth President of the United States, born at Kinderhook, N.Y., 1782.
— Walt Disney, American producer of animated cartoons and other motion pictures, born 1901.
— Amendment 21 to the United States Constitution, repealing prohibition, proclaimed, 1933.
— The AFL and CIO merged, 1955.
6 Families in Europe celebrate the Feast of St. Nicholas, often exchanging gifts.
— Columbus discovered Hispaniola, 1492.
— Warren Hastings, leader in India, born 1732.
— Dave Brubeck, American jazz pianist, born 1920.
7 Delaware ratified the Constitution, 1787.
— Japanese forces attacked Pearl Harbor, 1941.
8 Horace, Roman poet, born 65 B.C.
— Eli Whitney, inventor of cotton gin, born 1765.
— Jan Sibelius, Finnish composer, born 1865.
— The American Federation of Labor organized, 1886.
9 John Milton, English poet, born 1608.

9 Joel Chandler Harris, American author of the "Uncle Remus" stories, born 1848.
— The British captured Jerusalem, 1917.
10 William Lloyd Garrison, American journalist and abolitionist, born 1805.
— Mississippi admitted to the Union, 1817.
— Composer César Franck born 1822.
— Emily Dickinson, American poet, born 1830.
— The Territory of Wyoming authorized women to vote and hold office, 1869.
— Spain ceded Philippines to the United States, 1898.
— President Theodore Roosevelt awarded Nobel prize for mediation in the Russo-Japanese War, 1906.
11 Hector Berlioz, French composer, born 1803.
— Indiana admitted to the Union, 1816.
— Robert Koch, German bacteriologist, born 1843.
— Edward VIII of Great Britain abdicated, 1936.
12 John Jay, American diplomat, born 1745.
— Pennsylvania ratified the Constitution, 1787.
— Gustave Flaubert, French novelist, born 1821.
— Guglielmo Marconi received the first radio signal sent across the Atlantic Ocean, from England to Newfoundland, 1901.
13 The Council of Trent opened, 1545.
— Sir Francis Drake left England to sail around the world, attacking Spanish possessions, 1577.
— Heinrich Heine, German poet, born 1797.
14 Tycho Brahe, Danish astronomer, born 1546.
— George Washington died at Mt. Vernon, 1799.
— Alabama admitted to the Union, 1819.
— James Doolittle, American air pioneer and air force general, born 1896.
— Roald Amundsen, Norwegian explorer, reached the South Pole, 1911.
15 The first 10 amendments to the Constitution, including the Bill of Rights, ratified, 1791.

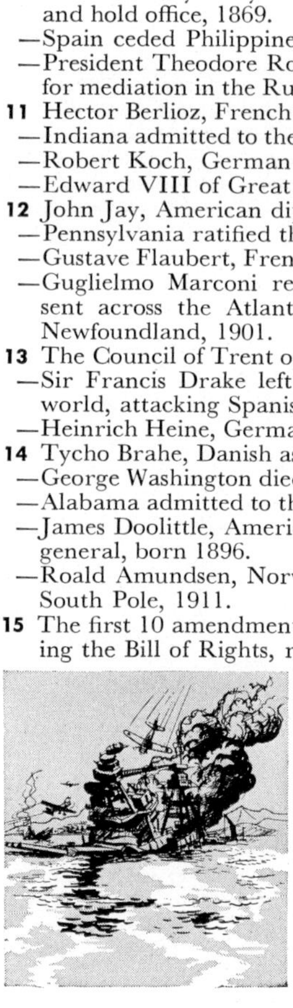

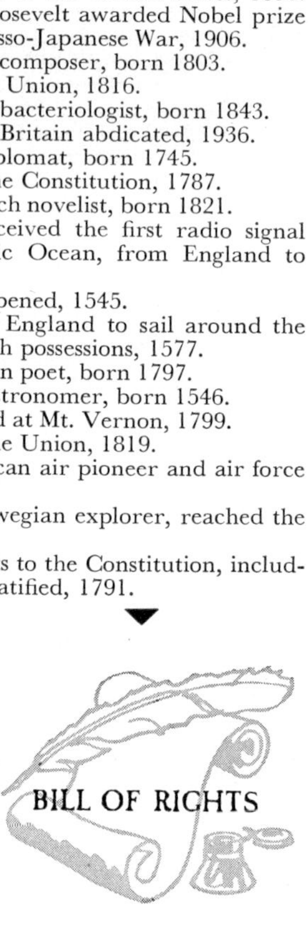

BILL OF RIGHTS

churches observe the Feast of Saint Stephen on December 26, the Feast of Saint John the Evangelist on December 27, and Holy Innocents' Day on December 28.

Popular Beliefs. A beautiful Bible story tells how the star of Bethlehem shone above the manger and guided the wise men to it. The star at the top of a Christmas tree symbolizes this star.

Symbols. Holly, narcissus, and poinsettia are regarded as special December flowers. People in many parts of the world use holly at Christmas celebrations. The turquoise and the zircon are the birthstones for December.
GRACE HUMPHREY

Quotations

'Twas the night before Christmas, when all through the house
Not a creature was stirring, not even a mouse;
The stockings were hung by the chimney with care,
In hopes that St. Nicholas soon would be there;
The children were nestled all snug in their beds,
While visions of sugar-plums danced in their heads.
Clement Clarke Moore

DECEMBER

Heap on more wood! The wind is chill;
But let it whistle as it will,
We'll keep our Christmas merry still.
Sir Walter Scott

The sun that brief December day
Rose cheerless over hills of gray,
And, darkly circled, gave at noon
A sadder sight than waning moon.
John Greenleaf Whittier

I heard the bells on Christmas Day
Their old, familiar carols play,
And wild and sweet
The words repeat
Of peace on earth, good will to men.
Henry Wadsworth Longfellow

Related Articles in WORLD BOOK include:

Calendar	Holly	Solstice
Christmas	Nicholas, Saint	Turquoise
Feasts and Festivals	Santa Claus	

IMPORTANT DECEMBER EVENTS

15 Maxwell Anderson, American playwright, born 1888.
15 or 16 Composer Ludwig van Beethoven born 1770.
16 English Parliament passed Bill of Rights, 1689.
— Boston Tea Party, 1773.
— Novelist Jane Austen born 1775.
— Actor-playwright Noel Coward born 1899.
— The Germans began the Battle of the Bulge, 1944.
17 Sir Humphry Davy, English chemist, born 1778.
— John Greenleaf Whittier, American poet, born 1807.
— William Lyon Mackenzie King, three times prime minister of Canada, born 1874.
— Orville Wright made first heavier-than-air flight at Kitty Hawk, N.C., 1903.
— Willard Libby, American chemist, born 1908.
18 Charles Wesley, English clergyman and author of many hymns, born 1707.
— New Jersey ratified the Constitution, 1787.
— Edward Alexander MacDowell, American composer and pianist, born 1861.
— Amendment 13 to the U.S. Constitution, ending slavery, proclaimed, 1865.
— Christopher Fry, British playwright, born 1907.
19 Continental Army camped for the winter at Valley Forge, Pa., 1777.
— Physicist Albert Michelson born 1852.
20 The United States took over Louisiana, 1803.
— Harvey Firestone, American industrial leader, born 1868.
21 The Pilgrims landed at Plymouth, Mass., 1620.
— Playwright Jean Baptiste Racine born 1639.
— Benjamin Disraeli, twice prime minister of Great Britain, born 1804.
— Joseph Stalin, Russian dictator, born 1879.
22 James Oglethorpe, founder of Georgia, born 1696.
— Opera composer Giacomo Puccini born 1858.

22 Poet Edwin Arlington Robinson born 1869.
23 Richard Arkwright, British inventor, born 1732.
— George Washington resigned his commission as commander in chief of the army, 1783.
— U.S. Federal Reserve System established, 1913.
24 "Kit" Carson, American frontier scout, born 1809.
— United States and Great Britain signed the Treaty of Ghent, ending the War of 1812, 1814.
— Matthew Arnold, British critic, born 1822.
25 Christmas, celebrated in Christian countries as the birthday of Jesus Christ.
— Isaac Newton, English mathematician who discovered laws of gravitation, born 1642.
— Washington and his men started across the Delaware River to Trenton, N.J., 1776.
— Clara Barton, "Angel of the Battlefield" and founder of the American Red Cross, born 1821.
26 Battle of Trenton, 1776.
— George Dewey, American admiral, born 1837.
27 Johannes Kepler, German astronomer, born 1571.
— Louis Pasteur, French chemist, born 1822.
28 Iowa admitted to the Union, 1846.
— Woodrow Wilson, 28th President of the United States, born at Staunton, Va., 1856.
29 Charles Goodyear, American inventor, born 1800.
— Andrew Johnson, 17th President of the United States, born at Raleigh, N.C., 1808.
— William E. Gladstone, four-time prime minister of Great Britain, born 1809.
— Texas admitted to the Union, 1845.
— American aviator Billy Mitchell born 1879.
30 The U.S. acquired the Gadsden Purchase from Mexico, 1853.
— Rudyard Kipling, British poet and storyteller, born 1865.
— Andreas Vesalius, the first anatomist to describe the human body completely, born 1514.
— Henri Matisse, French painter, born 1869.

DECEMBRIST UPRISING. See RUSSIA (Alexander I and Napoleon; Reaction and Reform).

DECEMVIRS, *dee SEHM vurz,* means a commission or official body of 10 members. The term commonly refers to the Roman commission of 10 members set up in 451 B.C. to replace the ordinary magistrates. They had absolute power to codify the laws, and draw up 10 tables of law. A second commission added two more tables the next year. The later decemvirs were violent. In 449 B.C., the army and people overthrew them. See also TWELVE TABLES, LAWS OF THE.

DECENTRALIZATION. See CENTRALIZATION.

DECIBEL, *DEHS ih bell,* is the unit used to measure the intensity of a sound. A decibel is a tenth of a larger unit, the *bel,* which was named for Alexander Graham Bell, the inventor of the telephone.

The decibel is not the unit of loudness. Loudness is often measured in *phons,* which depend on both the intensity and the *frequency,* or number of vibrations per second, of sound (see PHON).

The intensity of a sound depends on the energy it produces. The energy of sound is usually given in watts per square centimeter (see WATT). A sound of 0 decibels transmits 10^{-16} watts to each square centimeter of the ear. As a decimal fraction, this energy is written 0.000,000,000,000,000,1 watts. Zero decibels is about the least intensity of sound that the normal ear can hear. A sound of 10 decibels (1 bel) transmits ten times as much energy as a 0 decibel sound. A sound of 20 decibels transmits a hundred times as much energy as a 0 decibel sound and ten times as much as a 10 decibel sound. Ordinary speech measures approximately 60 decibels.   JOHN W. RENNER

See also SOUND (Measuring Sound).

DECIDUOUS TREE, *dee SID yoo us,* is the name for any tree which loses its leaves at a certain time each year and later grows new leaves. In northern temperate regions, most deciduous trees lose their leaves in the autumn (see LEAF). The twigs and branches stay bare all winter. The following spring they grow a new set of green leaves. Before the leaves die, some of the food material they contain is drawn back into the twigs and branches. There it is stored and used the following spring. Deciduous trees usually have broad leaves. These include oak, ash, beech, chestnut, and birch.

Scientists think that losing the leaves helps some trees to conserve water in the winter. Water normally passes into the air from tree leaves by a process called *transpiration* (see TRANSPIRATION).

Some trees, called *evergreens,* have a covering of leaves all year long (see EVERGREEN). A thick, outer layer of cells protects the leaves, or *needles,* of the evergreen from the cold. Some trees that lose their leaves in temperate climates keep them all year farther south.

Scientific Classification. Deciduous trees belong to phylum *Tracheophyta.* They are in both class *Gymnospermae* and class *Angiospermae.*   THEODORE W. BRETZ

See also TREE (The Broad-Leaf Trees).

DECILLION, *dee SILL yun,* is a thousand nonillions, or a unit with 33 zeros, in the United States and France. One decillion is written 1,000,000,000,000,000,000,-000,000,000,000,000. A decillion is a unit with 60 zeros in Great Britain and Germany. See also NUMBER.

DECIMAL NUMBER SYSTEM is the way we write numbers. The name *decimal* comes from the Latin word for *ten.* In this system, we use single number symbols, such as 1, 2, and 3, to write the numbers from one to nine. Then we use two symbols—1 and 0—and two places to write ten. The number 10 is the base of the system. We also write fractions with the decimal number system. For example, .6 is $\frac{6}{10}$ and .32 is $\frac{32}{100}$.

The decimal number system is one of the world's most useful ways of writing numbers. It uses only 10 simple symbols. A child can learn to write these symbols easily. In ancient Egypt, a child had to learn ⋂ for ten, ⌒ for one hundred, and ⚜ for one thousand. It is much easier to write 10, 100, and 1,000. We can use the system to write numbers as large or as small as we want. Some Australian tribes count from one to five, and then use a word that means *plenty* for any number larger than five. We can count in thousands, millions, billions, and much larger numbers. And we can write the tiniest parts of numbers with decimal fractions.

Prehistoric men counted on their fingers. This practice provided a natural base for a number system based on 10. Most civilizations of the ancient world—Egypt, Greece, and Rome—had separate symbols for 10 and 100. The Roman system, which used letters to stand for numbers, remained in use in Europe for many centuries. See ROMAN NUMERALS.

Mathematicians in India invented and developed zero and the place system between 100 B.C. and A.D. 150. The Arabs borrowed this new decimal system from India in the 800's. European merchants adopted the system from the Arabs and it began to spread through Europe in the 1200's. Most European countries now use the decimal system in all parts of their arithmetic. The English-speaking countries continue to use some measurements that are not based on the decimal number system. For example, the foot is divided into 12 inches.

Learning the Decimal System

Place Value. The decimal number system has only nine *digits* (number symbols) and *zero* [0]. However, you can write numbers larger than nine with these symbols. For example, you can write the number fourteen by using a system of *place value.* You do not need to invent a new symbol for fourteen. You can use two digits you already know, 1 and 4.

——————— **DECIMAL SYSTEM TERMS** ———————

Decimal or **Decimal Fraction** is a fraction whose denominator is 10 or some power of 10, such as 100 or 1,000. It is written with a decimal point.

Decimal Place is a number place to the right of the decimal point for tenths, hundredths, and so on.

Decimal Point [.] separates the two parts of a decimal number. Any number to the left of the point is a whole number. Any number to the right is a decimal fraction.

Digit is any one of the number symbols from 1 to 9.

Period is a group of three digits in a large number set off by commas for easier reading.

Place is the position of a digit with respect to other digits. The number 10 occupies two places.

Place Value means that the value of a digit—whether it is ones, tens, hundreds, or some larger number—depends on the place it occupies.

Repeating Decimal is a digit or group of digits that repeats itself indefinitely. For example, 1 ÷ 3 is .333333333....

Zero [0] means no thing or no number.

DECIMAL NUMBER SYSTEM

By counting, you can see that fourteen consists of a group of ten things and a group of four things. You can use 1 to stand for the group of ten things and 4 to stand for the group of four things. You can see that a digit occupies a space or *place* on the page. Two digits together, for example, 25, occupy two places. *You use the first place, on the right, for single things. You use the second place to the left for groups of ten things.* Here is the way you write sixteen: 16. When you see the number 16, you know that it means six single things and one group of ten things. The first place on the right is called *the 1's place*. It is for the numbers from one to nine. The second place to the left is called *the 10's place*. It is for the groups of ten from ten to ninety.

Suppose you want to write twenty-four. Twenty-four consists of two groups of ten things and four single things. So you must write a 2 in the 10's place and a 4 in the 1's place: 24. When you see the number 24, you know that it means two groups of ten (or two 10's) and four single things (or four 1's).

Place value means that the *value*, or the number of things for which a digit stands, depends on the place it occupies. In the first place on the right, a 2 means two 1's. In the second place to the left, it means two 10's. Number systems based on numbers other than 10 often help a beginner to understand place value. For example, the binary system uses only two symbols, 0 and 1, and the duodecimal system has a base of 12 (see BINARY ARITHMETIC; DUODECIMAL).

Zero. Most people learn that 10 stands for a group of ten things before they understand place value. Look at the number 10. Zero means *no thing* or *no number*. So zero in the first place on the right means no 1's. The 1 in the second place to the left means one 10, or one group of ten things. Look at the number 30. It means three 10's and no 1's. Zero does more than show no thing or no number. *Zero holds a number in place.* Without zero, you might mistake 10 for 1 or 30 for 3. This explains why zero is so important in making the decimal number system work. See ZERO.

Larger Numbers. Using two places, you can write the numbers from 10 to 99. To write one hundred, you must use the *third* place to the left. Look at the number 100. It stands for one group of a hundred things. Because there are no 1's or 10's, you must write zeros in the 1's and 10's places. The 1 in the third place to the left means one group of a hundred things. The two zeros mean no 10's and no 1's. Here are two more examples of three-place numbers:

617 = six 100's, one 10, and seven 1's
403 = four 100's, no 10's and three 1's

You use the fourth place to the left for thousands, the fifth for ten-thousands, and so on. Here is a chart that will help you learn the place values from one to one billion:

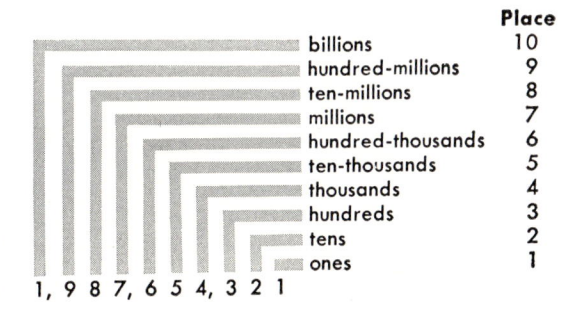

	Place
billions	10
hundred-millions	9
ten-millions	8
millions	7
hundred-thousands	6
ten-thousands	5
thousands	4
hundreds	3
tens	2
ones	1

1, 9 8 7, 6 5 4, 3 2 1

Look at the number 6,527,308,642. The chart shows you that this number means six billions, five hundred-millions, two ten-millions, seven millions, three hundred-thousands, no ten-thousands, eight thousands, six hundreds, four tens, and two ones. And there are numbers larger than a billion (see NUMBER).

When you write large numbers, such as one million, you should set off every three digits with a comma starting from the right and counting to the left. For example, there are two commas within 1,000,000. These groups of three digits set off by commas are called *periods*. The commas make large numbers easier to read.

DECIMAL NUMBER SYSTEM

Operations. You should always remember place value when you add, subtract, multiply, or divide numbers. For example, suppose you want to add 32, 18, and 21. First, you write the numbers to be added so there is a column for 1's and a column for 10's.

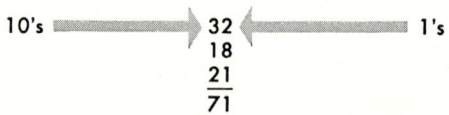

```
10's ━━━━▶ 32 ◀━━━━ 1's
           18
           21
           ──
           71
```

To be correct in arithmetic, you should always keep columns of numbers straight. If you are careless, you may forget whether the number with which you are working is a 10, a 100, or a 1,000. If you add the 1's column in the example above, you will find there are eleven 1's and that you must transfer ten 1's to the 10's column. Each operation in arithmetic has a regular method you can learn for transferring numbers from one place to another. See ADDITION (How to Carry); SUBTRACTION (How to Borrow); MULTIPLICATION (How to Carry); DIVISION (Short Division).

Decimal Fractions

Decimal fractions are fractions such as $\frac{1}{10}$, $\frac{1}{100}$, and $\frac{1}{1,000}$ (see FRACTION). You always write decimal fractions *without a denominator* as part of the decimal number system. For example, $\frac{25}{100}$ is written .25. In the United States and Canada, everyone deals with decimal fractions when using the system of dollars and cents. The amount $1.25 includes a decimal fraction, because .25 means $\frac{25}{100}$ of a dollar, or 25 cents.

Decimal Places. Look at the fraction $\frac{1}{10}$. Ten $\frac{1}{10}$'s are 1, a whole number. To write $\frac{1}{10}$ as part of the decimal system, place a *decimal point* [.] to the right of the 1's place. The decimal point means that anything to the right of the point is a fraction of 1. Then the first place to the right of the decimal point is for $\frac{1}{10}$'s. Suppose you want to write $6\frac{2}{10}$, using the decimal system. You write 6 in the 1's place and place a decimal point on its right. Then you write a 2 in the tenths place to the right: 6.2. Here is the way you write $\frac{9}{10}$: .9 . Places to the right of the decimal point are called *decimal places*.

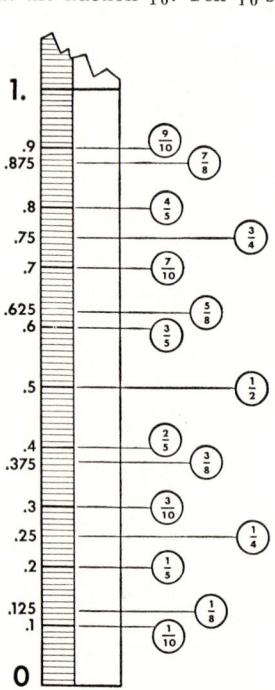

The second place to the right of the decimal point is for hundredths. Here is the way you write $1\frac{34}{100}$: 1.34 . If you add a dollar sign, 1.34 becomes a dollar and thirty-four cents: $1.34. You will find decimal fractions easier to learn if you think of decimal places in terms of money. Each dime or ten cents is a tenth of one dollar. The dimes are the first place to the right of the decimal point. Each cent, or penny, is a hundredth of one dollar. The cents are the second place to the right of the decimal point.

You use zero as a place holder. For example, suppose you want to write $\frac{6}{100}$ as a decimal fraction. The decimal fraction .6 means $\frac{6}{10}$, so you must use a zero to show there are no tenths when you write $\frac{6}{100}$: .06 . Here is the way you write $3\frac{7}{100}$: 3.07 .

You use the third decimal place to the right for thousandths, the fourth for ten-thousandths, and so on. Here is a chart that will help you learn the decimal places from tenths to billionths. Notice that the chart is for fractions, such as tenths and hundredths, and *not* for whole numbers, such as tens and hundreds.

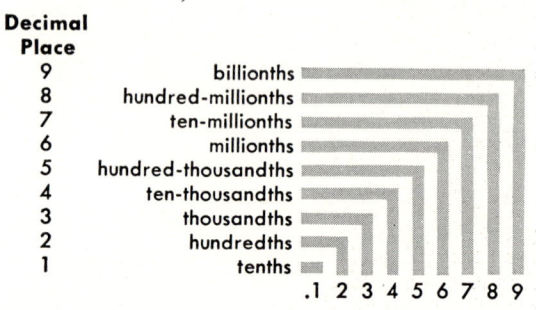

Decimal Place	
9	billionths
8	hundred-millionths
7	ten-millionths
6	millionths
5	hundred-thousandths
4	ten-thousandths
3	thousandths
2	hundredths
1	tenths

.1 2 3 4 5 6 7 8 9

Look at the decimal fraction .0007 . The chart shows you that this is seven ten-thousandths, or $\frac{7}{10,000}$. The zeros in the decimal fraction show that there are no tenths, hundredths, or thousandths.

Changing Fractions. People call fractions such as $\frac{1}{4}$, $\frac{5}{6}$, and $\frac{7}{8}$ *common fractions*. Suppose you want to change $\frac{7}{8}$ to a decimal fraction expressed in thousandths. *To change a common fraction to a decimal fraction, divide the numerator by the denominator.* To change $\frac{7}{8}$ to a decimal fraction, divide 7, the numerator, by 8, the denominator:

$$\frac{.875}{8 \overline{)7.000}}$$

First, add a decimal point and as many decimal places (zeros) as necessary to 7, the number being divided. Second, place the decimal point in the *quotient*, or answer, directly above the decimal point in the number being divided. Then complete the division. The common fraction $\frac{7}{8}$ becomes the decimal fraction .875 .

Some common fractions produce *repeating decimal fractions*. Suppose you want to change $\frac{1}{3}$ to a decimal fraction:

$$\frac{.333333}{3\overline{)1.000000}}$$

In a repeating decimal fraction, one digit or a group of digits repeats itself indefinitely. For practical purposes, this means you cannot complete the division. Most people use as many decimal places as necessary for their particular problem and attach a common fraction to the decimal fraction. For example, one choice you can use for $\frac{1}{3}$ is $.33\frac{1}{3}$.

To change a decimal fraction to a common fraction, remove the decimal point and write in the proper denominator. For example, .005 is $\frac{5}{1,000}$, .67 is $\frac{67}{100}$, and .1004 is $\frac{1,004}{10,000}$.

Common Fractions can be written as decimal fractions. The scale shows decimal and common fraction equivalents.

1.	
.9	$\frac{9}{10}$
.875	$\frac{7}{8}$
.8	$\frac{4}{5}$
.75	$\frac{3}{4}$
.7	$\frac{7}{10}$
.625	$\frac{5}{8}$
.6	$\frac{3}{5}$
.5	$\frac{1}{2}$
.4	$\frac{2}{5}$
.375	$\frac{3}{8}$
.3	$\frac{3}{10}$
.25	$\frac{1}{4}$
.2	$\frac{1}{5}$
.125	$\frac{1}{8}$
.1	$\frac{1}{10}$
0	

Then, if possible, reduce the fraction. For example, .75 becomes $\frac{75}{100}$, which can be reduced to $\frac{3}{4}$. See FRACTION (Converting and Reducing Fractions).

Rounding Off. When you work with decimal fractions, you must often *round off* your answer. For example, .354 rounded off to the nearest hundredth is .35, because .354 is nearer to .35 than to .36. Similarly, .354 rounded off to the nearest tenth is .4, because .354 is nearer to .4 than to .3. But .365 rounded off to the nearest hundredth is .37. *A number halfway between two values is usually rounded off to the greater value.*

Rounding off is useful in practical problems, particularly in measuring things. But you must be careful about attaching zeros to decimal fractions. When workmen measure things, they often do not make the most precise measurement. Instead, they use the most practical unit. For example, the measurement of a piece of wood might be recorded as .6 of a foot. This does not mean that the piece of wood is .60 or $\frac{60}{100}$ of a foot. It might be .59 or .61 of a foot. So if you wanted to add .6 and, for example, .29, you must either change .29 to .3 or find a more precise measurement for .6.

Operations with Decimal Fractions. You add and subtract decimal fractions just as you do whole numbers. For example, suppose you want to add 4.63, 5.02, and 4.80. Arrange the numbers so that there are columns for tenths and hundredths as well as for whole numbers.

```
 4.63
 5.02
 4.80
-----
14.45
```

The decimal point in the answer is placed directly below its position in the columns of numbers to be added or subtracted. The decimal point makes no difference in "carrying" or "borrowing" numbers from one place to another. In the example above, the sum of the tenths column is 14 tenths. Fourteen tenths is the same as 1.4, so you write a 4 in the tenths column and "carry" the 1 to the 1's column. The decimal point stays unchanged.

When you multiply exact decimal fractions, the operation itself is the same as the multiplication of whole numbers. But you must learn where to place the decimal point in the product, or answer. *The number of decimal places in the product is the sum of the decimal places in the two numbers multiplied.* Here are two examples:

```
234.62           18.972
  ×2             ×3.13
------           ------
469.24           56916
                 1 8972
                 56 916
                 --------
                 59.38236
```

In the example on the left, count the decimal places in the multipliers. There are two: tenths and hundredths in 234.62, and no decimal places in 2. So the product will have two decimal places. Count two places from the right in the product and place the decimal point between the 2 (tenths) and the 9 (1's). Use the same method in the example on the right. In this case, both multipliers include decimal fractions. They contain a total of five decimal places. So the decimal point in the answer appears five places from the right.

There is a regular method for dividing decimal fractions, but you must learn its steps in detail. See DIVISION (Division of Decimal Fractions).

LEE E. BOYER

Related Articles in WORLD BOOK include:

Abacus	Division	Multiplication
Addition	Duodecimal	Number
Arithmetic	Fraction	Percentage
Binary Arithmetic	Metric System	Subtraction
Dewey Decimal System		

Practice Decimal Examples

Write the following numbers and decimal fractions.
(1) One hundred, no tens, and six ones.
(2) Three ten-thousands, one thousand, no hundreds, four tens, and four ones.
(3) Seven thousands, no hundreds, two tens, and no ones.
(4) One million, three hundred-thousands, no ten-thousands, six thousands, two hundreds, no tens, and two ones.
(5) Six tenths and two hundredths.
(6) No tenths, no hundredths, and nine thousandths.
(7) No tenths, three hundredths, and two thousandths.
(8) No tenths, no hundredths, no thousandths, four ten-thousandths, and four hundred-thousandths.

Change into decimal fractions.
(9) $\frac{4}{5}$ (10) $\frac{3}{8}$ (11) $\frac{2}{3}$ (12) $\frac{1}{2}$ (13) $\frac{1}{16}$ (14) $\frac{5}{8}$

Change into common fractions.
(15) .40 (16) .02 (17) .125 (18) .66$\frac{2}{3}$ (19) .175 (20) .003

Place the decimal point in the answer.

```
(21)  8.67    (22)  6.45    (23)  7.28    (24)      4 3 2
     +3.22        -3.31          ×.3         10/ 4 3 2.0
     -----        -----         -----
     1 1 8 9      3 1 4         2 1 8 4
```

Answers to the Practice Examples

(1) 106	(9) .8 or .80	(17) $\frac{1}{8}$
(2) 31,044	(10) .375	(18) $\frac{2}{3}$
(3) 7,020	(11) .66$\frac{2}{3}$	(19) $\frac{7}{40}$
(4) 1,306,202	(12) .5 or .50	(20) $\frac{3}{1,000}$
(5) .62	(13) .0625	(21) 11.89
(6) .009	(14) .625	(22) 3.14
(7) .032	(15) $\frac{2}{5}$	(23) 2.184
(8) .00044	(16) $\frac{1}{50}$	(24) 43.2

DECIMAL SYSTEM. See DECIMAL NUMBER SYSTEM.
DECIMETER. See METRIC SYSTEM.
DECIPHER. See CODES AND CIPHERS.
DECK TENNIS is a game similar to tennis, in which the players use a 6-inch rope or rubber ring instead of racket and ball. They toss the ring back and forth over a net that is 4 feet 8 inches high. There is a 3-foot neutral zone on each side of the net. The court is 40 feet long and 18 feet wide. Inside alley lines narrow the singles court to 12 feet in width.

To serve, a player tosses the ring underhand over the net into the service court. The receiver must catch the ring in the air with one hand, and immediately return it over the net beyond the neutral zone. Only one serve is allowed, but serves that touch the top of the net are made again. Only the server scores. He receives points if an opponent fails to catch the ring or fails to return it to the server's court. The server continues to serve as long as he makes points. The game is usually 15 points. If a tie of 14-all occurs, a player must make two consecutive points to win. Two out of three games make up a match. Sometimes tennis scoring is used (see TENNIS).

HELEN I. DRIVER

DECLARATION OF HUMAN RIGHTS. See HUMAN RIGHTS, UNIVERSAL DECLARATION OF.

DECLARATION OF INDEPENDENCE

DECLARATION OF INDEPENDENCE. On every Fourth of July, the United States celebrates its birthday. On that date, in 1776, representatives of 13 British colonies in North America adopted an eloquent statement setting forth the reasons for declaring their independence from Great Britain.

No one was much surprised at the news. War against England had already begun. Battles had been fought at Lexington, Concord, and Breed's Hill. Colonial troops had seized Ticonderoga and Crown Point. George Washington had been named to head the colonial army. The spirit of independence was abroad in the land. Many men were asking, with Samuel Adams, "Is not America already independent? Why not then declare it?"

The actual birthday of the country was much quieter than later celebrations of its anniversary. No Liberty Bell rang out the glad news to a waiting crowd (see LIBERTY BELL). The great decisions for independence had really been taken much earlier.

On June 7, Richard Henry Lee of Virginia moved in the Continental Congress that "These United Colonies are, and of right ought to be, free and independent States." Three days later, Congress voted to name a special committee to draft a declaration supporting Lee's resolution. On June 11, it named John Adams, Benjamin Franklin, Thomas Jefferson, Robert Livingston, and Roger Sherman to the committee. Jefferson was given the task of preparing the draft. The committee titled its draft "A Declaration by the Representatives of the United States of America in Congress Assembled."

Congress approved the Lee resolution on July 2. Strictly speaking, this act became the official declaration of independence. On July 4, Congress adopted the final draft of the declaration in Independence Hall in

(Article continued on page 69)

The Declaration of Independence

In Congress, July 4, 1776. The unanimous Declaration of the thirteen united States of America,

When in the Course of human events, it becomes necessary for one people to dissolve the political bands which have connected them with another, and to assume among the powers of the earth, the separate and equal station to which the Laws of Nature and of Nature's God entitle them, a decent respect to the opinions of mankind requires that they should declare the causes which impel them to the separation.—

We hold these truths to be self-evident, that all men are created equal, that they are endowed by their Creator with certain unalienable Rights, that among these are Life, Liberty and the pursuit of Happiness.—

That to secure these rights, Governments are instituted among Men, deriving their just powers from the consent of the governed,—

That whenever any Form of Government becomes destructive of these ends, it is the Right of the People to alter or to abolish it, and to institute new Government, laying its foundation on such principles and organizing its powers in such form, as to them shall seem most likely to effect their Safety and Happiness. Prudence, indeed, will dictate that Governments long established should not be changed for light and transient causes; and accordingly all experience hath shown, that mankind are more disposed to suffer, while evils are sufferable, than to right themselves by abolishing the forms to which they are accustomed. But when a long train of abuses and usurpations, pursuing invariably the same Object evinces a design to reduce them under absolute Despotism, it is their right, it is their duty, to throw off such Government, and to provide new Guards for their future security.—

Such has been the patient sufferance of these Colonies; and such is now the necessity which constrains them to alter their former Systems of Government. The history of the present King of Great Britain is a history of repeated injuries and usurpations, all having in direct object the establishment of an absolute Tyranny over these States. To prove this, let Facts be submitted to a candid world.—

He has refused his Assent to Laws, the most wholesome and necessary for the public good.—

He has forbidden his Governors to pass Laws of immediate and pressing importance, unless suspended in their operation till his Assent should be obtained; and when so suspended, he has utterly neglected to attend to them.—

He has refused to pass other Laws for the accommodation of large districts of people, unless those people would relinquish the right of Representation in the Legislature, a right inestimable to them and formidable to tyrants only.—

He has called together legislative bodies at places unusual, uncomfortable, and distant from the depository of their public Records, for the sole purpose of fatiguing them into compliance with his measures.—

He has dissolved Representative Houses repeatedly, for opposing with manly firmness his invasions on the rights of the people.—

He has refused for a long time, after such dissolutions, to cause others to be elected; whereby the Legislative powers, incapable of Annihilation, have returned to the People at large for their exercise; the State remaining in the mean time exposed to all the dangers of invasion from without, and convulsions within.—

He has endeavoured to prevent the population of these States; for that purpose obstructing the Laws for Naturalization of Foreigners; refusing to pass others to encourage their migrations hither, and raising the conditions of new Appropriations of Lands.—

He has obstructed the Administration of Justice, by refusing his Assent to Laws for establishing Judiciary powers.—

He has made Judges dependent on his Will alone, for the tenure of their offices, and the amount and payment of their salaries.—

He has erected a multitude of New Offices, and sent hither swarms of Officers to harrass our people, and eat out their substance.—

He has kept among us in times of peace, Standing Armies without the Consent of our legislatures.—

He has affected to render the Military independent

The Declaration of Independence was signed in Independence Hall, Philadelphia. The American artist John Trumbull painted this scene.

Yale University Art Gallery

of and superior to the Civil power.—

He has combined with others to subject us to a jurisdiction foreign to our constitution, and unacknowledged by our laws; giving his Assent to their Acts of pretended Legislation:—

For quartering large bodies of armed troops among us:—

For protecting them, by a mock Trial, from punishment for any Murders which they should commit on the Inhabitants of these States:—

For cutting off our Trade with all parts of the world:—

For imposing Taxes on us without our Consent:—

For depriving us in many cases, of the benefits of Trial by Jury:—

For transporting us beyond Seas to be tried for pretended offences:—

For abolishing the free System of English Laws in a neighbouring Province, establishing therein an Arbitrary government, and enlarging its Boundaries so as to render it at once an example and fit instrument for introducing the same absolute rule in these Colonies:—

For taking away our Charters, abolishing our most valuable Laws, and altering fundamentally the Forms of our Governments:—

For suspending our own Legislatures, and declaring themselves invested with power to legislate for us in all cases whatsoever.—

He has abdicated Government here, by declaring us out of his Protection and waging War against us.—

He has plundered our seas, ravaged our Coasts, burnt our towns, and destroyed the lives of our people.—

He is at this time transporting large Armies of foreign Mercenaries to compleat the works of death, desolation and tyranny, already begun with circumstances of Cruelty & perfidy scarcely paralleled in the most barbarous ages, and totally unworthy the Head of a civilized nation.—

He has constrained our fellow Citizens taken Captive on the high Seas to bear Arms against their Country, to become the executioners of their friends and Brethren, or to fall themselves by their Hands.—

He has excited domestic insurrections amongst us, and has endeavoured to bring on the inhabitants of our frontiers, the merciless Indian Savages, whose known rule of warfare, is an undistinguished destruction of all ages, sexes and conditions.

In every stage of these Oppressions We have Petitioned for Redress in the most humble terms: Our repeated Petitions have been answered only by repeated injury. A Prince, whose character is thus marked by every act which may define a Tyrant, is unfit to be the ruler of a free people.

Nor have We been wanting in attentions to our British brethren. We have warned them from time to time of attempts by their legislature to extend an unwarrantable jurisdiction over us. We have reminded them of the circumstances of our emigration and settlement here. We have appealed to their native justice and magnanimity, and we have conjured them by the ties of our common kindred to disavow these usurpations, which, would inevitably interrupt our connections and correspondence. They too have been deaf to the voice of justice and of consanguinity. We must, therefore, acquiesce in the necessity, which denounces our Separation, and hold them, as we hold the rest of mankind, Enemies in War, in Peace Friends.—

We, therefore, the Representatives of the united States of America, in General Congress, Assembled, appealing to the Supreme Judge of the world for the rectitude of our intentions, do, in the Name, and by Authority of the good People of these Colonies, solemnly publish and declare, That these United Colonies are, and of Right ought to be, Free and Independent States; that they are Absolved from all Allegiance to the British Crown, and that all political connection between them and the State of Great Britain, is and ought to be totally dissolved; and that as Free and Independent States, they have full Power to levy War, conclude Peace, contract Alliances, establish Commerce, and to do all other Acts and Things which Independent States may of right do.—

And for the support of this Declaration, with a firm reliance on the protection of divine Providence, we mutually pledge to each other our Lives, our Fortunes and our sacred Honor.

In CONGRESS, July 4, 1776.

The unanimous Declaration of the thirteen united States of America.

[Full handwritten text of the Declaration of Independence, followed by signatures including John Hancock, Rob Morris, Benjamin Rush, Benj. Franklin, John Morton, Geo. Clymer, Ja. Smith, Geo. Taylor, James Wilson, Geo. Ross, Caesar Rodney, Geo. Read, Tho. M:Kean, Josiah Bartlett, Wm Whipple, Saml Adams, John Adams, Robt Treat Paine, Elbridge Gerry, Step. Hopkins, William Ellery, Roger Sherman, Sam^{el} Huntington, Wm Williams, Oliver Wolcott, Matthew Thornton, Abra Clark, and others.]

Historical Documents Co.—Frank H. Fleer Corp.;
Insurance Co. of North America Companies, Philadelphia

The Original Declaration of Independence is displayed in an upright case in the National Archives Building in Washington, D.C., above the United States Constitution and Bill of Rights. The priceless documents are sealed under glass. Any visitor can inspect them.

Signers of the Declaration of Independence

A biography of each signer of the Declaration of Independence appears in THE WORLD BOOK ENCYCLOPEDIA. Fifty members of Congress signed the engrossed copy of the Declaration on Aug. 2, 1776.

In the order they signed, they were:

John Hancock (Mass.)	William Williams (Conn.)
Josiah Bartlett (N.H.)	Benjamin Franklin (Pa.)
Philip Livingston (N.Y.)	William Paca (Md.)
Robert T. Paine (Mass.)	Francis Hopkinson (N.J.)
William Floyd (N.Y.)	Thomas Stone (Md.)
John Adams (Mass.)	Charles Carroll (Md.)
Francis Lewis (N.Y.)	Thomas Jefferson (Va.)
George Walton (Ga.)	George Taylor (Pa.)
Samuel Adams (Mass.)	Edward Rutledge (S.C.)
Richard Stockton (N.J.)	Joseph Hewes (N.C.)
Samuel Huntington (Conn.)	James Smith (Pa.)
Stephen Hopkins (R.I.)	George Ross (Pa.)
John Hart (N.J.)	George Clymer (Pa.)
Abraham Clark (N.J.)	Thomas Heyward, Jr. (S.C.)
Lewis Morris (N.Y.)	Button Gwinnett (Ga.)
John Morton (Pa.)	George Read (Del.)
Francis Lightfoot Lee (Va.)	James Wilson (Pa.)
John Penn (N.C.)	Thomas Lynch, Jr. (S.C.)
Roger Sherman (Conn.)	Samuel Chase (Md.)
William Whipple (N.H.)	Carter Braxton (Va.)
John Witherspoon (N.J.)	Benjamin Rush (Pa.)
William Ellery (R.I.)	Lyman Hall (Ga.)
William Hooper (N.C.)	Caesar Rodney (Del.)
Robert Morris (Pa.)	Thomas Nelson (Va.)
Benjamin Harrison (Va.)	Arthur Middleton (S.C.)

George Wythe (Va.) signed on August 27. On September 4, the document was signed by Richard Henry Lee (Va.), Elbridge Gerry (Mass.), and Oliver Wolcott (Conn.). Matthew Thornton (N.H.) signed on November 19. Thomas McKean (Del.) signed in 1781.

Philadelphia. This draft was largely Jefferson's work. John Hancock signed the document "by order and in behalf of Congress." Charles Thomson, secretary of Congress, attested Hancock's signature.

The public did not learn the actual words of the Declaration until July 8. The final version was called a "unanimous" declaration. But the word "unanimous" could not be properly used until July 19, when the New York delegation to Congress, which had not voted on July 4, reported that it favored the Declaration. Congress then ordered a copy of the Declaration engrossed on parchment and signed by all members of Congress. Fifty members signed the document on Aug. 2, 1776.

The ideas contained in the Declaration were not new. The English had used many of the same ideas to justify their revolution of 1688. But the simple beauty of the Declaration of Independence stirred the hearts of men and women from New Hampshire to Georgia.

When the British raided Washington in the War of 1812, the government hid the Declaration in Leesburg, Va. The Library of Congress in Washington held the original document from 1921 to 1952. Then the government moved the Declaration to the nearby National Archives Building. The text of the Declaration given in this article follows the spelling and punctuation of the parchment copy. RICHARD B. MORRIS

See also ADAMS, JOHN (National Politics); CONTINENTAL CONGRESS; JEFFERSON, THOMAS; UNITED STATES, GOVERNMENT OF (color picture).

DECORATION DAY

DECLARATION OF RIGHTS. See BILL OF RIGHTS; CONTINENTAL CONGRESS.

DECLARATORY ACT. See REVOLUTIONARY WAR IN AMERICA (Events Leading to the Revolution).

DECLENSION is a listing of the different case forms of a noun or pronoun. Some languages, such as Latin, Greek, and Russian, have complicated case systems. They have many forms for each noun or pronoun, varying with the way the words are used in sentences.

In English, the declension of nouns is extremely simple. English nouns have only two cases, a *common* case and a *possessive* case. For example:

	SINGULAR	PLURAL
Common	boy, man	boys, men
Possessive	boy's, man's	boys', men's

Six English pronouns have three cases, usually called *nominative*, *possessive*, and *objective*. These pronouns are *I, he, she, we, they,* and *who*. Here are the singular forms for three of them:

Nominative	I	he	who
Possessive	my, mine	his	whose
Objective	me	him	whom

Some pronouns have two possessive forms. One is used when the possessive is a modifier, as in "*my* team won"; "*her* cup broke"; "*their* letters came." The other form is used when the possessive is not a modifier, as in "*mine* won"; "*hers* broke"; "*theirs* came."

The form *whom* is probably dying out in speech, but it is used in writing when it is the object, as in "Whom should we ask?" PAUL ROBERTS

See also CASE; INFLECTION.

DECLINATION. See COMPASS (Variation).

DECODE. See CODES AND CIPHERS.

DECOMPOSITION, in chemistry, is the breaking down of a substance into simpler products, or into the elements of which it is composed. Decomposition may be brought about in several ways. Heat decomposes red mercuric oxide into its elements of oxygen and bright metallic mercury. Heat breaks down limestone to form lime and carbon dioxide. Heat also decomposes many organic compounds. An electric current decomposes water into its elements hydrogen and oxygen. Many substances are decomposed by chemical action. Sodium carbonate is used to decompose silicate rocks. Starch is broken down into a simple sugar, called *glucose*, by the action of a boiling, dilute acid. Decomposition may also be caused by the action of light, bacteria, or enzymes. The enzymes in yeast ferment sugar into simple products.

A distinction is sometimes made between decomposition caused by man, as in chemistry, and decomposition that occurs in nature. For example, animal and vegetable matter, when attacked by certain microorganisms, are said to *decompose*, or decay. Decay that occurs naturally is also called *putrefaction*. The decomposition of animals and plants plays an important part in geology. For example, coal and petroleum are formed from ferns and other marsh plants that became buried in swamps and decayed. JAMES S. FRITZ

DECOMPRESSION SICKNESS. See BENDS.

DECORATION, INTERIOR. See INTERIOR DECORATION.

DECORATION DAY. See MEMORIAL DAY.

DECORATIONS AND MEDALS

DECORATIONS AND MEDALS honor persons who have performed outstanding deeds, usually through service to their country. Decorations and medals go most often to members of the armed forces, but sometimes civilians are honored in this way. *Decorations* recognize acts of heroism or valuable service, often in time of war. Decorations are sometimes presented *posthumously*, or after death, to the family of a person who has died as the result of a heroic act. *Service medals* are awarded for other deeds or services, not necessarily heroic.

Decorations are in the form of a metal pendant or fob, and sometimes have the word *medal* in their names. Decorations and medals hang from colored pieces of cloth called *suspension ribbons*. In peacetime, the honored person ordinarily wears the actual decoration or medal only on formal, full-dress occasions. At other times, he wears a metal bar covered with a ribbon, representing the decoration or medal. A person who is awarded the same United States decoration twice does not receive the actual medal the second time. He receives instead a small emblem which he pins to the suspension ribbon or to the ribbon bar of the original award. The army and air force emblem for a second decoration is an *oak leaf cluster*. The navy and marine corps award a *gold star*. The wearer usually pins decorations and medals, or the ribbon *bars* that represent them, above the left breast pocket of his uniform. Decorations are worn above medals.

Decorations of the United States

General George Washington established the first United States military decoration in 1782. He awarded his soldiers the *Badge of Military Merit (Purple Heart)* for acts of unusual bravery. The Purple Heart was not used after the Revolutionary War until 1932.

Decorations, arranged in order of the degree of valor or achievement, are described below.

Medal of Honor. This decoration, often called the *Congressional Medal of Honor*, represents the nation's highest award. The President of the United States presents this decoration in the name of Congress. Only members of the armed forces who have risked their lives to perform some act of outstanding bravery in the presence of an enemy can receive the Medal of Honor. This decoration calls for gallantry "above and beyond the call of duty." The Medal of Honor entitles the winner to a $10-a-month pension at the age of 65. Only about 3,100 heroes have received the decoration. The medal hangs on a ribbon worn around the neck. Congress first authorized the medal for the navy in 1861, and for the army in 1862. The present form of the army medal, which the air force also uses, was created in 1904. It includes the head of Minerva, the Roman goddess of war.

Distinguished Service Cross of the army, the **Navy Cross,** and the **Air Force Cross** rank as the second highest decorations. They are awarded only to persons who have performed outstanding acts of heroism against an armed enemy. The Distinguished Service Cross was established in 1918. It also went to members of the air force until 1960, when Congress authorized the Air Force Cross. The Navy Cross was adopted in 1919.

In 1955, Congress created an organization of winners of the Medal of Honor, the Distinguished Service Cross, and the Navy Cross. It is called the Army and Navy Legion of Valor of the United States of America, Inc.

National Security Medal, established in 1953, is awarded to civilians or members of the armed forces for outstanding achievement in the field of intelligence relating to national security.

Distinguished Service Medal rates as the highest noncombat decoration. The decoration for the army and air force is of different design from that for the navy. The award goes to persons who perform exceptionally meritorious service to the government in a duty of great responsibility. The army's Distinguished Service Medal was authorized in 1918, and the navy's in 1919.

Silver Star is awarded for gallantry not great enough to merit the Medal of Honor or the Distinguished Service Cross. It was authorized in 1918. The army adopted the present design in 1932; the navy, in 1942.

Legion of Merit. Members of the armed forces of the United States, or of other friendly nations, can receive the Legion of Merit for performance of outstanding service. Members of the armed forces of another friendly nation may receive one of four degrees. These are *chief commander*, *commander*, *officer*, and *legionnaire*. The Legion of Merit was authorized in 1942.

Distinguished Flying Cross goes to persons who have distinguished themselves by heroism or outstanding achievement while flying. All members of the armed forces of the United States or other friendly countries are eligible. The Distinguished Flying Cross was authorized in 1926. The decoration has a four-bladed propeller on a bronze cross. President Coolidge awarded the first cross to Charles A. Lindbergh for his nonstop solo flight from New York to Paris in 1927.

Soldier's Medal, the **Navy and Marine Corps Medal,** and the **Airman's Medal** call for acts of heroism not involving conflict with an armed enemy. The Soldier's Medal, adopted in 1926, also went to air force members until 1960, when the Airman's Medal was adopted. The navy medal was authorized in 1942.

Bronze Star is awarded for heroism of a lesser degree than that required for the Silver Star. It is not given for heroism involving flight, because the Air Medal or the Distinguished Flying Cross is awarded for such service. The ribbon for the Bronze Star is red with narrow white borders and a blue center stripe edged with white. The Bronze Star was established in 1944.

Air Medal honors persons for meritorious achievement while flying. The degree of achievement is less than that required for the Distinguished Flying Cross. The bronze medal shows an eagle carrying two lightning flashes in its claws. The ribbon is blue with two broad gold stripes. The Air Medal was authorized in 1942.

Commendation Ribbon (navy), **Commendation Ribbon with Metal Pendant** (army), and **Air Force Commendation Medal** are awarded to members of the armed forces for meritorious achievement or service. These awards do not necessarily require combat with an enemy. The navy award was authorized in 1944, the army award in 1945, and the air force award in 1958.

Purple Heart is awarded to any member of the armed forces wounded in action against an enemy. The first purple heart decoration was simply a silk or cloth heart of purple trimmed with white lace. The decoration awarded today is a heart-shaped medal of purple en-

DECORATIONS AND MEDALS
Awarded by the United States

THE PURPLE HEART

MEDAL OF HONOR — Army and Air Force

MEDAL OF HONOR — Navy

DISTINGUISHED SERVICE MEDAL — Army and Air Force

DISTINGUISHED SERVICE MEDAL — Navy

DISTINGUISHED SERVICE CROSS — Army

NAVY CROSS

LEGION OF MERIT — Officer

LEGION OF MERIT — Legionnaire

VICTORY MEDAL, WORLD WAR I

VICTORY MEDAL, WORLD WAR II

DISTINGUISHED FLYING CROSS

SILVER STAR

NAVY AND MARINE CORPS MEDAL

Awarded by Other Countries

CROIX DE GUERRE — France, WORLD WAR II

LEGION OF HONOR — France

VICTORIA CROSS — British Commonwealth

IRON CROSS — Germany

MILITARY CROSS — Belgium

MEDAL FOR VALOR — Italy

DECORATIONS AND MEDALS

amel on bronze with a profile head of George Washington in the uniform of a general of the Revolutionary army. The medal hangs from a ribbon of purple silk with a narrow white stripe along the edge.

Medal for Merit and **Medal for Freedom** are two medals awarded by the United States to civilians. Members of the armed forces of other friendly nations may also receive the Medal for Freedom.

Merchant Marine Awards. The Distinguished Service Medal is the highest award given in the United States Merchant Marine. It is awarded to any person in the merchant marine who distinguishes himself by "outstanding act, conduct, or valor beyond the line of duty." Seamen receive a Meritorious Service Medal for acts considered less outstanding and in the line of duty. Each officer, master, or crew member of a maritime vessel that sees service in time of war or national emergency receives a service ribbon bar. Congress authorized the merchant marine awards in 1956.

United States Service Medals and Badges

A number of awards, not considered decorations, indicate that the wearer served in the armed forces in a certain period or campaign. Some of these medals include:

American Defense Service Medal was awarded to all members of the armed forces who served honorably for a year or more between Sept. 8, 1939, and Dec. 7, 1941.

Armed Forces Reserve Medal honors ten years of service in one or more of the Reserve units of the armed forces.

Good Conduct Medal goes to enlisted men or women who have served with good conduct for three years.

Korean Service Medal honors members of the armed forces who served in Korea between June 27, 1950, and July 27, 1954.

Other Service Medals include the *Victory Medals* of World War I and World War II, the *European-African-Middle Eastern Campaign Medal* and the *Asiatic-Pacific Campaign Medal* of World War II, the *Medal for Humane Action* (Berlin Airlift), the *United Nations Service Medal* of the Korean War, and the *WAC Service Medal*.

Badges are awarded to members of the armed forces for certain abilities and skills. Among the army badges is the *Combat Infantryman Badge*, awarded for combat in a major battle. The badge has a silver musket or gun fixed to a blue bar with a silver wreath around it. See ARMY, UNITED STATES (color picture).

A pilot wears a typical air force badge. It is silver-colored and consists of a shield between a pair of wings. See AIR FORCE, UNITED STATES (picture).

Navy badges include a gold-colored one for submarine service. It shows a submarine on the surface of the water flanked by dolphin. See NAVY, UNITED STATES (color picture).

Unit Emblems represent citations awarded the wearer's military unit for heroic action or outstanding achievement. The four unit emblems are the *Distinguished Unit Citation* (air force and army), the *Presidential Unit Citation* (marine corps and navy), the *Meritorious Unit Commendation* (air force and army), and the *Navy Unit Commendation* (marine corps and navy). Military personnel may also wear five unit emblems of other nations. They are the *French Fourragère*, the *Belgian Fourragère*, the *Dutch Orange Lanyard*, the *Philippine Presidential Unit Citation Badge*, and the *Republic of Korea Presidential Unit Citation Badge*.

Decorations and Orders of Other Countries

The countries of Europe and Asia have always placed strong emphasis on military decorations and orders. Some of the well-known awards include:

Belgium. *Military Cross* is awarded to officers only. They receive the decoration after twenty years of honorable service.

British Commonwealth. *Victoria Cross* is the highest British military decoration. This award calls for extraordinary bravery in the presence of the enemy. Victoria Crosses were originally made from metal taken from guns captured in the Crimean War of 1854-1856. Queen Victoria authorized the decoration in 1856. The British Government grants a special income of ten pounds a year to each winner of the Victoria Cross below the rank of a commissioned officer.

Distinguished Service Order, a decoration awarded for gallantry, carries nearly as much honor as the Victoria Cross. The decoration is in the form of a cross, and bears the initials of the reigning king or queen. It was authorized in 1886.

Order of Merit, established by King Edward VII in 1902, represents excellence in military, scientific, artistic, or professional work. The medal is in the form of a cross with red and blue enamel. The words "For Merit" are engraved inside a laurel wreath.

George Cross, first awarded by King George VI during World War II, is given for civilian bravery.

France. *Legion of Honor* is a decoration indicating membership in an honor society established by Napoleon in 1802. Both military men and civilians may become members of the legion for outstanding military or civilian services. The legion has five classes in this order: grand crosses, grand officers, commanders, officers, and chevaliers or knights.

Croix de Guerre (krwah duh GAIR) is a military decoration awarded to soldiers of France or its allies for acts of bravery. The award's name means *cross of war*. A bronze palm pinned to a Croix de Guerre ribbon shows that a person has merited the award a second time. A silver palm indicates that the honor has been awarded five times. A number of heroes from countries other than France have been honored with the Croix de Guerre since it was established in 1915.

Médaille Militaire, or Military Medal, is a decoration established by Napoleon III in 1852. It honors distinguished service in combat.

Germany. The *Iron Cross* is a military decoration to honor outstanding bravery or service. King Frederick William III of Prussia established the award in 1813. The decoration originally bore a W in the center that stood for King Frederick William. The Nazis replaced the W with a swastika during World War II.

Russia established two military honor awards during World War II. The government awards high officers of the army the *Order of Victory* for successful campaigns. The Order of Victory decoration has a star-shaped medal studded with diamonds and rubies. Junior officers and enlisted men receive the *Order of Glory* for heroism in battle.   ARTHUR E. DuBois and MADGE C. GRIFFIN

See also KNIGHTHOOD, ORDERS OF.

DECORATIVE ARTS is a term applied to objects used in decoration. It includes furniture, ceramics, silver, rugs, hangings, glass, small bronzes, carved woodwork, panels painted for decoration, and incidental objects for tables or cabinets. Decorative arts also include those often associated with churches, such as work in enamel, ivory, glass, gold, silver, bronze, and stained glass.

Decorative arts are often referred to as the *minor arts*. But this term does not mean that they are inferior. Some of the greatest objects created by man are called decorative arts. The term *fine arts* usually refers to the major works of painters, sculptors, and architects (see FINE ARTS). The *useful arts*, in combining beauty and practicality, are more closely related to the decorative arts (see USEFUL ARTS).

Decorative arts have always played an important part in the lives of peoples. Prehistoric man decorated his utensils, weapons, and clothing. Gorgeous objects of furniture and decoration created by Egyptian craftsmen have been found in tombs. The Greeks and Romans were intensely interested in the comforts of life. The decorative arts often accompanied these, and the greatest artists decorated everything from temples to ordinary pottery wine jugs. During the Middle Ages, men decorated their churches with ivory, enamel, and gold. The Renaissance produced many outstanding examples of the minor arts, including fine glassware from Venice and enamels from France.

Museums exhibit decorative arts of the past. Contemporary designers study these objects and express the present in new applications or in new ideas. Now many decorative arts are simple and useful in accordance with present-day styles. WILLIAM M. MILLIKEN

Related Articles in WORLD BOOK include:

Beadwork	Inlay	Paperwork,
Carving	Interior Decoration	Decorative
Ceramics	Ironwork, Decorative	Pottery
Enamel	Ivory	Pyrography
Furniture	Jewelry	Stained Glass
Gilding	Lace	Tapestry
Glassware	Mosaic	

DECORATOR. See INTERIOR DECORATION (Careers).
DECRESCENDO. See MUSIC (Terms).
DEDUCTIVE METHOD is the process of reasoning by which we draw conclusions by logical inference from given premises. If we begin by accepting the propositions that "All Greeks have beards" and that "Zeno is a Greek," we may validly conclude that "Zeno has a beard." We refer to the conclusions of deductive reasoning as *valid*, rather than *true*, because we must distinguish clearly between *that which follows logically* from other statements and *that which is the case*.

Starting premises may be articles of faith or assumptions. Before we can consider the conclusions drawn from these premises as valid, we must show that they are consistent with each other and with the original premise. Mathematics and logic are examples of disciplines that make extensive use of the deductive method. The scientific method requires a combination of induction and deduction. S. I. HAYAKAWA

See also INDUCTIVE METHOD; SCIENCE (The Scientific Method; Logic and Organization).

DEE, RIVER, is a picturesque stream in England and Wales. It is mentioned for its beauty in the works of English writers and poets. The River Dee rises in Lake Bala, Merionethshire, Wales. Near Chester, England, the Dee widens into a broad stream which empties into the Irish Sea. The river is about 70 miles long. See also BORE. FRANCIS H. HERRICK

DEED in common law was a written contract or agreement which had been properly signed under legal seal. The term deed is so used in the broadest sense today. But in its more restricted meaning it refers to a written agreement covering the sale or gift of real estate. It must be signed and delivered. When a deed is signed, it must usually be witnessed by one or more persons. Laws vary on the number and necessity of witnesses. A deed must be *acknowledged* before some official who has power to administer oaths. The seller or giver of the real estate acknowledges a deed when he swears that he is selling or giving the property of his free will.

The person who receives the property has the deed *recorded*, usually in the office of the registrar of deeds for the county in which the property is located. Every purchaser should ask for an *abstract of title*, which is a condensed history of title with mention of all liens or liabilities to which it may be subject (see ABSTRACT). A simplified method of property transfer, called the Torrens system, is used in some parts of the United States and other countries (see TORRENS SYSTEM).

There are two principal kinds of deeds, *quitclaim* and *warranty*. By a *quitclaim deed*, the purchaser acquires only the seller's rights to a piece of property. If the title is not clear, the purchaser is liable for any claims brought against the property, unless he can prove fraud on the part of the seller. By a *warranty deed*, the purchaser is guaranteed a clear title to the property he buys. The seller assumes responsibility for any later claims.

United States law requires that revenue stamps be attached to deeds. WILLIAM TUCKER DEAN

See also ESCROW; TITLE.

DEEP refers to any ocean area with a depth of more than 18,000 feet. More than 100 deeps have been found in ocean floors. Contrary to popular belief, they are not found in the center of the ocean. Most of them occur close to mountainous islands where steep shores plunge down to the bottom of the sea.

Challenger Deep, in the Mariana Trench 200 miles southwest of Guam, ranks as the deepest known ocean deep. The ocean floor at this point is 35,800 feet below the surface. Milwaukee Deep, north of Puerto Rico, has the greatest recorded depth in the Atlantic. It was found in 1939, and has a depth of 30,246 feet. ROBERT O. REID

See also ATLANTIC OCEAN (The Ocean Bed); EARTH (color picture, Heights and Depths); OCEAN (The Ocean Bed; picture, Characteristics of the Ocean Floor); PACIFIC OCEAN (Location and Size).

DEEP-SEA ANIMALS. See FISH (picture, Unusual Fishes); OCEAN (pictures).

DEEP-SEA DIVING. See DIVING, DEEP-SEA.

DEEP-SEA FISHING. See FISHING; FISHING INDUSTRY.

DEEPING, WARWICK (1877-1950), an English novelist, wrote his most famous book, *Sorrell and Son*, as a result of his experiences in World War I. He wrote more than 40 novels, including *Old Pybus*, which also gained wide popularity. His characters were drawn from real people, and his novels have happy endings. Deeping was born in Essex, England. R. W. STALLMAN

DEER

Wisconsin Conservation Dept.

DEER are among the most graceful of all hoofed animals. They are noted for their swift running and their ability to jump. Male deer, especially the male of the European red deer, are called *stags*. They are also known as *bucks*. Female deer are called *does*, and the young are known as *fawns*. The male deer have solid branching horns that are called antlers. They usually shed these horns every year. When attacked, deer use their antlers and their sharp front hoofs as weapons, although they usually prefer to run away.

Deer belong to the group of animals which have even numbers of toes. They run on two toes. They also belong to a smaller group of even-toed animals called *ruminants*, which have four stomach sections. The food is partly digested in one section of the stomach and then returned to the mouth. Returned food, called a *cud*, is chewed again before passing to the other sections. Deer are also classified as *ungulates*, or mammals with the last joint of the toe encased in a hoof.

Deer often cannot see stationary objects, but quickly detect motion. Smell is their keenest sense.

Deer live in nearly all parts of the world, except central and southern Africa and Australia. There are about sixty different kinds of deer. The largest deer is the giant moose, which lives in the Kenai Peninsula in Alaska. It is often more than six feet tall at the shoulder. The smallest deer is the pudu, or rabbit deer, which lives in Chile and is less than one foot tall. The American key deer, named for the Florida Keys where it lives, is only 27 inches tall. These deer can survive only in the Keys region. About a hundred live on game reservations in the area. Other deer include the caribou, elk, mule deer, red deer, and roebuck. The three important deer living in North America are the mule deer, the Columbian black-tailed deer, and the Virginia white-tailed deer.

The White-Tailed Deer

The white-tailed deer is perhaps the most important deer in North America. It is called the Virginia white-tailed deer because the first specimen described scientifically was killed in Virginia in 1784. This deer is the most widely distributed big game animal in America. This animal was once found from the Atlantic to the Pacific oceans, and from southern Canada to Peru.

The tail of this deer is feathery and snow-white. When the deer is startled and begins to run, its tail stands straight up. The deer's coat is sleek and shining. Its slender legs end in black hoofs. Its face has sharp features and its eyes are large and brown. In midsummer, the white-tailed deer has a red coat. When winter approaches, the coat turns to a light bluish gray. The largest white-tailed deer live along the Canadian border, where males sometimes weigh more than 275 pounds. Farther south, the deer are smaller. A small white-tailed deer known as the Coues deer is found in Arizona and New Mexico. It has a light brown coat in summer and a gray coat in winter. The males usually do not weigh more than 100 pounds.

The deer breed in late September to November. The white-tailed deer bears one to three young in the late spring. The young are covered with white spots, which disappear when the new fall coat of hair is grown. The male sheds its antlers in winter. By spring it has grown new ones. At first these new antlers are very tender and are covered with a soft, velvetlike covering of hair. The antlers gradually become hard as stone. When the horns are fully grown, the male can fight any rival. In autumn,

A Male Deer Grows New Antlers Each Year. These pictures show the stages of growth. The deer shed their antlers each winter. The following spring, the buds of new ones appear. The buds soon grow into small, blunt antlers. Later, during the summer, they grow more and begin to develop branches called *tines*. A soft, velvety hair covers the antlers until they are full-grown. By autumn, the hair is shed, leaving the antlers tall and sharp. During the autumn mating season, rival males fight duels in which they push against each other's antlers until the weaker deer turns and runs away.

Wisconsin Conservation Dept.

March 25 **April 15**

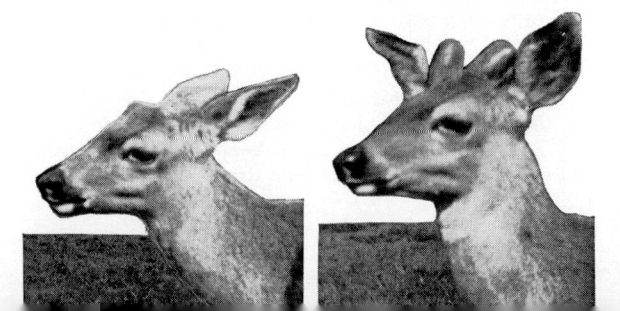

A Fawn, or baby, white-tailed deer has a reddish-brown coat with white spots. Their coats blend with the natural color of their surroundings and help conceal them from their enemies. The fawn's white spots resemble flecks of bright sunlight.

A Powerful Buck, or male, mule deer has large, full-grown antlers in autumn. His keen sense of smell warns him of danger, and his strong legs enable him to run faster than 30 miles an hour. Mule deer are so named because their large ears resemble those of mules.

Josef Muench

during the breeding season, rival bucks frequently engage in duels. They rarely hurt each other, however, because they fight by pushing against one another with their antlers. Eventually, the weaker buck turns and runs. But, occasionally, the rivals lock antlers and cannot break away from each other. Usually when this happens, both deer die of starvation.

White-tailed deer browse for their food like most other members of the deer family. They do not graze as domestic cattle do. They eat buds and twigs of wild shrubs and trees, such as willow, maple, and young aspen shoots. They generally live at the edges of woods and forests, where they can feed on berries and young second-growth trees.

The white-tailed deer was the most important deer to the early pioneers in North America. Deer were second only to the beaver in supplying the pioneers with much of their meat and clothing. Deerskin was used in making clothing such as moccasins, leggings, pants, coats, shoelaces, hats, and gloves. The colonists not only ate deer meat, but also shipped large numbers of deerskins to England. During 1756, the Province of Georgia alone shipped about 600,000 deerskins to England. The deer were killed mainly by guns, but they were often captured in camouflaged pits dug deep along the paths they took through the forest, or at places where they came to drink water or lick the salt that cropped out of the ground. Even today, deerskin is considered valuable for clothing.

Lewis and Clark might never have been able to finish

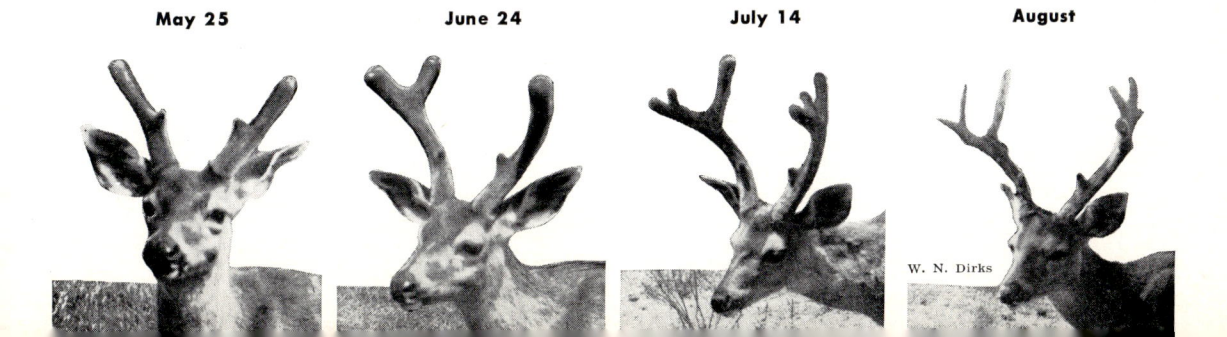

May 25   **June 24**   **July 14**   **August**

W. N. Dirks

Chital, or Axis Deer

Columbian Black-Tailed Deer

Red Deer

National Zoological Park, Washington, D.C.; New York Zoological Society

pampas deer lives on the plains and savannas of South America. It is a small deer which gives off a musk odor that can be smelled at considerable distances. The Chilean *pudu* has short legs, small spike antlers, and a tiny tail. It has a crest of hair across its forehead. The *huemul* of Peru stands about three feet tall at the shoulder. It lives on the upper slopes of the Andes Mountains. The *marsh deer* is the largest deer of South America. It stands about four feet high. Its coat is red in summer, brown in winter. This deer lives in the marshes along the eastern side of the continent from the Guianas south to Argentina.

The *fallow deer* is kept in many parks in Southern Europe for its beauty. The fallow deer is about three feet high. Its coat is brownish with white spots during the summer, and dark brown in winter.

The barasingha and the sambar live in India. The *sambar* resembles the American elk. It is over five feet high and may weigh as much as 700 pounds. The *barasingha* is also a large deer. It is nearly five feet high at the shoulder and weighs between 400 and 500 pounds. The *barking deer*, or *muntjac*, also lives in India, and is found in the Malay Peninsula, Thailand, and islands of the East Indies. When the muntjac is excited, it barks like a dog. It stands no more than 20 inches high, and at most weighs about 40 pounds. The *Japanese sika* is another small Asiatic deer. It stands about two and a half feet high and weighs up to 180 pounds. In winter its coat is brown, and in the summer it is red with white spots. The London Zoological Society has reintroduced *Père David's deer* to China, their native territory. The deer, named after the French Lazarist missionary who first saw them in 1865, have been extinct in China since 1921. A few of the animals, shipped to England, have multiplied.

Protection of Deer

The main causes of death among deer are disease, starvation, other animals, and man. Laws protecting deer against man have been in force in many places for a long time. At the end of the colonial period, all the colonies except Georgia had laws protecting deer. Massachusetts passed its first deer law in 1694. Open seasons, when hunters are permitted to kill deer, are established from time to time. Open seasons often depend upon the number of deer in an area. See GAME (Game Laws).

Deer are also protected in game refuges which have been set aside for them by national and state or province governments in the United States and Canada. Pennsylvania is particularly noted for its refuges. Deer and elk often become so accustomed to having their food brought to them by human beings that they seem unable to search for food themselves. Therefore conservationists believe the best way to protect deer is by keeping the deer population down to the point where the deer can live on the local food supply.

Scientific Classification. Deer are in the family *Cervidae*. The white-tailed deer belong to the genus *Odocoileus*, the brocket to genus *Mazama*, and the moose to genus *Alces*. Reindeer and caribou are in the genus *Rangifer*. Elk belong to the genus *Cervus*.   STANLEY P. YOUNG

their journey from St. Louis to Oregon if the hunters they took along had not furnished them with deer meat along the way. For four months, while they wintered in Oregon, they had little to eat except deer meat. Deer meat, called *venison* in North America, is useful because it can be preserved by "jerking" and saved for future use. *Jerking* means *smoking* or *sun-drying*. When deer meat is jerked, it is light in weight and a large supply can easily be carried. See PIONEER LIFE (Food).

The Indians had also found the deer useful in their daily living before the white men appeared. They ate venison, and used the bones of the deer to make harpoons, picks, and needles.

Other Important Kinds of Deer

The *mule deer* is described under its own title in the Encyclopedia. It is larger than the *Columbian Black-tailed deer*, which seldom weighs more than 150 pounds. The Columbian black-tailed deer is found along the Pacific Coast, from Sitka, Alaska, to San Diego, Calif. Its black tail is faced with white underneath. The *brown brocket* is a small deer about 20 inches high with an arched back and a spike horn that has no branches. It lives in most of tropical and subtropical America, from sea level to 16,000 feet up in the mountains. The

Related Articles in WORLD BOOK include:

Animal (color pictures)	Horn	Musk Deer
Buckskin	Moose	Red Deer
Caribou	Mule Deer	Reindeer
Elk		

DEER FLY is an insect related to the horse flies. It has blotched or banded wings, some of them beautifully colored. Only the females bite man. In the west, the name *deer fly* is given also to the *snipe fly*. These flies have two wings and six long legs. Some have long beaks shaped like the bill of the bird called a snipe. Snipe flies and deer flies suck blood from men and animals. Several botflies and ticks that attack deer are also called deer flies. Sometimes they carry diseases. A person may use mosquito repellents to avoid deer fly bites.

Scientific Classification. The deer fly belongs to the family *Tabanidae*. It is genus *Chrysops*. Snipe flies make up the family *Rhagionidae*. ROBERT L. USINGER

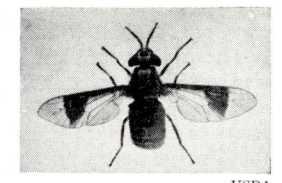

The Deer Fly bites both deer and men. Deer flies often carry a serious blood disease. USDA

See also BOTFLY; FLY (Flies That Harm Men).

DEER MOUSE. See WHITE-FOOTED MOUSE.

DEERE, JOHN (1804-1886), invented in 1837 the first steel plow that efficiently turned the heavy American prairie sod. He became one of the greatest plowmakers in the world.

Wood or iron plows, used before the steel plow was invented, were fragile and dulled easily. The heavy, gummy prairie soil stuck to the rough surface of the wood or iron instead of falling away from the moldboard cleanly in even furrows (see PLOW [Parts of a Plow]). Other inventors tried to solve the problem by changing the shape of the plow.

Deere, a skilled blacksmith, beat a moldboard out of an old circular saw. He hoped the hard-tempered steel would present a self-polishing and self-cleaning surface to the soil. The plow was a spectacular success. His first shop was at Grand Detour, Ill. Within ten years, his factory was producing one thousand plows a year. In 1846, he moved to Moline, Ill., where he built a new farm implement factory. To improve the quality of his iron plows, he used English steel in 1847.

Deere was born in Rutland, Vt., and received a common school education. He became a blacksmith's apprentice at the age of seventeen. RICHARD D. HUMPHREY

DEERHOUND is a Scottish breed of dog, close to the Irish wolfhound in ancestry. It was named for its skill at deer hunting, but it is now seldom used for hunting. The deerhound is a member of the hound class of dogs. It is a rugged, but graceful, dog with a keen sense of smell. It measures from 28 to 32 inches tall at the shoulder, and weighs from 75 to 110 pounds. The coat of the deerhound is 3 to 4 inches long, and is coarse and wiry. It may be gray, brindle, or wheaten in color. The deerhound makes an excellent pet. JOSEPHINE Z. RINE

DE FACTO GOVERNMENT. The government of a country can change quickly as a result of invasion or revolution. Other countries may refuse to recognize such a new government officially, but they may find it necessary to deal with it informally. These countries recognize the new government as a *de facto government* (government in fact). Later, the countries may recognize the new government as a *government de jure* (legal and official government). ROBERT G. NEUMANN

DE FALLA, MANUEL. See FALLA, MANUEL DE.

DEFAMATION. See LIBEL.

DEFENDANT. See COURT (How a Court Works).

DEFENESTRATION OF PRAGUE. See THIRTY YEARS' WAR (The Bohemian Period).

DEFENSE, CIVIL. See CIVIL DEFENSE.

John Deere Co., Moline, Ill.

John Deere, above, produced the first riding plow, the Gilpin Sulky, at Moline, Ill., in 1875. The invention saved farmers from many back-breaking hours of work guiding walking plows.

DEFENSE, DEPARTMENT OF

DEFENSE, DEPARTMENT OF, is an executive department of the United States government. The Secretary of Defense, a member of the President's Cabinet, heads the Department. The Department of Defense coordinates the work of its three military departments, which handle matters for the army, navy, and air force. It integrates the armed services into a team of land, sea, and air forces. It advises the President on matters of national defense and international security.

Functions. The Department of Defense provides civilian control for the armed services and civilian direction of their strategic plannings. It prepares the plans and provides the manpower and equipment for any military operations. The Secretary administers the military budget. He has authority to eliminate unnecessary duplication in personnel, supply, and other fields. He maintains direct contact with the Department of State, Atomic Energy Commission, and other government agencies.

The Secretary of Defense is appointed by the President with the approval of the Senate. He must be a civilian. He is the principal assistant to the President on defense matters. All functions in the Department of Defense are performed under his direction and control. The Secretary serves as a member of the National Security Council, the Civil and Defense Mobilization Board, the National Aeronautics and Space Council, and the North Atlantic Council.

Organization. The Department of Defense consists of the Office of the Secretary and the three separately organized military departments. It has headquarters in the Pentagon Building, Washington, D.C. The Deputy Secretary of Defense is the Secretary's chief aide, and serves as Acting Secretary in his absence.

The Director of Defense Research and Engineering is the principal adviser and assistant to the Secretary of Defense in all scientific and technical matters. He coordinates military research and development, and directs the activities of the Advanced Research Projects Agency and the Weapons Systems Evaluation Group.

Six Assistant Secretaries of Defense supervise other activities within the department. These activities include (1) finance, (2) international security affairs, (3) logistics and installations, (4) manpower, (5) public affairs, and (6) civil defense. Other aides to the Secretary of Defense include a General Counsel and assistants who are in charge of atomic energy and legislative affairs.

The Military Departments of the Army, Navy, and Air Force are subordinate divisions of the Department of Defense, with their own secretaries. The military heads of the services include the Chiefs of Staff of the Army and Air Force, Chief of Naval Operations, and the Commandant of the Marine Corps.

The military services provide forces for the unified and specified combatant commands under the President and the Secretary of Defense. These combat and service forces are organized, trained, and equipped to defend the United States from enemy attacks and to guard American interests at sea and in other countries.

Joint Committees advise the Secretary of Defense on policy and operations. The *Armed Forces Policy Council* considers broad defense policies. The Secretary, Deputy Secretary, military department secretaries, Joint Chiefs of Staff, and Director of Defense Research and Engineering serve as members of the Armed Forces Joint Policy Council.

The *Joint Secretaries* advise the Secretary on administration. They include the Deputy Secretary of Defense and the secretaries of the military departments.

A chairman and the military chiefs of the army, navy, and air force make up the *Joint Chiefs of Staff*. These men function as the principal military advisers to the President, the Secretary of Defense, and the National Security Council.

History. From 1798 to 1947, the separate departments of War and the Navy carried out defense activities. The army and navy built up their own organizations, and developed great rivalry. They competed with each other for money from Congress, and each service sometimes duplicated the work of the other.

World War II clearly showed the need for unified direction of the armed services and of production facilities. During the war, the services cooperated through joint committees, such as the Joint Chiefs of Staff, and through unified military commands in overseas theaters of military operations.

The National Security Act of 1947 created a *National Military Establishment*, headed by a Secretary of Defense with three executive departments. The Department of War became the *Department of the Army*. Congress made the army air forces a separate service under a new *Department of the Air Force*. The navy and marine corps continued under the *Department of the Navy*. The law also established the Joint Chiefs of Staff, Munitions Board, Research and Development Board, and War Council as permanent agencies within the new organization.

The Secretary of Defense became a member of the Cabinet in place of the secretaries of the military services. He exercised general direction of his agency. The Secretaries of the Army, Navy, and Air Force administered their own departments.

In 1949, Congress broadened the authority of the Secretary of Defense, because he did not have the powers to coordinate the services fully and eliminate overlapping functions. It provided him with a Deputy and three Assistant Secretaries. It also reduced the Departments of the Army, Navy, and Air Force from executive to military departments.

In 1952, Congress created a Defense Supply Management Agency and a Directorate of Installations within the Department of Defense. The following year, the President abolished these agencies and the Munitions Board and Research and Development Board. He gave the Secretary their functions, and authorized him to have six additional Assistant Secretaries and a General

SECRETARIES OF DEFENSE

Name	Year Appointed	Under President
*James V. Forrestal	1947	Truman
Louis A. Johnson	1949	Truman
*George C. Marshall	1950	Truman
Robert A. Lovett	1951	Truman
*Charles E. Wilson	1953	Eisenhower
Neil H. McElroy	1957	Eisenhower
Thomas S. Gates, Jr.	1959	Eisenhower
*Robert S. McNamara	1961	Kennedy

*Has a separate biography in WORLD BOOK.

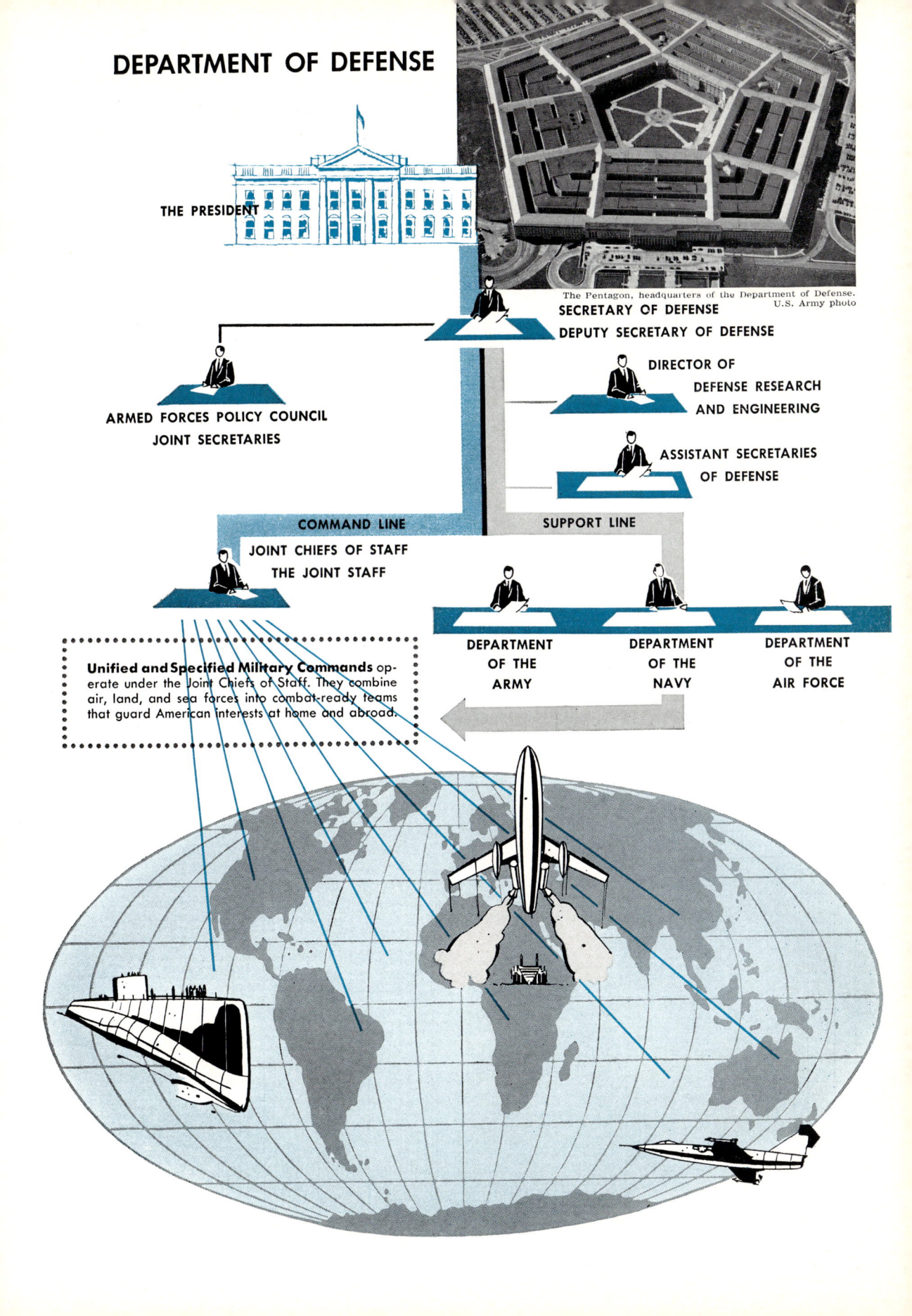

DEPARTMENT OF DEFENSE

The Pentagon, headquarters of the Department of Defense.
U.S. Army photo

THE PRESIDENT

SECRETARY OF DEFENSE
DEPUTY SECRETARY OF DEFENSE

ARMED FORCES POLICY COUNCIL
JOINT SECRETARIES

DIRECTOR OF DEFENSE RESEARCH AND ENGINEERING

ASSISTANT SECRETARIES OF DEFENSE

COMMAND LINE   SUPPORT LINE

JOINT CHIEFS OF STAFF
THE JOINT STAFF

DEPARTMENT OF THE ARMY

DEPARTMENT OF THE NAVY

DEPARTMENT OF THE AIR FORCE

Unified and Specified Military Commands operate under the Joint Chiefs of Staff. They combine air, land, and sea forces into combat-ready teams that guard American interests at home and abroad.

DEFENSE, NATIONAL

Counsel. In 1958, Congress increased the powers of the Secretary and reduced those of the military secretaries. It created the office of Director of Defense Research and Engineering, and decreased the number of Assistant Secretaries of Defense to seven. The Department employs more than 1,100,000 civilians. JOHN C. BOLLENS

Related Articles in WORLD BOOK include:
Air Force, Department of the
Air Force, United States
Army, Department of the
Army, United States
Civil Defense (Civil Defense in the United States)
Flag (color picture, Flags of the United States Government)
Joint Chiefs of Staff
Marine Corps, United States
National Defense
National Security Agency
Navy, Department of the
Navy, United States
Pentagon Building

DEFENSE, NATIONAL. See NATIONAL DEFENSE.

DEFENSE COMMAND. See AIR FORCE, UNITED STATES (Combat Commands); ARMY, UNITED STATES (The Continental Army Command); NAVY, UNITED STATES (The Shore Organization).

DEFERRED PAYMENT is a means of spreading a payment over a period of time by breaking it up into small payments. See INSTALLMENT PLAN.

DEFICIENCY DISEASE. See NUTRITION; DISEASE (Nutritional Diseases).

DEFLATION. See INFLATION AND DEFLATION.

DEFOE, *duh FOH,* **DANIEL** (1660-1731), wrote *Robinson Crusoe*, one of the best-known adventure stories in the western world (see ROBINSON CRUSOE). It was one of the first English novels. Defoe wrote his most famous works, *Robinson Crusoe* (1719), *Moll Flanders* (1722), and *A Journal of the Plague Year* (1722), late in life. Though they were fiction, Defoe presented them as true stories. His readers were completely taken in because the stories were so full of convincing details that seemed as true as real life.

The Novel *Moll Flanders* was written by Daniel Defoe in 1722. It is the story of an unwanted English girl.

Daniel Defoe — Brown Bros.

Lee De Forest — RCA

Defoe was born in London, the son of James Foe, a butcher and candlemaker. His earliest writings dealt with controversial subjects in politics and religion. One of these was *The Shortest Way with the Dissenters* (1702). It proposed ironically that Dissenters (Protestants who thought the state should not control religion) be punished by hanging. The Dissenters thought he meant what he said. The Tories believed that he was criticizing them for their desire to punish Dissenters.

Defoe's essay angered both groups. He was tried and imprisoned. He was later released when he agreed to write for the Tories, who recognized his skill. He changed his name to Defoe about this time. In his "Essay on Projects" (1697), he proposed such reforms as building insane asylums, improving highways, and establishing an "academy for women." For about 25 years he made his living by writing for newspapers, including his own *Review of the Affairs of France*. This was a four-page Whig paper published three times a week for 10 years. He was hired frequently by politicians to write for various newspapers. At times he was secretly writing for the Whigs in one paper and the Tories in another.

Defoe's early sympathies were with the Whig party. This group opposed the Church of England and the divine right of kings. When he was 25, Defoe fought in the unsuccessful Monmouth Rebellion against James II. He escaped punishment for this act. Defoe wrote more than 400 books and tracts during his life. SCOTT ELLEDGE

DE FOREST, LEE (1873-1961), an American inventor, pioneered in wireless telegraphy and radio broadcasting. He obtained patents on more than 300 inventions. He invented a vacuum tube called a *triode*, or *audion*, in 1907. It often is described as an invention as great as radio itself (see ELECTRONICS [Triode]). The tube, which amplifies weak sounds, is basic to long-distance radio and television communication.

De Forest staged the first musical radio broadcast in history from the Metropolitan Opera House in New York City in 1910. He designed and supervised construction of the United States government's first high-powered naval radio stations.

De Forest moved to the Pacific Coast in 1911. He became interested in sound pictures and diathermy machines. He worked on methods for photographing sound waves on motion-picture films.

He was born on Aug. 26, 1873, in Council Bluffs, Iowa. He was graduated from Sheffield Scientific School of Yale University in 1896. W. RUPERT MACLAURIN

80

Edgar Degas (self-portrait)
Brown Bros.

The Millinery Shop illustrates Degas' love of scenes from everyday life. He painted people impersonally, much as they would appear in candid photographs.

The Art Institute of Chicago; Mr. and Mrs. Lewis Colburn, Memorial Collection

Degas' Dancing Class is an example of the delicate sense of composition and beauty of line that characterize his work.
Archives Photographiques

DEGAS, *duh GAH,* **EDGAR** (1834-1917), was a French painter, pastelist, and sculptor. His explorations in color, composition, and form greatly influenced contemporary art. Degas developed his own style of painting out of the neoclassical tradition of painting (see PAINTING [In the 1800's]). He slowly incorporated into his art a sense of composition developed from his study of Japanese prints. He learned to use more vivid colors from Édouard Manet (see MANET, ÉDOUARD). He also took up pastels and developed the medium to a new brilliance of color and daring in composition.

Degas liked certain subjects, such as jockeys, ballet dancers, milliners, laundresses, women ironing, and women bathing. He painted and drew these subjects in many series, developing his composition toward more abstract pattern and flat color. His painting, *On the Stage,* appears in color in the PAINTING article.

Degas was born in Paris into a wealthy family. His full name was HILAIRE GERMAIN EDGAR DEGAS. He followed his own career without the necessity of pleasing critics or the public. Always a difficult person in friendships, Degas broke with Impressionist painters in 1886, and became a virtual recluse. He then did sculptures of horses and dancers. ROBERT GOLDWATER

DE GASPERI, *GAHS pay ree,* **ALCIDE** (1881-1954), leader of the Italian Christian Democratic party, was premier of Italy from 1945 to 1953. His leadership saved Italy from falling under control of the communists in the years after World War II. He served in the Austrian parliament from 1911 to 1918. After his home city of Trento became part of Italy in 1919, De Gasperi led the Popular party in the Italian Chamber of Deputies. He was imprisoned by Benito Mussolini in 1926. He was Italian foreign minister in 1944 and 1945. R. JOHN RATH

CHARLES DE GAULLE

DE GAULLE, *duh GOHL,* **CHARLES ANDRÉ JOSEPH MARIE** (1890-   ), became the outstanding French patriot, soldier, and statesman of the 1900's. He led French resistance against Germany in World War II, and restored order in France after the war. He guided the formation of France's Fifth Republic in 1958, and became its president.

As president of France, De Gaulle led his country through a difficult period in which Algeria and other parts of France's overseas empire won independence. He fashioned a new role in Europe for France based on close association with a former enemy, Germany. His leadership restored French political and economic stability, and again made the nation one of Europe's leading powers.

Charles de Gaulle became a symbol of France to Frenchmen and to people in other parts of the world. Even his name suggested *Gaul,* the ancient Roman name for France. An imposing figure 6 feet 4 inches tall, De Gaulle was stern and aloof. Some thought him rude, stubborn, and arrogant. But De Gaulle had a deep love for France and great confidence in himself. He firmly believed that he was the one man who could make France a world power again.

Early Life. Charles de Gaulle was born Nov. 22, 1890, at Lille. Charles' father, Henri, served as an officer in the Franco-Prussian War, then taught philosophy, literature, and mathematics. His mother, Jeanne Maillot de Gaulle, came from a literary and military family.

With his sister and three brothers, Charles grew up in an atmosphere that was both military and religious. As a boy, he enjoyed reading stories of famous French battles. When he played soldiers with his friends, Charles always had to be "France."

After studying at the College Stanislas in Paris, De Gaulle served a year in the infantry. There his height won him the nicknames *Big Charles* and *Asparagus.* He was graduated with honors in 1911 from the famous French military school, St. Cyr.

During World War I, De Gaulle was wounded four times. He was captured at Verdun in 1916. After the war, he served with the French army in Poland, then taught military history at St. Cyr for a year.

In 1921, he married Yvonne Vendroux. They had a son and two daughters. Yvonne de Gaulle followed her husband wherever his duties took him, but she rarely appeared in public.

Between World Wars I and II, De Gaulle held various military commands and taught at the French War College. His book *The Edge of the Sword* (1932) stressed the importance of powerful leadership in war. In *The Army of the Future* (1934), he outlined the theory of a war of movement, in which tanks and other mechanized forces would be used. Most French military leaders ignored this theory. But the Germans studied it carefully and used it in World War II.

Leader of the Free French. After the Germans invaded France in May, 1940, De Gaulle was put in charge of one of France's four armored divisions. He became under-secretary for war in June. But just days later, on June 22, France surrendered to Germany.

De Gaulle, now a general, escaped to London. He refused to accept the surrender. Nor would he recognize the authority of Marshal Pétain, his old regimental commander, who headed the Vichy government that cooperated with the Germans (see PÉTAIN, HENRI PHILIPPE). For this, a French military court sentenced him to death.

De Gaulle declared that France had lost a battle but not the war. He broadcast such messages to France as: "Soldiers of France, wherever you may be, arise!" His broadcasts stirred French patriotism and kept French resistance alive.

De Gaulle organized the Free French forces in Great Britain and in some of the French colonies. In September, 1941, he became president of the French National Committee in London. By 1943, the Allies had accepted him as the unquestioned leader of France.

Peacetime Leader. De Gaulle entered Paris triumphantly when the Allies liberated the city in August, 1944. In September, he became head of the provisional government.

De Gaulle got the machinery of government working again during the next 14 months. But France's left-wing parties did not support him, and he resigned in January, 1946. He bitterly opposed the constitution of 1946 because it did not provide a strong executive power. In 1947, he organized a new party, the Rally of the French People (R.P.F.) to reform the constitution. But it lost strength in the 1951 and 1956 elections.

He lived at his country home during his retirement. He wrote his World War II memoirs and watched the political situation in France go from bad to worse. In 1957, though he was 67, De Gaulle still hoped that France would recall him to solve the country's problems. But early in 1958 he admitted, "Now I begin to fear that it is too late."

The Fifth Republic. Finally, in May, 1958, the call came. France stood on the verge of civil war. Dissatisfied French officers, afraid they would lose the government's support against the Algerian rebels, seized power at Algiers. They demanded that De Gaulle head a new government. In June, De Gaulle accepted President René Coty's request to form a government on the condition that he have full powers for six months.

De Gaulle drew up a new constitution establishing the Fifth Republic. It provided broad powers for the president, who was to be elected for seven years by an electoral college of 80,000 public figures. French voters overwhelmingly approved the plan in October, 1958. In December, the electoral college chose De Gaulle as president. He received over 62,000 of the 80,000 votes.

As president, De Gaulle acted with great firmness. After another revolt in Algeria in 1960, he arrested French officers there who had formerly supported him. He negotiated with Algerian nationalist leaders for a cease-fire agreement. The agreement they reached in March, 1962, ended more than seven years of bloody war. At De Gaulle's urging, the French people voted almost 10 to 1 in April, 1962, for Algerian independence.

The French Assembly ousted the De Gaulle-sponsored government in October, 1962. But De Gaulle dissolved the Assembly. The election that followed made history. For the first time in France, one party— De Gaulle's Union for a New Republic—won an absolute majority. In a separate referendum, the voters also approved De Gaulle's proposal to elect future French presidents by direct popular vote.

During 1961 and 1962, De Gaulle worked closely with Chancellor Konrad Adenauer of West Germany. He had supported friendship between France and Germany since 1950. Now he declared that the long conflict between the two countries was over. In January, 1963, De Gaulle and Adenauer signed a treaty providing for political, scientific, cultural, and military cooperation between France and Germany. De Gaulle called the new friendship, "The great revolution, the turning point, in our history as yours."   ERNEST JOHN KNAPTON

DEGAUSSING. See MINE, MILITARY (Influence Ground Mines).

De Gaulle, Leader of the Free French, led a triumphant parade down the Champs Élysées in August, 1944, to mark the liberation of Paris after the German occupation of World War II.

De Gaulle, President of France, ended the seven-year Algerian war in 1962. He supported Algerian demands for freedom, and was warmly greeted during a 1959 tour of the country.

De Gaulle, European Statesman, promoted friendship and cooperation between France and Germany. He and West German Chancellor Konrad Adenauer signed an alliance in 1962.

DEGENERATION

DEGENERATION, dee JEN uhr AY shun, means the state of falling below a normal condition or quality. Any living thing may suffer from degeneration. In man, degeneration may be caused by old age, by lack of sufficient nourishment, by inactivity, by poisons, and by infectious diseases. These conditions cause changes in body tissues and organs and make it impossible for the affected parts to work properly. The accumulation of fat in or around the heart, arteries, and liver interferes with the work of these organs. Doctors call such conditions *fatty degeneration*. In some kinds of degeneration, such as *osteoarthritis*, a disease of the bones, the body tissues themselves may change. See ARTHRITIS.

In plants and animals, poor environment and improper breeding may cause degeneration. Plants that grow for many years in poor soil or an unsuitable climate show signs of degeneration. After several years, new plants will be smaller than those from which the seed was originally taken. Seeds from these smaller plants will produce inferior plants.

Man has used degeneration in animals to advantage. He sacrificed speed in the horse to develop a strong draft horse. He reduced the beef-producing qualities of cattle to obtain the dairy cow. BENJAMIN F. MILLER

DEGREE is a name given to various small units of measure. In mathematics, degrees are used to measure angles and also arcs of circles. An angle of 1 degree (1°) is $\frac{1}{90}$ of a right angle. An arc of 1° is $\frac{1}{360}$ of a whole circle. Because longitude and latitude lines are circles, they are also measured in degrees. Degrees in geometry are divided into 60 units called *minutes*. See ANGLE; CIRCLE; LATITUDE; LONGITUDE; MINUTE.

In science, 1 degree of temperature on the Fahrenheit scale is $\frac{1}{180}$ of the difference between the temperatures of melting ice and boiling water. One degree on the Centigrade scale of temperature is $\frac{1}{100}$ of the same difference. See THERMOMETER. HOLMES BOYNTON

DEGREE, COLLEGE. A university or college awards a *degree* to a person who has completed a required course of study. The institution presents the degree in the form of a *diploma*, a document which certifies the award. The four basic kinds of degrees are called *associate*, *bachelor*, *master*, and *doctor*. An honorary degree may be awarded for an outstanding contribution in a certain field.

The Associate Degree is awarded by many colleges and universities in the United States and most junior colleges (see JUNIOR COLLEGE). It usually indicates successful completion of two years of college work. The most commonly awarded associate degrees are the *Associate in Arts* and the *Associate in Science*.

The Bachelor's Degree. In the United States, a college student normally receives a bachelor's degree after four years of study in a university or college. He usually specializes in a field of study called his *major subject*. The institution often requires other types of study outside his major field in order to ensure a liberal education. There are many kinds of bachelor's degrees, but the two most common are the *Bachelor of Arts* (*B.A.*) and the *Bachelor of Science* (*B.S.*). The B.A. usually includes majors in such subjects as history, literature, and fine arts, and, in certain cases, science and mathematics. The B.S. usually includes majors in the physical and natural sciences. Most engineering students receive B.S. degrees. Many colleges offer specialized degrees, such as the *Bachelor of Education* or *Bachelor of Architecture*. Law students obtain the *Bachelor of Laws* after a longer period of training. Outstanding achievement in a bachelor's degree may be designated by the Latin phrases *cum laude* (*with praise*), *magna cum laude* (*with great praise*), or *summa cum laude* (*with the highest praise*).

British colleges and universities offer two types of bachelor's degrees, an ordinary, or *pass*, degree and an *honors* degree which requires more extensive and more advanced work. Canadian colleges and universities usually follow British or French tradition in their systems of degrees. See CANADA (Education).

ABBREVIATIONS USED FOR COLLEGE DEGREES

A.A. Associate in Arts
A.S. Associate in Science
B.A., A.B. Bachelor of Arts
B.A. in Ed. Bachelor of Arts in Education
B.Arch. Bachelor of Architecture
B.B.A. Bachelor of Business Administration
B.Ed. Bachelor of Education
B.E.E. Bachelor of Electrical Engineering
B.D. Bachelor of Divinity
B.F.A. Bachelor of Fine Arts
B.M., B.Mus. Bachelor of Music
B.M.E., B.Mus.Ed. Bachelor of Music Education
B.S. Bachelor of Science
B.S. in B.A., B.S.B.A. Bachelor of Science in Business Administration
B.S. in C.E., B.S.C.E. Bachelor of Science in Civil Engineering
B.S. in Ch.E., B.S.Ch.E. Bachelor of Science in Chemical Engineering
B.S. in Chemistry, B.S.Chem. Bachelor of Science in Chemistry
B.S. in Ed., B.S.Ed. Bachelor of Science in Education
B.S. in E.E., B.S.E.E. Bachelor of Science in Electrical Engineering

B.S. in Elem.Ed. Bachelor of Science in Elementary Education
B.S. in H.E., B.S. in H.Ec. Bachelor of Science in Home Economics
B.S. in M.E., B.S.M.E. Bachelor of Science in Mechanical Engineering
B.S. in Med.Tech. Bachelor of Science in Medical Technology
B.S.N. Bachelor of Science in Nursing
B.S.Pharm. Bachelor of Science in Pharmacy
D.B.A. Doctor of Business Administration
*D.D. Doctor of Divinity
D.D.S. Doctor of Dental Surgery
*D.Mus., Mus.D. Doctor of Music
D.V.M. Doctor of Veterinary Medicine
Ed.D., D.Ed. Doctor of Education
*L.H.D. Doctor of Humane Letters
*Lit.D., D.Lit. Doctor of Literature
*Litt.D. Doctor of Letters
LL.B. Bachelor of Law(s)
*LL.D. Doctor of Laws
LL.M. Master of Law(s)
M.A., A.M. Master of Arts
M.A. in Ed. Master of Arts in Education

M.A.T. Master of Arts in Teaching
M.B.A. Master of Business Administration
M.D. Doctor of Medicine
M.Ed. Master of Education
M.F.A. Master of Fine Arts
M.M., M.Mus. Master of Music
M.M.Ed., M.Mus.Ed. Master of Music Education
M.R.E. Master of Religious Education
M.S. Master of Science
M.S. in C.E., M.S.C.E. Master of Science in Civil Engineering
M.S. in Ch.E. Master of Science in Chemical Engineering
M.S. in Ed. Master of Science in Education
M.S. in E.E., M.S.E.E. Master of Science in Electrical Engineering
M.S. in M.E. Master of Science in Mechanical Engineering
M.S.W. Master of Social Work
Ph.D. Doctor of Philosophy
*Sc.D., D.Sc., D.S. Doctor of Science
S.T.M. Master of Sacred Theology
Th.M. Master of Theology

*Honorary Degree Only

The Master's Degree. In the United States, students who desire a master's degree must complete one or two years of advanced study beyond the bachelor's degree. Many institutions require a *thesis*, a written report of a special investigation in the student's major field. The two most common master's degrees are the *Master of Arts* and the *Master of Science*.

In Great Britain, the master's degree is usually considered the highest requirement for an academic career, but a number of British universities also offer the doctorate. In Scotland, a student proceeds directly to the master's degree without taking a bachelor's degree.

The Doctor's Degree is the highest earned degree in the United States, France, Germany, and many other countries. There are two distinct types of doctor's degrees. One is a professional degree required to practice in certain professions, such as medicine. The other is a research degree that indicates the candidate has acquired mastery of a broad field of knowledge and the technique of scholarly research.

In the United States, the research doctorate requires at least two or three additional years of study beyond the master's degree. Most doctoral students are expected to have a reading knowledge in two foreign languages. The candidate must also complete a series of examinations and present a written thesis or *dissertation*. The doctoral thesis represents an original contribution to knowledge, and is a more detailed study of a research problem than that required for the master's degree.

The *Doctor of Philosophy* degree is the most important research doctorate and may include specialization in almost any academic subject. The *Doctor of Education*, *Doctor of Medicine*, and *Doctor of Dental Science* degrees represent advanced professional training. Students in certain professions, such as medicine and dentistry, can obtain a doctor's degree without first receiving a bachelor's or master's degree. However, most students acquire a bachelor of science degree before entering medical training.

Honorary Degrees. Many colleges and universities have adopted the custom of awarding honorary degrees to persons for achievement in their chosen fields. Chief among these are the *Doctor of Letters* and the *Doctor of Laws*. These are often given to prominent authors, scholars, and leaders in the professions, business, government, and industry.

History. College degrees date from the 1200's when schools in Europe won the right to examine and license their graduates. The system of degrees, which took form by the 1300's, was modeled on the guild system. A student spent a sort of apprenticeship as a candidate for a bachelor's degree. Receiving the bachelor's degree resembled becoming a journeyman in a craft. The master's degree represented the status of a master craftsman, and served as a license to teach. The student's thesis was his "masterpiece," just as a journeyman submitted an example of his work to become a master craftsman. If the student continued to study and teach in law, medicine, or theology, he might earn the title of doctor. The medieval system remained largely unchanged until the impact of science on education in the 1700's and 1800's. During the last hundred years, college degrees in the United States have been extended to include many new fields of knowledge. HAROLD A. HASWELL

See also CAPS AND GOWNS; GRADUATION.

DE GROOT, HUIG. See GROTIUS, HUGO.

DE HOOCH, *duh hoke,* **PIETER** (1629-1684?), a Dutch artist, made noted paintings of middle-class subjects. They include housewives with maids or children, ladies and gentlemen in conversation or playing games, and soldiers in camp. He liked to show open doors which permitted glimpses of other rooms or of streets and gardens. His pictures were done in warm colors, and he was especially skillful in painting sunlight. One of his paintings, *The Mother*, appears in color in the PAINTING article. His best pictures come close to those of Jan Vermeer in quiet charm and technical perfection. De Hooch was born in Rotterdam, and became a member of the Guild of Painters at Delft in 1655. JULIUS S. HELD

DEHYDRATION, *DEE hy DRA shun*, is the process of preserving foods by drying them. In this process, most of the water is removed. Drying was one of the earliest means of preserving food. The North American Indians dried fish and pieces of meat in the sun to keep them from spoiling. Dried food was shipped to Union Army camps during the Civil War, but the soldiers complained of its poor flavor and bad odor. Nearly 9,000,000 pounds of dried vegetables and soups were used in World War I, but methods of dehydration were not yet well developed. Dehydration was greatly improved during World War II. Hundreds of millions of pounds of

50 QUARTS OF FRESH MILK equals 6¼ QUARTS OF DRIED MILK

Dehydration saves shipping and storage space. Such foods as dried milk retain their original taste when water is added.

dehydrated milk, eggs, vegetables, soup, meat, and fruit were consumed each year of the war.

Food which is to be dehydrated must be clean and sanitary. Drying agents in use today include sunshine, artificial heat, circulated air, and vacuums. The color and texture of foods are better retained in modern drying processes than by older methods. Cabbage which is treated with a bisulfite solution before dehydration retains its vitamin C. The vitamin C in tomatoes is retained if the tomatoes are first exposed to sulfurdioxide fumes, or are dipped in bisulfite solution. Blanching, or scalding, vegetables before drying also helps to preserve them.

Still in the laboratory stage is a process for dehydrating foods by microwave energy in a below-freezing vacuum. Thus it will be possible to store foods at room temperature for indefinite periods. The food may be restored to its original fresh condition, with no loss of texture or food value, by merely soaking it in water a few minutes. GUDRUN CARLSON

See also FOOD PRESERVATION (Drying).

DEIANIRA. See HERCULES.

DEIMOS

DEIMOS. See MARS (Moons of Mars).

DEISM is a theory about the nature and existence of God. It asserts that God exists, and that He created the world, but that He has no present relation to the world. The deist makes this assertion to harmonize science and free will with the existence of such a being as God. He feels that there is no real conflict between the idea of an all-powerful God and the idea of science studying a law-abiding world, or the idea of a person who makes real choices. The deist does not have to believe that no miracles are possible. Instead, he believes that God, being apart from the world, performs no miracles. The deist usually proves the existence of God from the order and harmony that exist in the universe. The deist also tends to reject revelation as the test of religious truth, accepting reason instead. LOUIS O. KATTSOFF

See also GOD; PANTHEISM.

DEJONG, *deh YAHNG,* **MEINDERT** (1906-), an author of children's books, won the 1955 Newbery medal for *The Wheel on the School,* a story about life in a Dutch seashore village. His works include *Hurry Home, Candy* (1953), *Shadrach* (1953), and *House of Sixty Fathers* (1956). He was born in Wierum, The Netherlands, and came to the United States at 8. DeJong graduated from Calvin College in 1928. GEORGE E. BUTLER

DE KALB, *duh KAHLP,* **JOHANN** (1721-1780), BARON DE KALB, was a German soldier who won distinction in the American Revolutionary War. He added "Baron" to his original name. He joined the French Army in 1743, and became a brigadier general in 1761. He came to America with the Marquis de Lafayette in 1777, and the Continental Congress appointed him a major general. He served under General George Washington at Brandywine, Germantown, Valley Forge, and Monmouth. He fought under General Horatio Gates in the Carolinas, and died in the battle of Camden, S.C. Lafayette laid the cornerstone of the De Kalb monument at Camden in 1825. He was born in Bavaria, Germany. ROBERT G. L. WAITE

Baron de Kalb — Brown Bros.

DEKANAWIDA. See NEW YORK (Famous New Yorkers).

DE KOONING, WILLEM (1904-), became one of the leading abstract expressionist painters in the 1940's (see PAINTING [After 1900]). Bold outlines and areas of textured color characterize his painting. His powerful abstractions, and later his series of *Woman* paintings, have influenced many artists. The subjects of De Kooning's works are not often recognizable, except in the *Woman* series. But the strong oppositions of flatness and depth in his canvases arouse emotions of anxiety, joy, or despair.

De Kooning was born and educated in Rotterdam, The Netherlands. He came to the United States in 1926, and worked as a house painter. His painting, *Woman I,* appears in color in the PAINTING article. GEORGE D. CULLER

Collection Mr. and Mrs. Earle Ludgin, Chicago

Willem de Kooning, left, is a leading abstract expressionist painter. He often uses intense colors. But his bold, strong lines, in such works as the untitled black and white painting, above, characterize his style.

Courtesy Sidney Janis Gallery, N.Y.

DE KOVEN, REGINALD (1859-1920), an American composer, became known for his light operas (see OPERA [Forms of Opera]). He wrote more than 400 songs. His greatest success was his light opera *Robin Hood,* which includes his two most popular songs, "Brown October Ale" and "Oh, Promise Me." He also wrote a grand opera, *The Canterbury Pilgrims,* and a folk opera, *Rip Van Winkle.*

De Koven was born in Middletown, Conn., and was graduated from Oxford. His full name was HENRY LOUIS REGINALD DE KOVEN. GILBERT CHASE

DE KRUIF, *duh KRIFE,* **PAUL** (1890-), an American writer, specialized in scientific and medical subjects. He publicized many medical discoveries and background facts about medical scientists at work. His books include *Microbe Hunters, Hunger Fighters, Men*

Reginald de Koven — Brown Bros.

Paul de Kruif — Don Wallace, Harcourt Brace

84

Archives Photographiques

Women of Algiers Is One of Many Scenes of Harem Life by Eugène Delacroix.

Against Death, and *Life Among the Doctors*. He supplied material for Sinclair Lewis' novel *Arrowsmith*.

De Kruif was born in Zeeland, Mich. He received a Ph.D. in bacteriology from the University of Michigan in 1916. He was a bacteriologist there from 1912 to 1917, and at the Rockefeller Institute from 1920 to 1922. He served as an officer in the Army Sanitary Corps in World War I. CARL NIEMEYER

DELACROIX, *duh lah KRWAH,* **FERDINAND VICTOR EUGÈNE** (1798-1863), was the leader of the Romantic movement in French painting. The writings of William Shakespeare, Lord Byron, and Sir Walter Scott inspired many of his pictures. Dante's *Inferno* provided the subject matter for his first successful painting, *The Bark of Dante*, exhibited in the Salon of 1822, and now in the Louvre in Paris.

The colorist tradition of the Venetian painters and the dynamic baroque art of the painter Peter Paul Rubens influenced Delacroix's style of painting. He used dashing brushwork, emotional line, and bold color. He was a master of tragic subjects, and his paintings show an intense feeling unknown in works of his day. The classical painters of his time condemned his paintings because he disregarded established traditions. Delacroix's highly individual style and independence as an artist made him a forerunner of modern art.

After his visit to Morocco in 1832, Delacroix's canvases often dealt with harem subjects, lion hunts, and other scenes from Arab life. His paintings include *Women of Algiers, Jewish Wedding in Morocco, Christ on the Cross,* and *The Murder of the Bishop of Liège*. He was born at Charenton, near Paris, on April 26, 1798. JOSEPH C. SLOANE

DE LACY, WALTER WASHINGTON. See WYOMING (Famous Wyomingites).

DELAGOA BAY, DEL *uh GO uh,* is an inlet of the Indian Ocean which cuts into the coast of Mozambique (Portuguese East Africa). The port of Lourenço Marques is located on Delagoa Bay. For location, see SOUTH AFRICA (color map).

DE LA MARE, DEL *uh MAIR,* **WALTER** (1873-1956), a British writer, became famous for his poetry of childhood and for his novel, *Memoirs of a Midget*. Much of his poetry and prose is dreamlike and full of fantasy. His works include *Songs of Childhood* (which he wrote under the pen name of Walter Ramal); *Crossings,* a play; *The Burning-Glass;* and *Collected Stories for Children.*

De la Mare was born in Charlton, Kent. He attended St. Paul's School, and then worked for an oil company. King George VI of Great Britain made him a Companion of Honor in 1948, and Queen Elizabeth II appointed him to the Order of Merit in 1953. JOSEPH E. BAKER

DE LA ROCHE, *rawsh,* **MAZO** (1879-1961), a Canadian novelist, was best known for her long series of books about the Whiteoak family. *Jalna,* first of the series, won the *Atlantic Monthly*'s $10,000 prize in 1927. She also wrote *Portrait of a Dog, The Master of Jalna, Young Renny, Whiteoak Harvest, Whiteoak Heritage,* and *Whiteoaks of Jalna.* Her books are noted for their description of simple and ordinary people. She was born in Toronto, Ont. GEORGE J. BECKER

DE LAVAL, CARL GUSTAF. See MILKING MACHINE; SEPARATOR; TURBINE (History).

DELAWARE
The First State

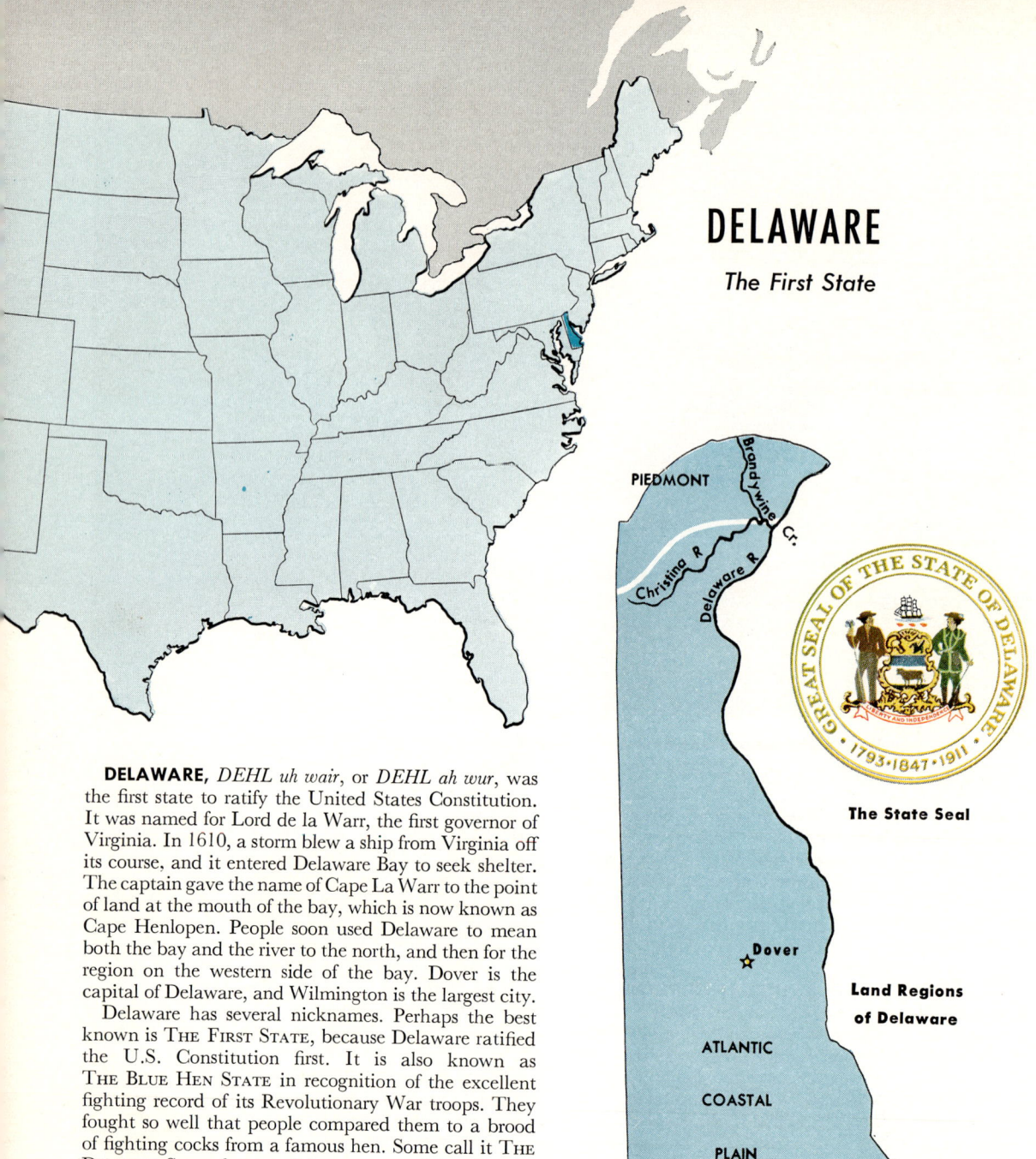

Land Regions of Delaware

The State Seal

DELAWARE, *DEHL uh wair,* or *DEHL ah wur,* was the first state to ratify the United States Constitution. It was named for Lord de la Warr, the first governor of Virginia. In 1610, a storm blew a ship from Virginia off its course, and it entered Delaware Bay to seek shelter. The captain gave the name of Cape La Warr to the point of land at the mouth of the bay, which is now known as Cape Henlopen. People soon used Delaware to mean both the bay and the river to the north, and then for the region on the western side of the bay. Dover is the capital of Delaware, and Wilmington is the largest city.

Delaware has several nicknames. Perhaps the best known is THE FIRST STATE, because Delaware ratified the U.S. Constitution first. It is also known as THE BLUE HEN STATE in recognition of the excellent fighting record of its Revolutionary War troops. They fought so well that people compared them to a brood of fighting cocks from a famous hen. Some call it THE DIAMOND STATE because it has so many riches, in spite of its small size. Only Rhode Island is smaller.

Networks of canals, railroads, and highways carry Delaware's farm and industrial products to New York City, Philadelphia, Baltimore, and Washington, D.C. Farms and orchards cover more than two thirds of the state. Chickens and poultry have been the chief agricultural product since the 1930's. In 1899, Delaware adopted laws that made it easy for businesses to incorporate in the state. Since then, some of the largest corporations in the country have located their home offices in Delaware. Wilmington serves as one of the country's three great centers for the manufacture of glazed kid leather for gloves. Éleuthère Irénée du Pont established the state's first gunpowder mill near Wilmington in 1802. Today, the great E. I. du Pont de Nemours chemical industry and other chemical companies have their headquarters in the state.

The Swedish and Finnish settlers who came to the Delaware region in 1638 built the first log cabins in America. Delaware is the only state with part of its boundary an *arc* (curve), and with units of local government called *hundreds*. The Delaware constitution, unlike that of any other state, may be amended by the legislature without the voters' approval.

For Delaware's relationship to other states in its region, see SOUTHERN STATES.

The Land and Its Resources

Location and Size. Most of Delaware lies on the Delmarva Peninsula. The name *Delmarva* comes from *Del*aware, *Mar*yland, and *V*irginia, which share the peninsula. The *Color Map* shows that New Jersey, the Delaware River, Delaware Bay, and the Atlantic Ocean form Delaware's eastern boundary. Maryland lies to the south and west, and Pennsylvania to the north.

The western boundary of Delaware follows a part of the historic Mason and Dixon's Line (see MASON AND DIXON'S LINE). The curved northern boundary was established in 1681 when King Charles II of England granted Pennsylvania to William Penn. The King was not sure how far south his grant to Penn would extend, but wanted to make sure that it did not include the city of New Castle. A year later, however, Penn got

--- **FACTS IN BRIEF** ---

Capital: Dover (since 1777). *Earlier capital*, New Castle (1704-1777).
Government: *Congress*—U.S. Senators, 2; U.S. Representatives, 1. *Electoral votes*, 3. *State Legislature*—senators, 17; representatives, 35. *Counties*, 3. *Voting Age*, 21.
Area: 2,057 square miles (including 79 square miles of inland water), 49th in size among the states. *Greatest distance:* (north-south) 110 miles; (east-west) 35 miles. *Coast line*, 28 miles.
Elevation: *Highest*, 450 feet above sea level at Centerville; *Lowest*, sea level along the coast.
Population: 446,292 (1960), 46th among the states. *Density*, 217 persons to the square mile. *Distribution*, urban, 66 per cent; rural, 34 per cent.
Chief Products: *Manufacturing and Processing*, chemicals, clothing, food products, leather goods, machinery, textiles. *Agriculture*, corn, dairy products, hogs, poultry, vegetables, wheat. *Mining*, gravel, kaolin, sand. *Fishing Industry*, clams, crabs, menhaden, oysters, trout.
Statehood: Dec. 7, 1787, the 1st state.
State Seal: The sheaf of wheat, ear of corn, and ox on the shield symbolize the farming activities of early Delaware. The rifleman and farmer standing at the sides of the shield represent the duties of Delawareans both as productive workers and as defenders of their rights. A ship sails above the shield, and a banner bearing the state motto waves beneath it. Original design adopted in 1777. Three dates on present seal—1793, 1847, and 1911—represent years in which variations of the original design were adopted by legislative action.
State Flag: A buff-colored diamond bearing the state seal stands in the center of a blue background. Below the diamond is the date "December 7, 1787," when Delaware became the first state to ratify the Constitution of the United States. Adopted in 1912.
State Motto: *Liberty and Independence.*
State Song: "Our Delaware." Words by George B. Hynson; music by William M. S. Brown. Adopted in 1925.

Flag and bird illustrations, courtesy of Eli Lilly and Company

The State Flag

The State Flower
Peach Blossom

The State Bird
Blue Hen Chicken

The State Tree
American Holly

DELAWARE

New Castle and all the land that is now Delaware by a grant from the King's brother, the Duke of York. This grant described Delaware's northern boundary as all the territory within 12 miles of "ye end of ye horse dyke" in New Castle. Part of this line ran into the Delaware River, and the state claimed control over navigation on a 24-mile stretch of the river. In 1934, the Supreme Court of the United States confirmed Delaware's right to the river by establishing the boundary at low-water mark on the New Jersey shore. Delaware covers 2,057 square miles.

Land Regions. Delaware has two natural regions. The Atlantic Coastal Plain covers the entire state except for a small strip in the northwestern corner. This northwestern corner forms a part of the Piedmont.

The Atlantic Coastal Plain includes all of Kent and Sussex counties, and most of New Castle County. The land seldom rises to more than 60 feet above sea level. Forests once blanketed most of this low, flat plain, and large areas of less desirable land are still wooded. A large swamp lies in the center of the southern boundary of the region. This swamp has various names, including Burnt Swamp, Pocomoke Swamp, and Cypress Swamp. It covers about 30,000 acres.

The Piedmont covers a small part of Delaware northwest of the Christina River. Farms and large estates lie among the rolling hills and fertile valleys of the region. Centerville is the highest point in the state, 450 feet above sea level. Most early settlers made their homes on the edge of the Piedmont, because its rivers provided power for the state's first industries.

Coast Line. Most of the smooth shore line along Delaware Bay and the Delaware River consists of marshes, except at the northern tip of the state. There, firm land forms the riverbank. A long sand reef faces the Atlantic Ocean in the southeastern part of the state. An inlet breaks the reef near its center, leading into Rehoboth and Indian River bays. This dune-covered strip is a popular vacation region.

Rivers, Bays, and Lakes. Most of the state's many streams flow eastward from a long, low ridge near the western boundary. Rivers in the southwest flow south and west across Maryland and into Chesapeake Bay. The Nanticoke is the most important of these rivers.

The broad Delaware River links the state with the Atlantic Ocean. Ships sail up the river to dock at Wilmington, where the mouth of the Christina River forms the harbor. Barges carry cargo up the Christina as far as Newport. Brandywine Creek is the chief tributary of the Christina. Other streams that flow into the Delaware River include the Smyrna River and Appoquinimink and Duck creeks. In southeastern Delaware, many streams empty into Delaware Bay and the Atlantic. The most important include the Broadkill, Indian, Mispillion, Murderkill, and St. Jones rivers.

Delaware Bay serves as an avenue of trade for ocean shipping, and provides abundant supplies of sea food. Rehoboth and Indian River bays lie behind the great sand reef in southeastern Delaware. Many of Delaware's more than 50 small lakes and ponds have excellent fresh-water fishing, and some have good beaches.

Natural Resources. Rich soil and abundant water supplies are Delaware's most important natural resources. The state cooperates with its neighbors in using the Delaware River to the best advantage.

Soil of Delaware is generally fertile, but somewhat sandy. Patches of gravel and coarse red sand cover the rocky hills in the Piedmont. Soil in the region just to the south is a mixture of clay and loam. Sandy soil covers most of the rest of the state.

Water from the Delaware River is shared by Delaware, New Jersey, New York, and Pennsylvania. The four states promote water conservation through the Interstate Commission for the Delaware River, or *Incodel*. Wilmington helped reduce pollution of the river by building a new sewage-treatment plant in 1955.

Minerals. The northern part of the state produces some gravel, feldspar, kaolin, mica, and quartz. Stone quarries produce Brandywine blue granite, which architects prize as a decorative building material.

Forests covered most of Delaware in the early 1600's. Most of the forests today are second-growth wood lots that cover about a third of the state. Lumbermen cut beech, black gum, cedar, hickory, loblolly pine, oak, shortleaf pine, and sweet gum. White cedar and bald cypress grow in the southern swamp. Smaller trees include the magnolia, sassafras, wild cherry, and willow.

Plant Life includes a wide variety of wild flowers. The swamp blooms with magnolias and pink lady's-slippers. Water lilies and floating hearts dot the surfaces of ponds and lakes. White and pink hibiscus rise from the sea marshes. Blueberries and cranberries form almost impassable thickets in many areas. A water lily that resembles the lotus of Egypt grows in the St. Jones River.

Animal Life in the fields and forests includes minks, otters, rabbits, red and gray foxes, and some beavers and deer. Commercial trappers take muskrats from the marshes and swamps. A few diamondback terrapins live on the coast, and snapping turtles live in every swamp.

Birds include bald eagles, blue herons, cardinals, ducks, hawks, orioles, ruby-throated hummingbirds, sandpipers, snowy egrets, and wrens. Sportsmen hunt such game birds as partridges, pheasants, quail, and woodcocks. Game fish include bass, pike, and trout.

Climate of Delaware is generally mild. Most winter winds come from the northwest, and are moderated by the mountains in Pennsylvania. Summer winds usually come from the southwest. Temperatures seldom vary more than 3°F. from one end of Delaware to the other. But on hot summer days, the beaches along the Atlantic are about 10 degrees cooler than the inland towns. Autumn is an especially pleasant season. Frost seldom comes until the middle of October. July temperatures average 76°F. Summers are humid, with the climate often foggy and unsettled. The average January temperature is 36°F. Millsboro reported the state's record high of 110°F. in July, 1930, and had the coldest temperature, −17°F., in January, 1893.

Rainfall totals about 45 inches a year in most of the state. Snowfall in the north averages 18 to 20 inches annually. Most of southern Delaware has 14 to 17 inches of snow each winter. The Atlantic Coast seldom receives more than 12 inches.

Life of the People

The People. The U.S. Bureau of the Census reported that the population of Delaware was 446,292 in 1960, or about 217 persons to the square mile. This repre-

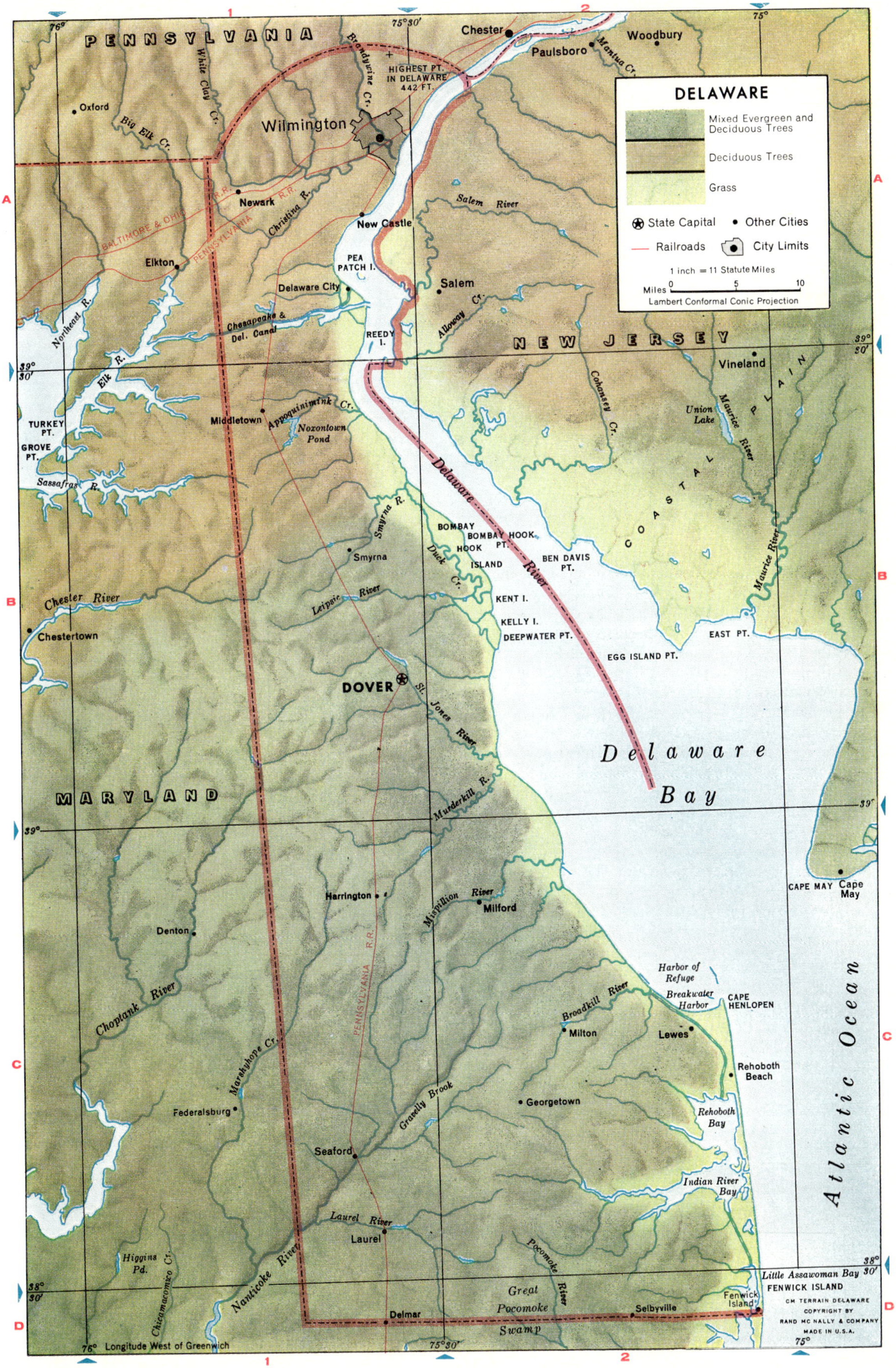

Especially created for **World Book Encyclopedia** by Rand McNally and World Book editors

DELAWARE

sented an increase of 40 per cent over the 1950 figure, 318,085. Two-thirds of the people live in cities.

More than 80 of every 100 Delawareans are American-born descendants of settlers from Finland, Germany, England, Scotland, Wales, Ireland, Italy, The Netherlands, Poland, and Sweden. About one-seventh of the people are Negroes. Two groups of mixed race, who call themselves Moors and Nanticokes, live in the state. The Moors live mainly in eastern Sussex County and around Cheswold, in Kent County. They claim descent from Spanish sailors who had Indian wives. According to legend, a Spanish ship exploring North America hundreds of years ago sank off the coast of Delaware. Seven sailors survived, and married Indian women. The Nanticokes are Sussex County neighbors of the Moors. They claim descent from the Nanticoke Indians.

The Methodist Church in America developed especially rapidly on the Delmarva Peninsula. In 1771, a British Methodist preacher named Francis Asbury came to America. He traveled throughout the colonies, but had especially great success in Delaware. Asbury met another Methodist leader, Thomas Coke, at Barratt's Chapel, near Frederica, in 1784. This meeting led directly to the organization of the American Methodist Church. Circuit riders and camp meetings brought Methodism to farmers who lived too far from towns to attend church. As a result, Methodism is particularly strong in rural Delaware. Roman Catholics are especially numerous in the cities. Other large religious groups include the Episcopalians and Presbyterians.

Cities. About two-thirds of the people live in or near Wilmington, the only large city in Delaware. Many factories in the city line the banks of the Christina River and Brandywine Creek. Wilmington is famous chiefly as the headquarters of chemical companies. Several cities have populations of over 4,000, including Dover, Elsmere, Milford, New Castle, Newark, and Seaford. Delaware is so small that most people in the cities and towns can travel quickly to the bay or ocean shore for such recreations as swimming, sailing, fishing, and crabbing. See the separate articles on Delaware's cities listed in the *Related Articles* at the end of this article.

Country Life. Quiet little market towns and villages dot the countryside south of the Chesapeake and Delaware Canal. They often lie beside creeks or rivers that once provided water highways for traders. Some towns, such as Clayton and Wyoming, grew up at railroad junctions. Delaware's friendly farmers like to gather at church suppers, family reunions, camp meetings, and carnivals and fairs.

Work of the People

About 33 of every 100 employed persons in Delaware work in manufacturing, 17 in wholesale and retail trade, and 5 in agriculture.

Manufacturing and Processing. Delaware is known as THE HOME OF CORPORATIONS. A state law passed in 1899 made it easy for businesses to be incorporated. Corporations can operate in Delaware even if they have nothing there except a mailbox. The law encouraged many companies to incorporate in Delaware, even though they do most of their business in other states.

More than 11 of every 100 employed Delawareans work in the chemical industry, and Wilmington is called "The Chemical Capital of the World." E. I. du Pont de Nemours and Company, the world's largest manufacturer of chemicals, has its headquarters in Wilmington, and also operates several plants in the state. Du Pont's chemical-research center near Wilmington is one of the largest in the world. Other large chemical companies also have offices, research laboratories, and factories in Delaware. The state's chemical plants manufacture only nonexplosive products, including nylon and paint pigments. Delaware's leading position in the chemical industry comes from its being a center for management and research, rather than a manufacturing center.

Food processing ranks second among Delaware's industries. Several plants pack fruits. Dover has canning plants for chicken, and Seaford packs cucumbers. Factories at Lewes manufacture oil and fertilizer from menhaden (see MENHADEN). Wilmington produces many leather products, including glazed kid, used to make gloves. Wilmington also has been the center of Delaware's shipbuilding industry since early colonial days. Other Delaware manufactures include automobiles, baskets and crates, clothing, electrical equipment, machinery, paper, petroleum products, plumbing supplies, and vulcanized fiber.

Agriculture. Delaware sends farm products to many Eastern cities. Farmers in the north supply milk and other dairy products. Central and southern Delaware farmers raise poultry and grow fruits and vegetables. The state's mild climate allows a growing season of about 190 days, from mid-April to mid-October. Cropland and pastures cover nearly half the state. Delaware has about 6,300 farms, averaging 130 acres in size.

Broilers (chickens between 6 and 13 weeks old) are the chief cash farm product. Delaware ranks among the 10 leading broiler states. Broiler production has made Sussex County one of the richest agricultural counties in the United States. The county's broilers often provide over half the state's farm income. Farmers in the south raise most of the hogs, and New Castle and Kent counties lead in beef cattle.

New Castle and Kent counties are the largest milk producers. The region around Wilmington once led in milk production, but refrigeration and fast transportation encouraged development of the dairy industry in the southern part of the state.

Farmers in New Castle and Kent counties grow wheat. Most farmers also raise corn, hay, and soybeans. Potatoes grow well in Kent County. New Castle County has an important mushroom industry. Sussex County produces fine vegetables and melons, including asparagus, beans, cantaloupes, cucumbers, peas, and tomatoes. Orchards in Kent County produce Stayman, Delicious, and Rome apples. Farmers throughout the state raise peaches and strawberries.

Forest and Mining Products. Delaware's forests supply wood for construction and for boxes and crates. Most of this timber comes from Sussex County.

There are few mineral resources. The iron deposits worked in colonial times no longer have commercial importance. Northern New Castle County produces sand, gravel, and rock.

Fishing and Fur Industries. Schools of menhaden along the Atlantic Coast provide the most valuable

DELAWARE

The maps and graphs on this page show the variations in rainfall, population, and growing season. They also tell the chief ways the people earn their living and the average yearly value of the state's main products.

TOTAL PRODUCTION $487,000,000

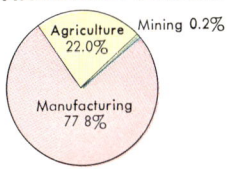

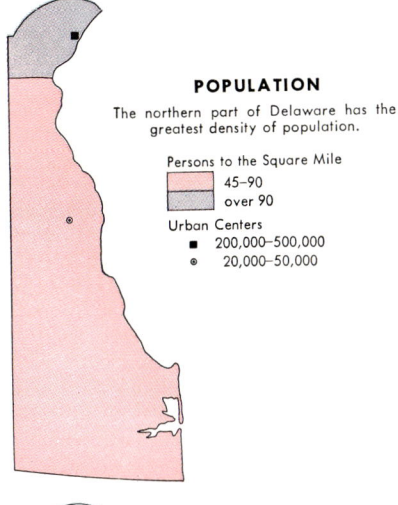

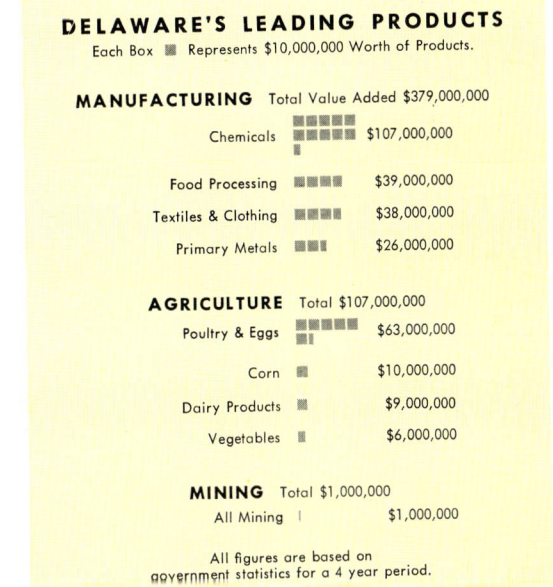

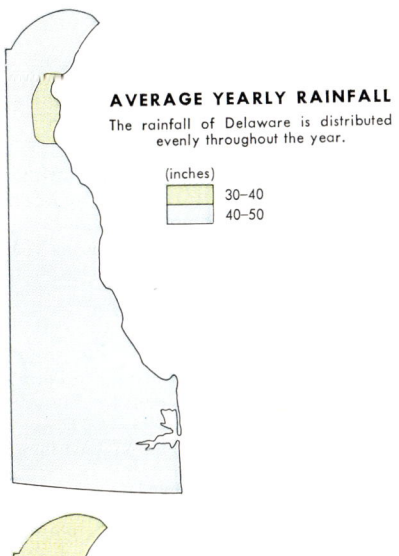

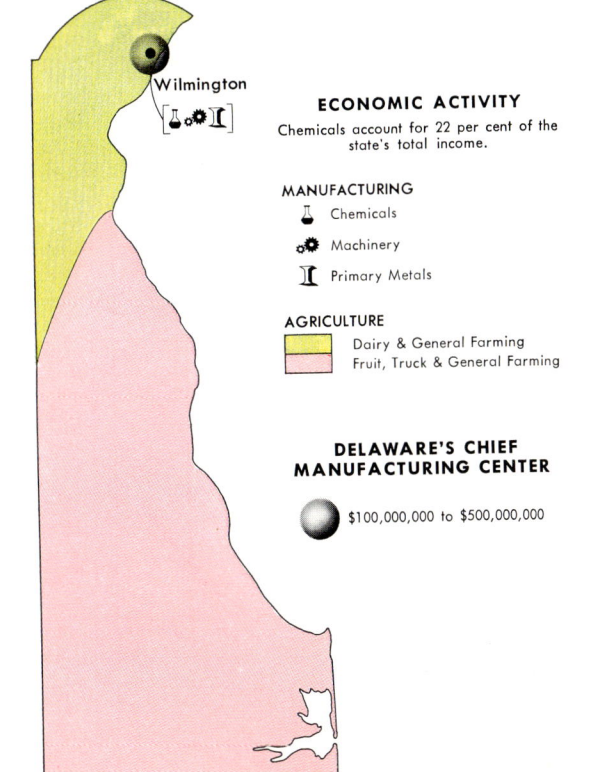

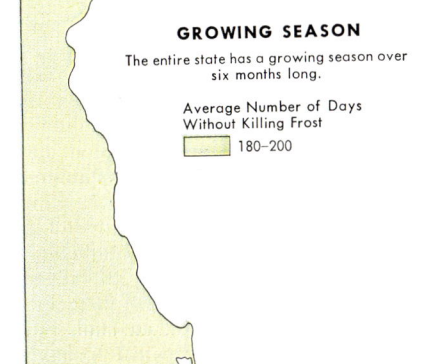

- Agriculture 22.0%
- Mining 0.2%
- Manufacturing 77.8%

POPULATION
The northern part of Delaware has the greatest density of population.

Persons to the Square Mile
- 45–90
- over 90

Urban Centers
- ■ 200,000–500,000
- ◉ 20,000–50,000

DELAWARE'S LEADING PRODUCTS
Each Box ▦ Represents $10,000,000 Worth of Products.

MANUFACTURING Total Value Added $379,000,000
Chemicals	▦▦▦▦▦▦▦▦▦▦▦	$107,000,000
Food Processing	▦▦▦▦	$39,000,000
Textiles & Clothing	▦▦▦▦	$38,000,000
Primary Metals	▦▦▦	$26,000,000

AGRICULTURE Total $107,000,000
Poultry & Eggs	▦▦▦▦▦▦	$63,000,000
Corn	▦	$10,000,000
Dairy Products	▦	$9,000,000
Vegetables	▦	$6,000,000

MINING Total $1,000,000
All Mining	▮	$1,000,000

All figures are based on government statistics for a 4 year period.

AVERAGE YEARLY RAINFALL
The rainfall of Delaware is distributed evenly throughout the year.

(inches)
- 30–40
- 40–50

ECONOMIC ACTIVITY
Chemicals account for 22 per cent of the state's total income.

MANUFACTURING
- Chemicals
- Machinery
- Primary Metals

AGRICULTURE
- Dairy & General Farming
- Fruit, Truck & General Farming

GROWING SEASON
The entire state has a growing season over six months long.

Average Number of Days Without Killing Frost
- 180–200

DELAWARE'S CHIEF MANUFACTURING CENTER
- ● $100,000,000 to $500,000,000

Especially created for **World Book Encyclopedia** by Rand McNally and World Book editors

DELAWARE

catch of Delaware fishermen. Factories at Lewes process the menhaden for industrial oils and fish meal. In addition, commercial fishermen catch sea trout, striped bass, crabs, and snapping turtles. They also dredge or dig up large quantities of oysters and clams. Fresh-water fish include bass, catfish, yellow perch, and pike.

In autumn, men along the coast of New Castle and Kent counties trap muskrats in the marshes. Delaware is one of the nation's chief sources of muskrat pelts.

Electric Power. The state depends on coal-burning steam generators for most of its electric power. Private companies produce most of the power. A few cities own and operate their own plants, but most municipal plants receive additional power from commercial companies. For Delaware's kilowatt-hour production, see ELECTRIC POWER (table).

Transportation. The Delaware River and its tributaries formed the first transportation system for colonists in the region. Today, networks of waterways, highways, railroads, and airlines serve all parts of the state.

Shipping. Wilmington is Delaware's chief port. In 1954, the city increased its foreign trade by enlarging warehouses for exported and imported goods. Industries have wharves for freighters and tankers at Edge Moor and Delaware City.

The marshy shores of Delaware Bay and the sandy Atlantic beaches offer few harbors except at Lewes, the home of ocean-fishing vessels. The granite Delaware Breakwater, completed in 1835, protects Lewes Harbor. In 1901, the United States government added the Harbor of Refuge to the breakwater to protect vessels from ocean storms.

The Chesapeake and Delaware Canal crosses northern Delaware. It cuts 361 miles from the trip for ships traveling between Wilmington and Baltimore. The $13\frac{1}{2}$-mile-long canal was completed in 1829. The Lewes and Rehoboth Canal connects Lewes with Rehoboth Bay.

Roads and Highways help provide swift transportation for perishable farm products. T. Coleman du Pont started Delaware's modern highway program in 1911 by beginning construction of a paved road from Wilmington south to the Maryland border. Delaware has about 4,100 miles of highways, two-thirds of which are paved. The Delaware Memorial Bridge over the Delaware River provides a link with the New Jersey Turnpike.

Aviation and Railroads. The state has about 20 airports. Greater Wilmington Airport near New Castle, the state's chief commercial air terminal, serves the Wilmington area. Dover has a large military airport. Railroads run on about 300 miles of track in Delaware.

Communication. James Adams set up Delaware's first printing press at Wilmington in 1761. He began publishing the state's first newspaper in the 1760's, but no copy of it exists. Delaware has three daily newspapers and about 20 weeklies. The dailies are Dover's *Delaware State News* and Wilmington's *Journal-Every-Evening* and *Morning News*. The *Milford Chronicle* has the largest circulation among the weekly newspapers.

The state's oldest radio stations, WDEL and WILM, were established in Wilmington in 1922. The first television station broadcast in Wilmington in 1949. It no longer operates. At Bethany Beach and Cape Henlopen, the U.S. Navy operates radio stations that help ships determine their exact location at sea.

Education

Schools. "Let us go and buy a schoolmaster!" was an expression commonly heard at New Castle and other Delaware ports whenever a ship bearing newcomers arrived from overseas during the 1700's. Many passengers from Europe who owed money for their fares taught school until they had worked out their debts. Some colonists sent their children to England or to Scotland to be educated.

In 1818, the state legislature gave $1,000 to each county for the education of poor children. The Delaware public-school system grew out of the work of Willard Hall, who proposed "An Act for the Establishment of Free Schools." The state legislature approved the bill in 1829. This act provided that the state would give as much money as each school district, up to $300. In 1907, school attendance became compulsory for children between the ages of 7 and 16.

Delaware abolished county school boards in 1921, and established a state board of education. This board consists of six voting members and two nonvoting members. The governor appoints the voting members to three-year terms. The two nonvoting members are the presidents of the University of Delaware and Delaware State College. They act as advisers. The board appoints the state superintendent of public instruction to a one-year term. The state provides over four-fifths of the funds for the public schools. Local school districts provide most of the remainder. For the number of students and teachers in Delaware, see EDUCATION (table).

Universities and Colleges. The University of Delaware, a state-supported school at Newark, is Delaware's only university (see DELAWARE, UNIVERSITY OF). The state also operates Delaware State College at Dover, founded in 1891. The Methodist Church supports Wesley College at Dover.

Libraries. The people of Wilmington organized the state's first library in 1754. From it grew the Library Company of Wilmington, founded in 1788. This library still operates as the Wilmington Institute Free Library. The state also has 17 smaller city and town libraries. The New Castle County Library supplies books to many farm communities in the county. The State Library Commission in Dover operates a bookmobile service in Kent and Sussex counties. The Historical Society of Delaware, in Wilmington, and the State Archives, at Dover, have excellent collections on local history. The Memorial Library of the University of Delaware is the chief research library.

Museums emphasize colonial life in the state. The Old Dutch House, built in New Castle in the late 1600's, offers a glimpse into the lives of Dutch families in colonial Delaware. The Dickinson Mansion, near Dover, was once the home of the writer and statesman John Dickinson, who became famous during the Revolutionary period. The state keeps the collections of the Delaware State Museum in two old Dover church buildings. These collections include displays of colonial furnishings and Indian relics, and exhibits of the region's natural history. Wilmington's Old Town Hall, built in 1798, displays material of the Historical Society of Delaware. The Henry Francis du Pont Winterthur Mu-

Ragsdale, F.P.G.

The Hagley Museum, devoted to U.S. industrial history, stands beside Brandywine Creek. It was built in 1814 as a cotton mill by E. I. du Pont.

Roy Pinney

The Du Pont Plant at Newport is one of many factories that make the state a leader in the chemical industry.

Delaware Memorial Bridge, near New Castle, links the state with New Jersey. The span crosses the Delaware River.

DELAWARE (Map Index)

Population
446,292 1960
318,085 1950
266,505 1940

Physical Features

Appoquinimink
  Creek .... B 1
Bombay Hook Isl. .. B 2
Bombay Hook Pt. ... B 2
Brandywine Creek .. A 1
Breakwater Harbor .. C 2
Broadkill Beach ..... C 2
Broadkill R. .... C 2
Browns Brook .... A 1
Cape Henlopen ..... C 2
Cedar Creek .... C 2
Chesapeake and
  Delaware Canal .. A 1
Christina R. .... A 1
Deep Creek .... C 1
Deepwater Pt. .... B 2
Delaware Bay .... B 2
Delaware R. .... B 2
Duck Creek .... B 2
Goose Pt. .... B 2
Gravelly Brook ...... C 1
Great Pocomoke
  Swamp .... D 2
Gum Brook .... C 1
Highest Point in
  Delaware .... A 1
Indian R. .... C 2
Indian River Bay .... C 2
Kelly Isl. .... B 2
Kent Isl. .... B 2
Laurel R. .... C 1
Leipsic R. .... B 1
Little Assawoman
  Bay .... D 2
Marshyhope Creek .. C 1
Mispillion R. .... C 2
Murderkill R. .... C 2
Nanticoke R. .... C 1
Noxontown Pond ... B 1
Pea Patch Isl. .... A 1
Pocomoke R. .... C 2
Red Lion Creek ..... A 1
Reedy Isl. .... A 1
Reedy Pt. .... A 1
Refuge, Harbor of .. C 2
Rehoboth Bay .... C 2
St. Jones R. .... B 1
Smyrna R. .... B 1
White Clay Creek ... A 1

Counties

Kent, 65,651 .... B 1
New Castle, 307,446 . A 1
Sussex, 73,195 ...... C 1

Cities

Andrewsville, 25 .... C 1
Angola, 90 .... C 2
Arden, 1,500 .... A 2
Bacon, 30 .... C 1
Bayard .... C 2
Bear, 75 .... A 1
Bellefonte, 1,536 ... A 2
Belltown, 200 .... C 2
Belvidere,* 1,000 ... A 1
Bethany Beach, 170 . C 2
Bethel, 28 .... C 1
Big Stone Beach,
  20 .... B 1
Bishops Corner, 120 . B 1
Blackbird, 30 .... B 1
Blades, 729 .... C 1
Bowers, 324 .... B 2
Brandywine Springs,
  400 .... A 1
Bridgeville, 1,469 ... C 1
Brookland Terrace,*
  900 .... A 1
Brookside, 4,000 ... A 1
Camden, 1,125 ..... B 1
Cannon, 75 .... C 1
Canterbury, 75 ..... B 1
Capitol Green, 900 . B 1
Capitol Park,* 750 . B 1
Carpenter, 100 ..... A 2
Carpenters Corner,
  100 .... C 2
Carrcroft, 87 .... A 1
Centerville, 42 ...... A 1
Cheswold, 281 ..... B 1
Christiana, 400 ..... A 1
Clarksville, 200 ..... C 2
Claymont, 12,000 .. A 2
Clayton, 1,028 ..... B 1
Collins Park, 2,600 . A 1
Concord, 130 .... C 1
Dagsboro, 477 ..... C 2
Delaware City,
  1,658 .... A 1
Delmar, 934 .... D 1
Dewey Beach, 150 . C 2
Dover, 7,250 .... °B 1
Downs Chapel, 20 . B 1
Duruss Heights, 800 . A 1
Eden Park, 425 .... A 1
Edge Hill, 800 ..... B 1
Ellendale, 370 ..... C 2
Elsmere, 7,319 .... A 1
Fairfax,* 1,000 ..... A 1
Farmington, 142 .. C 1
Farnhurst, 350 .... A 1
Felton, 422 .... B 1
Fenwick Island, 48 . D 2
Frankford, 558 .... C 2
Frederica, 863 .... B 2
Georgetown, 1,765 . °C 2
Greenwood, 768 .. C 1
Gumboro, 75 .... C 2
Hamilton Park,* 300 . A 1
Harbeson, 270 .... C 2
Harrington, 2,495 . C 1
Hartly, 164 .... B 1
Hazlettville, 25 .... B 1
Hearns Mill, 150 .. C 1
Hickman, 100 ..... C 1
Hillcrest, 300 ...... A 1
Hockessin, 400 .... A 1
Holloway Terrace,*
  1,100 .... A 1
Holly Oak, 1,000 .. A 2
Hollyville, 40 ...... C 2
Houston, 421 ..... C 1
Jimtown, 60 .... C 1
Kent Acres, 750 .. B 1
Kenton, 249 .... B 1
Kirkwood, 430 .... A 1
Kitts Hummock, 15 . B 2
Kynlyn,* 1,600 ... A 1
Laurel, 2,709 ..... C 1
Lebanon, 110 ..... B 1
Leipsic, 281 .... B 1
Lewes, 3,025 ..... C 2
Liftwood,* 800 ... A 1
Lincoln, 400 ...... C 2
Little Creek, 306 . B 2
Lowes Crossroads, 25 . C 2
Lynch Heights, 100 . C 2
Magnolia, 310 ... B 1
Marshallton, 3,000 . A 1
Masten, 30 .... C 1
McDaniel Heights,*
  486 .... A 1
Middleford, 50 ... C 1
Middletown, 2,191 . B 1
Midvale, 200 ..... A 1
Midway, 85 ...... C 2
Milford, 5,795 ... C 2
Millsboro, 536 .. C 2
Millside,* 1,000 . A 1
Millville, 231 .... C 2
Milton, 1,617 ... C 2
Minners Corner, 35 . C 1
Minquadale, 1,330 . A 1
Montchanin, 400 . A 1
Mount Pleasant, 50 . A 1
Nassau, 75 .... C 2
New Castle, 4,469 . A 1
Newark, 11,404 . A 1
Newport, 1,239 . A 1
North Hills,* 400 . A 1
Oak Grove, 100 . C 1
Oak Orchard, 50 . C 2
Ocean View, 422 . C 2
Odessa, 526 ..... B 1
Ogletown,* 175 . A 1
Penny Hill,* 1,000 . A 1
Pinetown, 75 .... C 2
Plymouth, 100 ...... B 2
Port Mahon, 20 .... B 2
Port Penn, 271 ..... A 1
Quakertown, 150 .. C 2
Red Lion, 40 .... A 1
Rehoboth Beach,
  1,507 .... C 2
Reliance, 75 .... C 1
Rising Sun, 150 ... B 1
Rockland, 300 .... A 1
Rodney Village,
  1,200 .... B 1
Rose Hill,* 670 ... A 1
Roxana, 100 ...... C 2
St. Georges, 339 . A 1
Seaford, 4,430 ... C 1
Selbyville, 1,080 . D 2
Silverbrook, 35 .. A 1
Silview, 519 ...... A 1
Slaughter Beach,
  107 .... C 2
Smyrna, 3,241 .. B 1
Smyrna Landing,
  175 .... B 1
Stanton, 2,000 .. A 1
Summit Bridge, 50 . A 1
Sycamore, 400 .. C 2
Talleyville, 2,000 . A 1
Taylors Bridge, 40 . B 1
The Cedars,* 800 . A 1
Townsend, 434 .. B 1
Vernon, 60 .... C 1
Viola, 159 .... B 1
Welshire,* 400 .. A 1
Whitesville, 25 .. D 2
Willowgrove, 100 . B 1
Wilmington, 95,827 . °A 1
Wilmington Manor,
  1,440 .... A 1
Winterthur, 200 .. A 1
Woodland, 50 .... C 1
Woodland Beach,
  125 .... B 2
Woodside, 189 .. B 1
Worthland,* 500 . A 2
Wyoming, 1,172 . B 1
York Beach,* 500 . C 2
Yorklyn, 500 ..... A 1

°County Seat.
*Does not appear on the map; key shows general location.

Source: Latest available census figures.

---

seum, near Wilmington, owns a collection of early American household furnishings. The Hagley Museum has old industrial displays as well as modern push-button exhibits.

The Arts

Painting. The first outstanding artist in Delaware, Gustavus Hesselius, came from Sweden in 1712. He specialized in portrait painting. Henry Lea Tatnall, a Quaker, became Delaware's first native-born painter of note. His landscapes, painted in the early 1800's, showed the beauty of rural Delaware. Robert Shaw portrayed historic Delaware buildings in his etchings. Felix O. C. Darley of Claymont was famous for his illustrations of books by James Fenimore Cooper, Charles Dickens, and other leading writers. Howard Pyle of Wilmington became the state's most famous illustrator and painter. He taught several gifted pupils, including N. C. Wyeth, Frank Schoonover, and Stanley Arthurs.

Literature. Delaware has produced a number of distinguished writers. John Dickinson vigorously supported the colonists during the 1760's and early 1770's, and gained fame as "The Penman of the American Revolution." George Alfred Townsend, a Civil War correspondent from Sussex County, wrote a group of short stories called *Tales of the Chesapeake*. Howard Pyle wrote *The Merry Adventures of Robin Hood*. Other distinguished writers include Robert Montgomery Bird, Henry Seidel Canby, Anne Parrish, and Max Adeler.

Interesting Places to Visit

The white sands of Bethany and Rehoboth beaches draw thousands of swimmers and sun bathers each summer. Yachtsmen sail the sparkling blue waters of the Indian River and Delaware Bay. Hunters find small animals and birds in the salt marshes. Fox hunters with their hounds dash across the countryside each autumn in the region around Middletown. The lakes, streams, and bays offer excellent fishing.

Following are brief descriptions of some of Delaware's interesting places to visit.

Amstel House, at New Castle, was built in 1730 or earlier. It houses the museum of the New Castle Historical Society. Exhibits include complete colonial furnishings for the kitchen and music room.

Churches. *Barratt's Chapel*, near Frederica, has been called "The Cradle of Methodism in America." Francis Asbury and Thomas Coke agreed to organize the American Methodist Episcopal Church at a meeting in this chapel on Nov. 14, 1784. *Christ Episcopal Church* stands on the wooded shore of Chipman's Pond near Laurel. Built in 1771, the pine church has never been painted, but remains remarkably well preserved. *Immanuel Church*, an Anglican church in New Castle, was built about 1704. Its churchyard holds the graves of many men famous in Delaware's early days, including governors Gunning Bedford, Thomas Stockton, and Nicholas van Dyke. *Old Drawyers' Presbyterian Church*, built near Odessa in the 1770's, stands on the site of a church where Presbyterians worshiped as early as 1711. *Old Swedes Church*, at Wilmington, was consecrated as a Swedish Lutheran church in 1699. It is one of the oldest churches in the United States, and now serves as a chapel of Trinity Episcopal Church. *Welsh Tract Baptist Church*, built near Newark in 1746, stands on a tract of land purchased from William Penn in 1703 by Welsh immigrants.

Cooch's Bridge, near Newark, was the site in 1777 of Delaware's only battle during the Revolutionary War. The Stars and Stripes may have flown in a land battle for the first time at this bridge.

Delaware Art Center, at Wilmington, has historical paintings by Howard Pyle, and a fine collection of Pre-Raphaelite paintings.

De Vries Monument, at Lewes, marks the supposed site of a fort built in 1631 by Dutch colonists sent to America

Especially created for **World Book Encyclopedia** by Rand McNally and World Book editors

Zwaanendael Museum in Lewes was built in 1931 in honor of the Dutch men and women who settled in Delaware in 1631.

A Colonial Kitchen in New Castle is part of Amstel House museum. The old-fashioned fireplace, utensils, firearms, and spinning wheel date from the days when Delaware was a colony.

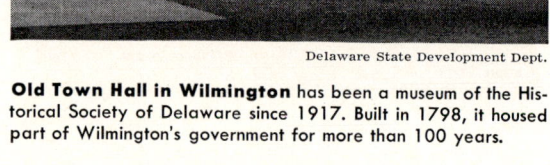

Delaware State Development Dept.

Old Town Hall in Wilmington has been a museum of the Historical Society of Delaware since 1917. Built in 1798, it housed part of Wilmington's government for more than 100 years.

by David Pietersen de Vries, a Dutch navigator and adventurer. Indians destroyed the colony.

Eleutherian Mills-Hagley Foundation Historic Site and Museum Area, near Wilmington, covers 185 acres on Brandywine Creek. The Du Ponts built their first gunpowder mill there. An industrial museum and several restored mills show the activities of early industries.

Henry Francis du Pont Winterthur Museum, near Wilmington, has more than 100 rooms, each furnished in the styles of periods between 1640 and the early 1800's. Visitors must write for permission to go through the museum, except during May.

Iron Hill, near Newark, is one of the highest points in Delaware, reaching an elevation of 334 feet. The Delaware River and Chesapeake Bay can be seen from its summit on clear days.

Old Court House, in New Castle, became Delaware's first capitol in 1704. According to tradition, William Penn took possession of his lands in Delaware here in 1682.

State House, in Dover, is one of the oldest state capitols. This colonial brick building dates from 1792. It houses several state administrative agencies.

Zwaanendael Museum, in Lewes, exhibits Indian relics and mementos of seafaring days in southern Delaware. The building is modeled after a wing of the Town Hall at Hoorn, in The Netherlands.

State Parks and Forests. The state forestry department controls about 4,600 acres of state forests. The largest is Redden State Forest (2,820 acres), near the village of Redden. Ellendale State Forest, near Milford, has an area of 993 acres. Other state forest areas are Blackbird Tract (676 acres), Appenzeller Tract (45 acres), and Red Lion Tract (5 acres). The following list describes the five state parks.

Brandywine Springs (57 acres), near Marshallton, occupies the site of the Brandywine Springs Hotel, a popular summer resort from 1827 to 1845. Fire destroyed the old hotel building in 1853. Established in 1951.

Delaware Dunes (5,000 acres) extends from Rehoboth Beach south to Maryland. Its beaches separate the Atlantic Ocean from Rehoboth, Indian River, and Little Assawoman bays. The park offers excellent swimming and fishing. Established in 1940.

Fort Christina (2 acres), at Wilmington, honors New Sweden, the first permanent settlement in Delaware. The park includes "The Rocks," a natural wharf where the first Swedish colonists landed in 1638. A monument of black Swedish granite commemorates the event. Carl Milles, a Swedish-American sculptor, designed the monument as a token of friendship between the Swedish and American people. Established in 1938.

Fort Delaware (178 acres) is on Pea Patch Island in the Delaware River, near Delaware City. A water-filled moat surrounds the massive five-sided fortress which held thousands of Confederate prisoners during the Civil War.

Trap Pond (1,000 acres), near Laurel, has bathing beaches and picnic areas. Established in 1952.

Annual Events in Delaware

Delaware Day is probably the state's most important holiday. The governor proclaims this holiday on December 7 to commemorate the day in 1787 when Delaware became the first state to ratify the Constitution of the United States. The following are the most important events in Delaware.

March, Delaware Swedish Colonial Day, in honor of

92b

the first permanent settlement, state-wide, March 29.

May, Delaware Festival of Arts, state-wide, first two weeks; A Day in Old Dover, featuring open house in the old homes of the city, first Saturday and Sunday; A Day in Old New Castle, with open house, third Saturday; horse racing at Delaware Park in Stanton, Memorial Day through July; Old Swedes Church Anniversary at Wilmington, May or June.

June, Old Drawyers' Church Anniversary near Odessa, first Sunday; start of yacht races on Indian River at Oak Orchard, no fixed date; boat races by Wilmington Power Squadron at Wilmington, no fixed date.

July, Kent and Sussex Fair and harness racing at Harrington, last week.

August, Big Thursday, a holiday for Kent County farmers, at Bowers, second Thursday; Big Quarterly, a Negro religious reunion, at Wilmington, last Sunday.

September, Barratt's Chapel Anniversary near Frederica, last Sunday.

December, Delaware Day, state-wide, Dec. 7.

Government

Constitution. Delaware has had four state constitutions, adopted in 1776, 1792, 1831, and 1897. Constitutional amendments require a two-thirds vote of the members of each house of the state legislature in two successive sessions. Delaware is the only state in which a constitutional amendment does not have to be submitted to the public for a vote.

Executive. Delawareans elect their governor for a term of four years. He may serve only two terms. Other elected executive officials include the lieutenant governor, attorney general, treasurer, auditor of accounts, and insurance commissioner. The treasurer and auditor serve two-year terms, and the others hold office for four years. The State Board of Health and other special boards carry on many administrative functions. The governor usually appoints members of these boards to terms of from 1 to 10 years. The governor appoints the secretary of state, who serves until the governor replaces him. The secretary of state grants all charters for corporations.

Legislature, which is called the *general assembly*, consists of a senate and a house of representatives. It meets in Dover on the first Tuesday in January of each year. The legislature usually continues in session until the summer. Kent and Sussex counties elect five senators each, and New Castle elects seven, two of whom come from Wilmington. Senators serve four-year terms. Kent and Sussex counties elect 10 representatives each, and New Castle elects 15, five of whom come from Wilmington. Representatives serve two-year terms.

Courts. The state supreme court, which meets in Dover, consists of a chief justice and two associate justices. Seven judges handle the work of the state's superior court, which meets in all three counties. Either the chancellor or vice-chancellor presides over the court of chancery. The governor appoints all these judges, with the consent of the senate, to 12-year terms.

The general assembly determines the maximum number of justices of the peace who may be appointed for each county. With the consent of the senate, the governor appoints these officials to four-year terms. The governor also appoints a judge for the Wilmington Municipal Court, two judges of the Family Court of New Castle County, judges of the common pleas for each county, and a judge of the Juvenile Court of Kent and Sussex County. Most of these judges serve 12-year terms.

Local Government. Delaware is the only state in which each county is divided into hundreds. A *hundred* is an old English unit of local government that corresponds to townships in other states. It has no government of its own, but serves as a basis for taxation and frequently for representation. See HUNDRED.

The voters of each county elect three levy-court commissioners to manage county finances. Commissioners serve six-year terms in New Castle and Sussex counties, and two-year terms in Kent County. The levy court sets the tax rate for the county, and administers such services as the collection and disposal of rubbish and garbage. Other elected county officials include the sheriff, coroner, comptroller, register of wills, and the receiver of taxes, who is also the county treasurer. All serve four-year terms except the sheriff and coroner, who serve two-year terms. Most of the cities and towns use some form of the mayor-council or council-manager system of government.

Taxation. The chief sources of revenue are individual income, state franchise, corporation income, and cigarette taxes. Delaware is the only state that requires its citizens to file a state income report, whether

Delaware State Development Dept.

Legislative Hall, the state capitol, opened for use in 1933. The architects designed this red brick Georgian-style building to resemble State House, Delaware's previous state capitol.

DELAWARE

or not they pay an income tax. There is no general retail sales tax. Corporation license fees provide almost a sixth of the state's revenue.

Politics. The Federalist party held power in Delaware until after 1830, when most of the Federalists became Whigs. The Democrats gained power after 1865. The Republicans have enjoyed an advantage in national elections since 1890, but state elections are close and uncertain. For the state's voting record in national elections since 1804, see ELECTORAL COLLEGE (table).

Although more than two-thirds of the people live in New Castle County, the other two counties have a majority in the legislature. By custom, both parties divide the candidacies for the major state offices almost equally among persons from all three counties. This gives farmers a strong voice in Delaware politics. Candidates for state and national offices are nominated in party conventions without primary elections.

Any citizen who is 21 years old and who has lived in Delaware for one year has the right to vote. A special provision in the state constitution requires that every voter who reached the age of 21 after 1900 must be able to read the constitution in English and to write his name if physically capable.

National Defense. The Delaware National Guard has about 3,400 men. Dover Air Force Base is the state's chief military installation.

History

Indian Days. The Delaware, or Leni-Lenape, and the Nanticoke Indians lived in the Delaware region when the first white settlers arrived. Both tribes spoke dialects of the Algonkian language. The Delaware tribe lived on both banks of the Delaware River, north from New Castle County to the Delaware Water Gap (see DELAWARE WATER GAP). These Indians had friendly relations with the early settlers. Most of them moved to the western United States and to Canada during the late 1600's and 1700's when white men moved into their lands. The Nanticoke lived in southwestern Delaware along the Nanticoke River. White men crowded most of them northwest to Pennsylvania before the Revolutionary War.

Dutch and Swedish Settlement. The English explorer Henry Hudson discovered Delaware Bay in 1609 while seeking a passage to the Far East for the Dutch East India Company (see HUDSON, HENRY). He did not go far inland because he saw it was a river estuary. In 1610, a ship from the Virginia colony sought shelter from a storm in the bay, but the crew did not attempt any exploration. The Dutch established the first settlement in Delaware at Zwaanendael (then called Swanendael) in 1631. The site of this settlement now is in the city of Lewes. Indians killed most of the colonists and burned the fort at Zwaanendael in 1632.

Some members of the Dutch West India Company became angry with the Dutch government, because it was more interested in immediate profits than in permanent colonization. These men brought settlers from Sweden to Delaware in 1638. They founded the colony of New Sweden, and built Fort Christina at present-day Wilmington. The Swedish government appointed Peter Ridder as the colony's governor in 1640. He served until 1643, when Johan Printz replaced him. New settlers from Sweden and Finland expanded the colony north.

The Dutch government, in turn, became angry with the Swedes for settling in what it considered Dutch territory. Peter Stuyvesant, the Dutch governor of New Netherland (New York), established a post at New Castle in 1651. The Swedes captured New Castle in 1654. The next year, the Dutch struck back, captured all New Sweden, and made it part of New Netherland.

English Rule. An English fleet seized all New Netherland in 1664. For the next 18 years, the English ruled Delaware as part of their colony of New York. The Dutch recaptured the colony briefly in 1673, but returned it peacefully in 1674. New Castle flourished as a kind of secondary capital, because Delaware was so far from New York City.

William Penn wanted to establish a connection between his colony of Pennsylvania, founded in 1681, and the ocean. In 1682, the Duke of York granted Delaware to Penn. That same year, Penn established the first representative government in the colony. He called a general assembly of elected delegates to meet at Chester, Pa. For 19 years, the same governor and general assembly served both Pennsylvania and Delaware. Each colony had an equal number of counties and an equal number of delegates in the assembly. During this period, people called Delaware "The Three Lower Counties," because the Delaware counties were down the river from Pennsylvania.

The Delaware colonists began to fear that they would become a minority in the colonial government as Pennsylvania grew and added new counties. In 1701, the Delaware delegates refused to meet with those from Pennsylvania. They asked Penn to give them a separate assembly. Penn consented, and Delaware's first general assembly met in New Castle in 1704. Delaware con-

---
RED-LETTER DATES IN DELAWARE

1609 Henry Hudson visited Delaware Bay.
1610 A ship from Lord de la Warr's Virginia colony visited Delaware Bay.
1631 The Dutch established Zwaanendael at the present site of Lewes.
1638 Swedish colonists established New Sweden, Delaware's first permanent settlement.
1655 The Dutch captured New Sweden.
1664 The English seized Dutch territory on the Delaware River for the Duke of York.
1682 William Penn took over the Delaware counties.
1704 Delaware's first separate general assembly met at New Castle.
1777 The British army invaded Delaware.
1787 Delaware became the first state of the Union on December 7.
1802 Éleuthère Irénée du Pont began manufacturing gunpowder on Brandywine Creek.
1829 The Chesapeake and Delaware Canal opened.
1865 Amendment 13 freed the last slaves in Delaware.
1897 Delaware adopted its present constitution.
1919 The Chesapeake and Delaware Canal was deepened and widened for ocean-going vessels.
1936 Delaware joined New York, New Jersey, and Pennsylvania to control pollution of the Delaware River.
1941 The general assembly amended the state's Sunday blue laws to allow more Sunday activities.
1951 The Delaware Memorial Bridge opened.
1957 The state began providing funds for needy students to attend the University of Delaware.

HISTORIC DELAWARE

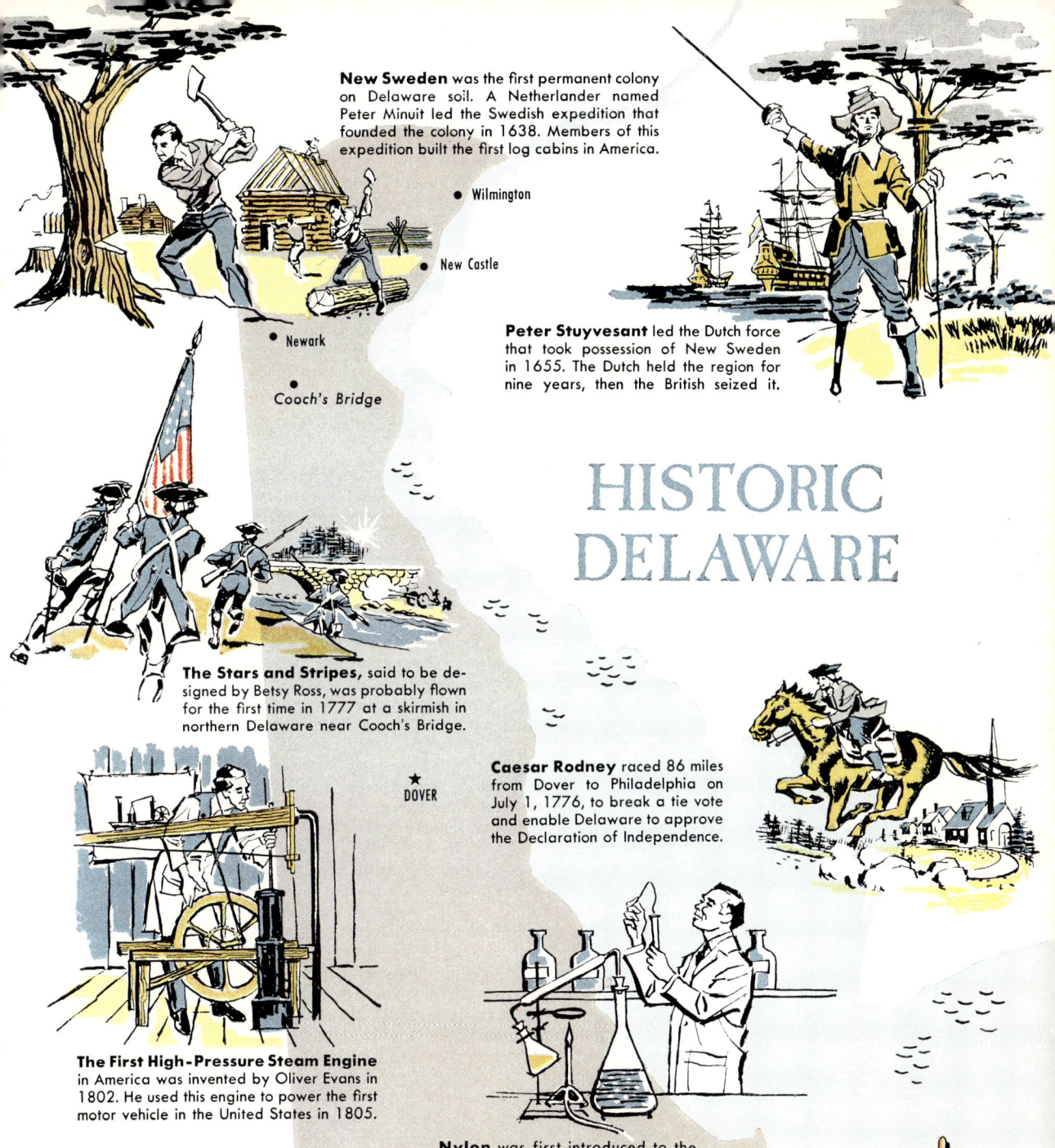

New Sweden was the first permanent colony on Delaware soil. A Netherlander named Peter Minuit led the Swedish expedition that founded the colony in 1638. Members of this expedition built the first log cabins in America.

- Wilmington
- New Castle
- Newark
- Cooch's Bridge

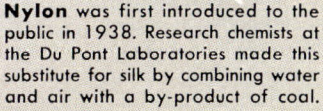

Peter Stuyvesant led the Dutch force that took possession of New Sweden in 1655. The Dutch held the region for nine years, then the British seized it.

The Stars and Stripes, said to be designed by Betsy Ross, was probably flown for the first time in 1777 at a skirmish in northern Delaware near Cooch's Bridge.

★ DOVER

Caesar Rodney raced 86 miles from Dover to Philadelphia on July 1, 1776, to break a tie vote and enable Delaware to approve the Declaration of Independence.

The First High-Pressure Steam Engine in America was invented by Oliver Evans in 1802. He used this engine to power the first motor vehicle in the United States in 1805.

Nylon was first introduced to the public in 1938. Research chemists at the Du Pont Laboratories made this substitute for silk by combining water and air with a by-product of coal.

The Christmas Seal first appeared in a local tuberculosis fund-drive in Delaware in 1907. Emily Bissell adapted the idea from a custom popular in Europe.

First State of the Union. Delaware won the title of "the First State" when it became the first of the original 13 states to ratify the U.S. Constitution.

DELAWARE

tinued to share Pennsylvania's governor until the Revolutionary War. Penn, or his heirs, appointed the governors, and the British government approved them.

The Revolutionary War. Delaware joined the other 12 American colonies to fight for independence, and formed an independent state government in 1776. John McKinly was elected the first president (governor) of the state. The state constitution of that year called The Three Lower Counties "The Delaware State."

In September, 1777, British troops landed in Maryland and prepared to capture Philadelphia. General George Washington moved his army to Wilmington to face the British. Advance units of the two armies skirmished at Cooch's Bridge near Newark. The British changed the direction of their advance and marched through Newark and Hockessin to Kennett Square in Pennsylvania. They defeated Washington at the Battle of the Brandywine in Pennsylvania, just beyond the Delaware boundary. The British occupied Wilmington for a few weeks after the battle. Their ships constantly threatened the state, and raiding parties often raced ashore to terrorize the countryside.

Statehood. On Dec. 7, 1787, Delaware became the first state to ratify the Constitution of the United States. Delegates at the state convention voted unanimously to adopt the Constitution. The state had a population of about 59,000 at this time. Delaware adopted a new state constitution in 1792, and changed its name from "The Delaware State" to "The State of Delaware." The title of the chief executive was changed from president to governor. Joshua Clayton became the first chief executive to have the title of governor.

Wilmington became the center of the country's flour-milling industry during the 1790's, because the swift streams offered cheap sources of power. In 1802, Éleuthère Irénée du Pont began manufacturing gunpowder on the banks of Brandywine Creek near Wilmington. The War of 1812 made new industries prosper because British ships could not bring goods to America. A brief depression followed the war. But many new industries opened around Wilmington after 1830.

The Civil War. Delaware was a slaveholding state, but only about 1,800 slaves remained by 1860. The state had so many ties with the North that it did not secede from the Union during the Civil War. But many Delawareans opposed the war. They felt that the South should have been allowed to leave the Union peacefully.

President Abraham Lincoln's Emancipation Proclamation had no effect in Delaware, because the state had remained loyal to the Union. The few slaves still in the state were not freed until Amendment 13 of the Constitution went into effect in December, 1865. Delaware and Kentucky were the last slaveholding states.

The Late 1800's. Delaware enjoyed increasing industrial prosperity after the Civil War. The extension of railroads made downstate farmlands more valuable, because crops could easily be moved to market. Wilmington grew rapidly during this period. Thousands of workmen were employed in the city's shipyards, iron foundries, machine shops, and manufacturing plants.

The state's present constitution was adopted in 1897. It carefully outlined the boundaries for each district from which a state legislator could be elected, so that the growing industrial areas would not be able to outvote the farming regions.

The Early 1900's. Delaware established its State Highway Department during the administration of Governor John G. Townsend, Jr., a Republican who served from 1917 to 1921. During this same period, the legislature established a state income tax, a pension system for needy mothers, an industrial accident board to award money to workmen injured on the job, and a state board of charities.

Governor Townsend's most important achievement was the large-scale revision of the public-school system that began during his administration. Pierre S. du Pont became interested in the improvement of the state's schools. He gave several million dollars to build new public schools and to aid the improvement of education in other ways. Du Pont also served as state tax commissioner. This enabled him to see that funds were collected to run the schools.

The economic depression of the 1930's put thousands of Delawareans out of work. But no major bank failures occurred. Probably as a result of the depression, the people elected Richard C. McMullen as governor in 1936. McMullen was the first Democratic governor to be elected since before 1900. In 1941, the state legislature amended its Sunday blue laws, placing fewer restrictions on Sunday activities (see BLUE LAWS).

Recent Developments. During World War II, Delaware industries turned to war work, and the Dravo Shipyards at Wilmington became the largest employer in the state. During the 1950's, Delaware's population increased by a greater percentage than that of any other state east of the Rocky Mountains except Florida. Industries grew with the population. The Du Pont, Hercules, and Atlas chemical companies enlarged their research laboratories. The Tidewater Oil Company built a gigantic $130,000,000 oil refinery near Delaware City in 1956. General Motors Corporation opened an automobile-assembly plant at Woodcrest, and Chrysler Corporation built one at Newark.

As industries and the population grew, public schools had to be enlarged. Most of the money for expansion came from the state, but private gifts proved especially helpful. Public schools in northern Delaware integrated their classes after the Supreme Court declared school segregation unconstitutional in 1954. In 1957, Republican Governor J. Caleb Boggs signed a "Right to Education" bill providing scholarship funds for needy students to attend the University of Delaware. The voters elected Boggs to the United States Senate in 1960, and chose Democrat Elbert N. Carvel as governor. Carvel had served as governor from 1949 to 1953.

Famous Delawareans

This section contains short biographies of persons important to the history of Delaware. A statue of Caesar Rodney, an American Revolutionary leader, represents Delaware in Statuary Hall in the Capitol in Washington, D.C. Other Delawareans who have separate biographies in WORLD BOOK are listed in the *Related Articles* at the end of this article.

Bayard, James Asheton (1767-1815), served as a Federalist member of the U.S. House of Representatives from 1797 to 1803, and in the U.S. Senate from 1805 to 1813. He was one of the commissioners who negotiated the Treaty of Ghent, ending the War of 1812. Bayard was born in Philadelphia.

Bayard, Thomas Francis (1828-1898), grandson of James Asheton Bayard, was the first U.S. Ambassador to Great Britain, serving from 1893 to 1897. He became a Democratic member of the U.S. Senate in 1869, and served until 1885. President Cleveland appointed him Secretary of State in 1885. He was born in Wilmington.

Bissell, Emily (1861-1948), a writer and editor, originated the sale of Christmas seals in the United States. She issued seals for the first time in 1907 to raise funds for the Delaware Tuberculosis Association. She was born in Wilmington.

Clayton, Joshua (1744-1798), a physician and politician, served as the last president of Delaware from 1789 to 1793, and as the first governor of Delaware from 1793 to 1796. He was elected to the U.S. Senate in 1798, but died that year. He was born in Maryland.

Hall, Willard (1780-1875), was the father of free public education in Delaware. He served as Delaware's secretary of state from 1812 to 1814, and again from 1821 to 1822. He was elected to the U.S. House of Representatives in 1817, and served until 1821. Hall, a Democrat, was appointed as a federal district judge in 1823, and served until 1871. He was born in Westford, Mass.

McKinly, John (1724-1796), a physician and statesman, was elected as the first president (governor) of Delaware in 1777. British troops captured him after only a few months in office. He later resumed the practice of medicine. He was born in Ireland.

McLane, Louis (1784-1857), a lawyer, businessman, and statesman, served as a Federalist member of the U.S. House of Representatives from 1817 to 1827, and as a U.S. Senator from 1827 to 1829. He was U.S. Minister to Great Britain from 1829 to 1831, and again from 1845 to 1846. He also served as Secretary of the Treasury from 1831 to 1833, and as Secretary of State from 1833 to 1834. McLane was born in Smyrna, Del.

Printz, Johan Björnsson (1592-1663), was the most important governor of the colony of New Sweden. He served from 1643 to 1653, and organized the colony's government into a workable form. He was born at Bottnaryd, Sweden.

Williams, John James (1904-   ), became a Republican member of the U.S. Senate in 1947. Beginning in 1951, he exposed several cases of corruption in the Internal Revenue Service. His exposures resulted in the discharge or imprisonment of several tax officials on charges of accepting bribes. Williams was born near Frankford.   JOHN A. MUNROE. *Critically reviewed by* PAUL DOLAN.

Related Articles in WORLD BOOK include:

BIOGRAPHIES

Bassett, Richard	Du Pont de Nemours
Bedford, Gunning	Evans, Oliver
Broom, Jacob	Marquand, John P.
Canby, Henry S.	McKean, Thomas
Cannon, Annie J.	Pyle, Howard
Carothers, Wallace H.	Read, George
Clayton, John M.	Rodney, Caesar
Dickinson, John	

CITIES

Dover	Lewes	Newark	Wilmington

HISTORY

Colonial Life in America	Hudson, Henry
Delaware, Lord	Mason and Dixon's Line
Delaware Indians	Penn, William
Revolutionary War in America	Stuyvesant, Peter

PHYSICAL FEATURES

Delaware Bay	Delmarva Peninsula
Delaware River	Piedmont Region

UNCLASSIFIED

Chicken	Log Cabin
Delaware, University of	Oyster
Du Pont Company	Southern States

DELAWARE

Outline

I. The Land and Its Resources
 A. Location and Size
 B. Land Regions
 C. Coastline
 D. Rivers, Bays, and Lakes
 E. Natural Resources
 F. Climate

II. Life of the People
 A. The People
 B. Cities
 C. Country Life

III. Work of the People
 A. Manufacturing and Processing
 B. Agriculture
 C. Forest and Mining Products
 D. Fishing and Fur Industries
 E. Electric Power
 F. Transportation
 G. Communication

IV. Education
 A. Schools
 B. Universities and Colleges
 C. Libraries
 D. Museums

V. The Arts
 A. Painting
 B. Literature

VI. Interesting Places to Visit
VII. Annual Events in Delaware
VIII. Government
IX. History
X. Famous Delawareans

Questions

Why do so many large corporations have their headquarters in Delaware?
Why does Delaware have a curved northern boundary?
What is *Incodel*? Who belongs to it?
With what other state did Delaware once share its governor and legislature? Why?
Why did the Emancipation Proclamation have no effect in Delaware?
Why did the Dutch conquer New Sweden?
Who first built log cabins in America? When?
How does the Delaware Constitution differ from all other state constitutions?
Why is Delaware often called the Blue Hen State?

Books for Young Readers

ANDERSON, FLORENCE S., and BOVAIRD, K. F. *The Delaware River and Valley*. Franklin Publishers & Supply Co., Philadelphia, Pa., 1960.
BAILEY, BERNADINE F. *Picture Book of Delaware*. Whitman, 1960.
MEG, ELISABETH (pseud. of E. W. Goepp and M. W. Sanders). *Packet Alley: A Magic Story of Now and Long Ago*. Putnam, 1951.

Books for Older Readers

Delaware: A Guide to the First State. New and rev. ed. Hastings, 1955. (American Guide series.)
DOLAN, PAUL. *The Government and Administration of Delaware*. Crowell, 1956.
DORIAN, MAX. *The Duponts: From Gunpowder to Nylon*. Little, Brown, 1962.
ELEUTHERIAN MILLS-HAGLEY FOUNDATION, INC. *The Hagley Museum: A Story of Early Industry on the Brandywine*. The Museum, Wilmington, Del., 1957.
LIBERMAN, CY, and ROSBROW, J. M. *The Delaware Citizen: The Guide to Active Citizenship in the First State*. 2nd. ed. Elsevier Press, 1954.
MUNROE, JOHN A. *Federalist Delaware, 1775-1815*. Rutgers Univ. Press, 1954.

DELAWARE, LORD

DELAWARE, LORD, or DE LA WARR (1577-1618), THOMAS WEST, became the first governor of the Virginia colony. Delaware River, Delaware Bay, the colony of Delaware, and the state of Delaware were named for him. He became a member of the Privy Council of Queen Elizabeth I. He also served as a member of the Virginia Company Council.

He arrived with supplies at Jamestown in June, 1610, in time to prevent the discouraged settlers from deserting the colony. He returned to England in 1611 and died on a second trip to America in 1618. J. CARLYLE SITTERSON

See also DELAWARE; JAMESTOWN; VIRGINIA (Early Settlement).

DELAWARE, UNIVERSITY OF, is a coeducational, land-grant state university at Newark, Del. It has schools of arts and science, agriculture, engineering, home economics, education, and graduate studies; and an agricultural experiment and extension division. The university's programs lead to bachelor's, master's, and doctor's degrees.

The university was founded as an academy in 1743. It became Newark College in 1833, and a university in 1921. It offers graduate programs in industrial history and early American decorative arts in cooperation with two museums. For enrollment, see UNIVERSITIES AND COLLEGES (table). JOHN A. PERKINS

DELAWARE BAY is a large inlet of the Atlantic Ocean. It separates New Jersey and Delaware. The deep channel of the bay connects with the Delaware River, making it possible for ocean-going vessels to reach Philadelphia, which lies about 100 miles above the entrance of the bay. Delaware Bay is about 50 miles long and about 35 miles wide at its widest point. The channel is from 30 to 60 feet deep through its entire length. At Cape Henlopen near the bay entrance, the federal government has built a $3,000,000 breakwater to provide shelter for ships. Lighthouses have been built in the bay to warn approaching vessels of shallow water. LOYAL DURAND, JR.

See also DELAWARE (color map); DELAWARE RIVER.

DELAWARE INDIANS, also called LENI-LENAPE, were one of the most advanced and civilized tribes of the eastern United States. Other members of the Algonkian language family respectfully called them "grandfathers." Their villages once occupied the whole Delaware River Basin. Delaware Indians near the present site of Philadelphia signed several treaties with William Penn. A famous political organization in New York City was named for Tamenend, or Tammany, a Delaware chief.

The Delaware lived in rectangular, bark-covered houses. They ate wild game, and raised corn and other vegetables. The *Walam Olum*, a tribal chronicle, describes early Delaware traditions.

The Delaware began very early to take on the ways of white men, and many became Christians. But they preferred to live by themselves, and their story is one long history of flight from the whites and the warlike Iroquois Indians. They moved from Pennsylvania to Indiana under pressure from the whites. Part of one band called *Munsee* settled there permanently, and gave their name to the town of Muncie, Ind. (see MUNSEE INDIANS). The rest fled to Missouri, to Texas, and then to Kansas. Finally they settled in Oklahoma. Many became scouts for white pioneers. "Kit" Carson considered them among his best helpers in his travels through the western United States. WILLIAM H. GILBERT

See also INDIAN, AMERICAN (Eastern Forests Indians); PENNSYLVANIA (Famous Pennsylvanians [Tedyuskung]).

DELAWARE RIVER is part of a waterway from the Middle Atlantic States to the Atlantic Ocean. The Delaware rises in the Catskill Mountains of New York. It flows between New York and Pennsylvania, Pennsylvania and New Jersey, and Delaware and New Jersey, to empty into Delaware Bay. The Delaware's most important branches are the Schuylkill and Lehigh rivers. It passes Delaware Water Gap near Stroudsburg, Pa.

The Delaware serves as a water transportation route for Philadelphia, Trenton and Camden, N.J., and Wilmington, Del., which lie in one of the great industrial areas of the United States. The Chesapeake and Delaware Canal connects the river with Chesapeake Bay. In 1961, the Delaware Basin Compact created a regional administrative agency to develop and control the water resources of the Delaware River Basin. LOYAL DURAND, JR.

See also DELAWARE BAY; DELAWARE WATER GAP.

The Delaware River Is Pennsylvania's Eastern Boundary.

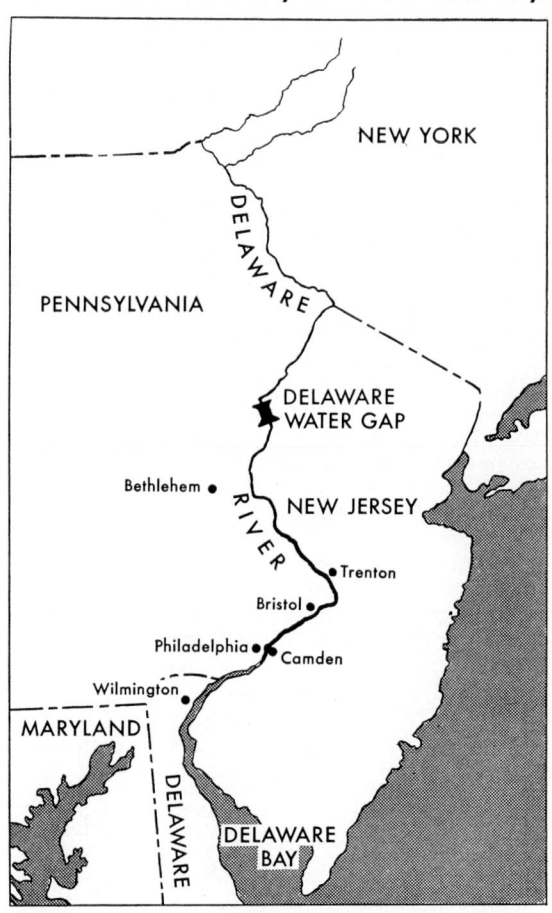

DELAWARE STATE COLLEGE is a state-controlled, coeducational college at Dover, Del. It offers liberal arts and teacher preparatory courses leading to bachelor's degrees. It was founded in 1891. For enrollment, see UNIVERSITIES AND COLLEGES (table).

The Delaware Water Gap is a scenic gorge that separates New Jersey from Pennsylvania. The Delaware River carved this gorge in the Kittatinny Mountains hundreds of years ago.

Gendreau

DELAWARE WATER GAP is a deep, narrow gorge cut by the Delaware River in the Kittatinny Mountains, 65 miles west of New York City. This gorge was worn through the solid rock of the mountains hundreds of years ago when the Delaware River was slowly forcing its way to the sea. The gorge is three miles long, with steep, rocky walls which rise as high as 1,400 feet on each side. Mount Tammany is located on the New Jersey side of the gorge and Mount Minsi on the Pennsylvania side. The beautiful scenery around Delaware Water Gap makes it a popular summer resort. See also DELAWARE RIVER. LOYAL DURAND, JR.

DE LEE, JOSEPH BOLIVAR (1869-1942), an American obstetrician and gynecologist, was noted for his work in improving obstetrical methods. He devised 40 instruments to help the obstetrician, including an incubator for premature infants. De Lee founded the Chicago Lying-in Hospital in 1895 and the Maternity Center in 1932. His films on obstetrics have been shown all over the world. De Lee taught obstetrics at Northwestern University and the University of Chicago. He was born in Cold Springs, N.Y. NOAH D. FABRICANT

DELEGATE is a representative chosen by a group to speak or act in its interests. National governments send delegates to international meetings. A delegate to a national political convention is chosen by the state he represents. The states determine the method of selection. They generally use either the primary (popular election) or the state party convention. More delegates may be chosen than the state has votes, in which case there are fractional votes. The word *delegate* is derived from the Latin *delegatus*, the past participle of the verb which means *to send*, or *appoint*. DAVID FELLMAN

DE LEÓN, JUAN PONCE. See PONCE DE LEÓN, JUAN.

DE LESSEPS, FERDINAND MARIE (1805-1894), was a French canal builder and diplomat. In 1854, Said Pasha, Viceroy of Egypt, invited him to start preparatory work on the Suez Canal. De Lesseps' plans provided for a canal without locks, extending from Port Said to Port Tewfik, connecting the Mediterranean Sea with the Gulf of Suez and the Red Sea. The company he organized started work on the Canal in 1859, and completed it 10 years later (see SUEZ CANAL).

De Lesseps was born in Versailles. From 1825 until his resignation in 1849, he worked in the French consular and diplomatic service. He was a member of the French Academy and the Academy of Science. At 74, De Lesseps reluctantly agreed to head the French company formed to build the Panama Canal (see PANAMA CANAL [The French Failure]). ROBERT W. ABBETT

DELFT, *dehlft* (pop. 74,500; alt. 6 ft.), is a Dutch town near The Hague. For its location, see NETHERLANDS (color map). It is a crossing point for many canals, and has about 70 bridges. One of its famous buildings, the Prinsenhof, now a museum, is the place where William I of Orange was assassinated in 1584. The Nieuwe Kerk (New Church), built in the 1400's, contains the tombs of William I and other rulers of the House of Orange. Jan Vermeer, the Dutch painter, lived and worked in Delft.

The city once was famous for the manufacture of blue pottery. The industry declined in the late 1700's because less care was put into its production. The art has since been revived by pottery makers. They call the new product "New Delft" pottery. BENJAMIN HUNNINGHER

Corcoran Gallery of Art

A Delft Vase by Jacobus Rynaker. The beautiful color and design in this octagonal vase is typical of world-famous Delft pottery. Many of the finer works are blue on a white background.

99

DELGADO, JOSÉ MATÍAS

DELGADO, *dehl GAH doh,* **JOSÉ MATÍAS** (1767-1832), a Salvadoran priest and patriot, is called the *Father of His Country.* He led the people of El Salvador in three revolutions for their freedom, and became the nation's hero.

Many Latin-American countries revolted against Spain in 1810. Father Delgado directed the revolt in El Salvador in 1811. The Spaniards quickly put it down. The Central American countries finally won their independence from Spain in 1821. When Mexico tried to include them in its empire in 1822, Father Delgado headed the resistance movement in El Salvador. He was president of the congress that drew up a constitution for the Republic of the United States of Central America (1823-1838). Disappointed in the Republic, Father Delgado began a campaign against neighboring countries, but died before the battle ended. He was born in San Salvador. HARVEY L. JOHNSON

DELHI, *DEHL ih* (pop. 2,051,622; met. area, 2,644,058; alt. 770 ft.), was once the capital of India. It lies on the Jumma River in the territory of Delhi. For location, see INDIA (color map).

Delhi has marble towers and domes, and the sunlight gleams on carved stone and silverwork. But it also has dirt and poverty, with narrow dark streets never touched by the sun.

The poor people of Delhi live in tiny, dark houses crowded into streets so narrow a person can almost reach from one side to the other. Sometimes as many as 20 persons live in one room, with no windows and no light. Many low-caste Indians work in the city's mills and factories. The wealthy people of Delhi live in large homes on wide streets. Gardens often surround the houses, which may be built around an inner courtyard.

Industry and Trade. Delhi is a center of manufacturing and trade. Railroads and caravan routes cross in the city, and merchants on camels sell their wares to traders from other countries. Flour mills grind the grain brought in from the farms of East Punjab. Cotton is woven into cloth in Delhi's cotton mills. Handcraftsmen make jewelry and other lovely objects of gold and silver, embroidered silk shawls, and wood carvings.

Many of the products of Delhi's hand industry are sold in the shops of the city's famous "Silver Street," the Chandni Chauk. It stretches a mile through the center of Delhi and is the busiest street in India. Open-face shops line the sides of the street, and a bazaar, or open trading place, runs down the center.

History. Other cities rose and fell in ruins on this site for hundreds of years before Delhi was built. Their ruins cover an area of about 45 square miles around the city. Some of these earlier cities were built by Moslem emperors. The present city was started by Shah Jahan, a Mogul emperor, in 1638 (see SHAH JAHAN). A wall surrounds the palaces and temples built for the Shah in the eastern part of the city.

Many of the buildings of old Delhi, surrounded by a stone wall, were built at the direction of Shah Jahan during the middle 1600's. The Pearl Mosque is a small temple where the emperor worshipped. It is made of white and gray marble, and covered with delicate carving. The Halls of Public and Private Audience are marble buildings where the emperor greeted his guests of state in all the jeweled splendor of an Eastern court. Over the city towers the Great Mosque, built from 1648 to 1650 by order of Shah Jahan. It is made of white

The 238-Foot Kutab Minar, a red sandstone and white marble tower of victory, stands at Delhi, India. It is more than 500 years old. Many of the buildings of old Delhi were built at the direction of Shah Jahan, a Mogul emperor, in the 1600's.

Fritz Henle, Black Star

marble and red sandstone. Three domes of white marble rise above the building. Many other mosques and minarets are scattered throughout Delhi.

Delhi was the scene of great ceremonies in 1877, when Queen Victoria was declared Empress of India. There were many days of great celebration again after Edward VII became Emperor in 1901, and in 1911, when George V assumed the title (see DURBAR). Delhi was made the capital of India in 1912, when the seat of government was moved from Calcutta. Then the capital was moved to New Delhi, a suburb of Delhi, where the seat of government was established in 1931. In 1947, New Delhi became the capital of independent India (see NEW DELHI). ROBERT I. CRANE

DELIAN LEAGUE. See ARISTIDES; PERICLES.

DELIBES, *duh LEEB*, **LÉO** (1836-1891), a French composer, became known for his opera *Lakmé* and two ballets, *Coppélia* and *Sylvia*. He saw the ballet as a blending of symphonic music, dramatic action, and pantomime, instead of its being simply a series of conventional dance movements. He opened the path for an important revival of that form. His ballets inspired such composers as Peter Tchaikovsky and Maurice Ravel. He was born at St. Germain du Val and went to Paris as a chorus singer and student at the Conservatory. He composed music for the theater from the age of 19 until his death. THEODORE M. FINNEY

DELILAH, *dee LIE luh*, was the Philistine mistress of the Israelite hero, Samson, a man famed for his tremendous strength. The Philistines bribed her to find out the secret of his power so that they might take him prisoner. After much coaxing, Samson told her that his strength lay in his long, thick hair which, because of a vow, he had never cut. Delilah had his head shaved while he was asleep. He became weak and helpless. His enemies easily captured him, blinded him, and made him work as a slave. This story is told in Judges 16. See also SAMSON. JOHN BRIGHT

DELINQUENCY, JUVENILE. See JUVENILE DELINQUENCY.

DELIRIUM TREMENS, *dee LIHR ih um TREE muhnz*, is a nervous and mental disturbance that results from acute alcoholism. A person often becomes markedly disturbed after unusually prolonged or heavy drinking of alcoholic beverages. He develops insomnia and a dislike for food, and becomes irritable and restless. He may then have visual illusions and hallucinations that are brief but terrifying. The condition itself may last from 3 to 10 days. Death sometimes results, often because pneumonia or heart failure develops. Doctors usually treat delirium tremens by taking alcohol away from the patient and giving him sedative and tranquilizing drugs. See also ALCOHOLISM. LOUIS D. BOSHES

DELIUS, *DEE lih us*, **FREDERICK** (1862-1934), was an English composer whose works reflect the influences and color of the places in which he lived. *Over the Hills and Far Away* (1895), *Brigg Fair* (1907), and *On Hearing the First Cuckoo in Spring* (1912) are orchestral landscapes describing England. *Appalachia* (1902) sings of American mountains and forests, and *Sea Drift* (1903), of the Atlantic Ocean. He subtitled an orchestral nocturne *Paris: the Song of a Great City* (1899). He was born in Bradford, England. WILLIAM FLEMING

DELLA FRANCESCA, PIERO. See PIERO DELLA FRANCESCA.

Alinari
Madonna and Child Jesus Is by Luca Della Robbia.

DELLA ROBBIA, *DELL uh RAHB ih uh*, was the family name of an uncle and his nephew who were Italian sculptors of the early Renaissance.

Luca Della Robbia (1400-1482) made the famous marble sculpture, the *Singing Gallery*, for the cathedral of Florence. He is better known for his work in terra cotta, a type of hard, durable earthenware. Della Robbia covered his terra cottas with glazes in white and brilliant colors. These terra cottas were less expensive than marble, and the glazed colors more durable than paint. Born in Florence, he began his career as a goldsmith, then turned to sculpture.

Andrea Della Robbia (1435-1525), the nephew, carried on the process of glazing terra cottas successfully. His uncle's will left the secret to him. He made a wider use of terra cotta than his uncle. One of his outstanding works is the infants on the Hospital of the Innocents in Florence. Della Robbia's work can be seen in the National Gallery, in Washington. He was born in Florence. See TERRA COTTA (picture). MARVIN C. ROSS

DELLO JOIO, *JOY oh*, **NORMAN** (1913-   ), an American composer and pianist, won the Pulitzer prize in 1957 for his *Meditations on Ecclesiastes* for orchestra. He has produced musical compositions in many forms: ballets; operas; chamber, choral, and orchestral music. His opera about Joan of Arc, *The Trial at Rouen*, was produced on television in 1956. He won the 1949 Music Critics Circle award for his *Variations, Chaconne, and Finale* for orchestra. Dello Joio also composed *Psalm of David*, for chorus and small orchestra; and *Lamentation of Saul*, for baritone and orchestra.

Dello Joio was born in New York City. While still in his teens, he became an organist and choirmaster. He has taught at Sarah Lawrence College and at Mannes College of Music, New York City. HOMER ULRICH

DELLS. See DALLES.

DELMARVA PENINSULA is in the eastern part of the United States. It lies between the Chesapeake and Delaware bays. The name is derived from *Del*aware, *Mar*yland, and Virginia (*Va*). Most of the state of Delaware, and parts of Maryland and Virginia, are on the peninsula.

DELOS. See CYCLADES.

DELPHI, *DEL fye,* was a town situated on the southern slope of Mount Parnassus. The town had the oldest and most influential religious sanctuary in ancient Greece. It was in the district of Phocis.

The ancient Greeks believed that the site of Delphi was sacred to the god Apollo. It gained importance as early as the 1100's B.C. Later, it became an international Greek shrine. Its sanctuary contained the main temple of Apollo, a stadium, a theater, and many small buildings and monuments. The Greeks held the Pythian Games in Delphi (see PYTHIAN GAMES).

The temple contained the famous *oracle*, or prophet (see ORACLES). A woman oracle, called Pythia, would utter weird sounds while in a frenzy. People believed these were the words of Apollo. Temple priests interpreted these to the public. Cities, as well as private individuals, sought her advice. As a result, the oracle greatly influenced Greek religion, economics, and politics. This influence gradually waned in later Greek and Roman times. The Christian Roman emperor Theodosius closed the sanctuary in A.D. 390.

French scholars began excavations in 1880. The present-day village of Kastri occupies the site of Delphi. JOHN H. KENT

See also GAS (Early Uses; picture, The Breath of Apollo); GREECE, ANCIENT (color picture, The Ruins of Delphi); PYTHON (mythology).

DELPHINIUM. See LARKSPUR; FLOWER (color picture, Summer Garden Flowers).

DEL SARTO, ANDREA (1486-1531), was an outstanding painter of the Italian Renaissance. He worked in his home city of Florence. During his time, Florence was declining in power, and the greatest artists who had been trained there, such as Leonardo da Vinci and Raphael, lived elsewhere. Del Sarto worked in the style that they had developed. It is marked by balanced designs with easy movements, and by gradual shadows and soft colors. Though not original, his work maintained the great Florentine tradition. CREIGHTON GILBERT

DELTA is a stretch of land, usually shaped like a rough triangle, built up by mud and sand at the mouth of a river. It is so named because it is shaped like *delta* (△), the fourth letter of the Greek alphabet. The name is applied to the mouths of rivers where they empty into gulfs, inland seas, bays, or lakes, and where one river joins another.

The main stream of a river usually divides into two or more branches near its mouth. Each of these branches often divides again. The strength of current in the river determines the size of the delta. A swiftly flowing current carries off the silt and sand to form sand bars or coastal islands. A slow current will generally build a large delta.

The delta area of the Mississippi River covers more than 15,000 square miles. The delta area contains thousands of acres of rich, fertile land. The Nile Delta covers an area of 10,000 square miles, and is also fertile. Both the Nile and Mississippi deltas produce valuable crops of high-grade cotton. ERNEST L. THURSTON

The Mississippi Delta, *above left,* grows farther into the Gulf of Mexico at the rate of one mile every 16 years. The river's slow current continuously deposits fertile soil there. The Mississippi delta has gradually assumed the shape of a bird's foot, *top inset*. The name *delta* was first given to the deposits formed in the Mediterranean Sea by the Nile River, *lower inset*.

See also RIVER (Estuaries and Deltas); EROSION; ALLUVIAL FAN; ALLUVIUM.

DELTA RAY. When a heavy cosmic ray particle, such as an alpha ray, falls on matter, the atoms of matter may give off slow electrons from their nuclei. These electrons, called *delta particles*, show up on a detecting medium such as photographic film. They appear as thin, wavy tracks, called *delta rays*, that branch off the track of the alpha particle. Scientists can measure the charge on the alpha particle from the number of delta rays in the track.

See also ALPHA RAY; COSMIC RAYS; WILSON CLOUD CHAMBER.

DELTA STATE COLLEGE is a coeducational teachers college at Cleveland, Miss. Courses include education, music, vocational home economics, social science, liberal arts, business, and medical technology. The college was founded in 1924. For enrollment, see UNIVERSITIES AND COLLEGES (table).

DELTA WING. See AIRPLANE (Wings).

DELTIOLOGY is the hobby of collecting post cards. See HOBBY (tables, Ten Favorite Hobbies, Fifty Popular Collection Hobbies).

DELTOID MUSCLE. See ARM.

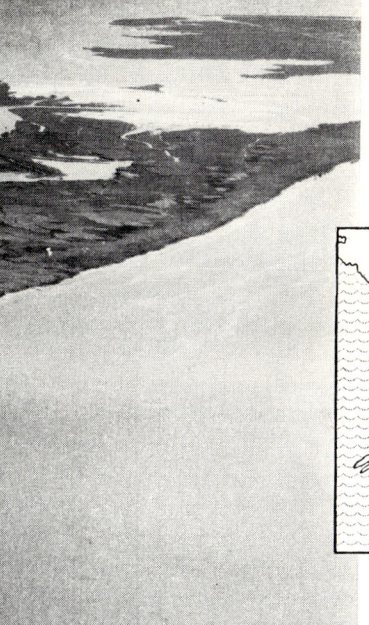

BIRD-FOOT DELTA OF THE MISSISSIPPI RIVER

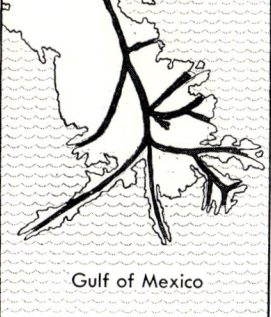

Gulf of Mexico

DELTA OF THE NILE RIVER

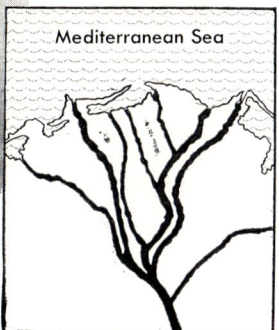

Mediterranean Sea

Fairchild Aerial Surveys, Inc.

DELUGE, *DEL yooj,* according to the Bible, was a great flood that covered all the earth with water thousands of years before Christ. All living things were destroyed except those that had been permitted to go into the ark which Noah had built.

The story is one of the most familiar of all Biblical tales (Gen. 6-8). The Deluge was sent to punish the wickedness of men, according to the account. Only Noah and his family were thought to be worth saving. They took with them at least one male and one female of each animal. The story of the Deluge resembles the flood story in the Babylonian epic of Gilgamesh. Many scholars believe that the Biblical story is simply a retelling of this poem. Flood legends occur in the tradition of many peoples.

Famous paintings of the Deluge are those of Poussin, in Paris, and of Raphael, in Rome.   CYRUS H. GORDON

See also ARARAT; ARK; DEUCALION; NOAH.

DELUSION, *dee LYOO zhun,* is a false belief. Persons with mental illness often have delusions. A common delusion is that of *grandeur,* in which a person has an exaggerated idea of his importance. Other delusions include those of *persecution,* in which a person believes he is being mistreated, and of *reference,* in which he falsely believes he is being talked about.

DEMAND. See SUPPLY AND DEMAND.
DEMAND BILL. See BILL OF EXCHANGE.
DEMARCATION, LINE OF. See LINE OF DEMARCATION.

DE MAUPASSANT, *duh MOH pah SAHN,* **GUY** (1850-1893), wrote vivid, brutal stories that made him one of the most popular French writers with the English-speaking public. His short stories are dramatic, restrained, concrete, and rich in effects of surprise. De Maupassant is often called the father of today's short story because he wrote in a tense, impersonal, and biting style.

Many of his most memorable stories present greedy Norman peasants, thrifty farmers, and women of low moral character. "The Ball of Fat," "The Piece of String," and *The House of Mme. Tellier,* a collection of short stories, treat brutally such forces in human life as hunger, fear, greed, envy, and sex.

De Maupassant wrote the novels *A Life, Pierre and Jean,* and *Bel Ami* after he had become a successful short-story writer. These novels pale today beside his dramatic short tales. He was born in Normandy, France. He died in an insane asylum.   HENRI PEYRE

Culver
Guy de Maupassant

DEME. See ATHENS (History).
DEMENTIA. See MENTAL ILLNESS (Schizophrenia).
DEMETER. See CERES.
DE MILLE, AGNES (1908-   ), an American choreographer, won fame for the dramatic ballets she staged for such musical comedies as *Oklahoma!, Carousel,* and *Brigadoon.* She prefers American themes, and her works tell realistic stories. A distinguished character dancer, Miss De Mille created the leading role in *Rodeo.* She was born in New York City and studied ballet under Theodore Kosloff. Miss De Mille made her professional debut in 1928.   LILLIAN MOORE

DE MILLE, CECIL BLOUNT (1881-1959), a pioneer American motion-picture producer, specialized in spectacular films, using giant settings and employing thousands of actors. De Mille received a special award for 35 years of motion-picture pioneering in 1949. His *The Greatest Show on Earth* won an Academy Award in 1952. *The Ten Commandments* achieved great success as a silent motion picture in 1923 and again with sound in 1957. His other outstanding motion pictures include *The Sign of the Cross, The Crusades,* and *Union Pacific.*

De Mille was born in Ashfield, Mass. He also acted on the stage and wrote two plays.   BARNARD HEWITT

Paramount Pictures
Cecil B. de Mille

DEMOBILIZATION. See ARMY, UNITED STATES (World War II).

103

MILESTONES IN DEMOCRACY

Athenian Constitution drawn up in 508 B.C. helped strengthen democracy in ancient Greece.

Bettmann Archive

Magna Carta, accepted by King John of England in 1215, guaranteed basic rights and liberties for the English people.

DEMOCRACY

DEMOCRACY means rule by the people. Abraham Lincoln defined democracy as "government *of* the people, *by* the people, *for* the people."

The word *democracy* usually refers to a form of government. But democracy is also a way of life. True democracy recognizes the rights of all men. It states that all persons are equal before the law. It refuses to allow the government to grant special favors because of a person's birth, wealth, race, or religion. Democracy provides freedom of speech, freedom of the press, and freedom of religion. Finally, democracy permits citizens to peacefully oppose actions by their government.

The citizens of a democracy take part in government in two ways, directly and indirectly. People take part *directly* when they gather together to work out laws, plans, and programs. This is *pure democracy*. People take part in government *indirectly* when they elect representatives who act for them. The United States has this *representative*, or *republican*, form of democracy (see REPUBLIC). In such a large nation, it would be impossible to call all the citizens together.

Representative government has a democratic spirit. All the people may not agree on a certain political issue or candidate for office. But democracy depends on the majority of the people deciding among issues and candidates. The people express their decisions by voting in free elections with secret ballots.

Kinds of Democracy

In addition to being a political system, democracy is an economic system and a social system. Economic and social democracy usually exist where political democracy is strong.

Political Democracy is a system of government in which the people govern themselves. They may criticize the leaders of their government, and they can choose new ones in an election. Democratic government rests on public opinion.

A basic belief of political democracy is that people of different interests and backgrounds have different political opinions. Political democracy accepts these opinions. It allows their free expression. In an election, the majority of the people show what policies they want their government to follow. The people accept the choices made by the majority of the voters.

A country with political democracy has at least two political parties, and may have many more. A dictatorship permits only one party. Under political democracy, parties represent the opinions of great numbers of people. The United States, Great Britain, and Canada each have two major parties. Other parties may appear from time to time. The "other side" always has the right to make its opinions known to the people.

Economic Democracy gives every person a chance to improve his economic standing. He may choose a job according to his likes and dislikes. He may change jobs if he wishes to. He may advance in his job as far as his abilities permit. A dictatorship forces many persons to do work that the government selects for them. They must accept wages that are set by the dictatorship.

Most economists believe that economic democracy grows out of political democracy. Voting and other democratic processes protect economic freedom. If a voter approves the economic ideas of a candidate for office, he can vote for that candidate in an election. There are also other ways in which the individual can influence economic affairs in a democracy. Any person may own stock in a company. As a *stockholder*, he may help form the policies of the company. Individual workers may join labor unions. By cooperating with other employees in one factory or one industry, workers gain *bargaining* power. They can ask for higher wages and various benefits. See LABOR.

Businessmen can also influence economic life in a democracy. The owner of a store may join businessmen's associations. The work of such groups can affect the economic life of an entire community. In the United States, the owner of a large corporation may support a lobbying action to gain greater benefits for his corporation or his industry (see LOBBYING).

Economic democracy is also called *free enterprise*. Under a free enterprise system, a nation's means of production and distribution are privately owned. The government regulates economic activity. But this regulation aims primarily to keep individuals and corporations from taking unfair advantage of each other. See FREE ENTERPRISE SYSTEM.

Social Democracy is sometimes called *social equality*.

The Declaration of Independence stated the democratic belief in "Life, Liberty and the pursuit of Happiness" in 1776.

National Historical Wax Museum

Storming the Bastille, a Paris prison symbolic of royal tyranny, began the French Revolution in 1789.

Jean Speiser

The United Nations was founded in 1945 as a step toward world democracy.

A democratic nation tries to give all citizens equal rights under the law. All laws apply equally to all citizens regardless of their birth, wealth, race, religion, or sex. A dictatorship usually favors one class of people or one political party. Social democracy cannot exist under such conditions.

Social democracy helps people in a material way. It encourages both governmental and private efforts to gain equality for all. In the United States, the Social Security Act protects most workers against the risks of unemployment and old age. Other laws enable more and more persons to have better housing, medical care, and education. State and local governments support similar aid programs. At the same time, private organizations serve society in various ways. For example, the Ford Foundation spends millions of dollars every year to support programs of welfare, education, and international aid. Other organizations work to solve such problems as crime and juvenile delinquency.

The goal of social democracy is not perfect equality for all. Democracy recognizes that a person's way of life is determined by his background, his abilities, and his efforts. The goal is to assure everyone an opportunity to make full use of his abilities.

Responsibilities in a Democracy

Obligations of Citizenship. Democratic laws and institutions do not guarantee that democracy will succeed. People must work constantly for democratic freedom. In many countries, democracy has been lost because the citizens did not help govern themselves by taking part in public affairs. Two conditions must exist if a person is to take part intelligently in his government. First, he must be informed. Second, he must act on his knowledge.

An informed citizen knows the important issues in his community, state or province, and country. Only if he knows these issues can he intelligently choose one policy or candidate over another. He can obtain information through newspapers, magazines, books, radio, and television.

After he has become informed, the citizen must act. He may help the political party of his choice. Or he may run for an elective office in his local government.

A good citizen does more than vote every few years. He remains active between elections. The results of an election, and the type of candidate who wins, depend on what citizens do during these periods. Many persons also work with groups that deal with community problems and are not connected with any political party. These groups include the Red Cross, the Boy Scouts and Girl Scouts, the Community Chest, and schools and hospitals.

Obligations of Government. The most important obligation of a government official in a democracy is to look upon public office as a trust. A dictator believes that his power is his as long as he can keep it by force. Under democracy, all political power comes from the people. A public official in a democracy receives his power for a limited time. He must use it honestly. He must work constantly for the growth of democracy.

The second major duty of a government official in a democracy is to do what is best for the most people. Even though he represents one political party, he must work for the common good after he takes office. The President of the United States is the leader of all the people—Democrats, Republicans, members of other parties, and nonvoters. It is not easy for an elected official to be completely neutral. But officials in a democracy must try to achieve both these ideals.

The Role of Education. A democracy needs educated citizens who can think for themselves. They must be able to make decisions on public issues and to vote intelligently. Education can strengthen democracy by teaching students *how* to think, rather than telling the student *what* to think. Children who learn to respect the views of others will, in later years, more easily respect different social and political opinions.

In a dictatorship, the student is taught to accept without question the policies and decisions of the individual or group in power. He learns to ignore moral and human issues, if necessary, in obeying the orders of the rulers. He becomes a servant of the state.

A democracy tries to give every person a chance to receive the type of education that suits him best. A student who wants to study engineering can usually do so at the college of his choice, if he can pass the entrance examinations. Most schools also give scholar-

DEMOCRACY

ships to needy students of exceptional ability.

Democratic education usually works best in a democratic atmosphere. Many schools encourage student experiences in self-government. Teachers try to follow democratic principles of fair play, respect, and mutual cooperation in their relations with students.

Challenges to Democracy

Most threats to democracy come from rival governmental systems, such as communism and fascism. Democracy may also be threatened by such internal problems as civic neglect and depression. History has shown that inefficiency may sometimes endanger democracy. A *bureaucracy* (class of government officials) may take over much of the work of governing, reducing the authority of the elected representatives of the people. Or a democracy may have so many political parties that no party can speak for the majority of the people.

Communism works to destroy democracy. A dictator heads a communist government. He keeps himself in power by using force to crush opposition. A communist government usually takes over all means of production and distribution. The government controls the press, radio, television, and all other means of communication. Communists claim that they seek equality for all citizens. But people have no way to protect their rights under communism. The interests of the individual are less important than the interests of the communist government. See COMMUNISM.

Communism began to threaten democracy after the second Russian Revolution of 1917. The revolution brought communism to power in Russia. Lenin and other communist leaders called for worldwide revolution to establish communism everywhere. But communism did not begin to challenge democracy seriously until after World War II. The communist government of Russia installed communist regimes in East Germany and in many countries of eastern Europe. Communists also worked to take over nations in Africa, Asia, and South America.

Fascism teaches that the government, not the people, is the source of all power. According to fascist doctrine, the people are too ignorant and emotional to rule themselves. Under fascism, a special group of leaders, supposedly superior in mental ability, governs the country. A dictator uses force to control the people. A fascist government usually does not own the nation's means of production and distribution. But it controls them completely. See FASCISM.

Fascism became a threat to democracy after fascists seized power in Italy in 1922. Led by Benito Mussolini, they destroyed all other political parties in Italy. The Nazi party in Germany, led by Adolf Hitler, expanded the ideas of fascism. The Nazis took over the German government in 1933. They immediately began to persecute many persons for religious or political reasons. Nazism taught that the Germans were superior to all other peoples. See NAZISM.

Civic Neglect. Some historians believe that an exaggerated desire for easy living can be a serious threat to democracy. If the majority of persons concentrate too much on their houses, clothing, wealth, and property, they may forget to perform their duties as citizens. Under these conditions, some historians say, democracy could die. A communist or fascist leader in a democratic country might use the right of free speech to win followers. He would conceal his real aim—to work for the overthrow of the government. If the people were not alert, they might not know their government was being destroyed.

Economic Depression may also endanger democracy. Some economists and political scientists believe that communism or fascism can take over a government more easily if the country becomes economically weak. Communism or fascism might become popular if many people were suffering from hunger or poverty. Many citizens might decide that communism or fascism could solve their individual problems.

The Development of Democracy

Origins of Democracy appeared in ancient Greece between the 600's and 400's B.C. The word *democracy* comes from the Greek words *demos*, meaning *people*, and *kratein*, which means to *rule*.

Ancient Athens and some other Greek city-states had democratic governments. Each citizen of Athens had the duty to serve in the assembly, which passed the laws of the community. The assembly also decided on important government policies in diplomacy, finance, foreign trade, and war. Every citizen was expected to serve on juries which heard and decided court trials. The Athenian system had many weaknesses. It permitted slavery. Women and slaves were not allowed to vote. But it showed that a large group of men could govern themselves efficiently.

Athenian democracy contrasted strongly with the government of Sparta, another Greek city-state. In Sparta, the citizen was regarded mainly as a soldier who had to obey his superiors. The happiness of the individual did not matter. No kindness could be shown toward persons who were weak or sick. The government tried to control the thoughts and actions of every citizen.

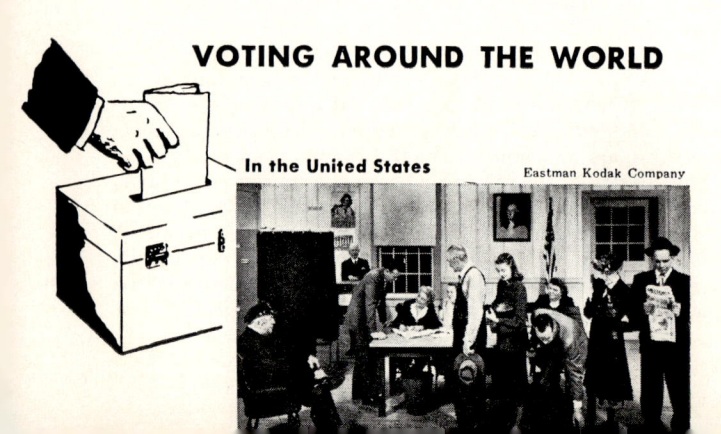

VOTING AROUND THE WORLD

In the United States
Eastman Kodak Company

In Nigeria
Wide World

DEMOCRACY

No one was allowed to criticize the government. Both fascism and communism have followed many Spartan ideas of government. See GREECE, ANCIENT.

The ancient Romans experimented with democracy. But they never practiced it as fully as the Athenians and some other Greeks did. At first, only the *patricians* (wealthy men) could vote or run the Roman government. After hundreds of years of struggle, the *plebeians* (men of the lower classes) won the right to vote. They also gained other rights of citizenship. The Roman *concilium plebis* (council of the people) provided a forum for discussing civic problems. But the patricians kept firm control of the government. Even under the emperors, the Romans acted as if the ruler governed with the consent of the people. See ROMAN EMPIRE.

Renaissance and Reformation. The Roman Empire broke up during the A.D. 300's and 400's. European civilization entered a period of decline that lasted about a thousand years, until the late 1400's. The Middle Ages blossomed into the Renaissance. Men began to take political and cultural ideas from ancient Greece and Rome. See MIDDLE AGES; RENAISSANCE.

The Renaissance developed most fully in Italy, where the links to ancient Rome were strongest. Art, science, and literature reached new heights. A new spirit of independence and individualism developed. This spirit influenced political thinking, and hastened the growth of democracy. People began to seek greater freedom in many fields. In religion, the Renaissance led to the Reformation. Martin Luther, a leader of the Reformation, declared in the early 1500's that all men are equal before God. Luther stated that all religious authority came from God, not from the popes or bishops of the Roman Catholic Church.

The Reformation led to the rise of a number of Protestant churches. Eventually, it contributed to the growth of democracy in two ways. First, the self-government practiced in some Protestant churches trained many persons for political self-government. Second, Protestants and Roman Catholics had to learn to live together in spite of religious differences. A desire for representative government spread. Historians believe this desire led to the Puritan Revolution in England during the 1600's. See PURITAN; REFORMATION.

Democracy in England. In 1215, English nobles forced King John to approve the Magna Carta (Great Charter). This historic document opposed taxation without representation, forbade unlawful arrests, and called for trial by jury. It became a symbol of human liberty for later generations. See MAGNA CARTA.

English democracy developed slowly during the next several hundred years. In 1628, Parliament passed the Petition of Right. This document protested the violation of some basic liberties by King Charles I. The petition called on the king to stop collecting taxes without the consent of Parliament. It also demanded an end to martial law. The Puritans, led by Oliver Cromwell, rebelled in 1642 when Charles claimed that the king ruled by divine right. Those who favored constitutional government fought the king's followers. Civil war broke out from time to time for more than 40 years. But neither side could win final victory. See DIVINE RIGHT OF KINGS; PETITION OF RIGHT.

Gradually, the English people came to believe that Parliament should have supreme power. John Locke (1632-1704), a great English writer and thinker, declared that final authority in political matters belonged to the people. The main function of government, Locke said, should be to protect the lives, liberty, and property of the people. The historic Bill of Rights of 1689 stated that Parliament, not the king, had political authority. The bill also stressed the importance of individual freedom in religion, law, and politics. See BILL OF RIGHTS (English Bill of Rights).

American Democracy took root in traditions brought to North America by the first English colonists. The Pilgrims, who settled in Massachusetts in 1620, joined in the Mayflower Compact to obey "just and equal laws" (see MAYFLOWER COMPACT). More than 150 years later, the American Revolution began. The colonists protested against British violations of democratic principles that were recognized in England itself. The most important of these violations was taxation without representation. The colonists also wanted more local government.

The Declaration of Independence, adopted by the Continental Congress in 1776, is a classic document of democracy. It established a doctrine of human rights as an ideal by which government must be guided. Thomas Jefferson, who wrote the Declaration, sought to show that America would offer a new way of life. See DECLARATION OF INDEPENDENCE.

People throughout the world saw the Declaration of Independence as the beginning of a daring experiment in government. The United States Constitution and the Bill of Rights were also hailed as great democratic documents. Millions of persons came to the United States in search of equal opportunity. The nation grew as American settlers moved westward. A pioneer spirit developed. It stressed self-reliance, individual liberty, and the right to improve one's economic standing. See BILL OF RIGHTS; UNITED STATES CONSTITUTION.

In Malaya
Federation of Malaya Information Services

In Algeria
Kay Lawson, Rapho-Guillumette

DEMOCRACY

The French Revolution. The success of representative government in England aroused interest in France. The American Revolution also inspired French patriots. By the 1700's, French intellectuals were fighting censorship and thought-control in religion, morals, and philosophy. These intellectuals included Denis Diderot and Voltaire.

At first, leading French thinkers proposed moderate reform and limited voting rights. Montesquieu, for example, spoke out for reform without violence in his *The Spirit of Laws* (1748). But his views and those of others failed to persuade the rulers of France that more democratic government was necessary. Frenchmen who wanted democracy turned to revolutionary leaders to achieve it. Jean Jacques Rousseau's *The Social Contract* (1762) further stirred the revolutionary spirit. This book declared that people "have a duty to obey only legitimate powers." Rousseau meant that power should come only from the people.

The French Revolution, a landmark in the history of democracy, began in 1789. In part, the revolution was an attack on the French monarchy and aristocracy. For hundreds of years, the kings and nobles of France had lived well while most of the people lived in poverty. In part, the revolution was an effort to achieve more democratic government. It did not succeed at once in achieving democracy. But the French Revolution paved the way for the first democratic government ever established by a major nation on the mainland of Europe. See FRENCH REVOLUTION.

The Spread of Democracy. During the 1800's and 1900's, democracy developed steadily in many parts of the world. Many countries followed the American, British, and French examples. In Europe, most governments introduced social reforms. Democratic institutions such as elections and legislatures became common. Where kings still ruled, they lost their absolute power.

With the Industrial Revolution of the 1800's, many people in Europe and the United States demanded safeguards of democratic rights. New laws gave more citizens the right to vote. Freedom of the press and of religion developed. Political parties grew stronger as more citizens took part in political life.

However, democracy did not take root everywhere. Some countries that adopted constitutions modeled on the United States Constitution later became dictatorships. These nations found that a constitution alone did not guarantee the survival of democracy. For example, dictators who took control of many Latin-American countries often kept national constitutions but ignored the people's rights. In Russia, a small group of revolutionists set up a communist dictatorship in 1917 that halted all progress toward democracy in that country. Germany adopted a democratic form of government during the 1920's, but it became a fascist dictatorship in the 1930's.

During World War II, communist Russia fought alongside the democracies against Germany, Italy, and Japan. But after the war, communist dictatorship began to threaten democracy throughout the world. Communists took over the governments of Czechoslovakia, China, and other countries of eastern Europe and Asia.

The struggle between democracy and communist imperialism came to be called the *cold war* (see COLD WAR). The democracies freed dozens of countries in Africa and Asia from colonial rule. These new nations sought to preserve their independence and political freedom. But they came under increasing pressure from both the democracies and the communist countries to join one side or the other. WILLIAM EBENSTEIN

Related Articles. See the GOVERNMENT article for a comparison of democracy and dictatorship. Other related articles in WORLD BOOK include:

DEMOCRATIC RIGHTS

Assembly	Freedom
Civil Rights	Freedom of Religion
Due Process of Law	Freedom of Speech
Four Freedoms	Freedom of the Press

GREAT DOCUMENTS OF DEMOCRACY

Bill of Rights	Human Rights, Universal Declaration of
Declaration of Independence	
Emancipation Proclamation	Magna Carta
Gettysburg Address	Petition of Right
	United States Constitution

THREATS TO DEMOCRACY

Bolshevik	Fifth Column
Communism	Imperialism
Dictator	Nazism
Espionage	Totalitarianism
Fascism	

TOOLS OF DEMOCRACY

Absentee Voting	Jury and Trial by Jury
Ballot	Plebiscite
Citizenship	Recall
Election	Woman Suffrage
Fifteenth Amendment	Voting
Habeas Corpus	Voting Machine
Initiative and Referendum	

Outline

I. Kinds of Democracy
  A. Political Democracy
  B. Economic Democracy
  C. Social Democracy

II. Responsibilities in a Democracy
  A. Obligations of Citizenship
  B. Obligations of Government
  C. The Role of Education

III. Challenges to Democracy
  A. Communism
  B. Fascism
  C. Civic Neglect
  D. Economic Depression

IV. The Development of Democracy
  A. Origins of Democracy
  B. Renaissance and Reformation
  C. Democracy in England
  D. American Democracy
  E. The French Revolution
  F. The Spread of Democracy

Questions

What does the word *democracy* mean?
Why is education important in a democracy?
What two political systems are the greatest threats to democracy?
What are two major duties of a citizen in a democracy?
How did the French Revolution help democracy grow?
What is *representative* democracy? *Direct* democracy?
In what ways did the governments of Athens and Sparta differ?
How can the citizen of a democracy take part in public affairs between elections?
What are the two major duties of a public official in a democratic society?
How may civic neglect threaten a democratic government?

DEMOCRATIC PARTY

DEMOCRATIC PARTY is one of the two major political parties of the United States. It is older than the other major party, the Republicans. As in the Republican party, early political divisions in the country influenced its origins and policies.

Some writers believe that the Democratic party began with the group called Anti-Federalists, who opposed the federal Constitution as it was originally drafted (see ANTI-FEDERALIST). The Anti-Federalists favored a national government of limited power. Under the leadership of Thomas Jefferson, they blocked acceptance of the Constitution until the opposing political group, the Federalists, promised that Congress would propose constitutional amendments that would guarantee certain liberties to the people (see BILL OF RIGHTS). Other writers find the origin of the Democratic party in the Democratic-Republicans, who elected Jefferson to the Presidency in 1800. Another group believes that the Democratic party really began with the election of Andrew Jackson in 1828. The party took its present name at that time.

Jackson, like Jefferson before him, built his political strength on the support of small farmers and workers. Businessmen and large planters opposed Jackson's party. In recent years, the chief support of the Democratic party has come from working-class groups in large cities, from many farmers, and from the southern states. But the Democratic party, like the Republican party, draws some support from people in all walks of life, in all parts of the country.

Before 1860. From the time of Andrew Jackson until the Civil War, the relation of the states to the national government was an issue in every national election. This issue was not merely a question of political theory, as it appeared on the surface. It was related to a bitter struggle over economic issues, particularly slavery and the tariff.

The cotton-growing states in the South depended heavily on the institution of slavery, and wanted to protect it at all costs. But the facts of geography made it clear that, as the United States expanded to the West, most of the new territories would be unsuitable for growing cotton. Because of this, the slaveholding interests could expect to find themselves outnumbered in the national government. The national government might then upset the economy in the southern states, either by passing tariffs that favored northern manufacturers at the expense of southern planters, or by taking direct action against the institution of slavery itself. The only complete safety for the cotton-growing states lay in the doctrine that each state had a right to declare national laws null and void, and to withdraw from the Union if the national government insisted on enforcing these laws.

The Democratic party had steadily favored the interests of farmers and planters, as against those of businessmen and manufacturers. Its greatest voting strength came from the grain farmers in the country back of the coastal areas, North and South. But some of the ablest Democratic leaders spoke for the states' rights interests of cotton planters, and planned a political alliance with them. The larger planters tended to become Whigs because of their dislike of small-farmer opposition to banks and other business enterprises. But the Democratic party pleased both the large planters and many small farmers

"A LIVE JACKASS KICKING A DEAD LION"
And such a Lion! and such a Jackass!

The Donkey was first used as a Democratic-party symbol in this political cartoon by Thomas Nast. It was published in the January 15, 1870, issue of *Harper's Weekly.* From the book *Thomas Nast,* by Albert Bigelow Paine (Harper and Brothers).

by trying to maintain the powers of the states against the national government. As a result of its leadership and its doctrine of states' rights, the party found itself compelled to defend slavery. During the 10 years before the Civil War, the southern wing of the Whig party moved closer to the Democratic party. As a result, the Democrats were even more strongly committed to the slaveholding class.

In the Minority. At the close of the Civil War, the Democratic party was in a difficult position. Up to that time, it had been the majority party, winning all presidential elections except three from 1800 to 1860. After the war, an overwhelming majority of white southerners were Democrats. Republican Reconstruction measures had firmly fixed their allegiance. But for a time, most of them were not allowed to vote because they had taken part in the war. In the North, many Democrats lost popularity because they had been indifferent toward the war, or had actively opposed it. Moreover, the party had lost its major issues. Slavery was dead, and the states' rights question was temporarily forgotten.

After 1865, the Democrats became a party of criticism and protest. They stood for lower tariffs or tariffs for revenue only. They attacked Reconstruction measures and government inefficiency and corruption. Led by Samuel J. Tilden, they almost won the election of 1876 by attacking corruption in President Ulysses S. Grant's administration and blaming it for an economic panic. Demands for civil-service reform, along with pledges to lower the tariff, were enough to win the election of Grover Cleveland in 1884 as the first Democratic president since the war. In 1892, after Benjamin Harrison's intervening Republican administration, Cleveland won a second term, largely on the tariff issue.

DEMOCRATIC PARTY
ADMINISTRATIONS IN OFFICE

The Democratic Party has held the presidential office during the periods shown in black, above. The donkey symbol represents Democratic administrations. The elephant stands for Republican administrations. The donkey symbol, though used for the period from 1801 to 1849, was not invented until later. The Democratic party did not use this name until 1828.

In the 1890's, the Democratic party took on a new character. President Cleveland had led the party into supporting the movement for the gold standard and hard currency. But unrest in the West and South threatened to move a large segment of the party toward the Populist program for free coinage of silver. William Jennings Bryan, a free-silver advocate, became the leader of the Democratic party in 1896. His advocacy of free silver failed to bring the party victory.

In 1912, a split in the Republican ranks led to Woodrow Wilson's election as a Democratic president. Lower tariffs and action against business monopolies were principal issues in his campaign platform. Important domestic legislation, such as the Federal Income Tax Act, the Clayton Antitrust Act, and the Federal Reserve Act, marked Wilson's first administration. But World War I overshadowed his domestic program. Wilson committed the Democrats to a strong international policy after the war. But the more conservative Republican party won the elections of 1920, 1924, and 1928. The landslide defeat of Alfred E. Smith, Democratic presidential candidate in the bitter 1928 campaign, brought the party to a low ebb. The depression that began the following year ultimately gave the Democrats a long and important period of leadership.

The New Deal. The election of Franklin D. Roosevelt in 1932 marked a sharp break in the history of the Democratic party. His administrations advanced policies to regulate banking and securities, expand public works, encourage labor organizations, improve working conditions, introduce social security, and subsidize agriculture. He appealed especially to labor, the farmer, and the middle class. Keeping the support of large sections of these groups and of the South, the Democratic party

DEMOCRATIC PRESIDENTIAL AND VICE-PRESIDENTIAL CANDIDATES

Year	President	Vice-President	Year	President	Vice-President
1828	*Andrew Jackson*	*John Calhoun	1904	Alton B. Parker	Henry G. Davis
1832	*Andrew Jackson*	*Martin Van Buren	1908	William Jennings Bryan	John W. Kern
1836	*Martin Van Buren*	*Richard M. Johnson	1912	*Woodrow Wilson*	*Thomas R. Marshall
1840	Martin Van Buren	*Richard M. Johnson	1916	*Woodrow Wilson*	*Thomas R. Marshall
1844	*James K. Polk*	*George M. Dallas	1920	James M. Cox	*Franklin D. Roosevelt
1848	Lewis Cass	William O. Butler	1924	John W. Davis	Charles W. Bryan
1852	*Franklin Pierce*	*William R. D. King	1928	Alfred E. Smith	Joseph T. Robinson
1856	*James Buchanan*	*John C. Breckinridge	1932	*Franklin D. Roosevelt*	*John Nance Garner
1860	Stephen A. Douglas	Herschel V. Johnson	1936	*Franklin D. Roosevelt*	*John Nance Garner
1864	George B. McClellan	George H. Pendleton	1940	*Franklin D. Roosevelt*	*Henry A. Wallace
1868	Horatio Seymour	*Francis P. Blair, Jr.	1944	*Franklin D. Roosevelt*	*Harry S. Truman
1872	Horace Greeley	Gratz Brown	1948	*Harry S. Truman*	*Alben W. Barkley
1876	Samuel J. Tilden	*Thomas A. Hendricks	1952	Adlai E. Stevenson	*John J. Sparkman
1880	Winfield S. Hancock	William H. English	1956	Adlai E. Stevenson	*Estes Kefauver
1884	*Grover Cleveland*	*Thomas A. Hendricks	1960	*John F. Kennedy*	*Lyndon B. Johnson
1888	Grover Cleveland	Allen G. Thurman			
1892	*Grover Cleveland*	*Adlai E. Stevenson			
1896	William Jennings Bryan	Arthur Sewall			
1900	William Jennings Bryan	*Adlai E. Stevenson			

Names of elected candidates are in italics.
Each presidential candidate has a biography in WORLD BOOK.
*Has a separate biography in WORLD BOOK.

broke all precedents by electing Roosevelt to a third term in 1940 and a fourth term in 1944.

Roosevelt demonstrated political skill which vastly strengthened the party. He retained the support of liberals in the cities and of many conservatives in the South. Democrats gained such strength in the North and West that southern Democrats, in key positions in Congress under the seniority system, could no longer exercise a firm negative voice in the selection of national Democratic candidates or platform policies. In 1936, the substitution of a simple majority vote requirement for the traditional two-thirds rule in Democratic national conventions also reduced the possibility of a sectional veto over selection of a Democratic presidential candidate (see POLITICAL CONVENTION).

Vice-President Harry S. Truman became President when Roosevelt died in 1945. He substantially carried on Roosevelt's policies, but the Democrats lost control of both houses of Congress in 1946. In the 1948 election, a group of southern Democrats, called *States' Rights Democrats* or *Dixiecrats*, broke away from the party. In a surprise victory over Republican nominee Thomas E. Dewey, Truman kept the presidency, and the Democrats won a majority in Congress. The States' Rights party carried four southern states. At the same time, many southern leaders became convinced that they would be in danger of political isolation if they left the Democratic party because of disagreement on programs.

In 1952 and 1956, the Democrats chose Adlai E. Stevenson of Illinois as their presidential candidate. Dwight D. Eisenhower, who ran well ahead of other Republicans, overwhelmingly defeated Stevenson. But the Democrats retained control over both houses of Congress for all of Eisenhower's administration except the first two years, 1953 and 1954.

In 1960, the Democrats nominated Senator John F. Kennedy of Massachusetts for President. He defeated the Republican candidate, Vice-President Richard M. Nixon. Campaign issues included foreign policy, civil rights, and medical aid to the aged. The Democrats retained control of Congress. FRANKLIN L. BURDETTE

See also DEMOCRATIC-REPUBLICAN PARTY; DIXIECRAT PARTY; NEW DEAL; POLITICAL PARTY; PRESIDENT OF THE UNITED STATES.

DEMOCRATIC-REPUBLICAN PARTY was an early political organization in the United States. It emerged as an opponent of the Federalist party during George Washington's first term as President. Its members followed the leadership of Thomas Jefferson in opposing *loose constructionism*, or a liberal interpretation of the Constitution. They also opposed the centralized national authority favored by Alexander Hamilton and the Federalists. They believed in a weak national government and strong state governments dominated by farming, rather than commercial, interests.

The Democratic-Republicans gained control when Thomas Jefferson was elected President in 1800, but practical politics forced them to adopt much of the centralized program of the Federalists. They dominated politics after 1816 until Andrew Jackson's administrations, when conflicts resulted in the formation of two new parties. The Democratic party succeeded the Democratic-Republican party, and the Whig party followed the Federalist principles. RAY ALLEN BILLINGTON

See also BUCKTAIL; FEDERALIST PARTY.

DEMOCRITUS, *dee MAHK rih tus* (460?-370? B.C.), a Greek philosopher, is sometimes called the father of modern science, because he gave a mechanical explanation for everything. He learned from his teacher, Leucippus, that everything was made up of tiny bits of matter called atoms. This theory said that countless atoms swirled around in empty space, and combined to form the universe, plants, animals, and even human beings. So Democritus concluded that when a tree, for example, comes into existence and grows, what happens is that more and more of these atoms are combining to form the tree. He decided that when the tree dies and decays, the atoms are not destroyed, but combine once again to make new things. Democritus lived at Abdera, in Thrace. LEWIS M. HAMMOND

See also ATOM (Development of the Atomic Theory).

DEMOGRAPHY, *dih MAHG ruh fih*, is the study of human population. *Demographers* (population experts) study the composition, distribution, changes, and movements in the population. They analyze trends in population and the relationship of a country's population to its standard of living. Population changes may be measured by birth rates, death rates, and migration. Demographers study the characteristics of population, such as age, sex, life span, and life expectancy. See also SOCIOLOGY (Demography); VITAL STATISTICS.

DE MOLAY, *DEE moh LAY*, **ORDER OF,** is an international organization of young men between the ages of 14 and 21. Since its founding in 1919, De Molay has initiated more than 2,500,000 members. The Order has 2,200 local chapters in the United States and several other countries. De Molay has international headquarters at 201 E. Armour Blvd., Kansas City 11, Mo.

The organization is under the guidance of the Masonic Order. Each chapter must have at least 25 members and be sponsored by a group of Masons or a Masonic body. Membership is open to boys of good character and of any faith who are recommended by two chapter members or a senior De Molay or a Master Mason.

The De Molay Emblem

The De Molay Order was founded in Kansas City in 1919 by Frank S. Land. Land asked a boy named Louis Lower to invite some of his friends to a meeting to discuss forming a club. When a name was needed, Land suggested some historical figures and the boys chose Jacques De Molay (1243?-1314?) as their namesake. De Molay was the last Grand Master of the Knights Templars, a famous group of French crusaders.

The ritual for the De Molay Order includes secret ceremonies and is based on seven points: filial love, reverence for God, courtesy, comradeship, fidelity, cleanness, and patriotism. RICHARD E. HARKINS

DEMONOLOGY. See WITCHCRAFT; DEVIL; DEVIL WORSHIP.

DE MORES, MARQUIS. See NORTH DAKOTA (Famous North Dakotans; Interesting Places to Visit).

DEMOSTHENES

A Statue of Demosthenes, a famous example of Greek Hellenistic sculpture, now stands in the Vatican.

DEMOSTHENES, *dee MAHS thuh neez* (384-322 B.C.), was a great Greek orator and patriot. He is best known for his *Philippics,* a series of speeches in which he violently attacked King Philip II of Macedon (see PHILIP II).

He was born in Attica. His father was a wealthy Athenian who, on his death, left his property and children to the care of three guardians. These men proved to be dishonest, and took the property. Demosthenes prosecuted them successfully when he came of age. He was so successful as a speaker in this lawsuit that he entered public life. He mastered Greek law and politics, and the art of oratory. Demosthenes had to overcome great difficulties to become an orator. He had a harsh, unpleasant voice, weak lungs, and an awkward manner. He is said to have trained himself by reciting as he climbed steep hills, and by shouting above the roar of ocean waves with his mouth full of pebbles.

Demosthenes worked unselfishly for Greek liberty from the age of 30 until he died. Philip of Macedon had gained a foothold at Delphi, in central Greece, by 346 B.C. Demosthenes created an alliance of the great Greek cities of Athens and Thebes to fight for Greek freedom. Philip defeated their combined armies in the battle of Chaeronea, 338 B.C. (see GREECE, ANCIENT [The End of the Classical Period]). Athens made peace, but Demosthenes kept up his opposition. Later he defended his policy in his greatest speech, *On the Crown.* Many critics consider this the most nearly perfect speech in history. Demosthenes poisoned himself in 322 B.C. when the last Greek effort to win freedom failed.   C. BRADFORD WELLES

DEMOTIC. See HIEROGLYPHIC.

DEMPSEY, "JACK," WILLIAM HARRISON (1895-   ), became one of the most popular heavyweight boxing champions of all time. Dempsey knocked out Jess Willard in 1919 to win the title. He lost it in 1926 to Gene Tunney. Their second fight, in 1927, was climaxed by the famous "long count." Dempsey knocked Tunney down in the seventh round. But he did not go to a neutral corner immediately, so the referee delayed starting the count over Tunney. Tunney rose at the count of 9, but it was estimated this was equivalent to a count of 14. Tunney went on to win the fight. Dempsey was born at Manassa, Colo., and started fighting in mining camps in 1912. He was called "the Manassa Mauler." See also BOXING (picture).   FRED RUSSELL

DEMPSTER, ARTHUR JEFFREY (1886-1950), was an American physicist. In 1935, he discovered uranium 235 (U-235), the rare isotope of the element uranium. U-235 is a key substance in the production of the atomic bomb.

Dempster's highly accurate determinations of the masses of many elements and isotopes are of fundamental importance in nuclear physics. They provide the means for measuring mass and energy transformations. He developed a *mass spectrograph,* an instrument for weighing and sorting out atoms by their mass. He made

United Press Int.

Jack Dempsey fought Gene Tunney in two heavyweight championship bouts. The famous "long count" occurred in Chicago in 1927 in their second fight. Dempsey knocked Tunney down, but did not go immediately to a neutral corner. The referee had to wave Dempsey away, *left,* before starting to count. Estimates on the length of the count vary from 14 to 21 seconds. Tunney won on a 10-round decision.

important contributions to the work of the Manhattan Project, a United States government agency that directed the development and production of the atomic bomb during World War II.

Dempster was born in Toronto, Ont., and was graduated from the University of Toronto. He moved to the United States in 1914, and was naturalized in 1918. In 1916, he took his doctor of philosophy degree at the University of Chicago. He became professor of physics there in 1927, and did pioneer work in discovering many isotopes. RALPH E. LAPP

See also ISOTOPE; U-235.

DEMURRER, in law, is a pleading which raises the question of whether the case being presented would win the lawsuit even if it were proved. For example, a man who had stored property in his neighbor's garage might sue the neighbor if his property was damaged by a lightning bolt. The garage owner could then reply with a *demurrer*, asking the court to consider whether the facts presented would entitle the man to win his case if they were proved. In meaning and in spirit, the demurrer is equivalent to the slang expression "So what!" When the court considers the demurrer, it must act as though the statements made by both parties in the case are true. But the demurrer does not admit that the statements are true. If the court rejects the demurrer, then it is still up to the property owner to prove his case. The demurrer has been abolished in many states of the United States. The same result is reached in other ways. THOMAS A. COWAN

DEMUTH, *duh MOOTH*, **CHARLES** (1883-1935), was an American painter and illustrator known for his oil, water-color, and tempera paintings of flowers, city scenes, and architectural subjects. His paintings were characterized by delicacy of touch and a remarkably sensitive feeling for the essence of the subject. He illustrated books by such authors as Émile Zola, Henry James, Edgar Allan Poe, and Honoré de Balzac. He was born in Lancaster, Pa., and studied in the United States and France. EDWIN L. FULWIDER

DEN. See LION (Habits); WOLF; BEAR (picture).

DEN, in scouting. See BOY SCOUTS (Cub Scouting).

DENARIUS, *dee NAIR ih us*, was a silver coin used by the Romans during the periods of the Republic and the Empire. The Romans first issued the coins about 187

The Denarius of Tiberius Caesar, which was issued from A.D. 14 to 37, carried the portrait of Tiberius on its front side.
Chase Manhattan Bank Money Museum

B.C. They disappeared from circulation in the A.D. 200's. The silver denarius by that time had been replaced by a copper one coated with silver. The value of the denarius first equaled 10, and later 16, of the coins called *asses*, or about 17 cents in United States or Canadian money. The standard gold coin of the Roman Empire was the *aureus*. This coin was about the same size as the denarius and was worth 20 denarii. The denarius was the penny referred to in the New Testament of the Bible. Its initial, *d*, is the English symbol for penny, or pence. LEWIS M. REAGAN

DENATURALIZATION. See NATURALIZATION (Denaturalization).

DENATURED ALCOHOL. See ALCOHOL (Ethyl Alcohol).

DENBY, EDWIN. See TEAPOT DOME.

DENDRITE. See NERVOUS SYSTEM (Nerve Cells).

DENDROCHRONOLOGY. See ARCHAEOLOGY (Absolute Chronology).

DENEB, *DEN eb*, is the brightest star in the constellation *Cygnus*. It is at the top of this crosslike constellation, so far from the earth that astronomers cannot accurately determine its distance. Deneb is 10,000 times as bright as the sun. Navigators use it as a guide.

DENEBOLA. See LEO (constellation).

DENGUE, *DEHNG gay*, is a fever that makes the head and eyes ache, and causes pain in muscles and joints. It may also cause a running nose and sore throat and make the skin break out in a rash. Dengue is caused by a *filtrable virus* that is carried by mosquitoes. Symptoms of the disease appear three to six days after a disease-bearing mosquito bites the victim. The rash breaks out on the fifth day of the illness. The fever subsides and then usually rises again. The disease is seldom fatal. Dengue occurs chiefly in Egypt, India, Iran, and the West Indies. BENJAMIN F. MILLER

See also MOSQUITO (Yellow Fever and Dengue); VIRUS.

DENIER, *duh NEER*, is a unit of weight used to measure silk or synthetic threads. It is the weight in grams of 9,842 yards of yarn. The term is most often used to describe the fineness of yarn in women's nylon hosiery, which ranges from 7 to 70 denier. A 7-denier nylon is so sheer that the hosiery made from it is almost transparent. CHARLES H. RUTLEDGE

DENIM is a durable twill fabric made of coarse, single, hard-twisted cotton yarns. The standard white-back denim is made with indigo-blue dyed *warp* (lengthwise) yarns and unbleached *filling* (crosswise) yarns. Solid-color face denims are made from yarns that are a blend of black and white fibers.

Denim is used chiefly for work clothes. But it is also woven for use in sportswear, usually in white, pastel shades, and stripes. Most denims are preshrunk in a process called *Sanforizing*. HAZEL B. STRAHAN

DENIS, SAINT (A.D. 200's), is the patron saint of France. Saint Gregory of Tours reported that Denis was sent to preach the gospel in Gaul during the reign of Emperor Decius (249-251), became bishop of Paris, and died a martyr. His feast day is October 9. Denis was sometimes confused with Denis the Areopagite, who was a convert of Saint Paul. WALTER J. BURGHARDT

DENISON UNIVERSITY is a privately endowed coeducational school of liberal arts and sciences at Granville, Ohio. Denison offers preprofessional training in medicine, dentistry, law, teaching, the ministry, business administration, and fine arts. It has an Air Force ROTC unit. Founded in 1831, it was incorporated as Denison University in 1856. For enrollment, see UNIVERSITIES AND COLLEGES (table). RUTH A. OUTLAND

113

DENMARK

Denmark lies in the northern part of Europe.

Denmark is smaller than Vermont and New Hampshire.

Soldiers of the Royal Bodyguard wear light blue trousers, dark blue jackets, and bearskin caps, as they guard the Danish king's palace.

Henri Cartier-Bresson

DENMARK is a small country in Northern Europe. It is made up of a peninsula and nearby islands. The official name of the country in Danish is KONGERIGET DANMARK, or KINGDOM OF DENMARK. Copenhagen is Denmark's capital and largest city.

The country covers an area slightly smaller than the combined areas of Vermont and New Hampshire. But Denmark has over four times as many people as those two states. Denmark is an important agricultural country, but more persons work in industry and handicrafts than in agriculture.

Denmark is a picture-book land of small green farms, blue lakes, and white beaches. The gently rolling countryside is neat and carefully tended. There are many parks and gardens. Old windmills, thatched farmhouses, modern homes, and ancient castles dot the countryside.

No other European country has had so long an unbroken rule by its own people as Denmark. It is one of the oldest kingdoms in the world. Danes honor their flag as the world's oldest. It has flown since the 1100's. The tiny kingdom has taught the world many lessons in freedom, education, and social legislation. The fairy tales of the Danish writer, Hans Christian Andersen, have delighted children in many lands.

The Land and Its Resources

Location, Size, and Surface Features. Denmark lies between the Baltic Sea and the North Sea. Water surrounds the country except for 42 miles in the south, where Denmark and Germany meet. The Skagerrak, an arm of the North Sea, lies between Denmark and Norway. The *Color Map* shows that the waters of the Kattegat, a strait, and the narrow Öresund separate Denmark from Sweden. Denmark covers 16,619 square miles.

Denmark consists of the peninsula of Jutland, which extends northward from Germany, and about 500

Storks Are Symbols of Good Luck in Denmark. Many Danes are happy to have storks pick their chimneys or roofs for summer nesting sites. Some even build special roosts for the storks.

A Huge Anchor, *right*, marks the entrance to the Nyhavn, considered the most colorful section of Copenhagen harbor. The anchor symbolizes the importance of shipping to the economy of Denmark.

nearby islands. People live on about 100 of the islands. Jutland covers 9,186 square miles. The western part of Jutland is a lowland covered by sand dunes and heaths. A low range of hills extends across the middle of the peninsula. The highest of these hills are less than 600 feet above sea level. Fertile lowlands and low, rolling hills lie along the east coast of Jutland and throughout the islands.

The largest Danish island is Sjaelland. It covers an area of 2,682 square miles and has an irregular coast line. Most of the island is fertile and easily cultivated. Bornholm is Denmark's only rocky island. Its granite cliffs rise abruptly out of the Baltic Sea, about 100 miles east of Sjaelland.

Rivers, Lakes, and Fiords. Denmark has many small lakes and gently flowing, winding streams. The 100-mile Gudenaa is the only river on which boats can travel. It rises in east-central Jutland and flows into the Kattegat near the city of Randers.

Many arms of the sea, called *fiords*, stretch across eastern Jutland. There also are many fiords in northern Sjaelland. The largest Danish fiord is the Limfjorden. It is so long that it almost cuts the northernmost tip of Jutland from the rest of the peninsula. A short canal, the Tyborön Canal, connects the Limfjorden with the North Sea.

Climate. Denmark is almost surrounded by water, and so has a mild, damp climate. The average summer temperature is 60°F., and the average winter temperature is about 32°F. The temperature varies greatly from day to day. Rain and mist are common all year, but the average annual rainfall of 21 to 27 inches is moder-

---
FACTS IN BRIEF

Type of Government: Constitutional monarchy.
Capital: Copenhagen.
Divisions: 25 counties (Faeroe Islands and Greenland not included). Counties are divided into parishes.
Head of State: Monarch.
Parliament: 179 members (four-year terms).
Official Language: Danish.
Area: 16,619 square miles. *Greatest distance:* (north-south) 223 miles; (east-west) Jutland, 108 miles; Sjaelland, 65 miles. *Coastline,* 4,622 miles.
Elevation: *Highest,* Ejner Bavnehøj, 566 feet above sea level; *Lowest,* sea level along the coasts.
Population: 4,700,000. *Density,* 283 persons per sq. mi. *Distribution,* urban, 50 per cent; rural, 50 per cent.
Chief Products: *Agriculture,* bacon, barley, beets, butter, eggs, ham, oats, potatoes, rye, wheat. *Manufacturing and Processing,* beer, bicycles, bricks, cement, diesel engines, electrical equipment, furniture, machinery, margarine, porcelain, powdered and condensed milk, ships, silverware, textiles. *Fishing Industry,* cod, herring, mackerel, oysters, plaice.
Flag: A large white cross appears on a red banner. The flag, adopted in 1219, is considered the oldest of any nation. See FLAG (color picture, Flags of Europe).
National Holiday: Constitution Day, June 5.
National Anthem: "Der Er Et Yndigt Land" ("There is a Lovely Country").
Money: *Basic unit,* krone. One hundred öre equal one krone. For its value in dollars, see MONEY (table, Values).

115

DENMARK

ate for a land constantly swept by winds from the Atlantic Ocean.

Natural Resources. Denmark's most important natural resources are the soil and the surrounding sea. About three fourths of the land produces crops. Nearly one tenth of Denmark is forest land. Most of the trees are beeches and spruces.

Denmark has few mineral resources. The marshes yield peat that is used as fuel. Some areas have clay that can be used to make pottery and tiles. Beds of soft rock that are rich in lime furnish raw materials for cement, fertilizer, and chalk.

Conservation. The thrifty Danes conserve and develop their few natural resources. They make the soil more productive by using fertilizers and by rotating crops. They plant trees in the sand dunes and on the heaths to keep the sand from drifting over the farm lands, and to improve the soil. They drain wet marshes and build dams to store floodwaters for use in dry seasons. Windmills pump water and generate electricity.

The People and Their Work

The People. The Danes are of Teutonic origin (see JUTE; TEUTON). About one fourth of the people live in Copenhagen, another fourth in the smaller cities and villages, and the rest on farms. The Danish language is much like Swedish and Norwegian. About 20,000 Germans live in south Jutland. They are the chief minority group in Denmark.

Way of Life. Danes are friendly, generous, and

DENMARK MAP INDEX

Counties

AABENRAA, 49,769 D 2
AALBORG, 239,041 .B 2
AARHUS, 221,895 ..B 3
ASSENS, 57,472 ....C 2
BORNHOLM, 48,373 D 7
FREDERIKSBORG, 181,663 ....C 5
HADERSLEV, 72, 153C 2
HJÖRRING, 177,778 A 2
HOLBAEK, 127,747.C 4
KÖBENHAVN, 1,321,805 ....C 5
MARIBO, 131,699 ..D 4
ODENSE, 207,273 ...C 3
PRAESTÖ, 121,976 .C 4
RANDERS, 170,231 .B 3
RIBE, 185,048 ......C 1
RINGKÖBING, 205,772 ....B 1
ROSKILDE, 90,337 .C 5
SKANDERBORG, 137,865 ....B 2
SÖNDERBORG, 56,267 ....D 2
SORÖ, 129,580 ....C 4
SVENDBORG, 149,163 ....C 3
THISTED, 84,955 ..B 1
TÖNDER, 42,457 ...C 1
VEJLE, 213,705 ....C 2
VIBORG, 161,232 ..B 2

Cities

Aabenraa, 14,219 ...C 2
Aabybro, 1,346 .....A 2
Aakirkeby, 1,461 ..C 7
Aalbaek, 877 ....A 3
Aalborg, 85,800 ...A 2
Aarhus, 119,568 (*177,234) ....B 3
Aars, 3,206 ....B 2
Aerösköbing, 1,273 .D 3
Allinge, 2,114 .....C 7
Alrö ....C 3
Als, 685 ....B 3
Asaa, 1,265 ....A 3
Assens, 4,937 .....C 2
Augustenborg, 1,926.D 2
Aulum, 1,253 ......B 1
Auning, 1,314 .....B 2
Bagenkop, 705 ....D 3
Ballerup, 9,392 ...C 5
Beder, 306 ....B 3
Bjerringbro, 3,582 ..B 2
Blokhus, ...A 2
Bogense, 2,968 ....C 3
Borre ....D 5
Bramminge, 2,900 ..C 1
Brande, 4,151 .....C 2
Broager, 1,601 ....D 2
Brönderslev, 9,454 ..A 2
Byrum, 395 ....A 4
Christiansfeld, 819 (*1,562) ....C 2
Copenhagen (Köbenhavn), 721,381 (*1,350,000) ....C 5
Dragör, 6,986 .....C 5
Dronninglund, 1,647 A 3
Ebeltoft, 2,227 ....B 3
Ejstrupholm, 913 ..C 2
Esbjerg, 55,171 ...C 1
Faaborg, 5,135 ....C 3
Fakse, 2,002 ......C 5
Fjerritslev, 1,925 ..A 2
Fredericia, 29,870 .C 2
Frederikshavn, 22,522 ....A 3
Frederikssund, 5,722 C 5
Frederiksvaerk, 4,435 (*6,155) ....B 5
Gedser, 1,262 .....D 4
Gilleleje, 2,219 ....B 5
Give, 1,800 ....C 2
Gjerrild, 300 ......B 3
Glyngöre, 930 ....B 1
Görlev, 1,379 .....C 4
Graasten, 2,414 ...D 2
Graested, 1,078 ...B 5
Grenaa, 9,088 .....B 3
Grindsted, 5,289 ..C 1
Haderslev, 19,735 ..C 2
Hadsten, 2,525 ....B 3
Hadsund, 3,424 ...B 3
Hals, 1,563 ....B 3
Hammel, 2,162 ....B 2
Hansted ....A 1
Harboöre, 1,028 ..B 1
Hasle, 1,487 ......C 7
Haslev, 6,155 .....C 5
Hejls, 292 ....C 2
Helsingör, 26,658 (*32,636) ....B 5
Herlufmagle, 496 ..C 4
Herning, 24,790 ..B 1
Hillerød, 11,605 (*18,147) ....C 5
Hirtshals, 4,177 ...A 2
Hjörring, 15,038 ..A 2
Hobro, 8,208 ......B 2
Höjer, 1,400 ......D 1
Holbaek, 15,475 ..C 4
Holstebro, 18,563 ..B 1
Holsted, 1,081 ....C 1
Höng, 1,950 ....C 4
Hörby, 462 ....A 3
Horsens, 37,261 ..C 2
Hörve, 906 ....C 4
Humlum, 548 .....B 1
Hundested, 3,806 ..C 4
Hurup, 2,160 .....B 1
Ikast, 5,797 ......B 2
Jellinge, 1,228 ...C 2
Juelsminde, 950 ..C 3
Jyderup, 2,305 ...C 4
Kalundborg, 9,763 .C 4
Kalvehave, 454 ....C 5
Karup, 1,137 .....B 2
Kellerup, 2,637 ...B 2
Kerteminde, 4,024 ..C 3
Klitmöller, 471 ...A 1
Knebel ....B 3
Köge, 12,294 ......C 5
Kolding, 35,101 ..C 2
Korsör, 14,276 ...C 4
Langaa, 2,119 ....B 2
Laurbjerg, 815 ...B 2
Lemvig, 5,783 ....B 1
Lögstör, 3,435 ....B 2
Lögumkloster, 1,907 .C 1
Lohals, 640 ....C 3
Lökken, 1,506 ....A 2
Lundby, 549 ......C 4
Mariager, 1,483 ..B 2
Maribo, 5,235 ....D 4
Marstal, 1,986 (*2,909) ....D 3
Martofte ....C 3
Middelfart, 8,801 (*11,701) ....C 2
Mou, 677 ....B 3
Naestved, 19,617 (*26,856) ....C 4
Nakskov, 16,639 ..D 4
Neksö, 3,220 .....C 8
Nibe, 2,494 ....B 2
Nordborg, 2,563 ..C 2
Nordby, 1,975 ....C 1
Nordby, 313 ......C 1
Nörre-Aaby, 1,844 .C 2
Nörre-Alslev, 1,062 .D 4
Nörresundby, 10,456 A 2
Nyborg, 11,667 ...C 3
Nyköbing, 9,326 ..B 1
Nyköbing, 4,803 ..C 4
Nyköbing Falster, 17,850 ....D 4
Nymindegab ......C 1
Nysted, 1,328 ....D 4
Odder, 5,562 .....C 3
Odense, 111,145 (*129,833) ....C 3
Orehoved, 424 ....D 4
Örsted, 1,031 .....B 3
Österby ....A 4
Praestö, 1,528 ...C 5
Randers, 42,238 (*54,780) ....B 3
Ribe, 7,809 ....C 1
Ringe, 2,936 .....C 3
Ringköbing, 4,869 .B 1
Ringsted, 9,694 ..C 4
Rödby, 3,551 .....D 4
Rönde, 1,384 .....B 3
Rönne, 13,195 ...C 7
Roskilde, 31,928 ..C 5
Rudköbing, 4,336 .D 3
Ry, 2,004 ....B 2
Ryomgaard, 861 ..B 3
Saeby, 3,669 .....A 3
Sakskjöbing, 2,526 (*4,035) ....D 4
Sandvig, 608 (part of Allinge-Sandvig) .C 7
Sejerö ....C 4
Selde, 411 ....B 2
Silkeborg, 24,465 ..B 2
Skaelsör, 2,889 ..C 4
Skaerbaek, 1,989 ..C 1
Skagen, 10,390 ..A 3
Skanderborg, 5,482 ....B 2
Skelde, 330 ....D 2
Skibby, 1,040 ....C 4
Skive, 15,558 ....B 2
Skjern, 5,349 ....C 1
Ködstrup, 390 ...B 3
Skörping, 1,461 ..B 2
Slagelse, 20,562 ..C 4
Slangerup, 1,638 ..C 5
Snedsted, 1,030 ..B 1
Söby, 728 ....D 3
Sönderborg, 20,653 .D 2
Sönderho, 410 ...C 1
Söndervig ....B 1
Sorö, 5,494 ......C 4
Spöttrup, 628 ....B 1
Stege, 2,620 (*3,816) ....D 5
Store-Heddinge, 2,082 ....C 5
Struer, 8,335 ....B 1
Stubbeköbing, 2,097 D 5
Sunds, 1,039 .....B 2
Svaneke, 1,167 ..C 8
Svendborg, 23,892 .C 3
Thisted, 8,768 ....B 1
Tinglev, 1,406 ...D 2
Tisvildeleje, 862 ..B 5
Toftlund, 1,814 ..C 2
Tönder, 7,192 ....D 1
Törring, 1,367 ...C 2
Tranebjerg, 729 ..C 3
Tversted ....A 3
Tybörön, 2,134 ..B 1
Ulfborg, 1,174 ...B 1
Vamdrup, 2,313 ..C 2
Varde, 9,577 .....C 1
Vejen, 4,582 .....C 2
Vejle, 31,362 (*39,498) ....C 2
Vesterö Havn, 517 .A 3
Vestervig, 573 ...B 1
Viborg, 23,265 ...B 2
Vojens, 3,563 ....C 2
Vordingborg, 11,780 C 4

Physical Features

Aabenraa Fjord .....C 2
Aalbaek Bugt (Bay) A 3
Aalborg Bugt (Bay) .B 3
Aarhus Bugt (Bay) .B 3
Aebelö (Isl.) ....C 3
Aerö (Isl.) ....D 3
Agersö (Isl.) ......C 4
Als (Isl.) ....C 2
Amager (Isl.) .....C 5
Anholt (Isl.) ......B 4
Baagö (Isl.) ......C 2
Baltic Sea ....C 5
Barsö (Isl.) ....C 2
Blaavands (Pt.) ..C 1
Bornholm (Isl.) ..D 7
Endelave (Isl.) ..C 3
Faejö (Isl.) ....D 4
Faemö (Isl.) .....D 4
Fakse Bugt (Bay) .D 5
Falster (Isl.) .....D 4
Fanö (Isl.) ....C 1
Fanö Bugt (Bay) ..C 1
Fehmarn Strait ..D 4
Fladsaa R. ....C 4
Flensburger Fjord .D 2
Fyn (Isl.) ....C 3
Gudenaa R. ......B 2
Helnaes (Isl.) ....C 2
Hesselö (Isl.) ....B 4
Ise Fjord ....C 4
Jammer Bugt (Bay) A 2
Jutland (Peninsula) .C 1
Kadet Channel ...D 4
Kattegat (Channel) .B 4
Köge Bugt (Bay) ..C 5
Kongeaa R. ......C 1
Laesö (Isl.) ....A 3
Langeland (Isl.) ..D 3
Langelands Belt (Strait) ....D 3
Langerak R. .....A 3
Lille Belt (Strait) .C 2
Limfjorden (Fjord) .B 2
Lindenborg R. ...B 2
Lolland (Isl.) .....D 4
Lyö (Isl.) ....C 3
Manö (Isl.) ......C 1
Mariager Fjord ..B 3
Möen (Isl.) ....C 5
Mors (Isl.) ....B 1
Nissum Fjord ....B 1
North Frisian Is. ..C 1
Odense R. ....C 3
Omö (Isl.) ....C 4
Öresund (Sound) .C 5
Orö (Isl.) ....C 4
Ringköbing Fjord ..B 1
Römö (Isl.) ......C 1
Rye R. ....A 2
Saltholm (Isl.) ...C 5
Samsö (Isl.) .....C 3
Samsö Belt (Strait) .C 3
Sejerö (Isl.) ......C 4
Sejerö Bugt (Bay) .C 4
Sjaelland (Isl.) ..C 4
Sjaellands Odde (Pt.) B 4
Skagen (The Skaw) (Cape) ....A 3
Skagerrak (Channel) A 1
Skive R. ....B 2
Skjern R. ....C 1
Smaalandsfarvandet (Bay) ....C 4
Sönder R. ....D 2
Storaa R. ....B 1
Store Belt (Strait) .C 3
Taasinge (Isl.) ...C 3
Tannis Bugt (Bay) .A 3
Tunö (Isl.) ....C 3
Turö (Isl.) ....C 3
Tybörön Canal ...B 1
Varde R. ....C 1
Venö (Isl.) ....B 1
Vigsö Bugt (Bay) ..A 1

*Population of metropolitan area, including suburbs.
*Does not appear on the map; key shows general location.

Source: Latest available official figures.

116

CM TERRAIN DENMARK
COPYRIGHT BY RAND McNALLY & COMPANY MADE IN U.S.A.
Longitude East of Greenwich
DENMARK
Mixed Evergreen and Deciduous Trees
Shrub
Grass
National Capital
Cities
Canals
Railroads
County Boundaries
1 inch = 31 Statute Miles
Miles 0 5 10 20 30
Lambert Conformal Conic Projection
Skagerrak
Kattegat
Baltic Sea
NORTH FRISIAN ISLANDS
Helgoland Bay
Jade Bay
Kiel Bay
Mecklenburg Bay
Fehmarn Strait
Kadet Channel
Öresund
Store Belt
Lille Belt
Samsö Belt
Smaalandsfarvandet
Limfjorden
Aalborg Bugt
Aarhus Bugt
Mariager Fjord
Ringköbing Fjord
Fanö Bugt
Sejerö Bugt
Köge Bugt
Fakse Bugt
Laholmsbukten
Skalderviken
Hanöbukten
Eckernförder Bucht
Hohwacht Bucht
Wismar Bucht
Lübeck Bay
Flensburger Fjord
SKAGEN (THE SKAW)
Skagen
Frederikshavn
HJÖRRING
Hjörring
Aalborg
AALBORG
THISTED
Thisted
VIBORG
Viborg
RANDERS
Randers
RINGKÖBING
Ringköbing
Herning
Silkeborg
Aarhus
SKANDERBORG
Skanderborg
Horsens
VEJLE
Vejle
Fredericia
Kolding
RIBE
Ribe
Esbjerg
HADERSLEV
Haderslev
AABENRAA
Aabenraa
TÖNDER
Tönder
SÖNDERBORG
Sönderborg
Flensburg
ODENSE
Odense
SVENDBORG
Svendborg
Nyborg
Faaborg
Assens
Middelfart
SJAELLAND
COPENHAGEN (København)
FREDERIKSBORG
Hilleröd
Helsingör
HOLBAEK
Holbaek
Kalundborg
ROSKILDE
Roskilde
SORÖ
Sorö
Slagelse
Korsör
PRAESTÖ
Praestö
Naestved
Köge
MARIBO
Maribo
Nakskov
LOLLAND
FALSTER
Nyköbing Falster
MÖEN
LANGELAND
Rudköbing
AERÖ
Aeröskobing
Marstal
SAMSÖ
ANHOLT (DENMARK)
LAESÖ
FANÖ
RÖMÖ
SYLT
Westerland
FÖHR
AMRUM
PELLWORM
FEHMARN
BORNHOLM (DENMARK)
Rönne
Nexö
Allinge
Svaneke
Göteborg
Halmstad
Helsingborg
Malmö
Kristianstad
Karlskrona
Falkenberg
Varberg
SWEDEN
WEST GERMANY
EAST GERMANY
GERMANY
Kiel
Lübeck
Hamburg
Neumünster
Schwerin
Wismar
Rostock
Especially created for World Book Encyclopedia by Rand McNally and World Book editors
©RMCN.

DENMARK

hospitable. Most of them have a keen sense of humor. Few Danes are very rich or very poor. The Danish standard of living is one of the highest in the world. Many persons own their own small homes. The roofs of houses generally are made of red or blue tiles, and some are thatched. Walls are usually made of red brick or reinforced concrete. Many farms have half-timbered buildings surrounding a square courtyard. Danish cities have huge apartment buildings. Each apartment in these buildings has its own plant-covered balcony.

Food. Danes enjoy eating, and they eat often and well. Almost everyone in Denmark has *smørrebrød* for lunch, and often again in the evening. Smørrebrød is a special kind of open-faced sandwich. A plate of smørrebrød often is a work of art. One sandwich, for example, is a pyramid-shaped pile of about 200 tiny shrimps on thin bread. Beer and ice-cold *snaps* (a kind of brandy) often accompany smørrebrød. Danish pastry is delicious. World-famous Danish restaurants include Oskar Davidsen's, De 7 smaa Hjem (The Seven Small Homes), the Nimb, and Wivex, all in Copenhagen.

Clothing. Danes wear about the same type of clothes as are worn in other European countries and in the United States. People in the rural districts sometimes wear colorful costumes on certain holidays. See CLOTHING (color picture, Europe).

Recreation. Copenhagen is one of the gayest cities in the world, with its Tivoli amusement park and other forms of entertainment. Many Danish towns hold annual festivals or pageants.

Danish Silverware is prized throughout the world. Skilled craftsmen hammer the pieces into the desired shapes.

Denmark celebrates the United States' Independence Day. This holiday is observed on July 4 in a national park at Rebild. A group of Danish-born Americans bought Rebild Hills in 1911. They gave the area to the Danish government in 1912, with the stipulation that the American Independence Day be observed there every year. This celebration helps strengthen the ties between Denmark and the United States.

Soccer is the Danish national sport. Danes also enjoy bicycling, tennis, horse racing, and golf. Swimming, sailing, rowing, and fishing are popular sports in Danish waters.

Cities. Copenhagen is Denmark's capital and largest city. Most of it lies on the eastern coast of Sjaelland Island. But parts of it lie on Amager Island. Odense stands near the center of Fyn Island. Except for Esbjerg, all other large cities lie along the eastern coast of Jutland, away from the fury of storms sweeping across the North Sea from the Atlantic Ocean.

See the separate articles on Danish cities listed in the *Related Articles* at the end of this article.

Agriculture. The chief occupation of Danish farmers once was growing wheat. In the 1880's, cheaper wheat from other countries began to threaten Denmark's agricultural economy, so the Danes switched to other farm products. Today, about one Dane out of every four works in the dairy-farming or stock-raising industries. Danish farmers produce some of the world's best bacon, ham, butter, cheese, and eggs. They grow large crops of beets, potatoes, oats, barley, and rye. Most of these crops are used for livestock feed.

Since the 1780's, Danish law has forbidden anyone to build up a large country estate. As a result, most farmers own and tend their own small farms. The average size of the Danish farm is from 50 to 125 acres.

Danish farmers have organized cooperative dairies and slaughterhouses, and many other cooperative groups. Through cooperatives, the farmers are able to use the most scientific machinery and farming methods. No farmer could afford to buy all the machinery that is owned cooperatively. The farmers set their own standards for products, require all members to keep careful production records, and set the prices at which products are sold. Each farmer in a cooperative receives his share of the profits. See COOPERATIVE.

Manufacturing. Denmark has few minerals or natural fuels. But the sea that surrounds much of the country provides the cheapest transportation medium in the world, and has enabled Denmark to build up a prosperous manufacturing industry. About one out of every three Danes works in manufacturing. Danish factories produce electrical equipment, bicycles, bricks, textiles, furniture, margarine, and beer. There are large cement factories in northern Jutland. Denmark is famous for its ships, diesel engines, dairy and slaughtering machinery, leatherware, metal goods, porcelain, and condensed and powdered milk.

Fisheries are an important part of the Danish economy because of the fish found along the country's long coastline. Thousands of Danish fishing boats bring in fish from the Kattegat, Skagerrak, North Sea, and Baltic. The Danes eat some of the fish. Some is shipped fresh in refrigerated trucks to other countries in Europe. The rest is canned and shipped to countries around the world. The most important seafoods are cod, herring, mackerel, plaice, oysters, shrimps, eels, and haddock.

Trade. Denmark's position on the sea and its large merchant fleet have given the country advantages in commerce. Great Britain, Germany, Sweden, the United States, and Norway are good markets for Danish products. These nations also supply Denmark with many of the products it needs. The excellent quality of Danish bacon, ham, butter, and eggs is well-known in world markets. Denmark also exports many manufactured products and farm animals, such as cattle and horses. Imports include grain, coal, iron goods, and textiles.

Transportation and Communication. Denmark has excellent railroads. The government owns 1,600 miles of the country's 3,100 miles of railways. The government-owned railways carry many more passengers and much more freight than the private railways. Roads and highways, many of them lined with trees, cover 15,000 miles. The longest bridge in Europe, the Storstrøm Bridge, connects the islands of Sjaelland and Falster. It is 10,499 feet long. Many roads have separate bicycle lanes. This is a necessary safety measure because at least one out of every two Danes owns a bicycle.

Small steamboats travel between the islands and the mainland, and from island to island. Ferries transport trains across the narrow waterways. Denmark has a large merchant fleet. In 1912, Denmark built the world's first seagoing diesel ship, the *Selandia*. Airlines connect Denmark with other nations. Almost every Danish family has a radio, and more than half have telephones. Telegraph service is country-wide. Denmark also has television.

Social and Cultural Achievements

Universities: University of Copenhagen, at Copenhagen, founded 1479; University of Aarhus, at Aarhus, founded 1928.

Museums: National Museum, National Art Gallery, Thorvaldsen's Museum, the New Carlsberg Glyptotek, and Rosenborg Castle, all in Copenhagen; Frederiksborg Castle in Hillerød; Hans Christian Andersen's House in Odense; Old Town in Aarhus.

Education. Educational standards are high in Denmark, and everyone has at least a grade-school education. Education is compulsory between the ages of seven and fourteen.

Denmark is famous for its unique Folk High Schools. A Danish churchman and poet, N.F.S. Grundtvig (1783-1872), realized that the young people in the farming districts needed more education. Through Grundtvig's efforts, the Folk High Schools were founded. They are unlike high schools in the United States, because they admit persons over 18 and they give no diploma. Their aim is to give young persons a general education by teaching history, literature, and methods of solving social problems. Some schools also teach farming subjects, domestic science, and gymnastics. Students live at the schools. Courses last five months in the winter and three months in the summer. Most schools have only men students in the winter, when there is little work on the farms, and women students in the summer.

Besides the Folk High Schools, Denmark has many agricultural schools. These two types of schools have helped the Danes become excellent farmers, and have contributed to their social and political knowledge.

DENMARK

Instruction in Denmark's two universities is free. Other educational institutions include technological schools, business schools, teacher-training schools, and evening schools.

Denmark has a fine library system. The government supports all public libraries, and there is much cooperation among them. If a person wants to borrow a book which his local library does not have, his library obtains it from another library. Danes use about 19,000,000 books a year from the libraries. The Royal Library in Copenhagen is the largest library in Scandinavia. Other important libraries include the University Library in Copenhagen and the State Library in Aarhus.

Religion. The Lutheran Church is the church of Denmark. About 98 of every 100 Danes are Lutherans, but there is complete freedom of religion for all faiths.

The Arts. Danes enjoy many beautiful ballads that date back to the 1200's. Danish ballads were handed down through many generations by word of mouth before they ever were written down.

Ludvig Holberg (1684-1754) often is called the father of Danish literature. He wrote books on many subjects, but was most famous for theatrical comedies that poked fun at the Danes. Adam Oehlenschläger (1779-1850) wrote beautiful nature poems and many tragedies, with heroes drawn from Danish and Norwegian history. His writings helped teach the people to love their country. Hans Christian Andersen wrote charming fairy tales. Søren Kierkegaard was a well-known philosopher and writer. Isak Dinesen (Karen Blixen) is another noted Danish writer. Danish authors who have won Nobel prizes for literature include Henrik Pontoppidan, Karl Gjellerup, and Johannes V. Jensen.

Among the most important Danish composers is Carl Nielsen (1865-1931). He composed symphonies, operas, ballads, songs, and other music. Well-known Danish painters include C. W. Eckersberg (1783-1853) and Peter Hansen (1868-1928). Bertel Thorvaldsen (1770-1844) was a well-known sculptor. He molded many handsome statues of the human figure. "Jason and the Golden Fleece" and "Ganymede Feeding the Eagle" are considered two of his best works (see GANYMEDE [picture]). Another Danish sculptor, Kai Nielsen (1882-1924), created many statues of children and young women.

Danes are proud of their craftsmanship in ceramics, silverware, and home furnishings. The Royal Porcelain Factory, and Bing and Grøndahl's Porcelain Factory, both in Copenhagen, produce fine porcelains. Georg Jensen is the best-known silversmith establishment. There is a permanent exhibition of Danish arts and crafts in a store in Copenhagen. Craftsmen from every part of the country display and sell their work there.

Government

National Government. Denmark is a constitutional monarchy. The monarchy is hereditary, but until 1953 when the country adopted a new constitution, no woman in modern history could inherit the throne. The powers of the ruler are restricted. He shares executive power with a council of ministers, which he appoints. The Parliament, or *Folketing*, makes the laws by which the kingdom is governed. Members of

DENMARK

Parliament are elected by popular vote on a proportional basis. Greenland and the Faeroe Islands each elect two members to Parliament. Denmark has had a *unicameral* (single-house) Parliament since 1953.

All Danish citizens who are 21 years of age or older may vote in national elections. Leading political parties are the Social Democrat, the Moderate Democrat, the Conservative, and the Social Liberal.

Local Government. Each *amt* (county) is administered by a council and governor. The state appoints the governor, but the council is elected locally. The parishes also are governed by elected councils.

History

Early Days. Scientists believe people lived in the region now called Denmark as much as 11,000 years ago. Little is known about these early people, except that they were fishermen and hunters.

For thousands of years, Denmark consisted of small communities governed by local chieftains. In the A.D. 800's, Danish vikings conquered southwestern England and settled the region of Normandy in France. Harald Bluetooth (?-985?) united Denmark about 950. His son, Sweyn Forkbeard (?-1014), attacked England and conquered the whole country by 1013. He was succeeded by his son Canute the Great, who reigned from 1019 to 1035. Canute conquered Norway in 1028. After his death in 1035, Denmark lost its possessions in other countries. It also went through a period of domestic disputes, because several men claimed the throne.

The Danish Empire. Valdemar the Great (who reigned from 1157 to 1182) and Valdemar the Victorious (who reigned from 1202 to 1241) built an empire on the Baltic Sea. It included much of northern Germany, the island of Gotland, and Estonia. Valdemar the Victorious gave the country its first system of laws, known as *The Jutland Code*. This code remained in force until 1683, and became the model for many later Danish laws. The empire built by the Valdemars gave way in the 1330's to the strong Hanseatic League, a group of cities that united for mutual protection of trade. Most cities of the league were German, and the Danes acquired many German customs from them. See HANSEATIC LEAGUE.

Toward the end of the 1300's, Denmark again became a great power. A strong monarch, Queen Margaret (reigned 1387-1397), united Denmark, Norway, and Sweden under Danish rule by 1397. The union began to crumble after Margaret's death. The empire broke apart when the Swedish nobles rebelled against King Christian II of Denmark (reigned 1513-1523) and won independence for Sweden in 1523.

King Christian III (reigned 1534-1559) adopted Lutheranism as the state religion of Denmark in 1536. He took over the vast lands and wealth that previously had been held by the Roman Catholic Church.

Wars with Sweden occurred frequently during the next two hundred years. For the first hundred years, the Danes tried to force Sweden back into a Scandinavian union under the Danish king. Sweden wanted control of the Baltic Sea so that it could trade with Germany, and it also wanted an outlet to the Atlantic Ocean. Danish and Norwegian possessions interfered with both these Swedish ambitions. But, between 1649 and 1660, Sweden won access to the ocean, and Denmark lost all its possessions on the Swedish mainland.

For the next hundred years, the Danes fought to win back the territories they had lost. During this period, the Swedes tried to obtain even more territory from

Danish Information Office
Kronborg Castle, famed as the scene of Shakespeare's tragedy, *Hamlet,* stands in the northern Danish town of Helsingör.

RED-LETTER DATES IN DENMARK
---

c. 950 Denmark became a united country.
1013-1042 Denmark ruled England.
1380 Iceland became a Danish possession.
1397 Denmark, Norway, and Sweden were united under the Danish Queen Margaret.
1536 Protestantism was established in Denmark.
1660 Danish and Norwegian territory was lost to Sweden. The Danish monarchy became hereditary.
1721 Denmark began to colonize Greenland.
1788 Serfdom was abolished.
1814 Denmark gave Norway to Sweden.
1849 Denmark adopted its first liberal constitution.
1864 Denmark lost Schleswig-Holstein to Prussia and Austria.
1920 Northern Schleswig voted to return to Danish rule.
1940-1945 Germany occupied Denmark.
1944 Iceland became independent of Denmark.
1953 Denmark adopted a new constitution, which made Greenland a county.
1961 Denmark applied for membership in the European Common Market.

DENMARK

Denmark. Finally, in 1814, at the end of the Napoleonic Wars, Denmark was forced to give Norway to Sweden.

Absolute Monarchy. After Denmark's great losses to Sweden, the power of the nobles declined, and that of the middle classes increased. In 1660, King Frederick III (reigned 1648-1670), helped by the merchants, made the monarchy absolute and the throne hereditary.

Many improvements followed. Commerce and the arts flourished. Danes settled Greenland in 1721. Denmark abolished serfdom in 1788. This cleared the way for the breakup of large land holdings, and eventually brought prosperity to the people.

The Schleswig Wars. In the 1830's and 1840's, the Danes demanded a liberal constitution which would give more rights to the people and take away the absolute power of the king. It became necessary to decide whether the constitution should apply only to Denmark, or to Schleswig-Holstein as well. Schleswig was a Danish dependency and Holstein was a German dependency, but Denmark ruled both. The German inhabitants of Holstein wanted their area and that of Schleswig to be united within the German Confederation. Open revolt against Denmark broke out in 1848 in Holstein and southern Schleswig. Prussia, and later Austria, helped the rebels. After two wars (1848-1850 and 1864), Denmark was forced to give the regions to Prussia and Austria.

Social Reforms. The period between 1864 and World War II was a time of the greatest economic, social, and cultural development in Danish history. The Danes improved their agricultural methods, developed cooperative enterprises, and expanded industry and commerce. They also introduced social measures such as old-age pensions and health insurance.

Denmark remained neutral during World War I. In 1918, Denmark recognized the independence of Iceland. But the king of Denmark also continued to be the king of Iceland until 1944, when Iceland became a republic. In 1920, the people of northern Schleswig voted to join Denmark again.

World War II. Germany attacked Denmark on April 9, 1940, and conquered the country in a few hours. For the first time in its thousand-year history, Denmark was completely conquered by an invader.

For a while, the Germans allowed the Danes to manage their own affairs under what was called "German protection." But the Danes worked secretly against the Germans, and sabotage and strikes spread. In August, 1943, King Christian X (reigned 1912-1947) was placed under military guard. Parliament ceased to function, and the army was disbanded. Danish naval officers sank their fleet in Copenhagen harbor. A resistance movement, directed by the "Freedom Council," operated against German shipping and communications.

The Germans tried to arrest and send to Germany the 6,000 Jews living in Denmark. But the Danes helped more than 5,000 Jews reach safety in Sweden. In 1944, the Germans disarmed the Danish police force and imprisoned the men in concentration camps. Denmark was liberated by Allied troops on May 5, 1945.

Recent Developments. Frederick IX (born 1899-) inherited the throne in 1947. Denmark became a charter member of the United Nations in 1945, and of the North Atlantic Treaty Organization in 1949.

The country adopted a new constitution in 1953. The constitution changed the status of Greenland from that of a colony to a full member of the Danish Commonwealth. An atomic research center opened at Roskilde in 1958. In 1961, Denmark applied for membership in the European Common Market. JENS NYHOLM

Related Articles in WORLD BOOK include:

BIOGRAPHIES

Andersen, Hans Christian
Anne (Anne of Denmark)
Bering, Vitus
Bohr, Niels
Brahe, Tycho
Canute
Christian (kings)
Fibiger, Johannes A. G.
Finsen, Niels R.
Frederick (Danish kings)
Gjellerup, Karl
Haakon VII
Hardecanute
Hevesy, Georg von
Jensen, Johannes V.
Kierkegaard, Søren A.
Melchior, Lauritz L. H.
Nielsen, Carl A.
Oersted, Hans C.
Pontoppidan, Henrik
Rasmussen, Knud J. V.
Thomsen, Christian J.
Thorvaldsen, Bertel
Wilfrid, Thomas

CITIES

Aalborg   Aarhus   Copenhagen   Odense

HISTORY

Anglo-Saxon
Danegeld
Europe, Council of
European Monetary Agreement
Jute
Norway (History)
Schleswig-Holstein
Seven Weeks' War
Sweden (History)
Viking

PHYSICAL FEATURES

Baltic Sea
Belt, Great and Little
Faeroe Islands
Kattegat
North Sea
Skagerrak

UNCLASSIFIED

Barley (table)
Cheese (table)
Christmas (color picture, Christmas Is Children's Time)
Easter (In Scandinavian Countries)
Greenland
Iceland
Krone
Scandinavia
Ship and Shipping (table)
Virgin Islands

Outline

I. The Land and Its Resources
　A. Location, Size, and Surface Features
　B. Rivers, Lakes, and Fiords
　C. Climate
　D. Natural Resources
　E. Conservation

II. The People and Their Work
　A. The People
　B. Way of Life
　C. Cities
　D. Agriculture
　E. Manufacturing
　F. Fisheries
　G. Trade
　H. Transportation and Communication

III. Social and Cultural Achievements
　A. Education　B. Religion　C. The Arts

IV. Government

V. History

Questions

Why is each of the following famous: Hans Christian Andersen? Queen Margaret? N. F. S. Grundtvig?

How does Denmark's geography differ from that of its Scandinavian neighbors, Norway and Sweden?

How do cooperatives help Danish farmers?

What are the aims of the Folk High Schools?

What are the leading farm products of Denmark?

How does life in Denmark compare with life in the United States?

How did the Danes react to the German occupation of their country during World War II?

Why is Denmark a strong nation in commerce?

To what church do most Danes belong?

DENNY, ARTHUR A.

DENNY, ARTHUR A. See WASHINGTON (Famous Washingtonians).

DENOMINATE NUMBER, *dee NAHM uh nayt*, is a number with a name, such as 5 miles, 10 inches, 3 pounds, or 6 ounces, rather than just 5, 10, 3, or 6. Denominate numbers are usually measurements. Parts of denominate numbers are sometimes indicated by decimals, such as $4.30, 8.14 inches, or 5.41 miles. When they are written this way, they can be added, subtracted, multiplied, or divided, as any other decimals are.

Many denominate numbers contain irregular subdivisions. For example, 1 rod contains $5\frac{1}{2}$ yards, 1 yard contains 3 feet, and 1 foot contains 12 inches. A denominate number which contains two or more irregular subdivisions is called a *compound denominate number*. 6 yards 4 feet 9 inches is an example. Such compounds are more difficult to add, subtract, multiply, or divide, because the subdivisions must first be changed or *reduced* to the same denomination or unit of measure before the operations are performed. HOWARD F. FEHR

DENOMINATOR. See FRACTION (Writing Fractions with Numbers); ARITHMETIC (Working With Fractions).

DENSITY is the relation between the weight, or *mass*, of a substance and its size, or *volume* (see MASS; VOLUME). A concrete block weighs more than a block of wood the same size because it has a greater density. Density is usually measured in pounds per cubic foot in the English system. In the metric system, density is usually expressed in grams per cubic centimeter. To find the density of a substance we divide its weight by its size.

The term *specific gravity* is related to density. It is the ratio between the density of any substance and the density of water at 4°C. For example: if we have a concrete block that is 10 cubic feet in size and weighs 1,500 lbs., we divide 1,500 by 10 to get its density of 150 lbs. per cubic foot. To find the specific gravity of the concrete, we divide 150 lbs. per cubic foot (density) by 62.4 lbs. per cubic foot, which is the density of water. The specific gravity of the concrete would be 2.403. LOUIS MARICK

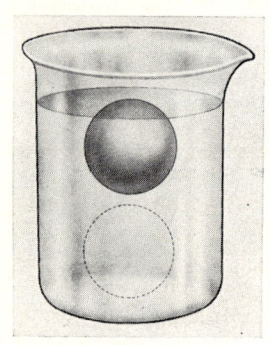

W. M. Welch Mfg. Co.
The Density of Water changes if the temperature is increased. The loaded ball will sink in warm water. The same ball will rise to the top in cold water, however.

See also GRAVITY, SPECIFIC.

DENSITY OF POPULATION. See POPULATION; WORLD (Population Distribution and Growth).

DENT, JOHN CHARLES (1841-1888), was a Canadian journalist and historian. He is best known for *The Last Forty Years*, a history of Canada from 1841 to 1881. He also wrote *The Canadian Portrait Gallery* and *The Story of the Upper Canadian Rebellion*.

Dent was born at Kendal, England, but came to Canada as an infant with his parents. He became a lawyer, but practiced for only a short time. He returned to England and served as a journalist with the *London Daily Telegraph*. He became editor of the *Toronto Evening Telegraph* in 1876, and later joined the editorial staff of the *Toronto Globe*. DESMOND PACEY

DENTAL ASSOCIATION, AMERICAN, is a national organization of dentists. Its purpose is to improve public health and promote the science and art of dentistry. It has 54 societies with 450 branches in the United States and its possessions. It has over 90,000 members. The association was founded in 1859. Headquarters are at 222 E. Superior St., Chicago, Ill.

DENTAL EROSION. See TEETH (Defects and Diseases).
DENTAL PULP. See TEETH (picture, The Parts of a Tooth).
DENTAL SCHOOL. See DENTISTRY (Careers).
DENTIFRICE. See TOOTH PASTE; TEETH (Daily Care).
DENTIN. See TEETH (picture, The Parts of a Tooth).

DENTISTRY is the art and science of treating diseases of the teeth and of other parts of the mouth. Dentists help to keep people healthy in many ways. They correct deformities of the teeth and mouth. Some specialize in making replacements for teeth and other parts of the mouth. They prescribe medicines and may perform operations on the mouth and jaws.

Fields in Dentistry

General Dental Practice includes mouth examination, diagnosis, treatment planning, treatment, and prevention of disease. The dentist frequently uses X rays and other equipment to insure correct diagnosis and treatment planning. Treatment may include filling cavities, removing the nerves of teeth, treating diseases of the gums, removing teeth, and replacing lost teeth with *bridges* and *dentures*, or dental plates. Anesthesia is often used in removing teeth as well as in any other treatment that would be painful without it. Teeth may be filled with gold, silver, amalgam, or cements, and with fused porcelain inlays. General dentists treat diseases of the mouth and gums such as trench mouth and pyorrhea. Perhaps one of the most important parts of a dentist's work is preventive dentistry. If a dentist examines a patient's teeth at regular intervals, he may find and treat a disease before it becomes serious.

Oral Surgery includes treating diseases, injuries, and deformities of the mouth and teeth by surgery. Broken jaws, injuries caused by automobile accidents, and harelips are among the conditions treated by the oral surgeon. He removes tumors from the mouth. He also extracts teeth, including impacted wisdom teeth, which might prove too difficult for the general dentist.

Orthodontics is concerned with deformities that develop during the growth of the teeth and jaws. Such malformations often cause teeth to be crowded and irregularly placed. This results in *malocclusion*, or "bad bite." These deformities detract from personal appearance, tend to make the teeth decay more readily, and often make chewing difficult. The orthodontist corrects these conditions by mechanical devices such as braces, and by other means which stimulate the growth of bones and bring teeth into a correct position in the mouth. Orthodontic treatment is sometimes put off until the child has grown the second, or permanent, set of teeth. See ORTHODONTICS.

Prosthodontics is the branch of dentistry that specializes in replacing lost teeth. The three most common ways of replacing lost teeth are by *bridgework*, which replaces one or more missing teeth; *partial dentures*,

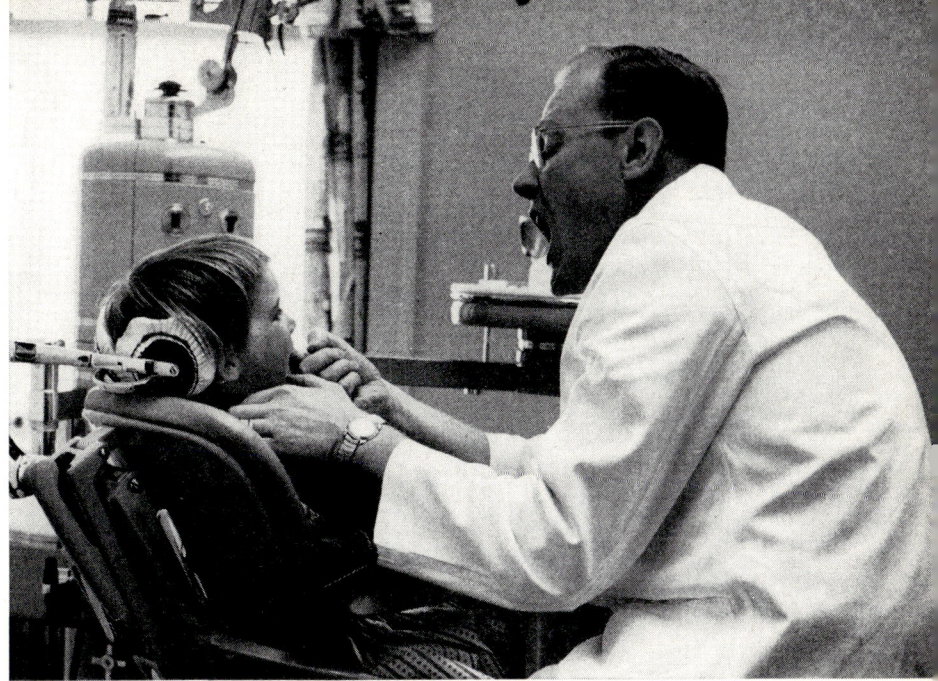

A Visit to the Dentist becomes an interesting adventure to a child. Periodic trips to a dentist should begin when a child's first set of teeth have come in, and should continue throughout a person's life.

Dorothy Reed

which replace several lost teeth; and *full dentures*, or plates, which are used when all the teeth in either jaw or both jaws are missing. The development of plastics and the use of various alloys have changed many of the methods of prosthodontics and improved the function and appearance of artificial teeth.

Periodontics is concerned with treating the gums and the parts of the jaws that support the teeth. More teeth are extracted during adult life because of the periodontal disease *pyorrhea* than for all other reasons combined (see PYORRHEA). Periodontal diseases destroy gum tissue and the supporting bone around the teeth. Once these tissues are destroyed, they cannot be restored. But usually dentists can prevent further destruction through proper treatment.

Pedodontics concentrates on the prevention and treatment of dental disease in children. Tooth decay is common during childhood. The pedodontist pays special attention to the diet of children, especially limiting the use of refined sugars.

Other Fields of dentistry are *public health dentistry*, which promotes dental health, and *oral pathology*, which deals with tumors and injuries of the mouth.

History of Dentistry

No one knows exactly when dentistry began, but it certainly is as old as any of the branches of science that treat disease. Prehistoric man used both magic and medicine to treat pain, including that caused by teeth. After writing was invented, both the Egyptians and the Babylonians recorded their methods of treatment.

Greek medical texts written in the 500's and 600's B.C. contain references to teething difficulties, oral symptoms found in such diseases as malaria, and to "pincers for pulling out teeth." But the first gold dental bridges are older than the Greek texts. These bridges, which show a high degree of technical skill, have been found in the ruins of the Etruscan civilization in Italy.

Dentistry developed slowly. During the Middle Ages

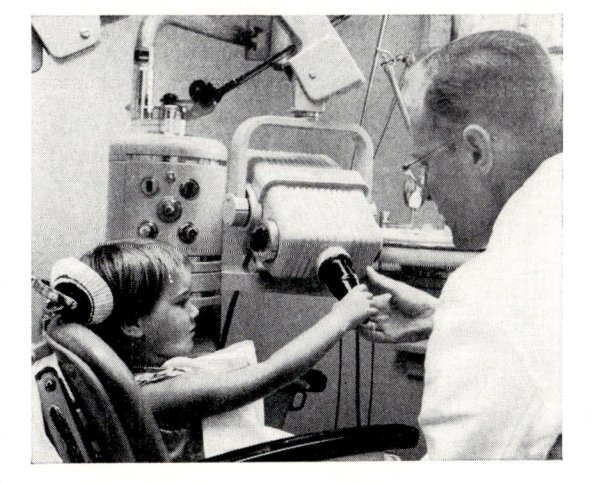

The X-Ray Machine, *above*, is important to the dentist. It works like a camera and takes pictures of the insides of the teeth. X-ray pictures are studied through a special viewer, *below*.

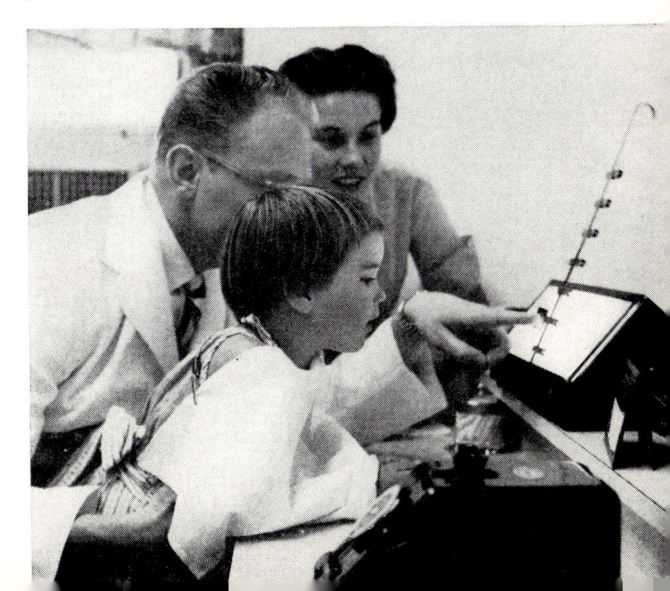

120a

DENTISTRY

barbers served as doctors and dentists. Jewelers and other craftsmen made dentures. It was not until 1840 that dentistry became a profession. In that year the first dental school was organized in Baltimore.

Since 1840, dentistry has made important progress in the United States. Josiah Flagg of Boston was the first native-born American dentist. He began practicing after his discharge from the army in 1783. Flagg was one of the first to use gold foil in filling teeth. The discovery of the X ray in 1895 gave dentistry a way of looking inside teeth to discover their defects. In 1910 Sir William Hunter and Sir Kenneth Goodby of England pointed out that infected teeth could cause infection to spread throughout the entire body.

The discovery of anesthesia was one of the most important forward steps in the history of dentistry. On Dec. 11, 1844, Dr. Horace Wells (1815-1848), a dentist, took laughing gas before having a tooth extracted. The tooth was pulled without pain. Laughing gas, or nitrous oxide, combined with oxygen, is still used to make tooth extraction painless.

Two years after Wells' discovery, William Morton, also a dentist, gave a public demonstration of the use of ether as an anesthetic during a surgical operation. See MORTON, WILLIAM THOMAS GREEN.

Quieter, faster drilling equipment, aimed at taking discomfort out of drilling, was developed in the 1950's. These drills worked at such high speeds that they reduced pain caused by heat and pressure.

Careers in Dentistry

Because tooth decay is the most common disease of man, the field of dentistry is constantly expanding as the population grows. There are about 100,000 licensed dentists in the United States. About 89,000 engage in active practice. Ten thousand work in dental education and research, dental public health, or for other dentists' organizations. Dentistry ranks as one of the highest paid professions in the United States.

In Canada, dentistry also ranks as one of the best-paid professions. There are about 5,800 dentists in Canada. They must meet the same personal and professional qualifications as dentists in the United States. They must also pass examinations given by a board of examiners in their provinces before they receive a license to practice.

Many women make good dentists. In the United States, women make up only about 1 per cent of the dental profession. But in certain countries in Europe, Asia, and South America, they constitute about 80 per cent of the profession.

Personal Requirements. Dentistry requires manual skills and a high level of intelligence. All dental schools participate in an aptitude testing program. On the basis of these tests, dental educators can predict quite accurately whether a prospective student will successfully complete dental training.

Educational Requirements. Every student preparing to enter a dental school must have at least two years

FILLING A CAVITY

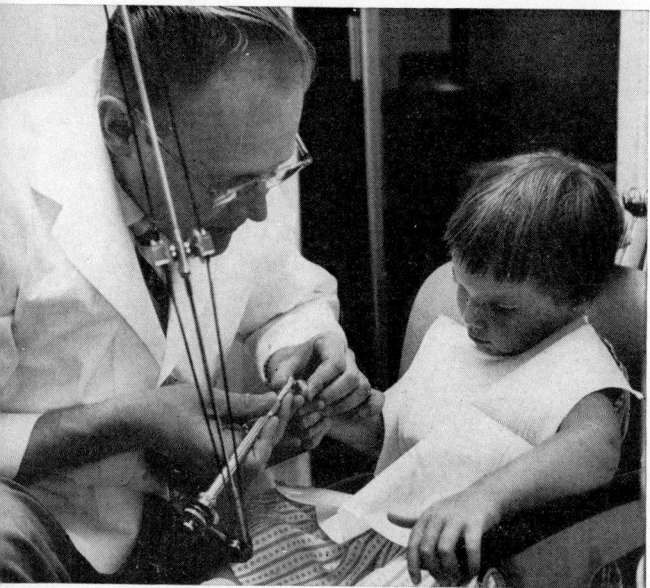

Dorothy Reed

The Dentist's Drill has many uses. The dentist explains to a young patient that a buffer attachment helps clean teeth.

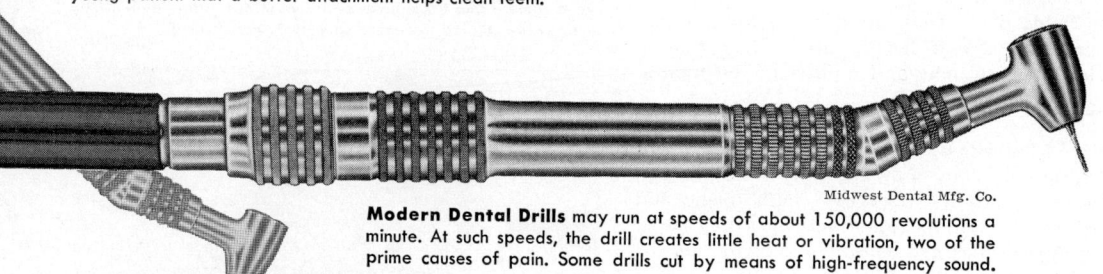

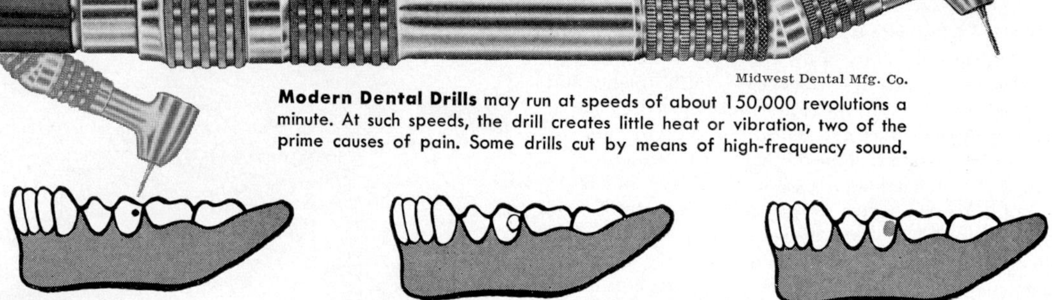

Midwest Dental Mfg. Co.

Modern Dental Drills may run at speeds of about 150,000 revolutions a minute. At such speeds, the drill creates little heat or vibration, two of the prime causes of pain. Some drills cut by means of high-frequency sound.

Filling a Cavity requires much skill. The dentist attaches a dental *bur*, or cutting tool, to the drill head. The bur cuts away the decayed part, *left*. After the decay is removed, *center*, the dentist fills the tooth by pressing gold, silver, or amalgams into the hole. He smooths the surface to remove rough spots and makes sure the finished filling, *right*, matches the shape of the tooth.

120b

ACCREDITED DENTAL SCHOOLS

U.S. SCHOOLS

ALABAMA	Univ. of Alabama	Birmingham
CALIFORNIA	Coll. of Physicians and Surgeons	San Francisco
	Univ. of California	San Francisco
	Univ. of Southern California	Los Angeles
	Loma Linda Univ.	Loma Linda
DISTRICT OF COLUMBIA	Georgetown Univ.	Washington
	Howard Univ.	Washington
GEORGIA	Emory Univ.	Atlanta
ILLINOIS	Loyola Univ.	Chicago
	Northwestern Univ.	Chicago
	Univ. of Illinois	Chicago
INDIANA	Indiana Univ.	Indianapolis
IOWA	State Univ. of Iowa	Iowa City
KENTUCKY	Univ. of Louisville	Louisville
LOUISIANA	Loyola Univ.	New Orleans
MARYLAND	Univ. of Maryland	Baltimore
MASSACHUSETTS	Harvard School of Dental Medicine	Boston
	Tufts Univ.	Boston
MICHIGAN	Univ. of Detroit	Detroit
	Univ. of Michigan	Ann Arbor
MINNESOTA	Univ. of Minnesota	Minneapolis
MISSOURI	Univ. of Kansas City	Kansas City
	St. Louis Univ.	St. Louis
	Washington Univ.	St. Louis
NEBRASKA	Creighton Univ.	Omaha
	Univ. of Nebraska	Lincoln

U.S. SCHOOLS

NEW JERSEY	Fairleigh Dickinson Univ.	Teaneck
	Seton Hall Univ.	Jersey City
NEW YORK	Columbia Univ.	New York
	New York Univ.	New York
	Univ. of Buffalo	Buffalo
NORTH CAROLINA	Univ. of North Carolina	Chapel Hill
OHIO	Ohio State Univ.	Columbus
	Western Reserve Univ.	Cleveland
OREGON	Univ. of Oregon	Portland
PENNSYLVANIA	Temple Univ.	Philadelphia
	Univ. of Pennsylvania	Philadelphia
	Univ. of Pittsburgh	Pittsburgh
TENNESSEE	Meharry Medical Coll.	Nashville
	Univ. of Tennessee	Memphis
TEXAS	Baylor Univ.	Dallas
	Univ. of Texas	Houston
VIRGINIA	Medical Coll. of Virginia	Richmond
WASHINGTON	Univ. of Washington	Seattle
WEST VIRGINIA	West Virginia Univ.	Morgantown
WISCONSIN	Marquette Univ.	Milwaukee
PUERTO RICO	Univ. of Puerto Rico	San Juan

CANADIAN SCHOOLS

ALBERTA	Univ. of Alberta	Edmonton
MANITOBA	Univ. of Manitoba	Winnipeg
NOVA SCOTIA	Dalhousie Univ.	Halifax
ONTARIO	Univ. of Toronto	Toronto
QUEBEC	McGill Univ.	Montreal
	Université de Montréal	Montreal

of college education. Professional education requires another four years of study at an accredited dental school.

The students in a dental school concentrate on three main areas of study: (1) academic, (2) dental sciences, and (3) professional matters. *Academic* work emphasizes the basic sciences. The study of *dental sciences* allows each student to learn and develop actual skills he needs to practice dentistry. The study of *professional matters* includes courses in the history of dentistry, management of a practice, professional ethics, and the legal aspects of dentistry. Students who successfully complete all these courses are awarded a degree of D.D.S. (Doctor of Dental Surgery), or D.M.D. (Doctor of Dental Medicine).

Postgraduate courses are offered for dentists who want to specialize, teach, or enter research, and for those who want to keep up with advances in dentistry.

Licensing. All states and Canadian provinces require that a dentist be licensed before he can practice. Applicants must be graduates of a school approved by the Council on Dental Education of the American Dental Association, or, in Canada, the Canadian Dental Association. Each must pass an examination given by a board of examiners. Most licenses allow dentists to practice as either general practitioners or specialists. But nine states require additional examinations for specialists. Few states allow a dentist from another state to begin practice without taking another examination.

Organizations. The professional organization of dentists in the United States is the American Dental Association (see DENTAL ASSOCIATION, AMERICAN). In Canada, it is the Canadian Dental Association, which maintains headquarters at 234 St. George St., Toronto 5, Ont.

ROBERT G. KESEL

See also TEETH; ORTHODONTICS; PROSTHETICS; HYPNOTISM (picture).

A DENTAL BRIDGE

After a tooth has been pulled, the dentist may fill the space with a *bridge*, or false tooth. He prepares the teeth on each side to hold plates that will keep the new tooth in place.

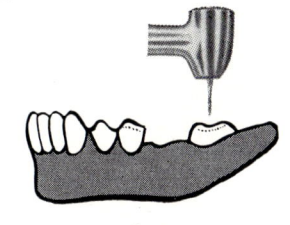

The dentist makes the new tooth the same shape as the one that was pulled. He fastens a plate in the false tooth. He puts the bridge in place, with a plate capping the teeth on each side.

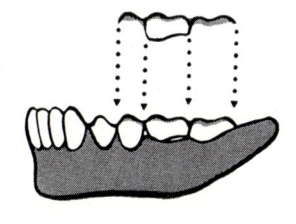

D'ENTRECASTEAUX ISLANDS

D'ENTRECASTEAUX ISLANDS, *DAHN truh KAHS TOH,* lie in the Pacific Ocean, north of the eastern tip of New Guinea. Three large islands (Goodenough, Fergusson, and Normanby) and more than a dozen small ones have a total land area of 945 square miles. For location, see AUSTRALIA (inset on color map). The islands are mountainous, some reaching 8,000 feet, and covered with forests. They have excellent harbors. Evidence of their volcanic origin is seen in extinct craters, geysers, and hot springs on Fergusson Island. The islands are governed as part of the Australian Territory of Papua. The 40,000 inhabitants of the islands are Melanesians. The island group is named for Bruni d'Entrecasteaux, a French explorer of the late 1700's. Allied military forces were based there during World War II. See also NEW GUINEA. EDWIN H. BRYAN, JR.

DENVER, Colo. (pop. 493,887; alt. 5,280 ft.), is the capital of Colorado, and one of the leading distribution and wholesale centers of the West. It ranks as one of the largest cities between Kansas City and the West Coast, and is widely known for its dry and healthful climate. Denver is often called the *Mile High City,* because the state Capitol stands on land that is one mile above sea level.

Location, Size, and Description. Denver lies almost in the center of Colorado, 10 miles east of the Rocky Mountains. It has an area of about 66 square miles. The South Platte River winds its way through the business district of the city. Many government buildings, parks, fountains, and monuments add beauty to the city. The Capitol dome, plated with gold leaf worth more than $14,000, towers above the gray-granite Capitol in the heart of Denver. It is a symbol of the city's history as a mining town. For location, see COLORADO (color map).

Cultural Life. Denver has more than 90 elementary and high schools and an evening vocational school. The Emily Griffith Opportunity School offers vocational training to adults of all ages. The city is the home of the University of Denver, Regis College, Westminster Law School, Colorado Woman's College, Iliff School of Theology, and University of Colorado medical school.

The Denver Public Library circulates more than 400,000 books every year. The Denver Museum of Natural History has excellent displays of prehistoric animals, minerals, and plant life. Other museums include the Colorado State Historical Museum and the Denver Art Museum. The Denver Symphony Orchestra plays an annual concert schedule. Summer concerts are held at the beautiful outdoor Theater of the Red Rocks.

Recreation. Many tourists visit Denver every year. The city has many parks, tennis courts, playgrounds, bathing beaches, and golf courses. It operates a chain of over 20 mountain parks that cover more than 32 square miles in the Rocky Mountains. Highways wind through the mountains to these parks. These parks have facilities for picnicking and camping. The highest automobile road in the United States leads to the peak of nearby Mount Evans, 14,264 feet high. The Cosmic Ray Laboratory of the University of Denver stands on top of the mountain.

Industry and Commerce. Denver is a distribution and wholesale center, serving about one quarter of the United States. The city also serves as the industrial and financial center of the Rocky Mountain region. The Denver Union Stockyards is one of the most important meat-handling centers in the country. Denver has one of the country's largest sheep markets. The city's leading industries include flour and grain milling, meat packing, the manufacture of mining equipment, printing and publishing, and rubber manufacturing. Shwayder Brothers, one of the largest luggage manufacturers in the world, has its factory in Denver.

The city is also the national or regional headquarters of more than 200 government agencies. The Denver mint produces millions of coins of various denominations every year. Nearby military installations include Lowry Air Force Base, Fort Logan, and Fitzsimons Army Hospital.

In the early 1900's, many people came to Denver to receive medical treatment for tuberculosis. The city is still a center of medical research and treatment.

Transportation. Seven major railroads serve the city. Six leading airlines provide air transportation at nearby Stapleton Airfield. Modern highways carry much bus, automobile, and truck traffic to Denver.

Government. In 1902, Denver led a home-rule movement among the cities of Colorado. A constitutional amendment resulting from this movement made Denver both a city and a county. The amendment allows the people to adopt laws that have force above most state laws within the city limits. Denver has a mayor-council form of government.

History. Denver was founded during the Pikes Peak gold rush of 1858, after prospectors found gold at Cherry Creek in what is now the Denver area. The settlement was named in honor of James W. Denver, then territorial governor of Kansas. Denver and a neighboring community, Auraria, consolidated on April 3, 1860. Denver was incorporated as a city in 1861 by the first Colorado Territorial Assembly. In 1881, the people of Colorado passed a constitutional amendment that made the city of Denver the permanent capital of the state.

HAROLD H. DUNHAM

Denver *Post*

Santa Fe Railway

Denver's City and County Building is shown from the door of the Colorado State Capitol. Thirty-five of Denver's leading architects combined to design the City and County Building. It houses many public offices. The sidewalks, grass, and trees in the foreground form what is known as the Civic Center.

Downtown Denver stands out against a background of snow-capped mountains. The City and County Building, *left foreground*, and the Colorado State Capitol Building, *right foreground*, are at the two ends of the Civic Center. Denver is sometimes called "the Western Capital," because it has headquarters of more than 200 federal agencies, including a mint which makes coins.

DENVER, UNIVERSITY OF

DENVER, UNIVERSITY OF, is a privately endowed coeducational school at Denver, Colo. It has colleges of arts and sciences, business administration, engineering, law, and graduate studies. It also has schools of art, communication arts, education, hotel and restaurant management, librarianship, music, nursing, public administration, social work, and speech. Its research activities include the Denver Research Institute, and the Bureau of Business and Social Research, the Bureau of Educational Research, and the Social Science Foundation. School colors are crimson and gold. The university was founded in 1864. For enrollment, see UNIVERSITIES AND COLLEGES (table). CHESTER M. ALTER

DEODAR. See CEDAR.

DEODORIZER is a substance that removes bad odors or changes them to pleasant ones. Odors can be a real problem in homes, factories, and hospitals.

Odors are carried by particles in the air. Many deodorizers therefore work by attacking odors in the air. Some are chemicals that react with the particles. Potassium permanganate, hypochlorous acid, and ozone destroy odors by a reaction called *oxidation*. Borax and lime *neutralize* unpleasant acid odors. Porous materials like charcoal and silica gel will collect vapors on their surface. They are said to *adsorb* the vapors.

Bad air is sometimes forced through a liquid such as water, alcohol, glycerin, or mineral oil. The particles in the air dissolve in the liquid. This is called *scrubbing* the air. Electricity can be used to remove dust that is carrying odors (see AIR CLEANER). Some deodorizers mask an offensive odor with a pleasant or perfumed one that is stronger. This method is called *reodorization*.

Some disinfectants deodorize at the same time they disinfect (see DISINFECTANT). They remove unpleasant odors formed by living things in the air, such as bacteria, molds, or fungi. Phenol and formaldehyde are often used in this way. Formaldehyde also combines with other chemicals to form new, odorless substances. Hydrated lime is a cheap disinfectant used for outhouses and stables. Chlorinated lime, called *bleaching powder*, and sodium hypochlorite also act as deodorizers. Phenol, creosote, and carbolic acid are disinfectants made from coal tar, and are used in barns, pens, and stables.

Deodorizers, often called *deodorants*, are also made for use on the body. Deodorizers applied to the body may mask the odor of perspiration. Creams made of petrolatum act by absorbing the odor. Other creams and powders contain a chemical such as aluminum chloride, which stops the perspiration for a time. These are not strictly deodorizers, a more correct name being *antiperspirants*. Liquid deodorizers may contain formaldehyde or vinegar. Deodorizers are also made in the form of solid sticks and aerosol sprays. Some body and breath deodorizers contain *chlorophyllins*, which are derivatives of chlorophyll, the green coloring matter of plants. GEORGE L. BUSH

DE OÑATE, JUAN. See OÑATE, JUAN DE.

DE PALMA, *duh PAHL muh,* **RALPH** (1883-1956), was a pioneer American automobile race driver. He won the Indianapolis Speedway 500-mile race in 1915 and the national driving title in 1912 and 1914. De Palma set a world record of 149.875 mph in 1919. He claimed 2,557 victories in 2,889 races. Many of these were match races against another driver, rather than open competition. De Palma was born in Italy and began racing on a bicycle in the 1890's. FRED RUSSELL

DEPARTMENT is the largest administrative and territorial subdivision of France. It corresponds somewhat to a state in the United States or to a province in Canada. At the time of the French Revolution, the existing subdivisions, the old provinces, were abolished. The National Assembly created the new areas in February, 1790. They were based on population, area, and amount of taxes paid. Geographical features gave each department its name.

There are 90 departments within France. Algeria and such French possessions as Martinique also have departmental government.

At first, the departments were largely self-governing and officials were elected. But the administration became highly centralized under Napoleon. A *prefect* is now in charge of each department. Departments are divided into *arrondissements*, each under a *subprefect*. The central government appoints these officials. There are also electoral districts in each arrondissement called *cantons*. *Communes* are the smallest administrative units in the French government. ROBERT B. HOLTMAN

See also ARRONDISSEMENT; CANTON; COMMUNE; FRANCE (Government); NAPOLEON I (Crowned Emperor).

DEPARTMENT STORE is a store which sells many different kinds of goods, each arranged in a separate department. Modern department stores serve the needs of entire families. People enjoy shopping in such stores because they can make all their purchases under one roof. Department stores depend on many customers in order to exist. Therefore, companies usually open them in large cities. Some companies open chain stores in different cities (see CHAIN STORE). Many department

Department Store Economist

A Department Store sells articles of almost every kind, including dry goods, clothing, hardware, furniture, sporting goods, and food. Some department stores even sell airplanes and houses.

stores have branch stores in large suburban communities.

Arrangement of a Department Store. The typical department store occupies one large building, with separate departments located on a number of floors. Small articles, which people often request, are usually placed on the first floor. The stores often sell less expensive grades of merchandise in the basement. Sometimes stores have several levels of sub-basement sales floors. A number provide special services, such as that of a shopping adviser. Others have sewing centers where women learn to cut, fit, and sew clothing. Some department stores hold special exhibitions to attract new customers.

Department stores employ hundreds of people for different jobs. Many employees, under the merchandise manager, buy, price, and sell the goods. The sales promotion manager and his staff promote the sale of merchandise through advertising and other techniques. The comptroller heads the section that keeps records and manages store financial affairs. The personnel staff hires employees and handles other employment problems.

Origin of the Department Store. Since the early 1800's, stores that handle a variety of merchandise have existed in the United States. These *general* stores still operate in many small towns. After 1870, several large American stores began to offer different types of merchandise arranged in separate departments.

Today, department stores can be found in almost every American city. Among the best-known department stores in the United States are Marshall Field (Chicago), R. H. Macy (New York City), I. Magnin (San Francisco), Nieman-Marcus (Dallas), and John Wanamaker (Philadelphia). In addition, several mail-order companies also operate department stores (see MAIL-ORDER BUSINESS). Department stores in the United States sell more than $12,700,000,000 worth of merchandise every year. FRED M. JONES

See also WINDOW DISPLAY.

DE PAUL UNIVERSITY is a coeducational school in Chicago. It is controlled by the Vincentian Fathers of the Roman Catholic Church. It accepts students of all denominations in its day and evening classes. The university has a graduate school, and colleges of liberal arts and sciences, law, commerce, and music. It grants B.A., B.S., B.Mus., LL.B., and master's degrees. Schools of nursing are affiliated with the university. De Paul has an army ROTC unit. The school's colors are red and blue. Its athletic teams are called the Demons. De Paul was founded in 1898. For enrollment, see UNIVERSITIES AND COLLEGES (table). LAWRENCE A. RAGAN

DEPAUW UNIVERSITY is a coeducational school at Greencastle, Ind., founded by the Methodist Church. DePauw has a liberal arts college and schools of music and nursing.

It grants B.A., B.Mus., B.S. in nursing degrees, and M.A. degrees. It has an Air Force ROTC unit. The school color is old gold. The Rector Scholarship Foundation annually provides tuition for several hundred men students. It was established in 1919 by the largest single scholarship grant given to any American undergraduate institution. The university was founded in 1837 as Indiana Asbury, so named in honor of Francis Asbury, a pioneer Methodist bishop. The name was changed in 1883 to honor Washington C. DePauw

(1822-1887), an American manufacturer who established an endowment for the school. For enrollment, see UNIVERSITIES AND COLLEGES (table). FREDRICK L. BERGMANN

DEPEW, CHAUNCEY MITCHELL (1834-1928), was an American lawyer and statesman. He served as a Republican U.S. Senator from New York from 1899 to 1911. Depew gained renown as a corporation lawyer. His main clients were railroads. He served as president of the New York Central Railroad from 1885 to 1899. Depew was born in Peekskill, N.Y., and was graduated from Yale College. Depew became well known for his witty after-dinner speeches, and spoke at many public and private banquets. H. G. REUSCHLEIN

DEPILATORY. See HAIR (Excess Hair).

DEPORTATION is the action a government takes when it forces an alien to leave the country and return to the place where he was born or had lived. It may deport him because he entered the country illegally, or because it is believed that he may harm the nation's interests in some way.

In the United States, the attorney general has the power to deport aliens as part of his responsibility to enforce immigration laws. Aliens may be deported if they become public charges, stay longer than their visas permit, or engage in subversive or criminal activities. A naturalized citizen who loses his citizenship may be deported by the Department of Justice.

Deportation also means banishing, or sending a convict to a penal settlement outside the country as punishment for a crime. ROBERT RIENOW

DEPOSIT, in banking. See BANKS AND BANKING (How Banks Receive and Lend Money).

DEPOSIT, in geology. See ROCK (Sedimentary Rock).

DEPOSIT INSURANCE CORPORATION. See FEDERAL DEPOSIT INSURANCE CORPORATION.

DEPOSITION. See GEOLOGY (Some Terms).

DEPOSITION, DEP oh ZISH un, in law, is the testimony of a witness who is unable to appear in court. The witness testifies under oath before a judicial officer. He makes a statement in answer to questions, either oral or written, asked by the officer. The second party in a lawsuit must also have a chance to question the witness. A deposition differs from an *affidavit*, which is a one-sided statement given voluntarily under oath (see AFFIDAVIT). THOMAS A. COWAN

DEPOT is a storehouse or a transportation station such as a bus or railroad depot. See also ARSENAL.

DEPRECIATION, dee PREE she AY shun, is the loss of value. Buildings, machines, vehicles, and other property *depreciate* (lose value) through use or accident, because they grow older, or because a new, better product replaces them. In accounting, depreciation is figured as a normal cost of doing business. The term *depreciation* is also used to mean the loss of value or purchasing power of money.

DEPRESSANT is a substance that slows the activity of the nervous system. It slows other functions of the body as well. Alcohol, often thought of as a stimulant, is actually a depressant. Many drugs, such as *ataractics* (tranquilizers), calm upset people without causing mental depression. Other depressants include anesthetics, anticonvulsants, sedatives, hypnotics, and soporifics. See also SEDATIVE; TRANQUILIZER. WALTER MODELL

125

U. S. DEPRESSIONS AND

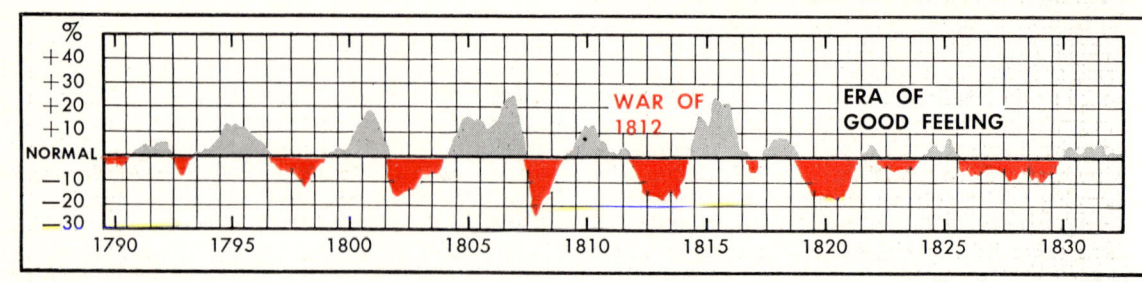

Business Activity in the United States has gone through many periods of prosperity and many periods of depression. These graphs show the average ups and downs of the economy as a whole, but do not attempt to show its overall expansion.

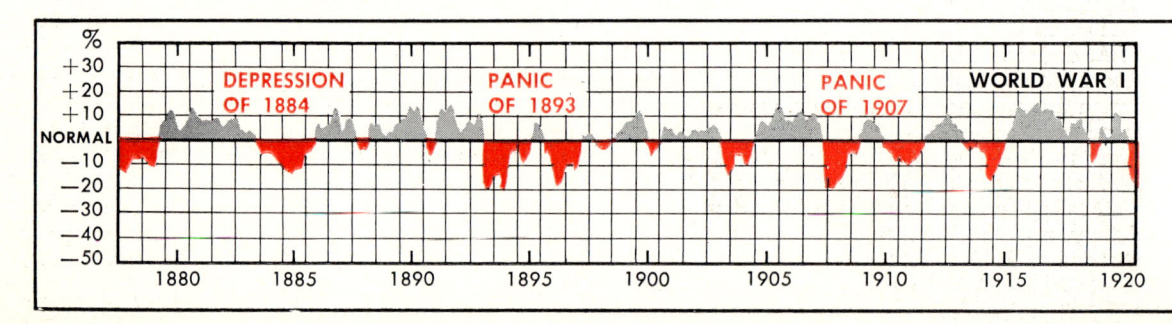

DEPRESSION is a condition in economic life in which a great many men have no work, machines stand idle, and the general level of economic activity is low, or *depressed*. A depression is the low part of the business cycle, or the opposite of *prosperity*. The *business cycle* refers to the waves of good and bad times that have plagued modern, industrialized economics.

The Seriousness of the Problem. Depression may well be the most serious problem facing our free enterprise economic system (see FREE ENTERPRISE SYSTEM). During a depression, people often follow any man who promises a change—the socialist, the communist, the fascist, or the crackpot with an impossible scheme to cure all the ills of society. Frequent depressions could be a danger to our way of life.

To one man, depression means standing in bread lines or walking the streets looking for work. To another, it means business failure and the necessity for a new start. To still another, it means the loss of his life's savings in a bank failure. To the nation, it means economic paralysis. To the world, it usually means a breakdown of friendly trade relations, as each nation tries to solve its own problems at the expense of other nations. In extreme cases, depression may set in motion the forces that lead to war. The effect of depression on Germany in the early 1930's made the German people more willing to follow Adolf Hitler into World War II as a fancied "cure" for their economic ills.

What Can Be Done to Avoid Depressions. In spite of the importance of the problem, economists cannot agree on what causes depression, or how to prevent it. A modern, highly industrialized economy is a very complex machine. When it breaks down, the causes of the trouble are difficult to identify. Each expert has his own diagnosis, and each diagnosis suggests a different cure. Some of the more widely-accepted explanations of the business cycle, and of the remedies associated with each explanation, are discussed below.

Underconsumption or Over-Saving Theories. Some men insist that depressions come because people spend too little of their incomes, which is the same as saying that they save too much. These men say such a practice leads to a lower demand for goods and services, and to unemployment. *The remedy they suggest:* redistribute income from the rich, who have high rates of saving, to the poor, who can be depended on to spend most of the dollars they receive. High taxes on the rich, to pay for a dole to the poor, would accomplish this.

Saving-Investment Theories. Another version of the theory presented above says depressions are caused by changes in the amount of spending for *capital goods*, such as tools, machinery, and buildings, which are used for producing other goods. Such spending is called *investment*. When people invest, they put their savings back into circulation. If there are not enough investment opportunities for all the dollars saved, the extra dollars do not get back into circulation. People hoard them. Hoarding reduces the number of dollars being spent for goods and services, and, in this way, leads to depression and unemployment.

Remedies the theorists suggest: (a) reduce the number of dollars saved, for instance, by redistributing income; and (b) increase the number of dollars invested by business firms. Most of the men who support this theory do not believe that these two remedies will be enough. They propose as well (c) that the government offset the hoarded dollars by borrowing money and spending it for such things as relief payments and public works projects. This remedy, and the saving-investment theory itself, is closely associated with the name of the English economist John Maynard Keynes. If it is thought that government spending will get the economy rolling and that deficit spending can then be stopped, proposal (c) is called "pump-priming." The Roosevelt administration acted on this idea in an attempt to lift the United States out of the depression of the 1930's.

PROSPERITY SINCE 1790

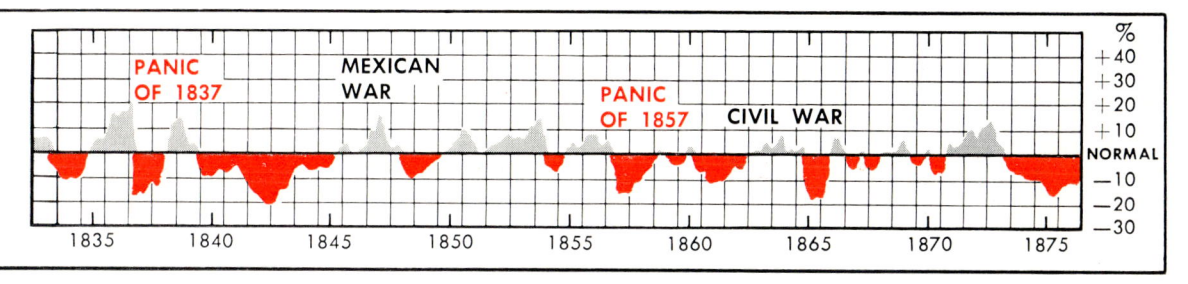

Quantity-of-Money Theories. Other economists argue that "booms" and "busts" are caused by the violent *fluctuations* (changes) in the money supply of the economy, particularly in the supply of check money. Checks are drawn on demand deposits in banks. When the total of demand deposits changes, it is just as if the government had increased or decreased the amount of its own coins and currency in circulation. According to this theory, changes in the total of demand deposits are largely responsible for the business cycle. *The suggested remedy:* control or change the banking system so as to prevent violent fluctuations in the supply of check money.

Price-of-Progress Theories. Some economists believe that the business cycle is the price a modern economy pays for progress, particularly for technological progress. According to this theory, progress never comes about smoothly, but rather by a process of "three steps forward and two backward." The "two backward" take the form of depression. *The suggested remedy:* all that can be done is to soften the effects of the low part of the business cycle. To stop the business cycle would be to stop progress.

Price "Stickiness" Theories. Other economists insist that the business cycle comes because prices and wages are not permitted to move up and down in free response to changes in supply and demand conditions. They argue that in a free market the price would always seek that level which would "clear the market." No goods would ever be unsold and no workers would ever be unemployed. Unemployment comes, they say, because markets are not free. *The proposed remedy:* restore free markets by curbing the activities of monopolists, trade unions, and all other groups which prevent the free movement of prices and wages.

Other Explanations. Some people say the business cycle is caused by changes in the *direction*, as distinguished from the *amount*, of spending. Others blame variations in farm crops, psychological waves of optimism and pessimism, and even sunspots.

The Outlook for the Future. The great number of explanations and remedies might seem to mean that nothing can be done about depressions. But most economists agree on the steps that should be taken to prevent a severe depression such as the one that occurred in the United States during the 1930's.

Most economists feel that in order to avoid serious depressions we must avoid extremes in the economic system during the prosperity periods. This usually means (1) that the quantity of check money should not be permitted to increase in a runaway fashion during prosperity; and (2) that the price-fixing activities of monopoly groups should be curbed to avoid upsetting the *price structure*, or the relationships among the prices for different types of goods.

Most economists—but certainly not all—agree that a depression can be held within reasonable limits by the use of government deficit spending to offset a drop in private spending, at least partially. How soon the government should do this and how far it should go are still hotly disputed questions. Actually, certain features of our present economic system automatically produce government deficits during a depression. The social security system, including unemployment insurance, and the income-tax system both are set up so that government revenues fall off while government expenditures increase as a depression gets under way. These are called *built-in stabilizers*. Finally, there is now general agreement that the government must provide all citizens with basic necessities during a depression.

Many economists hesitate to recommend stronger action than that outlined. They fear that a stronger remedy might "cure the disease but kill the patient" (the free enterprise system). They fear also that severe remedies might bring other serious problems such as continuous inflation or slower economic progress (see INFLATION AND DEFLATION). BENJAMIN A. ROGGE

Critically reviewed by JAMES WASHINGTON BELL

See also HOOVER, HERBERT CLARK (The Great Depression); ROOSEVELT, FRANKLIN DELANO (Roosevelt's First Administration); UNEMPLOYMENT; UNITED STATES, HISTORY OF (The Great Depression).

Adapted courtesy The Cleveland Trust Co.

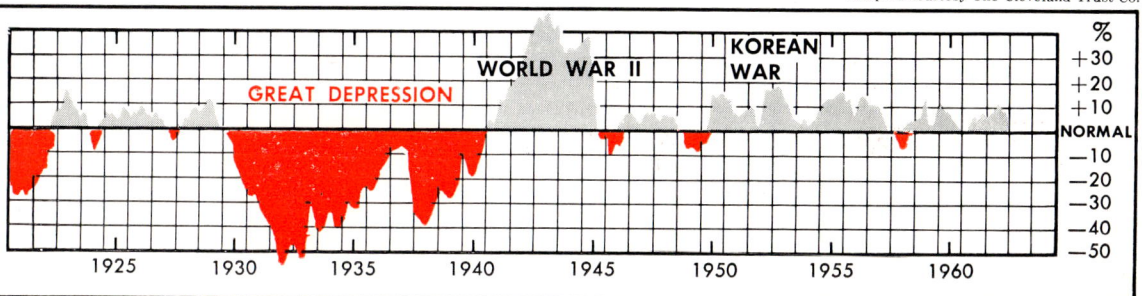

A Coast Guard Cutter Drops a Depth Charge in its hunt for enemy submarines in the Atlantic Ocean during World War II.

DEPTH CHARGE is a weapon designed to destroy submarines. It acts by exploding under water and creating a shock wave of tremendous pressure which will cause the submarine to collapse.

Depth charges during World War II consisted of light metal cases filled with an explosive such as TNT. Sailors called depth charges *ash cans* because they were about the size and shape of ordinary ash cans. Destroyers usually laid a pattern of charges over a submarine, rolling some off the deck and firing others out to the side.

In 1957, the United States Navy announced the development of atomic depth charges, to be dropped by antisubmarine planes. These consist of a core of fissionable material surrounded by heavy casing (see FISSION [Nuclear]). The weapon has a mechanical time device to control its firing time and can be preset to explode at varying depths. The atomic depth charge eliminates the need for knowing the exact location of a submarine in the depths of the ocean. It can destroy a target within a square mile of ocean and is particularly effective against submarines located at great depths. PAUL D. STROOP

The *Lulu* is the U.S. Navy's atomic depth charge.

DEPTH FINDER. See FATHOMETER; SONAR.
DEPTH PERCEPTION. See EYE (Stereoscopic Vision).
DEPTHS. See DEEP; EARTH (picture, Heights and Depths).
DE QUINCEY, *deh KWIN sih,* **THOMAS** (1785-1859), was a British essayist. His famous work, *Confessions of an English Opium-Eater*, is a masterpiece of imaginative, rhythmical prose.

De Quincey was born on Aug. 15, 1785, in Manchester, England. He attended grammar schools there and at Bath, but was so unhappy that he ran away. He spent several months in the hills of Wales and in London before his family found him, half-starved. He attended Worcester College, Oxford, for five years. While he was in college, he started to take opium to relieve neuralgia pains, and he was never able to break the drug habit.

De Quincey settled in the Lake country, near William Wordsworth, Samuel Taylor Coleridge, and Robert Southey, in 1809. He moved to London in 1820, and to Edinburgh in 1828. There he wrote for *Blackwood's* Magazine. His best-known essays include "On Murder Considered as One of the Fine Arts," "On the Knocking at the Gate in *Macbeth*," "The English Mail Coach," and "Suspiria." G. E. BENTLEY

Thomas De Quincey

DERBY, *DUR bih,* or (British) *DAHR bih,* is a stiff felt hat with a dome-shaped crown. The British usually call it a *bowler*. The name derby may come from England. The Earl of Derby, who established the Derby horse races at Epsom in 1780, often wore such hats. They were popular among men who attended the races. Derbies were first made in the U.S. in 1850 at South Norwalk, Conn. See also HAT (Felt Hats). WARREN S. SMITH

DERBY, *DAHR bih,* is a famous horse race begun in 1780 by the Earl of Derby at Epsom, England. The race, called "Epsom's Derby" in England, is known as "the English Derby" in other countries. The horse race at Churchill Downs, Louisville, Ky., was copied after the Derby (see KENTUCKY DERBY).

DERBY, or **CROWN DERBY** is a famous china made at Derby, England. See PORCELAIN (picture).
DERBY, SOAP BOX. See SOAP BOX DERBY.
DE RESZKE, JEAN and **EDOUARD.** See RESZKE.
DERINGER, HENRY, JR. See PISTOL (Early Pistols).
DERMAPTERA is an order of insects commonly called *earwigs*. These insects have a hard shell that covers their bodies like armor. A pair of strong pincers extends from the end of the abdomen. Scientists believe the insects use these pincers to defend themselves and to kill prey. Dermaptera live in moist places and usually come out only at night. See also EARWIG.

DERMATITIS is an inflammation of the skin that itches or burns. It shows redness, swelling, blisters, oozing, crusting, or scaling. It may be produced by friction, heat, cold, or the sun's rays. However, chemical agents most frequently cause dermatitis. These may be strong poisons that affect anyone's skin, or chemicals that irritate the skin of a person especially sensitive to the chemicals. These chemicals may be found in certain plants, foods, fabrics, dyes, cosmetics, and medications. See also ALLERGY; ECZEMA. MARCUS R. CARO

DERMATOLOGY deals with diseases of the skin. Dermatologists are physicians trained to diagnose and treat these diseases. When a disease of the whole body also affects the skin, dermatologists may help diagnose the disease from clues the affected skin provides. See also DERMATITIS; SKIN.

DERMIS. See SKIN.

128

DERRICK

A Huge Barge Derrick, *right,* raises a 3,000-ton, sunken oil-drilling barge.

Guy Derrick, *below,* has a long boom that can move heavy loads from side to side.

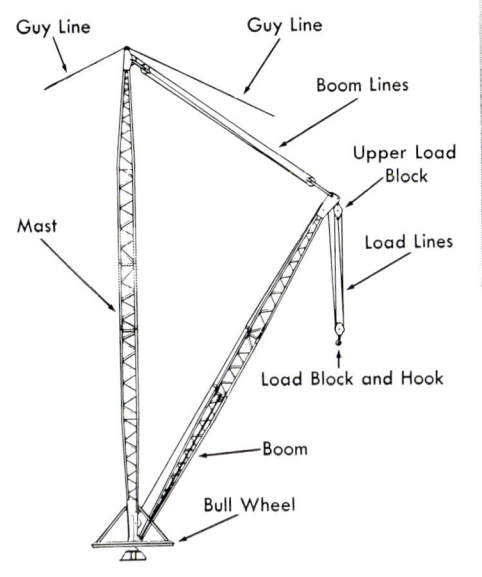

DERRICKS AND CRANES are hoisting machines used to lift and move heavy loads in such places as shipyards, factories, and at construction sites. Most *cranes* can move from place to place under their own power, while most *derricks* are stationary. However, engineers sometimes use either name to describe the same machine.

Derricks. The *gin-pole* is the simplest form of derrick. It has a *mast,* or pole, supported by four *guys,* or cables, staked to the ground. A pulley at the top of the mast supports ropes to lift the weight. The *sheers derrick* has two crossed masts and two guys. Other derricks have a long *boom,* or pole. The boom slants out from the base of the mast and supports the hoisting cable that carries the load. A cable attached to the top of the mast supports the boom. *Oil derricks* are tall steel structures that raise and lower the equipment used to drill an oil well.

Cranes. The *hand-operated jib crane* is the simplest type of crane. It has a long *jib,* or arm, that extends several feet from a heavy base. The base keeps the crane from tipping over. The end of the jib has a pulley. A rope or a cable, with a lifting hook in the end, runs from

American Hoist & Derrick Co.

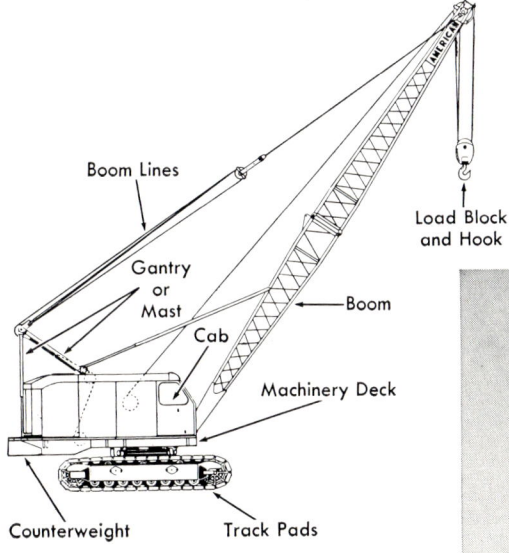

CRANE

Tractor-Mounted Crawler Crane, above, can carry loads from place to place. Track pads allow the crane to travel over rough or muddy ground.

Truck Crane, *right,* lowers a palm tree. The crane operator has controls to move the truck forward and backward.

Self-Propelled Locomotive Cranes can lift weights as heavy as 30 tons. They can also move other railroad cars.

this pulley to a *winch*, or crank, in the foundation. The operator turns the winch to lift or lower the hook. The arm of the crane can be swung in a circle before the weight is lowered. Thus, a jib crane can move a weight to any point around the circumference of the circle its jib makes. The *pillar jib crane* has a pillar rising from its base. A cable attached to the top of the pillar raises and lowers the end of the jib so the jib can be moved up and down as well as from side to side. When the jib moves up, it carries the load toward the base. When lowered, it moves the load away from the base.

Factories and foundries often use *bridge cranes*, sometimes called *overhead traveling cranes*. This type of crane moves back and forth on a bridge extending across the width of a factory room. The bridge travels the length of the room on overhead rails.

Locomotive cranes mounted on self-propelled railroad cars have long, power-operated booms. *Crawler cranes* are mounted on tractors.

Building contractors frequently use *truck cranes* mounted on gasoline-powered trucks. These cranes can be moved from place to place. R. G. HENNES

See also BLOCK AND TACKLE; BUILDING AND WRECKING MACHINES (pictures); PETROLEUM (pictures).

DERRINGER. See PISTOL (Early Pistols; picture).

DERVISH, DUR *vish,* is a term applied to members of various Islamic religious orders. They lead solitary, self-denying lives, beg for alms, and practice religious frenzies. The word *dervish* comes from the Persian, and means *door-seeker,* or *beggar.* Their origin dates back to the earliest days of Islam. Various orders exist with different rituals. Some dervishes repeat certain prayers to Allah. The dancing dervishes whirl and twist. The howling dervishes shriek, cut their bodies, and swallow hot coals and snakes. Some Moslems believe that the dervishes can perform miracles of healing or predict the future. They exercise considerable influence over the lower classes. Kemal Atatürk banned them in Turkey in 1925.

Fanatics similar to dervishes are called *fakirs*. See also DANCING (The Arabs); FAKIR; ISLAM. NABIA ABBOTT

DERWENT, RIVER, is a beautiful stream in west Cumberland County, England. The River Derwent rises in the Cumbrian Mountains and flows for 33 miles through the Cumberland Lake district. Here the river widens to form Derwentwater, a wooded, oval lake containing falls and several isles. The Derwent empties into Solway Firth, an inlet of the Irish Sea, at Workington. Three other English rivers bear the same name, in north Derbyshire, Yorkshire, and between Durham and Northumberland. The word *derwent* means *clear water* in ancient Celtic. JOHN D. ISAACS

DESCARTES, day KAHRT, RENÉ (1596-1650), was a French philosopher, scientist, and mathematician. The period in which he lived was a time of great political, social, and religious change. At this time the foundations of present-day physical science were laid down. Descartes supported the new physics enthusiastically, but he was a conservative in other respects. He saw that all the old, traditional bases for men's beliefs were being undermined, and he sought a new method by which men could attain certainty.

He tells us, first, to accept nothing until we see its truth "clearly and distinctly." We must divide any difficult problem into smaller and smaller parts until we come to some proposition so simple that we see its self-evident truth. We can then build on this sure basis, always proceeding by small, self-evident steps.

But what is to be the self-evident starting point? Descartes thought that it was the certainty of his own existence. It was possible to doubt everything else, but not one's own existence. As soon as you try to doubt your existence, you see that you must exist as the doubter. You cannot doubt that you are doubting.

René Descartes

From this line of reasoning, Descartes proved the existence of God. He argued that the idea of a perfect being cannot originate in the mind of a doubting, imperfect creature like man. A perfect idea must have a perfect cause, and this is God. Descartes proved the existence of the physical world on the ground that a good God would not allow men to believe in its existence unless it really existed. Descartes was born at La Haye. As a mathematician, he invented analytic geometry (see GEOMETRY). W. T. JONES

See also PHILOSOPHY (The Appeal to Reason).

DESCHUTES RIVER. See OREGON (Rivers).

DESCRIPTION, in literature. See LITERATURE (Kinds of Discourse).

DESENSITIZATION. See ALLERGY (Treatment).

DESERET, DEZ ur EHT, is a word meaning *honeybee* in the Book of Mormon. The Mormons adopted the honeybee as the symbol of hard work necessary for the success of their Salt Lake Valley settlement. In 1849, they organized the State of Deseret. Congress refused to admit it as a state, and created instead the Territory of Utah. See also MORMONS. HAROLD W. BRADLEY

SCENES FROM DESERT LANDS

The Wind Forms Sand Dunes in the Scorching Wastes of Death Valley in Eastern California.

Ewing Galloway; American Mus. of Nat. History

DESERT, *DEHZ ert*, is land where few plants can grow. Usually a lack of rainfall causes a lack of plant life. "Cold deserts" are places where it is too cold for plants to grow. A desert is seldom a flat, changeless waste of bare sand. It may have mountains and boulders. Parts of it may be deeply cut by the torrents that follow occasional bursts of rain. A desert may be hot, like the Sahara, or cold, like the *tundras* of Siberia. But, if a place has very little water and vegetation, people usually call it a desert.

All living things need water in order to live. The few plants and animals that live in deserts have become *adapted* (changed) so that they require less water than most plants and animals. Camels can drink a great amount of water at one time (one drank 30 gallons in 10 minutes). The reason that camels can go for long periods of time between drinks is that they do almost no sweating. Man and the so-called warm-blooded animals must keep their body temperatures constant. They sweat when it gets hot, and this cools the body. But camels can stand large increases in body temperature. They let their body temperatures soar, and retain the water they drink for long periods of time.

The smaller desert animals do not drink water. They usually burrow underground to get away from the sun during the hot days, and come out at night to eat. Some of them eat other animals, and get the water they need from the moisture in the meat. Others, like the kangaroo rat, eat plants and seeds. These plant eaters get the water they need from plant juices.

Desert plants also are adapted to the life they lead. Cactus plants store water in their thick stems. Their roots lie close to the surface of the ground, and quickly absorb the moisture from the light rains that occasionally fall. Most plants have broad, food-manufacturing leaves, from which moisture constantly evaporates into the air. Cactus plants have no wide leaves, so they lose little water through evaporation. The green stem manufactures the food in a cactus plant.

Some deserts are almost totally without water. In such places, winds may blow the sand into hills, or *dunes*, that shift and move endlessly across the desert. Few plants can live on such dry, shifting sands.

A Burro Is Fed in the Mongolian Desert.

Moslems Pause for Evening Prayer in the Sahara.

Sawders

The Mojave Desert Lies Northeast of Los Angeles.
Statile, Black Star

An *oasis* in the desert is a place where a spring, or irrigation from deep wells, gives plants a better chance to grow. Oases are like green islands in the middle of the bare desert wasteland. Some oases are big enough for two million people or more.

Modern irrigation is making many deserts grow abundant and useful crops where once nothing but cacti and sagebrush grew. Such desert regions have soil that is rich in the minerals that plants need to grow well. One of the best examples is the Imperial Valley of central California (see IMPERIAL VALLEY).

The greatest desert in the world stretches across Africa and Asia, and different parts of it have different names. Its various parts include the Sahara, the Arabian and Central Asian deserts, and the Gobi desert. All continents except Europe have large deserts. Much of northern Mexico is desert land. This land continues northward into the United States. R. WILL BURNETT

Related Articles in WORLD BOOK include:

DESERTS

Arabian Desert	Great Victoria	Painted Desert
Atacama Desert	Desert	Qattara
Australian Desert	High Desert	Depression
Colorado Desert	Kalahari Desert	Sahara
Death Valley	Kara Kum	Sechura Desert
Gobi	Kyzyl Kum	Syrian Desert
Great Basin	Libyan Desert	Takla Makan
Great Salt Lake	Mojave	Desert
Desert	Negev	Vizcaíno Desert

DESERT PLANT LIFE

Cactus	Date and Date Palm	Mesquite
Century Plant	Flower (color pictures,	Sagebrush
Creosote Bush	Flowers of the Desert)	Succulent

UNCLASSIFIED

Arab	Chuckwalla	Irrigation	Oasis
Bedouin	Climate	Kangaroo Rat	Rain
Camel	Dune	Mirage	Sand
Caravan	Horned Toad	Nomad	Sandstorm

DESERT FOX. See ROMMEL, ERWIN.

DESERTION, *dee ZUR shun,* is the military crime of running away from one of the armed forces with the intention of staying away. A member of the forces who runs away for only a short time to avoid dangerous duty also may be court-martialed as a deserter. During wartime, the death penalty may be imposed. During peacetime, the penalty may be any punishment except death. A lesser military crime is Absence Without Official Leave (AWOL). A deserter who joins the enemy commits the higher crime of *treason* (see TREASON).

Desertion is also a term used to describe a cause for divorce in most states of the United States. A husband or wife who intentionally leaves the other, without consent or adequate reason, and stays away for a certain length of time, has given grounds for divorce. The time necessary for legal desertion in various states ranges from one to seven years. JOHN W. WADE and ROBERT COLBORN

See also ABANDONMENT.

DE SEVERSKY, ALEXANDER PROCOFIEFF (1894-), is a pilot, aircraft designer, and military authority. His fighter plane designs were among the most advanced of the 1930's, and were exported widely. He invented an automatic bombsight, skis for aircraft, amphibian landing gear, and hydraulic shock absorbers for aircraft. His theories about the proper use of air power attracted wide attention.

De Seversky was born in Tiflis (now Tbilisi), Russia, and received his education at Russia's Imperial Naval Academy. He served in World War I, and lost a leg in aerial combat.

He came to the United States in 1918, after the Bolshevik revolution in Russia. In 1927 he became a naturalized American citizen. De Seversky founded his own aircraft manufacturing firm, the Seversky Aero Corporation,

Alexander de Seversky

in 1922. He operated it in New York until 1931 when it was reorganized as the Seversky Aircraft Corporation. He headed this company until 1939 when it became Republic Aviation. Later, he lectured on air power. He wrote *Victory Through Air Power* (1942). ROBERT B. HOTZ

DESIDERIO DA SETTIGNANO. See SCULPTURE (Italy; picture, Laughing Boy).

DESIDERIUS. See LOMBARD.

DESIGN is the intended arrangement of materials to produce a certain result or effect. The principles of design can be seen most clearly in the visual arts of drawing, painting, sculpture, and architecture.

The painter works with *lines, shapes,* and *colors.* He is also concerned with the *direction* of lines, the *size* of the shapes, and the *shading* of the colors. He tries to arrange all these elements into a pattern that will seem emotionally satisfying to the spectator. If this effect is obtained, his design will have *unity.*

Repetition is an important principle of design. It consists in the repeating of lines or shapes. Japanese color prints are noted for their handling of repetition. Many of them have fine slanting lines of rain, or scenes with reflections on water repeated over and over.

Harmony, or Balance, is as important as repetition. Harmony can be obtained in many ways in design. It may be either *symmetrical* (in balance) or *asymmetrical* (out of perfect balance, but still pleasing to the eye). Or a small area may balance a large area if the small area has an importance to the eye (because of treatment or color) that is equal to that of the larger area.

Contrast, or Discord, is the opposite of harmony. The colors red and orange harmonize, since orange contains red. A circle and an oval harmonize, because they both are made up of curved lines. But a line one-half inch long is not in harmony with a line twelve inches long. It is in contrast. The use of yellow with purple is also an example of contrast.

Rhythm and Movement are obtained by the use of wavy lines, or motifs placed in contrast to *static* (set) patterns which give interest to a design.

Unity occurs when all the elements in a design combine to form a consistent whole. Unity resembles balance. A design has unity if its masses are balanced, or if its tones and colors harmonize. But unity differs from balance because it implies that all these balanced elements form harmony in the design as a whole.

Design in Other Arts is always present. In music, sounds heard in a sequence of time provide the design materials. A sonata follows a set pattern. A symphony consists of several themes which are repeated in changing forms throughout the composition. In poetry, words are heard or read in a designed time sequence. A sonnet has a fixed form, or design, of fourteen lines. In architecture and sculpture, the design is usually called *structural*. The size and shape of a statue are the chief design concern of the sculptor, just as the architect's concern is with the size and shape of his building. The surfaces of buildings are sometimes decorated. Then the design is known as *decorative*, in contrast to structural design.

Industrial design has become more and more important. The kind of industrial design called structural design is used in mass production of commodities such as automobiles, fountain pens, and the many other things people enjoy using.   HARRY MUIR KURTZWORTH

Related Articles in WORLD BOOK include:

Airplane (Design and Testing)	Clothing	Industrial Arts
Architecture	Decorative Arts	Industrial Design
Automobile (Design)	Fashion	Interior Decoration
	Furniture	Painting
	Geometric Style	Sculpture

DE SITTER, WILLEM (1872-1934), was a noted Dutch astronomer. From his studies of Jupiter's satellites and his calculation of their elements and masses, he contributed to the theoretical understanding of satellites. He is most famous for his work on the age, size, and structure of the universe, and for his early realization of the importance of the Einstein theory of relativity in cosmology. In 1917, he proposed an extension of the theory. He suggested that distant galaxies might be receding rapidly from us and that, as a result, space might be expanding. His ideas were later proved by observation. De Sitter was born at Sneek in The Netherlands.   HELEN WRIGHT

PRINCIPLES OF DESIGN

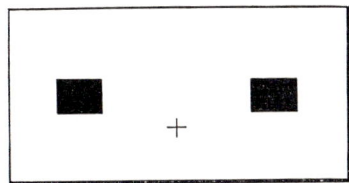

Symmetrical Balance is accomplished by placing two identical objects the same distance from the center.

Asymmetrical Balance is possible because the smaller object is twice the distance from the center.

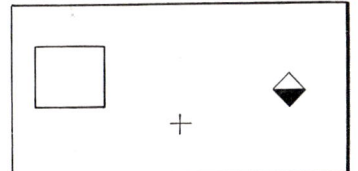

Visual Balance is gained when a design has a small important object opposite a big uninteresting object.

Unity of design may place stress on equally spaced straight lines, such as a row of identical soldiers.

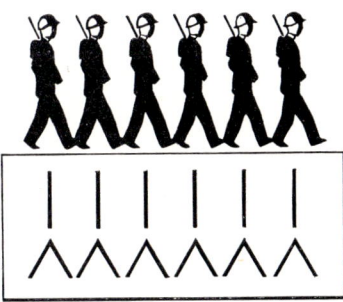

Movement gives interest to unity because it brings variation to the monotonous straight lines.

Rhythm is added to design by interrupted horizontal and vertical lines. The waving flags also add emphasis.

DE SMET, PIERRE JEAN

Father De Smet
Chicago Historical Society

DE SMET, PIERRE JEAN (1801-1873), was a Roman Catholic missionary who worked among the Indians of the United States for 50 years. De Smet was a Belgian who went to America at the age of 20. There he entered the Society of Jesus. In 1838 he went to the Potawatomi Indians, and succeeded in making peace between the Potawatomi and the Sioux. Later, he was sent west to the Flathead and Pend d'Oreille tribes. After a visit to the Blackfoot tribe in 1846, he returned to St. Louis and remained there to do other work. But he never lost interest in the Indians. The government asked him to go to the West Coast in 1851 and again in 1858. The purpose of these trips was to calm the Indians who were angered by the coming of white men to California and Oregon.

Father De Smet crossed the ocean many times and sought aid in European countries during the long years of his work. At the age of 67, he went alone into the camp of the Sioux, who had sworn to kill all white men. He was able to open the way to peace. His many writings give important facts about the American Indians. The Indians called De Smet "Blackrobe" because of his clerical dress. FULTON J. SHEEN

DES MOINES, *duh MOIN,* Iowa (pop. 208,982; alt. 805 ft.), is the capital and largest city in the state. It has earned wide recognition as an insurance center. Des Moines is located in central Iowa at the junction of the Des Moines and Raccoon rivers. For location, see IOWA (color map).

Industry and Commerce. About 50 insurance companies have home offices in Des Moines. The vast amount of printing required by the insurance business has helped make Des Moines a large printing center. Farm, home, fraternal, and commercial journals printed here have circulations totaling several million. Other industries include meat packing, and the manufacture of clothing, cosmetics, food products, agricultural implements, and cement.

Cultural Life. Des Moines is the home of Drake University and other schools and colleges. In 1948, the city opened a new Art Center, designed by Eliel Saarinen (see SAARINEN [Eliel]).

History. A military post called Fort Des Moines was established on the site of the city in 1843. As the Indians left the surrounding country, new settlers came to this post. The great flood of 1851 nearly washed away the pioneer community, but in the fall of that year a town government was formed. Four years later, this frontier settlement was made the state capital, but the state government was not actually transferred from Iowa City until 1857. During the following 25 years Des Moines grew to be the largest city in the state. In 1907, the "Des Moines plan" of municipal government was adopted. This followed the Galveston (Tex.) commission form of government, but added such features as nonpartisan elections, career service for city workers, direct legislation, and provision for the recall of elected officials. In 1949, the people of Des Moines voted to adopt the council-manager form of government. The heart of the city has a beautiful civic center which contains the principal city, state, and federal government buildings. The city now covers an area of about 55 square miles.

A cavalry post, reviving the name of Fort Des Moines, was established at Des Moines in 1903. This post was used during World War I as a training camp for Negro officers. Later it became a hospital. During World War II, Fort Des Moines was used to train WAC officers, and became known as *The West Point for Women.* Camp Dodge, a few miles north, was an induction center in World Wars I and II. WILLIAM J. PETERSEN

See also IOWA (picture, The Iowa Capitol).

DES MOINES RIVER. See IOWA (Rivers and Lakes).

DE SOTO, *dee SOH toh,* **HERNANDO** (1500?-1542), a Spanish explorer, was the first white man to cross the Mississippi River. He had become wealthy in the Spanish conquest of Peru. He arrived in Cuba as governor in 1538. He decided to explore Florida, which had been described to him as "a land of gold."

De Soto landed with 600 soldiers at Tampa Bay in May, 1539. His expedition moved north to an Indian town called Apalache. A party that he sent west from there discovered Pensacola Bay. The explorers then crossed Georgia to the Savannah River, and followed the river to the Blue Ridge mountains. Crossing these mountains, De Soto descended the Alabama River to a place called Mavilla. There he defeated an Indian tribe, but suffered heavy losses.

Hernando de Soto
Brown Bros.

Unwilling to abandon his search for gold, De Soto turned northwest. He sighted the Mississippi River near the present city of Memphis, Tenn., in May, 1541. The

Downtown Des Moines has a number of tall buildings. This view down Walnut Street shows the Iowa state capitol, faintly visible in the background.
Greater Des Moines Chamber of Commerce

De Soto and His Men discovered the Mississippi River on May 8, 1541, *above*, during their search for treasure. The map, *below*, traces the route De Soto's expedition followed.

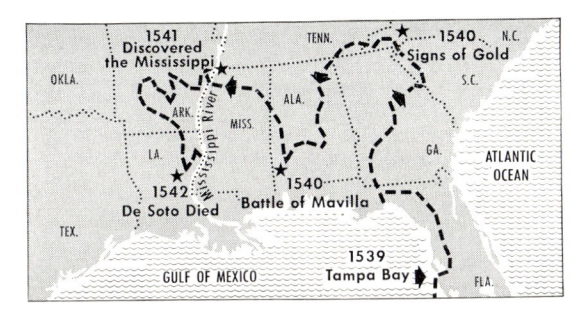

expedition crossed into Arkansas, explored the Ozark mountains, then returned to the Mississippi River, where De Soto died of fever. His men weighted his body and buried it in the river. Altogether, De Soto's tour had taken him through territory that later became Florida, Georgia, South Carolina, North Carolina, Tennessee, Alabama, Mississippi, Arkansas, and Louisiana. After De Soto's death, his men traveled as far west as Texas.

The survivors, under the leadership of Luis de Moscoso, built crude boats and floated down the Mississippi River. Indians attacked them constantly. But they found refuge in Tampico, Mexico, then a Spanish settlement. De Soto was born at Barcarrota, Spain. When he was about 19, he went to Central America and took part in the Spanish conquest there. CHARLES E. NOWELL.

See also MISSISSIPPI RIVER.

DE SOTO NATIONAL MEMORIAL is a national memorial at Shaw's Point, four miles west of Bradenton, Fla. It covers an area of 30.0 acres. It was established in 1949 to commemorate Hernando De Soto's landing place in his expedition of 1539 (see DE SOTO, HERNANDO). The National Park Service controls it.

DESPERADO. See WESTERN FRONTIER LIFE (Crime).

DESPIAU, CHARLES (1874-1946), a French sculptor, carved some of the finest portraits of his time. His portrait sculptures include *Mrs. Charles Lindbergh* and *Madame Derain*, wife of a painter-friend. Like Edgar Degas, Despiau worked to catch the specific character of the body and its movement. Born in Mont-de-Marsan, in the south of France, Despiau decided to become a sculptor when he was 16. He studied chiefly in Paris, and came under the influence of Auguste Rodin. He worked with Rodin for a time. CHARLES SEYMOUR, JR.

DESPOTISM is a form of government in which the ruler has unlimited power over the lives of the people. Despots are not necessarily harsh or cruel. They may be kindly and considerate, and they may even put the welfare of the people above their own private wishes. As a rule, however, a despot can keep his absolute power only by the use of force.

The late 1700's are often called the Age of the Enlightened Despots. During this period, Frederick the Great of Prussia, Catherine the Great of Russia, and Joseph II of Austria did their best to reform the laws, to promote education and the arts, and to conduct the affairs of the country efficiently. Charles III of Spain, Leopold of Tuscany, Joseph of Portugal, and Gustavus III of Sweden also deserved the name of "enlightened despots." Some of these rulers learned that freedom and education make rebellious subjects, and gave up enlightenment. Nearly all were followed by weak rulers who undid whatever good the "enlightened despots" had accomplished. WILLIAM EBENSTEIN.

See also CATHERINE (II); FREDERICK (II) of Prussia; GOVERNMENT (When Tyrants Rule; The National State).

DESSALINES, DAY SAH LEEN, **JEAN JACQUES** (1758?-1806), is the national hero of Haiti. He was an illiterate slave who freed Haiti from France and became the country's emperor. He was born on a plantation at Grande Rivière, Haiti, and took the name of his French master. He joined the 1791 Negro revolt that resulted in the abolition of slavery in 1793. He fought under Toussaint l'Ouverture against the invasion of the British, and became a general (see TOUSSAINT L'OUVERTURE).

After Toussaint was seized and sent to France, Dessalines led a successful rebellion against the French. This made Haiti the second independent nation in the Western Hemisphere, the United States being the first. Dessalines became president of Haiti on Jan. 1, 1804, but soon proclaimed himself emperor. He was murdered two years later. DONALD E. WORCESTER.

See also HAITI (Independence); CHRISTOPHE, HENRI.

DESTROYER is the smallest seagoing combat ship. It is generally from 300 to 400 feet long, and displaces from 2,000 to 4,000 tons. Destroyers are used mainly to screen other ships, to picket certain areas, and to escort ships. Destroyers are long-range, high-speed, hard-hitting ships. For protection, they rely on watertight compartments and speed. Sailors call destroyers "tin cans" because of their light steel hulls.

The most common type of destroyer in the U.S. Navy is known as the *710 Class* or *long hull*, developed during World War II. They have two main engine groups of high-pressure steam turbines that total over 60,000 horsepower. A newer and larger version of the destroyer, the *Forrest Sherman* class, includes the most powerful craft of this size afloat. Engines, boilers, and other machinery for propulsion occupy nearly three-fourths of their length below the main deck. The ships are capable of speeds above 35 knots. Some destroyers of other navies are able to steam at nearly 40 knots, but they do not have the long cruising range that U.S. Navy destroyers of the *Forrest Sherman* class possess.

Destroyers are armed with torpedoes in tubes on deck, multipurpose five-inch guns, and depth charges. Torpedoes are a destroyer's main weapon against surface ships, but the five-inch guns can be used against ships as well as against aircraft. On the newest destroy-

DESTRUCTIVE DISTILLATION

ers, guided missile systems replace deck guns. The missiles make the destroyers even more versatile. They are capable of supporting invasion forces and striking land targets, as well as fighting other ships at sea and providing antiaircraft protection.

The *destroyer escort* is a smaller ship developed during World War II primarily for slower speed convoy duties. These 1,300-ton to 1,500-ton ships are armed primarily with torpedoes, depth charges, and three-inch and five-inch guns.   T. C. GILLMER

See also NAVY, UNITED STATES (table, Names of Naval Ships; picture, Warships of the Navy); WARSHIP.

DESTRUCTIVE DISTILLATION. See DISTILLATION.

DE SUCRE, ANTONIO JOSÉ. See SUCRE, ANTONIO JOSÉ DE.

DETECTIVE. See POLICE (The Detective Division); DETECTIVE AGENCY.

DETECTIVE AGENCY provides private investigation, crime detection, and crime prevention services for the general public. Anyone can hire a private detective. A detective agency may vary from a one-man concern to a large company. Men who work for such agencies are often former police officers. Much of the work they do resembles official police work. They help their clients gain information to use in lawsuits. They may also investigate kidnapings, thefts, or blackmail attempts. Banks, hotels, theaters, and other businesses often hire private detectives to prevent theft. Private detectives often cooperate closely with various law enforcement agencies.

DETECTOR. See RADIO (Vacuum Tubes; color diagram, How Radio Works).

DETERGENT is any cleansing substance. Water, soap, or even abrasives such as sand may be called detergents. But today, the term usually means a synthetic compound that acts like soap. Such compounds are often called *synthetic detergents*. Unlike soaps, synthetic detergents do not react with the calcium and magnesium salts in hard water to form scum of the kind that makes rings on bathtubs. Synthetic detergent formulas can also be "tailored" so that detergents produce the desired amount of suds for any use. Because of these advantages, synthetic detergents have many industrial and home uses.

Household synthetic detergents contain sulfates or sulfonates made from animal and vegetable fats or petroleum compounds. These ingredients are called *surface-active agents* or *surfactants*. They help give detergents a cleansing action similar to that of soap (see SOAP [How Soap Works]). The first such agent was sulfated olive oil developed in 1834.   JAMES C. ERVIN

DETERMINANT, in mathematics, is a single number related to a square *array* (arrangement) of numbers called *elements.* For example, the array

$$\begin{vmatrix} 3 & 1 \\ 2 & 6 \end{vmatrix}$$

is related to the single number 16. You can compute the value of this determinant in three steps. (1) Multiply the upper left element *3* by the lower right element 6: $3 \times 6 = 18$. (2) Multiply the lower left element *2* by the upper right element *1*: $2 \times 1 = 2$. (3) Subtract the product of step 2 from the product of step 1: $18 - 2 =$ 16. The word *determinant* is also used for the square array itself.

Mathematicians use determinants to state formulas for the solution of many problems. Such problems include the solution of equations and the calculation of certain areas and volumes.

Using 2 by 2 Determinants. The array above is called a *2 by 2 determinant* because it has two *rows* (3,1 and 2,6) and two *columns* (3,2 and 1,6).

In general, the symbols a_1, b_1, a_2, b_2 can be used to represent the numbers of any 2 by 2 determinant. The value of the determinant is stated as follows:

$$\begin{vmatrix} a_1 & b_1 \\ a_2 & b_2 \end{vmatrix} = a_1 b_2 - a_2 b_1$$

The 2 by 2 determinant can be used to solve linear equations in two variables (see ALGEBRA [Solving Linear Equations in Two Variables]). For example, suppose you wanted to solve the following equations:

$$3x + 1y = 5$$
$$2x + 6y = 14$$

To find the value of the variable *x*, eliminate the variable *y* by multiplying the first equation by 6, and then subtracting the second equation:

$$\begin{array}{r} 18x + 6y = 30 \\ -2x - 6y = -14 \\ \hline 16x = 16 \end{array}$$

$$x = \frac{16}{16} = 1$$

The above operations could also be written as follows:

$$\begin{array}{r} 6 \times 3x + 6 \times 1y = 6 \times 5 \\ -2x - 6y = -14 \\ \hline (6 \times 3 - 1 \times 2)x = 6 \times 5 - 1 \times 14 \end{array}$$

$$x = \frac{6 \times 5 - 1 \times 14}{6 \times 3 - 1 \times 2}$$

The last expression can be written as the ratio of two determinants:

$$x = \frac{\begin{vmatrix} 5 & 1 \\ 14 & 6 \end{vmatrix}}{\begin{vmatrix} 3 & 1 \\ 2 & 6 \end{vmatrix}} = \frac{5 \times 6 - 14 \times 1}{3 \times 6 - 2 \times 1} = \frac{30 - 14}{18 - 2} = \frac{16}{16} = 1$$

You could solve the original equations in a similar way for *y* and get

$$y = \frac{\begin{vmatrix} 3 & 5 \\ 2 & 14 \end{vmatrix}}{\begin{vmatrix} 3 & 1 \\ 2 & 6 \end{vmatrix}} = \frac{3 \times 14 - 2 \times 5}{3 \times 6 - 2 \times 1} = \frac{42 - 10}{18 - 2} = \frac{32}{16} = 2$$

Note that the same determinant appears as the denominator in the formulas for both *x* and *y*. This determinant is called the *determinant of the system.* It is made up of the coefficients of *x* and *y* in the original equations

(3,1,2,6). The numerator in the formula for x is the determinant of the system with the coefficients of x replaced by the constants in the original equations (5,14). Similarly, these constants replace the coefficients of y in the numerator of the formula for y.

In general, equations in x and y can be written in the form

$$a_1x + b_1y = c_1$$
$$a_2x + b_2y = c_2$$

You can solve these equations for x as follows: (1) multiply the first equation by b_2; (2) multiply the second equation by b_1; (3) subtract the product of step 2 from the product of step 1. The result is:

$$(a_1b_2 - a_2b_1)x = c_1b_2 - c_2b_1$$

$$x = \frac{c_1b_2 - c_2b_1}{a_1b_2 - a_2b_1} = \frac{\begin{vmatrix} c_1 & b_1 \\ c_2 & b_2 \end{vmatrix}}{\begin{vmatrix} a_1 & b_1 \\ a_2 & b_2 \end{vmatrix}}$$

You could solve for y in a similar way and get:

$$y = \frac{a_1c_2 - a_2c_1}{a_1b_2 - a_2b_1} = \frac{\begin{vmatrix} a_1 & c_1 \\ a_2 & c_2 \end{vmatrix}}{\begin{vmatrix} a_1 & b_1 \\ a_2 & b_2 \end{vmatrix}}$$

Using Higher Order Determinants. The order of a determinant is the number of rows or columns it has. A 2 by 2 determinant is of the *second* order, a 3 by 3 of the *third*, and so on. Determinants of an order higher than the second appear, for example, in the solution of three or more simultaneous equations.

You can use third order determinants to solve the following three equations:

$$3x + 2y + z = 10$$
$$4y - z = 5$$
$$5x + y - 2z = 1$$

The formulas for x, y, and z are similar to the ones used to solve only two equations. The denominator of each formula is the determinant of the system. The numerators are the determinant of the system with the coefficients of x, y, or z replaced by the constants. For example, the formula for x is:

$$x = \frac{\begin{vmatrix} 10 & 2 & 1 \\ 5 & 4 & -1 \\ 1 & 1 & -2 \end{vmatrix}}{\begin{vmatrix} 3 & 2 & 1 \\ 0 & 4 & -1 \\ 5 & 1 & -2 \end{vmatrix}}$$

Third order determinants such as the one above can be computed in several ways. One method is to reduce the determinant to a series of 2 by 2 determinants. With this method, the denominator in the above formula can be reduced as follows:

DETONATOR

$$\begin{vmatrix} 3 & 2 & 1 \\ 0 & 4 & -1 \\ 5 & 1 & -2 \end{vmatrix} = 3\begin{vmatrix} 4 & -1 \\ 1 & -2 \end{vmatrix} - 2\begin{vmatrix} 0 & -1 \\ 5 & -2 \end{vmatrix} + 1\begin{vmatrix} 0 & 4 \\ 5 & 1 \end{vmatrix}$$

$$= 3(-7) - 2(5) + 1(-20)$$
$$= -21 - 10 - 20 = -51$$

In this operation, each 2 by 2 determinant is multiplied by a number that appears in the first row of the 3 by 3 determinant (3,2,1). The 2 by 2 determinants are called *minors* of these first row elements. For example, the determinant

$$\begin{vmatrix} 4 & -1 \\ 1 & -2 \end{vmatrix}$$

is the minor of 3. It consists of the elements that remain in the 3 by 3 determinant after the row and column in which 3 appears are crossed out. Similarly, the minor of 2 includes the elements that remain after the first row and second column are crossed out.

This series of 2 by 2 determinants is called an *expansion in terms of the minors of the first row*. It consists of the products of the first row elements and their respective minors. The value of the 3 by 3 determinant is computed by alternately adding and subtracting these products. In general terms, the formula for expanding a 3 by 3 determinant in this way is

$$\begin{vmatrix} a_1 & b_1 & c_1 \\ a_2 & b_2 & c_2 \\ a_3 & b_3 & c_3 \end{vmatrix} = a_1\begin{vmatrix} b_2 & c_2 \\ b_3 & c_3 \end{vmatrix} - b_1\begin{vmatrix} a_2 & c_2 \\ a_3 & c_3 \end{vmatrix} + c_1\begin{vmatrix} a_2 & b_2 \\ a_3 & b_3 \end{vmatrix}$$

Determinants can be expanded similarly in terms of the minors of any row or column if the signs of the minors are properly chosen.

Determinants of orders higher than the third also can be computed by reducing them to 2 by 2 determinants. However, the minors of these determinants are not 2 by 2 determinants. (The order of a minor is always one less than the order of the determinant from which it is formed.) The minors themselves must be repeatedly expanded until 2 by 2 determinants are finally obtained. Such expansions may be quite long if the order of the determinant is high. Mathematicians use several other methods for simplifying high order determinants.   PHILLIP S. JONES

DETERMINISM. See FREE WILL.

DETONATOR, *DET oh NAY tur*, is a small metal or plastic capsule that contains an easily explodable charge. It is used to *detonate*, or set off, larger explosive charges, such as dynamite, mines, and bombs. It contains a heat-sensitive *priming charge*, such as lead azide, and a *base charge* of some more powerful explosive, such as RDX. Flame from a fuse or heat from an electric wire ignites the priming charge which ignites the base charge. The explosion of the base charge sets off the dynamite, mine, or bomb. Detonators for dynamite are called *blasting caps*.   JULIUS ROTH

DETROIT, *dee TROYT,* Mich., produces more automobiles and trucks than any other city in the world. It is often called the *Automobile Capital of the World* or the *Motor City.* Detroit is the fifth largest city in the United States, and the largest in Michigan.

The city lies on the Detroit River. Like a strait, this short stream connects Lakes Erie and St. Clair. The French word *Detroit* means *strait.* The river is one of the busiest in the country, and Detroit ranks as one of the nation's leading ports. The gleaming white buildings of the Civic Center stand on the riverbank in the downtown area.

Location, Size, and Description. Detroit is on the southeastern border of Michigan, where the Detroit River separates the United States and Canada. Because of a bend in the river, Detroit lies directly north of Windsor, Ont., its Canadian neighbor. A bridge, two tunnels, and a ferry line for freight trains connect the cities. See MICHIGAN (color map).

Wharves, warehouses, railroad stations, and power and industrial plants line most of the water front. The Civic Center borders the river at the foot of Woodward Avenue, the main north-south street. Gardens set off its handsome buildings. These structures include the Veterans Memorial Building, a meeting place for veterans' organizations; the 20-story City-County Building, which houses government offices; the circular Convention Arena, which can seat 12,500 persons; the Henry and Edsel Ford Auditorium, with a seating capacity of 3,000; and Cobo Hall, featuring more than nine acres of exhibit space. Albert E. Cobo served as mayor of Detroit from 1949 to 1957.

Inland from the water front, the downtown area includes hundreds of stores and offices in an area five blocks long and four blocks wide.

Detroit is built in the general form of a half circle, with the base lying on the river. The principal streets extend from the center toward the west, north, and east like the spokes of a wheel. The older part of the downtown area is laid out with flower-filled circles, squares, and triangles at street intersections. Most of the rest of the city follows the familiar checkerboard pattern of east-west and north-south streets.

Industrial and residential suburbs border Detroit on three sides. They include Wyandotte, Lincoln Park, River Rouge, Dearborn, Livonia, Pontiac, Royal Oak, Ferndale, Warren, East Detroit, Roseville, St. Clair Shores, and five towns with Grosse Pointe as part of their names. Two cities—Hamtramck and Highland Park—lie entirely within Detroit. See HAMTRAMCK; HIGHLAND PARK.

The People. Only about a third of the people living in Detroit were born there. Many persons came from other parts of the United States seeking job opportunities. More than half the residents were either born abroad or have parents from other countries. The largest number came from Canada. The Detroit area has about 35,000 Arabic-speaking persons, the largest such group in the United States. Over a third of the city's people belong to the Roman Catholic Church, the biggest religious group in Detroit.

Industry. Detroit is one of the most important manufacturing cities in the world. Its 6,000 factories produce

Downtown Detroit lies on the north bank of the Detroit River. The Canadian city of Windsor, Ont., is on the south bank. A new Civic Center, begun in 1950, borders seven blocks of Detroit's riverfront. One of its buildings is the Henry and Edsel Ford Auditorium, *center.*

--- **FACTS IN BRIEF** ---

Population: 1,670,144; metropolitan area, 3,762,360.
Area: 140 square miles; metropolitan area, 1,965 square miles.
Altitude: 585 feet above sea level.
Climate: Average temp., Jan., 26° F.; July, 73° F.
　　　　　Average annual rainfall, 32 inches.
　　　　　Average annual snowfall, 32 inches.
Government: Mayor-council (four-year terms).
Founded: 1701. Incorporated as a village, 1802; as a city, 1815.
City Seal: The seal shows two women, one weeping and looking at a burning city, the other pointing to a new city. The city mottoes appear left and right of the figures. The seal commemorates the fire of 1805 and the rebirth of Detroit.
City Flag: The seal in the center is surrounded by golden French fleurs-de-lis, golden British lions, and American stars and stripes, representing the three countries that have controlled Detroit.
City Mottoes: *Speramus Meliora* (We hope for better things); *Resurget Cineribus* (It shall rise again from the ashes).

more than $5,700,000,000 worth of goods each year. About a third of the workers in the metropolitan area are employed in the automobile industry. The automobile companies not only assemble cars and trucks, but also manufacture many of their parts. In addition, automobile companies in the Motor City have built technical centers for research and experimental engineering.

Other products of the city include aluminum castings, brass and bronze products, chemicals, drugs and medicines, foundry and machine-shop articles, furnaces, machinery, machine tools, paint and varnish, rubber products, stampings, steel, and stoves. One of the largest salt mines in the United States lies beneath Detroit. It has about 200 miles of corridors. See SALT (picture, An Underground Salt Mine).

Transportation. Detroit is a gateway for commerce between eastern and western Great Lakes ports. Exports are a significant factor in Detroit industry. The average yearly value of exports exceeds $1,375,000,000. Imports total about $800,000,000. More than 700 foreign ships dock at the port of Detroit every year.

The automotive capital depends largely on cars and buses for transportation. The Edsel Ford Expressway cuts across the city from east to west, and other expressways run northwest and northeast. These freeways speed the movement of automobiles and trucks. The city owns and operates a fleet of buses. Two major airports serve

Joe Clark, Pix; Detroit Convention and Tourist Bureau

The City-County Building, near the east end of Detroit's Civic Center, includes the 20-story Courts Tower and a 14-story office building.

Detroit is shown in black, and the metropolitan area in light gray.

DETROIT

DETROIT

Detroit. The Metropolitan Airport lies 21 miles west of the city, and Willow Run Airport is 31 miles west. Several major railway lines enter the city.

Communication. The city's major newspapers are the *Free Press* and the *News*. They have a combined daily circulation of about 1,300,000. Radio station WWJ, founded in 1920, was the first in Michigan. In 1947, WWJ-TV became the state's first television station. The Detroit metropolitan area has about 20 radio stations and 5 television stations.

Education. The Detroit public school system has more than 280,000 students and 280 schools. About 160 parochial and private schools serve 90,000 pupils. Universities and colleges in Detroit include Marygrove College, Mercy College, the University of Detroit, and Wayne State University.

The Cultural Center, two miles north of the river on Woodward Avenue, includes the following activities. Its largest institution is Wayne State University. The main Detroit Public Library has more than 1,400,000 volumes, and administers about 30 branch libraries throughout the city. The Detroit Institute of Arts owns a notable collection of sculptures and paintings, including murals by the Mexican artist Diego Rivera. The Cultural Center also includes the Children's Museum, the Detroit Historical Museum, the International Institute, and the Society of Arts and Crafts.

Recreation. Detroit's park system covers more than 5,700 acres. Belle Isle, a 985-acre park in the Detroit River, has a children's zoo, a conservatory, an aquarium, and a beach. The Nancy Brown Peace Carillon, dedicated to world peace, is also on Belle Isle. River Rouge Park covers 1,203 acres, and features golf, tennis, and swimming. The Detroit Zoo has wide moats, rather than bars, between visitors and the wild animals.

The Detroit Symphony Orchestra plays in the Henry and Edsel Ford Auditorium in the Civic Center. A number of nationality groups in Detroit have musical organizations.

The Detroit Tigers of the American League play baseball in Tiger Stadium, and the Detroit Lions of the National Football League also play there. Other professional athletic teams are the Detroit Red Wings of the National Hockey League and the Detroit Pistons of the National Basketball Association. Both these clubs play in Olympia Stadium.

Government. Detroit has a mayor-council form of government. The people elect the mayor and nine councilmen to four-year terms. All elections are nonpartisan. That is, party labels do not appear on ballots. Detroit is the seat of Wayne County.

History. French explorers and adventurers visited the site of Detroit as early as 1648. In 1701, Antoine de la Mothe Cadillac established Fort Pontchartrain, com-

The *Automobile Capital of the World* held its first National Automobile Show in Cobo Hall, *below*, in 1960. Visitors may drive up a circular ramp and park on the roof. Detroit's people depend largely on cars and buses for transportation.

Detroit Convention and Tourist Bureau

monly called Fort Detroit. The British, under Major Robert Rogers, seized the fort in 1760, during the French and Indian Wars. Chief Pontiac led a group of Indians in an attack on the fort in 1763, but failed to capture it. The British built Fort Lernoult at the site in 1778, during the Revolutionary War in America. The Treaty of Paris ended the war in 1783, but the British held the fort until 1796. They wanted to keep their valuable fur trade in the region as long as possible. General "Mad Anthony" Wayne was the fort's first American commander.

Detroit was incorporated as a village in 1802. It became the seat of the new territory of Michigan in 1805. The entire settlement burned to the ground that same year because of a fire that spread quickly from a stable. In rebuilding their community, the people completely replotted the streets, following a pattern suggested by the layout of Washington, D.C.

British forces captured and held Detroit briefly during the War of 1812. Fort Lernoult was renamed Fort Shelby at this time. Detroit became a city in 1815. It served as the first capital of the state of Michigan, from 1837 until 1847, when Lansing became the capital.

Until the 1870's, Detroit was primarily a commercial center for the farming trade of the surrounding territory. Then manufacturing took over as the city's chief activity.

Several factors in the early 1900's led to Detroit's leadership in automobile manufacturing. The chief factor was a determined group of Detroit men who believed they could make good automobiles. These men, including Henry Ford, Walter P. Chrysler, and Ransom E. Olds, were convinced that the cars would be financially successful. Detroit also had a surplus labor supply because the city's railroad-equipment industry had fallen in importance. In addition, land and lake routes made it easy and inexpensive to bring raw materials to the city.

During World War I, Detroit produced thousands of trucks and armored vehicles, and Liberty motors for Allied airplanes. The city converted its automobile industry entirely to war production during World War II. Military products included airplanes, artillery, aviation engines, jeeps, munitions, ships, tanks, and tank destroyers. Detroit earned the nickname of the *Arsenal of Democracy*.

Detroit's plans for the 1950's and 1960's included a program of downtown conservation and improvement. A 75-acre site along the river was cleared of old structures and dedicated to public use. The Veterans Memorial Building, completed in 1950, was the first structure in the $106,000,000 Civic Center. It stands on the site of Fort Pontchartrain. The city's plans also include new public schools, huge housing developments, and miles of new expressways. HENRY D. BROWN

Related Articles in WORLD BOOK include:

Cadillac, Antoine de la Mothe	Highland Park
Detroit, University of	Marygrove College
Detroit River	Mercy College
Ford (family)	Michigan (color picture)
General Motors Corporation	Pontiac (Indian chief)
Greenfield Village	Wayne State University
Hamtramck	

DETROIT, UNIVERSITY OF, is a coeducational school located in Detroit, Mich. It is controlled and conducted by members of the Roman Catholic Society of Jesus, but students of all faiths are admitted. The university includes colleges of arts and sciences, engineering, commerce and finance, law, and dentistry, and a graduate division. The university was founded in 1877 as Detroit College. For enrollment, see UNIVERSITIES AND COLLEGES (table). HUGH F. SMITH

DETROIT DAM stands on the North Santiam River about 45 miles southeast of Salem, Ore. It is a concrete gravity-type dam 454 feet high and 1,528 feet long. The reservoir holds 455,000 acre-feet of water. The dam's powerhouse has a capacity of 100,000 kilowatts. Completed in 1953, the dam is used for flood control, navigation, and power purposes. T. W. MERMEL

DETROIT RIVER connects Lake Saint Clair and Lake Erie. It carries more shipping than almost any other river in North America. This river forms part of the boundary between Michigan and the province of Ontario, Canada. The Detroit is sometimes called the *Dardanelles of America* because it serves the same purpose as the Dardanelles, which connects the Aegean Sea and Sea of Marmara. Boats passing through the Detroit River carry much of the grain shipped from the northwestern United States. They also carry iron ore shipped from Minnesota, Wisconsin, and northern Michigan. The Detroit River is 28 miles long, and from one-half mile to three miles wide. The upper section of the river contains a number of islands which have been used as summer resorts. The banks of the river are lined for many miles with warehouses and factories of Detroit, Mich., and Windsor, Ont. An international bridge spans the river at Detroit. LOYAL DURAND, JR.

DEUCALION, *doo KAY lih un,* was the "Noah" of Greek mythology. He was the son of Prometheus, and, according to some authorities, his mother was Pandora (see PANDORA; PROMETHEUS). When Zeus (Jupiter) decided to destroy mankind by floods because of its wickedness, Prometheus warned Deucalion and his wife Pyrrha. He told them to build a wooden ark. They floated in this ark for nine days, until they landed on the top of Mount Parnassus. When the water went down, they were the only creatures left alive on earth.

Deucalion and Pyrrha asked the oracle at Delphi how they might restore mankind (see DELPHI). The Oracle told them to "throw the bones of their mother." They guessed this to mean stones, the bones of mother earth. The stones Deucalion threw became men, and those that Pyrrha threw became women. Deucalion became the ancestor of the Greeks through his son Hellen, for whom the Hellenes (Greeks) were named. The grave of Deucalion was said to be visible at Athens in the ancient temple of Zeus. H. LLOYD STOW

DEUTERIUM, *doo TEER ih uhm,* also called HEAVY HYDROGEN, is a stable isotope of hydrogen (see ISOTOPE). Its chemical symbol is D or H^2. Deuterium is an important part of the hydrogen bomb, and is used in research in biochemistry and atomic physics. About 1 part in 6,000 of all normal hydrogen is deuterium.

Properties. The mass of an atom of deuterium is about twice that of a normal hydrogen atom. The nucleus of an ordinary hydrogen atom contains only a proton. A

DEUTERON

hydrogen atom has the atomic weight, 1.00797. The nucleus of a deuterium atom, called a *deuteron*, contains a proton and a neutron. Deuterium has an atomic weight of 2.01410. Deuterium and ordinary hydrogen have one electron. Chemically, deuterium reacts in the same way as ordinary hydrogen. But it generally reacts more slowly and less completely. Deuterium combines with oxygen to form *deuterium oxide* (D_2O), commonly called *heavy water* (see HEAVY WATER). Deuterium oxide may be used as a *moderator* in atomic reactors to reduce the speed of neutrons in a nuclear chain reaction.

Uses. Scientists frequently use deuterium to study organic and biochemical reactions. The heavy hydrogen atom serves as an *isotopic tracer*. A carbon atom can be *tagged* (labeled) by substituting the deuterium isotope for one or more of the associated hydrogen atoms. After the organic or biochemical reaction is completed, the deuterium can be located by the density of water produced, or by spectroscopic studies. This enables scientists to tell exactly how the reaction took place.

Atomic scientists use deuterons as bombarding particles in atomic reactors. A cyclotron may accelerate their energy up to many millions, or even billions, of electron volts. When these particles hit the target material, they alter the composition of its atoms and form another element or a new isotope of the original element (see CYCLOTRON; TRANSMUTATION OF ELEMENTS).

Deuterium is an important ingredient in the hydrogen bomb. *Tritium*, an isotope of hydrogen with an atomic weight of 3, is unstable. When a mixture of deuterium and tritium is triggered by an atomic explosion, a *thermonuclear* (heat-induced) chain reaction takes place. The atoms of the hydrogen isotopes fuse with each other and release energy (see FUSION; HYDROGEN BOMB).

Discovery. Harold C. Urey, an American chemist, announced his discovery of deuterium in 1932. Urey applied Niels Bohr's theories of the atom to the hydrogen atom (see BOHR, NIELS). He distilled liquid hydrogen and detected deuterium in the liquid remaining. Urey received the Nobel prize in 1934 for his discovery. Gilbert N. Lewis, a chemist at the University of California, first separated deuterium oxide from ordinary water in 1932.   HAROLD C. UREY

See also HYDROGEN; ISOTOPE; TRITIUM; UREY, HAROLD C.

DEUTERON. See DEUTERIUM.

DEUTERONOMY, *DYOO ter AHN oh mih*, is the fifth book of the Bible, and the last of the Pentateuch, or Five Books of Moses. Its name comes from a Greek word meaning *the second law*. The book contains Moses' last words to the Israelites as they prepared to enter the Promised Land. In this important hour, Moses repeated and added to many of the laws found in the earlier books of the Bible. The most famous example is the Ten Commandments, which appear in Exodus (20: 3-17) and in Deuteronomy (5: 7-21) with several changes.

Deuteronomy contains four main sections: (1) *The orations* (chapters 1 to 11) review the history of the Hebrew people in order to emphasize God's love for them and to urge them to be loyal to His Law. (2) *The laws* (12-25) deal with all areas of life. They range from rituals for religious festivals to regulations concerning family living. (3) *The great warning* (26-29) emphasizes that only obedience to God's Law can bring national well-being, and that disobedience brings disaster. A description of Moses' preparations for his death follows this section. (4) *The song of Moses* (32) stresses the relationship of love and loyalty between God and Israel, and *the blessing of Moses* (33) tells the future destiny of the tribes of Israel. The book ends with a moving account of Moses' death.

Many scholars believe that the book of Deuteronomy, or a part of it, was the book of the Law found in the Temple in Jerusalem in 621 B.C. The book of Kings tells how this book of law became the basis for a great religious reformation during the reign of King Josiah of Judah (about 639-608 B.C.).   ROBERT GORDIS

See also PENTATEUCH; MOSES; JOSIAH.

DEUTSCHLAND. See GERMANY.

DEUTSCHLAND ÜBER ALLES is the name of a famous German song that is the national anthem of West Germany. The English translation is "Germany above all." The song was written by Hoffmann von Fallersleben in 1841. He intended to express only the idea of patriotic love of country. But Germany's many wars of conquest later led to the interpretation of the song as "Germany above the whole world."

DEUTZIA, *DYUT sih uh*, is a shrub related to the hydrangea. It has clusters of white, pink, or purplish flowers. They bloom in spring or early summer, and usually have five petals. The leaves, which are new each year, have small teeth along the edges and are covered with a rough fuzz. Deutzias came from Asia, but grow well in North America and other northern regions. They thrive in well-drained soil, and make fine garden borders.

Scientific Classification. Deutzia belongs to the saxifrage family, *Saxifragaceae*. One dwarf variety is classified as genus *Deutzia*, species *D. gracilis*.   J. J. LEVISON

See also SAXIFRAGE.

J. Horace McFarland
Deutzia Gracilis

DE VALERA, *DEV uh LAIR uh*, **EAMON** (1882-   ), a leader in Ireland's fight to win independence, served three times as Prime Minister after 1937, and was elected President of Ireland in 1959. He also was President of the Irish Free State from 1932 to 1937.

De Valera was born in New York City, of a Spanish father and an Irish mother. He spent his childhood in Ireland and became a leader in the unsuccessful Easter Rebellion in 1916. A British court sentenced him to death, but the sentence was changed to life imprisonment because he was American-born. He was released in 1917, and was elected to the British Parliament because he was one of the survivors of the rebellion. The

Eamon De Valera
Miller Services, Ltd.

Sinn Féin convention in 1917 elected him "President of the Irish Republic," a paper organization (see SINN FÉIN). He was sent to prison in 1918. He escaped in 1919 and went to the United States.

In 1921, De Valera took part in negotiations with the British government that established the Irish Free State. But this settlement divided Ireland, and he opposed it. He was imprisoned for 10 months in 1923 and 1924. In 1926, De Valera resigned as president of Sinn Féin because the party refused to recognize the *Dáil Éireann* (Assembly of Ireland). The Dáil Éireann still owed partial allegiance to England. He then formed the *Fianna Fáil* (Soldiers of Destiny) party, which won control of the government in 1932. De Valera was prime minister from 1937 to 1948, from 1951 to 1954, and from 1957 to 1959. ALFRED F. HAVIGHURST

See also IRELAND (History).

DEVALUATION is a method of reducing the value of a currency. Many countries have devalued their currencies in attempts to stop falling prices at home and to improve their competitive positions in world trade. Great Britain devalued the pound from $4.03 to $2.80 in 1949, thus cutting the price of British goods in the United States by one third (see EXCHANGE). Great Britain hoped to increase its sales to the United States and to earn enough dollars to pay for its imports from the United States. The United States devalued the dollar by 41 per cent in 1934. This enabled the government to establish a fund to stabilize the dollar in terms of the value of money in other countries. LEONARD C. R. LANGER

See also MONEY (History).

DEVELOPING. See PHOTOGRAPHY (Darkroom Processes).

DEVIATION OF THE COMPASS. See COMPASS.

DEVIL is an evil spirit. The word *devil* comes from the Greek, and means *slanderer* or *false accuser*. The ancient Hebrew word for *devil* was Satan.

Early men discovered that some forces of nature were helpful, but others were harmful. To them, the dangerous forces became demons and evil spirits. They blamed demons for all their troubles.

In the Old Testament, Satan is not God's opponent. Instead, he searches out men's sins, and accuses mankind before God. In the Apocrypha, Satan is the author of all evil, and rules over a host of angels. In the New Testament, Satan has other names, such as devil, enemy, and Beelzebub. In the Middle Ages, he was usually represented with horns, a tail, and cloven hoofs.

Most religions have a devil or devils. Early Buddhists called the devil *Mara*. Zoroastrians first called the devil *Angra Mainyu*, or *lying mind*. Later, they personified him as Ahriman. They believe that Ahura-Mazda, their god, will defeat Ahriman at the end of history. The Moslem devil, *Iblis*, was an angel who rebelled when Adam was created, refusing to bow down to a creature made of earth. Moslems believe Iblis became the tempter and enemy of man. FLOYD H. ROSS

See also BEELZEBUB; DEVIL WORSHIP; LUCIFER; MEPHISTOPHELES.

DEVIL-IN-THE-BUSH. See LOVE-IN-A-MIST.

DEVIL WORSHIP is part of the religion of certain tribes in Africa, Asia, and South America. Devil dances played a large part in demon worship in Tibet, both before and after the coming of Buddhism. Devil worshipers believe that the powers of evil are as great as those of good. They believe that the devil is an evil god who can do great harm to those who refuse to worship him.

Devil worship seems to arise out of two human needs. One need is for men to deal with the evil forces they feel to be present in the world. The other is to "act out" some of the evil forces that they vaguely sense in themselves, but cannot deal with consciously.

People have often used the phrase *devil worshipers* to describe people who worship gods different from their own. The early Christians regarded most other religions as the worship of devils, indicating a lack of understanding of these religions. FLOYD H. ROSS

See also ANIMISM; DEVIL.

DEVILLE, HENRI ÉTIENNE SAINTE-CLAIRE. See ALUMINUM (Henri Etienne Sainte-Claire Deville).

DEVIL'S-DARNING-NEEDLE. See DRAGONFLY.

DEVIL'S DEN. See OKLAHOMA (Interesting Places to Visit).

DEVIL'S HOPYARD. See CONNECTICUT (Interesting Places to Visit).

DEVILS ISLAND. See FRENCH GUIANA.

DEVILS LAKE, N. Dak. (pop. 6,299; alt. 1,465 ft.), stands 54 miles east and 15 miles south of the geographic center of North America. It is a distribution and trade center for the north-central part of North Dakota. The State School for the Deaf is located in Devils Lake. South of the city is the region called Devils Lake, a park of about 100 square miles. The region contains North Dakota Military Park and the Fort Totten Indian Reservation, a state historic site. For location, see NORTH DAKOTA (color map). RUSSELL REID

DEVIL'S-PAINTBRUSH is a wild flower also called *orange hawkweed*. A cluster of orange-red flower heads grows on a slender leafless stem, sometimes 28 inches high. Oblong leaves grow around the bottom of the stem. The whole plant is covered with long hairs. The paintbrush appearance comes from a row of bristles attached to the ripening seeds. Devil's-paintbrush grows in Europe and eastern North America.

Scientific Classification. Devil's-paintbrush belongs to the composite family *Compositae*. It is genus *Hieracium*, species *H. aurantiacum*. JULIAN A. STEYERMARK

DEVILS POSTPILE NATIONAL MONUMENT is in northeastern California, surrounded by the Sierra Nevada National Forest. The monument contains a spectacular mass of blue-gray, many-sided basalt columns. It towers 60 feet above the San Joaquin River, and resembles an immense pile of posts. The 798.46-acre monument was established in 1911.

See also BASALT (picture).

DEVIL'S-SNUFFBOX. See PUFFBALL.

DEVILS TOWER NATIONAL MONUMENT is in northeastern Wyoming. It contains a natural rock tower of volcanic origin, 865 feet high. The tower rises from the hills bordering the Belle Fourche River. The 1,347-acre monument, established in September, 1906, by President Theodore Roosevelt, was the first national monument in the United States. See also WYOMING (color picture, Devils Tower).

DEVLIN, ARTHUR. See SKIING (History).

DEVOLUTION, WAR OF. See AIX-LA-CHAPELLE, TREATIES OF.

DEVON. See CATTLE (Other Beef Cattle).

DEVONIAN PERIOD

DEVONIAN PERIOD, *dee VO nih un,* in geology, is a period of the earth's history. It began approximately 330,000,000 years ago and lasted for 40,000,000 years. During this time, seas covered the continents, laying down thick sediment that became rock. The Devonian Period has been called *the age of fishes.* See also GEOLOGY (table, Outline of Earth History).

DEVONSHIRE, DUKE OF (1868-1938), VICTOR CHRISTIAN WILLIAM CAVENDISH, served as governor-general of Canada from 1916 to 1921. He was treasurer to the household of Queen Victoria in 1900, and of King Edward VII from 1901 to 1903. He served as British Secretary of State for the Colonies from 1922 to 1924. He was born in England. LUCIEN BRAULT

DE VOTO, BERNARD AUGUSTINE (1897-1955), an American editor and critic, became well known for his histories of the western frontier. He won the Pulitzer prize for *Across the Wide Missouri* in 1948. He also wrote a history, *The Year of Decision: 1846,* and *Literary Fallacy,* a criticism of fiction writing. He wrote fiction under the name John August. He wrote his books like a straight-talking frontiersman. De Voto promoted conservation in a column, "The Easy Chair," in *Harper's* magazine. He served as editor of *The Saturday Review of Literature* from 1936 to 1938. De Voto was born in Ogden, Utah, on Jan. 11, 1897. EDWIN H. CADY

DE VRIES, HUGO (1848-1935), a Dutch botanist and student of organic evolution, was known primarily as the author of the "mutation theory" (see MUTATION). This theory states that new species of plants and animals arise by *mutations* (sudden transformations) which might appear at any time and are then continued from generation to generation. De Vries' work stimulated research on heredity and evolution. However, mutations as conspicuous as those he described in the evening primrose were later proved to be the exception rather than the rule. Born at Haarlem, The Netherlands, De Vries became famous with the publication of *The Mutation Theory* (1900-1903). ROGERS McVAUGH

DE VRIES MONUMENT. See DELAWARE (Interesting Places to Visit).

DEW is the name given to the tiny, glistening drops of water that often appear on plants and blades of grass early on clear mornings.

Formation of Dew. Dew forms when moist air is cooled by direct contact with cold objects out in the open. Such things as blades of grass, leaves, or outside wires receive heat from the sun during the day by direct radiation (see RADIATION [How Radiation Affects Life on the Earth]). The heat also evaporates moisture into the air. These objects lose the heat again at night, also through radiation. Since radiation is most effective on clear nights, objects in the open cool down faster when the sky is clear than when it is cloudy. As the objects cool, the air next to them cools too. When this air reaches the *dew point,* it can no longer hold all the moisture present (see DEW POINT). It deposits this excess moisture as dew. When the temperature falls below the freezing point, *frost* forms instead of dew.

Dew forms best on still, clear nights. When the wind is blowing, the air cannot stay in contact with cool objects long enough to cool to the dew point. When the sky is cloudy, the earth and objects in exposed places lose heat more slowly than when it is clear.

Where Dew Forms. Dew forms better on dark objects than on light-colored ones because dark objects radiate heat best. Dew also forms more readily on materials that conduct heat well, such as metal car tops, than on poor heat conductors, such as wooden poles.

Importance of Dew. In some parts of the world where rainfall is very light, dew is extremely important to plant growth. In Lima, Peru, for example, dew supplies more water than rain. Dew is often heavy in tropical regions where the air is extremely moist and the nights cool. GEORGE F. TAYLOR

See also AIR (Moisture in Air); FROST.

DEW LINE, or DISTANT EARLY WARNING LINE, protects the U.S. and Canada against air attack from the north. It has 64 radar stations and extends 4,500 miles from the Aleutian Islands, across Canada, to Iceland. The original 3,000 miles of the DEW line is operated by the U.S. and Canada from North American Air Defense (NORAD) headquarters at Colorado Springs, Colo. NORAD and Space Surveillance (SPASUR) control the rest. SPASUR tracks objects in earth orbit. See RADAR (Radar Warning Systems).

Dew Looks Like Jewels on the Strands of a Spider Web. Hugh Spencer

HOW DEW IS FORMED

The Heat of the Sun causes moisture from the earth to evaporate into the warm air. | **After Sunset,** the air and the earth cool, moisture condenses, and dewdrops form.

DEW POINT is the temperature at which moisture in the air begins to condense. The dew point is either lower than the air temperature, or the same as the air temperature, when the relative humidity is 100 per cent. Dew forms when a thin film of air, in contact with the surface, is cooled to below the dew point. Cooling the air below its dew point causes dew on the surface or fog in the air, when the dew point is above the freezing temperature. If the air temperature and dew point are below freezing, frost may form on the surface, or ice crystals may form in the air. Fog and clouds occur when large volumes of air are cooled to below the dew point. P. E. Church

See also CONDENSATION; DEW; FOG; FROST; HUMIDITY.

DEWAR, SIR JAMES (1842-1923), was a British chemist and physicist. He invented the Dewar flask, a type of vacuum bottle, commonly known today as the *thermos bottle* (see VACUUM BOTTLE). Dewar was born in Kincardine-on-Forth, Scotland, and studied at Edinburgh University. He did much of his experimental research at the Royal Institution in London, where he was professor of chemistry.

DEWBERRY is a trailing blackberry. It is not an erect bush, like other blackberries, but a bramble of long and willowy branches that trail on the ground or climb over other shrubs and fences. The dewberry is

The Dewberry Has a Wine Color and a Sweet Taste.

also called *running blackberry* and *ground blackberry*. The fruit is similar to that of the erect blackberries. However, dewberries tend to ripen earlier than most erect ones. New plants are raised from the tips of branches, which grow roots when they come in contact with the soil. The roots grow for many years, but the tops live only two years. The fruit grows on branches during the second year. Both wild and cultivated varieties grow well in the southern states, in parts of the North, Midwest, and East, and along the Pacific. Cultivated varieties include *Young*, *Logan*, *Boysen*, and *Lucretia*.

Scientific Classification. The dewberry belongs to the rose family, *Rosaceae*. The southern variety is genus *Rubus*, species *R. trivialis*. REID M. BROOKS

DEWEY, GEORGE (1837-1917), an American naval officer, won fame as "the hero of Manila." He was the only American ever to become Admiral of the Navy.

Dewey was in Hong Kong in command of the Asiatic Squadron when war broke out between Spain and the United States in 1898. He received orders on April 26 to go to the Philippine Islands and capture or destroy the Spanish fleet. Late on April 30, Dewey's six ships, led by the U.S.S. *Olympia*, approached Manila Bay.

DEWEY, JOHN

Early the next day Dewey gave the captain of the *Olympia* the famous command, "You may fire when you are ready, Gridley," and attacked the Spanish fleet of 10 cruisers and gunboats. By noon Dewey's force had destroyed the Spanish fleet without the loss of a single American life. This victory made the United States an important power in the Pacific Ocean, and inspired the confidence of the American people in the U.S. Navy. After his victory Dewey remained in Manila Bay until troops arrived to capture Manila. When Dewey returned to New York City in 1899, he received a great welcome. The people of the country donated funds to buy a home for him in Washington, D.C. The Congress presented Dewey with a sword, and all his men were awarded medals.

Dewey was born on Dec. 26, 1837, in Montpelier, Vt. He studied at Norwich Military Academy and at the United States Naval Academy at Annapolis. Dewey saw his first wartime naval service in the Civil War. As a lieutenant, he became the executive officer of the U.S.S. *Mississippi* in David Farragut's fleet in 1861. He took part in the famous run past the forts that guarded New Orleans. Later, Dewey served on Farragut's flagship (see FARRAGUT, DAVID G.). He became president of the newly created General Board of the Navy Department in 1900, and the next year he served as president of the Schley court of inquiry (see SCHLEY, WINFIELD S.). He served as an honored adviser on all naval matters until his death. In 1925, eight years after his death, Dewey's body was placed in the Cathedral of Saints Peter and Paul in Washington, D.C. DONALD W. MITCHELL

See also PHILIPPINES (War with Spain).

DEWEY, JOHN (1859-1952), was a widely known and influential American philosopher and educator. His philosophical beliefs have been described as (1) radical empiricism, (2) instrumentalism, (3) experimentalism, and (4) pragmatism.

Radical empiricism means that Dewey's philosophy sticks close to the standpoint of human experience. To find out the meaning of things, one has to see how they are presented in experience. Things *are* what they are experienced to be. See EMPIRICISM.

Instrumentalism is a term usually applied to Dewey's theory of reason. He held that ideas are plans of action. They arise in response to a problem, and serve their purpose by solving the problem. Ideas are *instruments* in the reconstruction of experience.

Admiral George Dewey
Brown Bros.

John Dewey
G. P. Putnam's Sons

DEWEY, MELVIL

Dewey's philosophy also might properly be called *experimentalism*, because it insists that ideas must always be tested by experiment. He believed that no knowledge is ever so certain that it is not subject to new evidence which experimentation and experiences might provide.

Dewey's philosophy is practical in character, like that of William James. James believed that an idea must be judged by how it works. Because of this, his philosophy is frequently called *pragmatism*. See PRAGMATISM.

Dewey applied these basic concepts to nearly every aspect of philosophy and education. His notion that ideas are plans of action determines his theory of truth. If an idea does what it intends as a plan of action, it is true. If it fails, it is false. Dewey's experimental beliefs carried over into his educational philosophy, and became the basis for what is usually described as *progressive education* (see PROGRESSIVE EDUCATION). His influence on public schools has been great, both in the United States and in other nations.

Among Dewey's most important books are *The School and Society* (1899), *Essays in Experimental Logic* (1916), *Experience and Nature* (1925), *The Quest for Certainty* (1929), *Art as Experience* (1934), and *Logic, the Theory of Inquiry* (1938).

Dewey was born on Oct. 20, 1859, in Burlington, Vt. He was graduated from the University of Vermont in 1879, and received his Ph.D. from Johns Hopkins University in 1884. He became a professor of philosophy at the University of Minnesota in 1888, and served in the same position at the University of Michigan from 1889 to 1894. He served as head of the department of philosophy and pedagogy at the University of Chicago from 1894 to 1904. From 1904 until his retirement in 1930, Dewey was a professor of philosophy at Columbia University. EUGENE T. ADAMS.

DEWEY, MELVIL (1851-1931), an American librarian, began the decimal library-classification system (see DEWEY DECIMAL SYSTEM). He founded the American Library Association and the *Library Journal* in 1876 (see AMERICAN LIBRARY ASSOCIATION). He became chief librarian of Columbia University in 1883, and established the first library school there in 1887. He served as director of the New York State Library from 1889 to 1906. He was born in Adams Center, N.Y. See also EXTENSION SERVICE. R. B. DOWNS.

DEWEY, NELSON. See WISCONSIN (Famous Wisconsinites).

DEWEY, THOMAS EDMUND (1902-), a successful prosecuting attorney and Republican politician, served as governor of New York from 1943 to 1955. He ran unsuccessfully for President of the United States on the Republican ticket in 1944 and 1948. His running mates for Vice President were John Bricker and Earl Warren.

Dewey was born on March 24, 1902, in Owosso, Mich. He was graduated from the University of Michigan, and finished his law course at Columbia University in two years. In 1933, he became United States attorney for the southern district of New York state. Governor Herbert Lehman appointed him special prosecutor for vice and racket investigations in New York City in 1935. Dewey's vigorous and successful prosecution of organized crime brought him wide recognition.

He was defeated for the New York governorship in 1938, but was elected in 1942, the first Republican governor of the state in 20 years. He was re-elected in 1946 and 1950, but did not seek office in 1954. Dewey's defeat in the 1948 presidential election was considered a major political upset. Dewey returned to his private law practice in 1955. RICHARD L. WATSON, JR.

United Press Int.
Thomas E. Dewey

DEWEY DECIMAL SYSTEM is the most widely used method of classifying books in a library. It is named for Melvil Dewey, who developed it in 1876 (see DEWEY, MELVIL). This system classifies books by dividing them into 10 main groups. Each of these different classes is represented by figures, as in the following table:

000-099 General Works (encyclopedias, bibliographies, periodicals, journalism)
100-199 Philosophy, Psychology, Ethics (conduct)
200-299 Religion and Mythology
300-399 Social Sciences (economics, sociology, civics, law, education, vocations, customs)
400-499 Philology (language, dictionaries, grammar)
500-599 Science (mathematics, astronomy, physics, chemistry, geology, paleontology, biology, zoology, botany)
600-699 Useful Arts (medicine, engineering, agriculture, home economics, business, radio, television, aviation)
700-799 Fine Arts (architecture, sculpture, painting, music, photography, recreation)
800-899 Literature (novels, poetry, plays, criticism)
900-999 History, Geography, Biography, Travel

Each of these 10 main classes is broken up into more specialized fields. For example, class 600-699, Useful Arts, is subdivided into 10 special classes. Each of these divisions is further subdivided. The numbers 630-639, for example, represent Agriculture, and are subdivided into such classes as Field Crops, Garden Crops, and Dairy Products. When the classification becomes very fine, decimals are used. For example, books on useful insects, such as bees and silkworms, would be grouped together under 638. Books on beekeeping would be in 638.1, and those on silkworms in 638.2.

Some libraries do not use the Dewey Decimal System, but have their own classifications. RALPH A. ULVELING.

DE WITT, JAN. See NETHERLANDS (Wars with England and France).

DEXTRIN, *DEKS trin*, is a sticky substance obtained from starch. Its chemical make-up is very much like that of starch. They are both *carbohydrates* (see CARBOHYDRATE), but dextrin is the simpler of the two and more easily digested. Dextrin causes the slightly sweet taste of a crust of bread. In the human body, dextrin forms during digestion by the action of saliva and other body liquids on starch. For use in industry, dextrin can be made by heating starch or by treating it with an acid. It is used as an adhesive on postage stamps. Manufacturers also use dextrin in *sizing* (stiffening) textiles, and in cosmetics, glues, paints, and varnish. RICHARD A. HAVENS.

See also STARCH.

DEXTROSE is a white, grainy sugar. It is found in fruits such as grapes and in the bodies of human beings and animals. Dextrose, sometimes called *grape sugar*, or *glucose*, is not as sweet as ordinary sugar. Dextrose dissolves more easily in water than sugar does, and is easily absorbed by the intestines. Because it is already a *simple sugar*, it does not need to be digested. This quality makes dextrose a source of quick energy and an emergency food. Dextrose is often dissolved in liquid and forced into the blood system of a patient who has just had a surgical operation. If too much dextrose is taken into the body it becomes either fat or waste. In the case of a person who has diabetes, dextrose passes into the blood because the body tissues do not burn it up. Dextrose is manufactured from cornstarch for commercial use. It is usually made in the form of corn sirup. The starch is treated with steam, under pressure, in the presence of hydrochloric acid. Dextrose is used in candymaking, in soda-fountain mixtures, in the preserving of fruits, and in making soap and tanning fluids. See also GLUCOSE. RICHARD A. HAVENS

DHAULAGIRI. See HIMALAYA; MOUNTAIN (table, Famous Mountains of the World).

DHOLE is a wild dog of India.

DHOTI. See INDIA (Costume).

DHOW is an Egyptian sailboat. See EGYPT (Transportation; picture, The Great Nile River).

DIABASE. See BASALT.

DIABETES, *DY uh BEE teez*, is the name of two diseases that have the same sign, excessive urination. *Diabetes mellitus*, the more common of the two, occurs when the pancreas does not produce enough of the hormone *insulin* (see PANCREAS). *Diabetes insipidus* results when the posterior (rear) lobe of the pituitary gland does not function normally.

Diabetes Mellitus is characterized by the presence of abnormal amounts of sugar in the blood and by sugar in the urine. Insulin enables the body to store and burn the sugar in food properly. When the pancreas does not produce enough insulin, the body cannot use or store sugar normally. Excess sugar accumulates in the blood. The kidneys give off some of this sugar into the urine. The way fat and protein are used is also abnormal in diabetes mellitus, and excessive amounts of the products of their breakdown appear in the blood and urine.

The Signs and Symptoms, besides the presence of too much sugar and other products in the blood and urine, may include great thirst, passing large amounts of urine, loss of weight, and loss of strength. Untreated diabetics have a tendency toward attacks of boils, carbuncles, and other infections. The disease also causes decreased blood circulation in the limbs. This may result in gangrene.

Treatment. Most cases of diabetes cannot be cured. But almost all may be controlled by injections of insulin and careful attention to diet. Diabetics often live as long as people in normal health. Every diabetic should be under a doctor's care. The patient should learn to test his urine for sugar, and keep a record of his diet, weight, and urine sugar.

Some mild cases of diabetes can be controlled by diet alone. The diabetic should not eat foods high in sugar, such as candy, cake, and jam. Special foods that contain little or no added sugar are available. The diet can be pleasing and varied if the patient is careful about the food he chooses. He should carefully select foods that contain needed vitamins and minerals.

Even when a diabetic uses insulin, he must watch his diet carefully. The amount of insulin given depends on weight, diet, amount of exercise, severity of the disease, and general health. Most diabetics, including small children, give themselves injections of insulin.

Insulin, the natural antidiabetic hormone, must be given by injection, because if taken by mouth it is destroyed in the digestive system. Scientists have developed several drugs that diabetics can take by mouth. The safest drug tested, *tolbutamide*, lowers the blood-sugar level in some diabetics. Some people who develop diabetes when they are adults are able to use tolbutamide instead of insulin. But these people must be under a doctor's care.

Diabetes Insipidus is characterized by the excessive passing of urine. Because the patient loses so much water, he becomes very thirsty. This condition results from injury or disease of the posterior lobe of the pituitary gland. The injured gland does not produce its *antidiuretic hormone*. Without this hormone, the kidneys cannot hold back water that passes to them from the blood. Diabetes insipidus cannot be cured. But treatment with *pitressin*, an extract of the posterior lobe of the pituitary gland, lets the kidney reabsorb water.

The American Diabetes Association sponsors research and conducts public education primarily in the field of diabetes mellitus. Its headquarters are at 1 E. 45th St., New York City. CHARLES H. BEST

See also CORI; DISEASE (table, Diseases Most Important in Causing Death); FEHLING'S SOLUTION; GLAND (The Endocrine Glands); INSULIN.

DIABLO DAM is part of the Seattle power system on the Skagit River in northwestern Washington. This power project lies in the high, wooded slopes of Mount Baker National Forest near Pyramid Peak. Diablo is an arch dam, 389 feet high and 1,180 feet long. The reservoir holds 90,000 acre-feet of water. It was completed in 1930. The powerhouse was completed in 1936, and has a capacity of 122,400 kilowatts. T. W. MERMEL

See also DAM; ROSS DAM.

DIACRITICAL MARK is a sign used to show differences, usually in sounds and pronunciation. For example, the *e* sounds in *eve* and *end* are different, so they have been given separate signs. The names of the most common signs are: *macron* (ēve), *detached bar* (ĕvent), *breve* (ĕnd), *italic breve* (silĕnt), and *tilde* (makēr). Diacritical marks are also used on many foreign personal and place names. Examples are: Müller (German), Dvořák (Czech), Noël (French), Ångerman (Swedish), Blasco-Ibáñez (Spanish), and Bragança (Portuguese). See also PRONUNCIATION; and the Key to Pronunciation, in the front of the A volume. MARTHA F. SIMMONDS

DIADEM. See CROWN.

DIAGHILEV, or DIAGHILEFF, *DYAH gih lef*, **SERGEI PAVLOVICH** (1872-1929), was a Russian impresario. He presented *Les Ballets Russes* in Paris in 1909 and electrified Europe. The company later became famous as the *Diaghilev Ballets Russes*. Diaghilev introduced Russian ballet to the United States in 1916. Diaghilev was born at Perm, Novgorod, Russia. DORATHI BOCK PIERRE

See also BALLET (Russian Ballet).

145

DIAGNOSIS

DIAGNOSIS, DIE ug NO sis, is the art by which doctors determine which diseases are affecting their patients. The X ray may be used to give a diagnosis of tuberculosis. A chemical analysis of the patient's urine is often taken to see if the patient has diabetes. Diagnosis is one of the most important branches of medicine.

There are many different types of diagnosis. A *biological* diagnosis is made by performing tests on animals with a sample of one of the patient's body fluids. A *clinical diagnosis* is made completely from symptoms. A *differential diagnosis* is one that compares symptoms of several diseases to see which one is most likely to be causing the trouble. One way of deciding what is wrong with a sick person is to decide what disease he does *not* have. The doctor compares the sick person's symptoms with the known symptoms of various diseases. All the diseases are weeded out until it is fairly certain that the patient could have only one disease. This is called *diagnosis by exclusion*. A *laboratory diagnosis* is made by studying the blood, urine, or other liquids of the body in a laboratory, as in the case of anemia and diabetes.

A *physical diagnosis* is made by looking at the patient for signs of disease apparent to the eye, such as rashes or broken bones, and examining the patient with the hands. Sometimes doctors will actually try to induce symptoms or make them worse, when they think a disease is present but cannot be sure because the symptoms are not definite enough. Another type of bacteriologic diagnosis involves the injection of sera and observing the change of appearance in the skin at the site of injection. For example, an injection of tuberculin is often given as a test for tuberculosis. The patient is susceptible to the disease if the injection makes him develop a local "rash." A *tentative diagnosis* is sometimes made when the symptoms are not definite. The diagnosis is made, and the doctors give treatment for what they decide the disease to be, but they watch closely for new symptoms.

When a patient is first seen, the doctor usually checks a few basic things immediately. He may look into the mouth to see if the patient's tongue is coated, or if his throat shows signs of an infection. He may listen to the patient's heart and lungs with a stethoscope, take his pulse, and examine his ears and eyes. All these things are part of a simple diagnosis. If the doctor hears something unusual in the heart action, for example, he may make further heart diagnosis with an electrocardiograph machine. Terminals of wire conducting very small amounts of electricity are fastened to the patient's arms and legs so that they register the way the heart functions and record the movement on a graph. Any irregular heart action will make an irregular line on the graph.

Modern methods of diagnosis have been aided by the invention of such devices as the stethoscope and the electrocardiograph, and by improvements in laboratory technique. If cancer is suspected, a small piece of tissue may be cut from the diseased part and examined in the laboratory to see if cancerous cells are present. Smears of body fluids can be examined underneath the microscope to identify the germ of a disease. In some cases, fluids from the person's body may be injected into a laboratory animal to see if it develops a disease.

A diagnosis for anemia is made by taking a sample of the patient's blood and examining it to see if it has a sufficient number of red blood corpuscles, and if it contains sufficient iron in the form of hemoglobin.

Every disease has certain symptoms. Mumps causes an increase in the size of glands in the lower part of the face and upper part of the neck creating an appearance of swollen jaws. Infantile paralysis frequently begins with signs of a bad cold, moderately increased temperature, pains in the back and joints, and weakness of muscle. People with diabetes usually urinate more frequently than is normal.   AUSTIN EDWARD SMITH

Related Articles in WORLD BOOK include:
Biopsy	Gastroscope	Ophthalmoscope
Bronchoscope	Manometer	Spirometer
Electrocardiograph	Metabolimeter	Stethoscope
Fluoroscope		

DIAGNOSTIC TEST. See TESTS AND MEASUREMENTS (Diagnostic Tests).

DIAL. See CLOCK; SUNDIAL.

DIALECT, DIE uh lekt, is the way people talk in a certain district of a country, or in a certain social class. Dialect differs from accepted speech patterns of the language. The people of New England will usually say "idear" instead of *idea*, "caah" instead of *car*, or "Bahstun" for *Boston*. This localized usage in pronunciation is part of the *dialect* of the people in that district. The use of certain words or expressions in a locality is also considered as part of the dialect.

Once it was not so easy to move about and talk with others as it is now. People living only a few miles apart spoke differently. Sometimes a group of people, such as cowboys, rivermen, or thieves, would develop a dialect as important as that of a region. Newspapers and the radio of today, by following standard usages, are helping to reduce these differences in speech.

Dialects have been preserved in literature for readers to enjoy and study. They are as much a part of local color as are geography and customs. Many authors have recognized this fact and become famous as a result. Among stories told in dialect are Mark Twain's stories of the Mississippi, Joel Chandler Harris' *Uncle Remus* stories of the Southern Negro, and Bret Harte's tales of the Western mining camps.

Dialects are even more marked in Great Britain. Some of them are London Cockney, Yorkshire, and Scottish. Rudyard Kipling immortalized the British soldiers' dialect in his stories and poems. Sir James Barrie was a master of Scottish dialect. The French language has several dialects, including Picard, Norman, Lorrain, and Walloon.   CLARENCE STRATTON

See also IDIOM; JARGON; LANGUAGE; SLANG.

DIALECTICAL MATERIALISM. See MATERIALISM; METAPHYSICS (Doctrines); PHILOSOPHY (Philosophy and Government).

DIAMETER, die AM uh tur, in geometry, is the length of a straight line that crosses through the center of a circle or a sphere and touches its boundaries. *Diameter* is also the name of the line itself. The *radius* runs from the center to the boundary of a circle or sphere. It is half as long as a diameter.

When a microscope or telescope enlarges the apparent size of an object, the degree of magnification is expressed in *diameters*. For example, a microscope that makes a line appear 10 times longer has enlarged the line 10 diameters, usually written *10X*.   HOLMES BOYNTON

See also CIRCLE; MICROSCOPE; SPHERE.

FLORENTINE

DRESDEN GREEN

SANCY

STAR OF ESTE

Diamond Mining in South Africa takes place in shafts and tunnels sunk hundreds of feet underground. The diamonds come from *blue ground* rock found in or near extinct volcanoes. Miners drill and blast out huge chunks of this rock. Machines on the surface crush the rock to free the diamonds, which must then be cut and polished.

KOH-I-NOOR

A Fortune in Diamonds is represented by these world-famous gems, whose value totals millions of dollars.

ORLOFF

TIFFANY

CULLINAN I

HOPE

DIAMOND is the hardest naturally occurring substance known to man, and one of the most valuable. Because of its hardness, it is the most enduring of all gem stones. In Europe and America the diamond is the traditional jewel for engagement and wedding rings. In addition to its use as a gem, the diamond is used in many industries for cutting, grinding, and boring.

What Diamonds Are. In composition, diamonds are almost pure carbon, with small amounts of impurities that give color to the stones. They form in crystals. (See CRYSTAL AND CRYSTALLIZATION.) Most diamonds have eight sides, which form a double pyramid. Some diamonds have as many as twelve sides, all exactly alike. Others have six sides, forming a cube. Scientists believe diamonds were formed millions of years ago when carbon was subjected to great heat and pressure.

A diamond can be used to cut another diamond. The only other material that can cut a diamond is *borazon*, an artificial substance first produced in 1957. But diamonds can be separated or broken with a severe blow, since in certain directions they lack toughness. A diamond will not dissolve in acid. But it can be destroyed when it is subjected to intense heat. If it is heated in the presence of oxygen, it will vaporize as carbon dioxide. If it is heated without oxygen, it will turn to graphite, a mineral so soft that it is used as a lubricant. Some diamonds can be made to glow when they are subjected to X rays or to ultraviolet light.

Where Diamonds Are Found. Diamonds are among the most costly jewels in the world, partly because they are rare. Only three important diamond fields have been found in the world, in India, South America, and Africa. The earliest diamonds came from India where they were found in the beds of streams, but India produces few diamonds today. Valuable fields were discovered in Brazil about 1725, and today Brazil provides about 4 per cent of the world's diamonds. The largest yield comes from Africa, which produces about 95 per cent of the world's supply. Many of the African diamonds are suitable only for industrial use.

The first diamonds were found in the sand and gravel of stream beds. These were called *alluvial* diamonds. Later, diamonds were found deep in the earth, in rock formations, called *pipes*, that resemble the throats of extinct volcanoes. The rock in which diamonds are found is called *blue ground*. But even in the South African mines, which are the richest source of gem diamonds in the world, many tons of blue ground must be taken from deep in the earth, crushed, and sorted to obtain one small diamond. Of the ore taken from these mines, *only one part in thirty-five million is diamond*. In 1955, De Beers Consolidated Mines announced a new and cheaper method of mining diamonds, called *block caving*. A large cone-shaped excavation is dug beneath the blue ground and lined with concrete. Above the cones, the miners cut a slot, causing the ground to cave in and settle in the cones. When the ground settles, it breaks into small pieces which then go to lower tunnels to be processed.

The diamond fields of South Africa were discovered in 1866, when a Boer farmer's children found "a pretty pebble" in the sandy bed of the Vaal River.

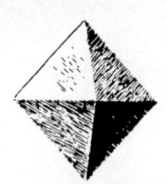

A rough, uncut and unpolished diamond before cutting begins.

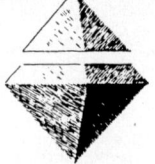

Before polishing, a worker saws the rough diamond in two.

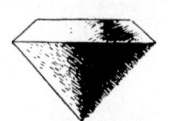

Experts next grind off the diamond's corners so it is shaped like a top.

Now workers begin to polish the tiny facets.

A finished diamond usually has a total of 58 facets.

Cutting and Polishing transforms rough diamonds into sparkling gems in the steps shown above. Craftsmen polish tiny *facets* (sides) on the diamonds with machines resembling phonographs, *right*. An arm clamps the diamond at the proper angle to grind a facet against a revolving disk coated with diamond dust.

The "pebble" proved to be a diamond worth $2,500. Stones worth more than $1,000,000,000 have been taken from these mines. In 1956, Russia announced the discovery of a large diamond deposit in Siberia.

In the United States, single alluvial diamonds have been found in widely separated places. The only diamond mine in the United States is located near Murfreesboro, Ark. See ARKANSAS (color picture).

How Diamonds Are Cut to Make Jewels. Most diamonds look dull when they are taken from the ground. Many are covered with a sort of grayish film. Diamonds have great power to reflect light, bend rays of light, and to break light up into all the colors of the rainbow. But to produce the greatest possible brilliance in a diamond, many little sides, or *facets*, must be cut and polished on it, and each tiny facet must be exactly the right size and shape and must be placed at exactly the right angle.

At first, the cutters simply polished the rough stone to take off the dull surface, by rubbing one stone against another. Later, during the 1400's, the cutters learned how to shape and polish a diamond by use of an iron wheel coated with diamond dust. As man learned more about diamonds, he discovered the shapes which would give the greatest brilliance. The style of cut which is most often seen today is the round shape with fifty-eight facets, which is called the *brilliant cut*. This style of cutting was begun in the 1600's. In recent years, diamond saws have been developed. They are used to saw the diamond crystals into parts. A diamond is polished from each part. See LAPIDARY.

How Diamonds Can Be Judged. Gem diamonds are graded according to weight, purity, color, and cut. The

De Beers Consolidated Mines, Ltd.; U&U

weight of a diamond is measured by the *carat*, one carat weighing 200 milligrams. The *purity* of a diamond can be lessened by various kinds of flaws. These flaws include the presence of foreign minerals and uncrystallized carbon, small *pores* caused by gas or moisture, and small cracks, or *fissures*, which jewelers sometimes call *feathers*. The color of most diamonds used in jewelry consists of a faintly yellowish tint. A small percentage of gem diamonds are colorless, and a few possess a faint tinge of blue. There are also red, yellow, brown, green, and even black diamonds, although only yellow and brown diamonds are common. The *cut* of the diamond affects its value, because a stone that is not accurately cut, or is not properly proportioned, does not have as much brilliance as a stone that is well cut.

In buying a diamond, the buyer should have the ad-

The Size of Diamonds is determined by their weight in carats. One carat equals one fifth of a gram. Each circle represents a diamond of a certain size. The figures above each circle give the approximate weight and approximate diameter in millimeters.

Gemological Institute of America

.02	.03	.05	.06	.08	.09	.11	.13	........Carat
1.55	2.0	2.35	2.6	2.75	2.9	3.0	3.2	........Millimeter

.25	.33	.50	.75	1.0	2.0	4.0	........Carat
4.1	4.4	5.2	5.8	6.4	8.0	10.5	........Millimeter

MAN-MADE DIAMONDS

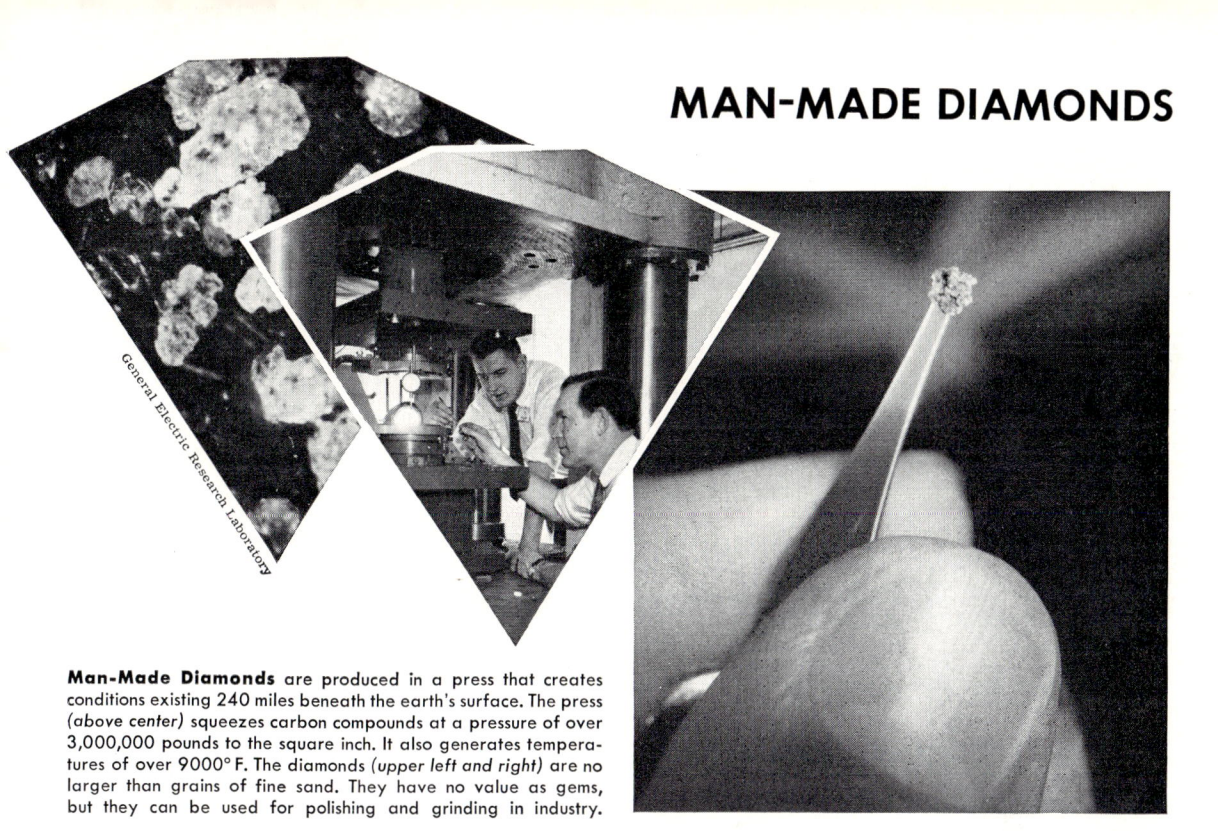

Man-Made Diamonds are produced in a press that creates conditions existing 240 miles beneath the earth's surface. The press (above center) squeezes carbon compounds at a pressure of over 3,000,000 pounds to the square inch. It also generates temperatures of over 9000° F. The diamonds (upper left and right) are no larger than grains of fine sand. They have no value as gems, but they can be used for polishing and grinding in industry.

vice of a reliable dealer. Terms used to describe gem diamonds vary considerably. A *flawless* diamond should have no physical defects, such as cracks, spots, scratches, blemishes, or cloudy texture. But a flawless diamond may not have the right color. Some dealers use the term *perfect* to describe a diamond that has no flaws, and also is the right color. Both these terms are sometimes used to mean that the diamond is perfectly or flawlessly cut and shaped.

One of the reasons why diamonds are so expensive is that cutting and polishing the rough diamond is a slow and costly process. It must be done by highly trained workers, who take many years to learn to do their work skillfully.

Famous Diamonds. Many large diamonds of rare quality are the property of royalty or of a government. The largest stone ever discovered was the *Cullinan*. This diamond, found in 1905 in the Premier mine of South Africa, weighed 3,106 carats, or about one and one-third pounds. It was purchased by the Transvaal Government and presented to King Edward VII of England. Amsterdam cutters trimmed the Cullinan into nine large stones and ninety-six smaller stones. The largest of these is the largest cut diamond in the world. In 1934 the *Jonker* diamond was found. It weighed 726 carats, and was said to be unequalled in purity. In 1935-1937 the Jonker was cut into twelve flawless stones. The *Orloff* is a magnificent Russian crown jewel which was bought by Prince Orloff for the Empress Catherine II. This huge diamond is said to have been stolen from the eye of an idol in a Hindu temple. The *Koh-i-noor*, now in the British crown jewels, was for many centuries in the possession of Indian and Persian rulers. It came into the possession of Great Britain when the British annexed the Punjab in 1849. The *Regent*, or *Pitt*, diamond is an Indian gem and is regarded as one of the most beautiful of the large stones. The Regent is owned by France and exhibited in the Louvre Museum. The most famous of Brazilian diamonds is the *Star of the South*. The blue, $44\frac{1}{2}$-carat *Hope* diamond became the property of the Smithsonian Institution in 1958.

Industrial Uses. Diamonds are widely used today for industrial work. They are necessary because manufacturers of automobiles, airplanes, and other kinds of engines and machinery began to use harder metals and to design engines and motors which required greater accuracy in shaping the parts. Often it is now necessary to shape very hard metal to an accuracy of one ten-thousandth of an inch or less. Diamonds are used in such work because they are harder than nearly any other substance and can cut, grind, and bore very hard metal more quickly and more accurately than any other material. Sometimes whole rough diamonds are set into industrial tools. Sometimes the diamonds are crushed and the diamond dust is baked into the industrial tools. Occasionally, the diamonds are cut to some special shape before they are set into tools. Diamonds are set in the ends of drills used in mining. Very fine wire is drawn to size through diamonds in which tapering holes have been cut. A permanent, indestructible diamond needle is used in some makes of record machines.

The diamonds used in industry are stones which are imperfectly formed, contain flaws, or have poor color.

In 1955, the General Electric Research Laboratory announced that a team of its scientists had made diamonds from a carbonaceous material under extreme pressures and temperatures. FREDERICK H. POUGH

Related Articles in WORLD BOOK include:

Borazon	Carbon	Hardness
Carat	Gem	Lapidary

DIAMOND CAVE

DIAMOND CAVE. See Arkansas (Interesting Places).

DIAMOND HEAD is an extinct volcano, 760 feet high, located on the Hawaiian island of Oahu, 5 miles southeast of Honolulu. The crater contains a National Guard base, and a highway runs along its top. See also Hawaii (picture, The Punchbowl).

DIAMOND HORSESHOE. See Metropolitan Opera Association.

DIAMOND STATE. See Delaware.

DIANA, *dy AN uh,* was the Roman goddess of hunting and the moon. Her Greek name was Artemis. She was the daughter of Jupiter and Latona (Zeus and Leto) and the twin sister of Apollo. Diana was the goddess of wild animals and especially protected young creatures. She looked after maidens and helped women in childbirth. Her temple at Ephesus in Asia Minor was one of the most splendid in the ancient world.

Diana in her usual form is represented as a beautiful young woman, dressed in hunting clothes. She has a bow and arrows, and is often pictured with a deer or hunting dogs.

She was often confused in ancient myths with Hecate, a goddess of sorcerers, witches, and ghosts. In this form Diana was worshiped at crossroads in the dark of the night (see Hecate). O. M. Pearl

See also Actaeon; Apollo; Arethusa; Iphigenia.

Statue of Diana stands in the Vatican Museum.

DIAPHRAGM, *DIE uh fram,* is the large muscular structure which separates the chest from the abdomen. Only man and the group of animals called *mammals* have complete diaphragms. The diaphragm is the chief muscle used in breathing. It is shaped like a dome. When we take a breath, the diaphragm moves downward and becomes flat. This increases the space above it in the chest. At the same time, the small muscles attached to the ribs cause these ribs to move outward, expanding the chest. All this expansion makes room for more air to come into the lungs from the outside. When the air rushes in, we say we are taking a breath. This action is called *inspiration.* Breathing out is *expiration.* In expiration, the diaphragm curves up toward the chest again and the air is forced out of the lungs.

The *phrenic nerve* carries to the diaphragm the stimuli which make it work. This nerve extends from the neck through the chest down to the diaphragm.

Besides its work in breathing, the diaphragm often helps an animal to support itself. If a person wants to pull or lift a heavy object, he will usually take a deep breath and then hold it while he acts. This contracts the diaphragm until it is firm and hard. The diaphragm is

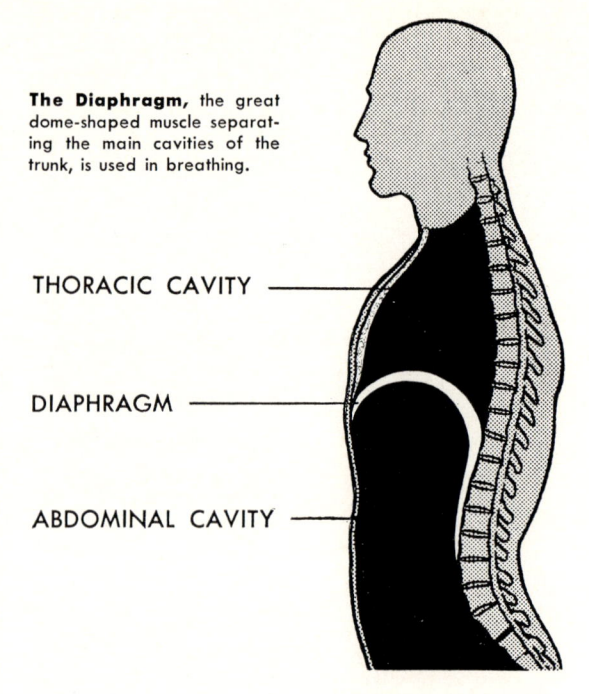

The Diaphragm, the great dome-shaped muscle separating the main cavities of the trunk, is used in breathing.

THORACIC CAVITY

DIAPHRAGM

ABDOMINAL CAVITY

attached to the ribs, and it holds them in one position. This action is called "fixing" the ribs. It is very important in doing heavy work, because many large muscles of the back and abdomen are attached to the ribs. If the ribs are firmly fixed, these muscles can pull against them with great force. The word diaphragm comes from two Greek words that mean through, and to fence or enclose. Andrew Conway Ivy

See also Abdomen; Chest; Respiration.

DIARRHEA, *DIE uh REE uh,* is an intestinal disorder suffered by men and animals. It is characterized by frequent bowel movements. The stools may be soft or watery, and may contain either mucus or pus. In severe cases the stools may contain blood. The victim of diarrhea often has cramping pains in the abdomen. In severe cases, the victim may have a constant thirst.

Diarrhea is often a symptom rather than a disease itself. It accompanies bacillary or amebic dysentery, and ulcerative colitis. It also occurs in regional enteritis and chronic pancreatic disease. Diarrhea is sometimes caused by infected food. It occurs when intestinal parasites infest the body. Poisons, such as arsenic, silver salts, and mercury, can cause an attack. Diarrhea may also come with emotional disturbances, such as fear and grief. E. Clinton Texter

See also Cholera; Colitis; Dysentery; Enteritis; Thrush (disease).

DIARY is a notebook containing a day-by-day account of personal experiences. Diaries are also known as *journals.* Keeping a diary is a valuable activity for young persons. It helps them learn to express their beliefs, their experiences, and their desires. The rereading of a diary which has been kept for several years helps the writer to realize how his attitudes may have changed and how his mind has grown. A diary also serves as a factual record of events that might otherwise be difficult to recall.

Samuel Pepys, an Englishman, kept a diary over a period of nine years, from 1660 to 1669. Pepys' diary has become one of the most notable in the world. In it the author gives a full and realistic portrayal of his own character, as well as much valuable information about the society of his time, all in a chatty, delightfully informal manner. Later, Jonathan Swift, the English satirist, contributed his remarkable *Journal to Stella*. John Wesley, who founded the Methodist Church, wrote a set of journals. In the 1800's, diaries appeared more frequently. Sir Walter Scott's *Journal* and the diary of Henry Crabb Robinson (1775-1867) are among the best examples from this period.

France also produced a number of good diarists. The Marquis de Dangeau (1638-1720) kept a diary which is the source of a great deal of knowledge about the reign of Louis XIV. The *Mémoires Secrets* of Petit de Bachaumont is also valued for its historical information. Another famous French diary is that of the brothers Jules and Edmond de Goncourt, who recorded the doings of Parisian artistic circles in the 1800's. MARTHA F. SIMMONDS

See also PEPYS, SAMUEL; SWIFT, JONATHAN; WESLEY (JOHN).

DIAS, *DE ush*, or **DIAZ, BARTOLOMEU** (1457?-1500), was a Portuguese sea captain who discovered the Cape of Good Hope in 1488 (see CAPE OF GOOD HOPE). He made several voyages to the west coast of Africa. In 1487, King John II of Portugal ordered him to try to sail around Africa. Dias, with a fleet of several ships, followed the African coast to the mouth of the Orange River. Heavy winds blew the fleet far to the south. He rounded the Cape of Good Hope without sighting it, and landed at Mossel Bay in South Africa.

Dias sailed on until the northward bend of the continent showed that he had entered the Indian Ocean. He would have sailed to India, but his weary crews staged a sit-down strike which forced him to return to Portugal. He discovered the Cape of Good Hope on the way home.

In 1497, Dias sailed as far as West Africa with Vasco da Gama, who was looking for a sea route to India by way of the Cape of Good Hope. In 1500, Dias commanded a ship in the fleet of Pedro Álvares Cabral, who discovered Brazil while trying to follow da Gama's route to India (see CABRAL, PEDRO ÁLVARES). Dias died when his ship went down in a storm. CHARLES E. NOWELL

Bartolomeu Dias Discovered the Cape of Good Hope.
Courtesy of *Salvat* Editores, S.A.

DIASTASE, *DIE uh stace*, is an amylase, or enzyme, found in germinating seeds and in animal secretions and tissues. See ENZYME; DIGESTION.

DIASTOLIC PRESSURE. See BLOOD PRESSURE.

DIASTROPHISM, *dy AS troh fiz'm*, is the uplifting of the earth's crust, forming continents, ocean basins, mountains, and *faults* (see FAULT). It causes a rearrangement of existing physical features. Most of the movements are very slow. See also GEOLOGY (Movements of Sea and Land).

DIATHERMY, *DIE uh THUR mih*, is a method of treating ailments by passing an electric current through the body. An oscillating current is used, with the very high frequency of 10,000,000 to 100,000,000 cycles per sec-

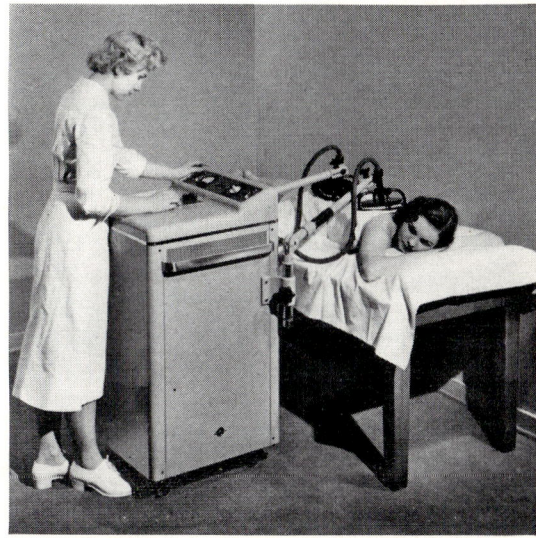

X-Ray Department, General Electric Co.
Diathermy Machines produce heat by electromagnetic induction and treat patients by warming tissues inside the body.

ond. This means it changes direction so quickly that the nervous system does not have time to react as it would in low-frequency electric shock. The tissues grow warm because of their resistance as the high-frequency current passes through them. By using diathermy, doctors can warm parts inside the body beneath the surface. It would be much more difficult, if not impossible, to do this with baths or hot pads. In *medical diathermy*, the heat is kept low enough so it will not injure the tissues. In *long-wave diathermy*, the current flows between two metal conductors which fit against the patient's leg or any part of the body to be treated. When using *short-wave diathermy*, short-length radio waves are passed through the tissues from one rubber-covered electrode to the other. Diathermy is used for conditions which require heat, such as inflammation, muscle strain, neuritis, and arthritis. In *surgical diathermy*, a point of wire takes the place of one of the electrodes. The electric current is concentrated at the point and sufficient heat is generated to destroy the tissues. The point can then be used to cut tissues or remove growths, such as warts and cancer. It can also be used inside the body to remove growths endangering internal organs. HOWARD A. CARTER

151

DIATOM

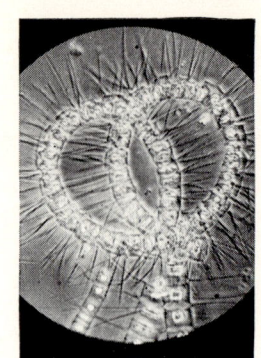

Chaetoceros Debilis, a diatom of the sea, forms these spiral chains.

Roman Vishniac; Roy M. Allen

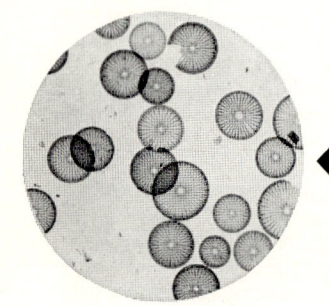

This Circular Pattern is in an *Arachnodiscus* diatom.

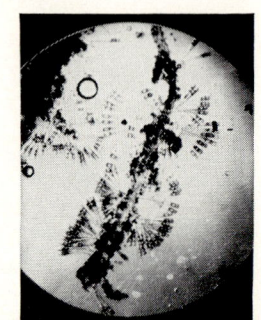

Fanlike Patterns of great beauty mark this fresh-water diatom of the *Pennatae* group.

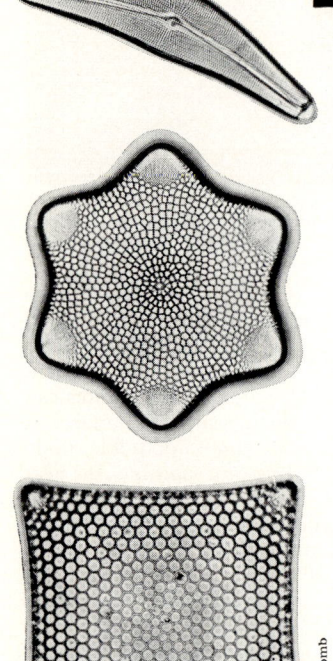

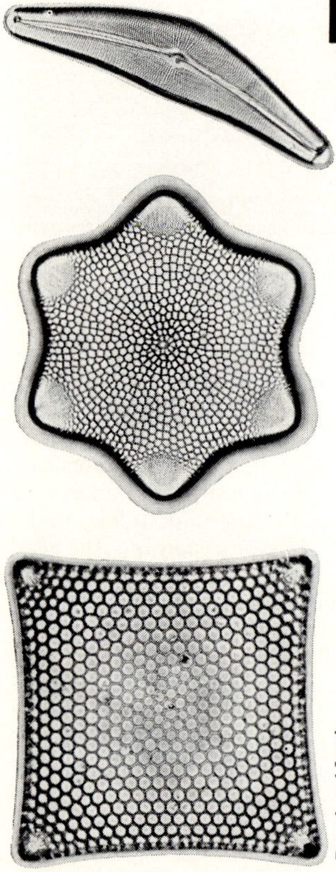

Bausch and Lomb

The Delicate Shells of Diatoms, *above left,* reveal only a few of the many different shapes of these one-celled plants. The top photograph, an edgewise view, shows how the two shells or "valves" of the diatom fit together. The lower two are flat views.

DIATOM, *DIE uh tahm,* is a tiny water plant of the kind called algae. Unlike some of the other algae, which include large seaweeds, a diatom consists of only one golden-brown cell. There are several thousand species of diatoms, including both salt- and fresh-water types. Some appear as brown, slimy coatings on stones and piles in water. Many of these one-celled plants may hang together in chains, and in various other arrangements. Still others float free. Diatoms can move by themselves through the water with jerky, creeping, or pendulumlike motions. The cell wall of the individual diatom is made up of two nearly equal halves, called valves. They are joined together somewhat as the two halves of a pillbox. The "glassy" cell wall is largely made up of silica, and forms a shell. Often the shell is very beautiful. Silica will not dissolve in water, so large masses of the tiny shells may be found at the bottom of seas, lakes, and ponds. The free, floating diatoms which grow in midocean and in lakes are a very important food for small sea animals. These, in turn, are eaten by fishes. If there were no diatoms, most of the fish of the world would die.

An earthy material composed largely of diatom shells is called *diatomite*. It is mined in California, Oregon, Washington, Nevada, Arizona, and Florida. Diatomite is used as a polishing powder, abrasive, plastic filler, insulator, filter, and in manufacturing explosives.

Scientific Classification. Diatoms are in phylum *Chrysophyta*. The many kinds of diatoms make up the class *Bacillariophyceae*. LEWIS HANFORD TIFFANY

See also ALGAE; WATER PLANT.

Johns-Manville

Diatomite, taken from diatom shells, has many industrial uses. Each load of this power shovel contains millions of tiny diatom shells. Each shell is from 12,000,000 to 28,000,000 years old. This huge deposit of diatom shells is located at Lompoc, Calif.

DIATONIC SCALE. See MUSIC (picture, The Scale).

DIATRYMA, DIE uh TRY muh, was a primitive bird that lived probably about 55,000,000 years ago. Scientists found a diatryma fossil in Wyoming. The bird stood about 7 feet high and had a huge head and bill. It had small wings and could not fly. But its strong legs made it a swift runner.

DÍAZ, ARMANDO. See ITALY (Italy and World War I).

DIAZ, BARTOLOMEU. See DIAS, BARTOLOMEU.

DÍAZ, DEE ahs, **PORFIRIO,** pawr FEE rih oh (1830-1915), served as president of Mexico from 1877 to 1880 and from 1884 to 1911. He gained fame as a general in the war against French invaders that lasted from 1863 to 1867. Overthrowing President Lerdo de Tejada in 1876, he acted as provisional president until his election in 1877. His policies encouraged railroads, large-scale agriculture, banking, and industry. But conditions improved little for most of the people. A popular uprising broke out in 1910, and forced him into exile in France, where he died. Díaz was born in Oaxaca, Mexico. See also MEXICO (Dictatorship). HAROLD E. DAVIS

Frank Cassidy
Dice are used in gambling. They are also used in many children's games to determine the number of moves a player may make.

DICE are small cubes of ivory, bone, wood, or other material, used in games of chance. A single such cube is called a *die*. Each face of a die carries from one to six dots. The sum of the dots on any two opposite faces of a die always equals seven. The player shakes the dice in a box or in his hands and then tosses them on a level surface. The numbers showing on the top faces form the basis for deciding the game. How many times any combination of numbers will appear depends entirely on chance, and thus a game of dice is a gamble. Since a player cannot throw by skill, dice games are often regarded as gambling and are forbidden by law in parts of the United States. LILLIAN FRANKEL

DICENTRA, dy SEN truh, is the name of a group of plants which include bleeding heart, Dutchman's-breeches, and squirrel corn. These plants produce a heart-shaped flower. They are abundant in Asia and America. Bleeding heart is a favorite garden plant. Squirrel corn and Dutchman's-breeches are early spring wild flowers.

Scientific Classification. Dicentras are in the fumitory family *Fumariaceae*. They are genus *Dicentra*. DONALD WYMAN

See also BLEEDING HEART; DUTCHMAN'S-BREECHES.

DICKCISSEL

DICHOTOMY, die KAHT oh mih, in biology, means a branching into two parts. In astronomy it describes that phase of the moon in which only half of its disk appears.

DICK, GEORGE FREDERICK and **GLADYS.** See DICK TEST; SCARLET FEVER.

DICK TEST is a test used to determine whether or not a person is immune to scarlet fever. A small amount of substance containing scarlet fever toxin is injected under the skin of one arm (see TOXIN). This substance is prepared by making a culture of scarlet fever bacteria in laboratory media and filtering off the liquids which contain the toxin. If the person is not immune to scarlet fever, tender, red, swollen spots will appear on the skin after 24 hours. Since the person's skin may be sensitive to other substances in the filtrate besides the toxin, a comparison, or control, injection is usually made on the other arm. This is done by injecting a small amount of filtrate in which the toxin has been neutralized. In this way a positive reaction to the Dick test can be seen immediately. The Dick test was developed by the American bacteriologists George and Gladys Dick in 1923. They also developed an antitoxin for the treatment of scarlet fever. AUSTIN EDWARD SMITH

See also SCARLET FEVER.

DICKCISSEL, dik SISS ul, is a bunting of the finch and sparrow family (see BUNTING). The dickcissel is a bird about 6 inches long. Its plumage is a streaked grayish-brown, varied by a yellow breast and bright chestnut wing patches. There is a conspicuous black crescent on the throat. Dickcissels are common in the central United States, and are sometimes seen in the eastern states. Their favorite haunts are along railroads and roadsides. The birds eat insects and seeds. The female lays from 3 to 5 eggs. The nest is built of leaves, grass, and hair, and is on or near the ground.

Scientific Classification. The dickcissel belongs to the family *Fringillidae*. The bird is in the genus *Spiza*, and is species *americana*. GEORGE J. WALLACE

The Dickcissel is named for its loud, persistent call. This suggests the syllables, "Dick, dick, dick, cis-cis-cis-cis." The last four notes of the bird's call are sounded rapidly.

DICKENS, CHARLES

DICKENS, CHARLES (1812-1870), was one of the greatest English novelists, and the most popular writer of his time. Dickens had a genuine love for people. He wrote mostly about the lower classes in England, but all classes read and enjoyed his books. His 15 novels created many distinctive characters who became immortal in literature, and presented an unrivaled picture of England, especially London.

His imaginary characters seem more real to many people than the real characters of history. Dickens exposed the social wrongs of his time in his novels. His books were responsible for many reforms in behalf of children and the poor. He had a keen eye for every detail of scene and behavior. Humor, absurdities, mystery, and tender pity characterize his works.

Early Life. CHARLES JOHN HUFFAM DICKENS was born on Feb. 7, 1812, at Landport, Portsmouth. He moved with his family to Chatham about 1816, and to London in 1821. Dickens had an unhappy childhood, and it furnished the background for some of his books. For example, his father was a happy-go-lucky man who fell deeply in debt and served a term in a debtors' jail called the Marshalsea. Dickens later made this prison famous in *Little Dorrit*.

Dickens had to go to work in a warehouse, pasting labels on blacking bottles, at the age of 10. His unhappy experiences and the people he met in his unpleasant surroundings were stored in the boy's memory. Later, he went to school for two years, then worked in a lawyer's office. He studied shorthand in his spare time, and became a reporter in the House of Commons at the age of 19.

He began writing sketches of London life for newspapers and magazines. These were reprinted as *Sketches by Boz* in 1836. George Cruikshank, the famous illustrator and caricaturist, illustrated two of Dickens' books, beginning with *Sketches by Boz* (see CRUIKSHANK, GEORGE). These sketches were so popular that a publisher asked for a new series. *Pickwick Papers* began to appear in monthly issues in 1836. This loosely woven story was so amusing that one of its main characters, Sam Weller, became famous throughout the world. Dickens married Catherine Hogarth in the same year. They had nine children.

Champion of the Poor. Dickens attacked what he believed were the most serious abuses of the poor. He described the sufferings of children realistically. *Bleak House* attacked the long-drawn-out law suits in the court of chancery. *Little Dorrit* showed the evils of the debtors'-prison system. The vivid word pictures he created impressed his readers, and convinced many of them that such conditions had to be corrected.

Oliver Twist exposed the abuses of children in the workhouse system and the slums. He based *David Copperfield* on his own experiences during his warehouse days (see DAVID COPPERFIELD). Mr. Micawber, in this novel, is a good-natured exaggeration of Dickens' own father. The severe punishment children suffered in schools, especially cheap boarding schools, impressed Dickens. The readers could almost feel the sting of Mr. Creakle's cane in *David Copperfield*. Dickens' description of the monstrous schoolmaster Squeers in *Nicholas Nickleby* is almost too vicious to be real, but too convincing not to be taken seriously by his readers.

Dickens believed "cramming" in schools was an evil. In *Dombey and Son*, he spoke of the "mental green peas," "intellectual asparagus," and "mathematical gooseberries" that were "common at untimely seasons." He felt that if students learned anything under this system, they should get the credit, not their masters.

Dickens had great influence in changing the general attitude toward children. Most parents and teachers of the day considered children troublesome little beings that should be treated sternly. He attacked this unsympathetic strictness and the way the individuality of children was ignored. Many of his ideas were ahead of his time. But they later became common, and Dickens

Brown Bros.

Charles Dickens, a great English novelist, wrote books that helped bring many reforms in behalf of children and the poor.

is credited with helping to bring about changes that improved child training and education.

Hard Times criticized adults for robbing children of a real childhood and for preventing them from developing their imaginations. It was also a bitter picture of the heartlessness of industrialists toward laborers.

A Christmas Carol was published shortly before Christmas in 1843. It sold 6,000 copies on the first day. This little book has spread its glad influence throughout the world for more than 100 years. Lord Jeffrey, Dickens' friend, once said that it had done more good than all the pulpits in Christendom. Novelist William Makepeace Thackeray declared that it was a national benefit, and A. Edward Newton once called it "the best book of its kind in the world."

Critics consider *A Tale of Two Cities* Dickens' most dramatic and artistic story. Sidney Carton, the hero in this historical novel of the French Revolution, is perhaps the most heroic character in all his works. Dickens wrote only one other historical novel, *Barnaby Rudge*.

UNFORGETTABLE CHARACTERS FROM THE DICKENS NOVELS

Mr. Pickwick and His Friends have many laughable experiences in *The Pickwick Papers*. The novel is made up of a group of separate stories about Mr. Pickwick's adventures.

Sidney Carton plays a leading part in *A Tale of Two Cities*.

Wilkins Micawber is the optimistic ne'er-do-well in *David Copperfield*. He is always waiting cheerfully "for something to turn up."

Bob Cratchit Carries Tiny Tim through wintry London streets in *A Christmas Carol*.

Mr. Brownlow saves Oliver Twist from a gang of thieves, and then adopts him, in the novel *Oliver Twist*.

Great Expectations, one of Dickens' best novels, was made into a motion picture in the 1940's. In this scene, Lawyer Jaggers (Francis L. Sullivan), *right,* tells Pip (John Mills), *left,* of a gift from an anonymous benefactor.

United World Films, Inc.

His other works include *Our Mutual Friend; The Old Curiosity Shop,* which introduced the famous characters Little Nell and Dick Swiveller; *Great Expectations,* which critics regard as his best-rounded story; and *The Mystery of Edwin Drood,* which he left unfinished at his death. Readers have puzzled ever since over how it was to end. Many solutions of the mystery have been published.

Dickens met the detective novelist, Wilkie Collins, in 1851 (see COLLINS, WILKIE). They became close friends and often worked together. Critics agree that they had great influence on each other. Dickens admired Collins as a master of plot, and Collins admired Dickens as a master of characterization.

A Visit to America. Dickens visited the United States and Canada in 1842. He wrote *American Notes* and *Martin Chuzzlewit* after this trip. *Martin Chuzzlewit* included a humorous satire on Midwestern frontier life that stirred up feeling against Dickens in the United States. But large audiences attended Dickens' readings from his books when he visited the United States again in 1867.

Dickens made popular personal appearances in the last years of his life. He could keep audiences enthralled for an entire evening with readings of comic and dramatic scenes from his books. In his *Letters* he described amusingly the crowds that flocked to see and hear him. But the strain of the performances damaged his health, and he died at the age of 58 in his home at Gadshill, near Rochester. As a small boy he had picked out this house as the one he wanted to own and eventually he had been able to buy it. His friend, John Forster, wrote the first biography of Dickens.   LIONEL STEVENSON

DICKINSON, EMILY (1830-1886), the most important woman poet of the United States, was almost entirely unknown to the people of her own time. All seven of the poems that appeared during her lifetime were printed anonymously, and most of them were published against her wishes.

Miss Dickinson was born in Amherst, Mass. She attended Amherst Academy for three years, then spent one year at Mount Holyoke Seminary. In 1854, she met a brilliant Philadelphia preacher, Charles Wadsworth, and fell in love with him. He was 40 years old and happily married. The story that he was also in love with her and proposed elopement is based on interpretation of her poems, and Miss Dickinson herself warns us not to take them literally.

Whatever actually happened, the experience seems to have been the most important fact in Miss Dickinson's development as an artist. Before she met Wadsworth, she had been a sprightly and original verse writer. Her personal emotional problem and its solution played a large part in making her a great lyrical poet of love, death, and immortality.

Miss Dickinson withdrew more and more from the world. She had poor health, and spent much time in writing. She was also shy and fastidious. As she wrote:

> The soul selects her own society,
> Then shuts the door;
> On her divine majority
> Obtrude no more.
> I've known her from an ample nation
> Choose one;
> Then close the valves of her attention
> Like stone.

In 1862, at about the same time this poem was written, Miss Dickinson wrote to Thomas W. Higginson, a critic and essayist. She sent him some poems and asked for advice. He suggested that she needed to polish some of her lines. Instead of making changes, she gave up all thought of publication.

After her death, her sister Lavinia turned over all the poems she could find to Higginson and Mrs. Mabel Loomis Todd to be edited. Their first volume appeared in 1890, and more poems were published in the 1900's. Emily Dickinson became known as one of the chief influences on present-day poetry.   JOHN TYREE FAIN

See also POETRY (What Makes a Poem Great?).

Emily Dickinson
Little Brown & Co.

156

DICKINSON, JOHN (1732-1808), an American statesman, served in the Delaware and Pennsylvania assemblies, the Stamp Act Congress, and the Continental Congress. Dickinson favored conciliation with England. He expressed his calm political views in his *Letters from a Farmer in Pennsylvania to the Inhabitants of the British Colonies*. As a delegate from Delaware, he helped to draft the United States Constitution. He was not present when the Constitution was signed, but he asked another delegate to add his name.

Dickinson was born in Talbot County, Maryland, and became a lawyer. Dickinson College at Carlisle, Pa., was named for him. The John and Samuel Dickinson mansion near Dover, Del., was opened to the public as an historic shrine in 1956. KENNETH R. ROSSMAN

DICKINSON COLLEGE is a coeducational liberal arts college at Carlisle, Pa. Students may follow either a four-year course or an accelerated plan. Dickinson was founded in 1773 and is one of the country's oldest colleges. It's the only college ever to have had a graduate as President and another as Chief Justice of the United States at the same time. This was when James Buchanan was President and Roger Taney was Chief Justice. For enrollment, see UNIVERSITIES AND COLLEGES (table). W. W. EDEL

DICKSON MOUNDS. See ILLINOIS (Interesting Places to Visit).

DICOTYLEDON, *die CAHT uh LEE dun*, is a type of flowering plant that has two seed leaves, or *cotyledons*. The cotyledons store reserve food for the embryo plant. Dicotyledon foliage leaves have netted veins. Their flower petals usually grow in multiples of 4 or 5. See also COTYLEDON.

DICTATING MACHINE records speech and then reproduces it, like a phonograph. The person who dictates speaks into a microphone. The microphone is connected to a recorder that makes a record. When the typist is ready for the record, she places it on a transcribing machine. Then she listens through a hearing device to the voice from the record. The records used include plastic belts, wax cylinders, plastic disks, wire, and tape.

Dictating machines save time because a person can dictate at any time without calling a stenographer. After the stenographer has typed the letter, she can check it with the record to make sure the letter is correct. Some dictating machines are light enough in weight to be carried easily on business trips. Dictations can then be mailed to the office to be typed.

Electronic devices have made dictating machines extremely sensitive. A small two-stage vacuum-tube amplifier can magnify sounds from two to three million times. No matter how rapidly a person dictates, the dictating machine can keep up with him. It can reproduce the dictation at any speed desired.

"Remote control" dictating systems carry several messages at once by direct wire to a central recording machine beside a typist's desk. RAYMOND F. YATES

See also BUSINESS MACHINES.

DICTATOR is any ruler whose power is not limited either by law or by the acts of any official body.

Dictators usually have come to power under conditions of turmoil and confusion. Governments, unable to provide their people with security, may turn to a dictator who promises to achieve it. Often the dictator seizes power through political trickery.

Once in control, the dictator and his followers retain their positions through force or threat of force. They abolish or closely control the legislature, and quickly suppress freedom of speech, assembly, and the press. They set up an elaborate secret-police system to detect opponents of the government. Those who openly object to dictatorship are persecuted.

Familiar examples of the dictator have included Benito Mussolini in Italy, Adolf Hitler in Germany, and Joseph Stalin in Russia.

In ancient Rome, the senate often met national emergencies by appointing one consul to select a dictator. The Roman dictator held office for 6 months and could be reappointed if the emergency still existed. The dictator had power of life and death without appeal to the people or the senate, but he could not leave the country and had no control of the treasury. Julius Caesar was appointed dictator by the Roman Senate on three different occasions. WILLIAM EBENSTEIN

See also AUTOCRACY; GOVERNMENT (When Tyrants Rule; A Comparison of Democracy and Dictatorship).

Dictaphone Corporation

Dictating Machines save valuable business hours. An executive can dictate his correspondence at his own convenience, *above*. Later, a typist can listen to the recorded message, *right*, type it, and check it with the recording to be sure of accuracy.

DICTIONARY

DICTIONARY is a book that contains a selected list of words arranged in alphabetical order. It explains their meanings and gives information about them. With a dictionary, a person can look up a word quickly, discover what it means, and learn how it is pronounced. A good dictionary puts down the facts of a language as educated speakers and writers use that language. A dictionary editor cannot change the facts of a language any more than a map maker can change the position of mountains, rivers, or cities when making a map.

What Dictionaries Contain

Dictionaries contain the meanings of many kinds of words. Most dictionaries include (1) the ordinary words of everyday life, such as *bread*, *run*, and *with*; (2) literary words used in formal writing, such as *aggregation*, *despoil*, and *incontrovertible*; (3) technical words, such as *starboard*, *gene*, and *ratio*; (4) words used chiefly on informal occasions, such as *gab* and *razz*; (5) words used in writing to give an old-fashioned flavor, such as *aweary* and *avaunt*; (6) words not used today but found in the writings of some authors, such as *plaister* for *plaster*; (7) words or phrases from other languages, such as *coup d'état* from French and *troika* from Russian; (8) *idioms* (groups of words with meanings different from their literal meanings), such as *split hairs* and *under the thumb of*; (9) abbreviations, such as *U.S.A.*, *Kans.*, and *p.*; and (10) important proper names, such as *Juno* and *Jupiter*.

No dictionary records all the words of our language. In fact, no one knows exactly how many English words there are. Besides ordinary words used in everyday speech, the English language includes thousands of geographical names. There are thousands of words that are no longer used. And there are hundreds of thousands of technical terms, including more than 750,000 names of insects alone. New words are coined for new scientific and technical discoveries, and slang words and special vocabularies constantly spring up. As nations draw closer together through trade and travel, languages tend to borrow more and more words from each other. That is why a dictionary editor must be selective in the words he decides to include.

Most dictionaries tell us much more than just the meanings of words. Many list pronunciations, derivations, illustrative quotations, synonyms and antonyms, and other information. The color illustration with this article shows in detail what dictionaries tell us.

Kinds of Dictionaries

Dictionaries may be classified as *general dictionaries* and *specialized dictionaries*. A general dictionary contains information on everyday words such as *it* and *the*. But it also defines many technical terms such as *chromatography* and *columella*. A specialized dictionary omits most everyday terms, and limits itself to information on words used in a particular field, such as biology.

General Dictionaries range in size from small pocket dictionaries to large multivolume or table dictionaries.

The number of entries in a general dictionary depends on its purpose. Each dictionary is designed to answer the questions of a certain type of reader. A sixth-grade student, for example, would not want all the information given in a dictionary a college professor would use. For this reason, dictionary editors work hard to design their products to suit the needs of their intended audiences. They know that the usefulness of any dictionary depends on the education of the user and the kind of information he wishes to find.

A general dictionary may be designed for use by elementary-school students, high-school students, or college students. It may also be designed for use by the general reader, or even by the entire family. *The World Book Encyclopedia Dictionary* is an example of a dictionary designed for family use.

The largest general dictionaries may contain over 400,000 entries. When a dictionary has this many entries, many obsolete and technical terms must be included. Other general dictionaries may range in size from those with about 15,000 entries to those with about 200,000 entries.

Specialized Dictionaries are designed to give more information in particular fields than general dictionaries can. A *gazetteer* (geographical dictionary) lists the names of cities, countries, islands, lakes, and other places. It gives the pronunciation of each name and a brief description of the place. A *biographical dictionary* lists and gives the pronunciation of the names of famous people. Each entry includes the dates the person lived, his nationality, and why he is remembered. A *thesaurus* contains lists of synonyms and antonyms. Other specialized dictionaries are devoted exclusively to English usage; idioms; Old English; pronunciations; slang; spelling; and various aspects of science and technology. There are dictionaries of all the major languages of the world. *Bilingual* dictionaries translate the words of one language into another. They include French-English,

Don Stebbing

A Dictionary, such as *The World Book Encyclopedia Dictionary*, contains valuable information on thousands of words and phrases.

WHAT A DICTIONARY TELLS YOU

In addition to defining words, a dictionary provides much useful information about them. You can get the most out of a dictionary by learning what its abbreviations and symbols stand for. These examples come from THE WORLD BOOK ENCYCLOPEDIA DICTIONARY.

Word Entries begin in bold black type. Proper nouns are capitalized. Other words begin with small letters. The first letter of the entry extends into the margin for easy location.

Other Forms of the word may include verb tenses, unusual spellings for plurals, and comparative forms of adjectives. This example shows principal parts of the verb *alembicate*.

Pronunciation, given in phonetic symbols, appears immediately after the word entries. Sometimes several correct pronunciations are listed. This dictionary has a key to its phonetic symbols at the bottom of each right-hand page, and more detailed explanations at the front of the book.

Parts of Speech notations describe the word's grammatical use. Words that may be used as more than one part of speech are defined accordingly. The parts of speech are abbreviated, as in *adj.* for *adjective* and *n.* for *noun*. Verbs are shown as transitive or intransitive by the initials *v.t.* and *v.i.*

Synonyms that have the same or nearly the same meaning as the word defined appear in a separate paragraph. This note gives the synonyms for the adjective form of *alert*.

Levels of Usage labels, such as *slang* and *informal*, tell whether the word is acceptable English usage. The meaning of the labels is explained at the front of the dictionary.

Usage Notes discuss spelling and grammar, and advise on how to use the word in speaking and writing.

---

a·lem·bic (ə lem′bik), *n.* 1. a glass or metal container, formerly used in chemistry for distilling. 2. something that transforms or refines: *Imagination is the alembic of the mind.* [< Medieval Latin *alambicus* < Arabic *al-'anbīq* the still < Late Greek *ámbīx, -īkos* alembic < Greek, vessel narrowing toward the brim]

Alembic (def. 1)

a·lem·bi·cate (ə lem′bə kāt), *v.t.,* **-cat·ed, -cat·ing.** to distill in an alembic.
A·len·çon lace (ə len′sən, -son), 1. a fine needle-point lace made by hand in France.

a·lerce (ə lèrs′), *n.* 1. a large pine that resembles the California redwood. 2. the wood used by the Moors in their buildings, obtained from the sandarac tree of Morocco. [< Spanish *alerce* < Arabic *'al-'arz* the cedar]

a·lert (ə lèrt′), *adj.* 1. keen and watchful; wide-awake: *A good hunting dog is alert to every sound and movement in the field.* 2. quick in action; nimble: *A sparrow is very alert in its movements.*
—*n.* 1. a signal warning of an attack by approaching enemy aircraft or other threatened danger. 2. the period of time after this warning until the attack is over or the danger has passed: *The rest of the coast as far north as Massachusetts should stand by on a hurricane alert, the bureau said* (Wall Street Journal). 3. a signal to troops, etc., to be ready for action.
on the alert, watchful; ready at any instant for what is coming: *A sentry must be on the alert. The Government is on the alert and will take the necessary steps to maintain security and stability* (London Times).
—*v.t.* 1. to warn against an air attack, a hurricane, etc. 2. to call to arms; notify (troops, etc.) to get ready for action, 3. to make alert; warn: *Despite alerted antiaircraft and fighter defenses, the Liberators pressed home low-level attack through oil fires and intense smoke, wrecking the refineries* (Time).
[< French *alerte* < Italian *all'erta* on the watch] —**a·lert′ly,** *adv.* —**a·lert′ness,** *n.*
—**Syn.** *adj.* 1. attentive, vigilant. See *watchful.* 2. brisk, active. —**Ant.** *adj.* 1. heedless.

à l'es·pa·gnole (à les pà nyōl′), *French.* in the Spanish style.

all-right (ôl′rīt′), *adj. U.S. Slang.* very good or excellent of its kind; very dependable: *Don't worry about him; he's an all-right fellow.*
all right, 1. without error; correct. 2. yes: *All right. I'll come.* 3. without doubt; certainly. 4. in good health: *I was ill for a week, but I'm all right now.* 5. satisfactory; accceptable: *The substitute material should be all right.*
→ See **alright** for usage note.

al·right (ôl rīt′), *adv. Informal.* all right.
→ **All right** is the correct spelling of both the adjective phrase (*He is all right*) and the sentence adverb meaning yes, certainly (*All right, I'll come*). The spelling **alright** is not used in formal and in most informal writing. Occasionally it is found in advertising and in comic strips, but it is not as yet generally acceptable.

Definitions give the exact meanings of words. When a word has more than one meaning, the definitions are numbered. This dictionary lists the most common meaning first. Some dictionaries present definitions in historical order, beginning with the earliest-known meaning.

Illustrations clarify the definitions. A label shows which meaning of the word is being illustrated. Here, the drawing illustrates the first definition of the word *alembic*.

Derivations tell what language or languages a word comes from, and its meaning in the original language. The symbol < means *comes from*.

Examples point out how to use the word in actual phrases and sentences.

Phrases that include the key word but have special meanings of their own are explained separately.

Quotations from well-known authors or publications often illustrate the meaning of the word. The source of the quotation appears in parentheses.

Antonyms that have the opposite or nearly the opposite meaning as the word defined are included in many entries. *Heedless* is the antonym for the most common definition of *alert*.

Foreign Words and Phrases in common use are identified, and their pronunciation and translation given.

Cross References refer to additional information elsewhere. An arrow marks the note for attention.

DICTIONARY

English-German, Spanish-Italian, Italian-French, Greek-Latin, Russian-Polish, and Hebrew-Arabic dictionaries.

How To Use a Dictionary

Before you use a dictionary, try to become familiar with the methods, principles, and scope of the book. You will find that various dictionaries are arranged in different ways. Most American dictionaries arrange all entries in a single alphabetical list. Others put abbreviations, geographical names, and biographical names in separate lists, usually at the end of the book. All good dictionaries today have introductory sections that explain what the book contains and how it is arranged.

The first thing a dictionary entry shows you is how to spell a word and how to divide it into syllables. Accent marks and symbols that are explained in the book tell you how to pronounce the word. Many dictionaries also tell what part of speech the word is. For example, they list *boy* as a *noun*, and *speak* as a *verb*.

Definitions of the word usually follow. Some dictionaries list the most commonly used meaning of the word first. Others arrange the meanings historically, so that the first meaning listed is the one that occurred first in the language. Most dictionaries use the word in a sentence or quotation to help define it. Sometimes they add pictures or drawings to tell more about the entry.

After the definitions, many dictionaries include a list of *synonyms*, or words having about the same meaning as the word being defined. Sometimes a list of *antonyms*, words with opposite meanings, follows the synonyms.

History

The word *dictionary* comes from the medieval Latin word *dictionarium*, which in turn came from the Latin *dictio*, meaning *saying*. The ancient Greeks and Romans were the first to produce these works. But most Greek and Latin dictionaries were either lists of rare and difficult words or specialized lists of words.

During the Middle Ages, scholars made much use of Latin dictionaries which explained hard Latin words in easier Latin. Toward the end of the Middle Ages, as Latin began to lose ground to English, French, German, and other national languages of Europe, scholars began to rely on *glossaries* to understand Latin manuscripts (see GLOSSARY). The glossaries usually gave the meanings of hard Latin words in the words of the national language. As these languages became accepted in each country, people needed new dictionaries to explain the hard words of their own language in terms of simpler words in the same language.

Early English Dictionaries. In 1604, Robert Cawdrey, a schoolmaster, prepared the first English dictionary. Called *The Table Alphabeticall of Hard Words*, it defined about 3,000 hard English words that had been taken from other languages. Larger dictionaries that offered more information about the words they contained were produced in the 1600's. In 1721, Nathan Bailey published a dictionary containing about 60,000 words. This was the first English dictionary that tried to include all English words instead of hard words only.

In the early 1700's, Jonathan Swift, Alexander Pope, Joseph Addison, Samuel Johnson, and other literary men of England wanted to prepare a dictionary that would set the standard for good usage in English. French and Italian scholars had already published dictionaries in their languages, and the success of those works influenced the literary men of England. Samuel Johnson undertook the task of preparing an English dictionary. He spent several years selecting quotations from the best writers to illustrate the meanings of words. He finally published his great work, *A Dictionary of the English Language*, in 1755. With John Walker's *Critical and Pronouncing Dictionary and Expositor of the English Language* (1791), it served as the standard for information about English words until the middle of the 1800's.

In 1806, Noah Webster published a small school dictionary in the United States. Webster wanted to set up an American standard of good usage to compare with the British standard set by Johnson and Walker. He had received encouragement from Benjamin Franklin, James Madison, and other American leaders. In 1828, he published a dictionary containing 70,000 entries. Since then, Webster's dictionaries have been frequently revised and are widely used today. See WEBSTER, NOAH.

The period of national dictionaries gave way to scholarly dictionaries in the 1880's. The first scholarly dictionary was *A New English Dictionary on Historical Principles*, often called *The Oxford English Dictionary*. It was published from 1884 to 1928 and has more than 414,000 entries. This great dictionary gives a historical record of each meaning. It lists the date the word first occurred in written English and other dates that show how it was used through the years, or the date it probably disappeared from use. A supplement to the dictionary appeared in 1933. No other dictionary in English or in any other language approaches this one in wealth and authority of historical detail. *The Century Dictionary* is its nearest American counterpart.

Current Dictionaries. Two large dictionaries sold in the United States and Canada are *Webster's Third New International Dictionary*, with about 450,000 words, and *Funk and Wagnall's New Standard Dictionary of the English Language*, with about 600,000 words. The two-volume *World Book Encyclopedia Dictionary*, a Thorndike-Barnhart work with more than 180,000 entries, is designed for family use. It is the first dictionary especially planned and developed to be used with a specific encyclopedia. College dictionaries containing from 125,000 to 150,000 words include *Webster's Seventh New Collegiate Dictionary*, *Webster's New World Dictionary*, *The American College Dictionary*, and *The New College Standard Dictionary*. High school dictionaries with about 80,000 words include *Webster's Student Dictionary* and the *Thorndike-Barnhart High School Dictionary*. Elementary dictionaries include *The Winston Dictionary for Children*; *The New Winston Dictionary for Young People*; *Webster's Elementary Dictionary*; and three Thorndike-Barnhart works, the *Beginning Dictionary*, the *Junior Dictionary*, and the *Advanced Junior Dictionary*.

CLARENCE L. BARNHART

Related Articles. See the separate articles in WORLD BOOK on each letter of the alphabet. See also the following articles:

Abbreviation	Etymology	Philology
Antonym	Grammar	Pronunciation
Apposition	Index	Punctuation
Capitalization	Language	Spelling
Cross Reference	Lexicographer	Synonym
Encyclopedia	Parts of Speech	Syntax

DIDEROT, *dee* **DROH, DENIS** (1713-1784), a French philosopher and writer, spent 20 years editing his *Encyclopedia*. Rousseau, Voltaire, and other prominent men contributed to it. It stressed the value of objective, scientific knowledge as opposed to tradition and orthodoxy. The French government was deeply suspicious of the project and interfered repeatedly in his work. Diderot was born at Langres, France. W. T. JONES

See also ENCYCLOPEDIA (After 1700).

DIDO, *DI doh*, or ELISSA, was the legendary founder and queen of Carthage. She was the daughter of King Belus of Tyre, and the wife of Acerbas, or Sychaeus. She fled to Africa with many devoted followers after her brother, Pygmalion, murdered her husband. There she was offered as much land as might be surrounded by a bull's hide. She cut a hide into thin strips, pieced them together, and surrounded a large area. This became the site of Carthage (see CARTHAGE).

Hiarbas, or Iarbas, an African prince, wished to marry Dido and threatened war if she refused. Dido hated and feared him. She built a large funeral fire, threw herself upon it, and stabbed herself.

In his *Aeneid*, Virgil changed this story. He had Dido commit suicide because Aeneas, the Trojan hero, deserted her (see AENEAS; AENEID). VAN JOHNSON

DIDRIKSON, *DID rik sun*, **"BABE," MILDRED ELLA** (1914-1956), was one of the greatest woman athletes in history. She won fame as an outstanding golfer. She set world records in the 1932 Olympic Games in the woman's 80-meter hurdles and javelin throw. The Amateur Athletic Union (AAU) named her to its All-America woman's basketball team in 1930 and 1931. She also played baseball, football, pocket billiards, and tennis, did some boxing, and competed in swimming events.

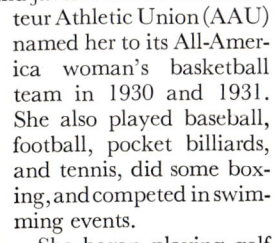

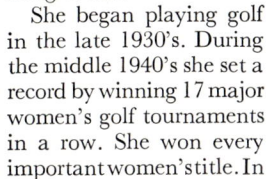

She began playing golf in the late 1930's. During the middle 1940's she set a record by winning 17 major women's golf tournaments in a row. She won every important women's title. In 1947, she became the first woman from the United States to win the British Women's Amateur golf tournament.

Babe Didrikson survived a 1953 cancer operation, and came back to win the National Women's Open and the Tam O'Shanter All-America tournaments in 1954. In 1950, the Associated Press named her the outstanding woman athlete of the first half of the 1900's. She was born in Port Arthur, Tex., and married George Zaharias, a professional wrestler, in 1938. FRED RUSSELL

DIDYMUS. See THOMAS, SAINT.

DIE AND DIEMAKING. A *die* is a block or plate used to shape metal. *Diemaking* is the process of molding the dies. Dies have to be made with great precision, and diemakers are among the most highly skilled workers in factories and machine shops.

Manufacturers use dies as molds in casting and drop forging, to stamp articles from metal, and to draw metal into wire, tubes, or other shapes. Engraved plates that

Wide World
"Babe" Didrikson

DIE AND DIEMAKING

reproduce ornamental designs or letters on paper, leather, and other material are also called dies. Dies for metalworking are usually made of cast iron or hardened steel. The metal is often chromium plated. Dies may also be made partly or entirely of hard rubber or plastics.

In the process of *die-casting*, metals are melted in a machine that forces the liquid metal into steel dies. These dies replace the molds used in ordinary casting (see CAST AND CASTING). The metal hardens into the design of the dies and comes out of the machine as a solid casting that may be used without any more finishing. In this way, manufacturers can make many small articles of intricate shapes cheaply and at high rates of speed. Zinc mixed with other metals is often used in die-casting machines to make such automobile parts as door handles, radiator grilles, and instrument panel frames. Other articles made by die-casting include gears, locks, and cash-register parts. Aluminum alloys are also frequently used in die-casting. Manufacturers do not die-cast steel and iron because these metals do not melt at low temperatures. Brass and other copper

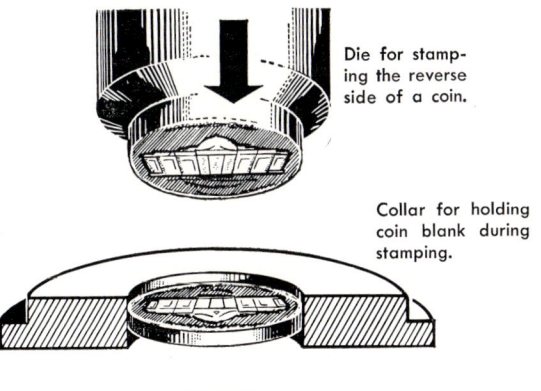

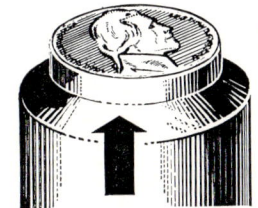

Die for stamping the reverse side of a coin.

Collar for holding coin blank during stamping.

Die for stamping the obverse, or dated, side of a coin.

Dies Are Used in Stamping Coins. The smooth disks of coin metal, or "blanks," are fed into a power-driven stamping press. Here they are stamped on both sides at once.

alloys are die-cast, but are hard to work with because they also do not melt at low temperatures.

In *drop-forging*, heated metal is placed between two halves of the die. A powerful hammer drives the halves together, forming the metal into the desired shape.

In *stamping*, punch presses use dies to stamp unheated sheets, plates, or strips of metal. Some stamping dies simply punch a hole in the metal or cut it to a desired shape. Others shape and form the metal. Some stamping dies do both jobs.

In *drawing* and *extrusion*, hot or cold metal is forced through an opening in a die to form the material into wires, tubes, or bars (see EXTRUSION). ALLISON BUTTS

See also FORGING; TOOLMAKING.

161

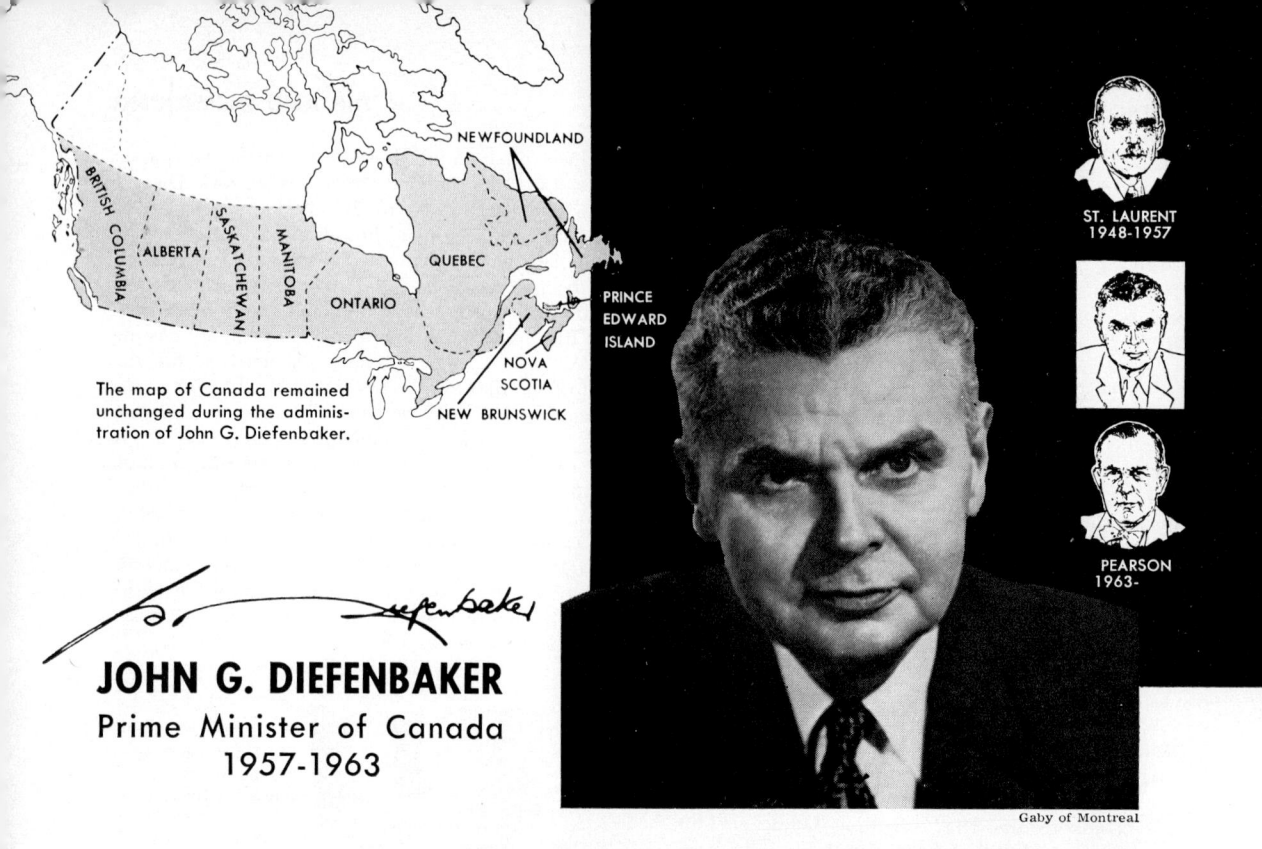

The map of Canada remained unchanged during the administration of John G. Diefenbaker.

ST. LAURENT
1948-1957

PEARSON
1963-

JOHN G. DIEFENBAKER
Prime Minister of Canada
1957-1963

Gaby of Montreal

DIEFENBAKER, *DEE fen bayk ur,* **JOHN GEORGE** (1895-   ), served as Prime Minister of Canada from 1957 to 1963. One of the reasons for the defeat of Diefenbaker's Conservative government was his refusal to accept atomic warheads for defense missiles supplied by the United States. The Liberals won the election of April, 1963, and Liberal leader Lester B. Pearson became Prime Minister.

The Conservatives elected Diefenbaker as party leader in 1956. Diefenbaker led his party to victory in the 1957 election, and became the first Conservative Prime Minister in 22 years. In 1958, Canadians re-elected the Conservatives with the largest parliamentary majority in the nation's history. The Conservatives won again in the 1962 election, but they did not have an absolute majority in parliament. Diefenbaker's government stayed in power only with the support of the small Social Credit party.

As Prime Minister, Diefenbaker increased Canada's social welfare programs and speeded development of the nation's rich northland. Canada faced serious economic problems in the early 1960's, and Diefenbaker adopted austerity measures to fight them. Under Diefenbaker, Canada increased its trade with communist countries. The St. Lawrence Seaway was completed, and George P. Vanier became the first French-Canadian governor-general of Canada.

Tall and thin, with gray, curly hair and piercing blue eyes, Diefenbaker won friends and made enemies with his strong personality and fighting spirit. Diefenbaker made strong appeals to the national feeling of Canadians. "We are an independent country," he declared, "and we have the right to assert our rights and not have them determined by another country." Some persons called Diefenbaker's attitude "anti-American," but he disagreed. "The very thought is repugnant to me," Diefenbaker said. "I am strongly pro-Canadian."

Early Life

Boyhood and Education. John Diefenbaker was born on Sept. 18, 1895, in the village of Neustadt, Ont. The family of his father, William, had come to Canada from Germany. His mother, Mary Florence Bannerman Diefenbaker, was a granddaughter of George Bannerman, one of Lord Selkirk's Scottish settlers in the Red River Colony of Manitoba. John had a younger brother, Elmer.

John's father taught school for 20 years, then became a civil servant. As Prime Minister, Diefenbaker recalled: "My father was a person who had a dedicated devotion to the public service. Throughout the schools he taught, there were a great many who went into public life, because of his feeling that it was one field in which there was a need."

In 1903, when John was 8 years old, the family moved to a homestead in Saskatchewan. The boy loved stories of the early days on the prairie. He was particularly fascinated by tales about Gabriel Dumont, Louis Riel's right-hand man during the Saskatchewan Rebellion of 1885 (see SASKATCHEWAN REBELLION). John also studied the lives of such men as Abraham Lincoln, William Gladstone, and Napoleon.

John's interest later shifted to Canadian history. One night, according to a family legend, he looked up from reading a biography of Prime Minister Sir Wilfrid Laurier and announced: "I'm going to be Premier (Prime Minister) of Canada." But John most admired former Prime Minister Sir John A. Macdonald.

In 1910, the Diefenbakers moved to Saskatoon, Sask., so John could attend high school there. John

DIEFENBAKER, JOHN G.

went on to the University of Saskatchewan, where he was active in campus politics. The college magazine predicted that someday he would lead the opposition in the house of commons. He received his bachelor's degree in 1915 and a master's degree in 1916.

Diefenbaker was commissioned a lieutenant in the Canadian Army during World War I. He arrived in France in 1916, but was returned to Canada the next year after being injured in training camp.

Young Lawyer. Diefenbaker had always planned to be a lawyer. "There was no member of my family who was a lawyer," he said, "but I never deviated from that course from the time I was 8 or 9 years of age." He studied law at the University of Saskatchewan and received his law degree in 1919. That same year, he opened a small office in the nearby town of Wakaw.

Diefenbaker developed an outstanding reputation as a defense lawyer. Some persons who heard him in court claimed he could hold a jury spellbound with his oratory. "I just chat with the jury," said Diefenbaker.

In 1923, Diefenbaker moved to Prince Albert, Sask. He became a King's Counsel in 1929, and was a vice-president of the Canadian Bar Association from 1939 to 1942.

Diefenbaker married Edna May Brower in 1929. She died in 1951. Two years later, he married Mrs. Olive Freeman Palmer, an old friend from Wakaw. Mrs. Palmer, a widow with a grown daughter, was assistant director of the Ontario Department of Education.

Member of Parliament

In 1925 and 1926, Diefenbaker ran as a Conservative candidate for the Canadian house of commons. He lost both times. He ran for the Saskatchewan legislature in 1929 and 1938, and again was defeated each time. He also ran for mayor of Prince Albert in 1934, and lost that election, too.

Diefenbaker's repeated defeats did not discourage him. He became leader of the Saskatchewan Conservative party in 1936 and served until 1940. He again ran for the house of commons in 1940, and this time he won.

As a lawyer, Diefenbaker had made a reputation by defending individual civil rights. As a member of parliament, he argued for a national bill of rights. Canada's first bill of rights was adopted in 1958 when Diefenbaker was Prime Minister.

The first bill Diefenbaker introduced in parliament provided for Canadian citizenship for Canadians. They were then British subjects. Diefenbaker denounced what he called "hyphenated citizenship." He meant that every Canadian was listed in the census by the national origin of his father, such as French or Italian.

In 1948, the Conservative party met to choose a leader to succeed John Bracken. Some members suggested Diefenbaker, but the party chose George Drew. In 1956, Drew became ill and had to give up politics. The Conservatives chose Diefenbaker as leader in December, 1956.

The Conservatives, discouraged after a long period of Liberal rule, held little hope for a victory in the 1957 election. But Diefenbaker waged a vigorous campaign. He charged that the Liberals had grown too powerful. He seemed to radiate vitality as he told of his plans for developing northern Canada.

In the 1957 election, the Conservatives won more seats in parliament than any other party, although they

---
IMPORTANT DATES IN DIEFENBAKER'S LIFE

- **1895** (Sept. 18) Born in Neustadt, Ont.
- **1919** Began to practice law in Wakaw, Sask.
- **1929** Married Edna May Brower.
- **1936** Became leader of Saskatchewan Conservative party.
- **1940** Elected to parliament.
- **1951** Mrs. Edna Diefenbaker died.
- **1953** Married Mrs. Olive Freeman Palmer.
- **1956** Chosen leader of Conservative party.
- **1957** (June 21) Became Prime Minister of Canada.
- **1958** Conservatives won largest parliamentary majority in Canadian history.
- **1962** Conservatives won re-election.
- **1963** Liberals defeated Conservatives. Diefenbaker resigned as Prime Minister on April 22.

IMPORTANT EVENTS DURING DIEFENBAKER'S ADMINISTRATION

Francis Miller for *Life* Magazine, © 1957 Time, Inc.

Campaigning in 1957, Diefenbaker visited his home town of Prince Albert, Sask.

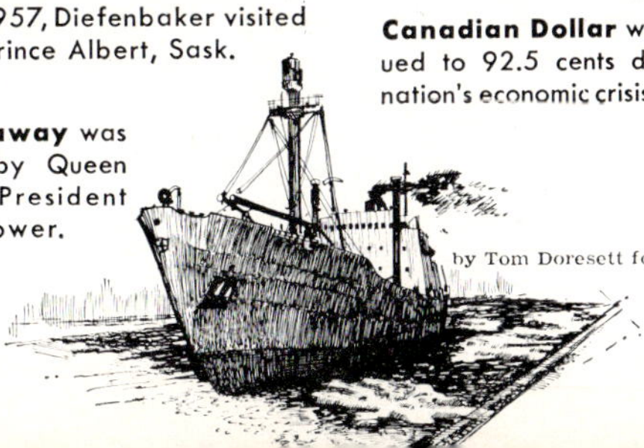

St. Lawrence Seaway was opened in 1959 by Queen Elizabeth II and President Dwight D. Eisenhower.

Hospitalization Insurance for all Canadians was set up by the government in 1961.

Canadian Dollar was devalued to 92.5 cents during the nation's economic crisis of 1962.

by Tom Doresett for WORLD BOOK

Atomic Weapons Dispute with the United States led to the downfall of Diefenbaker's government in early 1963.

Queen Elizabeth II conferred with Diefenbaker and opened a new session of parliament when she visited Canada in 1957.

United Press Int.

DIEFENBAKER, JOHN G.

did not win an absolute majority. Diefenbaker became the first Conservative Prime Minister since Richard B. Bennett, who served from 1930 to 1935.

Prime Minister (1957-1963)

John G. Diefenbaker, the first Prime Minister of Canada to come from a prairie province, took office on June 21, 1957. He succeeded Louis S. St. Laurent.

Parliament passed several bills sponsored by Diefenbaker's government. One bill increased old-age pensions. Other social welfare legislation provided cash loans to economically depressed areas. Another bill gave financial aid to expand hydroelectric power in the Atlantic provinces.

In 1958, Diefenbaker asked for a new election. He wanted more supporters in parliament to help him pass his legislative program. The Conservatives won 208 of the 265 seats in the house of commons—the largest parliamentary majority in Canadian history.

Much of Diefenbaker's social legislation soon became law. Parliament increased pensions for the blind and disabled, and approved a program of federal hospital insurance. In 1958, the government began to build roads into Canada's rich but undeveloped northland.

In 1960, Diefenbaker and President Dwight D. Eisenhower of the United States signed a treaty to harness the waters of the Columbia River. But the government of British Columbia refused to cooperate. Diefenbaker found himself unable to carry out the treaty.

Diefenbaker addressed the United Nations General Assembly in 1957 and 1960. He also attended the Commonwealth Prime Ministers' Conferences in London, England, in 1957, 1960, 1961, and 1962.

Economic Problems. During the early 1960's, Diefenbaker's government faced major economic problems. Canada had an unfavorable balance of trade with the United States. It imported far more from the United States than it sold there. In an effort to improve the trade balance, Diefenbaker urged Canadians to increase their trade with nations of the British Commonwealth. The government set up restrictions to discourage Canadians from investing abroad. It wanted such investment to take place in Canada, where it would aid the economy. But these measures did not solve the problem. Canada also faced major unemployment—up to 11 per cent of the work force in 1961 and 1962.

By the middle of 1962, Diefenbaker was forced to adopt austerity measures to boost the economy. The government lowered the value of the Canadian dollar. It reduced spending, raised tariffs on imports, and borrowed about $1,000,000,000 from foreign banks.

In the election of June, 1962, the Conservatives won the largest number of seats in parliament, but not an absolute majority. Diefenbaker remained Prime Minister only because the Social Credit party supported him.

Nuclear Controversy. In 1961, it was announced that the United States would supply Canada with missiles essential for the defense of North America. However, the Canadian government was not ready to accept atomic warheads for missiles received from the United States. By 1963, Canada had still not equipped the missiles with atomic warheads.

On Jan. 30, 1963, the United States charged that Canada had failed to propose a practical plan for arming its forces against a possible Russian attack. Diefenbaker angrily answered that the U.S. statement was "an unwarranted intrusion in Canadian affairs." He opposed acquiring nuclear warheads, saying that U.S. control of the missiles would threaten Canadian sovereignty. However, Liberal leader Lester B. Pearson declared that Canada should live up to its agreement and accept nuclear warheads. On Feb. 5, the house of commons passed a motion of no-confidence in Diefenbaker's government, and the government fell from power.

In the election of April, 1963, the Liberals won 129 seats in the house of commons. This was just short of an absolute majority of the 265 seats, but more than any other party won. The Conservatives won only 95 seats. Pearson succeeded Diefenbaker as Prime Minister on April 22, 1963. Diefenbaker became leader of the opposition in parliament.　　　　　　　　G. F. G. STANLEY

Related Articles in WORLD BOOK include:

Bennett, Richard B.	Political Party (Political
Canada, Government of	Parties in Canada)
Canada, History of	Saint Laurent, Louis S.
Pearson, Lester B.	Vanier, George P.

DIELECTRIC. See ELECTRICITY (Current Electricity).

DIELS, *deels,* **OTTO** (1876-1954), a German chemist, shared the 1950 Nobel prize for chemistry with his former pupil, Kurt Alder. They discovered and developed a process called *diene synthesis* for joining molecules containing carbon atoms. It yields complex natural molecules such as vitamins and hormones, and man-made materials such as synthetic rubber and fuels. He also discovered the gas *carbon suboxide.* Diels was born in Hamburg, Germany, and was graduated from the University of Berlin.

DIEM, NGO-DINH. See NGO-DINH-DIEM.

DIEMAKING. See DIE AND DIEMAKING.

DIEN BIEN PHU. See INDOCHINA (Indochina War).

DIEPPE, *dee EHP* (pop. 26,427; alt. 200 ft.), is a resort town on the north coast of France, 33 miles north of Rouen. For location, see FRANCE (color map). Tourists take over the town during the summer. They crowd the beaches and stay in the large hotels that stand along the waterfront. During the rest of the year, Dieppe is a quiet town where the people are busy with spinning, porcelain making, and shipbuilding. The town has a good harbor, bordered with white chalk cliffs. The English held Dieppe from 1420 to 1435. It was nearly destroyed by the bombardment of an Anglo-Dutch fleet in 1694. Dieppe became a fashionable resort for French society in the 1700's. Germans occupied the town during World War II. It was the scene of the largest commando raid of the war. Canadian and British troops landed at Dieppe on Aug. 19, 1942. They damaged German installations and emplacements in spite of heavy losses of men and equipment.　　　　　　　　EDWARD W. FOX

DIES, MARTIN (1900-　　), a lawyer, served as a Democrat from Texas in the United States House of Representatives from 1931 to 1945, and again from 1953 to 1959. Dies became a center of national controversy in the 1930's as chairman of the House Committee for the Investigation of Un-American Activities. He was born in Colorado City, Tex., and was graduated from National University, Washington, D.C. In 1940, Dies wrote *Trojan Horses in America.*　　　ERIC F. GOLDMAN

DIESEL, *DEE zul*, **RUDOLF** (1858-1913), a German mechanical engineer, developed an internal-combustion machine that used oil as fuel. Because of its simplicity of design and the economy of its fuel, the diesel engine is frequently preferred to the gasoline engine. It has greatly increased the efficiency of industry and transportation. See DIESEL ENGINE.

Diesel was born in Paris of German parents, and received his technical education in Munich. He became interested in designing an engine more efficient than steam and gas engines. He based his work on the theory of heat engines and on the designs of other engineers. He patented his design in 1892, and had completed and operated the first successful diesel engine by 1897. He also founded a factory to make diesel engines. In 1913, Diesel mysteriously disappeared from a German ship bound for London.   ROBERT E. SCHOFIELD

DIESEL ENGINE is a type of internal-combustion engine used chiefly for heavy-duty work. Most of the locomotives in the United States are diesel powered. Diesel engines drive huge freight trucks, large buses, tractors, and heavy road-building equipment. They are also used to power submarines and ships, and the generators of electric-power stations in small cities.

How a Diesel Engine Works. There are two main types of internal-combustion engines. One type, found in most automobiles, is called a *spark-ignition* engine. It uses electricity and spark plugs to ignite the fuel in the engine's cylinders (see GASOLINE ENGINE). The other type, the diesel engine, is a *compression-ignition* engine. When air confined in a cylinder is suddenly compressed, the temperature of the air rises. In a diesel engine, each piston compresses air in a cylinder. Fuel is injected and the heat of the air makes it ignite.

Diesel engines burn fuel oils, which require less refining and are cheaper than higher-grade fuels such as gasoline. During the combustion process, the stored chemical energy in the fuel is converted to *thermal*, or heat, energy. The temperature in each cylinder rises as high as 4,500°F. and creates pressures of 1,500 pounds a square inch. The pressure pushes against the tops of the pistons, forcing them to the other end of their cylinders. The pistons are connected by a rod or other suitable connecting mechanism to a crankshaft which they turn. In this way, a diesel engine supplies rotary power to drive vehicles and other machines.

In order for the compressed air inside the cylinders to ignite the fuel, it must have a certain temperature. The degree to which the temperature of the air rises depends on the amount of work done by the piston in compressing it. This work is measured in terms of the ratio between the volume of uncompressed air and the volume of the air after it is compressed. The compression ratio necessary to ignite the fuel depends on the size of the engine's cylinders. In large cylinders, the compression ratio is about 13 to 1. For small cylinders, it may be as high as 20 to 1. The average ratio is 14.5 to 1.

Near the end of the piston's compression stroke, the fuel is injected into a cylinder. In order to have the fuel and air mix well, the fuel is injected under high pressure as a spray. Combustion usually starts just before the piston ends its compression stroke. The power of diesel engines can be increased by *supercharging*, or forcing air under pressure into the cylinders. See FUEL INJECTION; SUPERCHARGER.

Diesel engines have a high *thermal efficiency*, or ability to convert the stored chemical energy in the fuel into *mechanical energy*, or work. They burn cheap fuel oils and can perform heavy work even under highly overloaded conditions. This is why they are favored for heavy-duty work.

Kinds of Diesel Engines. There are two main types of diesel engines. They differ according to the number of piston strokes required to complete a cycle of air compression, exhaust, and intake of fresh air. A *stroke* is the distance a piston travels in one direction. These engines are (1) the four-stroke cycle engine and (2) the two-stroke cycle engine.

In a *four-stroke engine*, each piston moves down, up,

The Diesel Engine operates in two or four cycles. This diagram shows how a single cylinder in a four-cycle engine operates. On Stroke 1, the piston moves down, drawing air into the cylinder. On Stroke 2, the rising piston compresses the air in the cylinder, raising the air temperature to about 900°F. When oil is sprayed into the cylinder, the heat causes it to burn explosively, forcing the piston down in Stroke 3. This is called the power stroke. On Stroke 4, the piston rises again, emptying the cylinder.

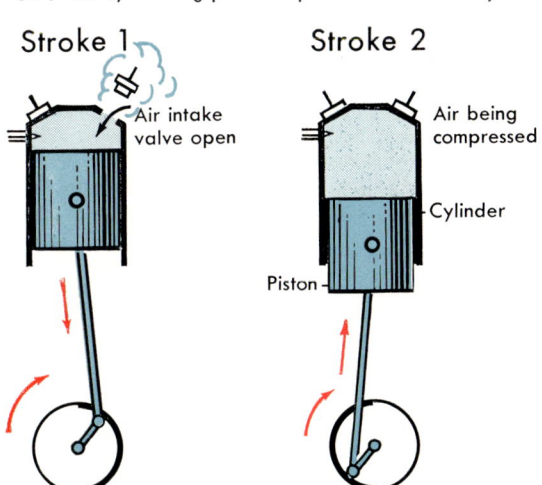

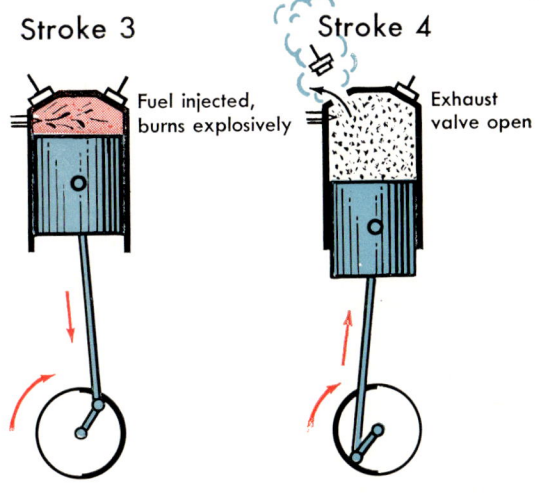

Stroke 1 — Air intake valve open
Stroke 2 — Air being compressed — Cylinder — Piston
Stroke 3 — Fuel injected, burns explosively
Stroke 4 — Exhaust valve open

163

DIET

down, and up to complete a cycle. The first downstroke draws air into the cylinder. The first upstroke compresses the air. The second downstroke is the power stroke. The second upstroke exhausts the gases produced by combustion. A four-stroke engine requires exhaust and air-intake valves.

In a *two-stroke engine*, the exhaust and intake of fresh air occur through openings in the cylinder near the end of the down-, or power, stroke. The one upstroke is the compression stroke. A two-stroke engine does not need valves. These engines have twice as many power strokes per cycle as four-stroke engines, and are used where high power is needed in a small engine.

History. The diesel engine is named for Rudolf Diesel, the German engineer who invented it. Diesel built his first engine in 1893. It exploded and almost killed him, but it proved that fuel could be ignited without a spark. He operated his first successful engine in 1897. Later, Sir Dugald Clerk of Great Britain developed the two-stroke diesel. OTTO A. UYEHARA

See also DIESEL, RUDOLF; ENGINE ANALYZER; LOCOMOTIVE; STARTER.

DIET, *DIE ut*, is the name of the parliament of Japan. The parliament of the Holy Roman Empire in Europe also was called the Diet. The parliament of Hungary, now the national assembly, formerly was called the Diet. The word was long applied in Europe to religious assemblies. In 1521, Martin Luther was judged by the Diet of Worms. See also JAPAN (National Government); LUTHER, MARTIN. WILFRID DYSON HAMBLY

DIET is the food and drink that a person takes regularly day after day. The word *diet* also refers to the amounts or kinds of food needed under special circumstances, such as losing or gaining weight. Diet needs vary according to age, weight, condition of health, climate, and amount of activity. *Dietetics* is the science of feeding individuals or groups. The money available and health and nutritional needs affect the type of feeding prescribed.

Normal Diet contains all the food elements needed to keep an average person in good health. To stay healthy, one needs *proteins* to build tissues, and *fats* and *carbohydrates* to provide energy and heat. *Minerals* and *vitamins* are needed for growth and to maintain tissues and regulate body functions. In the United States, calcium and iron are the minerals most often in short supply in the diet. Vitamins A and C are often eaten in smaller amounts than are recommended.

A diet that lacks any needed food element may cause certain *deficiency diseases*. For example, lack of vitamin A causes night blindness, and lack of vitamin C causes scurvy (see SCURVY).

Diets for Losing or Gaining Weight. Both the energy value of food and the energy spent in daily activity are measured in *calories*, or units of heat (see CALORIE). Diets for gaining or losing weight are based on the amount of calories taken into the body in food and the amount of calories used up in activity. If a person takes in more calories than he uses up, he will gain weight. He will lose weight if he takes in less calories than he uses up. A diet aimed toward gaining weight should include all the food elements. A doctor's advice should be sought before dieting to lose weight.

Special Diets may be prescribed for persons suffering from certain diseases. For example, the healthy body needs sugar, but a person with diabetes must limit the use of sugar unless he takes insulin (see INSULIN). Doctors may prescribe low-salt diets for patients with certain heart or kidney diseases.

Some persons suffer allergic or skin reactions from certain food products, such as milk, tomatoes, strawberries, wheat, potatoes, eggs, fish, nuts, chocolate, or pork. These persons should avoid such foods and consult a physician.

Certain groups of people, such as young children or older people, have special dietary needs. Because children grow rapidly, they need food not only to replace worn-out tissues and provide energy, but also to build new tissue.

A child's diet should include milk and milk products, eggs, lean meat, poultry, fish, fruits, vegetables, and cereals.

A well-balanced diet is as important to the older person as it is to the child. Older people need as many nutrients as young adults. But if their activity is reduced, they will need fewer calories. Expectant or nursing mothers and babies also need special diets (see BABY [The Baby's Heritage; Feeding]). JANICE M. SMITH

Related Articles in WORLD BOOK include:

Allergy	Fat	Milk (Food Values)
Calorie	Food	Nutrition
Carbohydrate	Fruit (Food Value)	Protein
Cooking	Health	Vitamin
Digestion	Metabolism	Weight Control

DIETETICS. See DIET; DIETITIAN.

DIETITIAN plans menus and supervises the purchasing, preparation, and serving of food in hospitals, schools, industrial cafeterias, restaurants, and institutions. She teaches others the importance of good nutrition and helps them plan diets and prepare meals. Dietitians must be trained in the science of nutrition, and in *dietetics*, the science that deals with the relation of diet to health.

Kind of Work. Many dietitians work in hospitals. They may plan diets for patients according to directions from doctors. They also help patients understand their diets. Administrative dietitians in hospitals, restaurants, schools, and other organizations manage the purchase of food and equipment. They may also supervise and train employees who prepare and serve meals. Public and private agencies employ dietitians to teach the principles of nutrition. Dietitians employed by food and kitchen appliance companies supervise test kitchens and help in public relations programs.

Qualifications. Dietitians must be intelligent, careful, patient, and healthy. They must be interested in food science, and be able to teach and get along with all kinds of people.

In high school, the prospective dietitian may discover an interest in science by taking such courses as chemistry and biology. She must study four years at college or university. Students of dietetics take courses in chemistry, biology, education, social sciences, foods, nutrition, institution management, and related subjects. Then most dietitians serve a one-year internship in a hospital, food clinic, or other institution. Here they learn to put their knowledge to practical use.

Opportunities and Advantages. Most dietitians are

women, although there are a few men, particularly in food administration and nutritional research. The field offers fine job opportunities, since the demand for trained dietitians exceeds the supply. A dietitian has the satisfaction of working with people, knowing that she is helping them to better health. Salaries for dietitians range from more than $3,600 for beginners, to over $10,000 for experienced workers. Opportunities are available for promotion to administrative and managerial positions in the field. Dietitians enjoy professional standing in their communities.

Information about a career as a dietitian can be obtained from the American Dietetic Association, 620 N. Michigan Ave., Chicago 11, Ill.

History. Interest in dietetics began in the late 1800's. Dietitians, who were trained only in college domestic science courses, prepared food for hospital patients on special diets. During the early 1900's, some dietitians extended their services to include the feeding of all the people in the hospital. Following World War I, opportunities arose outside hospitals. Industrial cafeterias, restaurants, and schools employed dietitians to supervise diet and menu planning. As knowledge increased in the field of nutrition, dietitians needed more education, and requirements were standardized. During World War II, the armed services commissioned almost 2,000 dietitians to supervise meal planning. Today, dietitians in many fields plan and teach others to plan nutritious meals.   THELMA POLLEN

See also DIET; NUTRITION.

DIFFERENTIAL is a system of gears mounted between the rear axles of a motor vehicle. These gears make it possible for one rear wheel to turn faster than the other when the vehicle goes around a corner.

The differential gears of an automobile are assembled inside a metal housing and are turned by the drive shaft from the engine. An axle extends from each side of the housing to a rear wheel. These axles are connected only by the gears of the differential.

When the vehicle moves straight ahead, the differential gears divide the driving force equally between the two axles. This keeps each of the rear wheels spinning at the same speed. But when the car turns a corner, the gears permit one axle to turn faster than the other. This makes it possible for the outer wheel, which has farther to go, to spin faster than the inner wheel. Therefore, the car does not skid. In the same way, when a car gets stuck in snow or mud, the differential gears allow one rear wheel to spin while the other does not move.

Racing cars are built without differentials because the gearing causes a loss of power on turns. That is the reason racing cars always skid around turns.

Charles S. Mott (1875-   ) and H. H. Timken (1831-1909) were pioneer developers of differential gearing in the United States.   FRANKLIN M. RECK

See also AUTOMOBILE (color picture, How Your Car Runs); GEAR.

DIFFERENTIAL ANALYZER is a calculating machine that works by electronics. It can solve advanced mathematical problems of physics, electrical engineering, aerodynamics, and other sciences. It was invented in 1931 by the American scientist Vannevar Bush. See also BUSH, VANNEVAR; COMPUTER.

DIFFERENTIAL CALCULUS. See CALCULUS.

DIFFRACTION

DIFFRACTION, *dihFRAK shun,* is the spreading out of waves, such as water waves, sound waves, or light waves, as they pass around an obstacle or through a hole or other opening. Water waves, sound waves, and light waves all show diffraction. Water waves spread out in every direction as they pass through an opening in a breakwater. Sound waves bend around a building, for we can hear a person shout on the other side

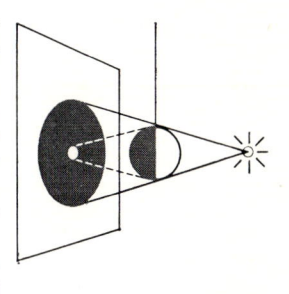

Light Diffraction. Light rays from a point source bend around a ball bearing and unite at a spot in its shadow.

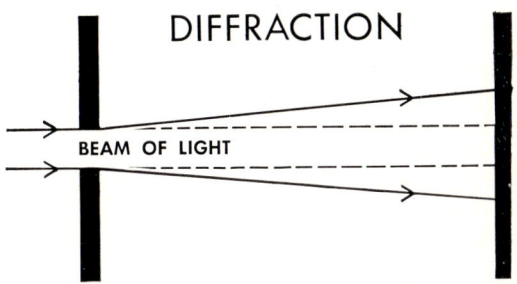

DIFFRACTION

BEAM OF LIGHT

Rays of light always bend outward and expand as they pass around obstacles or go through an opening.

even when we cannot see him. It is easy to observe diffraction of water and sound waves. But to detect it in light waves we must use very small obstacles as well as small distant sources of light. If you look through a silk umbrella toward a distant street light, you see a brilliant pattern of light spots. Each spot is stretched out in a *spectrum*. This is caused by the diffraction of light waves.

Light Diffraction. Scientists use laboratory demonstrations to show how light bends around objects. In one demonstration, the physicist uses a ball bearing and an electric arc lamp that produces a bright point of light. He places the arc lamp several feet away from a white screen. Then, using a thin thread or a magnetized needle, he suspends the ball bearing between the lamp and the screen. The ball's shadow, which falls on the screen, has a small white spot in its center. The shadow looks as though there were a small hole through the center of the ball.

The spot is caused by the diffraction of light waves as they pass the edge of the ball. The light waves bend around the edge of the ball and unite to give light at the screen. Scientists say that these waves are *in phase*. They are in phase because the center of the shadow is the same distance from all points on the edge of the ball. At other points in the shadow, the light waves are *out of phase*, so they cannot unite to produce light on the screen.

Diffraction Grating and the Diffraction Spectrum. A diffraction spectrum is formed by passing light through a diffraction grating. A diffraction grating consists of a system of many lines drawn very close together on a

165

DIFFUSION

plate of glass. They are parallel and equally distant, and there are usually thousands of lines to an inch. White light that passes through the grating is broken up into different colors. You can easily observe a diffraction spectrum by sighting along a phonograph record toward a strong source of light.

The diagram with this article gives a rough idea of the way a diffraction grating works. W is a wave of white light that is approaching grating G. The grating has two openings, A and B, through which the light passes and falls on screen S. When the light passes through the openings, it is diffracted, and bends in every direction. Light from both A and B reaches point R on the screen. But the distance from A to R is greater than the distance from B to R. The distance AC is the difference between the lengths of AR and BR, as indicated by the arc BC in the diagram. Suppose AC equals the length of one wave of red light. Then waves of red light coming from both A and B will unite to produce red light at R. This is because the waves of red light will be *in phase*. But each color has a different wave length, so light waves of other colors will not be in phase at R. They will be in phase at other points on the screen, between red at R and violet at V. The band of colors that appears on the screen between R and V is called the *diffraction spectrum*.

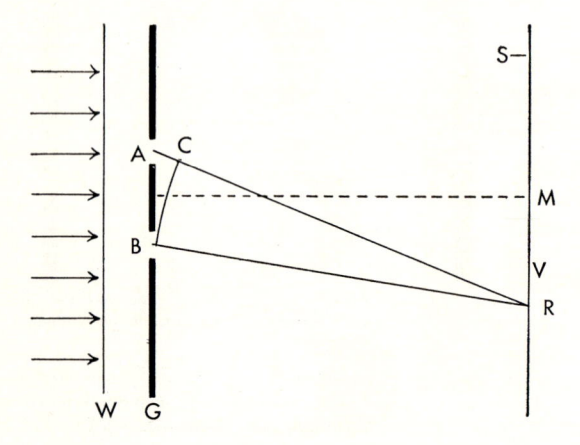

If the spectrum lies near point M, the colors will be spread out in an almost uniform pattern called a *normal spectrum*. This spectrum differs from the spectrum produced by a prism. The colors in a prismatic spectrum are not spread out evenly. The blue light spreads out more than red.

Crystals act as natural diffraction gratings because of the regular arrangement of their atoms. But scientists do not use crystals to diffract light because the wave lengths of light are too long. Instead, they use crystals to diffract X rays. Scientists send X rays through crystals and study the diffraction patterns to learn how the atoms are arranged in the crystal. SAMUEL W. HARDING

See also LIGHT (The Nature of Light).

DIFFUSION, *dih FYOO zhun*, is said to occur when the molecules of one substance mix with those of another. All substances—gases, liquids, or solids—are made of tiny particles called *molecules*. The molecules constantly move. Substances mix when their molecules move among each other. They can move most easily if they bump into each other as little as possible. The farther apart they are, the less danger they have of colliding, and the more rapid is the diffusion. The molecules in gases, such as air, are farther apart than the molecules

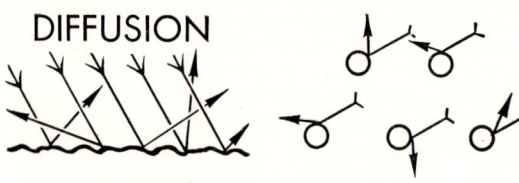

DIFFUSION

Light is scattered in all directions when it falls on an uneven surface.

The rays of the sun are spread by millions of dust particles in the air.

in liquids and solids. Therefore, diffusion occurs more rapidly in gases than in liquids.

If you uncork a bottle of smelling salts in a room, you can soon smell the odor all through the room. The same thing is true of the fragrance of flowers. These odors come from gases whose molecules have mingled with the molecules of the other gases in the air. We say the molecules of gases have *diffused*.

If you pour a little red ink through a tube to the bottom of a glass jar of water, all the water will soon turn red. The ink has diffused all through the water. In ammonia water, the gas ammonia has diffused through the liquid water. When a lump of sugar sweetens a cup of coffee, the solid sugar has dissolved in the coffee and diffused through it.

In the plant world, diffusion takes place when sap passes through cell walls (see OSMOSIS).

When light shines on a rough surface, the rays are diffused, or reflected in many directions. Diffused light makes good reading light because it does not give off any glare. LOUIS MARICK

See also GAS; MOLECULE.

DIGESTION, *dih JEHS chun*, is the process by which food is broken down into smaller particles, or molecules, for use in the human body. This breakdown makes it possible for the smaller digested particles to pass through the intestinal wall into the blood stream. The simple digested food particles in the blood stream are distributed to nourish all parts of the body. Digestion takes place in almost all parts of the alimentary canal (see ALIMENTARY CANAL). In these parts, the food is mixed with substances called *enzymes*, which speed up chemical reactions of the food.

The fats, proteins, and carbohydrates (starches and sugars) in foods are made up of very complex molecules and must be digested, or broken down. When digestion is completed, starches and complex sugars are broken down into simple sugars, fats are digested to fatty acids and glycerin, and proteins are digested to amino acids. Simple sugars, fatty acids and glycerin, and amino acids are the digested foods which can be absorbed into the blood stream. Other foods such as vitamins, minerals, and water do not need digestion.

From Mouth to Stomach. Digestion begins in the mouth. Chewing is very important to good digestion, for two reasons. When chewed food is ground into fine particles, the digestive juices, which contain enzymes, can

HOW FOOD IS DIGESTED

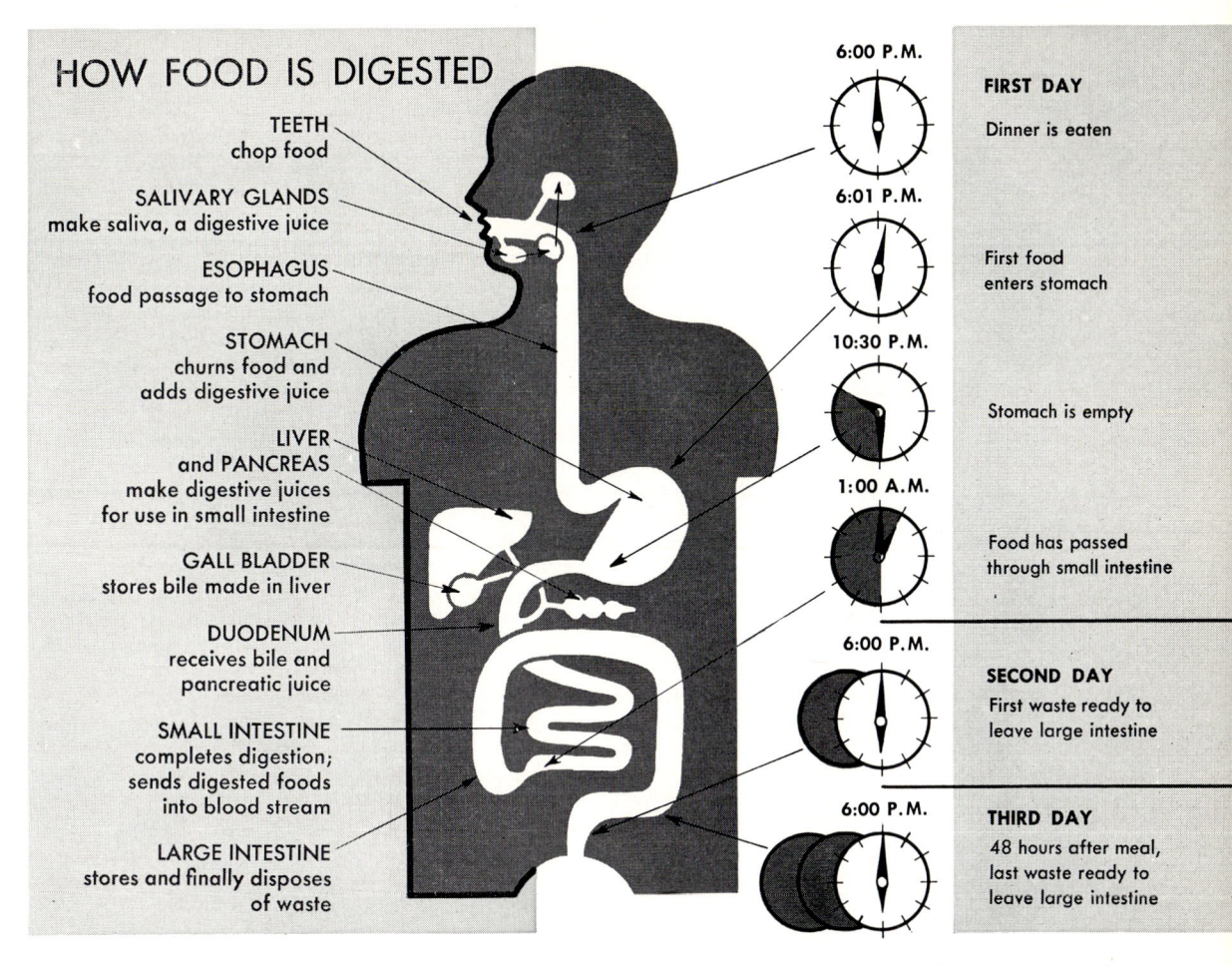

TEETH chop food

SALIVARY GLANDS make saliva, a digestive juice

ESOPHAGUS food passage to stomach

STOMACH churns food and adds digestive juice

LIVER and PANCREAS make digestive juices for use in small intestine

GALL BLADDER stores bile made in liver

DUODENUM receives bile and pancreatic juice

SMALL INTESTINE completes digestion; sends digested foods into blood stream

LARGE INTESTINE stores and finally disposes of waste

FIRST DAY
- 6:00 P.M. — Dinner is eaten
- 6:01 P.M. — First food enters stomach
- 10:30 P.M. — Stomach is empty
- 1:00 A.M. — Food has passed through small intestine

SECOND DAY
- 6:00 P.M. — First waste ready to leave large intestine

THIRD DAY
- 6:00 P.M. — 48 hours after meal, last waste ready to leave large intestine

---

react more easily. As the food is chewed, it is moistened and mixed with saliva which contains the enzyme *ptyalin*. Ptyalin changes some of the starches to sugar.

After the food is swallowed, it passes through the esophagus into the stomach. In the stomach it is thoroughly mixed with more digestive juices by a vigorous churning motion. This churning motion is caused by the contraction of strong muscles in the walls of the stomach. The digestive juice in the stomach is called *gastric juice*. It contains hydrochloric acid and the enzyme *pepsin*.

The gastric juice begins the digestion of protein foods such as meat, eggs, and milk. Starches, sugars, and fats are not digested by the gastric juice. The food remains in the stomach for two to five hours, depending on the type of food. Food which has been churned, partly digested, and changed to a thick liquid in the stomach is called *chyme*. Chyme passes from the stomach into the small intestine.

In the Small Intestine, the digestive process is completed on the partly digested food by pancreatic juice, intestinal juice, and bile. The pancreatic juice is produced by the pancreas and pours into the small intestine through a tube, or duct. The pancreatic juice contains the enzymes *trypsin, amylase,* and *lipase*. Trypsin breaks down the partly digested proteins, amylase changes starch into simple sugars, and lipase splits fats into fatty acids and glycerin. The intestinal juice is produced by the walls of the small intestine. It has milder digestive effects than the pancreatic juice, but carries out the same kind of digestion. Bile is produced in the liver, stored in the gall bladder, and flows into the small intestine through the bile duct. Bile helps the body digest and absorb fats.

When the food is completely digested, it is absorbed by tiny blood and lymph vessels in the walls of the small intestine. It is then carried into the circulation for nourishment of the body. Food particles are small enough to pass through the walls of the intestine and blood vessels only when they are completely digested.

Almost no digestion takes place in the large intestine. The large intestine stores waste food products and absorbs small amounts of water and minerals. The waste materials that accumulate in the large intestine are roughage that cannot be digested in the body. Such waste materials are eliminated from the body from time to time.

ANDREW CONWAY IVY

Related Articles in WORLD BOOK include:

Alimentary Canal	Enzyme	Mastication
Amino Acid	Esophagus	Pancreas
Assimilation	Fat	Pepsin
Beaumont, William	Gland	Starch
Bile	Indigestion	Stomach
Carbohydrate	Intestine	Sugar
Cellulose	Liver	Swallowing
Dyspepsia	Lymph	Teeth

The Digit Was a Measure used in ancient times. It was the breadth of a forefinger, usually from .72 to .75 of an inch.

DIGIT, *DIJ it*, means any one of the ten numerals from 0 to 9. The word *digit* comes from the Latin word *digitus*, meaning *finger*. We write numbers in the decimal number system by means of digits and place value. See ARABIC NUMERALS; DECIMAL NUMBER SYSTEM.

In astronomy, a digit is one-twelfth of the diameter of the sun or moon. Astronomers measure an eclipse with digits. For example, they speak of an eclipse of 8 digits. See ECLIPSE. HOWARD W. EVES

DIGITALIS, *DIHJ ih TAL is*, is a powerful drug made from the dried leaves of the purple foxglove, a common garden flower. It takes its name from the scientific name of the foxglove (see FOXGLOVE). In 1785, a British physician, William Withering, introduced it for the treatment of certain heart diseases. Doctors use digitalis when the action of the heart muscles is too weak to force blood out of the heart normally. They also use it to make the heart beat more regularly. It can be given as a powder, in tablets, as a liquid, or as a tincture.

Digitalis is very powerful and should never be taken except under a doctor's direction. The doses should always be small. Overdoses of digitalis cause nausea, vomiting, diarrhea, disturbance of the action of the heart, fainting, and even death. AUSTIN EDWARD SMITH

DIGRAPH. See CODES AND CIPHERS (Cryptanalysis).

DIHEDRAL WINGS. See AIRPLANE (Wings).

DIK-DIK is the smallest of the antelopes. It lives only in eastern Africa, except for one species in southwest Africa. The tallest dik-diks are 14 or 15 inches high at the shoulder. Females are sometimes larger than males, but have no horns. The slightly curved horns of the male are more than half as long as the head. Dik-diks are very slender animals, with tiny hoofs, short tails, and long hairy muzzles.

Scientific Classification. Dik-diks are in the family *Bovidae*. The two genera of dik-diks are *Madoqua* and *Rhynchotragus*. VICTOR H. CAHALANE

See also ANTELOPE.

DIKE. See GEOLOGY (Some Terms); LEVEE; NETHERLANDS (Reclamation).

DILI, *DIL ee* (pop. 1,795), is the capital, chief port, and commercial center of Portuguese Timor. It lies on the northern coast of the island. For location, see INDONESIA (color map).

Ships reach the port of Dili through a channel in the coral reef. Dili exports copra, tobacco, coffee, and sandalwood. The city's factories process coffee and make soap and pottery. JUSTUS M. VAN DER KROEF

See also TIMOR.

DILIGENTI QUINTUPLETS, *DILL uh JEN tih* (1943-), MARÍA ESTHER, MARÍA FERNANDA, MARÍA CRISTINA, CARLOS ALBERTO, and FRANCO, were the second set of quintuplets known to live more than a few hours after birth (see DIONNE QUINTUPLETS). They were born on July 15, 1943, in Buenos Aires, Argentina, to Franco and Ana María Aversano Vallota de Diligenti. Each of the five babies weighed 2 pounds. Fernanda and Esther were so frail that Diligenti had them placed in incubators at a sanitarium, and registered only three of the births. A year later, a reporter investigated a rumor of the quintuplets' birth, and Diligenti admitted he had falsely registered the births.

Diligenti wanted the children to grow up independently of each other, and he sent them to five different schools when they were 6. They were together only during vacations and holidays. HELEN E. MARSHALL

Clusters of Ripe Seeds grow on stalks of dill. The seeds and leaves of the plant flavor many foods. Dill is related to caraway, parsley, and several other common herbs and vegetables.

DILL is a small hardy plant related to parsley, anise, and caraway. It grows wild in southeastern Europe. The dill plant is light green and has an umbrellalike shape. People use the bitter seeds and tiny leaves to season foods, especially pickled foods. Several useful medicines are made from dill. Oil for use in perfumes can also be made from dill.

Scientific Classification. The dill plant is a member of the parsley family, *Umbelliferae*. It is genus *Anethum*, species *A. graveolens*. HAROLD NORMAN MOLDENKE

DILLARD UNIVERSITY is a coeducational undergraduate college at New Orleans, La. It was formed by a merger of New Orleans University and Straight College in 1935. The school provides courses in the humanities, social science, natural science, education, and nursing. For enrollment, see UNIVERSITIES AND COLLEGES (table).

DILLINGHAM, BENJAMIN F. and **WALTER F.** See HAWAII (Famous Hawaiians).

DILLON, CLARENCE DOUGLAS (1909-   ), became Secretary of the Treasury in 1961 under President John F. Kennedy. An investment banker, Dillon also served under President Dwight D. Eisenhower. He was Under Secretary of State for Economic Affairs in 1958-1959 and Under Secretary of State in 1959-1960.

Harris & Ewing
C. Douglas Dillon

Dillon was graduated from Harvard University in 1931. He entered his father's Wall Street firm, Dillon, Read, & Co. Inc., and became a vice-president and director in 1938. He served as chairman of the board from 1946 to 1953. During World War II, Dillon earned the rank of lieutenant commander in the U.S. Navy. He was ambassador to France from 1953 to 1957. Dillon was born in Geneva, Switzerland.   ERIC SEVAREID

DILLON, GEORGE (1906-   ), an American poet, published his first book, *Boy in the Wind*, in 1927. His second book of poems, *The Flowering Stone*, won the 1932 Pulitzer prize in poetry. With Edna St. Vincent Millay, he translated *Flowers of Evil* from the French. He worked 24 years on the staff of *Poetry* magazine. Dillon was born in Jacksonville, Fla.   JOHN HOLMES

DIMAGGIO, *dee MAH jih oh,* **JOSEPH PAUL** (1914-   ), was one of the greatest outfielders in baseball history. He played with the New York Yankees from 1936 to 1952. DiMaggio hit safely in 56 straight games in 1941, to set a major league record. He had a lifetime batting average of .325 in 1,736 games, and played in 10 World Series and 11 major league All-Star games. In 1939, 1941, and 1947, DiMaggio was the American League's most valuable player. He was elected to the baseball Hall of Fame in 1955. He was born in Martinez, Calif.   FRED RUSSELL

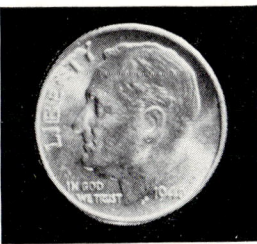

Chase Manhattan Bank Money Museum
U.S. Dime Pictures President Franklin D. Roosevelt.

DIME is a silver coin of the United States. The name comes from the Latin *decimus*, meaning *tenth*. The dime is so called because it has the buying power of one tenth of a dollar. But the silver in the dime could be sold for only about $3\frac{1}{2}$ cents. Before 1933, a dime was legal as payment in amounts of $10 or less. In that year, Congress made the dime legal tender in any amount. See also FASCES; MONEY (U.S. Coins).   LEWIS M. REAGAN

DIMETER. See METER (poetry).

DIMITY, *DIM uh tih,* is a sheer, plain-weave, lightweight cotton fabric. It often has a corded or checked effect that is achieved by weaving two or more yarns together. Dimity may be dyed or printed. The word *dimity* comes from the Greek *dimitos*, which means *double thread*.   HAZEL B. STRAHAN

DIMOND, ANTHONY J. See ALASKA (Famous Alaskans).

DINAR is the monetary unit of Iraq, Jordan, and Yugoslavia. In Iraq the dinar is a gold coin, while in Yugoslavia, where 100 para equal one dinar, the dinar is a copper-and-nickel coin. The dinar was once the chief coin of the Moslems and the territory they controlled. Its name comes from a silver Roman coin, the *denarius* (see DENARIUS). For values of the dinar, see MONEY (table, Values of Monetary Units).   LEWIS M. REAGAN

D'INDY, *dan DEE,* **VINCENT** (1851-1931), was a French composer, organist, and conductor. His compositions are noted for the way they express his love of nature. His works include *Poem of the Mountains*, a suite for piano and orchestra; *Istar Variations*, for orchestra; *Symphony on a French Mountain Air*, for orchestra and piano; and *Symphony No. 2 in B flat*.

D'Indy was born in Paris, and studied with the composer César Franck. He became widely known as a teacher of composition. In 1894, D'Indy helped found the *Schola Cantorum*, a school in Paris devoted to religious music. He directed the school from 1911 until his death. France, Spain, and Belgium honored D'Indy for his contributions to music.   JOYCE MICHELL

DINGLEY, NELSON, JR. See MAINE (Famous Maine Men and Women).

DINGO, *DING go,* is the wild dog of Australia. Dingoes are the only wild members of the dog family found in the country. Scientists believe that prehistoric men brought the first dingoes to Australia.

Dingoes are medium-sized dogs about as large as English setters. They have alert faces; sharp, erect ears; and brushlike tails. Most dingoes have yellowish-brown fur. But the animal's colors range from yellowish-white to black. Dingoes rarely bark, but howl instead. If caught as puppies, they make good pets.

Dingoes hunt alone or in family groups. Their chief food is the wallaby, or small kangaroo. Dingoes also catch sheep, and the Australian government has spent large sums of money in efforts to exterminate the dogs.

Scientific Classification. The dingo belongs to the dog family, *Canidae*. It is classified as genus *Canis*, species *dingo*.   WILLIAM O. PRUITT, JR.

See also ANIMAL (color picture, Australia).

DINMONT. See DANDIE DINMONT TERRIER.

The Dingo Is the Only Dog Native to Australia.
New York Zoological Society

Mighty Dinosaurs Once Roamed North America. The monster *Tyrannosaurus, right,* ranks as the largest meat-eating animal that ever lived. This 45-foot-long giant often attacked plant-eating dinosaurs, such as the bony-headed *Triceratops, left.*

Chicago Natural History Museum

DINOSAUR, *DIE no sore,* is the common name for two groups of reptiles that lived millions of years ago. Some of them were the largest, most terrifying animals that ever stalked the earth. The word *dinosaur* comes from the Greek words *dinos,* meaning *terrible,* and *sauros,* meaning *lizard.* Dinosaurs were not lizards, but the biggest flesh-eating dinosaurs were indeed "terrible." They stood as much as 20 feet high and had skulls 4 feet long, with huge, daggerlike teeth. The biggest plant eaters must have shaken the earth when they moved. Some were 80 feet long and weighed 50 tons! But not all dinosaurs were giants. One kind was only $2\frac{1}{2}$ feet long, about as big as a medium-sized dog.

Dinosaurs dominated the world during the *Mesozoic era*—from about 200,000,000 years ago to 60,000,000 years ago. The Mesozoic is divided into three *periods.* The oldest period, the *Triassic,* was from 200,000,000 to 170,000,000 years ago. The middle period, the *Jurassic,* was from 170,000,000 to 130,000,000 years ago. The most recent period, 130,000,000 to 60,000,000 years ago, was the *Cretaceous.* Dinosaurs appeared in the late Triassic and died out at the end of the Cretaceous period.

Scientists learn about dinosaurs from *fossils,* the records and remains of ancient living things. *Paleontologists,* scientists who study fossils, search for dinosaur bones and tracks. They study them and try to reconstruct the appearance and habits of the animals. This work requires a thorough knowledge of the body structure of living animals, and of the relation of body structure to habits. See FOSSIL (Studying Fossils).

Kinds of Dinosaurs

Dinosaurs were as varied in appearance and habits as are land animals of today. Some dinosaurs were large, some small. Some walked on two feet, some on four. Some ate plants, others ate meat. Some had smooth skin, others had scaly skin. Still others had skin studded with bony plates. But all dinosaurs had tiny brains. The dinosaurs, like other reptiles, laid their eggs on land. Scientists believe that large dinosaurs lived to be more than 100 years old.

Dinosaurs made up two great *orders,* or groups, of reptiles. The two groups differed in the structure of the *pelvis,* or hip bone. The *Saurischia* (pronounced *saw RISS ki uh*) had hips similar to those of modern lizards. The *Ornithischia* (pronounced *OR nih THIS ki uh*) had birdlike hips.

Lizard-Hipped Dinosaurs were divided into two groups: the *sauropods,* the gigantic plant eaters, and the *theropods,* including all the meat eaters.

Sauropods were the largest of all land animals. One of these monsters was *Brontosaurus,* which means *thunder lizard.* This 70- to 80-foot-long swamp dweller stood on four elephantlike legs. Another, *Diplodocus,* was almost 90 feet long, but more slender than *Brontosaurus. Brachiosaurus* was the largest of all dinosaurs, even though it had a rather short tail. It was 80 feet long and weighed 50 tons. It could have looked over the top of a three-story building.

All the sauropods had long necks and long tails. But their heads were only about 2 feet long. They had delicate teeth and must have eaten only tender plants. They probably spent most of their time in shallow water, which helped support their tremendous weight. Sauropods were fairly common in the late Jurassic period, but most of them died out at its close. A few survived in Asia and the southern continents during the Cretaceous Period. Scientists have found their fossils in Africa, Asia, Australia, Europe, Madagascar, and North and South America.

Theropods all walked on their hind legs and had small front legs that they used for grasping and tearing food. They had big heads with large, sharp teeth. The first theropod discovered, *Megalosaurus,* stood about 12 feet

── TRIASSIC 200,000,000 years ago ──

DINOSAUR FAMILY TREE

Dinosaurs ruled the earth for about 140,000,000 years. They ranged in size from creatures no bigger than chickens to huge animals such as *Brachiosaurus*. This monster, shown compared in size to a man, could look over the top of a three-story building. The two main groups of dinosaurs were the *ornithischians*, or bird-hipped dinosaurs, and the *saurischians*, or lizard-hipped dinosaurs. The dinosaurs illustrated are *not* drawn to scale.

THECODONTS, ancestors of all dinosaurs, grew to about 3 feet in length. These reptiles ran on their hind legs.

ORNITHISCHIAN DINOSAURS

SAURISCHIAN DINOSAURS

── JURASSIC 170,000,000 years ago ──

SAUROPODS, such as the clumsy, 80-foot-long *Brontosaurus*, ate huge amounts of plants.

STEGOSAURS, the first of the armored dinosaurs, were protected by triangular bony plates standing up along their backs.

── CRETACEOUS 130,000,000 years ago ──

ANKYLOSAURS had spikes and bony plates that protected their bodies. *Palaeoscinus* could use its mighty tail as a club.

ORNITHOPODS lived in shallow water along the shores of lakes and rivers. *Trachodon* grew to a length of about 40 feet.

THEROPODS, such as the terrible *Tyrannosaurus*, were flesh-eating dinosaurs. They preyed on the plant-eating dinosaurs.

CERATOPSIANS had horns or bony frills to protect their heads. *Triceratops*, the last ceratopsian, was 25 feet long.

American Museum of Natural History;
Chicago Natural History Museum

DINOSAUR

high. Its direct descendant, *Allosaurus*, was a 15-foot terror that preyed on the huge sauropods. The largest meat-eating animal that ever lived, *Tyrannosaurus*, measured about 45 feet from head to tail. It stood almost 20 feet high and had a 4-foot head. Its mouth was armed with 8-inch, daggerlike teeth. It had ridiculously small, useless front legs. Theropods also include the smallest well-known dinosaur, *Compsognathus*, which measured only 2½ feet, including its long tail. Its head was only 3½ inches long.

Theropods lived from the late Triassic through the Cretaceous periods. Their remains have been found in Africa, Asia, Australia, Europe, and North and South America.

Bird-Hipped Dinosaurs, the *Ornithischia*, were divided into four groups: (1) *stegosaurs*, armored dinosaurs of the Jurassic period; (2) *ankylosaurs*, armored dinosaurs of the Cretaceous period; (3) *ornithopods*, or duck-billed dinosaurs; and (4) *ceratopsians*, or horned dinosaurs. All these dinosaurs were plant eaters.

Stegosaurs were the first *Ornithischia* to appear on earth. *Stegosaurus*, a typical member of this group, was about 18 feet long and had a small head. Great bony plates set on edge protected its neck, back, and tail. It probably lashed out at attackers with these spikes. *Stegosaurus'* brain was about the size of a walnut. But near its hip it had a nerve center 20 times as large as the brain. This center controlled the action of its tail and hind legs. Stegosaurs lived until the early Cretaceous period, then died out. Their remains have been found in Africa, Europe, and North America.

Ankylosaurs generally resembled *Ankylosaurus*, a low, squat, powerful dinosaur. *Ankylosaurus* had almost solid armor, like an armadillo, with a row of large, sharp spikes down both its sides. Its tail was clublike, tipped with a heavy mass of bone. Ankylosaurs lived in Asia, Europe, and North America.

Ornithopods walked on two legs and had a long, balancing tail. They had no front teeth, and many of them had mouths that broadened into ducklike bills. Later ornithopods, such as *Trachodon*, had as many as 2,000 teeth. Preserved casts of the skin of a few of these dinosaurs show that they had webbed feet. This indicates that they were good swimmers. Ornithopods lived from the late Jurassic period through the Cretaceous period in Asia, Europe, and North America.

Ceratopsians looked much like rhinoceroses, but many, including *Triceratops*, were larger. Some had one horn, some as many as five. They all had big fringes growing back from their skulls to protect their necks. Paleontologists have found many fossils of *Protoceratops*, a small

RECONSTRUCTING A DINOSAUR SKELETON

Preparing the Skeleton may take months or even years of work. Scientists first clean the bones and glue together broken pieces. They make plaster substitutes for any missing parts. Then they drill holes in large bones and strengthen them with steel rods.

Chicago *Daily News*

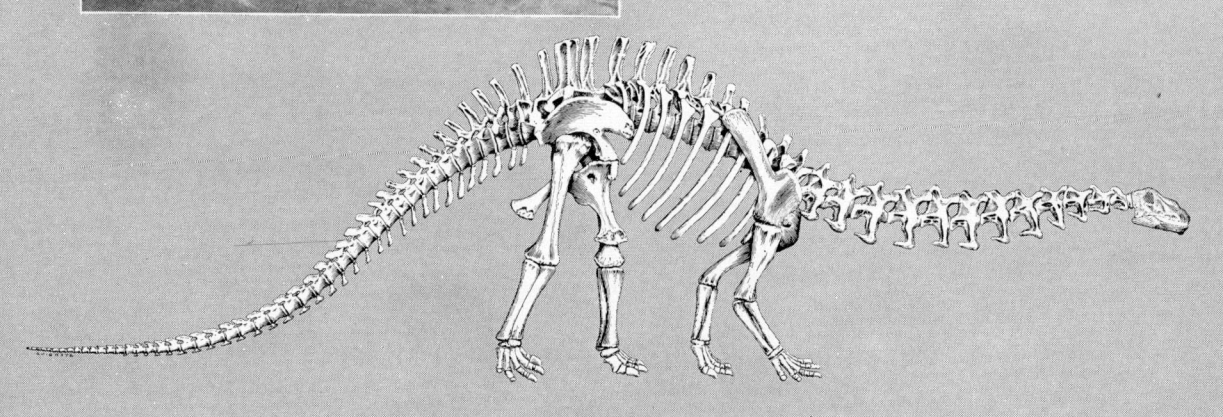

Chicago Natural History Museum

An Assembled *Brontosaurus* Skeleton looks like this drawing prepared by the Chicago Natural History Museum. The bones of the actual skeleton are supported and fastened together by steel rods. The scientists mount it in a natural position.

ceratopsian. These fossils range from adult animals to eggs. The eggs are about 6 to 7 inches long and 3 inches across (see FOSSIL [picture, Dinosaur Egg]). Ceratopsians, the last dinosaurs to appear, lived during the late Cretaceous period in Asia and North America.

How Dinosaurs Lived

Surroundings. When dinosaurs first appeared, North America was a low-lying continent with a great sea bordered by swamps where the Rocky Mountains now rise. The climate was warm, and forests of pines, redwoods, and cycads (a subtropical plant) grew on land (see CYCAD). Flowering plants appeared in the Cretaceous period.

Dinosaurs shared the swamps with other animals. Snakes glided through the water. Crocodiles as much as 40 feet long lived along the shores. *Pterosaurs*, flying reptiles, flew overhead on leathery wings. Birds appeared during the Jurassic period. Small mammals became numerous and varied. See also PREHISTORIC ANIMAL (Age of Dinosaurs).

Getting Food. The lush vegetation of the steaming swamps furnished food for the great sauropods. They moved slowly through the swamps with their ridiculously small heads working all the time to gulp down enough food for their huge bodies. Ornithopods swam in the *estuaries*, or river mouths, feeding on floating water plants. The stegosaurs, land dinosaurs of the Jurassic period, ate ferns, cycads, and pines. Ankylosaurs and ceratopsians of the Cretaceous period also ate these plants, along with flowering plants. Theropods preyed upon all the other kinds of animals.

Protection. Plant eaters developed many kinds of protection against the theropods. Some, including the sauropods and ornithopods, retreated into the water where the theropods could not go. The theropods were land animals and probably could not swim. Land-dwelling ornithischians had horns or armor, or both. Bony armor and spiked or clubbed tails protected the stegosaurs and ankylosaurs. Ceratopsians, like the modern rhinoceros, developed a counterattack. The charge of an enraged *Triceratops* must have put many a *Tyrannosaurus* to flight.

Why Dinosaurs Died Out

Scientists have advanced many reasons to explain why the dinosaurs died out. Probably the basic cause was the rise of mountain ranges during the Cretaceous period. When mountains formed, the great seaways drained from the continents and the vast swamplands dried up (see EARTH [How Mountains are Made]). This caused tremendous changes in the climate and food supply. But the dinosaurs had become specially adapted to the old conditions. When these conditions changed rapidly, the dinosaurs could not adjust. New plants appeared, and old ones died out. The plant eaters could not live on the new plants. As the plant eaters died out, the meat eaters that depended on them for food also died. This long, slow process took from 10,000,000 to 20,000,000 years. By the end of the Cretaceous period, all the dinosaurs had disappeared from the earth.

Other factors, including disease, probably affected the dinosaurs. Many scientists believe that the development of mammals also ranked as an important factor in the extinction of the dinosaurs. Mammals have better brains than the dinosaurs and better protection against cold. Some of the mammals probably ate dinosaur eggs and young dinosaurs. Although they were not the only cause, they almost certainly helped in the extinction of the great reptiles.   SAMUEL PAUL WELLES

Related Articles in WORLD BOOK include:

Alberta (Interesting Places to Visit)	Dinosaur National Monument
American Museum of Natural History	Fossil
Andrews, Roy Chapman	Geology (Outline of Earth History)
Arizona (Interesting Places to Visit)	Prehistoric Animal
	Reptile

Chicago Natural History Museum

Painted Restoration shows what *Brontosaurus* probably looked like when it lived. Scientists and artists work together to make the restoration as realistic as possible. They add plants and other animals that lived where the dinosaurs roamed.

DINOSAUR CANYON

DINOSAUR CANYON. See ARIZONA (Interesting Places to Visit).

DINOSAUR NATIONAL MONUMENT, located in Utah and Colorado, is a highly scenic region containing spectacular canyons cut by the Green and Yampa rivers. Its deposits of fossil remains of prehistoric reptiles are of scientific interest. The monument covers 205,136.31 acres. The U.S. government established it in 1915.

DINWIDDIE, *dihn WIHD ih,* **ROBERT** (1693-1770), was lieutenant governor of Virginia from 1751 to 1758. He served as the acting governor of the colony, because the governors usually lived in England. Greatly interested in the Ohio region, he decided to keep that area from the French. In 1753, he sent George Washington to demand that the French withdraw from western Pennsylvania, claimed by Virginia. In the war that followed, Dinwiddie urged the colonies to help the English drive the French from the Ohio Valley. He aided the expedition sent against Fort Duquesne in 1755. He quarreled continually with the Virginia Assembly because of its reluctance to vote funds for the war. He returned to England in 1758. He was born near Glasgow, Scotland. J. CARLYLE SITTERSON

Culver
Robert Dinwiddie

See WASHINGTON, GEORGE (Early Military Career).

DIOCESE, *DIE oh sees,* is the territory over which a bishop has authority. The Romans used this term for a time. They divided sections of their empire into *dioceses.* But later the word came to be used only in connection with the governing of churches. See also BISHOP.

DIOCLETIAN, *DY oh KLEE shun* (A.D. 245-313), was a Roman emperor. He was born in poverty at Dioclea in Dalmatia, and rose through the army to become a general. In A.D. 284, he was proclaimed emperor by the soldiers. Diocletian was an able organizer and administrator. He tried to bring peace and stability after 50 years of civil war and anarchy. Because of the size of the empire, he divided it into four administrative units, each under its own ruler. Diocletian resigned in 305. His reign was marred by persecutions of Christians and other religious groups when he attempted to restore the pagan Roman gods. ROBERT GEHLMANN BONE

DIODE. See ELECTRONICS (Diode).

DIOECIOUS PLANT. See FLOWER (Variations).

DIOGENES, *di AHJ ee neez* (412-323 B.C.), a philosopher of ancient Greece, was called the "Cynic." He belonged to the Cynic school of philosophy, which taught that a man ought to lead a life of self-control, and be free from all desire for material things and pleasures. Diogenes carried this view to extremes in his own life. According to tradition, he used a tub for shelter and walked the streets barefoot. Diogenes believed that good birth, riches, and honor were of little value. He felt they did not help a man lead a virtuous life.

He was born at Sinope, in Asia Minor. Pirates captured him during a journey from Athens to Aegina and

Brown Bros.
Diogenes, the Greek Philosopher, went through the streets of Athens, carrying a lighted lantern. He held this up to the faces of strangers and said he was looking for an honest man.

offered him for sale as a slave. He told his captors he knew no trade except how to govern men. Pointing to a wealthy Corinthian, he said: "Sell me to this man, he needs a master." The Corinthian bought Diogenes and made him tutor to his sons. When Alexander the Great came to see Diogenes, who was sunning himself, he said, "Ask any favor you wish." Legend says that Diogenes replied: "Please move out of my sunlight." To which Alexander commented: "If I were not Alexander, I would like to be Diogenes." LEWIS M. HAMMOND

See also CYNIC SCHOOL OF PHILOSOPHY.

DIOMEDE ISLANDS. See ALASKA.

DIOMEDES, king of Argos. See ULYSSES.

DIOMEDES, king of Thrace. See HERCULES.

DIONNE QUINTUPLETS, *dih AHN,* or *dih OHN,* CÉCILE, YVONNE, ANNETTE, MARIE (1934-   ), and ÉMILIE (1934-1954), are believed to be the first quintuplets to live more than a few hours after birth. The tiny babies, daughters of Oliva and Elzire Dionne, weighed a total of only 13 lbs. 6 oz. at birth. They were born in a seven-room family house near Callander, Ont., on May 28, 1934. Dr. Allan Dafoe, their physician, borrowed incubators and saved their lives by providing excellent scientific care.

Gifts poured in for the famous babies, and the Ontario legislature made them wards of the British king. For 10 years, they lived in a nursery built for them by the government. Then they went to live with their parents and brothers and sisters in a 20-room mansion. They had nuns as tutors. Their father received control of the girls by parliamentary act in 1944. The quintuplets earned a fortune from endorsing products and from their appearances in motion pictures. When they were a year old, they portrayed themselves in a film that was based on the life of their physician. A $1,000,000 reserve fund, set aside by their guardians, was given to the quintuplets when they became 21 years old.

The quintuplets began to lead separate lives in 1953. Three of the girls studied home economics at the Institut Familial in Nicolet, Que., and Yvonne studied art in Montreal. Marie entered a convent, but stayed there less than a year. Émilie died on Aug. 6, 1954. In October, 1957, Annette became the first of the quintuplets to be married. Cécile was married a month later, and Marie in August, 1958.   HELEN E. MARSHALL

See also DILIGENTI QUINTUPLETS.

The Dionne Quintuplets were wards of the British king until they were 10 years old. The girls, shown *below* at the age of 6, lived in a nursery built by the Canadian government.

King Features Syndicate

DIONYSIUS EXIGUUS. See CHRISTIAN ERA.
DIONYSIUS THE AREOPAGITE. See ANGEL.
DIONYSUS AND DIONYSIA. See BACCHUS.
DIOPHANTUS. See ALGEBRA (History).

DIOPSIDE, *die AHP side,* a mineral contained in igneous rock, belongs to the pyroxene group (see ROCK [Igneous Rock]). It is used as a gem stone. The crystals are often pale green or white. Diopside, found in marble deposits, is a calcium and magnesium silicate. It may be found with garnet and tourmaline.

DIOR, CHRISTIAN (1905-1957), a French fashion designer, created a "new look" in women's fashions in 1947. The "new look" featured long hemlines and full skirts. Dior was born at Granville, France, and became a fashion illustrator for the newspaper *Le Figaro Illustré*. He opened his own fashion salon, the House of Dior, in Paris in 1946, and became known as the leading designer in France.

DIORAMA, *DIE oh RAH muh,* is an exhibit showing modeled figures or objects in front of a painted or modeled background. The models become smaller toward the back of the exhibit and blend so skillfully with the background that the scene looks real. Dioramas showing outdoor scenes have curved backgrounds to help a feeling of distance. Museums use dioramas to show historical events and industrial methods.

DIPHTHERIA

School children sometimes make simple dioramas as educational projects.

The word *diorama* comes from Greek words meaning *a view through.* Louis Daguerre, a French inventor, first used the word about 1822 for transparent paintings he exhibited and for a theater he opened.   RALPH H. LEWIS

See also MONTANA (color picture, "Custer's Last Stand").

DIOSCURI. See CASTOR AND POLLUX.
DIP. See GEOLOGY (Some Terms).
DIPHTHERIA, *diff THEER ih uh,* is a severe contagious disease in which a false membrane grows over the mucous membrane, usually in the throat or nose. Most people can get diphtheria, but it is unusual in infants less than six months old. The disease most commonly occurs during autumn and winter. During the late 1800's, diphtheria epidemics swept Western Europe and the United States. But, since 1890, there has been a sharp decline in the number of cases of the disease in these regions.

How Diphtheria Spreads. Diphtheria is caused by a specific bacillus, *Corynebacterium diphtheriae*. The bacteria spread from one person to another. Because the bacteria usually live in the human nose and throat, doctors believe the most common method for spreading the disease is by coughing and sneezing. Persons called *carriers* may harbor the bacteria without showing any signs of the disease. Such persons may spread the disease to others.

Symptoms. The strong false membrane of diphtheria appears as a yellowish-gray patch on the mucous membrane of the victim's pharynx, tonsils, nose, or throat. In rare cases, the membrane may form over an open skin wound. When it forms in the throat, the membrane may obstruct it so completely that the victim cannot breathe. To save the patient's life, the doctor makes a temporary opening through the neck, directly into the windpipe.

In most cases of diphtheria, the microorganisms remain in the victim's throat and never enter the blood stream. But they produce a *toxin*, or poison, which the blood carries to all parts of the body.

Treatment. Doctors treat diphtheria by injecting an *antitoxin* into the patient's muscles. The antitoxin is a substance that neutralizes the toxin produced by the germs. It is made by concentrating the blood serum of horses or sheep that have been inoculated repeatedly with diphtheria toxin (see ANTITOXIN). The first effective diphtheria antitoxin was developed in 1890 by Emil von Behring, a German bacteriologist.

Prevention. Diphtheria can be prevented. Doctors give three injections of diphtheria toxoid at weekly intervals. Diphtheria toxoid is made from diphtheria toxins that have been treated with chemicals to prevent harmful effects. The toxoid stimulates a person's body to produce immune antibodies (see ANTIBODY).

A test to determine a person's immunity to diphtheria was introduced by the physician Béla Schick in 1913 (see SCHICK TEST). Doctors use this test during outbreaks of diphtheria to determine which persons need inoculations. They also use the test after an inoculation to make sure that the toxoid has made the person immune.   PAUL S. RHOADS

DIPHTHONG

DIPHTHONG, *DIHF thong*, is the sound produced by pronouncing two vowels as a single syllable. Examples are the *ou* in *out* and *oi* in *oil*. One sees readily how two sounds become a diphthong by pronouncing *ah* and *ee* together slowly, then more rapidly. They become the diphthong heard in *mine*, commonly described as *long i*. Diphthongs are often called *digraphs*.

DIPLODOCUS. See Dinosaur (Lizard-Hipped).

DIPLOMACY, *dih PLOH muh sih*, is the means of conducting negotiations between nations. Most nations send representatives to live in other countries. There, they help carry on day-to-day relationships between their country and the country where they serve. These *diplomats* work to gain political or economic advantages for their country and to promote international cooperation. They follow strict rules of procedure in official discussions and observe some customs hundreds of years old. Most customs emphasize dignity and ceremony.

Diplomatic Representatives observe strict rules about rank and importance. The highest rank is ambassador, followed by envoy extraordinary and minister plenipotentiary, minister resident, chargé d'affaires, secretary of legation, and, finally, attaché. Most large nations send ambassadors to each other, and to many smaller nations. Smaller countries send and receive diplomats of lower rank. Most governments also send *consuls* to cities in other countries to take care of international business relations. The pope sends *nuncios*, *legates*, and *delegates* to many countries to represent himself.

Each nation handles its diplomatic affairs through a foreign office. In the United States, the office that handles foreign relations is known as the Department of State. A foreign office usually forms the most important part of the executive branch of the government.

Diplomatic Duties. A diplomatic officer abroad is the accredited spokesman for his government. He gathers information on everything of value to his government and transmits it in formal reports, usually in code (see Codes and Ciphers). He protects the rights of his fellow citizens who are living or traveling abroad.

Diplomats maintain their headquarters in an embassy or legation. The only difference between an embassy and a legation is the rank of the diplomat in charge. An ambassador heads the staff of an embassy, while a minister leads a legation. A diplomat's staff may include special advisers, and attachés who report on industrial, agricultural, or social conditions.

Diplomatic Immunity. Diplomats enjoy several important privileges and immunities while serving abroad. These privileges arise partly because diplomats are the direct representatives of sovereign powers. Just as important, diplomats must have complete independence of action in order to perform their duties. A diplomat's privileges are based on the principle of *extraterritoriality*. This principle, used in international law, includes the guarantee that persons living in foreign countries will remain under the authority of their own governments (see Extraterritoriality). Four important diplomatic privileges and immunities include:

1. A diplomat cannot be arrested for any reason. His family and staff usually share this exemption.

2. His residence, papers, and effects cannot be searched or seized.

3. His personal belongings cannot be taxed by the country in which he serves.

4. He, his family, and his staff enjoy complete freedom of worship.

History. Nations have not always used diplomacy to settle international problems. The Greeks never used diplomatic representatives, and the Romans used them only for special purposes. But relations between countries grew more and more complex. Most nations eventually realized that they needed permanent representatives in other countries. Embassies first appeared in Italy during the 1200's and 1300's. At that time, they served as headquarters for spies and espionage agents, as well as for diplomats. Many historians believe that Cardinal Richelieu of France started the system of resident representatives during the 1600's.

Some scholars argue that diplomatic representatives are unnecessary today. They suggest that nations can take care of all diplomatic matters by letter, telegraph, or radio. They believe that diplomacy is kept alive only to satisfy the vanity of some governments. But personal diplomatic contact has many advantages. Diplomats take great care to make friends with government officials and influential citizens. When they present a formal

COUNTRIES TO WHICH THE UNITED STATES SENDS AMBASSADORS

Afghanistan	Germany, West	Nicaragua
Algeria	Ghana	Niger
Argentina	Great Britain	Nigeria
Australia	Greece	Norway
Austria	Guatemala	Pakistan
Belgium	Guinea	Panama
Bolivia	Haiti	Paraguay
Brazil	Honduras	Peru
Burma	Iceland	Philippines
Burundi	India	Poland
Cambodia	Indonesia	Portugal
Cameroon	Iran	Russia
Canada	Iraq	Rwanda
Central African Republic	Ireland	Saudi Arabia
	Israel	Senegal
Ceylon	Italy	Sierra Leone
Chad	Ivory Coast	Somalia
Chile	Jamaica	South Africa
China, Nationalist	Japan	Spain
Colombia	Jordan	Sudan
Congo (Brazzaville)	Korea, South	Sweden
Congo (Léopoldville)	Kuwait	Switzerland
Costa Rica	Laos	Syria
Cyprus	Lebanon	Tanganyika
Czechoslovakia	Liberia	Thailand
Dahomey	Libya	Togo
Denmark	Luxembourg	Trinidad and Tobago
Dominican Republic	Madagascar	
	Malaya	Tunisia
Ecuador	Mali	Turkey
Egypt (UAR)	Mauritania	Uganda
El Salvador	Mexico	Upper Volta
Ethiopia	Morocco	Uruguay
Finland	Nepal	Venezuela
France	Netherlands	Vietnam, South
Gabon	New Zealand	Yugoslavia

COUNTRIES TO WHICH THE UNITED STATES SENDS MINISTERS

Bulgaria	Hungary	Romania	Yemen

176

proposal, they can count on these friendships to help them. In addition, a diplomat can test reaction to ideas his government is considering by talking informally with his acquaintances.

Sometimes heads of various governments feel that they need personal conferences with leaders of other governments. They bypass their own diplomats in such "summit meetings."
CARTER L. DAVIDSON

Related Articles in WORLD BOOK include:
Ambassador	Extraterritoriality	Minister
Attaché	Foreign Policy	Nuncio
Chargé d'Affaires	Foreign Service	Protocol
Consul	Legate	State, Department of
Diplomatic Corps	Legation	

DIPLOMATIC CORPS includes all the men and women in the diplomatic service of one nation who live and work in the capital of another nation. Most governments make a distinction between members of the diplomatic corps and members of the *consular service*, although both belong to the *foreign service*. Diplomatic representatives deal primarily with political relations, while consular representatives deal with commercial relations.

Members of a diplomatic mission would include the ambassador, minister, or chargé d'affaires; and counselors, various attachés, and secretaries. Clerks and other employees also belong to the diplomatic corps. A mission maintains offices and living quarters in an embassy or a legation.
CARTER L. DAVIDSON

See also DIPLOMACY; FOREIGN SERVICE.

DIPLURA is an order of insects that have no eyes and no wings. They have slender, whitish bodies, and live in rotten wood or under leaves or stones. These insects shun light and move quickly to find a hiding place whenever they are disturbed.

DIPOLE. See ANTENNA.

DIPPER. See WATER OUZEL.

DIPPERS, BIG AND LITTLE. See BIG AND LITTLE DIPPERS.

DIPPING NEEDLE is a magnetic needle suspended so that it will dip toward the earth. It points toward magnetic substances. It is somewhat like a compass, but it is held on edge so that it points vertically instead of horizontally. In a compass, the north-seeking end of the needle will swing *around* horizontally until it points toward the North Magnetic Pole. But the north-seeking end of a dipping needle will swing *down* until it points toward the North Magnetic Pole.

The north-seeking end would point straight down if a dipping needle were held over the North Magnetic Pole. The other end of the needle, the south-seeking end, would point straight down if the dipping needle were held over the South Magnetic Pole. The needle remains horizontal at the magnetic equator. At all other places on the earth, the needle points down at an angle from the horizontal. A scale marked on the case shows the angle of dip from the true horizontal (see MAGNETIC EQUATOR).

W. S. Darley and Co.
A Dipping Needle is used to locate water pipes and other underground magnetic objects. It points down when held directly over the metal object.

Dipping needles are used to study the earth's magnetism, to locate iron and other magnetic objects just under the earth's surface, and to locate underground meter boxes and water pipes.
R. WILL BURNETT

DIPSOMANIA. See ALCOHOLISM.

DIPTERA, *DIP tur uh,* is the large order of insects that are true flies. *Diptera* means *two wings*. Diptera have only two wings and a pair of knobbed threads called *halteres* (balancers). All other winged insects have four wings in two pairs. Diptera mouth parts usually consist of a tube, called a *proboscis*, for piercing and sucking juices from animals and plants. The Diptera include crane flies, gnats, midges, mosquitoes, houseflies, horseflies, black flies, and deer flies. Insects such as May flies and dragonflies are not true flies, and therefore are not Diptera.
WILLIAM C. BEAVER

Related Articles in WORLD BOOK include:
Apple Maggot	Fruit Fly	Mediterranean Fruit Fly
Beefly	Gnat	
Blowfly	Hessian Fly	Mosquito
Bluebottle	Horsefly	Sand Fly
Botfly	Insect	Tachina Fly
Deer Fly	Maggot	Tsetse Fly
Fly		Warble Fly

DIRAC, *dih RACK,* **PAUL ADRIEN MAURICE** (1902-   ), is a British physicist noted for his prediction of the existence of the positive electron, or *positron*, and for other contributions to theoretical physics. He won the 1933 Nobel prize in physics with Erwin Schrödinger, an Austrian physicist, for his brilliant studies and research in the field of atomic physics.

Dirac and Schrödinger developed the science of wave mechanics, a mathematical system based on the *energy states* in atoms. Dirac predicted, as a result of this theory, the presence of a positively charged electron. The negative electron had been known and observed for many years (see ELECTRON). Carl D. Anderson observed the positron in 1932, thus proving Dirac's theory (see ANDERSON, CARL D.; LAMB, WILLIS E., JR.).

United Press Int.
Paul Dirac

Dirac was born on Aug. 8, 1902, in Bristol, England, and received degrees from Bristol and Cambridge universities. He became a fellow of the Royal Society in 1930, and won the society's Royal Medal in 1939 for the development of new quantum mechanics. Dirac joined the Cambridge University faculty in 1932. He wrote *Principles of Quantum Mechanics*, and papers on the quantum theory (see QUANTUM THEORY).
CARL T. CHASE

DIRECT CURRENT. See ELECTRIC CURRENT; ELECTRIC GENERATOR.

DIRECT-MAIL ADVERTISING. See ADVERTISING (Ways of Advertising).

DIRECT PRIMARY. See PRIMARY ELECTION.

177

An easy way to find direction is by means of a watch, a stick, and the sun. Hold the stick upright at the outer end of the hour hand. Turn the watch slowly until the stick shadow falls along the hour hand. South will lie halfway between the shadow and the 12 o'clock numeral. With this fixed, it will be easy to tell the other directions.

The sun rises in the east and sets in the west. By remembering this fact, it is possible to tell directions during the morning and afternoon. When facing the sun, the extended arms indicate the North and South. While facing the afternoon sun, the right arm points to the North. When facing the morning sun, the right arm points to the South.

HOW TO TELL DIRECTION

Giving accurate directions is not always an easy task. The best way to direct someone is to form a mental picture of the route they must follow. It is always helpful to remember prominent landmarks, such as the City Hall, a traffic stoplight, stores, or a church steeple.

DIRECTION. One of the first things a child must learn is how to find his way around his neighborhood. He first learns the direction of his home. No matter where he is, he knows whether he is walking toward his home or away from it. This knowledge is called a *sense of direction*. The older a child becomes, the more he moves about, and the more his sense of direction develops and becomes certain.

A child gains a sense of direction by comparing the location of things. When he faces the front of his house, his school is behind and to his right, for example. When he turns around and puts his back to the house, he knows the school is now in front and to his left. He learns the direction of the school by locating it in regard to his home and to himself. All directions are learned this way. In a short while, the child can leave his home and walk many blocks. He may change his direction many times, and always know the direction of his home and other places that he knew before. He learns how to use street signs, and how to use all the familiar landmarks in his town. He not only knows directions for himself, but he can give directions to others, by pointing out and describing objects along the way. If someone asks him how to reach the railroad station, he will tell the person which way to walk, how many blocks, when to turn, and what landmarks to observe.

If the child is in a strange area where there are no familiar objects, he will be "lost." Grown men, even sailors and explorers, would also be lost in strange places if they depended on familiar landmarks, for there would not be any. Some other landmarks must be used.

Men long ago divided direction into four main parts —north, south, east, and west. At all points of the world, north is in the same direction, and so are east, west, and south. When a man enters a strange country going north, he knows that east is to his right, west to his left, and south behind him. If he keeps track of the distance he travels in any direction he can always find his way back.

Direction can be told from the sun. In most parts of the northern half of the world, the sun is slightly to the south. It rises in the east and sets in the west. At noon the sun is directly south. When a man faces the sun at noon, north is behind him, east is on his left, and west is on his right. At night, he can find north by looking at the group of stars called the Big Dipper, which make the outline of a dipper. The last two stars on the dipper cup point to the North Star. When a man faces this star, he faces north.

Compasses tell the direction of north by magnetism (see COMPASS). With a compass and other instruments, sailors can tell exactly where they are, and which direction they are sailing even when the stars are not visible. Maps, compasses, astronomy are all based on direction and distance. Woodsmen do not need to see the stars to tell which way is north. They know that moss grows thickest on the north side of trees.   E. B. ESPENSHADE

See also NAVIGATION.

DIRECTION FINDER is a radio device that enables ships and airplanes to find their location. It is also used to determine the direction in which they are moving. It is simply a radio antenna wound in square or round form and arranged so that it can be turned on a pivot.

When the flat side of the finder faces the radio sending station, the radio wave strikes all four sides at the same time, and the volume of sound produced in the receiving set is reduced. When one of the edges is facing the sending station, the volume of sound response is loudest. The radio operator turns the antenna until his radio goes silent. Then he knows the flat side of the direction finder loop antenna is facing the sending station. When the signal is weakest, a line drawn through the antenna will be perpendicular to the direction of the broadcasting station heard.

The operator may use a vertical *sense antenna* with the loop antenna to determine on which side of the antenna the sending station is located. To find his geographical position, the operator uses a direction finder to find the direction of two or more other stations. Then he draws lines along those directions on a map. The spot at which the lines intersect is the location of his ship or plane.

Most direction finders on ships and planes have been replaced by more accurate devices (see AIRCRAFT INSTRUMENTS; ANTENNA; RADAR [Ships]; LORAN). Government agencies use direction finders to locate illegal radio stations. Direction finders are sometimes known as radio compasses.   RAYMOND F. YATES

DIRECTIONAL GYRO. See AIRCRAFT INSTRUMENTS (Navigation Instruments).

A Radio Direction Finder is operated from below deck by turning the antenna wheel. The earphones, plugged into the radio, allow the operator to hear the buzzing beacon signal.   R.C.A.

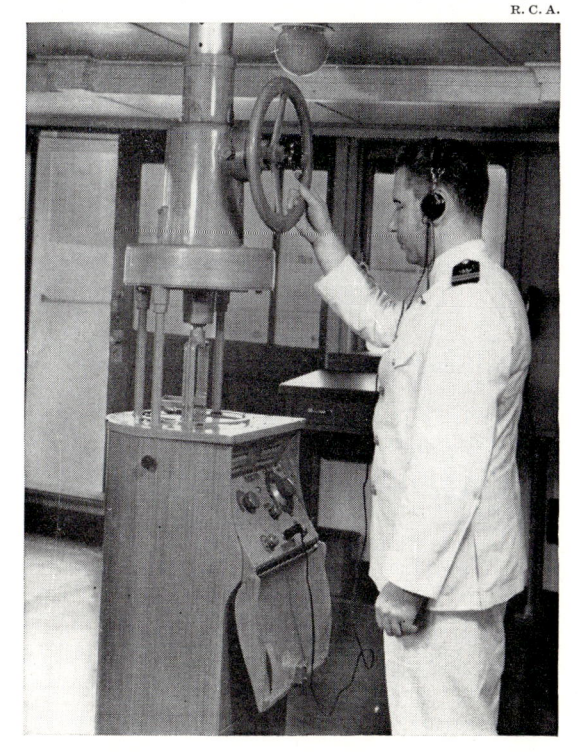

DIRECTIONAL RADIO BEAM. See AIRPLANE (picture, Radio Signals Mark the Airways).

DIRECTOR. See MOTION PICTURE (People Who Make Motion Pictures); also the list of Directors and Producers in the Related Articles of MOTION PICTURE.

DIRECTOR SYSTEM. See RANGE FINDER.

DIRECTORS, BOARD OF. See CORPORATION.

DIRECTORY (in French, *Directoire*, DEE reck TWAHR) was the conservative form of government established in France under the constitution of 1795. It was an executive body composed of five directors. One director retired each year. The Directory became unpopular because of its mismanagement of domestic and military affairs. It ended with Napoleon's seizure of power in November, 1799.   ROBERT B. HOLTMAN

See also NAPOLEON I (First Consul of France).

DIRIGIBLE, *DIHR ij uh b'l,* is a lighter-than-air airship. It is a cigar-shaped balloon that is driven by an engine and can be steered. It has a rudder and vertical fins to help control it in flight. It contains gas bags filled with hydrogen or helium to make it lighter than air. See also AIRSHIP; BALLOON.

DIRK. See DAGGER.

DIRKSEN, EVERETT McKINLEY (1896-   ), a Republican from Illinois, became minority leader of the United States Senate in 1959. Dirksen served in the House of Representatives from 1933 through 1948. He was elected to the Senate in 1950 and was re-elected in 1956 and 1962.

While in Congress, Dirksen earned a national reputation as an eloquent speaker. He was born in Pekin, Ill., on Jan. 4, 1896. He was graduated from the University of Minnesota.

Maurice Seymour
Everett M. Dirksen

DIS. See PLUTO (mythology).

DISABLED. See HANDICAPPED.

DISABLED AMERICAN VETERANS (D.A.V.) is an organization of men and women who have been disabled in line of duty during time of war. It was founded in March, 1920, by a group of disabled veterans under the leadership of Judge Robert S. Marx of Cincinnati, Ohio.

The purpose of the organization is to care for disabled veterans and to help them return to a useful way of living. Money for rehabilitation work comes from a yearly campaign in which the D.A.V. manufactures and sends out millions of miniature automobile license plates for identifying key chains. The D.A.V. has over 1,700 chapters in the United States and other countries. Headquarters are at 1423 E. McMillan St., Cincinnati, Ohio.   VIVIAN D. CORBLY

Disabled American Veterans
The D.A.V. Emblem

DISARMAMENT

DISARMAMENT, also called ARMS CONTROL, means reducing, limiting, controlling, or eliminating a nation's armed forces and weapons. International agreements usually form the basis for disarmament. Types of disarmament include (1) general and complete, (2) limited or partial, and (3) regional.

General and Complete Disarmament would allow nations to keep only those forces and non-nuclear armaments necessary to protect their citizens and support United Nations peace forces. General and complete disarmament would be planned so that no nation would achieve a military advantage during the disarmament process. The plan would include stronger methods for peacefully settling disagreements between nations.

Limited or Partial Disarmament describes agreements between nations that apply only to one or more parts of their total armed forces and weapons. A treaty among nuclear powers to ban the testing of nuclear weapons is an example of limited disarmament.

Regional Disarmament usually means limiting armed forces and weapons in a certain geographical area. Two or more nations may agree to limit their armed forces and weapons. Regional disarmament may also mean an agreement on how armed forces and weapons are distributed within a given region. Some nations have set up between them *demilitarized zones*, areas in which there are no troops or weapons.

The Argument for Disarmament

Persons favoring disarmament use these arguments:

The need for disarmament agreements became more critical in the 1950's and 1960's as nations developed powerful weapons of mass destruction. One Polaris submarine with its missiles and nuclear warheads contains more destructive power than all of the weapons used in World War II. Because of such weapons, nations can no longer think of total war as an effective way to attain national goals. Even if a nation attacked another nation with nuclear weapons, it would probably be destroyed by a counter-attack.

The high cost of missiles and nuclear weapons is another reason for disarmament. Any nation that tries to keep up in a nuclear armaments race must spend a large part of its resources to do so. In addition, countries in an arms race also must keep a large number of their scientists and engineers working on military projects instead of in peaceful industries.

As the number of nations that possess nuclear weapons increases, the chance increases that a nuclear war may begin. There can be no assurance of peace as long as large stocks of weapons exist in the world. Disarmament agreements would stop or slow down the arms buildup and reduce tension between nations.

The Argument Against Disarmament

Persons who oppose disarmament use these arguments:

Armed forces and weapons in themselves do not cause international disputes or tension. They merely reflect political, economic, and other kinds of disputes. These disputes must be settled before nations can agree on disarmament. Nations that first try to agree on disarmament raise false hopes among their peoples. False hopes may cause the people of a country to oppose spending the money necessary for adequate defense. A false sense of security can do more to bring on war than having armed forces and weapons ready to deter war. Disarmament also may damage a nation's military defense, which has been carefully worked out by military planners.

Without mutual inspection, disarmament agreements cannot work between a nation that has an open, free society and one that has a secret, totalitarian society. The closed society has the advantage because no one can be certain it is keeping its part of the agreement.

History of Disarmament

Until the 1900's, there were only a few limited disarmament agreements. One of these, the Rush-Bagot Agreement of 1817 between the United States and Great Britain, limited their forces along the Great Lakes.

The armistice signed after World War I disarmed Germany and limited the size of its army. France, Italy, Japan, Great Britain, and the United States held a conference on arms limitation in Washington, D.C., in 1921 and 1922. They agreed to limit the number, size, and guns of their battleships for 15 years. In 1930, at the London Naval Conference, Japan, Great Britain, and the United States consented to limit the size and guns of their cruisers, destroyers, and submarines. But these agreements lasted only until 1936. The League of Nations called a disarmament conference in Geneva, Switzerland, in 1932, but it failed.

The peace treaties signed at the end of World War II provided for the disarmament of Germany and Japan. In the years following World War II, the United Nations tried to obtain a general agreement limiting armaments. A 12-nation Disarmament Commission, set up by the General Assembly, began meeting in February, 1952. Two years later, a subcommittee was set up to speed the talks. But the members—Canada, France, Great Britain, Russia, and the United States—could not agree.

In 1957, the commission was enlarged to 26 members. It was expanded to include all UN members in 1959. Great Britain, Russia, and the United States then set up a 10-nation committee. It broke down in 1960. Talks in 1961 were limited to an effort to ban further testing of nuclear weapons. In March, 1962, a 17-nation committee began disarmament talks. These discussions were reconvened in 1963.

Both the United States and Russia made disarmament proposals, but they differed substantially. Russia said that U.S. inspection proposals amounted to spying. The United States said inspection helped guarantee that all nations were abiding by the treaty.

Nations also discussed ways to reduce the risk of war through accident; ways to prevent outer space from being used for military purposes; and agreements to prevent additional countries from obtaining nuclear weapons. A. S. FISHER

DISARMAMENT AGENCY, UNITED STATES, is an agency that coordinates government activities in international arms control. Its official name is the UNITED STATES ARMS CONTROL AND DISARMAMENT AGENCY. Congress set it up in 1961 to combine political, military, scientific, and technical skills to find ways of reducing armaments and to help promote peace. The agency coordinates study and research and develops policies. Its director is responsible to the Secretary of State and the President. A. S. FISHER

MAJOR DISASTERS

Year	Location	Dead	Disaster
1737	Calcutta, India	300,000	Earthquake
1865	Mississippi River	1,450	Steamboat Explosion
1867	West Indies	1,000	Shipwrecks (Hurricane)
1871	Chicago	300	Fire
1887	Central China	900,000	Flood
1889	Johnstown, Pa.	2,200	Flood
1893	Central U.S.	3,000	Tornadoes
1896	Ecuador; Peru	70,000	Earthquake
1903	Chicago	600	Theater Fire
1904	New York City	1,021	Steamboat Fire
1906	San Francisco	700	Earthquake; Fire
1911	Eastern China	100,000	Flood
1912	North Atlantic	1,517	Shipwreck (*Titanic*)
1913	Central U.S.	1,232	Floods
1917	Halifax, N.S.	1,635	Ship Explosion
1921	Swatow, China	1,000	Shipwreck
1930	Dominican Republic	2,000	Hurricane
1937	New London, Tex.	294	School Fire
1938	New England	488	Hurricane
1942	Bengal, India	21,000	Cyclone; Tidal Wave
1942	Boston	490	Night Club Fire
1942	Manchuria	1,549	Mine Explosion
1944	Hartford, Conn.	160	Circus Fire
1947	Texas City, Tex.	575	Explosion
1948	China Sea	1,100	Ship Explosion
1951	Manchuria	1,800	Flood
1951	Papua	3,000	Volcanic Eruption
1953	North Sea	2,000	Storm and Floods
1954	Japan	1,570	Typhoon
1955	India; Pakistan	1,700	Flood
1956	Cali, Colombia	1,290	Explosion; Fire
1956	China	1,960	Typhoon
1959	Japan	5,000	Typhoon
1960	Agadir, Morocco	15,000	Earthquake; Tidal Wave
1960	Chile	2,000	Earthquake; Tidal Wave
1960	New York City	134	Aircraft Collision
1961	Pakistan	2,000	Hurricane; Floods
1962	Peru	3,500	Avalanche
1963	Bali	1,500	Volcanic Eruption
1963	North Atlantic	129	Submarine *Thresher* Lost

DISASTER is a sudden and extremely unfortunate event that affects many people. Some of the world's greatest disasters are listed above.

Related Articles in WORLD BOOK include:
Earthquake (Famous Earthquakes)
Fire Fighting (Disastrous Fires in History)
Floods and Flood Control
Hurricane (Hurricanes That Made History)
Shipwreck
Volcano (Famous Volcanic Eruptions)

DISASTER RELIEF. See CARE; CIVIL DEFENSE; COAST GUARD, UNITED STATES; NATIONAL GUARD; RED CROSS; SALVATION ARMY.

DISCHARGE, MILITARY. See MILITARY DISCHARGE.

DISCIPLE. See APOSTLE.

DISCIPLES OF CHRIST. See CHRISTIAN CHURCHES, INTERNATIONAL CONVENTION OF.

DISCOBOLUS. See DISCUS THROW.

DISCOUNT is a term applied in business to a deduction from a stated price or from a payment due at some future date. The forms most commonly used in business include *bank discount*, *trade discount*, and *cash discount*.

Bank Discount is the deduction which a bank makes from the face value of a note. The bank does this when it cashes a note before it is due. Bank discount is determined in the same manner as simple interest. But it is taken in advance, by being deducted from the face value of the note. The difference between the face value of the note and the discount is called the *proceeds*. For example, the holder of a note may wish to turn it into cash, or have it *discounted*, before it becomes due. He may do so by presenting the note to the bank and receiving for it the amount of its face value, less the interest due during the term of discount. The *term of discount*, or *time to run*, is the period of time following the day the note is presented for payment through the day on which it matures. Bank discount creates a higher effective rate of interest than simple interest. The borrower pays the same amount in either case for the use of the money received, but with bank discount he receives only the proceeds instead of the face value of the note. Suppose a note for $5,000, dated February 26 and maturing on May 26, were presented to the bank on April 1. The number of days following April 1 through May 26 is 55. If the note bears interest at 6 per cent a year, the interest for this period of 55 days would amount to $45.83. The bank deducts, or discounts, this sum from the face value of the note as its charge for cashing it. Then the bank pays the balance, or $4,954.17, to the person who presented the note for payment. The bank, in turn, collects the full sum of $5,000 on the date the note matures.

Trade Discount is a term used by manufacturers and wholesale merchants when they take off a certain percentage of the price given in a price list. This price is called the *list price*. The list price less the discount is known as the *net price*. Market values may change after price lists are issued. Changes in list prices are often made by varying the trade discount.

Cash Discount is a deduction of a percentage of a bill for goods sold on credit. A cash discount is given when the bill is paid within a short period. Many merchants offer cash discounts to buyers to induce them to pay their bills quickly instead of waiting until the bill is due. Such a discount might be expressed as *2/10, n/30*, which is read as *two ten, net thirty*. This means that the buyer may deduct 2 per cent from the bill if he pays it within 10 days, or he may wait and pay the whole amount at the end of the 30 days.   ROBERT W. MERRY

DISCOUNT HOUSE is a retail store that sells products at prices lower than those usually charged by other retail stores. Discount houses sell in mass volume and make only a small profit on each item. They became an important form of mass distribution after World War II. Most discount houses operate on a self-service basis and their operating expenses are lower than those of other retail stores. Some discount houses specialize in certain products, such as electrical appliances or clothing. Others carry a wide variety of products similar to the variety that traditional department stores carry. Many discount houses are located in suburban shopping centers and offer shoppers ample parking space and long shopping hours.   NATHANIEL SCHWARTZ

See also DEPARTMENT STORE.

DISCOVERER, an earth satellite. See SPACE TRAVEL (table, Major Satellites and Probes).

DISCOVERY. See EXPLORATION AND DISCOVERY; INVENTION.

HOW TO THROW A DISCUS

The discus thrower stands in a circle measuring 8 ft. 2½ in. in diameter. He must not step outside this circle. He holds the discus flat against the palm of his hand, and swings within the circle with his arm outstretched. He releases the discus at the end of the second turn. The power comes from the body and from the follow-through of the thrower's arm.

DISCUS THROW is one of the oldest individual sports. It was a popular event with the ancient Greeks in their Olympic Games. The Greeks considered the discus-throwing champion the greatest athlete. Myron, a Greek sculptor, made a remarkable bronze statue known as the *Discobolus*, or *Discus Thrower*. Only copies remain. The finest is in the Vatican in Rome.

Athletes in ancient times threw a discus made of stone or metal. The discus used today is a round wooden plate with a smooth metal rim. It is $8\frac{5}{8}$ inches in diameter and $1\frac{3}{4}$ inches thick at the center, tapering slightly at the edge. It weighs 4 pounds, $6\frac{1}{2}$ ounces. The circular metal rim must be at least 2 inches and not more than $2\frac{1}{2}$ inches in diameter.

Athletes throw the discus from a circle that is 8 feet, $2\frac{1}{2}$ inches in diameter. The discus thrower holds the discus in the palm of one hand, the ends of his fingers curling around the metal rim. He whirls his body in a complete turn to gather speed and power, and hurls the discus at the end of his second turn. His fingertips spin the discus as it leaves his hand, and it flies through the air in a fairly flat position.

The thrower fouls if he touches the ground outside the circle with any part of his body before the discus strikes the ground, or if he steps on the circle. Judges measure the distance of his throw from the inside edge of the circle to the nearest point the discus struck the ground. Each competitor gets three throws, and his best mark counts. In big meets, the best seven competitors each receive three more throws.

Discus throwing requires less strain than shot-putting or the hammer throw. Good throwing is a matter of practice and form rather than great strength.

For the world discus-throwing record, see TRACK AND FIELD (table). FRED RUSSELL

DISCUSSION. See CONFERENCE; DEBATE; FORUM; PANEL DISCUSSION; SYMPOSIUM.

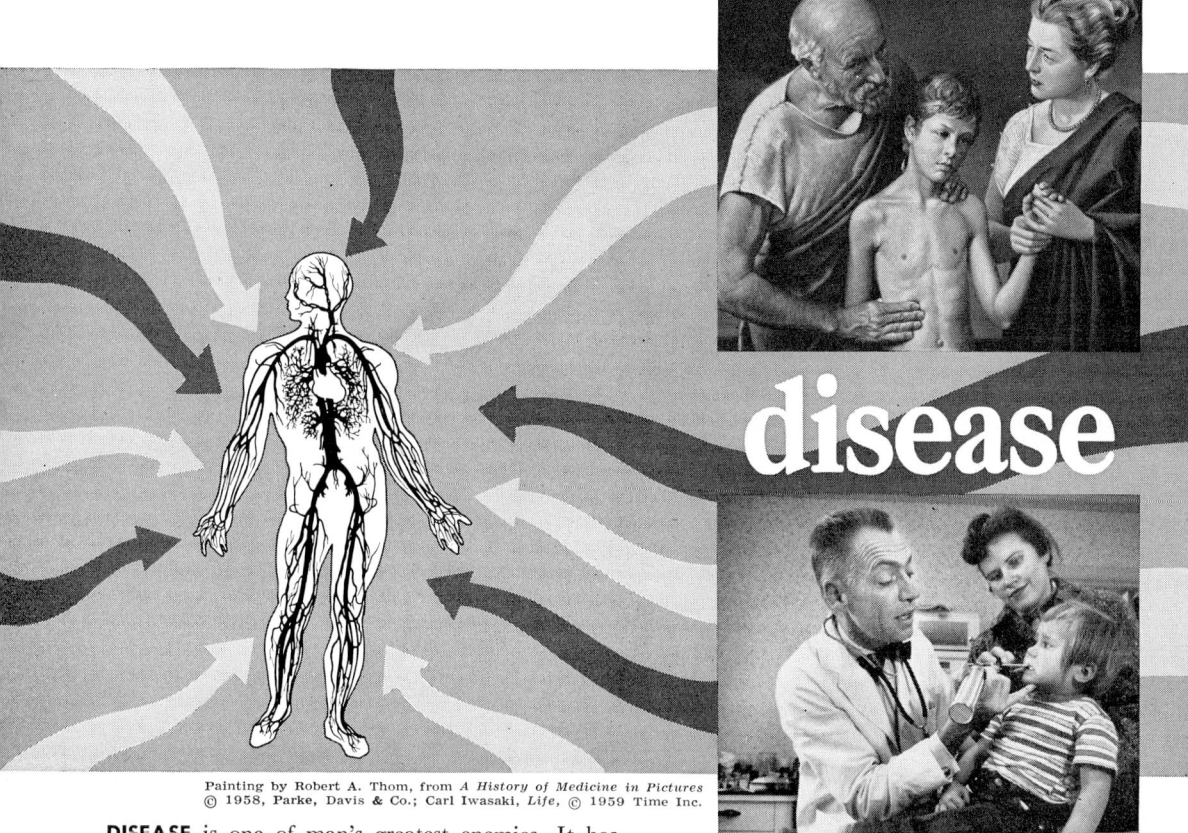

Painting by Robert A. Thom, from *A History of Medicine in Pictures* © 1958, Parke, Davis & Co.; Carl Iwasaki, *Life*, © 1959 Time Inc.

Throughout history, man has fought disease. Physicians have tried to prolong life since the time of Hippocrates, a famous doctor in Ancient Greece.

disease

DISEASE is one of man's greatest enemies. It has killed and crippled more persons than all the wars ever fought. It has even influenced the course of history. Man has conquered many diseases. But millions of persons in all parts of the world still become ill from diseases each day. All living things can get diseases—plants and animals as well as humans.

Human diseases include most conditions that interfere with the normal state of the body or of the mind. Originally, the word *disease* meant chiefly illnesses for which the cause was unknown. But scientists now know that diseases have many different causes. For example, some diseases, such as poliomyelitis, pneumonia, and scarlet fever, can be caused by germs. Other diseases, including scurvy and rickets, may result from poor diets. Still others may be caused by allergies, harmful fumes in the air, and even old age.

Some diseases, called *communicable* or *contagious* diseases, can spread from one person to another. An *epidemic* takes place when a communicable disease, such as diphtheria or typhoid fever, spreads widely through a community. Sometimes epidemics occur at the same time in many countries throughout the world, as did the influenza epidemic of 1957. Then they are called *pandemics*. In some countries, certain diseases are always present, as the bubonic plague in India and China. These are called *endemic* diseases.

North Americans are considered to be among the healthiest people in the world. But in Canada, experts have found that more than 10,000,000 persons have some kind of illness during a year. In the United States, a survey showed that two of every five persons has a *chronic*, or long-continued, disease. The survey also showed that the average person has two or more *acute*, or short and severe, illnesses each year.

Diseases affect the working efficiency of industries as well as of individuals. In the United States, persons absent because of the common cold cost industries about 120,000,000 days of work every year.

Diseases Caused by Germs

Men once believed that evil spirits made people sick. It was not until the 1400's that scientists began to suspect that some diseases were caused by tiny, invisible particles called *germs*. Early researchers called these germs "living seeds of disease." They believed that germs developed out of nothing in the blood streams of man and of animals. In the 1500's, doctors began to suggest that some germs could be passed from one person to another and spread disease.

Bacteria and other germs were first seen under a microscope in the 1600's. But the *germ theory* of disease was not proved until the late 1800's. Robert Koch, a German physician, and Louis Pasteur, a French chemist, both experimented with anthrax, an infectious disease of man and animals. Koch showed that animals injected with anthrax germs soon got the disease. Pasteur developed a vaccine to slow down the multiplication of the germs.

Today, scientists know that infectious diseases are caused by many kinds of germs, including bacteria, viruses, and protozoa. These microorganisms cause disease by attacking living tissue. Some germs live in the tissue and multiply so rapidly that the tissue dies. Others produce *toxins* (poisons) that kill tissue.

183

TYPES OF DISEASE GERMS

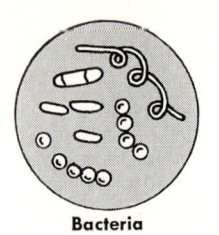

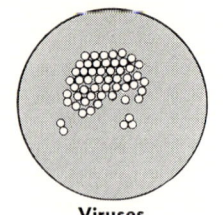

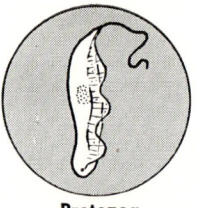

Bacteria **Viruses** **Protozoa**

Three common kinds of disease germs are bacteria, viruses, and protozoa. *Bacteria* have different shapes. They may be round, rod-shaped, or coiled. They cause such diseases as diphtheria and tuberculosis. *Viruses* are smaller than bacteria and multiply very rapidly. They cause mumps and smallpox. *Protozoa* are one-celled animals. Some kinds cause malaria and sleeping sickness.

Bacterial Diseases are caused by *bacteria*, or one-celled plants that can be seen only through a microscope. Scientists do not know exactly how many kinds of bacteria exist. But they do know that a single grain of soil may hold more than 100,000,000 bacteria of many different kinds. Fortunately, most bacteria do not cause disease, and many are useful. For example, bacteria cause milk to ferment so that dairies can use it to make buttermilk and cheese.

Some bacteria always live in the bodies of man and animals. They may be found on the skin; in the nose, mouth, and throat; and in the lungs, stomach, and intestines. These bacteria normally do no harm. But they may cause disease when the body's resistance is low for any reason. For example, bacteria called *streptococci* are often present in a person's throat. Disease or fatigue may lower the body's resistance to these bacteria, allowing them to multiply so rapidly that they harm the throat tissue. The person then suffers a *sore throat*.

Bacteria that pass from person to person cause many diseases, including scarlet fever, whooping cough, diphtheria, and tuberculosis. Bacteria from the soil may produce *tetanus* (lockjaw). Other kinds of bacteria cause leprosy and undulant fever. See BACTERIA.

Protozoan Diseases. Protozoa are one-celled animals found in great numbers almost everywhere in nature. Some protozoa harm man. One of these, the *Plasmodium*, causes malaria. Other protozoa cause sleeping sickness and amebic dysentery. See PROTOZOAN.

Worm Diseases. Some worms can cause diseases. One kind of worm, the *flatworm*, must spend part of its growing period in the bodies of humans or animals. Perhaps the best-known flatworm is the tapeworm, which causes an intestinal disease. Another group of worms, the *roundworms*, causes trichinosis, a disease in which the muscles become painful and swollen. See FLATWORM; ROUNDWORM.

Fungus Diseases. Fungi are tiny plants. They cause many skin diseases. Ringworm infections such as

---

DISEASE TERMS

Bacteria are tiny one-celled plants that may be shaped like spheres, rods, or spirals. Some cause diseases, but many do not.

Contagious Disease or **Communicable Disease** is a disease that can be passed from a sick person to a healthy person through direct or indirect contact.

Epidemic is the spread of disease throughout a community.

Germ, or **Microorganism,** is any tiny plant or animal that can only be seen through a microscope.

Incubation Period is the time between invasion of the body by a disease-producing germ and the appearance of the first symptoms of the disease.

Infectious Disease is a disease caused by organisms that destroy living cells. An infectious disease can be contagious. But the germs that cause it may also be carried in the air or in water.

Organism is any living plant or animal.

Pandemic is a widespread epidemic, as in the spread of a disease through a whole region, or through many countries of the world.

Parasite is an organism that feeds and lives in or on another organism.

Period of Communicability is the time during which contagious diseases are most easily passed from sick persons to healthy persons.

Viruses are microorganisms smaller than bacteria. Viruses can be seen only with the aid of an electron microscope. Many are called *filterable viruses* because they pass through filters that hold back bacteria.

MEANINGS OF DISEASE TERM ENDINGS

—itis means *inflammation*. It is usually associated with infection. Appendicitis is an inflammation of the appendix, and tonsillitis is an inflammation of the tonsils.

—emia refers to *blood*. Anemia is a deficiency in the blood. Septicemia, sometimes called blood poisoning, is the presence of disease germs in the blood.

—ism denotes *excess*. Morphinism means too much morphine in the body, and alcoholism too much alcohol.

—phobia means *fear*. Claustrophobia means fear of being confined, and hydrophobia is a fear of water.

—osis denotes a *diseased* or *abnormal condition*. Arteriosclerosis is a disease of the arteries. A psychosis is a severe mental illness.

U.S. DEATH RATES FROM MAJOR DISEASES
Death rate per 100,000 population

Diseases of the Heart
and Blood Vessels
513 deaths

Cancer
148 deaths

Diseases of
Early Infancy
39 deaths

Influenza and Pneumonia (except
of newborn)
34 deaths

Diabetes Mellitus
16 deaths

Based on a 4-year average of government statistics.

HOW GERMS ENTER THE BODY

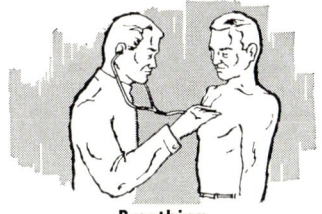

Breathing    **Eating**    **Skin Breaks**

Germs invade the body through the nose, the mouth, or breaks in the skin. The germs that cause the common cold "ride" on moisture in the air. They enter the nose and lungs when we breathe. Food carries the germs of dysentery and other diseases into the stomach and intestines. Germs that cause boils and blood poisoning can enter the body through a scratch or pin prick in the skin.

athlete's foot are caused by fungi, not by worms. Fungi also cause lung diseases such as histoplasmosis. See FUNGI; FUNGUS DISEASE.

Virus Diseases are caused by germs called *viruses*, which are even smaller than bacteria. Viruses are so small that scientists can see them only by means of a powerful electron microscope. There are hundreds of kinds of viruses. All are infectious and can cause diseases in most living things. Some even infect other germs. Scientists have found that viruses may sometimes remain inactive for years, but can quickly infect any defenseless cell. After they invade the cell, they multiply rapidly. For example, millions of polio viruses crowded together form only a speck. But a single one of these viruses can enter a human nerve cell and produce many new viruses in a few hours. Each new virus is as dangerous as the original one.

Viruses cause many common diseases, including mumps, measles, smallpox, chicken pox, and influenza. Some kinds of viruses cause cells to multiply rapidly and produce cancer. Other kinds of viruses, or a combination of several different kinds, cause the common cold. See VIRUS.

Diseases Present at Birth

Some babies are born with a disease. For example, a *blue baby* is born with a heart defect that prevents the blood from flowing properly to the lungs. Doctors use the term *congenital* for a defect or disease present at birth.

MAIN CONTAGIOUS DISEASES IN THE U.S.
Cases reported each year

Measles — 524,000 cases
Venereal Diseases — 359,000 cases
Scarlet Fever and Streptococcal Sore Throat — 285,000 cases
Tuberculosis — 79,000 cases
Whooping Cough — 29,000 cases

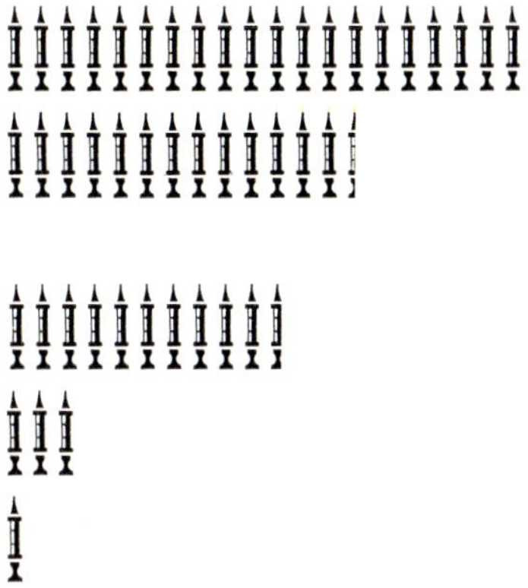

Based on a 4-year average of government statistics.

Congenital defects may result when a mother gets a serious disease while pregnant. If a woman has German measles during the first three months of pregnancy, there is an increased chance that her baby will be born with a defect. Certain types of malnutrition during the early months of pregnancy may have similar effects.

Perhaps the most important cause of congenital disease is heredity. Hemophilia, a disease in which the blood does not clot, is hereditary. Babies can get syphilis from their mothers. Doctors believe that persons may inherit a tendency toward some diseases, such as diabetes. See HEREDITY.

Diseases Caused by Environment

Our *environment*, or surroundings, contains many factors that may cause disease. Even the weather can be dangerous. Too much cold may result in frostbite. Excessive heat may produce heat exhaustion.

Sometimes man poisons his environment, producing a new source of disease. In many communities, factories and motor vehicles pollute the air with poisonous gas fumes that may cause lung diseases. Sometimes the poisonous fumes become so thick that they form a kind of fog called *smog*. In 1952, during a few days of smog in London, more than 5,000 persons died. Some doctors believe that air pollution may even cause cancer of the lungs and other parts of the body.

Our environment is filled with many forms of radiant energy which make life possible. Radiation from the sun provides us with heat, light, and food. But radiation from any source may be dangerous because it can destroy body tissues. Even the sun's rays which penetrate the atmosphere can cause serious burns. Most scientists believe that some effects of radiation may be delayed, and may later produce cancer. Experts also believe that radiation may cause unfavorable *mutations*, or hereditary changes (see MUTATION).

Man is learning to protect himself against damage from radiation. In atomic energy projects, thick concrete walls shield workers from the effects of radiation. In hospitals and laboratories, X-ray technicians stand out of the range of the radiation. When radium is used, lead shields protect workers from the rays. Scientists are seeking ways to protect man from the effects of radioactive fallout. See RADIATION (Learning to Live with High-Energy Radiation); RADIATION SICKNESS.

Nutritional Diseases

Improper diet can cause sickness and death. Diseases caused by not eating the right foods are called *nutri-*

DISEASE

tional diseases. A *deficiency*, or lack, of certain vitamins can cause rickets, scurvy, or pellagra. These deficiency diseases can be cured or prevented by eating foods containing the vitamins.

Poor nutrition remains a common cause of illness in spite of medical knowledge about proper diet. In some parts of the world, people do not get enough food, or can obtain food of only poor quality. Most difficult for them to obtain are the protein foods, such as meat, eggs, and milk. See NUTRITION.

Eating too much also can cause disease. Overweight may shorten a person's life by helping bring about heart disease, or by affecting the circulation of the blood. Overweight is usually caused by eating too much. See WEIGHT CONTROL.

Allergies

Some persons become sick when they eat certain foods, or when they come in contact with certain plants or animals. Such a sensitivity is called an *allergy*. Sometimes an allergy develops only after repeated exposure to a substance. Persons may develop allergies after exposure to almost any substance, such as cat hair, ragweed, or house dust. Doctors do not know why only some individuals develop allergies. See ALLERGY.

Functional Diseases

All parts of a healthy body work together in harmony. If anything disturbs the *function*, or work, of one part, other parts are usually disturbed, too. The nervous system and the hormones produced by glands act as a regulatory system. They control the development and function of all body parts. When this regulatory system operates properly, the composition of the body usually remains stable.

Diseases that affect the nervous system or the hormone glands may produce serious disturbances of the whole body. A nerve may be damaged in an accident or by a disease such as poliomyelitis. Then the body muscles that are controlled by that nerve may begin to *deteriorate*, or waste away. If glands that produce hormones, such as the thyroid and adrenal glands, do not work properly, disease also may result. When the thyroid gland is not active enough, a person may get *hypothyroidism*, a disease in which the mind and body suffer. See THYROID GLAND.

Doctors do not know exactly how all the regulating systems of the body work. One of the least known of these systems is the one that controls the production of cells and the growth of tissues. When this system is disturbed, one type of cell may grow unchecked and may destroy other cells. Such abnormal growths form *tumors*, including cancers. See CANCER.

Diseases of Children

Children in various parts of the world have different kinds of diseases. In regions where food and sanitation are poor, many children die during their first year from nutritional and infectious diseases. The most frequent ailments of American children are the common cold and other infections of the nose, throat, and lungs. Childhood diseases include whooping cough, measles, mumps, scarlet fever, and chicken pox. Adults also may get these diseases, particularly if they did not have them during childhood.

Some diseases, such as whooping cough and chicken pox, usually leave a child *immune*, or protected, for the rest of his life. A baby usually is protected from many diseases for a short time after birth by an immunity inherited from his mother. Antibodies pass from mother to baby before birth. These disease-fighting substances protect the infant for about three months. They give his body time to form its own *antibodies*, or protective substances, against some diseases. The doctor may vaccinate him for protection against others. See ANTIBODY; IMMUNITY.

Diseases of the Aged

Some doctors believe that the body organs gradually become weaker as a person grows older. *Geriatric diseases*, or diseases of old people, often result from the natural process of growing older. Common ailments of adults and the aged include cancer, high blood pressure, and damage to the blood vessels, heart, and brain. Mental illness usually strikes adults and the aged, but children may also suffer from it. Patients with mental illness occupy about half the hospital beds in the United States. See GERIATRICS; MENTAL ILLNESS.

Occupational Diseases

Persons who do certain kinds of work may get special kinds of diseases. Painters may suffer from lead poisoning as a result of exposure to the lead in paint. Coal miners and workers in the asbestos, iron, and cotton industries may breathe in dust, which can cause lung diseases. These workers often wear masks over their noses and mouths to keep the dust out. Silica dust causes a lung disease called silicosis. Glassmakers, grinders, granite cutters, and road builders may get silicosis. They wear nose filters, respirators, or masks to prevent the disease. In the chemical industry, workers' lungs may be irritated by gases, dust, or chemical fumes. Persons who handle insecticides may develop skin rashes. Most states have laws to provide safety measures for the prevention of industrial diseases.

Some occupational diseases result from physical causes. One of these diseases is called the bends. It results from rapidly lowering the air pressure surrounding the body. Bubbles of nitrogen form in the blood and body tissues, causing great pain. The bends may affect persons who must work in compressed air, as in constructing a tunnel under a river. Skin divers and deep-sea divers may also suffer from this illness.

How Diseases Spread

Diseases may spread from one person to another, from one animal to another, or from one plant to another. Some animal diseases also can be passed to humans. Occasionally, diseases may spread through whole communities and become epidemics. Scientists called *epidemiologists* study the spread of disease and search for ways to prevent it.

By Humans. Many infectious diseases pass from one person to another by direct contact. A healthy person can pick up the germs by touching infected areas on the sick person's body. Diseases that spread in this way include boils, abscesses, venereal diseases, and athlete's foot. Other diseases spread indirectly. When a person

SOME COMMON COMMUNICABLE DISEASES

DISEASE	SYMPTOMS	INCUBATION PERIOD	PERIOD OF COMMUNICABILITY	PREVENTIVE MEASURES
Chicken Pox	Headache, fever, recurrent skin rashes that form crusts.	14 to 21 days	From day before symptoms appear until 6 days after first rashes form.	None. Attack gives permanent immunity.
Diphtheria	Sore throat, hoarseness, fever.	2 to 5 days	About 2 to 4 weeks.	Diphtheria toxoid injections, started at 3 months of age. Repeated doses throughout childhood.
German Measles	Headache, enlarged lymph nodes, cough, sore throat, rash.	14 to 21 days, usually 18 days.	From 1 or 2 days before rash appears until 4 days after.	None. Attack gives permanent immunity.
Infectious Mononucleosis (Glandular Fever)	Sore throat, enlarged lymph glands, fatigue.	4 to 14 days	Unknown	None
Influenza	Fever, chills, muscular aches and pains.	1 to 3 days	When symptoms appear until 7 days after.	Influenza vaccine protects for only a few months.
Measles	Fever, body aches, cough, rash, eyes sensitive to light.	Fever, 10 days. Rash, 14 days.	From 4 days before rash appears until 5 days after.	Measles vaccines.
Mumps	Chills, headache, fever, swollen glands in neck and throat.	12 to 26 days, usually 18 days.	From 7 days before until 9 days after symptoms, or until swelling disappears.	None. Gamma globulin protects after exposure.
Poliomyelitis	Fever, sore throat, muscle pain, stiff back, paralysis.	Paralytic, 9 to 13 days. Nonparalytic, 4 to 10 days.	Last part of incubation period and first week of acute illness.	Poliomyelitis vaccines.
Scarlet Fever	Sore throat, rash, high fever, chills.	2 to 5 days	Beginning of incubation period until 2 or 3 weeks after symptoms appear.	None. Attack usually gives permanent immunity.
Smallpox	Chills, fever, headache, backache, rash that forms scabs.	7 to 16 days, commonly 12; rarely up to 21 days.	When symptoms appear until 2 or 3 weeks after, when scabs disappear.	Smallpox vaccination during the first year, and every 5 to 7 years thereafter. Attack gives permanent immunity.
Whooping Cough	Increased nose and throat secretion, violent cough, vomiting, fever.	7 to 10 days, rarely up to 21 days.	7 days after exposure to 3 weeks after coughing begins.	Whooping cough vaccine started at 3 months. Repeated doses during preschool years. Attack usually gives permanent immunity.

Each disease listed in this table has a separate article in WORLD BOOK.

with a cold sneezes or coughs, small drops of moisture containing germs are sprayed into the air. Another person may breathe in the droplets and catch a cold.

Humans and animals can spread disease even though they show no sign of illness themselves. These *carriers* have the disease germs within their bodies. Human carriers may spread such diseases as typhoid fever, diphtheria, syphilis, scarlet fever, and pneumonia. Public health laws require that certain known carriers have physical examinations and receive treatment. In addition, their activities are controlled by law. A carrier of typhoid fever, for example, would not be allowed to work in a restaurant. See PUBLIC HEALTH.

By Insects and Other Animals. Insects spread some of the most deadly diseases known to man. The germs that cause typhus and bubonic plague are carried by fleas and lice. These insects put the germs in a person's body when they bite. Certain mosquitoes spread malaria and yellow fever germs. They get the germs when they bite a person who has the disease. If they bite another person, they inject the disease germs into his blood stream. In the same way, the tsetse fly transmits the tiny organism that causes African sleeping sickness. The common housefly also spreads serious diseases. It may rest on human or animal wastes that contain typhoid and dysentery germs. Particles of the waste material cling to the fly's hairy legs and body, and may be brushed off on food.

Some animals, when infected with rabies, can pass the germs to a person whom they bite. These animals

DISEASE

include dogs, cats, and bats. Other animals spread disease to humans by direct contact. For example, a hunter may get tularemia, or rabbit fever, when he handles an infected rabbit or squirrel. Even the pelts of infected animals can be dangerous. Tanners and wool sorters sometimes get anthrax, a serious infectious disease, when they handle the hides of sick animals. Parakeets, parrots, and pigeons may spread psittacosis, a disease similar to pneumonia.

Animals also pass diseases to humans indirectly, usually through meat and other foods. The small worms that cause trichinosis, a hog disease, may stay alive in pork that is not thoroughly cooked. The worms enter the intestines of a person who eats the undercooked pork, and multiply rapidly.

Cows may spread two serious diseases in milk. One is bovine tuberculosis. The other is called Bang's disease when it affects cows, and undulant fever when it invades the human body. Before the discovery of the process of pasteurization, these diseases killed thousands of persons every year.

How the Body Fights Disease

The skin is often called "the body's first line of defense." It acts as armor, resisting many germs that might harm the more delicate parts of the body. Any break in the skin, even a pin prick, provides an opening for dangerous germs. Some germs enter the body through the nose and mouth and other natural openings. These areas provide warmth and moisture, in which germs thrive. But mucous membrane, the thin tissue that lines the body openings, has a high resistance to germs. It also produces *mucus*, a sticky liquid, that catches many germs. When the membrane of the nose and throat becomes irritated, we cough or sneeze, blowing out the unwanted substances.

Other body liquids also provide a defense against disease. Tears, for example, wash bacteria from the eyes. Tears also contain substances that fight bacteria. Acid in the stomach kills many germs before they can reach other parts of the body.

The various kinds of *tissue cells*, or the cells that make up the tissues of the body, and the white blood cells, form a second line of defense. Germs may attack tissue cells anywhere in the body. Then the body produces new cells to replace those that are destroyed by the invaders. These new tissue cells try to form a "wall" around the germs. The blood supply to the area increases, and white blood cells devour the germs and the dead tissue cells. The white blood cells then form *pus*, which may drain out of the body through a break in the skin. Or the pus may be carried away by the lymph and gradually be destroyed in the body. See BLOOD [White Blood Cells]; LYMPH; PUS.

Sometimes the invading germs cannot be killed where they enter the body. Then the body sets up a stronger defense that centers in the blood stream. The tissues and organs form different kinds of antibodies, each of which does a specific job. One kind, the *antitoxins*, neutralizes poisons produced by certain bacteria. Another type of antibody, the *agglutinins*, causes some bacteria to clump together in the blood. This clumping

HOW YOUR BODY FIGHTS GERMS

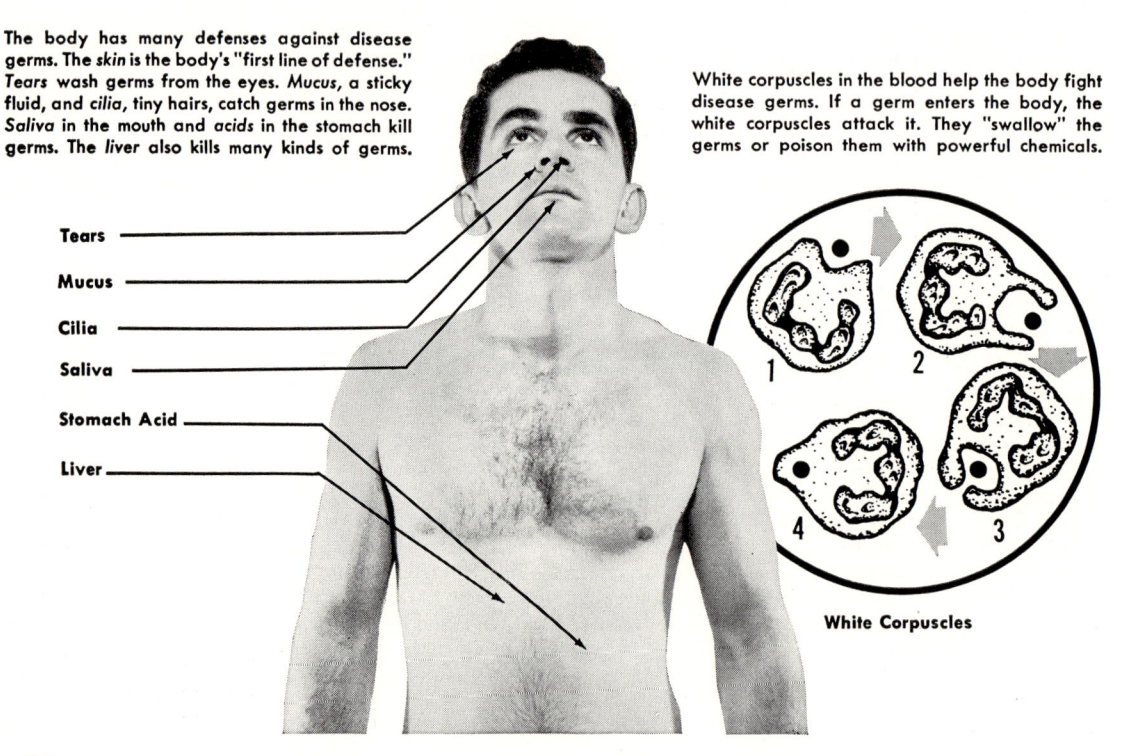

The body has many defenses against disease germs. The *skin* is the body's "first line of defense." *Tears* wash germs from the eyes. *Mucus*, a sticky fluid, and *cilia*, tiny hairs, catch germs in the nose. *Saliva* in the mouth and *acids* in the stomach kill germs. The *liver* also kills many kinds of germs.

Tears
Mucus
Cilia
Saliva
Stomach Acid
Liver

White corpuscles in the blood help the body fight disease germs. If a germ enters the body, the white corpuscles attack it. They "swallow" the germs or poison them with powerful chemicals.

White Corpuscles

process allows white blood cells to surround the bacteria and devour them. Other kinds of antibodies kill or weaken germs in different ways.

Man's Battle Against Disease

An epidemic was responsible for some of the earliest public health laws in Europe. From 1347 to 1350, about 60,000,000 persons in Asia, Africa, and Europe died from plague. As a result, governments began making laws regulating sanitary conditions.

Diseases have also affected the course of history. Smallpox, which European explorers brought with them, aided in the conquest of North and South America. The disease killed millions of Indians who had no immunity to smallpox. During the Civil War, more soldiers died of typhoid fever than were killed in battle. The influenza epidemic of 1917 and 1918 killed about 20,000,000 persons throughout the world—more than died during four years of battle in World War I. During World War II, Allied armies in the Pacific theater had five times as many casualties from malaria as from combat.

Until about 1870, two of every three children died during their first few years of life. This death rate still exists in many countries. But in the United States, Canada, and many other nations of Western civilization, every child has a good chance of living 60 to 70 years. The remarkable increase in life expectancy has resulted from two factors: (1) a higher standard of living, and (2) advances in medical science. An improved standard of living allows people to have good food and clean, comfortable homes, and to take care of their health. Advances in medical science make it possible to prevent and to treat many diseases that once caused death.

Detecting Disease. Only a hundred years ago, a doctor had little help in *diagnosing*, or determining, a patient's disease. He had to rely on symptoms that he could observe or those that the patient could tell him about. If the patient's body was hot, the doctor knew he probably had a fever. The doctor put his ear to the patient's chest to hear the heart and other body sounds. He felt the patient's pulse, and examined his tongue. See DIAGNOSIS.

A doctor still uses most of these physical signs to diagnose illness. But he also has many instruments that help him. He can examine blood cells through a powerful microscope. He can use X rays to study the lungs, the heart, and bones, and other parts of the body. Chemical tests tell him much about the blood, urine, and other body fluids. With such tools, the physician can detect the exact cause and location of a disease.

Treating Disease. One of the most important medical achievements has been the discovery of drugs to treat diseases. Drugs that attack one kind of germ may be useless against another kind. Penicillin and the sulfa drugs, for example, attack the germs that cause pneumonia, gonorrhea, and syphilis. But they do not harm the common viruses. See DRUG.

Another advancement in the treatment of disease was the use of substances that occur naturally in the body. Some of these substances are *hormones*, such as insulin for the treatment of diabetes. Other substances come from certain tissues, such as liver extract for the treatment of pernicious anemia. See HORMONE.

DISEASE

The development of surgical techniques has been still another great achievement in fighting disease. Surgeons can remove all or part of a lung or kidney. They can repair the heart or stomach. Surgeons can even replace bones with metal or plastic parts. See SURGERY.

Preventing Disease. Many diseases, even serious ones, can be prevented. Nutritional diseases such as rickets, scurvy, and pellagra may be avoided by eating well-balanced meals. When a person's diet does not supply enough vitamins, a doctor may prescribe additional vitamins. Other diseases, including cholera and typhus, may be prevented by proper sanitation and adequate housing. Most countries have laws that regulate sanitation, the purity of water and food, and working conditions in factories. Quarantine laws prevent the sick from coming in contact with healthy persons (see QUARANTINE).

Vaccines and serums can help build up a person's resistance to disease. Doctors use *inoculations*, or injections of killed or weakened disease germs, that cause the body to build up resistance to a disease. People are inoculated against many bacterial diseases, including diphtheria, whooping cough, typhoid fever, and cholera. See INOCULATION.

Vaccines cause the body to produce antibodies that fight certain diseases such as smallpox and poliomyelitis. Vaccines contain dead or weakened disease germs. When the doctor injects a vaccine, the body begins to form antibodies. The body continues to produce antibodies for several years. But just to make sure, doctors sometimes give "booster shots," or small additional doses of vaccine. See ANTIBODY; VACCINATION.

Doctors may give *serums* to persons who already have a disease, or to those who have been exposed to one. Serums injected into the body add antibodies to the blood. Unlike vaccines, serums do not cause the body to form antibodies. See SERUM.

Knowledge of the causes of disease enables scientists to find ways to prevent or control it. For example, swamps can be drained to prevent malaria mosquitoes from breeding. Insecticides are sprayed over infested areas to destroy flies and other insects that carry germs. Farmers inoculate cattle against Bang's disease. Milk is pasteurized to destroy germs it may contain.

Research. Throughout the world, research scientists seek ways to cure or prevent diseases. They also try to find what causes certain diseases. They may make thousands of experiments, and their findings must satisfy rigid tests. Chemists, biologists, physicists, and psychologists work with physicians in the study of disease.

Plant and Animal Diseases

Plant Diseases in the United States cause crop losses totaling about $3,000,000,000 every year. Some diseases kill plants, ruining entire orchards and fields of grain. Others weaken plants, causing them to produce poor quality crops and reducing the size of the crops. The greatest threat of plant diseases to man is that they destroy materials essential to life. Green plants manufacture *carbohydrates*, or starches and sugars, which all living things need for energy. Only plants, or animals that eat plants, can provide man with the carbo-

DISEASE

hydrates he must have. Serious outbreaks of plant diseases can cause famine and death. During the 1840's, more than 750,000 persons died in Ireland when a fungus blight destroyed the nation's potato crop, causing a famine.

Some plant diseases cause serious illness in humans. *Ergot*, a fungus that attacks wheat, barley, and rye, can produce *ergotism* in persons who eat bread made from infected grain. However, scientists use ergot from rye to make powerful drugs to help control bleeding, especially after childbirth. When ergot epidemics strike rye fields, the crop may become more valuable for drugs than for grain.

Plant diseases may also result from infection by other fungi, bacteria, and viruses. Rust fungi destroy many grains, fruits, and green plants. More than 170 kinds of bacteria can produce diseases in flowering plants. Viruses cause mosaic disease, which destroys many edible fruits and plants.

Scientists and farmers have developed various ways to control plant diseases. They breed new varieties of plants that resist disease. They also rotate their crops, add certain chemicals to the soil, and spray their fields with other chemicals. See FUNGICIDE; INSECTICIDE; ROTATION OF CROPS.

Animal Diseases kill more than $2,000,000,000 worth of livestock annually in the United States. Sometimes a serious disease kills most of the animals in a herd. Then the farmer must destroy all animals that have come in contact with the herd. He kills these other animals in order to prevent an epidemic in the entire region. One of the most dreaded animal diseases is foot-and-mouth disease. It attacks cattle, hogs, sheep, and goats. The disease spreads rapidly, and many of the infected animals die.

Animals suffer from many diseases caused by bacteria, viruses, and protozoa. Bacteria cause white diarrhea, which is often fatal to chicks. Distemper and hog cholera result from virus infections. Coccidiosis, a protozoan infection, is a destructive disease of poultry. It also attacks cattle, hogs, and cats.

Humans can get some diseases from animals. A person who drinks unpasteurized milk from cows that have tuberculosis or brucellosis may also develop these diseases.

Veterinarians, or animal doctors, work with other scientists and farmers to keep animals healthy. They study diseases, develop ways to keep them from spreading, and conduct research programs to find new cures. See VETERINARY MEDICINE.

RENÉ J. DUBOS

Related Articles in WORLD BOOK include:

ALLERGIES
Allergy	Conjunctivitis	Hay Fever
Asthma	Eczema	Hives

BACTERIAL DISEASES
Anthrax	Erysipelas	Scrofula
Bacteria	Leprosy	Tetanus
Bubonic Plague	Meningitis	Tuberculosis
Cholera	Osteomyelitis	Tularemia
Croup	Paratyphoid Fever	Typhoid Fever
Diphtheria		Undulant Fever
Dysentery (Bacillary Dysentery)	Pneumonia Scarlet Fever	Whooping Cough

ENVIRONMENTAL AND OCCUPATIONAL DISEASES
Airsickness	Gangrene	Red-Out
Altitude Sickness	Immersion Foot	Seasickness
Asphyxiation	Lead Poisoning	Silicosis
Bends	Radiation Sickness	Sunstroke
Frostbite		Trench Foot

FUNGUS DISEASES
Athlete's Foot	Jungle Rot	Thrush
Fungus Disease	Lumpy Jaw	

NUTRITIONAL DISEASES
Beriberi	Pellagra	Scurvy
Malnutrition	Rickets	

PARASITIC DISEASES
Dysentery (Amebic Dysentery)	Malaria	Schistosomiasis
	Parasite	Sleeping Sickness
Elephantiasis	Pinworm	Tapeworm
Hookworm	Ringworm	Trichinosis
Kala Azar	Roundworm	

VIRUS DISEASES
Chicken Pox	Infectious Mononucleosis	Poliomyelitis
Cold, Common		Rabies
Dengue	Influenza	Smallpox
German Measles	Measles	Virus
Herpes	Mumps	Yellow Fever

SYMPTOMS OF DISEASE
Abscess	Diarrhea	Hiccup	Neuralgia
Backache	Dizziness	Indigestion	Pain
Biliousness	Dyspepsia	Infection	Pus
Bleeding	Edema	Inflammation	Shock
Colic	Fainting	Insomnia	Sneezing
Constipation	Fatigue	Itch	Spasm
Convulsions	Fever	Jaundice	Squint
Cough	Headache	Lumbago	Vomiting
Cramp	Hemorrhage	Nausea	

UNCLASSIFIED
Appendicitis	Heart (Heart Diseases)	Quarantine
Arthritis		Relapsing Fever
Blindness (Diseases)	Kidney (Diseases of the Kidneys)	Rheumatism
Brain (Brain Diseases)		Rocky Mountain Spotted Fever
Cancer	Liver (Diseases of the Liver)	Senility
Colitis		Skin
Cystic Fibrosis	Lung (Diseases and Care of the Lungs)	Stomach (Diseases)
Diagnosis		Tick Fever
Enteritis		Typhus
Epidemic	Mental Illness	Vaccination
Eye (Defects and Diseases)	Myelitis	Venereal Diseases
Gland (Diseases of Glands)	Peritonitis	

Outline
I. **Diseases Caused by Germs**
   A. Bacterial Diseases   D. Fungus Diseases
   B. Protozoan Diseases   E. Virus Diseases
   C. Worm Diseases
II. **Diseases Present at Birth**
III. **Diseases Caused by Environment**
IV. **Nutritional Diseases**
V. **Allergies**
VI. **Functional Diseases**
VII. **Diseases of Children**
VIII. **Diseases of the Aged**
IX. **Occupational Diseases**
X. **How Diseases Spread**
   A. By Humans   B. By Insects and Other Animals
XI. **How the Body Fights Disease**
XII. **Man's Battle Against Disease**
   A. Detecting Disease   C. Preventing Disease
   B. Treating Disease   D. Research
XIII. **Plant and Animal Diseases**
   A. Plant Diseases   B. Animal Diseases

Questions

What is disease? What is an epidemic? A pandemic?
What is "the body's first line of defense"?
What are two reasons that people live longer than they did a hundred years ago?
What substances necessary for life can man get only from green plants or from animals that eat plants?
What two diseases can be caused by the weather?
Who proved the germ theory of disease?
How many bacteria have been found in a grain of soil?
What is the leading cause of congenital disease?
What disease do skin divers often get?
What is a carrier?

DISH. See PORCELAIN; POTTERY; STONEWARE.

DISINFECTANT, DIHS in FECK tunt, is a chemical substance used to kill bacteria and other organisms which cause disease. People use disinfectants to clean and sterilize instruments and utensils, clothes, and rooms. Disinfectants have a limited value in controlling the spread of epidemics of disease. They should not be confused with *antiseptics* which prevent or stop the growth of bacteria. Disinfectants are sometimes called *germicides* or *bactericides*. They sometimes include substances called *deodorants*, which neutralize odors.

Disinfectants are powerful chemicals which should be properly labeled. They should be carefully handled and always kept away from children.

Some of the most important disinfectants are the following:

Bleaching Powder, chloride of lime, or sodium hypochlorite, is widely used for purifying water. It also kills bacteria on contaminated objects which are scattered about an infected area.

Carbolic Acid, or phenol, disinfects body discharges and dirty rooms. Certain preparations of it can be used to sterilize clothing and utensils. Doctors once used carbolic acid to disinfect the skin, but this practice is no longer used. A disinfecting solution of carbolic acid should contain one part carbolic acid to 20 parts water.

Formaldehyde in water solution disinfects clothing and body discharges. In water solution it is called formalin. A 2 to 5 per cent solution of formaldehyde disinfects clothing. A 10 per cent solution kills germs in body discharges.

Mercuric Chloride, bichloride of mercury, or corrosive sublimate, is used to disinfect hands and other parts of the body which do not have cuts or openings. It should never touch a mucous membrane. Mercuric chloride is very poisonous and dangerous to use except under proper direction. It is used in a solution of one part of mercuric chloride to 2,000 parts of water.

Potassium Permanganate is used to disinfect sinks, drains, and water pipes. It can also destroy organic matter. Surgeons use water solutions of potassium permanganate to disinfect their hands. It should always be used greatly diluted in water. W. W. BAUER

Related Articles in WORLD BOOK include:

Antiseptic	Chlorine	Formaldehyde
Bichloride of Mercury	Creosote	Germicide
Carbolic Acid	Cresol	Lye
Chloride of Lime	Deodorizer	

DISLOCATION occurs when any part of the body moves from its normal position. The term usually refers to the movement out of normal position of the bones of a joint (see JOINT). When bones become dislocated, they do not meet properly at the joint. This usually results in pain and swelling.

Sometimes in dislocation the bones of a joint are pulled out of place only slightly. Physicians call this an *incomplete dislocation*. In other cases, the bones become completely separated from each other. This is a *complete dislocation*. A complete dislocation must be corrected immediately. In *simple dislocation*, the patient has no external wound. A *compound dislocation* is one accompanied by a wound opening from the body surface. When a dislocation occurs in the same joint many times, physicians say it is *habitual*.

Some types of dislocation are *congenital*, or present at birth. These may be hereditary, or may be caused by some factor before or during birth. An example is congenital dislocation of the hip. BENJAMIN F. MILLER

See also CONGENITAL DISLOCATION.

DISMAL SWAMP. This stretch of wild marshland covers nearly 750 square miles in northeastern North Carolina and southeastern Virginia. For location, see NORTH CAROLINA (color map). It is one of the largest swamps in the United States. It is a tangle of vines and cypress, black gum, and juniper trees. Many peat bogs lie in the area. Bears, deer, and snakes live in the swamp. Lake Drummond lies in Virginia at the north end of the large swamp. LOYAL DURAND, JR.

DISMAS, SAINT, is a saint of the Roman Catholic Church. The Bible tells us that two thieves were crucified beside Christ. One of them criticized the other severely for mocking Christ. He also asked Jesus to remember him. Hearing this, Christ said: "Today thou shalt be with me in Paradise." The name of this "good thief" was Dismas. Dismas is considered a saint, and his feast day is March 25. The thief who mocked Christ is said to have been called Gestas. FULTON J. SHEEN

Dismal Swamp's tangled tree roots and shallow marshland make navigation difficult even for small boats.

Virginia Chamber of Commerce

DISNEY, "WALT," WALTER E.

DISNEY, "WALT," WALTER E. (1901-   ), is an American producer of animated cartoons, motion pictures, and television shows. He became famous for his cartoon characters Mickey Mouse and Donald Duck. He made many technical advances in the use of sound, color, and photography in animated cartoons. Later, he made motion-picture history with his films of wild life in natural surroundings.

Disney's first success came in 1928 with a Mickey Mouse film called "Steamboat Bill." He used a sound track in it, and made Mickey talk. In 1932, he produced the first cartoons in technicolor. He also produced the *Silly Symphonies* and the *Three Little Pigs*.

Disney released his first feature-length animated picture, *Snow White and the Seven Dwarfs*, in 1938, and followed with *Fantasia* and *Pinocchio* in 1940. He used animated form and color in *Fantasia* to interpret orchestral music visually. His other feature-length cartoon motion pictures include *Bambi, Cinderella, Alice in Wonderland, Peter Pan*, and *Lady and the Tramp*. During World War II, Disney produced training and information cartoons for the United States government.

He combined characters played by live actors with cartoon characters in his feature-length picture, *Song of the South*.

Seal Island, the first of Disney's series of short True-Life Adventures, appeared in 1948. Another, *Nature's Half Acre*, won the Venice Film Festival documentary award in 1951. Disney released his first feature-length nature film, *The Living Desert*, in 1953. *The Vanishing Prairie* and others followed later.

Disney has also made conventional pictures, such as *Treasure Island, Robin Hood, 20,000 Leagues Under the Sea, The Great Locomotive Chase*, and *The Littlest Outlaw*. His films have won many Academy of Motion Picture Arts and Sciences Oscar awards.

He entered the television field in 1950, and produced the *Davy Crockett* films and the programs Mickey Mouse Club and Disneyland. In 1955, he opened Disneyland Park, a large amusement park for children near Los Angeles.

Disney was born in Chicago on Dec. 5, 1901. He attended the Chicago Academy of Fine Arts. He served as a World War I Red Cross ambulance driver in 1918. After the war, he worked for a time as a commercial artist in Kansas City, Mo. He did his first motion-picture cartoon work there in 1920. He went to Hollywood in 1923, and from 1926 to 1928 made the series Oswald, the Rabbit.   BARNARD HEWITT

See also CARTOON (Types of Cartoons).

Walt Disney Productions
"Walt" Disney

DISNEY COMBINES FACT AND FANTASY

Mickey Mouse
Minnie Mouse
Pluto
Donald Duck

Fantasia, a feature-length animated cartoon, showed these cupids in a scene picturing Beethoven's *Symphony No. 6 in F*, "Pastoral."

The Living Desert, Disney's first feature-length True-Life Adventure, featured desert creatures such as Sidewinder, the rattlesnake.

DISORDERLY CONDUCT. See BREACH OF THE PEACE.

DISPERSION. See GEM (Qualities of Gem Minerals).

DISPLACED PERSON (DP) is a European who has been forced to leave his home because of war or political or religious persecution. Nazi Germany moved millions of persons to slave-labor and concentration camps. Others fled from their homes. Western Europe had more than 8,000,000 DP's at the end of World War II. About 1,000,000 Russians refused to return home. Boundary changes and the reaction against communist rule swelled the number of DP's after the war.

On Dec. 15, 1946, the United Nations established the International Refugee Organization to care for and settle DP's. The U.S. Congress passed the Displaced Persons Act on June 25, 1948. This act and later amendments allowed more than 440,000 DP's to enter the United States between July 1, 1948, and July 1, 1952. The original act applied only to DP's entering Germany, Austria, or Italy before Dec. 22, 1945. Congress later admitted Hungarian and other DP's. Canada also admitted over 160,000 DP's after World War II. STEFAN T. POSSONY

See also IMMIGRATION AND EMIGRATION (After World War II); REFUGEE.

DISPLACEMENT means putting an object out of place. For example, rock formations may be *displaced* by faulting (see GEOLOGY [Some Terms (Fault)]). A ship or other object in water will *displace* an amount of water equal to its own weight (see GRAVITY, SPECIFIC; SHIP AND SHIPPING [Nautical Measurements; The Hull and Superstructure]).

DISRAELI, BENJAMIN

DISRAELI, *diz RAY lih,* **BENJAMIN** (1804-1881), EARL OF BEACONSFIELD, was the only man to be born a Jew who became prime minister of Great Britain. The eldest son of a noted Jewish author, he became a member of the Church of England in 1817. He gave up the study of law as a young man, and created a sensation by writing *Vivian Grey* and other novels. He tried several times to win a seat in the House of Commons before being elected as a Tory in 1837.

His extreme clothes and exaggerated speech made him stand out in the House of Commons. After almost 10 years he became the champion of high tariffs. He opposed Sir Robert Peel's bill to repeal the Corn Laws (see CORN LAWS). He became Chancellor of the Exchequer in 1852, and held that office three more times.

Disraeli was largely responsible for the 1867 Parliamentary Reform Act. He became prime minister for the first time in 1868. In his second term as prime minister, from 1874 to 1880, he introduced laws to improve slum conditions, to protect the factory worker, and to

Brown Bros.
Benjamin Disraeli

Perri, Disney's first "true life fantasy," told the story of the little pine squirrel, Perri, and her friends in Wildwood Heart.

Disneyland, a 180-acre amusement park at Anaheim, Calif., opened in 1955. Its five main sections are shown, *below.* The Sleeping Beauty Castle, *right,* is the entrance to Fantasyland.

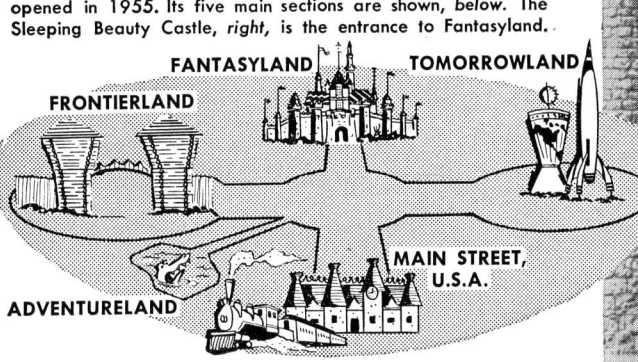

FANTASYLAND TOMORROWLAND
FRONTIERLAND
MAIN STREET, U.S.A.
ADVENTURELAND

DISSECTION

help the farm laborer, who was in economic distress.

The Disraeli government was imperialistic in its policy outside Great Britain. It defended and advanced the country's colonial claims in India and Africa. Disraeli thwarted Russia's claim to Turkey and confined Russia to the Black Sea. He also obtained a major interest in the Suez Canal for Great Britain by purchasing a large number of shares.

Disraeli believed in progress within the limits of traditionalism. He deeply impressed his country by insisting that conservative policy must provide for progress and the improvement of working-class conditions. He thought that Tories would have to favor laws designed to make the lower classes more comfortable in Great Britain, and the country more respected and powerful abroad. He described himself as "a conservative to preserve all that is good in our constitution, and a radical to remove all that is bad." He was the political opponent of William E. Gladstone. Disraeli was born on Dec. 21, 1804, in London. JAMES L. GODFREY

See also CONSERVATIVE PARTY.

DISSECTION. See ANATOMY.

DISSONANCE. See SOUND (Beats).

DISSTON, HAMILTON. See FLORIDA (Famous Floridians).

DISTANCE is the space between two points. It can be measured in miles, rods, feet, inches, meters, kilometers, centimeters, and many other units of measurement. The vast spaces between the stars and planets, or astronomical distances, are measured by the speed of light. Astronomers say, for example, that a star is six *light-years* away, which means that light reaches the earth six years after it leaves the star. Light travels 6,000,000,000,000 miles a year, so that a star six light-years away is 36,000,000,000,000 miles away.

Astronomers can see hundreds of thousands of miles through their powerful telescopes. A distance of 20 miles means little to them. Physicists and biologists can measure very short distances, such as the distance between two electrons, or the diameter of a cell. The *micron*, one-millionth of a meter, is their unit of measurement. Scientists also use a *millimicron*, which is a thousandth of a micron. PHILLIP S. JONES

Related Articles in WORLD BOOK include:

Astronomy (Distances in Space; How Astronomers Determine Distances)
Aviation (World Air Mileage Chart)
Measurement (Length and Distance)
Parallax
Telemetering
Visibility, Distances of
Weights and Measures (Linear Measure)

DISTANT EARLY WARNING LINE. See DEW LINE.

DISTEMPER is a common contagious disease of young dogs. It usually begins with loss of appetite, chill, fever, reddened eyes, and dry muzzle. Later there may be infections in the lungs, intestines, or nervous system. If the infection is in the lung there is discharging through the nose, coughing, and heavy breathing. An intestinal infection usually results in frothy and bloody diarrhea. If the infection is in the nervous system, the dog may suffer from convulsions and may die, or it may suffer from a muscular twitching called *chorea*.

Distemper can be prevented by vaccination with specially prepared vaccines. It can be treated by giving the dog antiserum and other drugs. The dog should be under the care of a veterinarian. Dogs which have recovered from one attack of distemper are immune to later attacks. Distemper is caused by a virus discovered by Louis Carré of France in 1904.

Distemper of young horses is called *strangles*. It is caused by *Streptococcus equi* bacteria, and differs from distemper in dogs. The horse suffers from a sore throat, fever, and infection in the lymph glands. Strangles can be treated with antibiotics such as penicillin.

Cats also contract distemper, different from that of dogs (see CAT [Cat Diseases]). D. W. BRUNER

DISTILLATION, DIHS *tuh* LAY *shun*, is a process to extract gas or vapor from a liquid or solid. The method employs heat and an apparatus called a *still*. Everyone has noticed that when water is exposed to air it will dry up. When the water disappears, it has not been destroyed, but changed to an invisible gas called *water vapor*. We say that it has *evaporated*. Boiling water forms the same gas, only more quickly, and we call it *steam*. When steam is formed, the water *vaporizes*. The clear space just above the spout of a boiling kettle is filled with steam. The cloud we see above this clear space, and usually call "steam," is not really water vapor, but droplets of water formed again when the gas cooled. We say the gas has *condensed* to water. If we want to condense a larger amount of the water vapor, we must invert a cold vessel, such as a milk bottle, above the spout. Droplets may then collect in the bottle, especially if it is kept cold.

Distillation is this process of boiling a liquid, such as water, and condensing the vapor which forms. So distillation really includes two processes, *vaporization* and *condensation*. The *distilled water* is purer than the original water, because the process leaves behind substances, such as salt, which do not evaporate at the boiling temperature of water. Water is constantly evaporating from sea, soil, and plants, and the naturally distilled water is rain or dew.

The apparatus for distilling is called a *still*. Its first essential part is the *boiler*, in which the mixture to be distilled is heated. Whichever substance in the mixture boils at the lowest temperature will be the first to turn to a vapor. The second part is the *condenser*, in which the vapor is cooled and condensed into a liquid again. The third part is the *receiver*, a vessel in which the distilled liquid, called the *distillate*, is collected. The receiver is not essential; any vessel may be used. Many liquids besides water are purified by distillation.

Fractional Distillation. When several liquids are mixed, it is usually impossible to separate them completely by simple distillation. For example, alcohol boils at 172° F., and water at 212° F., but even the water will evaporate fairly rapidly at 172° F. So the distillate from an alcohol-water mixture will contain some water. But the distillate collected at first will have a larger proportion of alcohol than the portions that condense later. So we remove this first batch before much water distillate has condensed. In the same way the remaining distillate is collected in *fractions*, and the whole process is called *fractional distillation*. Then each fraction can be redistilled, to get a much purer product. Fractional distillation is used to make distilled liquors, such as brandy and whisky. These always contain much more alcohol than

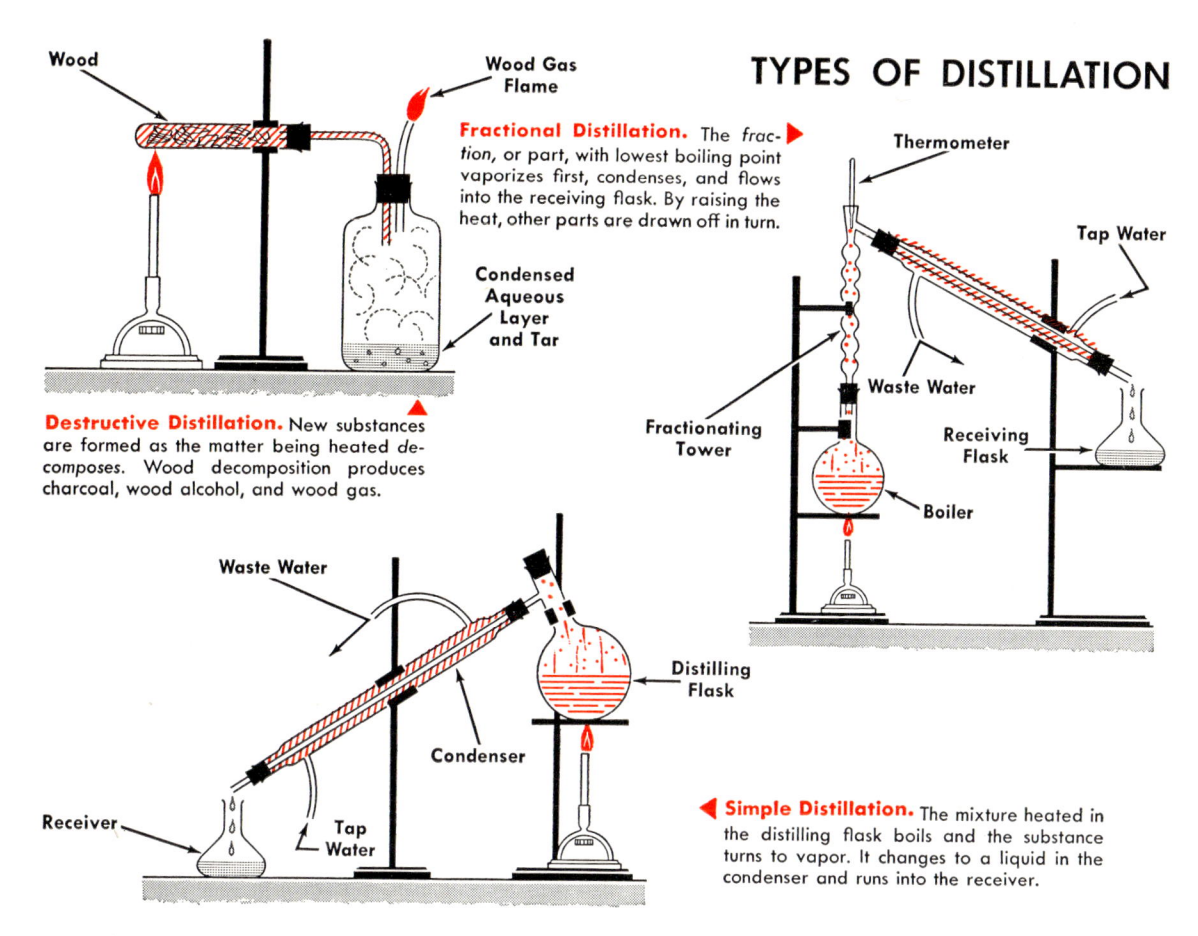

TYPES OF DISTILLATION

Fractional Distillation. The *fraction*, or part, with lowest boiling point vaporizes first, condenses, and flows into the receiving flask. By raising the heat, other parts are drawn off in turn.

Destructive Distillation. New substances are formed as the matter being heated *decomposes*. Wood decomposition produces charcoal, wood alcohol, and wood gas.

Simple Distillation. The mixture heated in the distilling flask boils and the substance turns to vapor. It changes to a liquid in the condenser and runs into the receiver.

---

wines and beers, which are not distilled. But fractional distillation of an alcohol-water mixture, no matter how far carried out, cannot yield alcohol which is more than about 95 per cent pure. The remaining 5 per cent of water must be removed with certain chemicals, such as metallic sodium or quicklime. Fractional distillation is also important in petroleum refining. Petroleum is a mixture of many substances which have to be separated to be useful. The earlier fractions give naphtha and benzine. Next comes gasoline, afterward kerosene, and then the heavier lubricating oils. Much of this separation is brought about in a single distillation by using huge *fractionating* towers. The substances which make up the earliest fractions are the ones that boil off at the lowest temperatures. Their vapors rise highest in the towers and are carried off by pipes high up. Separate pipes carry off the different fractions at different levels. Fractional distillation is also used to separate the different products obtained directly from coal tar.

Destructive Distillation. Neither simple nor fractional distillation forms new substances. Each merely separates substances that have been mixed together. But when a substance such as wood is heated in a closed vessel, it *decomposes*, and gives substances that were not there before. This is *destructive distillation*, and is a chemical process. GEORGE L. BUSH

Related Articles in WORLD BOOK include:
Acetic Acid   Condensation   Petroleum
Alcohol   Distilling   (Refining)
Alcoholic Drink Evaporation

DISTILLING is the process of manufacturing alcoholic beverages such as whisky, brandy, and rum. Manufacturers distill whisky from a fermented "mash" of corn, rye, wheat, or other small grains, malt, and water. They make brandy from the fermented juice of grapes and other fruits. Rum comes from fermented molasses and sugar-cane juices.

Liquors are first fermented, then put through several distillation processes (see FERMENTATION; DISTILLATION). This removes impurities such as fusel oil, aldehydes, and acids. By a process called *rectification*, some of the impurities remain in the beverage to add flavor. Liquors have no color when first made. Manufacturers add color to them either by storing them in charred wooden barrels, or by adding caramel coloring.

The distilling industry is one of the largest in the United States. People spend almost $4,000,000,000 a year for distilled liquors. The federal and state governments collect large sums from liquor taxes.

Leading companies in the distilling industry include Joseph E. Seagram & Sons; Schenley Industries, Inc.; National Distillers Products Corp.; Hiram Walker & Sons, Inc.; James B. Beam Distilling Co.; and Brown-Forman Distillers Corp. J. BERNARD ROBB

See also ALCOHOLIC DRINK (Distilled Liquors); INTERNAL REVENUE.

DISTINGUISHED. For medals beginning with the word *distinguished*, such as Distinguished Flying Cross, see DECORATIONS AND MEDALS.

DISTRIBUTARY. See RIVER (Parts).

DISTRIBUTION

DISTRIBUTION is the second step in a series of economic processes which bring goods and services from those who make them to those who use them. The making of such goods and services is called *production*. The use of the goods is called *consumption*. Distribution includes all methods by which the goods are sent from producers to consumers. Another part of this distribution process is the distribution of income. The distribution of income is the way in which the wealth of the nation is divided among those who produce, those who distribute goods and services, and those who consume goods. Nearly all consumers are also either producers or distributors. Without the process of distribution, people would have no way of obtaining useful services or products, such as food from a farmer, clothing from a tailor, or an automobile from a manufacturer.

Distribution of Goods. Many steps lie between the making of a product and its delivery to the consumer. The process of distribution enters into the production of a loaf of bread long before the loaf is baked. Wheat that is grown on the plains of Nebraska may be distributed to mills at Minneapolis, Minn., to be ground into flour. This flour may be sent to a bakery at Chicago, Ill., where it is baked into bread, sliced, and wrapped. Then it is delivered to a grocery store, where it is bought, taken home, and consumed.

Methods of distributing goods vary with the particular product and its industry. In colonial times, a shoemaker sold his shoes directly to the consumer, who ordered them before they were made. Today, most of our food, clothing, and other products are made in quantities long before any individual consumer has any thought of buying them. Goods usually go from the producer to a *wholesaler*, who is a person or a company dealing in large quantities of goods.

A wholesaler of potatoes buys potatoes from farmers in carload lots. Few grocers could handle such large quantities of potatoes, since they would spoil before they could be sold. The wholesaler sells smaller quantities to *retailers*. The grocer can buy a dozen sacks of potatoes from the wholesaler's carload and sell them to his customers, who are the consumers.

Storage is another process involved in distribution. Foods and other products which may spoil are stored in cold-storage warehouses. Eggs, meat, seafood, and fruits and vegetables are often stored for several months until they can be sold.

The wholesalers and retailers are sometimes called *middlemen*. Each middleman tries to make a profit on the goods he handles. These profits are added to the costs of the goods and are paid for by the consumer when he buys the product. Some methods of distribution do away with one or more of these middlemen. Farmers often sell their produce directly to the market through co-operative associations, which return part of their profits to the farmers. There are many consumer co-operatives which do away with the wholesaler's profit. Mail-order houses do away with both wholesaler and retailer by selling directly to the consumer, who selects the merchandise from a catalog. Other distributing

The Circles of Distribution—a greatly simplified diagram showing how goods, services, and income move from place to place and from person to person. The outer circle shows how wheat finds its way from the farmer to the workman, who consumes it in the form of bread. The workman helps to produce the tractor used by the farmer in growing wheat. The inner circle shows how the money involved in the various sales and purchases passes from hand to hand.

methods eliminate the expense of keeping up wholesale and retail stores by employing house-to-house salesmen. However, the elimination of middlemen does not always guarantee lower prices for the consumer. Sometimes it means only that the producer assumes the costs ordinarily paid by the middlemen. Occasionally, he may be able to reduce the costs of distributing his products, and thus be able to lower prices or even to make larger profits.

Advertising and *packaging* are parts of the distributing process which attempt to increase the flow of goods to consumers. Producers and distributors advertise their products in newspapers and magazines, over the radio, on television, and in outdoor advertising. By packaging their products in attractively designed and labeled boxes, wrappings, or other containers, they make the product more appealing to prospective buyers.

Distribution of Income. Money has been called the oil that makes the wheels of the distribution machine turn smoothly. The producer must have money to invest in plants, machinery, and labor to make his product. The wholesaler, retailer, and others involved in production and in distribution must have money to engage in their part of the distribution process. The consumer must have money to buy the products. Most consumers obtain their money by working to produce goods.

The total of all the incomes received in the distribution process is called the *gross national income.* A fair distribution of the national income is necessary for an even distribution of goods. If the consumers do not have enough money to buy the goods produced, the wholesalers, retailers, and producers do not make a profit. So workers, who are also consumers, may have to be laid off, and many plants may have to close. If farmers do not get enough money for their produce, they cannot buy manufactured goods. An economic depression may take place if the distribution process breaks down.

The proper distribution of income is a complicated matter. It involves not only fair profits and wages, but also fair prices, rent, and interest. High wages do not help the consumer to buy more goods if the price of goods is too high. Low prices are of no value to the distribution process if many persons are unemployed and cannot afford to buy goods.

Distribution of Services. Too many gasoline stations in the same neighborhood means that most or all of them will be unable to make a fair profit. This is a problem of *distribution of services.* Sometimes a new machine does away with the jobs of thousands of workers. This happened when the automatic teletypewriter replaced the skill of many Morse-code telegraphers. These men had to learn a new occupation before they could again take their place in the distribution system.

Problems of Distribution. In an ideal society, production, distribution, and consumption would be balanced so as to meet the needs of all the people. Many economists believe that we now have enough factories, machinery, and tools to come nearer to producing all the things that people would like to consume than we have ever done. These economists believe that the fact that many persons do not receive all the goods they can consume is the fault of distribution. Other economists believe that the fault lies with improper production—that not enough goods can be produced at all times at a profit to satisfy the people's needs. The solution of the

DISTRICT OF COLUMBIA TEACHERS COLLEGE

problem of distribution is one of the major tasks confronting modern society.   ROBERT D. PATTON

Related Articles in WORLD BOOK include:

Advertising	Economics	Profit
Banks and Banking	Good Will	Rent
Black Market	Investment	Retailing
Business	Money	Stock Exchange
Cold Storage	Packaging	Supermarket
Consumption	Parity	Trade
Cooperative	Production	Wages and Hours
Credit		

DISTRIBUTOR. See IGNITION; GASOLINE ENGINE (The Ignition System).

DISTRICT ATTORNEY is a public officer whose chief duties are bringing charges against and prosecuting persons charged with some crime or offense. He is the attorney for the people in criminal trials. He may act as attorney for the government in suits to collect taxes, to take property for public use, and the like. He also may appear for the defense in suits brought against the government. In many states, he is elected. In others, he is appointed.

United States district attorneys are appointed by the President and are responsible to the attorney general. A district attorney is appointed for each federal judicial district. His term of office is four years. He serves as attorney for the government when it prosecutes for crimes, sues, or is sued.   ERWIN N. GRISWOLD

DISTRICT COURT is the court in which most federal court cases are first heard in the United States. The district court ranks below the court of appeals. In a district court, questions of fact are decided by a jury, or, if the parties wish, by a judge. The first hearing of a case is called a trial, and the district court is called a *trial court.* The district court decides on the truth of contested events, and the court's decision is final. But the rules of law used by the district court may be reviewed by a higher court, on appeal. The appeal is usually to the Court of Appeals. Sometimes the decision of the Court of Appeals is reviewed by the Supreme Court of the United States.

There are about 90 district courts in the United States and its possessions. Each court has one or more judges, and a United States attorney. The courts hear most federal crime cases, as well as civil suits arising under postal, patent, copyright, internal revenue, and bankruptcy laws.   ERWIN N. GRISWOLD

See also COURT OF APPEALS; COURT (Federal Courts); SUPREME COURT OF THE UNITED STATES.

DISTRICT OF COLUMBIA (D.C.) is the seat of the United States government. This federal district covers 69 square miles along the Potomac River between Maryland and Virginia. It lies about 38 miles southwest of Baltimore. The city of Washington covers the entire District. For a history of the District of Columbia, see WASHINGTON, D.C. See also FEDERAL DISTRICT; FLAG (color picture, Flags of the States and Territories).

DISTRICT OF COLUMBIA TEACHERS COLLEGE is a coeducational college for teachers in Washington, D.C. It is part of the public school system of the district. It grants the B.S. degree. The college was organized in 1955 by the merger of Miner Teachers College and Wilson Teachers College. For enrollment, see UNIVERSITIES AND COLLEGES (table).

197

DITMARS, RAYMOND LEE

DITMARS, *DIT mahrz,* **RAYMOND LEE** (1876-1942), was a noted American authority on reptiles. His popular books included *The Reptile Book, Reptiles of the World, Snakes of the World,* and *Strange Animals I Have Known.* He became curator of reptiles at the New York Zoological Park in 1899, and remained at the park until his death. He pioneered in developing snake-bite serums which have saved many lives. Ditmars was born in Newark, N.J., and was graduated from Barnard Military Academy in 1891.   A. M. WINCHESTER

DIU. See INDIA (History).

DIURETIC, *DIE yu REHT ick,* is a drug or other substance that increases the secretion of urine by the kidneys. Many substances such as water, glucose solution, tea, coffee, mineral waters, and beer have a diuretic effect on the kidneys. Diuretics are used to treat many diseases in which the secretion and flow of urine are greatly affected, such as when the kidneys are damaged by poisons. They are also used to rid the body of extra fluid, as in edema.   AUSTIN EDWARD SMITH

DIVE BOMBER. See BOMBER.

DIVER, a bird. See LOON.

DIVERSIFIED FARMING. See AGRICULTURE (Kinds).

DIVIDE is a high place in the land, situated so that the streams on one side flow in the opposite direction to the streams on the other side. These streams then flow into different river systems, which may empty into different oceans. The little streams are called the *headwaters* of the river systems. The divide separates the headwaters of the systems. Another name for a divide is *watershed.* A divide may be rather low, like the height of land that runs from east to west across North America. This divide separates the rivers that flow generally northward into the Gulf of Saint Lawrence, Hudson Bay, and the Arctic Ocean from those that flow into the Mississippi basin. Some divides are very high with steep slopes, like the Rocky Mountains. This separates the rivers flowing into the Mississippi from those flowing into the Pacific Ocean. The watershed that runs north and south through the Rocky Mountains is called the *Continental Divide.* On Cutbank Pass in Glacier National Park, there are three brooks so close together that a person can pour water into all three. One brook carries water to Hudson Bay, another to the Pacific Ocean, and the third into the Gulf of Mexico. This point is actually the top of the North American continent. At several places, sources of streams flowing to the Pacific and to the Gulf lie only a few feet apart.   ELDRED D. WILSON

See also CONTINENTAL DIVIDE; GREAT DIVIDE.

DIVIDEND, in arithmetic, see DIVISION (Learning to Divide; table, Division Terms). In insurance and securities, see INSURANCE (How Life Insurance Policies Pay Benefits); STOCK, CAPITAL.

DIVIDER is a drafting instrument used to divide lines into equal parts. It also transfers dimensions from a ruler to a map or a drawing. A divider measures and plots small distances between two points more accurately than a ruler. It can be used on maps to check the distance between two points against the scale of miles.

A divider has two needle-pointed legs, joined together at the top. An adjusting screw changes the distance between the two legs. Dividers range in length from about 3 to 8 inches. They are a type of calipers (see CALIPER).   E. B. ESPENSHADE

CONTINENTAL DIVIDE

Diagram of a Typical Divide, *below,* shows how a ridge causes water to run in two different directions and form separate systems of streams and rivers. The Continental Divide runs the full length of the North American continent, from north to south. It passes through the Rocky Mountains, *right,* but it also extends as a smaller ridge across the relatively flat plains of the southwestern United States.

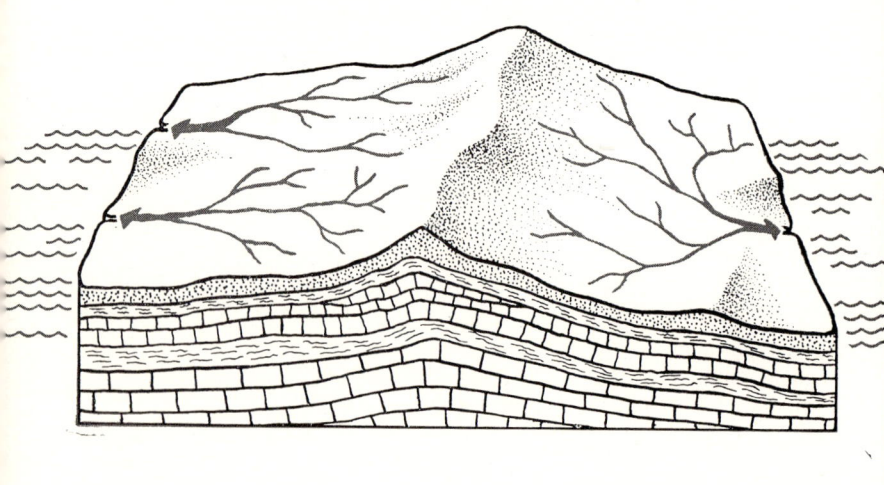

DIVINATION, DIV ih NAY shun, is the practice of foretelling events by means of signs or omens. Superstitious people have believed in divination from earliest times.

It is believed by many that natural occurrences such as a sudden storm or a falling star, have a hidden meaning. A flock of flying birds might mean that a fleet of ships was sailing to meet an enemy. The sight of a hawk later could mean that a victory had been won, or a crow could indicate defeat.

Many systems of artificial divination developed out of these beliefs. In Greek mythology, men appealed directly to oracles for advice, and were answered by the inspired words of the gods. Drawing lots grew up as a form of divination. When a man wanted a question answered, he drew lots, and thought the answer was directed by gods. Dreams have long been believed to foretell happenings, and many elaborate systems of telling their meaning have been thought up. Probably the best example of the art of divination is found in the fortunetellers, who "read" a person's future from a crystal ball, tea leaves, or playing cards. Astrology and numerology have many followers. Many people plan their daily actions only after consulting their horoscopes.

The more scientifically minded a man becomes, the less he believes in the infallibility of divination, magic, or spells. Science tries to give exact, rational explanations for natural happenings.

A *divining rod* is a forked stick, supposed to be attracted by water as a magnet is by steel. It is used to locate the best spot to dig a well. A person holds the stick parallel to the ground with the forked ends in his hands. The pointed end is believed to point toward the ground when it passes over water. Most people doubt its value.

Burlington Railroad

The *Ouija board* is a flat board on which are printed the letters of the alphabet, the digits 1 to 9 and 0, and the words *yes* and *no*. A small three-legged table, called a *planchette*, is placed on this board. The operator puts his fingertips lightly upon the table, which is then supposed to move toward the letters and spell out messages. Some persons think the operator moves the table without realizing he is doing so. WILSON D. WALLIS

See also ASTROLOGY; FORTUNETELLING; NUMEROLOGY; PALMISTRY.

DIVINE COMEDY is a long poem in three parts written by the Italian poet Dante Alighieri. Its subject is what happens to the soul after death. The first section is the *Inferno*, or *Hell*. The second section is the *Purgatorio*, or *Purgatory*, and the third is the *Paradiso*, or *Heaven*. Dante called the work *Comedy* in accordance with the custom of the times because the story ended in happiness. Appreciative readers added the *Divine*.

The hero of the poem is Dante, who tells the story. Dante visits Hell and Purgatory, guided by the spirit of the Roman poet Virgil (see VIRGIL). He finds many persons of past times and of his own time. Some are famous, some are ordinary citizens, but all are suffering punishment for their sins. In Hell, Dante finds those whose sins were the worst, and whose agony is therefore terrible and unending. But in Purgatory he finds those whose sins were forgivable, and whose torments are not severe and will not last forever. Dante pictures Hell as a pit leading deep into the earth. Purgatory is a mountain rising from the brink of the pit of Hell. Heaven begins at the top of the mountain of Purgatory. Here Virgil leaves Dante to the poet's beloved Beatrice, who leads him through the spheres of Heaven to the throne of God. For a brief instant Dante knows the ecstasy of being at one with God. But the brilliance of the light which streams from God is so intense that Dante cannot see Him.

The *Divine Comedy* is considered to be Dante's greatest work. It makes use of the poet's rich learning as well as of his religious beliefs. It is written in *terza rima*. This is a rhyme scheme in which the second of every three lines rhymes with the first and third lines of the next three: aba/bcb/cdc/ded, and so on. Dante probably began writing the *Divine Comedy* about 1300, the year when the poem says his personal visit to the afterlife supposedly took place.

See also DANTE ALIGHIERI.

DIVINE RIGHT OF KINGS is the belief that monarchs get their right to rule directly from God, rather than from the consent or wish of their subjects. According to this belief, it is up to God to punish a wicked king. So far as the people are concerned, "the king can do no wrong." This idea was at its height in England during the reign of the Stuarts and in France during the reign of Louis XIV. The first blow at divine right was the execution of the English king, Charles I, in 1649. The French Revolution completely repudiated the belief, and asserted the doctrine that the right to rule came from the people. But the divine-right doctrine lasted long after that time. It was asserted in the early 1900's by the German emperor, Wilhelm II, as king of Prussia, and by Czar Nicholas II of Russia. J. SALWYN SCHAPIRO

DIVINE SARAH. See BERNHARDT, SARAH.

Diving Is a Popular, Healthful Water Sport.
H. Armstrong Roberts

POPULAR DIVING STYLES

jackknife dive

DIVING is a water sport performed by plunging into water in various ways, usually head first. A diver needs long practice to become highly skilled. Diving techniques have become so varied and elaborate that competitive diving is known as *fancy diving*. Expert divers compete for world recognition in the Olympic Games every four years. The United States and many other nations choose national champions every year. But most swimmers learn diving only as a form of recreation.

Diving demands coordination, muscular control, and exact timing. The combination of relaxation and smooth execution of a properly performed dive makes it a thrilling sport to watch.

Forms of Diving

Dives are in five main groups. (1) The diver faces the water and enters it from a forward position in *forward dives*. (2) The diver stands with his back to the water and enters it from a backward position in *backward dives*. (3) The diver first faces the water but then turns in mid-air in *gainer dives*. (4) The diver stands with his back to the water but turns and enters it in a forward position in a *cutaway dive*, such as the back jackknife. (5) The diver twists before entering the water in a *twist dive*. Each dive is often combined with others.

Diving Positions. A diver may make a dive from a running or standing position. A diver may perform dives from three positions. (1) The body may be straight, or in *layout*. (2) The diver, when in the air, may bring his knees up close to or touching his chest in a *tuck*. (3) The diver may bend his body forward from the hips, keep his legs straight at the knees, and his toes pointed in a *pike*.

Styles of Fancy Diving. Three common styles of fancy diving are the *backward somersault*, the *half-gainer*, and the *swan dive*. These dives demand fine precision.

In the *backward somersault*, the diver starts the dive with his back to the water. His body makes one complete turn backwards, and he enters the water feet first, facing the springboard.

In the *half-gainer*, the diver faces the water and turns backward in the air. He enters the water head first, facing the springboard.

In the *swan dive*, the diver stretches his arms out sideways, in line with his shoulders in mid-air. He keeps his arms in this position until just before he enters the water. Then he brings them together above his head, in a straight line with his body.

Competitive Diving

Springboard Diving, in formal competition, is judged on four main points. (1) The diver's *approach* to the end of the springboard is important. In a running forward dive, for example, a diver takes three quick steps plus a jump, or *hurdle*, and finishes with both feet at the end of the board. From there, he springs into the air. (2) The *height of the spring* should be at least 3 feet above the board. (3) Judges rate the *execution* of the dive, or how smoothly it is performed, after it reaches full height. (4) They judge the diver's *entry into the water*.

FAMOUS U.S. DIVING CHAMPIONS

Name	Championship Held	Year	Where Won
Marjorie Gestring	Women's Olympic Springboard	1936	Berlin
Zoe Ann Olsen	U.S. Women's 3-Meter Springboard	1945—1949	San Antonio; Daytona Beach; San Diego; Jasonville, Ind.
Victoria Draves	Women's Olympic Springboard and Platform	1948	London
Patricia McCormick	Women's Olympic Springboard and Platform	1952; 1956	Helsinki; Melbourne
Paula Jean Myers	U.S. Women's 1-Meter, 3-Meter, and Platform	1957	Beverly Hills; Houston
Bruce Harlan	Men's Olympic Springboard	1948	London
Dr. Sammy Lee	Men's Olympic Platform	1948; 1952	London; Helsinki
David Browning	Men's Olympic Springboard	1952	Helsinki
Robert Clotworthy	Men's Olympic Springboard	1956	Melbourne
Gary Tobian	U.S. Men's Platform	1955—1957	Los Angeles; Detroit; Philadelphia
	Men's Olympic Springboard	1960	Rome
Robert Webster	Men's Olympic Platform	1960	Rome

swan dive

half-gainer dive

backward dive

The diver should enter the water nearly in line with the board, and his body should be almost at right angles to the surface of the water. The body should form a straight line, with arms and legs straight, toes pointed, and head in natural position. His arms should be straight above the head in headfirst dives, and at the sides in feet-first dives.

High-Platform Diving is judged in much the same way, but the judges do not consider the height of the spring to be so important. The firm surface of the platform permits little spring. The greater distance of the diver from the water also allows more time to complete the dive. Otherwise, such dives are the same as those from a high or low springboard. The diving rules of the Olympic Games are used as a guide for judging other springboard and platform diving contests.

Standard Springboard Equipment and Heights. The low board is 14 feet long and 20 inches wide. It is 1 meter, or 39.37 inches, above water level. The high board is 16 feet long and 20 inches wide. It is 3 meters, or 9.84 feet, above the water. Cocoa matting, or a suitable nonskid material, covers the board. The front edge of the board extends at least 5 feet beyond the edge of the pool. The degree of the board's slope should always be so that the forward edge is raised above the base end not more than 2 inches. A diver makes a platform dive from a platform that stands 10 meters, or 32.8 feet, above the water.

Diving for Fun

Learning to dive can be a pleasant and challenging experience. But diving should be learned only from a qualified diver or diving instructor at a properly supervised swimming pool. Many deaths occur each year because inexperienced divers have not learned how to protect themselves in diving, or because they dive into unknown waters that are too shallow or cover submerged objects.

An experienced high diver avoids striking the water flatly with his stomach or back. Such a dive might force the air from his lungs and stun him long enough to permit drowning. He also clasps his hands together by joining his fingers just before entering the water. This prevents the force of the water from separating the diver's extended arms and injuring his head. When diving feet first, he keeps his legs together to avoid a groin injury. If the dive gets out of control, the experienced diver tucks himself into a compact knot. He thereby receives less impact when he strikes the water.

History

Diving in its present highly organized form dates from about 1895. In that year, the Royal Life Saving Society of Great Britain became interested in a "graceful diving competition." A similar interest swept the United States about 1900. It started with dives from fixed platforms. Springboards developed later, and more difficult dives were invented. Diving enthusiasts set up scoring systems, and standardized the diving boards in size and height.

FRED RUSSELL

See also SWIMMING; SKIN DIVING.

DIVING, DEEP-SEA, is the art of working under water. Some people enjoy deep-sea diving as a sport. But for most divers it is a way of reaching jobs that must be done under water. For example, deep-sea divers raise sunken ships. They help build underwater foundations for bridges and piers. Sometimes, divers recover great treasures of gold and silver and other valuable cargoes from the holds of sunken ships.

A diver faces danger each time he goes under water. His life depends on a steady supply of air pumped to him through a hose from the surface. He usually wears a bulky waterproof suit and a metal helmet that make it difficult to move about. Often, a diver must grope his way through icy water filled with mud and silt that make it hard to see. Swift currents may hurl him against an obstacle and tangle his air hose. If a diver rises to the surface too rapidly, he may suffer a sickness called the *bends* (see BENDS).

There are four main kinds of deep-sea divers. *Commercial divers* salvage sunken ships, cargoes, and aircraft, and help build or repair docks, breakwaters, piers, bridges, and pipelines. *Open-sea divers* harvest sponges, pearl oysters, seaweed, and other products of the sea. *Research divers* search the bottoms of oceans for oil and conduct scientific investigations of sea life, geology, and oceanography. *Military divers* blow up harbor defenses, clear mines from harbors, scout shore lines, and also salvage sunken ships and aircraft. See SALVAGE.

Kinds of Diving Equipment

Helmet Equipment is used by most professional divers. This equipment provides divers with a steady air supply and a telephone for communication. But it is also bulky and expensive. The diver wears a large round

DIVING RECORDS

Depth (Feet)	Diver	Date and Location
Skin Diving (No Air Supply)		
127.95	Erminio Falco Alberto Novelli	1956—Mediterranean Sea, off Rapallo, Italy
Helmet Diving (Breathing Air)		
304	Frank Crilley	1915—Pacific Ocean, off Honolulu, Hawaii
SCUBA Diving (Breathing Air)		
328	Eduard Admetlla	1957—Mediterranean Sea, off Cartagena, Spain
Articulated Diving Bell		
400	Albert Gianni	1930—Atlantic Ocean, off France near Ushant Island
Helmet Diving (Breathing Oxygen-Helium)		
600	George Wookey	1956—Atlantic Ocean, off England
Bathysphere		
3,600	William Beebe	1934—Atlantic Ocean, off Bermuda
Benthascope		
4,500	Otis Barton	1949—Pacific Ocean, off California
Bathyscaphe		
35,800	Jacques Piccard Lt. Donald Walsh	1960—Mariana Trench, Pacific Ocean

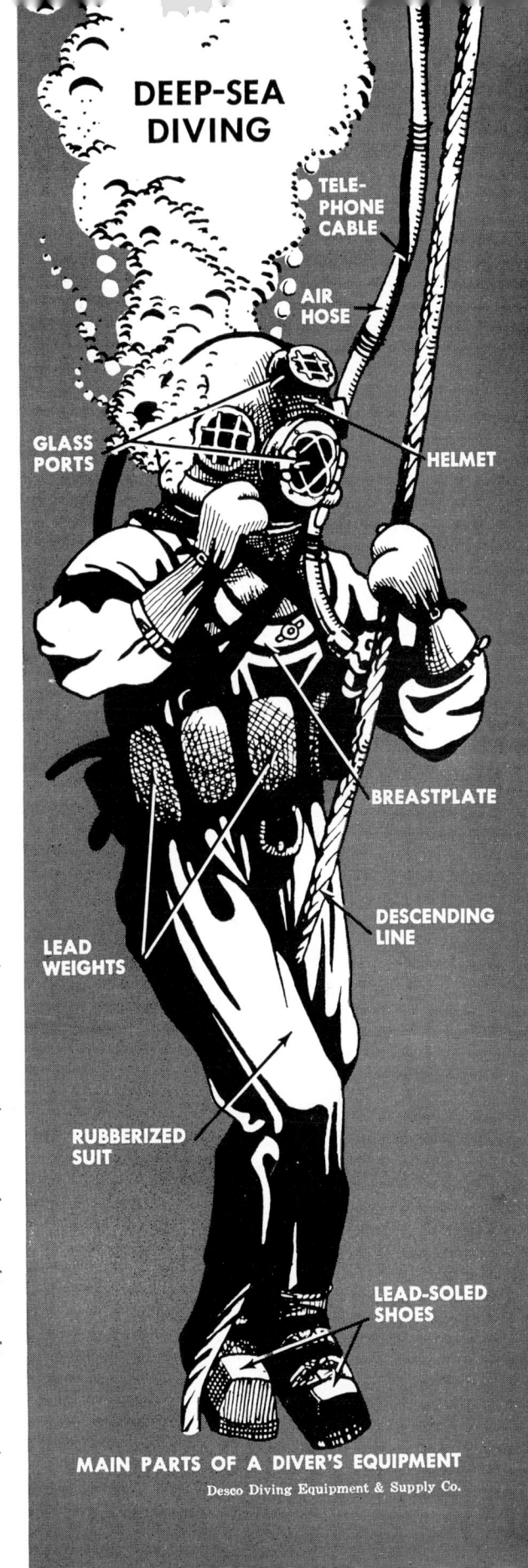

DEEP-SEA DIVING

TELEPHONE CABLE
AIR HOSE
GLASS PORTS
HELMET
BREASTPLATE
LEAD WEIGHTS
DESCENDING LINE
RUBBERIZED SUIT
LEAD-SOLED SHOES

MAIN PARTS OF A DIVER'S EQUIPMENT

Desco Diving Equipment & Supply Co.

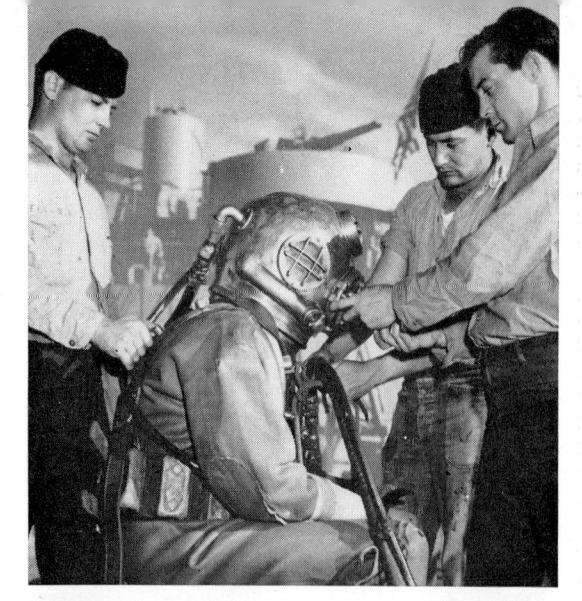

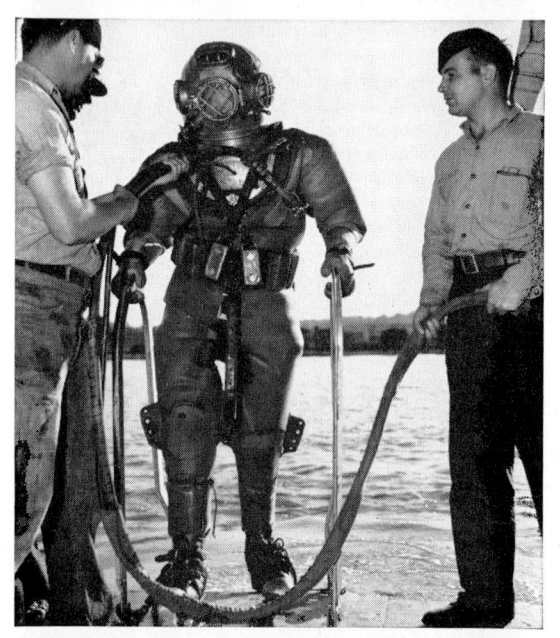

Deep-Sea Divers lead dangerous lives. If their equipment fails to work properly, they may suffocate or be crushed by water pressure. Before a diver goes down, his helpers, *top*, close the front glass port in his helmet and check his air hose and telephone cable. The helpers next assist the diver to a ladder, *center*, so he can climb into the water. After leaving the ladder, the diver, *bottom*, may descend by sliding down a heavy rope that guides him to the spot where he will work.

helmet made of copper, and a rubberized canvas suit usually called a *dress*. Rubber cuffs and a thick rubber collar are cemented to the dress. Heavy brass clamps bolt a copper breastplate to the collar. The helmet screws onto the breastplate. The diver can see out of the helmet through glass *ports*, or windows. Lead-soled shoes and a belt containing lead weights hold the diver under water and help him maintain his balance.

An air hose and a combination life line and telephone cable fasten to two outlets on the back of the helmet. The hose and life line loop under the diver's arms and pass across his chest, where they are lashed to brass loops on the breastplate. The telephone cable connects to a telephone inside the helmet and another one on the surface. A pump on the surface compresses air which travels through the air hose to the helmet, and also blows up the diver's dress. The air pressure inside the diver's dress helps him resist the tremendous pressure of water at great depths. The air the diver breathes escapes through a valve in his helmet. The diver can control the amount of air in his dress by adjusting this valve with his chin.

Ordinarily, a diver breathes only compressed air. But for dives to depths of 300 feet or more, the diver may breathe mixtures of oxygen and nitrogen or oxygen and helium. These mixtures enable divers to resist greater water pressures and to rise more quickly to the surface.

Divers who use helmet equipment usually descend from a barge or tugboat. The diver may climb down a ladder fastened to the side of the vessel or be hoisted over the side by a small crane. The diver can be pulled to the surface by his life line or on a small platform lowered from the surface vessel.

Mask Equipment can be used for shallow dives of less than 50 feet. The mask is made of rubber and metal, and covers the entire face of the diver. An air hose runs from the mask to a surface air supply. The diver may wear a light canvas-rubber suit with this equipment. Such suits usually have a hood that covers all the diver's head except the face.

Self-Contained Underwater Breathing Apparatus (SCUBA) is used by skin divers. The diver carries one or more tanks filled with compressed air strapped to his back. Tubes and valves connect the tanks to a face mask worn by the diver. Most skin divers use an *open-circuit* apparatus, such as the French *Aqua-Lung*. This type allows the air the diver breathes to escape as bubbles. Naval frogmen use *closed-* or *semiclosed-circuit* apparatus. No bubbles escape from these types of apparatus to warn an enemy of the frogmen's presence. Self-contained apparatus is light, inexpensive, and allows the diver more freedom of movement than helmet equipment. But the diver cannot stay under water so long nor dive so deep. See SKIN DIVING.

Diving Bells. Divers have used open and closed diving bells for hundreds of years. Such bells are made of thick steel. Water enters the bottom of *open* bells until the air pressure in the upper part of the bell equals the water pressure outside. No water enters *closed* diving bells. Such devices include the *bathysphere* used by American scientist William Beebe, the *bathyscaphe* developed by the Swiss physicist Auguste Piccard, and the *benthoscope* developed by Otis Barton. *Articulated* (jointed) *diving bells* look like huge armored suits, and permit limited movement by the diver. Scientists use these bells to make underwater observations and photographs at great depths. See BATHYSCAPHE; BATHYSPHERE; DIVING BELL.

History

Diving goes back thousands of years in history. Homer, the Greek poet, compared the fall of Hector's charioteer in the *Iliad* with the motion of a diver diving for oysters. Alexander the Great ordered divers to destroy the underwater defenses of Tyre when he attacked that island city in 333 B.C. In A.D. 77, Pliny the Elder described a breathing device similar to the *snorkel* used by today's skin divers.

For hundreds of years, inventors experimented with many kinds of crude diving devices and apparatus. But divers could not go very deep until the force pump, a machine for compressing air, was developed in 1788 (see PUMP). In 1819, Augustus Siebe of England invented the diving helmet. The pump and the diving helmet marked the beginning of modern diving.

Inventors designed the first crude self-contained breathing apparatus in 1825. The diver carried a limited supply of air compressed in a metal container strapped to his waist. Jacques-Yves Cousteau, a French naval officer, and Émile Gagnan, a French engineer, perfected such devices with the invention of the Aqua-Lung in 1943.

Career Opportunities

Most deep-sea divers are young men 20 to 30 years old. A diver must be in top physical condition for safe diving. He must also have many technical skills. Divers often weld and cut metal, pour concrete, and do similar technical tasks under water. The pay scales for commercial divers commonly range from $35 to $135 a day. However, a diver may earn as much as $600 a day when diving to depths of more than 200 feet. The United States probably has fewer than 700 full-time commercial divers. The Coastal School of Deep Sea Diving in Oakland, Calif., and the United States Navy's Deep Sea Diving School in Washington, D.C., train most persons who become commercial divers. E. R. CROSS

See also FISH (picture, Fish Flock for Food).

DIVING, SKIN. See SKIN DIVING.
DIVING BEETLE. See WATER BEETLE.
DIVING BELL is a bottomless metal chamber, made in the shape of a box or bell, and used as an underwater workroom. It protects men who lay the foundations of bridges, string telephone or telegraph wires under rivers, or do other work at the bottom of fairly shallow bodies of water. The diving bell is filled with compressed air through a tube in its roof. The pressure of the air prevents the water from rising inside the bell. When the diving bell comes to rest on the bottom of a river or lake, the workmen have space in which to work. Only their feet get wet. The diving bell is raised and lowered by heavy steel cables. It may be stopped and held at any

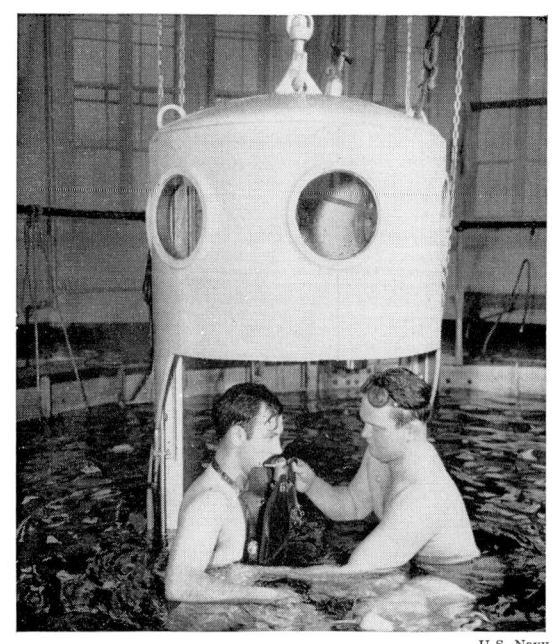

U.S. Navy
A Diving Bell Is Used at a Submarine Training School.

point on its trip up or down. The weight of the bell carries it to the bottom.

The diving bell is one of the oldest inventions designed to help men work under water. Alexander the Great is said to have used some sort of diving bell in the 300's B.C., and Roger Bacon made a similar device about the middle of the A.D. 1200's.   PAUL D. STROOP

See also DIVING, DEEP-SEA (Diving Bells).

DIVING LUNG. See AQUA-LUNG; DIVING, DEEP-SEA; SKIN DIVING.

DIVINING ROD. See DIVINATION.

DIVISION (military) is a unit in the armed forces. It is the major combat unit of the U.S. Army. The army has 16 divisions, each of which has about 15,000 men. There are four types of army divisions: (1) airborne, (2) armored, (3) infantry, and (4) mechanized. The army reorganized its divisions under the Reorganization Army Divisions (ROAD) program in 1962 to make them more flexible so each would be equipped for its location and mission. A division may have from 6 to 15 battalions depending on its mission. Most divisions have 10 battalions, as well as control and supply units. In each division, the battalions and other units are organized into three brigades. See ARMY, U.S. (table, Army Levels of Command).

The division is also a basic ground-fighting unit in the U.S. Marine Corps (see MARINE CORPS, U.S.). A Marine Corps division has about 19,000 men, organized into three regiments and support troops. A U.S. Air Force air division includes two or more *wings* (see AIR FORCE, U.S.). A wing is a mobile unit that can operate independently. The U.S. Navy groups two or more ships within a fleet to form a division for administrative purposes (see NAVY, U.S.). In naval aviation, a division, such as a carrier division, includes two or more sections. Division organization is also used by the armed forces of other countries.   MARK M. BOATNER III

H. Armstrong Roberts

DIVISION, *duh VIZH un,* is a way of separating a group of things into equal parts.

Suppose you had 16¢ to spend on postage stamps. They cost 4¢ each. You want to know how many stamps you can buy for 16¢. If you have 16 pennies, you can count out the pennies into equal groups of 4. There are four equal groups of 4. So you can buy four four-cent stamps for 16¢, as shown below.

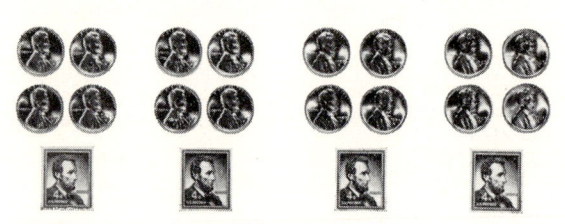

Separating a group of 16 things into four equal parts of 4 things is an example of division.

Division is one of the four basic operations in arithmetic. The others are addition, subtraction, and multiplication. You must learn how to add, subtract, and multiply before you begin to study division.

Learning to Divide

Once people learned division only by memorizing. Most teachers now agree that the best way to learn

––––––––– DIVISION TERMS –––––––––

Dividend. In 32 ÷ 8 = 4, 32 is the dividend.
Division Fact is a division in which the divisor and quotient are whole numbers not larger than 9. For example, 42 ÷ 7 = 6 is a division fact.
Divisor. In 32 ÷ 8 = 4, 8 is the divisor.
Long Division is a method of dividing numbers in which the work is written out.
Quotient. In 32 ÷ 8 = 4, 4 is the quotient.
Remainder is any amount left over after a division operation has been completed. The remainder is always less than the divisor.
Short Division is a method of dividing numbers in which much of the work is done mentally.

division is by understanding. You can learn to understand division without much difficulty.

Writing Division. One way of separating a group into equal parts is by counting it out into equal parts. But there is a much easier way to divide. To find how many groups of 3 there are in 12, you can subtract 3 from 12 until nothing is left:

$$\begin{array}{c}12\\-3\\\hline 9\end{array} \Rightarrow \begin{array}{c}9\\-3\\\hline 6\end{array} \Rightarrow \begin{array}{c}6\\-3\\\hline 3\end{array} \Rightarrow \begin{array}{c}3\\-3\\\hline 0\end{array}$$

This shows that there are four 3's in 12.

Each basic operation in arithmetic is indicated by a special symbol. The symbol for division is ÷. The statement 12 ÷ 3 = 4 means that when 12 things are separated into 3 equal groups, each group has 4 things in it. Or, that there are three 4's in 12. People who know division usually read 12 ÷ 3 = 4 as "12 divided by 3 is 4." When you actually work a problem in division, you will find it useful to write it this way:

$$3\overline{)12}^{4}$$

The parts of a problem in division have special names. The number being divided is called the *dividend*. The number by which the dividend is divided is the *divisor*. The answer, or result, of the division is called the *quotient*.

Divisor ⟹ $3\overline{)12}^{4}$ ⟸ Quotient / Dividend

Another way of writing a problem in division is the form used in writing fractions (see FRACTION):

$$\frac{12}{3} = 4$$

Division Facts. By using subtraction, you discovered that there are three equal groups of 4 things in a group of 12. Or, 12 ÷ 3 = 4. This is a *division fact*. You can find all the division facts by using subtraction.

The 64 Division Facts

$2\overline{)4}$ $\;$ $2\overline{)6}$ $\;$ $2\overline{)8}$ $\;$ $2\overline{)10}$ $\;$ $2\overline{)12}$ $\;$ $2\overline{)14}$ $\;$ $2\overline{)16}$ $\;$ $2\overline{)18}$

$3\overline{)6}$ $\;$ $3\overline{)9}$ $\;$ $3\overline{)12}$ $\;$ $3\overline{)15}$ $\;$ $3\overline{)18}$ $\;$ $3\overline{)21}$ $\;$ $3\overline{)24}$ $\;$ $3\overline{)27}$

$4\overline{)8}$ $\;$ $4\overline{)12}$ $\;$ $4\overline{)16}$ $\;$ $4\overline{)20}$ $\;$ $4\overline{)24}$ $\;$ $4\overline{)28}$ $\;$ $4\overline{)32}$ $\;$ $4\overline{)36}$

$5\overline{)10}$ $\;$ $5\overline{)15}$ $\;$ $5\overline{)20}$ $\;$ $5\overline{)25}$ $\;$ $5\overline{)30}$ $\;$ $5\overline{)35}$ $\;$ $5\overline{)40}$ $\;$ $5\overline{)45}$

$6\overline{)12}$ $\;$ $6\overline{)18}$ $\;$ $6\overline{)24}$ $\;$ $6\overline{)30}$ $\;$ $6\overline{)36}$ $\;$ $6\overline{)42}$ $\;$ $6\overline{)48}$ $\;$ $6\overline{)54}$

$7\overline{)14}$ $\;$ $7\overline{)21}$ $\;$ $7\overline{)28}$ $\;$ $7\overline{)35}$ $\;$ $7\overline{)42}$ $\;$ $7\overline{)49}$ $\;$ $7\overline{)56}$ $\;$ $7\overline{)63}$

$8\overline{)16}$ $\;$ $8\overline{)24}$ $\;$ $8\overline{)32}$ $\;$ $8\overline{)40}$ $\;$ $8\overline{)48}$ $\;$ $8\overline{)56}$ $\;$ $8\overline{)64}$ $\;$ $8\overline{)72}$

$9\overline{)18}$ $\;$ $9\overline{)27}$ $\;$ $9\overline{)36}$ $\;$ $9\overline{)45}$ $\;$ $9\overline{)54}$ $\;$ $9\overline{)63}$ $\;$ $9\overline{)72}$ $\;$ $9\overline{)81}$

It is important to learn the division facts so well that you can use them automatically. The facts are useful themselves. They are also necessary in learning how to divide larger numbers quickly and accurately.

Long Division

Long division is a method that can be used to divide large numbers. In long division, you write out the work carefully.

Suppose you want to find out how many 3's there are in 79, or 79 ÷ 3. Instead of subtracting one 3 at a time, you can shorten your work by subtracting several 3's at once. To begin, you might subtract five 3's, or 15, each time:

```
 79      64      49      34      19       4
-15     -15     -15     -15     -15      -3
---     ---     ---     ---     ---     ---
 64      49      34      19       4       1
```

All together, you subtracted 5 + 5 + 5 + 5 + 5 or twenty-five 3's from 79, leaving 4. You cannot take away five more 3's, but you can take away one more 3, leaving a *remainder* of 1. Thus, there are 25 + 1 or twenty-six 3's in 79 with 1 left over.

Subtracting five 3's at a time shortened your work. Next, you might try subtracting ten 3's, or 30, each time:

```
 79      49      19       4
-30     -30     -15      -3
---     ---     ---     ---
 49      19       4       1
```

This time, you subtracted 10 + 10 + 5 + 1 or twenty-six 3's from 79, and had 1 left as a remainder. A better form to use is this:

```
3)79
  -30      10    The number of 3's
  ---
   49      10    subtracted are re-
  -30
  ---
   19       5    corded in this column.
  -15
  ---
    4
   -3       1
   ---
Remainder 1     26    The total number
                      of 3's subtracted.
```

After some practice, you might subtract twenty 3's and then six 3's:

```
    26          The result is written
 3)79
  -60      20   above the dividend
  ---
   19
  -18       6   to complete the form.
  ---
    1      26
```

To gain further practice in long division, you might now try to find out how many 21's there are in 891, or 891 ÷ 21. First, you must decide how many 21's you will subtract at a time. Ten 21's, or 210, might prove to be useful. Using 10's, 100's, or 1,000's in multiplying the divisor makes division much easier.

```
      42
 21)891
  -210      10   Number of 21's
  ----
   681
  -210      10   subtracted.
  ----
   471
  -210      10
  ----
   261
  -210      10
  ----
    51
   -21       1
   ---
    30
   -21       1
   ---
Remainder  9     42
```

When you have subtracted four 210's or forty 21's, you find that the remainder, 51, is too small to subtract ten more 21's. You can, however, subtract one 21 at a time. This finally gives you 10 + 10 + 10 + 10 + 1 + 1 or forty-two 21's in 891, with a remainder of 9.

You could have used twenty 21's, or 420, as your first unit.

```
      42
 21)891
  -420      20   Number of 21's
  ----
   471
  -420      20   subtracted.
  ----
    51
   -42       2
   ---
Remainder  9     42
```

One last example will illustrate further the process of long division. Suppose you want to know how many 37's there are in 12,526, or 12,526 ÷ 37. Once again you must decide how many 37's to subtract at one time.

```
       338
 37)12526
   -7400    200   Number of 37's
   -----
    5126
   -3700    100   subtracted.
   -----
    1426
   -1110     30
   -----
     316
    -185      5
    ----
     131
    -111      3
    ----
Remainder  20    338
```

You may have to experiment on a sheet of scrap paper to find the units that you can use to solve the problem easily. You can use even larger units than 200.

```
       338
 37)12526
  -11100    300   Number of 37's
  -----
    1426
   -1110     30   subtracted.
   -----
     316
    -296      8
    ----
Remainder  20    338
```

207

DIVISION

Many persons use a form for long division even shorter than those outlined above. The three steps look like this:

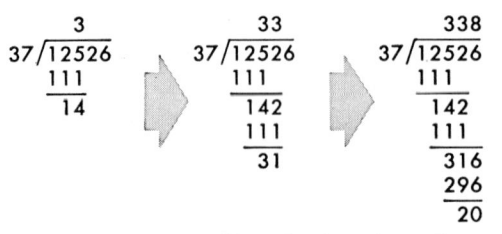

```
       3              33             338
37/12526        37/12526        37/12526
   111             111             111
    14             142             142
                   111             111
                    31             316
                                   296
                                    20
```

This form does the same things that have been discussed above, but by a different method. It does not illustrate the process of long division so well to a beginner.

When using this shorter form, it helps to notice that in all these examples you write the answer (quotient) above the proper places in the dividend. That is, when you subtract a unit of 100's, you record the number of 100's above the 100's place in the dividend.

Remainders in Division. There is often a remainder when you have completed a problem in division. What you do with this remainder depends on the kind of problem. If you want to know how many 3's there are in 79, you might have had 79¢ to spend on three-cent postage stamps. You would find that you could buy 26 stamps and have 1¢ left.

If you wanted to share 79 apples among three persons, you would also find that there are twenty-six 3's in 79 and a remainder of 1. This means that each person gets 26 apples and there is one left to share. If the sharing is to be absolutely equal, you would have to cut the remaining apple into three equal parts. Each person would receive $26\frac{1}{3}$ apples.

These examples show that what is done to a remainder depends on the problem. In some cases, further division into fractional parts is indicated. In other cases, the remainder merely tells how many are "left over."

Division of Decimal Fractions. You can also use long division to divide numbers that include decimal fractions. The statement 78.35 ÷ 3.6 is this kind of problem. In order to understand division of decimal fractions, you must learn an interesting feature of division.

You know that 15 ÷ 3 = 5 is a division fact. What would happen if both the 15 and 3 were multiplied by 10? That is, what is the result of dividing 150 by 30? Long division will show you that this quotient is also 5. Thus, 15 ÷ 3 = 5, and 150 ÷ 30 = 5. Similarly, 72 ÷ 6 = 12 and 720 ÷ 60 = 12. If the 72 and 6 are multiplied by 100, the quotient of 7,200 ÷ 600 is also 12. These examples illustrate a general rule: *multiplying both the dividend and divisor by 10, 100, 1,000, and so on, does not change the quotient.*

This rule can be used to divide 78.35 by 3.6. Both 78.35 and 3.6 can be multiplied by 10. Thus, 78.35 × 10 = 783.5 and 3.6 × 10 = 36. The quotient of 783.5 ÷ 36 will be the same as the quotient of 78.35 ÷ 3.6. But the decimal points now have new positions. A useful device is to use a caret mark (∧) to indicate the new position of the decimal points. The decimal point in the quotient will appear directly above the caret mark in the dividend.

$$3.6_\wedge \overline{)78.3_\wedge 5}$$

This shows that 78.35 and 3.6 have both been multiplied by 10. Sometimes it is necessary to multiply the dividend and divisor by 100, 1,000, or some larger multiple of 10. For example, 25.773 ÷ 17.94 should be multiplied by 100:

$$17.94_\wedge \overline{)25.77_\wedge 3}$$

You should multiply the dividend and divisor by a multiple of 10 large enough to change the divisor into a *whole number*, or a number that does not include a decimal fraction.

After you have learned to change the divisor into a whole number, you can solve problems in this new form, for example, 4.2 ÷ 3. Put in the form of a question, this is "how many 3's are there in 4.2?" The number 4.2 is the same as 42 tenths. You can restate the question as "how many 3's are there in 42 tenths?" You can find the answer by subtracting units of 3's:

```
    14 tenths
3/42 tenths
 −30 tenths        10 tenths
  12 tenths
 −12 tenths         4 tenths
                   14 tenths
```

Thus, 14 tenths, or 1.4, is the answer. When you have learned this process, you will not have to write out the names. This form is better:

```
    1.4
3/4.2
  3 0           10
  1 2
  1 2            4
                14
```

If the divisor is a whole number, you can disregard the decimal point in the dividend while you are working the problem. When you get a number for the quotient, put as many decimal places in the quotient as there are in the dividend.

In division problems, you often have to find the quotient to the nearest tenth, hundredth, and so on. You can do this easily. After you have placed the caret marks in the divisor and dividend, use just as many digits to the right of the dividend's caret mark as the number of decimal places wanted in the answer. Sometimes it is necessary to add zeros to the dividend. For example, you must first change $3.6\overline{)78.35}$ to $3.6_\wedge \overline{)78.3_\wedge 5}$ to make the divisor a whole number. Suppose the quotient must be correct to the nearest hundredth. Then you must add a zero to the dividend, making it $78.3_\wedge 50$.

```
          2 1.76
3.6∧/78.3∧50
 −72 0 00              2000
    6 3 50
   −3 6 00              100
    2 7 50
   −2 5 20               70
      2 30
     −2 16                6
         14             2176
```

You do not have to do anything with the remainder, because the problem asked you to be accurate only to the nearest hundredth.

Short Division

When dividing by a one-digit number such as 7, you can do some of the work in long division without writing it down. Division of this kind, which is usually done in the mind rather than on paper, is called *short division*. The method is the same as in long division, but you do the work mentally.

```
Long Division              Short Division
    212                       212   R(emainder) 1
 4/849                      4/849
 -800        200
   49
  -40         10
    9
   -8          2
    1        212
```

The only difference between these two examples is that in short division you do the work mentally and indicate the remainder next to the quotient. The letter *R* is often used to mean *Remainder*. In this example, you first see that you can subtract two hundred 4's from 849. You write the 2 in the 100's place over the 8 in the dividend. Next, you can take away ten 4's from the remaining 49. You write the 1 in the 10's place over the 4 in the dividend. Finally, you can take away two 4's from the remaining 9. You write the 2 in the 1's place over the 9 in the dividend. You show the remainder to the right of the quotient.

In more difficult problems in short division, you must use a new device. The problem 415 ÷ 7 will show this.

$$\frac{5}{7 \overline{)415}}$$

Your first step is to subtract fifty 7's or 350, which is thirty-five 10's. Write the 5 (for 50 or five 10's) over the 1 in the dividend. You do the subtraction mentally. Thirty-five 10's subtracted from forty-one 10's is six 10's. You write a little 6 to the left of the 5 in the dividend.

$$\frac{5}{7 \overline{)41^65}}$$

Now you are dividing six 10's and 5, or 65, by 7. You can subtract nine 7's or 63 from 65, leaving a remainder of 2.

$$\frac{5\ 9}{7 \overline{)41^65}} \quad \text{R 2} \quad \text{or } 59\tfrac{2}{7}$$

It is useful to see how this process is derived from long division.

```
   59                  5 9         R 2
 7/415               7/41 65
 -350       50
   65
  - 63        9
    2
```

DIVISION

Another example is 7,536 ÷ 9. As in the case of long division, you must decide how many 9's you can subtract at one time.

$$\frac{8\ 3\ 7}{9 \overline{)75^33^66}} \quad \text{R 3} \quad \text{or } 837\tfrac{3}{9} \text{ or } 837\tfrac{1}{3}$$

First, you subtract eight hundred 9's, or 7,200. You write the 8 (for eight 100's or 800) over the 5 in the dividend. Mentally you subtract 72 (hundreds) from 75 (hundreds): 75−72=3. You write a little 3 to the left of the 3 in the dividend to keep the three 100's in the work. From this new figure of 336, you can subtract thirty 9's or 270. You write the 3 for the thirty 9's over the 3 in the dividend. Next, 33−27=6. You write a little 6 to the left of the 6 in the dividend to keep the six 10's in the work. From this new figure of 66, you can subtract seven 9's, or 63. You write the 7 for the seven 9's over the 6 in the dividend. Finally, 66 − 63 = 3. You indicate the remainder of 3 to the right of the quotient. After some practice, you will be able to leave out the little numbers as reminders of figures that must be included in the work. You will soon be able to remember these numbers in your head.

How to Check Division

You will be wise to check the answer to a division problem to be sure you have solved it correctly.

Rounding Off. One way to check is to see whether or not the quotient is a sensible answer. You can estimate a quotient by rounding off the dividend and divisor. To estimate the quotient of 158 ÷ 76, you can round off 158 to 160 and 76 to 80. Because 160 ÷ 80 = 2, the quotient of 158 ÷ 76 should be about 2. To estimate the quotient of 5,124 ÷ 36, you can round off 5,124 to 5,000 and 36 to 50. You can see that 5,000 ÷ 50 = 100, and 5,000 ÷ 25 = 200. Thus, the quotient of 5,124 ÷ 36 should be somewhere between 100 and 200. Estimating the quotient will help you decide if your answer is sensible.

Checking by Multiplication. Another way of checking a quotient is to multiply the quotient by the divisor to see if the product is the dividend. If you have multiplied correctly, this method will catch any error. This is because multiplication is the opposite of division.

```
       13                 13
  24/312               × 24
                         52
                         26
                        312
```

The next example shows how to use the remainder in checking by multiplication:

```
       42      R 7        42
  21/889               × 21
                         42
                         84
                        882
                        + 7         R
                        889
```

209

DIVISION

The quotient is multiplied by the divisor, and the remainder is added to the product.

Four Key Division Ideas

Here are four important rules to remember for solving division problems.

1. Remember that division means breaking up a number into smaller equal groups. The divisor shows the size of these groups.

2. Learn the division facts so well that you do not have to stop and figure them out each time. You will use the division facts constantly in everyday arithmetic, and will need to know them to divide larger numbers.

3. Remember the method for dividing larger numbers used in long division. In long division, subtract the divisor from the dividend as many times as possible in a single step. In this way, you can reduce the number of steps in long division.

4. Always check the answer after finishing a division problem. You can do this by estimating or by multiplying the quotient by the divisor and adding any remainder.

Fun with Division

Space is a game played with cards much like those used in bingo. Each card has a square drawn on it. The square is subdivided into 25 smaller squares. The letters S P A C E are written across the top of the card. The squares are filled in with any arrangement of the numerals from 1 to 9. Each square has one number, except the one in the center which is marked *F* for "free." Each card should have a different pattern of numerals on it. Each player has a card and a set of small markers. The leader of the game calls out questions on the division facts, for example, "Under *A*, the 4's in 20." There are five 4's in 20. If the player has the number 5 under *A* on his card, he covers the number. The first player to completely cover all numbers in a row, a column, or a diagonal calls out "Space!" and wins the game. The leader keeps a record of the division facts as he calls them out. He uses this record to check the winner's card. For a new game, exchange the cards among the players.

S	P	A	C	E
2	1	3	4	5
3	4	5	5	3
5	6	F	6	4
6	8	6	7	6
8	9	8	9	8

Divide-Down is an arithmetic version of a spelldown. The players are divided into two teams. Each player is asked one of the division facts, such as "how many 6's in 42?" If he answers correctly, he stays in the game. If he misses, he must leave the game. When all the members of one team have missed, the other team is declared the winner.

HENRY VAN ENGEN

Related Articles in WORLD BOOK include:
Addition   Fraction
Arithmetic   Multiplication
Decimal Number System   Subtraction

Outline

I. **Learning to Divide**
   A. Writing Division   B. Division Facts
II. **Long Division**
   A. Remainders in Division
   B. Division of Decimal Fractions
III. **Short Division**
IV. **How to Check Division**
   A. Rounding Off   B. Checking by Multiplication
V. **Four Key Division Ideas**
VI. **Fun with Division**

PRACTICE DIVISION EXAMPLES

1. $4\overline{)56}$
2. $7\overline{)105}$
3. $5\overline{)625}$
4. $6\overline{)522}$
5. $9\overline{)387}$
6. $2\overline{)1146}$
7. $3\overline{)1008}$
8. $8\overline{)984}$
9. $23\overline{)483}$
10. $47\overline{)6281}$
11. $326\overline{)10457}$
12. $29\overline{)1201}$
13. $3.14\overline{)25.60}$
14. $.06\overline{)9.87}$
15. $1.26\overline{).00904}$

16. Miss Smith's class at school is going to visit the local newspaper. Some of the mothers have offered to drive. There are 35 children in the class, and each car can take 5 children. How many cars will be needed for the trip?

17. A certain kind of candy bar costs 6¢ each. How many of these candy bars can Sue buy with 48¢?

18. There are 7 days in a week. How many weeks are there in one year (365 days)?

19. Four boys wish to share equally 64 pieces of candy. How many pieces should each boy get?

20. Tom rides his bicycle at a speed of 6 miles an hour. At this rate, how many hours will it take him to ride 15 miles?

21. Jane's class in school wants to buy some sketchbooks that cost 23¢ each. Her class has $5.85 to spend for books. How many sketchbooks can Jane's class buy?

22. An airplane travels at the rate of 350 miles an hour. At this rate, how long will it take to fly 820 miles?

23. Bill and his father went on a trip in their car. They traveled 378.4 miles in 10.3 hours. What was their average rate of speed?

24. Mary's mother rents a house for $1,620 a year. How much rent would she have to pay for one month?

ANSWERS TO THE DIVISION EXAMPLES

1. 14
2. 15
3. 125
4. 87
5. 43
6. 573
7. 336
8. 123
9. 21
10. 133 R 30
11. 32 R 25
12. 41 R 12
13. 8.15
14. 164.5
15. .00717
16. 7 cars
17. 8 bars
18. 52 weeks and 1 day
19. 16 pieces
20. $2\frac{1}{2}$ hours
21. 25 books and 10¢ left
22. 2 hrs. and about 20 min.
23. 36.7 miles an hour
24. $135 a month

DIVISION OF LABOR. See Mass Production.

DIVORCE is the dissolution of a marriage relationship by the decree of a court. It is usually distinguished from *annulment*, which is a judicial declaration that a marriage is invalid because of incapacity, lack of consent of the parties, or some defect in the marriage formalities. Divorce is also distinguished from *legal separation*, which allows the parties to live apart, but does not legally dissolve the marriage in other respects.

Grounds for Divorce. In the United States, divorces may be granted only for grounds which are set out in laws. The common causes for which divorces are granted include adultery, cruelty, and desertion. Other causes, found in some states, include habitual drunkenness, drug addiction, failure to support, incompatibility, insanity, and imprisonment for felony. New York state grants divorces only on the ground of adultery. Several states, such as Nevada, list many grounds. The Roman Catholic Church and some Protestant churches consider divorces justifiable only in extreme cases.

Laws Governing Divorce. Because there are so many differences in the divorce laws of the different states, persons who cannot obtain a divorce in one state sometimes go to another state to obtain it. A problem which has frequently arisen is whether the first state must recognize the divorce decree granted in the second state. The Supreme Court of the United States has ruled that a state has authority to grant a divorce decree only if either the husband or wife has a *domicile* there. This means that the person must legally be regarded as living or having his home there. Nevada and other states which grant easy divorces have statutes requiring short periods of residence, such as six weeks. But residence alone is not enough. The court must make a proper finding of domicile. If one of the parties has a domicile in another country, a divorce obtained there will generally be recognized in the United States.

Effects of Divorce. When a divorce decree is granted, the court usually makes provision for the custody and support of the children, if there are any. A wife is often awarded *alimony*, a sum of money for her own support. The husband may be ordered to pay alimony either in one lump sum or in installments. An *absolute divorce* permits either party to marry again. But in some states the decree does not become final for a period of time. The parties are not free to marry until later.

There are two ways in which marriages may be dissolved, in the eyes of the Roman Catholic Church. One of these is called the *Pauline Privilege*. If two unbaptized persons marry, and one of them later becomes a Catholic, and if the unbaptized person is not willing to live with a Catholic, the marriage may be dissolved by the Congregation of the Holy Office of Rome. Unconsummated Catholic marriages may be dissolved by act of the Pope at the request of one or both of the parties, or if one or both intend to take religious vows. In the United States, this dissolution is not final in the eyes of the law until it has been decided in a court action.

History. In England in the 1800's, divorces were granted by acts of Parliament. At one time, some state legislatures in the United States granted divorces by special acts, but this practice has now died out.

The U.S. divorce rate is high in comparison with other countries. Many sociologists believe that divorce laws should be made stricter, and that this will reduce the divorce rate. Others believe that the way to reduce the divorce rate is to make the marriage laws stricter and the divorce laws more liberal.   John W. Wade

Related Articles in World Book include:
Abandonment   Alimony   Desertion
Alienation   Annulment   Marriage

DIVORCE RATE IN THE UNITED STATES

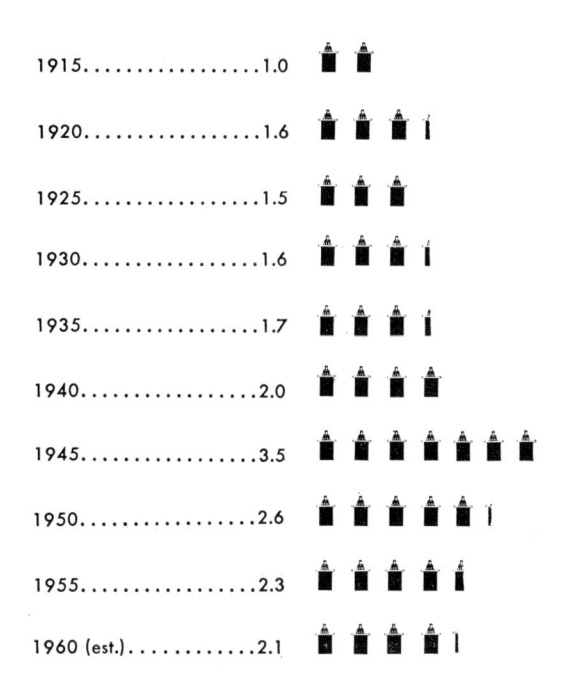

Year	Rate
1915	1.0
1920	1.6
1925	1.5
1930	1.6
1935	1.7
1940	2.0
1945	3.5
1950	2.6
1955	2.3
1960 (est.)	2.1

Each symbol stands for 0.5 divorces per 1,000 population. Based on latest available statistics.

DIX, DOROTHEA LYNDE (1802-1887), led the drive to build state hospitals for the mentally ill in the United States. She also improved prison conditions. She traveled through the U.S. and Europe for this cause until she was 80. She gained the support of wealthy people, educators, and statesmen.

She was born in Hampden, Me., but grew up in Massachusetts in her grandmother's home. She taught, and wrote children's books. She visited a Massachusetts house of correction in 1841, and was shocked by the treatment of mentally ill persons. She asked the legislature to provide better care for the mentally ill, and started the reform in that state. She served as Superintendent of Women Nurses during the Civil War.   Louis Filler

Dorothea Dix
Keystone View

DIXIE

DIXIE is the name of a famous song especially popular in the South. Daniel D. Emmett, member of a minstrel-show company, wrote the song in 1859 in New York City. He intended it to be a closing number because it permitted a parade of the entire company. The song became an immediate hit. Many publishers printed their own versions.

The original first stanza was as follows:
"I wish I was in de land ob cotton,
Old times dar am not forgotten,
Look away! Look away! Look away! Dixie Land."

When Abraham Lincoln ran for the presidency in 1860, "Dixie" was used as a campaign song against him. Five years later, after the Civil War, he asked a band at the White House to play "Dixie." CHARLES B. RIGHTER

DIXIE, or DIXIELAND, is a name often given to the southern part of the United States. There are different explanations for this name. A Louisiana bank once printed $10 bills bearing the French word *dix*, which means *ten*. According to one story, people called Louisiana "Dix's Land," and then shortened it to Dixie. In time, *Dixie* came to mean the entire South. In another story, a man named Dixie, or Dixy, who lived on Manhattan Island (New York City), was good to his slaves. He had to send some of his slaves south. They became homesick for "Dixie's Land." RAY ALLEN BILLINGTON

DIXIE HIGHWAY is a series of scenic automobile roads that lead from the Straits of Mackinac, at the northern tip of Lake Michigan, to Miami, near the southern end of the peninsula of Florida. It has two main routes, an east route and a west route. The east route passes through Detroit, Mich., Cincinnati, Ohio, and Jacksonville, Fla. The west route passes through South Bend, Ind., Louisville, Ky., and Atlanta, Ga.

Carl G. Fisher, a pioneer automobile manufacturer, originated the idea of the Dixie Highway. The building of the highway began in 1915. MATTHEW C. SIELSKI

DIXIECRAT PARTY is the nickname for the States' Rights Democratic party. In the national election of 1948, many Southern Democrats objected to their party's civil rights program. They formed the Dixiecrat party and nominated J. Strom Thurmond for President and Fielding L. Wright for Vice-President. The party won the electoral votes of four Southern States.

DIXON, JEREMIAH. See MASON AND DIXON'S LINE.

DIXON, JOSEPH (1799-1869), was an American inventor and manufacturer. He founded a factory to make lead pencils and stove polish from graphite at Salem, Mass., in 1827. In 1832, he patented a process of using colored inks to prevent counterfeiting. After moving his factory to Jersey City, N.J., Dixon patented and introduced graphite crucibles for making pottery and steel in 1850. He was born in Marblehead, Mass.

DIZZINESS is a condition in which a person feels that his surroundings are whirling about, or that he is falling. Dizziness also means lightheadedness, the sensation that comes before fainting. It causes a person to stagger or fall. Often there is nausea and vomiting. Dizziness is also called *vertigo*. Too large or too small a flow of blood to the brain may cause dizziness. It may also be caused by changes in the pressure of the fluid in the semicircular canals of the inner ear. Dizziness often accompanies such disorders as anemia, epilepsy, heart trouble, and diseases of the inner ear. Some people feel dizzy when they are whirled very rapidly or when they stand at great heights. R. B. CAPPS

DJAKARTA, *juh KAHR tuh*, or JAKARTA (pop. 2,922,000; alt. 16 ft.), is the capital and chief port of the Republic of Indonesia. *Djakarta* is an Indonesian word that means *important city*. The city was formerly called *Batavia*.

The city lies in the northwestern corner of the island of Java. For the location of Djakarta, see INDONESIA (inset on color map). Djakarta has wide paved streets and many modern buildings, such as the famous Hôtel des Indes, now named Duta Indonesia. It is a railroad and airline center. Its exports include spices, oils, rice, tea, bamboo, diamonds, and rubber.

The city was founded by the Dutch in the early 1600's, and soon became an important administrative center. It was the capital of Netherlands East Indies under the Dutch. JUSTUS M. VAN DER KROEF

DJAWA, or JAVA. See INDONESIA.

DJIBOUTI, *juh BOO tih* (pop. 25,000; alt. 15 ft.), is the capital of French Somaliland. It is also called *Jibuti*. It is a port on the Gulf of Aden, south of the Bab el Mandeb Strait. Djibouti is at the northern end of a railroad connecting Addis Ababa, capital of Ethiopia, with the sea. The port was created in 1888 and the city became the capital of the colony in 1892.

DNA. See NUCLEIC ACID.

DNEPR RIVER, *D'NYEH pr'*, or DNIEPER, *NEE per*, is the second longest waterway in European Russia. The Dnepr rises near Smolensk in central European Russia. It flows southward for 1,420 miles to empty into the Black Sea. The Dnepr drains an area of about 200,000 square miles in one of Russia's most important economic regions. For location, see RUSSIA (color map).

The Dnepr has been dredged so that boats can travel over almost the entire length of the river. Dams and reservoirs have deepened the Dnepr and removed obstacles caused by rapids. The Dneproges Dam is near Zaporozhye (see DNEPROGES DAM). Other dams on the Dnepr include those at Kiev, Kremenchug, Dneprodzerzhinsk, and Kakhovka. River vessels carry timber from the north and grain from the Ukraine along the lower course. Important tributaries of the Dnepr River are the Berezina, Desna, and Pripet rivers. The Pripet River and a canal connect the Dnepr with the Bug and Vistula rivers in Poland. THEODORE SHABAD

DNEPROGES DAM, *dun yep ruh JESS*, one of the large concrete dams in Russia, is located 200 miles from the mouth of the Dnepr River. It provides hydroelectric power for most of the mines and industries in the southern part of the country. The dam is 5,000 feet long and 200 feet high, and was completed in 1932. When the Germans invaded the Ukraine in 1941, the Russians blew up the dam and hydroelectric power plant. They rebuilt them after the war. The dam holds back 1,600,-000 cubic yards of water. Its power plant can generate 650,000 kilowatts of electricity. T. W. MERMEL

DNEPROPETROVSK, *NEP roh puh TRAWfsk* (pop. 707,000; alt. 210 ft.), formerly called *Ekaterinoslav*, is one of the most important industrial cities of Russia. It lies on the Dnepr River 250 miles northeast of Odessa. The city is a steel and machinery center. THEODORE SHABAD

DNESTR RIVER, *D'NYEHS tr'*, or DNIESTER, *NEES ter*, rises in the Carpathian Mountains in the dis-

A Dock and Pier in the port of Baltimore clearly show the difference between the two. The dock is the water in which the ship rides. A warehouse is on the pier, which extends into the harbor. The railway cars are on floating piers.

trict of Galicia, in central Europe, and empties into the Black Sea. The Dnestr flows to the southeast for 875 miles. For 500 miles of this distance, the Dnestr passes through part of Russia along the border of Bessarabia. Boats can travel up the Dnestr from the Black Sea to Khotin. M. KAMIL DZIEWANOWSKI

DO-IT-YOURSELF. See HOBBY (Do-It-Yourself and Handicraft; and the list of Related Articles).

DO-NOTHING KINGS. See MEROVINGIAN.

DOANE COLLEGE is a coeducational liberal arts college at Crete, Nebr. Founded in 1858 by the Congregational Church, it was the first college founded in Nebraska. For enrollment, see UNIVERSITIES (table).

DÖBEREINER, JOHANN. See FURFURAL.

DOBERMAN PINSCHER, *DOH ber muhn PIN sher,* is a very intelligent breed of dogs that was developed for police work. Its color and streamlined figure come from crossing it with the Manchester terrier. The Doberman has short glistening hair, usually black with rust-brown markings. Other colors are red or blue, with the same markings. It is a medium-sized dog, standing about 27 inches high at the shoulder, and weighing from 60 to 75 pounds.

The Doberman has rather long legs, and a lean, long head. Its tail and ears are usually cut short. The Doberman excels all other police dogs in speed. It is a high jumper and ranks next to the greyhound as a runner. It is graceful, lively, and extremely alert as a watchdog. In World War II, the Doberman served with American troops in the Southwest Pacific. The miniature pinscher weighs from 6 to 10 pounds. The breed is named after Louis Doberman, a German watchman, who first raised these dogs in the 1800's. HENRY P. DAVIS

See also DOG (color picture, Working Dogs).

DOBIE, JAMES FRANK (1888-   ), is an American author and professor, and a leading collector of Texas lore and folk tales. Dobie was born on a Texas ranch, was graduated from Southwestern University, and taught at the University of Texas. His books include *A Vaquero of the Brush Country, Coronado's Children, The Longhorns, Up the Trail from Texas, Tales of Old-Time Texas, On the Open Range, The Mustangs,* and *A Texan in England.* E. HUDSON LONG

DOBRUJA. See ROMANIA (Location).

DOCK is the water beside a wharf or pier (or between two wharves or piers) in which a ship floats. The term *dock* is often used incorrectly to mean a wharf or pier. The *wet* dock is a basin with gates to keep in or shut out water, and maintain the same water level while unloading and loading ships. Such docks are used in harbors where the tide rises and falls greatly. The river at Liverpool, England, is lined for miles with walled docks. The gates are closed when the tide goes out to keep the ships afloat. ALVIN F. HARLOW

See also DRY DOCK; MARINA.

DOCK is the name of several kinds of plants belonging to the buckwheat family. Three common perennial weeds brought into the United States and Canada belong to this family. They are the *narrow-leaf,* or *yellow, dock* (from the color of the taproot), the *sour dock,* and the *broadleaf dock.* These weeds infest meadowland, gardens, lawns, and pastures, and are common wayside weeds. These plants grow from 2 to 4 feet high, and they have long, large leaves with wavy margins. Their thick, tapering roots are used medicinally for tonics, astringents, and skin remedies. The leaves of sour dock are eaten as potherbs, or greens, but they may poison animals that have a diet low in calcium. Dock may be controlled with amino triazole sprays.

Dock usually is considered a weed. But some varieties are used as herbs and to make dyes.

Scientific Classification. The docks belong to the buckwheat family *Polygonaceae.* The narrow-leaf dock is genus *Rumex,* species *R. crispus.* The broadleaf dock is *R. obtusifolius.* The sour dock is *R. acetosa.* LOUIS PYENSON

See also BUCKWHEAT.

DOCKYARD. See NAVAL SHIPYARD.

213

DOCTOR

DOCTOR, in medicine. See MEDICINE (Careers).

DOCTOR is a degree awarded to a person by a college or university. Physicians have the *Doctor of Medicine (M.D.)* degree. Many scientists and teachers have the *Doctor of Philosophy (Ph.D.)* degree. Clergymen, dentists, lawyers, mathematicians, and other professional people may have doctors' degrees. See also CAPS AND GOWNS; DEGREE, COLLEGE.   HOLLIS L. CASWELL

DOCTOR DOLITTLE. See LOFTING, HUGH.

DOCTORFISH, one of the surgeonfishes, is a tropical marine fish, found in the East Indies. The doctorfish is sometimes called the *tang*. It is a brilliant metallic blue on top and turquoise below. It has a black tail, and its fins are outlined with bright blue. The fish gets its name because it has a sharp erectile spine in a little groove on each side of the body near the tail. This spine is shaped like a *lancet*, or surgeon's knife.

Scientific Classification. The doctorfish is a member of the family *Acanthuridae*. It is genus *Acanthurus*, species *hepatus*.   LEONARD P. SCHULTZ

DOCUMENTARY FILM. See MOTION PICTURE (Information).

DODD, THOMAS J. See CONNECTICUT (Famous Connecticut Men and Women).

DODD, WILLIAM EDWARD (1869-1940), a noted American historian, served as U.S. Ambassador to Germany from 1933 to 1937. He resigned in protest against Adolf Hitler's policies, and published the widely-read *Ambassador Dodd's Diary.*

He made lecture tours in the United States criticizing Nazi Germany. His works include the historical books *Life of Jefferson Davis, Expansion and Conflict, Statesmen of the Old South,* and *Woodrow Wilson and His Work*.

Dodd was born in Clayton, N.C. He was graduated from Virginia Polytechnic Institute. Dodd received his Ph.D. degree from the University of Leipzig, Germany. He taught history at Randolph-Macon College from 1901 to 1908, and at the University of Chicago from 1908 to 1933.   ERIC F. GOLDMAN

DODDER is a destructive weed found over most of the world. Most kinds of dodder are native to North and South America. The dodder plant twines or wraps itself around some other plant and then grows on it. It is called a *parasite* because it takes its food from the tissues of the plant on which it grows. The dodder plant grows from the ground in the spring, using the reserve food which is stored in the seed. Before long the tiny dodder twines around some nearby plant, and attaches itself by little suckers. The root and older part of the stem, which are in the soil, die, break off, and leave the dodder plant free.

The stems of dodder are very slender and look like yellow, orange, white, or brown threads. The stems twine around other plants and sprawl from one plant to another, forming tangled masses. Dodder flowers are small and whitish, and form in dense clusters.

Dodder destroys much flax, clover, and alfalfa. In regions where much dodder grows, seeds of such crops should be examined before sowing. Some dodder seeds are smaller than clover seeds and can be sifted out.

Scientific Classification. The dodder plants are members of the family *Convolvulaceae*. They make up the genus *Cuscuta*.   ARTHUR CRONQUIST

See also PARASITE.

DODDS, HAROLD WILLIS (1889-   ), an American educator, served as president of Princeton University from 1933 to 1957. He stated his educational philosophy in an essay: "We are not put into the world to sit still and know; we are put here to act." He served on the executive board of UNESCO (United Nations Educational, Scientific, and Cultural Organization) in 1946. Dodds was born at Utica, Pa., and was graduated from Grove City (Pa.) College and received his Ph.D. from the University of Pennsylvania. He taught at Purdue and Western Reserve universities before going to Princeton University.   JOHN S. BRUBACHER

DODECANESE, *doh DEK uh neece*, **ISLANDS** is a group of 13 islands in the Aegean Sea off the coast of Asia Minor. Only two of the islands, Rhodes and Cos, are really fertile, although all possess a mild and pleasant climate. The islanders raise sheep and goats, and grow wheat, vegetables, tobacco, grapes, olives, oranges, figs, and almonds. They also dive for sponges. Italy acquired the islands from Turkey in 1912. They were given to Greece after World War II. See also PATMOS; RHODES; GREECE (color map).   HARRY N. HOWARD

DODGE, GRENVILLE MELLEN. See IOWA (Famous Iowans).

DODGE, HENRY. See WISCONSIN (Famous Wisconsinites).

DODGE, JOHN. See AUTOMOBILE (Famous Men).

DODGE, JOHN W. See TENNESSEE (Famous Tennesseans).

DODGE, MARY ELIZABETH MAPES (1831-1905), an American author, wrote *Hans Brinker, or, The Silver Skates* (1865), a famous children's book about Holland. Within 30 years the book had appeared in more than

Grosset & Dunlap

An Illustration from Mary Dodge's Book, *Hans Brinker, or, The Silver Skates*. The burgomaster's daughter is shown persuading Hans to buy new skates for the important race.

100 editions and was translated into six languages. It also received a prize from the French Academy. Mrs. Dodge was recognized as a leader in the field of juvenile literature. She became editor of *St. Nicholas Magazine* when it was organized in 1873, and persuaded the best authors of the time to write for the magazine.

She was born in New York City, and grew up in a home that was a center for literary groups. William Cullen Bryant and Horace Greeley were frequent visitors. Her husband died when she was 27, leaving her with two small sons. Because she had to support them, she returned to her father's home in Newark, N.J., and started her literary career. EVELYN RAY SICKELS

DODGE CITY, Kans. (pop. 13,520; alt. 2,480 ft.), called *the Cowboy Capital of the World*, was a well-known "Wild West" frontier town. It lies on the Arkansas River, about 100 miles east of the Colorado border (see KANSAS [map]). Dodge City is the chief commercial center of southwestern Kansas. It is the seat of Ford County, and has a commission government.

Traders on the Santa Fe Trail traveled through the area in the 1800's. The town was established when the Santa Fe Railroad came in 1872. For about 10 years

Bettmann Archive

Dodge City, Kans., boasted a huge cattle market in the days of Wyatt Earp. Cowboys drove thousands of longhorn cattle through the streets to the railroad yards to load them on trains.

after 1875, it was the largest cattle market in the world. Many gunmen lived here, and such famous marshals as Wyatt Earp and "Bat" Masterson enforced the law. The present city hall stands on Boot Hill. It was called *Boot Hill* because many gunmen in the 1870's were buried there, still wearing their boots. WILLIAM F. ZORNOW

DODGSON, CHARLES LUTWIDGE. See CARROLL, LEWIS.

DODO, *DOH doh*, is an extinct bird. It died out in 1681. The dodo was about the size of a turkey. Its short legs, enormous beak, stubby flightless wings, and tuftlike tail of curly feathers gave it a strange appearance. The gray dodo lived on the island of Mauritius and the white dodo on the island of Réunion, both in the Indian Ocean. A related genus, known as the *solitaire*, lived on nearby Rodrigues Island. It was more slender than the dodo. These birds could not fly, and they were killed off by hogs and monkeys that early explorers brought to the islands. Sailors also killed many of them. Navigators of the 1600's left descriptions of the dodoes, and a specimen was taken to London in 1638. Its head and a foot are on exhibition in the British

American Museum of Natural History

The Dodo of Mauritius island had tiny wings that were so small the bird could not fly. This model of a dodo was constructed according to a painting made while the birds were still alive.

Museum. Experts have used the animal pictures of the Flemish painter Roelandt Savery (1576-1639) as a pattern for a model of the Mauritius dodo.

Scientific Classification. The dodo belonged to the order *Columbiformes*. It was in the family *Raphidae*. The gray dodo was genus *Raphus*, species *cucullatus*. The white dodo was *Raphus solitarius*. The solitaire was *Pezophaps solitarius*. ALDEN H. MILLER

DODONA, *doh DOH nuh*, was an ancient sanctuary in northwestern Greece. It was located near the present-day city of Ioannina. The sanctuary had an oracle of Zeus which was second in fame only to the oracle of Apollo at Delphi. People wrote their questions on lead tablets. They believed the rustling of the leaves of a sacred red oak tree answered them. Temple priests called *Selli* interpreted these rustlings. The Romans destroyed the sanctuary in 219 B.C. JOHN H. KENT

DOE. See DEER; GOAT.

DOE, JOHN, is the name used in legal documents to describe a person whose real name is unknown.

DOENITZ, *DUH nits,* **KARL** (1892-   ), a German admiral, became commander in chief of the German fleet in January, 1943, during World War II. Before this appointment, he directed development of the German submarine service. He invented the "wolf pack" technique of submarine warfare to penetrate convoy defenses. With the collapse of Germany in 1945, Adolf Hitler chose Doenitz to succeed him as head of the government. Doenitz concluded peace with the Allies. He was tried for war crimes at Nuremberg, and was sentenced to 10 years in prison. He was released in 1956. Doenitz was born at Berlin-Gruneau. LESTER B. MASON

215

dog

Kwiatkowski

DOG has been "man's best friend" for thousands of years. These friendly, obedient animals serve people throughout the world in work, play, and sport. Dogs live near the Eskimo's igloo, in jungle villages, in farm homes, and in city apartments. About 25,000,000 dogs live in the United States.

Dogs have earned man's love and respect with their faithfulness and devotion. Many dogs have given their own lives to save or protect their masters. Dogs guard the home, and herd cattle and sheep. Their keen sense of smell makes them fine hunting companions. Dogs like to be with people, especially children, and often howl sadly when left alone. One of the happiest sights is a dog greeting a child with joyful barks and wagging tail.

A dog can be taught to obey commands because it is intelligent and wants to please. Dogs rank fifth in intelligence among animals. They were the first animals to be tamed by man.

How Dogs Help Man

Most dogs can be trained to guard their masters' homes and property. Their barking and growling frighten burglars, and awaken sleeping families in case of fire. Fierce watchdogs protect stores and factories at night. Sometimes dogs accompany policemen on lonely beats. Bloodhounds track down criminals. Specially-trained Seeing Eye dogs lead blind persons (see SEEING EYE). German shepherds and other dogs are trained to find people buried under avalanches in the Alps.

About 8,500 dogs served in the "K9 Corps" of the United States Army during World War II. They located wounded soldiers on battlefields, and carried messages and medical supplies under fire. Other dogs helped the Coast Guard patrol the shore line of the United States.

Dogs tend cattle and sheep, and keep livestock from straying during the day. They drive the animals into the barn at night, and attack wolves and other wild beasts that might harm livestock. Dogs also kill rats and mice that eat grain.

In Belgium and some other countries, farmers use dogs to haul milk, vegetables, and other produce in small carts. Tribes that wander from place to place sometimes use dogs to drag or carry loads. A medium-sized dog can carry loads of 30 to 60 pounds on its back. In many Arctic regions, sleds pulled by dogs serve as the only means of transportation in winter (see DOG SLED).

Doctors often try out new medicines and operations on dogs before using them on humans. Frederick G. Banting and Charles H. Best used dogs in the experiments that led to the discovery of insulin (see INSULIN). Ivan P. Pavlov, a Russian doctor, discovered the conditioned reflex by experimenting with dogs (see REFLEX ACTION).

For hundreds of years, performing dogs have entertained audiences in circuses and theaters. The collies that played the role of Lassie, and the German shepherds that played the role of Rin-Tin-Tin, became famous motion-picture and television stars.

Breeds of Dogs

The American Kennel Club is the chief organization of dog breeders. It recognizes 115 breeds and varieties of purebreds. A *purebred* is a dog whose *sire* (father)

80 Breeds of Dogs are shown in color illustrations on the following pages. All color photographs are by Walter Chandoha, unless otherwise noted. All color paintings are by Edwin Megargee.

216

English Setter | Irish Setter | German Short-Haired Pointer

Brittany Spaniel

Weimaraner

Cocker Spaniel

Golden Retriever

sporting dogs

Chesapeake Bay Retriever

Irish Water Spaniel

English Springer Spaniel

English Cocker Spaniel

Pointer  | Labrador Retriever  | Gordon Setter

DOG

and *dam* (mother) belong to the same breed. When the ancestors of a purebred are known and registered by a breed club, the dog has a *pedigree*. Dog clubs and associations register only proven purebreds in their *studbooks*. The AKC registers all 115 pure breeds. Other organizations that keep studbooks include the National Coursing Association, the American Coonhunters Association, and sporting publications such as *American Field*.

The AKC divides the 115 pure breeds into six groups: (1) sporting dogs, (2) hounds, (3) working dogs, (4) terriers, (5) toy dogs, and (6) nonsporting dogs.

Sporting Dogs hunt chiefly by smelling the air to locate game birds. The sporting group includes 24 breeds of pointers, setters, retrievers, and spaniels. Pointers and setters smell the game, then "point" their bodies and noses toward it to guide the hunter. Setters take their name from dogs that were once trained to *set* (crouch) after locating game birds hiding in grass or bushes. The hunters then cast nets over the birds. Retrievers pick up birds that have been shot, and bring them back to the hunters. When sportsmen began using guns for hunting, they trained certain dogs to *spring* (scare) game birds into the air. Such dogs are called *springers*. Most spaniels hunt in this way.

Hounds include 19 breeds of dogs that hunt by smell or sight. Bloodhounds and other *scent hounds* follow an odor on the ground by running with their noses to the earth. Coonhounds and other breeds *bay*, or *give tongue*, when trailing game. When hounds bay, their barks become deep and prolonged. The basenji, an African hound, is the only dog that cannot bark. Tall, slender *sight hounds*, or *gazehounds*, watch game as they run after it. Sportsmen use such gazehounds as whippets and greyhounds for dog racing (see DOG RACING). Hounds are among the oldest known dogs. See HOUND.

Working Dogs serve man as herders, guards, sled dogs, and in other useful ways. The working group has the largest number of breeds, 29. Some of them, including Doberman pinschers and German shepherds, have become famous as war dogs. Collies, old English sheep dogs, Shetland sheep dogs, and Welsh corgis herd cattle and sheep. Siberian huskies, Alaskan Malamutes, and Samoyeds pull sleds.

Terriers hunt rats, mice, and other vermin, chiefly by digging in the ground. These dogs kill their prey by crushing it with their powerful jaws. The terrier group includes 20 breeds. Most have wire-haired coats, and bushy whiskers and eyebrows. See TERRIER.

Toy Dogs include 14 small breeds that are kept as pets. Breeders have developed some of the toys from much larger dogs. The pug, for example, might be called a small mastiff, and the miniature pinscher a pocket-size Doberman pinscher. See TOY DOG.

Nonsporting Dogs include nine breeds kept chiefly as pets. The Boston terrier is the only nonsporting breed developed in the United States. This breed is classed as a nonsporting dog, although it is partly descended from crossbreeding with an English terrier. The Lhasa apso guarded the monasteries of Tibet 800 years ago. The Chinese raised chow chows, commonly called *chows*, as hunters. Poodles once served French hunters as retrievers.

Other Breeds of dogs are not registered by the American Kennel Club, because so few are raised in the United States. These breeds include the Australian kelpie, British border collie, Mexican hairless, Russian owtchah, and Italian spinone. Breeders occasionally exhibit these dogs at shows as *miscellaneous* breeds.

Crossbreds and Mongrels make up the largest number of dogs throughout the world. A *crossbred* has parents that belong to different breeds. *Mongrels* have such mixed parentage that no one breed can be recognized. Crossbreds and mongrels often are as good pets as pure-

HOW BIG ARE DOGS?

Irish Wolfhounds rank as the largest dogs and Chihuahuas as the smallest. The Saint Bernard is one of the heaviest dogs. Other breeds range in size between these extremes.

Irish Wolfhound   Saint Bernard   Collie   Cocker Spaniel   Chihuahua

breds. They vary greatly in size and appearance.

Wild Dogs still roam in hungry packs in many parts of the world. They include wolves, coyotes, foxes, jackals, the dholes of eastern India, the South American bush dogs, the African hunting dogs, and the dingoes of Australia. Many of these dogs have great natural hunting abilities. Wild dogs sometimes mate with tame dogs. The puppies of some wild dogs have been tamed.

The Body of the Dog

Dogs range in size from the Chihuahua, which is not much larger than a pigeon, to the Irish wolfhound, which may stand nearly 3 feet high at the shoulders. Mastiffs and Saint Bernards, the heaviest dogs, weigh as much as 180 pounds.

Coat. Some dogs have long coats and others have short coats. The hair may be curly as on the poodle, or straight as on the Pekingese. The collie's coat feels rough, and the Kerry blue terrier's coat is soft. Most dogs have two coats. The outer coat protects the dog's body from rain and snow, and the undercoat keeps the animal warm. In winter, a dog's undercoat grows thick and furry. Dogs shed their undercoats in summer and grow them back in autumn.

Bones. All dogs have the same number of bones, but the length, shape, and size differ from breed to breed. Long leg bones and sloping ribs make the greyhound tall and slim. Stockier dogs, such as the German rottweiler, have rounder ribs and heavier bones. A dog's front leg bones are usually straight.

Dogs, like cats, have five claws on their front feet and four on their hind feet. But dogs cannot pull their claws inside their paws as cats can.

Nose. Dogs recognize objects by smell, much as man recognizes them by sight. A dog can detect the scent of an object which its master has held in his hand for only a second. Avalanche shepherd dogs of Switzerland can smell men buried under 20 feet of snow. Moisture helps a dog detect odors, and most dogs have moist noses. Dogs lick their noses to keep them moist. However, a healthy dog can have a warm, dry nose.

Mouth. The mouths of dogs differ in shape according to the breed. For example, bulldogs have broad jaws and collies have narrow jaws. Puppies have 32 temporary teeth, which they shed when they are about 5 months old. Adult dogs have 42 permanent teeth, including four large teeth, two in each jaw, called *fangs*.

DOG TERMS

Bitch is an adult female dog.
Canine means a dog or doglike. It comes from *canis*, the Latin word for dog.
Crossbred is a dog whose parents belong to different breeds.
Dog is an adult male dog. However, the term is generally used for all dogs, regardless of age or sex.
Litter is a group of puppies born at one time.
Mongrel is a dog of such mixed ancestry that no one breed can be recognized.
Pack is a group of dogs.
Pedigree is a record of a purebred dog's ancestors.
Puppy is a dog less than 1 year old.
Purebred is a dog whose parents belong to the same breed.
Studbook is a book in which breeders register the pedigrees of dogs.
Whelp is an *unweaned* puppy, or one that still drinks its mother's milk.

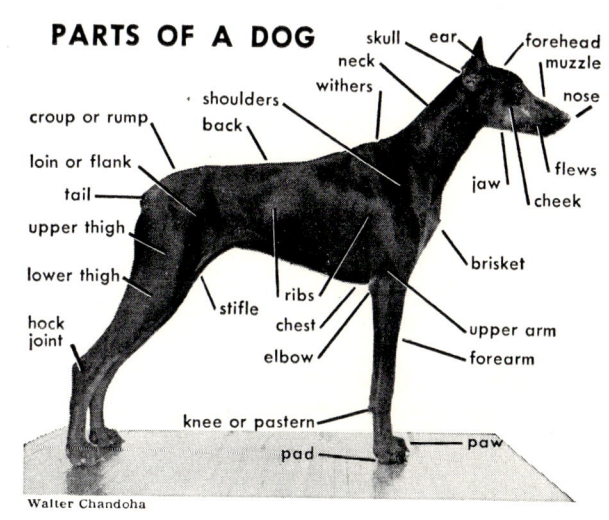

PARTS OF A DOG

Walter Chandoha

Dogs tear meat with their fangs. A dog drinks by lapping liquids with its tongue, a few drops at a time.

Ears. A dog can hear sounds 250 yards away that most people cannot hear beyond 25 yards. The human ear can detect sound waves that vibrate at frequencies up to 20,000 times a second. But dogs can hear sound waves that vibrate at frequencies of more than 30,000 times a second. Some persons signal to their dogs by blowing on high-pitched whistles that cannot be heard by humans.

The outsides of a dog's ears have flaps of skin called *leathers*. These protect the dog's ears, and can be moved to help catch and locate sounds. Small dogs can usually hear better than large dogs.

Eyes. Dogs cannot see as well as men. They have difficulty telling colors apart, except by the degree of brightness, and are considered color blind. A dog sees objects first by their movement, second by their brightness, and third by their shape.

Body Functions of a dog differ only slightly from those of a human. For example, a dog's normal body temperature is about 101° F., only a little higher than a human's normal temperature of 98.6° F. A dog's heart beats between 70 and 120 times a minute, compared with the human heart, which beats 70 to 80 times a minute. When a dog becomes excited or overheated, it sticks out its tongue and *pants* (breathes heavily). The extra air cools the inside of the animal's body. Dogs have sweat glands on their noses, foot pads, and hairy parts of the body. The glands on the hairy surfaces are not active in cooling the body, but protect the skin from an unusual increase in temperature.

Life History. A female dog carries its young about 60 days before the puppies are born. A puppy is born blind and helpless. Its eyes open about 10 to 14 days after birth. Dogs give birth to litters of 1 to 12 or more puppies. One Welsh foxhound gave birth to 23 puppies, the largest recorded litter. The mother provides milk for her puppies until they are 4 to 5 weeks old. Dogs become fully grown at 8 months to 2 years of age, depending on the size of the breed. Large dogs develop more slowly than small dogs.

The average dog lives for about 12 or 13 years. A 6-month-old puppy compares in development with a 6-year-old child. The first two years of a dog's life equal about the first 24 years of a man's life. After the second

nonsporting dogs

Dalmatian
Camera Clix

Schipperke

Boston Terrier

Keeshond

French Bulldog
Ira Haas, Photo Researchers

Poodle

Chow Chow

Bulldog

220

hounds

Basset Hound

Irish Wolfhound

Bloodhound

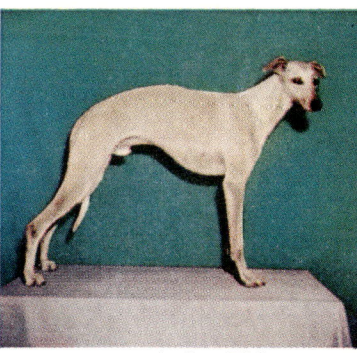

Greyhound

Basenji

Whippet

Borzoi

Rhodesian Ridgeback

Saluki

American Foxhound

Black and Tan Coonhound

Afghan Hound

Norwegian Elkhound

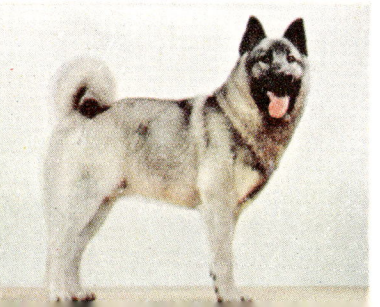

Dachshund

Beagle

HOW TO BUILD A DOGHOUSE

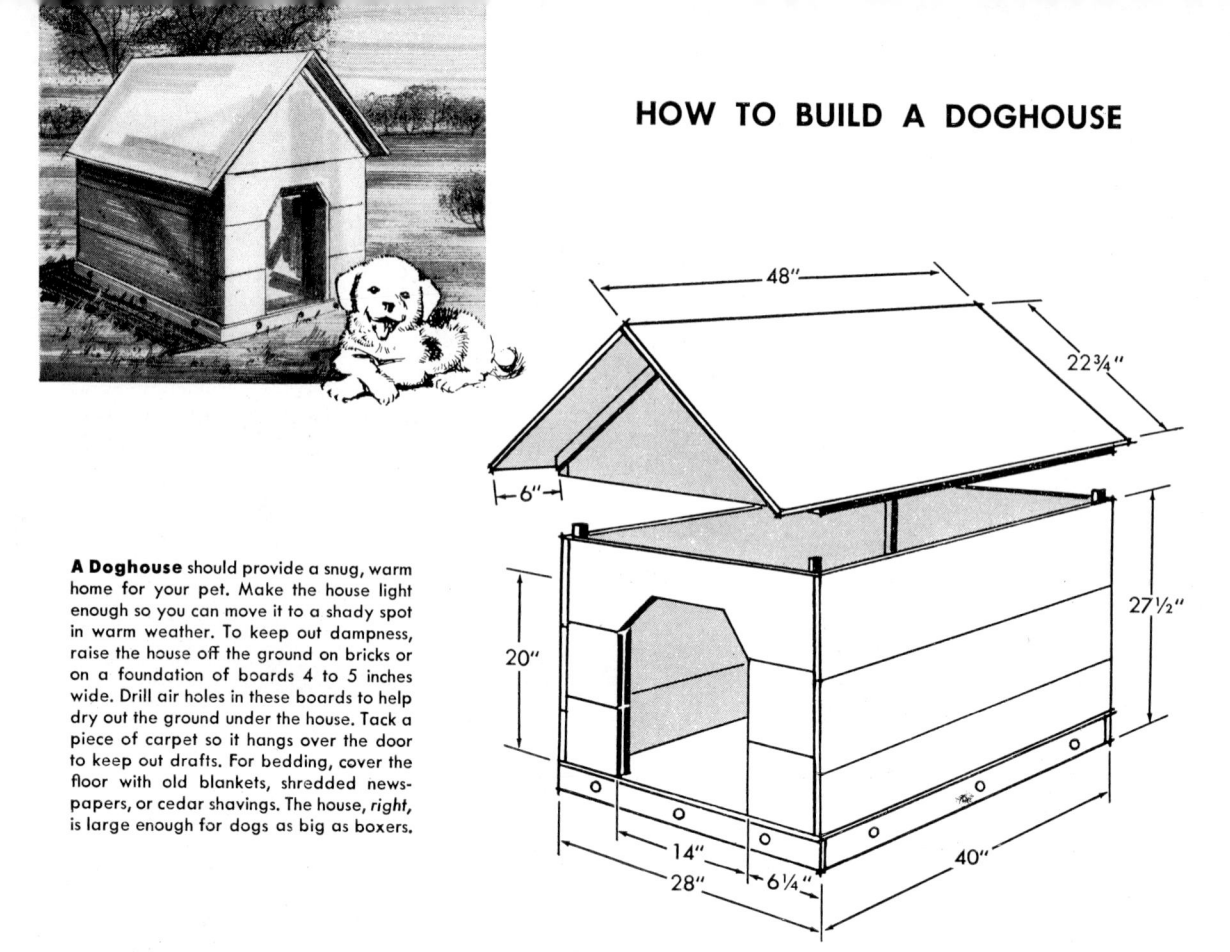

A Doghouse should provide a snug, warm home for your pet. Make the house light enough so you can move it to a shady spot in warm weather. To keep out dampness, raise the house off the ground on bricks or on a foundation of boards 4 to 5 inches wide. Drill air holes in these boards to help dry out the ground under the house. Tack a piece of carpet so it hangs over the door to keep out drafts. For bedding, cover the floor with old blankets, shredded newspapers, or cedar shavings. The house, *right*, is large enough for dogs as big as boxers.

year, each year of a dog's life equals about four years of a man's life. For example, a 13-year-old dog compares in age with a 70-year-old man.

Instincts and Intelligence. Dogs have many of the instincts of their wild ancestors. For example, all dogs gobble their food as though they were keeping other animals from grabbing it. They turn around several times before lying down, in much the same way that wild dogs trample grass to make a sheltered bed. A frightened dog curls its tail between its legs to keep it out of the reach of enemies. Male dogs urinate on trees to tell other dogs they have been there.

The ability of dogs to learn to obey commands is one mark of their intelligence. But for the first three weeks of a puppy's life, it knows nothing and needs only warmth and food. In the fourth week of life, the puppy can see, hear, and smell, and it begins to learn. From the fourth to the seventh week, the puppy starts playing and responds to humans. From the seventh to the twelfth week, the puppy can learn simple commands such as "Let's go for a walk." Such orders, if repeated several times, come to mean to the dog exactly what they mean to a person. Some dogs seem to have the power to reason, or solve problems such as how to get food from a box by pressing a lever.

How to Care for Your Dog

Before you buy a dog, consider the size of your house or apartment. Large dogs, such as great Danes and collies, need big yards in which to run and play. Smaller dogs can live in smaller homes. But even large dogs will be happy in small homes if you take them out regularly for long walks. All dogs need daily exercise.

A purebred usually makes a better choice for a pet than a mongrel. You can tell in advance what a purebred will look like and how big it will be when fully grown. Breeders raise purebreds to have good health and good tempers. A puppy's disposition depends partly on the way you treat it. If you treat your puppy roughly, it will grow into a rough dog. Treat it gently, and it will become a gentle pet.

A puppy should be about 8 weeks old before you take it home. It should appear lively and playful. Its eyes should be bright and clear, its skin clean, and its coat shiny. Your puppy, like a baby, depends upon you for everything—food, shelter, and training.

Feeding. No one can tell exactly how much any dog should eat. If your dog becomes fat, feed it less food. If it appears thin, feed it more food. Dogs of all ages need meat every day. You may give a fully grown dog table scraps that contain at least one-third meat. Do not give your dog bones. Bone splinters can injure him if he swallows them. Serve your dog warm food in a clean dish. Throw uneaten food away after about 20 minutes. Wash the food dish thoroughly every day. Keep cool, fresh drinking water available at all times in a dish that the dog cannot tip over. The feeding table with this article is based on figures from the National Research Council. It shows the estimated amounts of food a dog needs each day according to its weight.

Small daily amounts of vitamin-rich cod-liver oil help fortify puppies and adult dogs in cold weather. A veterinarian can prescribe the correct doses of cod-liver oil and other vitamins and minerals for your dog (see VETERINARY MEDICINE). Dog-food companies make a wide variety of dry meals and canned meat foods that supply most of the necessary vitamins and minerals.

A DOG'S MENU

Three Months Old

Breakfast—cereal and milk.
Lunch—meat and crumbled bread or toast.
Dinner—repeat breakfast.
Bedtime—repeat lunch.

Six Months Old

Breakfast—cereal and milk.
Lunch—meat or boiled egg, and meal.
Dinner—meat with cooked, mashed vegetables.

Ten Months Old and Adult

Breakfast—cereal or meal, soaked in milk.
Dinner—meat with vegetables or meal.

RECOMMENDED FOODS

Cereals: malt cereal, pablum, and dry breakfast foods such as corn flakes or shredded wheat.

Eggs should always be cooked.

Meal is a ground biscuit food sold for dogs. It should be soaked in milk or meat soup. Dogs also eat unground dog biscuits.

Meats: canned dog foods, chicken, fish, horsemeat, kidney, lamb, liver, pork, and raw chopped beef or cooked beef. Fish and chicken meat must be carefully boned.

Milk Foods: buttermilk, cottage cheese, fresh whole milk, and evaporated milk.

Vegetables: beans, carrots, onions, peas, spinach, and tomatoes. Except for tomatoes, vegetables should be cooked. Peas and beans should be mashed.

Shelter. A dog that lives indoors needs a clean sleeping box lined with blankets or shredded paper. Short-haired dogs need more warmth than long-haired ones. A dog should not sleep next to a radiator or on a cement floor. A dog that lives outdoors needs a weatherproof kennel, or doghouse, with a dry, warm floor covered with cedar shavings, sawdust, or blankets.

Grooming. A daily brushing cleans the dog's coat and stimulates the skin. It also stops a dog from scratching itself to remove loose hair. A dog should be washed as seldom as possible. Too much washing can cause a dog's skin to dry out and crack. If your dog needs a bath, wash it with warm water and soap. Rinse and dry the animal thoroughly. Puppies should not be washed until they are 6 months old. Trim your dog's toenails about once every two months. Clean its teeth weekly with a damp cloth dipped in salt. If your dog's eyes run, wipe

FEEDING TABLE

	Meal or Other Dry Foods		Canned Dog Foods	
Weight of Dog lbs.	Adult lbs.	Puppy lbs.	Adult lbs.	Puppy lbs.
5	¼	½	½	1
10	⅓	⅔	1	2
15	½	¾	1¼	2½
20	½	1	1½	3
30	¾	1½	2	4⅓
50	1⅓	2½	3½	7
70	1¾	3½	4¾	9⅔
110	2¾	—	7	—

DOG

them gently with cotton moistened with a weak boric-acid solution. Clean your dog's ears with cotton if they look brown or dirty inside or are filled with wax.

Diseases. Dogs suffer many diseases that attack humans, including colds, tonsillitis, and pneumonia. A veterinarian should always treat a sick dog. Signs of illness include fever, coughing, running eyes and nose, and excessive water drinking.

Distemper and hepatitis are two common virus diseases that attack dogs. Veterinarians can vaccinate puppies against them. Chills, fever, reddened eyes, and loss of appetite may be signs of these diseases. Dogs also suffer from rabies if they are bitten by an animal that has this rare but serious disease. Some communities require that dogs be inoculated against rabies. See DISTEMPER; HEPATITIS; RABIES.

Most puppies suffer from worms. Signs of worms include vomiting, bloating, and general unfitness. A veterinarian can provide pills to rid the dog of worms. Fleas are common pests in summer, and transmit tapeworms to dogs. Comb fleas off your dog, or dust it with flea powder. Use only flea powders made for dogs, or the animal may become poisoned by licking its coat. Dogs also may suffer from skin diseases such as mange.

Puppies often suffer fits, or convulsions. If a puppy has a fit, it should be shut in a box so that it cannot injure itself. A fit is not a disease, but a sign that something is wrong. A veterinarian should examine the dog.

Laws. Most cities and states have laws that require a dog owner to buy a license for his dog. Many communities also have laws that require dogs to be leashed outdoors. Laws usually make the dog owner responsible for any damage caused by his pet.

Other laws protect dogs, and punish persons who beat, starve, or are otherwise cruel to them. These laws have been passed largely through the work of such groups as the Society for the Prevention of Cruelty to Animals and other humane societies.

How to Train Your Dog

Dogs need to be taught good manners just as children do. Training makes a dog easier to care for, cleaner in the house, and safer on the street. An untrained dog that roams outdoors and barks constantly can annoy an entire neighborhood.

Housebreaking a puppy should start as soon as you bring it home. If the puppy must stay indoors, place newspapers on the floor of the kitchen or another room that will not be easily damaged. When the puppy wets, rush it to the papers. Always place the newspapers in the same spot. Take the puppy to its papers immediately after it eats, plays, and wakes up. Praise the pup when it wets where you want it to. Scold your pet when it has an accident. But do not rub its nose in the droppings. Use the same method when you are training the dog to go outdoors. Watch where the puppy wets. Then always take it to these places when you take the pet outside.

Obedience Training begins with teaching your dog to walk on a leash, to come when called, to sit, to lie down, and to heel. Training should start when your puppy is 8 weeks old. Give a 15-minute lesson several times a day. Use kind words and pats, and reward your dog when it does something right. Do not begin a

Shetland Sheep Dog
Ira Haas, Photo Researchers

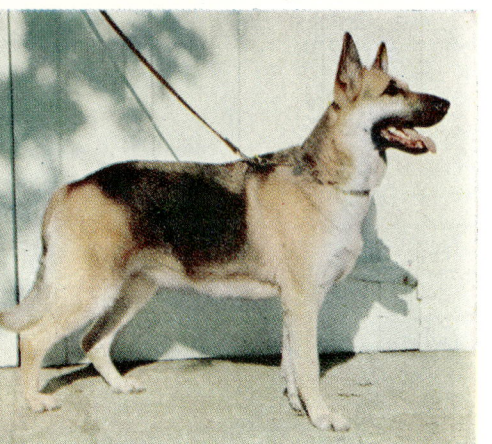

Welsh Corgi (Pembroke)

Siberian Husky

working

German Shepherd

Puli

Mastiff

Great Dane

Old English Sheep Dog

Saint Bernard

Three Lions

dogs

Samoyed

Boxer

Newfoundland

Collie

Alaskan Malamute

Doberman Pinscher

Standard Schnauzer

Great Pyrenees

DOG

COMMON SAYINGS ABOUT DOGS

Barking dogs never bite describes people who sound more dangerous than they really are.

Barking up the wrong tree means to look for something in the wrong place.

Dog in a manger describes a person who keeps others from using something that he himself cannot use. It comes from Aesop's fable of a dog that crawled into a manger of hay and prevented a horse from eating, even though dogs do not eat hay.

Every dog has his day is an expression used when something pleasant happens to a person, especially one who has been having bad luck.

Let sleeping dogs lie means to leave a situation undisturbed.

Tail wagging the dog means, for example, that an unimportant member of a group is actually directing everyone's activities.

You can't teach an old dog new tricks is often used to describe a person who refuses to change his ways, or to learn a new way of doing something.

---

second exercise until the first one has been learned. Be patient but firm. The dog must understand that a command means instant obedience.

Put a collar around your dog's neck before training it to walk on a leash. After the dog gets used to wearing a collar, take it out walking with a leash. Your dog will probably fight the leash at first. But it will soon learn that the leash means a walk. You may also want to teach your dog to *heel*, or walk by your side. To do this, hold the dog at your left side on a short leash. Then walk forward swiftly. Strike the dog lightly on the nose with a folded newspaper if it tries to run in front of you. At the same time give the command, "heel."

To teach your dog to come when called, fasten a light rope about 20 to 30 feet long to its collar. Let the dog romp at the full length of the cord for a while, and then call it. If your pet does not come, pull it toward you. Repeat this until the dog learns to come on command. To teach the dog to sit, hold it near you on a short leash and order it to sit. Hold the leash tightly to keep its head up. At the same time, push down on the animal's hindquarters with your hand until it is in a sitting position.

To break your dog of the habit of jumping up on people, bring your knee up against its chest when it leaps up to greet you. At the same time, repeat the order, "down." Your knee may knock the dog over, but this will teach it to stay down when told to do so. Puppies often howl and whine at night. A ticking clock placed next to a puppy's box will often keep him quiet.

Tricks. Many people enjoy teaching their pets to shake hands, play dead, roll over, sit up, and do other tricks. In general, follow the same methods to teach a dog tricks as you would to teach it obedience commands. For example, to teach a dog to shake hands, pick up one of its front paws, and at the same time say "shake hands." Keep repeating this until the dog learns to offer a paw when you ask it to shake hands.

Dog Shows. Hundreds of dog shows are held in the United States every year. The American Kennel Club licenses judges, and supervises most of these shows. They are usually called *bench shows*, because the dogs are exhibited in stalls mounted on benches. A dog must be registered with the AKC to be entered in such contests. The Westminster Kennel Club of New York City stages one of the most important shows on the second Monday and Tuesday in February at Madison Square Garden. This show, held every year since 1877, is one of the oldest regular sporting events in the United States.

The judges of a dog show pick the best dog of each breed. Next, the judges choose the best dog of its group

William Brown

Purebred Dogs, such as the poodle, *left,* receive expert grooming before appearing in shows.

The Westminster Kennel Club Show ranks as one of the most important dog shows in the United States. It is held every February in New York City. Only prize-winning purebreds, such as the hounds being judged *below,* can compete in the Westminster.

Evelyn M. Shafer

RECOGNIZED BREEDS OF PUREBRED DOGS

Breed	Country and Probable Date of Origin	Average Wt. in lbs.
SPORTING GROUP		
American Water Spaniel	United States, 1800's	25-45
Brittany Spaniel	France, 1800's	30-40
Chesapeake Bay Retriever	United States, 1800's	55-75
Clumber Spaniel	England, 1800's	35-65
Cocker Spaniel	England, 1800's	22-28
Curly-Coated Retriever	England, 1800's	60-70
English Cocker Spaniel	England, 1800's	26-34
English Setter	England, 1500's	50-70
English Springer Spaniel	England, 1800's	35-50
Field Spaniel	England, 1700's	35-40
Flat-Coated Retriever	England, 1800's	60-70
German Short-Haired Pointer	Germany, about 1900	45-70
German Wire-Haired Pointer	Germany, 1870	55-65
Golden Retriever	Scotland, 1870	55-70
Gordon Setter	Scotland, 1600's	45-75
Griffon (Wire-Haired Pointing)	The Netherlands and France, 1800's	50-60
Irish Setter	Ireland, 1700's	50-60
Irish Water Spaniel	Ireland, 1800's	45-65
Labrador Retriever	Newfoundland, 1800's	55-75
Pointer	Spain, Portugal, Eastern Europe, and England, about 1650	55-60
Sussex Spaniel	England, 1800's	35-45
Vizsla	Hungary, 1000's	50
Weimaraner	Germany, 1800's	55-85
Welsh Springer Spaniel	Wales, 1700's	40
HOUND GROUP		
Afghan Hound	Sinai Peninsula, Egypt, 4000-3000 B.C.	50-60
American Foxhound	United States, 1600's	60-70
Basenji	Africa, 3400 B.C.	22-24
Basset Hound	France, 1600's	25-45
Beagle	England, Wales, 1600's	18-30
Bloodhound	The Middle East, 100 B.C.	80-110
Borzoi	Russia, 1600's	60-105
Coonhound (Black and Tan)	England, 1700's	50-60
Dachshund	Germany, 1700's	5-20
English Foxhound	England, 1600's	60-75
Greyhound	Egypt, 4000-3500 B.C.	60-70
Harrier	France, 1000's	40-50
Irish Wolfhound	Ireland, 400's	105-140
Norwegian Elkhound	Norway, 5000-4000 B.C.	50
Otter Hound	England, 1300's	65
Rhodesian Ridgeback	Africa, 1700's	65-75
Saluki	Egypt, 7000-6000 B.C.	60
Scottish Deerhound	Scotland, 1500's	75-110
Whippet	England, 1800's	18-23
TOY GROUP		
Affenpinscher	Europe, 1700's	7-8
Brussels Griffon	Belgium, 1600's	6-12
Chihuahua	Mexico, 1500's or earlier	1-6
English Toy Spaniel	Japan or China, Ancient Times	9-12
Italian Greyhound	Italy, 100 B.C.	6-10
Japanese Spaniel	China, Ancient Times	7
Maltese	Malta, 800 B.C. or earlier	2-7
Miniature Pinscher	Germany, 1700's	6-10
Papillon	Spain, 1500's	5-11
Pekingese	China, 700's	6-10
Pomeranian	Pomerania, Poland, 1800's	3-7
Pug	China, 1700's	14-18
Silky Terrier	Australia, about 1900	8-10
Yorkshire Terrier	England, 1800's	4-8

Breed	Country and Probable Date of Origin	Average Wt. in lbs.
WORKING GROUP		
Alaskan Malamute	Alaska, 1000 B.C. or earlier	50-85
Belgian Malinois	Belgium, 1800's	50-55
Belgian Sheep Dog	Belgium, 1800's	55-60
Belgian Tervuren	Belgium, about 1880	55
Bernese Mountain Dog	Switzerland, 100 B.C.	50-75
Bouvier des Flandres	Flanders, 1800's	70
Boxer	Germany, 1800's	62-75
Briard	France, 1100's	70-80
Bull-Mastiff	England, 1800's	100-115
Collie	Scotland, 1600's	50-75
Doberman Pinscher	Germany, 1800's	60-75
German Shepherd Dog	Germany, 1800's	60-85
Giant Schnauzer	Bavaria, 1600-1800	75
Great Dane	Germany, 1500's	120-150
Great Pyrenees	France, 1800-1000 B.C.	90-125
Komondor	Hungary, 900's	90
Kuvasz	Tibet, 1200's	70
Mastiff	England, 55 B.C. or earlier	165-185
Newfoundland	Newfoundland, 1600's	110-150
Old English Sheep Dog	England, 1800's	50-65
Puli	Hungary, 1000's	30-35
Rottweiler	Germany, about A.D. 50	80-90
Saint Bernard	Switzerland, 1600's	165-180
Samoyed	Northern Siberia, 1000 B.C. or earlier	35-60
Schnauzer (Standard)	Germany, before 1400	35-40
Shetland Sheep Dog	Shetland Islands, 1600's	16
Siberian Husky	Siberia, 1000 B.C. or earlier	40-50
Welsh Corgi (Cardigan)	Wales, 1200 B.C. or earlier	15-25
Welsh Corgi (Pembroke)	Wales, 1107	18-24
TERRIER GROUP		
Airedale Terrier	England, 1800's	40-50
Australian Terrier	Australia, 1885	12-14
Bedlington Terrier	England, 1800's	22-24
Border Terrier	Scottish-English border, 1700's	11-15
Bull Terrier	England, 1800's	30-60
Cairn Terrier	Scotland, 1700's	13-14
Dandie Dinmont Terrier	England and Scotland, about 1700	14-20
Fox Terrier	England, 1700's	15-19
Irish Terrier	Ireland, 1700's	25-27
Kerry Blue Terrier	Ireland, 1800's	30-40
Lakeland Terrier	England, 1800's	15-17
Manchester Terrier	England, 1800's	5-22
Norwich Terrier	England, 1880	10-15
Schnauzer (Miniature)	Germany, 1800's	15
Scottish Terrier	Scotland, 1800's	18-22
Sealyham Terrier	Wales, 1800's	20
Skye Terrier	Scotland, 1600's	25
Staffordshire Terrier	England, 1800's	35-50
Welsh Terrier	Wales, 1700's	20
West Highland White Terrier	Scotland, 1600's	13-19
NONSPORTING GROUP		
Boston Terrier	Boston, Mass., 1870	12-25
Bulldog	England, 1200's	40-50
Chow Chow	China, 150 B.C.	50-60
Dalmatian	Dalmatia, Austria, 1700's	40-50
French Bulldog	France, 1400's	18-28
Keeshond	Holland, 1500's	35-40
Lhasa Apso	Tibet, about 1100	15
Poodle	Germany, 1500's	7-55
Schipperke	Belgium, 1600's	15

Source: American Kennel Club

Each breed listed in this table has a separate article in WORLD BOOK

terriers

Bull Terrier

Staffordshire Terrier

Kerry Blue Terrier

Airedale Terrier

Welsh Terrier

Miniature Schnauzer

Fox Terrier

Manchester Terrier

Scottish Terrier

Irish Terrier

Dandie Dinmont Terrier

Bedlington Terrier

Skye Terrier

Sealyham Terrier

Cairn Terrier

Toy Manchester Terrier

Miniature Pinscher

Pekingese
Ylla, Rapho-Guillumette

Chihuahua

Mexican Hairless

toy dogs

Toy Poodle

Pomeranian

Brussels Griffon

Maltese

Yorkshire Terrier
Camera Clix

Pug

229

DOG

in each of the six main groups of dogs. From these winners, the judges name the best dog in the show. Judges rate a dog on such points as color, posture, the condition of its coat and teeth, the shape and size of its body, and the way it moves about.

Field Trials test the hunting ability of sporting dogs and hounds. In bird-dog field trials, judges rate the dogs on such points as endurance, ability to scent game, obedience to a handler's commands, and the thoroughness with which the dogs cover the hunting area. In retriever field trials, judges rate the dogs on their ability to find quickly and return without damage the birds that hunters have shot.

Other events for dogs include sheep-dog trials, obedience trials, sled-dog racing, and coursing and racing contests. Sheep-dog trials test the ability of the animals to herd flocks of sheep. In obedience trials, judges rate dogs on their ability to obey commands. Coursing contests test the skill of greyhounds in running down rabbits.

History

All dogs are probably descended from an animal called *Tomarctus*. This animal lived about 15,000,000 years ago. It probably looked much like a wolf. It had a wedge-shaped head; long, low body; thick coat; and long, furry tail. Descendants of Tomarctus developed into wolves, jackals, coyotes, foxes, and other wild dogs that spread throughout the world.

Stone Age people who lived in Europe 10,000 to 20,000 years ago tamed dogs to help them track game. About 8,000 years ago, the ancient Egyptians raised greyhound-like dogs to hunt antelope. Several thousand years later, the Egyptians developed Saluki hunting

---
FAMOUS DOGS IN HISTORY AND LEGEND

Aibe was a wolfhound famed for its hunting ability. The King of Connacht in Ireland offered 6,000 cows for Aibe in the 1100's.

Argus, Ulysses' hunting dog, was the only creature that recognized the Greek hero when he returned home disguised as a beggar after 20 years of adventure.

Balto, an Eskimo dog, led a dog team that carried diphtheria serum 600 miles through an Alaskan blizzard from Nenana to Nome in 1925.

Barry, a Saint Bernard, rescued 40 persons when they became lost in the snows of Switzerland's Saint Bernard Pass about 1800.

Buddy, a German shepherd, in 1928 became the first seeing-eye dog for the blind.

Caesar, a terrier, was the pet of King Edward VII of Great Britain. He walked ahead of kings and princes in his master's funeral procession in 1910.

Cerberus, the three-headed dog of Greek mythology, guarded the gates to the underworld (see CERBERUS).

Fala, a Scottish terrier, became famous as the devoted pet of President Franklin Delano Roosevelt.

Greyfriars Bobby, a Skye terrier, accompanied his Scotch master to Edinburgh every market day. After the man died in 1858, Bobby lived about 10 years by his grave until he died at the age of 14.

Igloo, a fox terrier, was the special pet of Admiral Richard E. Byrd. He flew with Byrd on flights over the North and South poles.

Laika became the world's first space traveler. Russian scientists sent the small animal aloft in an artificial earth satellite in 1957.

---

dogs. *Saluki* is an Arabic word meaning *the noble one*. These dogs are probably the oldest known breed (see SALUKI). North American Indians tamed dogs as early as 4,000 years ago. The ancient Greeks raised large lion-hunting dogs called mastiffs. The Romans kept dogs as pets, and also used them to hunt and to herd sheep. The ancient Chinese bred watchdogs and hunting dogs.

In the Middle Ages, from about A.D. 400 to 1400, knights kept hounds for hunting deer, elk, and other game. English sportsmen in the 1500's developed the bulldog for the sport of *baiting*, or fighting, bulls. The various breeds of dogs gradually became fixed in size, color, and the ability to perform certain tasks. People named the breeds after the game they hunted, the work they performed, and the places where they developed.

Scientific Classification. All dogs belong to the family *Canidae*. Tamed dogs are in the genus *Canis*, species *familiaris*.   JOSEPHINE Z. RINE

Related Articles. All the dogs listed in the table of *Recognized Breeds and Varieties of Purebred Dogs* with this article have separate articles in WORLD BOOK. Other related articles include:

DOG FAMILY

Coyote	Fox	Wolf
Dingo	Jackal	

UNCLASSIFIED

Breeding	Pet	Spitz
Dog Racing	Police Dog	Terhune, Albert
Dog Sled	Seeing Eye	Payson
Hound	Sheep Dog	Terrier
Humane Society	Society for the	Toy Dog
Insurance (picture, Dogs Can Be Insured)	Prevention of Cruelty to Animals	

Outline

I. **How Dogs Help Man**
II. **Breeds of Dogs**
   A. Sporting Dogs   F. Nonsporting Dogs
   B. Hounds   G. Other breeds
   C. Working Dogs   H. Crossbreds and Mongrels
   D. Terriers   I. Wild Dogs
   E. Toy Dogs
III. **The Body of the Dog**
   A. Coat   E. Ears   H. Life History
   B. Bones   F. Eyes   I. Instincts and
   C. Nose   G. Body Functions   Intelligence
   D. Mouth
IV. **How to Care for Your Dog**
   A. Feeding   C. Grooming   E. Laws
   B. Shelter   D. Diseases
V. **How to Train Your Dog**
   A. Housebreaking   D. Dog Shows
   B. Obedience Training   E. Field Trials
   C. Tricks
VI. **History**

Questions

What is the only dog that cannot bark?
What is probably the oldest known breed of dog? Where did this breed originate?
Why do dogs turn around before lying down? Why do they gobble their food?
What are the six main groups of purebred dogs? What other kinds of dogs are there?
Why do purebred dogs usually make better pets than mongrels?
Why do most dogs have two coats?
How long does the average dog live?
Why does a dog *pant* when it is overheated?

DOG DAYS are hot, sticky summer days. The ancient Greeks originated the name *dog days*. They applied it to the period when the dog star, Sirius, rose with the sun, a period of about 40 days beginning in early July and ending near mid-August. The rising of Sirius does not actually affect the weather. But the middle part of the 40-day period happens to occur at the same time as most of the uncomfortably hot days. Some people once believed that "dog days" were so named because dogs were most likely to contract rabies during the hot weather. This belief is not true, and the superstition has largely disappeared. P. E. CHURCH

DOG RACING is a sport in which dogs chase a mechanical "rabbit" that runs around a race track on an electric rail. The track is oval, and usually is about 550 yards long. An American, Oliver B. Smith, invented this type of dog racing in 1919. Eight dogs usually compete in a dog race. The races usually feature two breeds of dogs, the greyhound and the whippet (see GREYHOUND; WHIPPET).

DOGBANE

on the ground in these areas during the winter. The sleds are usually made of wood and are from 6 to 13 feet long and from 12 to 24 inches wide. They have either wooden or metal runners.

The stocky, hardy dogs harnessed to the sleds can move over ice and snow easily because of their size and agility. Dog teams generally include from 7 to 10 dogs. Each team has a lead dog that guides the others. It obeys commands given by the driver.

In an average day, a dog team can pull a load twice the team's weight about 25 miles, at a speed of from 2 to 5 miles an hour. Sled dogs weigh between 50 and 100 pounds. One team of dogs can haul more than 1,000 pounds. ELMER HARP, JR.

See also ALASKA (color picture); ESKIMO (Transportation); ESKIMO DOG; MANITOBA (Annual Events; color picture [Dog-Sled Races]); SLED.

DOG STAR. See SIRIUS.

City of Miami News Bureau

Racing Greyhounds round a turn at one of the four dog tracks in Miami, Fla. Dog racing attracts many fans during the Miami racing season, which runs from November until summer.

The sport is popular in Florida, Massachusetts, and certain other areas in the United States. Large crowds also attend dog races in Great Britain. The annual Waterloo Cup race, held in Liverpool, England, is perhaps the most important dog race.

In ancient times, dogs were trained to race after live game. This sport is called *coursing*. The Saluki, a popular racing dog in ancient Egypt, is still used in some European dog races (see SALUKI). FRED RUSSELL

DOG SHOW. See DOG (Dog Shows).

DOG SLED is used for transportation in such Arctic regions as Alaska, northern Canada, and Siberia. Dog sleds often provide the only means of carrying supplies

DOGBANE is the name of 11 closely related plants. They grow in the north temperate zone, mostly in the United States and Canada. All the dogbanes are poisonous green plants which contain a milky bitter juice. But they are not very dangerous because most grazing animals dislike the bitter juice and will not eat them.

A common dogbane called the *spreading dogbane*, or *honeybloom*, has light-green leaves and clusters of pale pink flowers. It has a bitter root which physicians sometimes use to cause vomiting. Another dogbane called the *Canada* or *Indian hemp* has greenish-white flowers that grow in clusters. These clusters are followed by long, slender pods. The bark of this dogbane produces

Three Lions

Dog-Sled Racing is a popular sport in Canada and the northern United States. When one driver overtakes another, he must be given unlimited right of way to pass. This race was run at Lake Placid, N.Y.

The Dogbane Blossoms grow on the ends of thin spreading branches. The flower has the shape of a tiny bell.

a long, strong white fiber that is used to make nets.

Scientific Classification. Dogbanes belong to the dogbane family, *Apocynaceae*. The spreading dogbane is genus *Apocynum*, species *A. androsaemifolium*. The Indian hemp is *A. cannabinum*. HAROLD NORMAN MOLDENKE

DOGE, *dohj*, was the title of the rulers of Venice from 697 to 1797. *Doge* comes from the Latin word *dux*, meaning *leader*. Genoa also had doges.

The doges of Venice were elected for life from among the richest and most powerful families. They enjoyed almost absolute power in governmental, military, and church affairs until 1032. Then they tried unsuccessfully to make the office hereditary. After this the doges were closely supervised. In 1310, the doge became subordinate to the Council of Ten, and from then on this *oligarchy* (small, powerful group) really ruled Venice. The Council ruled Venice until 1797, when Napoleon suppressed the Republic of Venice. He abolished the

The Doge's Palace, built during the Middle Ages, was the home of medieval rulers of Venice. A striking example of early Italian architecture, it borders the Grand Canal, *background*.
May, Black Star

Council and the *dogate* (office of the doges) in the same year. WILLIAM H. MAEHL

See also GENOA (History); VENICE (History).

DOGFISH are small sharks. They live in temperate and warm seas. The *spiny dogfish* has spines in front of the *dorsal* (top) fins, but the *smooth dogfish* lacks these spines. Dogfish have no bones. Their skeleton is made of cartilage. They seldom grow more than 3 feet long. Americans rarely eat dogfish, but Europeans consider the fish an important food. Dogfish skin can be dried and used to polish wood. Fishermen once caught dogfish for their vitamin-rich livers, but synthetic vitamins have replaced the need for dogfish livers.

The *bowfin*, or *mudfish*, is sometimes called dogfish. It lives in the rivers of the United States and Canada, but it is not related to the salt-water dogfish. The bowfin lays its eggs in a nest, and bravely defends its young. See BOWFIN.

Scientific Classification. Spiny dogfishes belong to the family *Squalidae*. The common spiny dogfish is classified in the genus *Squalus*, species *S. acanthias*. Smooth dogfishes belong to the family *Carcharhinidae*. They are classified as *Mustelus canis*. LEONARD P. SCHULTZ

See also LIFE (table, Length of Life of Animals).

The Spiny Dogfish Is a Member of the Shark Family.
State of Calif. Dept. of Fish and Game

DOGGER BANK is a large area of shallow water located in the middle of the North Sea between England and Denmark. Dogger Bank is a famous fishing ground, chiefly because the water is only 50 to 120 feet deep. In 1915, the British navy won an important battle against the German fleet off Dogger Bank. A German battle cruiser was sunk and another was seriously damaged in this battle. FRANCIS H. HERRICK

DOGTOOTH. See TEETH (Permanent Teeth).

DOGTOOTH VIOLET, or **ADDER'S-TONGUE,** is an attractive spring wildflower of the eastern United States and Canada. It is not really a violet, but belongs to the lily family. It breaks through the ground early, and catches the sunshine before leaves appear on the trees and darken the ground. Dogtooth violet has been oddly misnamed because it does not resemble a dog's tooth. The young shoots are sharply pointed. The two smooth, grayish-green leaves, mottled with brown, spring from the bulb. The yellow, white, or pink bell-shaped flower nods on a stem 6 to 12 inches long, between the two leaves. The flower has a faint fragrance. Dogtooth violet may be found in early spring along the banks of brooks. It is sometimes called *trout lily*.

Scientific Classification. The common dogtooth violet belongs to the lily family, *Liliaceae*. It is genus *Erythronium*, species *E. dens-canis*. GEORGE H. M. LAWRENCE

See also PLANT (color picture, Some Members of the Lily Family).

The Flowering Dogwood blooms in early spring before the leaves appear. The blossom is really a tiny cluster of flowers surrounded by four white leaves that look like petals.

J. Horace McFarland

DOGWOOD is the common name for a group of shrubs and small trees. About 40 kinds of dogwood exist. Fourteen kinds are native to the United States.

The best-known is the *flowering dogwood*. It has four large whitish *bracts*, or leaflike structures, beneath its small, greenish-white flowers. The bright-red fruits, or *drupes*, usually have two seeds. The leaves have parallel veins, and are quite rich in calcium. The neat bark pattern and the gray, urn-shaped flower buds make the dogwood an attractive winter tree. Flowering dogwood rarely grows more than 40 feet high or 18 inches in diameter. Its wood is hard and heavy.

Scientific Classification. The dogwood belongs to the family *Cornaceae*. Flowering dogwood is genus *Cornus*, species *florida*.   T. EWALD MAKI

See also BRITISH COLUMBIA (color picture, Provincial Flower); LEAF (picture, Kinds of Leaves); TREE (color picture, Ornamental Trees).

DOHA, *DOH huh* (pop. 27,500; alt. 5 ft.), is the capital of Qatar. It is also the largest city, major port, and commercial center of that Arab sheikdom. It lies on the east side of the Qatar Peninsula on the Persian Gulf. The city's industries include fishing, pearling, and metalworking.

DOHENY, EDWARD L. See TEAPOT DOME.

DOHNÁNYI, *DOH nah yih*, **ERNST VON**, or **ERNÖ** (1877-1960), a Hungarian composer and conductor, became one of the outstanding pianists of his time. He was appointed director of the Budapest Conservatory in 1919, and director of Hungarian radio in 1931. He became noted for his piano compositions, including *Ruralia Hungarica*, *Four Rhapsodies*, and *Humoresques*. Dohnányi was born in Pressburg (now Bratislava in Czechoslovakia). In 1949, he moved to Tallahassee, Fla., where he became a professor of music at Florida State University.   JOYCE MICHELL

DOISY, EDWARD ADELBERT (1893-   ), an American chemist, determined the nature of vitamin K, which helps the liver produce prothrombin, one of the clotting factors in blood. He isolated and synthesized pure vitamin K_1. Its use saves many lives each year. Doisy shared the 1943 Nobel prize for this work and for the isolation of the female sex hormone. He was born at Hume, Ill., and was graduated from the University of Illinois and Harvard University.   HERBERT S. RHINESMITH

See also VITAMIN (Vitamin K).

DOLBEAR, *DOHL beer*, **AMOS E.** (1837-1910), an American physicist and inventor, might be known today as the inventor of the telephone and radio, if he had only had better luck. In 1864, he made a "talking machine" much like the telephone Alexander Graham Bell patented in 1877. Dolbear insisted the idea was his. After a long, bitter court fight, Bell was declared the true inventor. Dolbear produced radio waves in 1882, but the discovery is usually credited to the German scientist Heinrich R. Hertz in 1888. Dolbear was born in Norwich, Conn.   IRA M. FREEMAN

DOLDRUMS, *DAHL drums*, is a belt of calms, light breezes, or sudden squalls near the equator, mainly over the oceans. Meteorologists call it the *intertropic convergence zone*. The name *doldrums* means *listlessness*. Seamen were the first to use this name because their sailing ships often were *becalmed*, or unable to sail, in the region.

In the doldrums, the air moves upward, causing sudden thunderstorms and gusty winds. The region is one of the rainiest in the world. It is also dangerous to airplanes because the turbulent clouds build up higher than most aircraft can fly.   WALTER J. SAUCIER

See also CALMS, REGIONS OF; HORSE LATITUDES.

DOLE. See UNEMPLOYMENT INSURANCE.

DOLE, JAMES D. See HAWAII (Famous Hawaiians).

DOLE, SANFORD BALLARD (1844-1926), an American lawyer, was a leader of the group that brought about the annexation of Hawaii to the United States. He joined a revolutionary movement in 1893 that deposed Queen Liliuokalani and sought annexation by the United States. He headed the Revolutionary Provisional Government.

He became president of the Republic of Hawaii when President Grover Cleveland opposed annexation. But the U.S. annexed Hawaii in 1898 after Cleveland left office. Dole then served as the first territorial governor from 1900 to 1903, and as U.S. district judge for Hawaii from 1903 to 1915.

He was born in Honolulu of American parents, and was educated in Hawaii and at Williams College in Massachusetts.   ERIC F. GOLDMAN

See also HAWAII (History); LILIUOKALANI, LYDIA KAMEKEHA.

DOLIN, ANTON (1904-   ), an English ballet dancer, founded and directed the London Festival Ballet. He first starred with the Diaghilev Ballet, then joined Alicia Markova in the Markova-Dolin company. Dolin danced with Ballet Theatre in America, appearing in *Giselle*, *Swan Lake*, *Bluebird*, *Aleko*, and other ballets. He was born PATRICK HEALEY-KAY, in Slinfold, England. His Russian ballet teacher, Serafima Astafieva, renamed him Dolin.   LILLIAN MOORE

DOLL

DOLL. In almost every part of the world, children play with dolls. They may be made of anything from cooky dough and candy to cloth and rubber. They may be made in factories and bought in shops, or they may be made at home and cost nothing. It makes little difference what they look like or how much money is paid for them. Dolls are loved the world around.

The doll is a favorite playmate of most girls. All the secrets of its owner are poured into its ears. Girls can play grownup to their heart's content with the cuddly child dolls of today. They sew for their dolls and keep them neat and clean. Singing to them and rocking them to sleep is part of the fun of playing mother. Now and then, girls will pretend their dolls are sick, so that they may nurse them.

Dolls are the playthings of rich and poor alike. They comfort the sick and amuse the well. They are the hobby of young and old. Even boys may like dolls that look like clowns, policemen, or Indians.

Costume dolls from foreign lands show how other peoples dress. From old dolls, we can find out how people of long ago lived and what they wore.

The word *doll* was first used about 1750. There was no such word in earlier days. The dolls of different lands were called by different names. In the American colonies they were called puppets, babes or babies, and "little ladies." Dolls at that time were usually made to look like women or girls. In an ancient language of India, the only word for dolls was "little daughter."

Dolls of Early Days

Nobody is sure who made the first doll. Perhaps somebody found a stone or root or piece of wood that looked like a human being. The first dolls were believed to bring good luck to their owners. No child was allowed to touch the dolls because they were thought to have magic powers.

Good-Luck Dolls were supposed to bring rain or food when they were needed, to make goats give more milk, or to help win wars. Some people thought dolls could even make sick people well. Some tribes who believed this made wooden dolls that looked like ugly elves. They were supposed to frighten people. Only the medicine men, or *witch doctors*, were allowed to handle them.

Paddle Dolls are perhaps the oldest dolls. They were made by the Egyptians three thousand years ago and may be seen today in the British Museum in London. They are called paddle dolls because they were made from thin pieces of board carved in the shape of canoe paddles. Lines were carved and painted on them to look like clothes. Hair was made of short strings of beads. The figures were made without legs so they could not run away. When an important person died in old Egypt, many such doll figures were buried with him. They looked like barbers, bakers, cooks, clowns, maids, actors, and musicians. They were supposed to be friends and servants for the dead person in the spirit world.

Doll-Size Figures have been found among old Roman and Greek tombs. Most of these are also believed to have been funeral figures. They were usually made of wood or clay of some kind. The oldest-known Greek play doll is a clay rattle in the form of a woman. The Greek or Roman girl often played with her dolls until shortly before her marriage. Then the Greek girl would leave them on the altar of Artemis, the goddess of unmarried girls. The Roman girl took them to the altar of Diana. The girls did this to show that they were no longer interested in childish things. The best Roman

UNUSUAL DOLLS

EGGSHELL DOLLS

Eggshell dolls are often used as Easter favors. Cotton is stuck in the empty end of the eggshell for hair. The eyes, nose, and mouth are painted on, and the bottom end is glued.

SACRED INDIAN DOLL

The "Katcina" doll was used by the Hopi Indians who lived in the southwestern part of the United States. From it, and from the designs on its clothes, the Hopi children learned about the ancient spirits of the tribe.

CORNHUSK DOLL

Pioneer and Indian boys and girls were very clever in making cornhusk dolls. They braided the cornhusks for hair and for arms. They stuck bright bird feathers in the braids.

SPOOL DOLL

Big and little spools are strung together to make a loose-jointed doll. A face is drawn on the top spool, and other trimmings may also be added.

WITCH DOLL

The "Kalifa" doll is found in the Egyptian Sudan. Its body is made from the stalk of a plant. The head is of black wax and beads are used for eyes.

CRAB-CLAW DOLL

A crab-claw doll is made from the claw of a hard crab. For a headdress, seagull or other bright bird feathers are put in the open end of the claw.

TUMBLE DOLL

The first tumble doll was an image of Buddha, a Chinese god. Such dolls were weighted at the bottom, for the Chinese believed Buddha could not fall. Push this doll over and it bobs up again. The Chinese name for it means, "struck, not falling."

COSTUME DOLLS FROM MANY LANDS

DUTCH

SCOTTISH

SWEDISH

JAPANESE

RUSSIAN

SPANISH

Different countries, different dolls! Katrinka of Holland wears wooden shoes and a stiff-starched cap. Sandy of Scotland has kilts, a bonnet, a plaid over his shoulder, and a sporran (fur pouch). Greta of Sweden has long puffed sleeves and a striped apron. Sonia of Russia wears a bright tunic and hat. Dolores, the Spanish senorita, is very gay with shawl, high comb, and red rose. Little Butterfly of Japan has on her best silk kimono, ready for the Festival of Dolls.

ESKIMO

SWISS

MEXICAN

CHINESE

FRENCH

INDIAN

The Eskimo doll is clothed in fur-lined parka. Heidi of Switzerland, in her flowered apron and puffy sleeves, is in holiday dress. Pedro, in his sombrero (hat) and sash is from Mexico. Nanette of France wears a dainty dress and wooden shoes. Little Eagle, the Indian doll, looks brave in beads and feathers. Ling Fu, the Chinese doll, is in holiday clothes of silk cap, trousers, and colorful tunic. Such dolls as these are loved the world around.

DOLL

dolls were made of clay. Strips of carved wood served for legs and arms. Even in these early times, the limbs of some dolls could be moved by pulling strings.

Dolls have also been used by the Christian church. Not so many years ago they were used to take the parts of saints in church plays. Even today, at Christmastime, dolls made to look like Mary, Joseph, and baby Jesus may be seen in the churches and homes of many lands.

Fashion Dolls were first used in France about six hundred years ago. These were large dolls dressed in the latest fashions. These "fashion babies" were sent to other lands to show what fine clothes the French could make. They took the place of fashion magazines. They had wardrobes complete even to hats, shoes, and undergarments. Only the rich could afford these dolls. But, strangely enough, these beautifully dressed dolls had the crudest kinds of bodies. Their legs were often no more than a pair of sticks.

Kings and queens sent these fashion dolls as gifts to one another. About 1390, the queen of England received a group of French dolls dressed in the rich costumes of court ladies. Two fashion dolls which were sent to King Gustavus Adolphus of Sweden about three hundred years ago may still be seen at the University of Uppsala in Sweden.

Later, fashion dolls forty inches tall were sent to far-off India to show the women how to wear their English clothes. Before the dolls were sent, the people of India had been folding up their English-made wraps and wearing them as head coverings. Fashion dolls also made a great stir among the well-to-do in the American colonies. Newspapers announced their arrival and told what it would cost to see them.

Pantin Dolls were popular in France about two hundred years ago. These pasteboard dolls were somewhat like the jumping jacks or puppets of today. For years men and women played with them no matter where they were, in their homes, on the streets, in their shops, and at parties. By pulling strings, the French made their funny pantins dance and act.

Dolls in America

Indian Dolls were usually made from the skins of animals. The skins were sewed together with strong strips of leather. Then they were stuffed with moss, animal hair, or dried grass. Their clothes were made of soft deerskin, and they wore necklaces and bracelets of tiny beads, shells, or seeds. Wigs made from the hair of goats, buffaloes, or horses were sewed to the tops of their leather heads. Other Indian dolls were made from cornhusks, grass, or apples. As the funny apple-headed dolls grew older, their faces began to dry up. In only a few days they looked like old squaws, with dark, dry, and wrinkled faces.

Colonial Dolls were usually whittled from wood or cut from cloth and dressed like their owners. Others were made from pine cones, corncobs, or other materials at hand. Though crude, they were treasured friends.

The oldest doll in America is probably the one called *Letitia Penn*. William Penn brought it from England in 1699 for a friend of his little daughter, Letitia. Its gown has a tight waist and sleeves, and the skirt is wider than the doll is high. The doll has only one arm now, and its face seems to us to look somewhat unfriendly.

Another famous doll is *Mehitable Hodges*, sometimes called the *Salem Doll*. She was brought to America in 1724 by Captain Gamaliel Hodges as a gift for his daughter. Still another of the very old colonial dolls is a stumpy, homemade rag doll. Even her name sounds homemade. It is *Bangwell Putt*. Bangwell had no face. But for eighty years she did her rag-doll best to brighten the life of her blind mistress, Clarissa Field of Northfield, Mass.

Improvements in Dolls. For many years, little girls in America continued to play with dolls that had been brought from Europe. Little by little, better dolls began to be made. Soft kid was used for their bodies, and they took on a more lifelike shape. Stuffings improved. Bran and sawdust were common for many, many years. Later, hair, shavings, and seaweed were used.

At first most dolls belonged to grownups, not to children. But by 1800, dolls had become the child's own toy. Factories did not make enough dolls for all the little girls, so the homemade rag doll became popular.

Marshall Field & Co.
What the Well-Dressed Doll Will Wear is seen from the large display of clothes in her "doll-sized" wardrobe trunk.

In order to get to an American girl from Europe, a factory-made doll had to travel by boat, stagecoach, and perhaps by saddlebag or covered wagon.

For a long time, doll heads were made of china. Their faces were round and rosy and were not supposed to look like real people. Penny china dolls about two inches high also became very popular. Many girls owned whole families of them.

Doll hands and feet were of leather, china, or wood. It was fashionable for women to have small feet, so doll feet were made much too small for their bodies. China heads, hands, and feet were sold in stores to those who wished to make dolls at home.

Until about 1870, American girls played with dolls that looked like serious, grown-up ladies. They wore bustles, jackets, and the quaint dresses of these days. Only a few dolls were made to look like children. Some had wax heads, which broke if the dolls were dropped. The wax cracked in cold weather and melted in hot weather. The finest wax dolls came from England. Other dolls had heads made of *papier-mâché*, a mixture of pulped paper and glue.

DOLL

The best doll heads then were made of *bisque*, a kind of hard earthenware. Such dolls had kid bodies and jointed necks, arms, and legs. They also had real curls, and eyes which opened and closed. Most of them came dressed only in cotton slips and had to have their clothing made for them by their owners.

Modern Dolls

Beginning about 1900, new developments occurred in the world of dolls. Manufacturers made more dolls that looked like babies. Many of them, called *ma-ma dolls*, had built-in devices that made them seem to cry. Johann Maelzel of Germany had invented this mechanism about 1825, but few manufacturers used it until around 1900. Dolls that opened and shut their eyes became popular. Factories made remarkable mechanical dolls that could walk, do tricks, or play music.

Europe. Germany, especially the cities of Nuremberg and Sonnenberg, made most of the best dolls between 1870 and 1914. Käthe Kruse was one of the first to make dolls that looked like real children. Her husband did not want their children to play with the ugly dolls of the time, so she made new ones. The first ones had heads made of raw potatoes, with faces drawn on with a burnt match. Later ones were made of waterproof cloth stuffed with *kapok*, a light fiber. Madame Lenci of Italy became famous for her felt dolls, many of them dressed in gay costumes. France and England also made good dolls.

United States factories first began making dolls in the 1900's. They used unbreakable materials such as rubber and *composition*, a mixture of wood flour, starch, rosin, and water. The first really successful American doll, *Billiken*, became popular around 1910. Many American dolls appeared during World War I, when children could not get German dolls. The plump *Kewpie Doll* found a large audience. Other American dolls included the *Bye-Lo Baby*, which looked like a tiny baby; the little girl *Patsy;* and *Ginny*, with her many clothes. *Character Dolls* included Mickey and Minnie Mouse, Raggedy Anne and Raggedy Andy, and comic-strip figures. *Portrait Dolls* resembled real persons like Shirley Temple.

American dolls grew more and more lifelike. Dolls that cried followed the *Dy-Dee Doll* of the 1930's. Later dolls had nylon "hair," make-up kits, roller skates, and even mink coats. "Teen-age" dolls and giant "walking dolls" also became popular.

Homemade Dolls

No child need be without a doll when she can make her own. Dolls can be made from almost anything. Forest dwellers use wood, bark, and roots. People of the plains wrap grasses, straws, or cornhusks into doll shapes. Those who live near the sea use shells and seaweed. In hot countries, strips of palm leaf are woven into dolls.

Swedish girls make pretty dolls of rolled-up birchbark. Birchbark is fringed for hands, and clothes are scraps of neatly hemmed birchbark. Hungarian children make rag dolls with oats for eyes and a grain of corn for a nose. They also make poppy dolls by pulling down the flower petals and binding them with a blade of grass. The seed pod is the poppy doll's head, and the petals are her skirts. To the Russian girl, no doll is more dear than a painted woodsman cut from wood. Arms are pine cones, hair is moss, and dresses and shoes are woven from fibers.

In Bermuda, doll bodies are made from the heart of the banana stalk. Large round nuts are used as heads. In South Africa, children make their dolls from corncobs. A small home-woven blanket serves as clothing. In England and many other lands, dolls are baked from bread dough and dressed in long, white baby dresses.

Mexican children play with rag dolls or wooden ones covered with cloth. The potter's children model tiny dolls of clay and paint them with homemade colors. Still other Mexican dolls are braided leaf fibers. Very sturdy dolls are made of straw, cornhusks, and pieces of cornstalk. These are painted in brilliant colors.

In Chile and Brazil, yarn is wrapped around pieces of wire to make dolls. Heads are of cork or wood. Odd little woven woolen dolls are made in Peru.

Zylstra
Two Lifelike Dolls are modeled on the kind first made in Germany by the famous woman dollmaker, Käthe Kruse.

Eskimo play dolls have long been made from skins. They are dressed in fur scraps and stuffed with reindeer hair or fur. Many doll figures are carved from bone or walrus tusk.

In the United States, all kinds of materials may be used for making dolls. Scraps of cloth, old stockings, or pieces of felt or leather are excellent. Corncobs and cornhusks are good, and so are peanuts and acorns. A clever person can make a doll of a spool, clothespin, or tenpin. Other materials are paper, cardboard, hairpins, wires, raffia, string, and rubber from old inner tubes.

Stocking Dolls are about the easiest to make. The only materials needed are old stockings, stuffing, and thread. Stuffing can be cotton, old rags, or even some finely torn bits of newspaper. The best stockings are those of heavy silk or smooth cotton. Pert little faces can be made by stitching on eyes, mouth, and nose with colored thread. Buttons make good eyes.

Rag Dolls are the most popular of all homemade dolls. They are almost as old as history. One in Egypt was probably used about two thousand years ago. It is made of linen and stuffed with coarse grass. The features are embroidered on. Its hair is linen threads.

239

DOLL

Two-in-One Dolls are rag dolls, each with a black face and a white face. They can be easily made by making two bodies that go only to the waist. One is of black material and the other of white material, and each has a matching pair of arms. A blue dress looks well on the white doll and a red dress on the black one. Each dress should be twice as long as the body. Paints or colored threads can be used to make the faces. Raveled yarn will do for hair, and soft caps or bonnets may be made for each head. When both dolls are finished, they are sewn tightly together at the waist. When the white head is held up, the black one hangs beneath the full blue skirt. When the black head is up, the white one hangs under the red dress.

Cork Dolls are made with two corks, a large one for the body and a smaller one for the head. Matchsticks are stuck into the larger cork to serve as arms and legs and to hold head and body together. Thumbtacks in the leg-ends make these dolls stand up easily.

Making the Doll's Clothes is as much fun as making the doll itself. Soft, thin materials are best for small dolls. Scraps of old clothing may be used. A single tiny piece of cloth will make a whole outfit for a spool doll. Where old light bulbs are used for dolls' heads, the faces are painted on and crepe paper is often used for clothing.

Dollhouses

Even three hundred years ago, fine dollhouses were the fashion in Europe. Fancy Dutch houses were made in the form of cupboards. When the doors were open, one could peep into every room in the house, from basement to attic. The houses were sometimes six, seven, or eight feet high, and were made for grownups. A few of these old dollhouses may still be seen in the museums of Europe.

One of the finest was the Utrecht (Holland) Dollhouse, made in 1670. It had fifteen rooms. One of these was full of tiny vases and other small treasures. These great dollhouses were furnished exactly like the homes of wealthy persons. Anyone who studies them can learn a great deal about how people lived long ago.

A dollhouse usually had doll people in it, too. Doll lords and ladies sat in the drawing rooms. Cooks, butlers, maids, and laundresses were at work in other rooms. In one of these houses, a tiny nurse is seen holding a baby doll whose long dress almost sweeps the floor. In the best dollhouses, every tiny article is perfectly made. Kitchens are complete with pots and pans, knives, dishes, candlesticks, baskets, brushes, and tiny brooms.

These houses cost so much that only the wealthy could own them. Peter the Great, the ruler of all Russia, once ordered one. When it was finished, he refused to pay for it, because he felt that it cost too much even for him. Mary of Teck, the wife of King George V of Great Britain, was also interested in dollhouses. She found enjoyment in an elaborate dollhouse that cost nearly a million dollars. In it are real pianos, and works of noted composers, authors, and painters. The eleven-room dollhouse of the American actress Colleen Moore is twelve feet high and nine feet square. It, too, cost a million dollars. One drawing-room chandelier is decorated with real diamonds and other precious stones. But dollhouses for children are not so big or so costly. Some have six or seven rooms, and others only one. There are also one-room doll stores.

Homemade dollhouses are simple to make. A square hatbox or a grocery carton makes a cozy one-room apartment. A great favorite is an orange box stood on end. This becomes a two-story house with an upstairs. Fringed rugs for the floors may be cut from old cloth. Spools and pieces of cardboard make fine tables and benches. Chairs may be made from old salt boxes, round ice-cream cartons, or other small boxes. A cracker carton becomes a davenport, a cigar box makes a bed, and a raisin box is a chest of drawers.

Gay furniture can be created by using colored paper or cloth, or paint. Leftover scraps of wallpaper will help to make the walls seem real. Oval cocoa-can lids become tiny, framed pictures when colored cutouts are pasted on them. Old purse mirrors are dollhouse size. The table may be set with bottle caps.

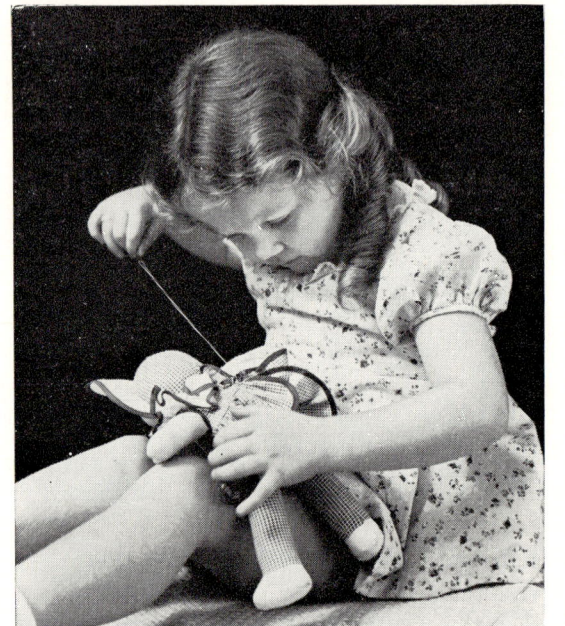

Repairing Her Doll's Dress gives this little girl practice in sewing which may prove useful later in her life. *H. Armstrong Roberts*

Many stores sell dollhouse furniture, but it is more fun to make one's own.

Doll Collections

Thousands of people, young and old, in all parts of the world, make a hobby of collecting dolls. Some collectors own a thousand or more dolls. Many persons collect antique dolls. Others specialize in costume dolls that represent all countries and times. Instead of buying dolls for their collections, some persons make their own. A few dolls stand as high as adults, while others can fit in a thimble. Doll collections often travel from place to place to be exhibited in libraries, schools, clubs, and museums.

Famous Collectors include the Aztec emperor Montezuma. More than 400 years ago, Cortes, the Spanish conqueror of Mexico, found the emperor amusing himself with his doll collection. Before Victoria became queen of England, she owned dozens and dozens of dolls. She put her best needlework into their tiny silken gowns, and named them after the ladies and actresses

HOW DOLLS HAVE CHANGED

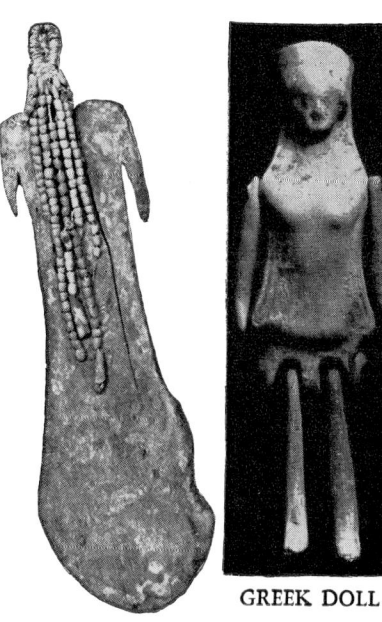

GREEK DOLL

EGYPTIAN DOLL

The paddle doll of Egypt and the terra cotta (baked clay) doll of Greece are more than three thousand years old. They were put in the tombs of dead people to keep them company. They were never used as playthings.

Photos: Brooklyn Museum

OLDEST AMERICAN DOLL

"Letitia Penn" is probably the oldest doll in America. It was brought from England to Philadelphia by William Penn in 1699. Made of wood, it is dressed in a gown of brocade and velvet like a lady of the English Court.

Photo: Smithsonian Institution

CHINA DOLL

China doll heads were being made and sold during the nineteenth century. The bodies, made of kid or cloth, were stuffed with bran and sawdust.

Photo: Thayer Museum of Art

FASHION DOLL

Photo: Brooklyn Museum

Fashion dolls were used to carry the latest dress and hair styles to other countries. France used such "fashion babies" five hundred years ago. They were brought to this country before and after the War of Independence.

TODAY'S DOLL

The doll of today is made to look just like a real child, with silky hair.

HOW TO MAKE

PAPER DOLL

Pocahontas is a sitting doll made from paper. Cut out a newspaper pattern and outline it on stiff wrapping paper. Draw the eyes, nose, and mouth. Paste on the feathers, braids, and headband. Use crayon to put on the bright colors, as water colors might wrinkle the paper.

Little Miss Muffet, Goldilocks, and other dolls may be made in the same way. In making curly-headed dolls, cut the hair longer at the sides. Snip into the fringe and curl it by putting fringes across a blunt knife blade.

STOCKING DOLL

Cut the pieces as shown. Sew up the bottom of the body and stuff it with cotton, kapok, or rags. Then tie it at the neck. If the head seems too wide, gather it at the back.

Sew on the arms and legs and tie the body at the waistline. Use buttons for eyes and red chainstitching for the nose and mouth. Over-and-over stitches at the center of the mouth improve its shape. Sew on a stocking wig. Then braid it or leave it hanging. If you prefer, the doll may be dressed as Red Riding Hood, Little Bopeep, Cinderella, Little Miss Muffet, or anyone else.

HOMEMADE DOLLS

ACORN DOLLS

To make funny little acorn dolls, use acorns and matchsticks. With a nail, punch tiny holes in the acorns for the arms, legs, and neck. Then cement them into the holes. Punch holes for eyes, nose, and mouth, or draw them. For hair, use the fuzzy-edged acorn cup of a burr oak. The top of the cup makes a fine cap.

CORNCOB DOLL

For hair, use the silk on the corncob. The arms, skirt, and kerchief are made of cornhusks. Draw the eyes, nose, and mouth.

CORNSTARCH DOLL

The head of this 9-inch wire doll is made of cornstarch, salt, and water. Mix 2 tablespoonfuls of salt, 1 tablespoonful of cornstarch with 1 tablespoonful of boiling water. Heat over the fire for a moment. When cool, knead it into a ball the size of a walnut and press it over the head wire. Model the head and hair. Shape the hands and feet out of the leftovers. Let these dry for two days, and then color with water colors.

Wire for body and legs, 18 inches long. Arm wire, 9 inches. Stuff body slightly and wrap with cloth.

DOLL

whose costumes she copied. She especially liked small wooden dolls with jointed limbs. Queen Marie of Romania had a collection of more than a thousand dolls, most of them dressed in various costumes. The people of The Netherlands gave their queen, Wilhelmina, a large collection of costume dolls. Another famous doll collection belonged to Eugene Field, the poet who wrote "Little Boy Blue" and "Wynken, Blynken, and Nod."

Noted Collections of dolls include a large one at the Metropolitan Museum in New York City. Another fine collection, dressed in various European costumes, is found in the New York Children's Museum. Noted collections may also be seen in the Smithsonian Institution in Washington, D.C.; Essex Institute at Salem, Mass.; the Museum of Art in Toledo, Ohio; the children's library in Hartford, Conn.; Pennsylvania Museum at Philadelphia, Pa.; children's museums at Detroit, Mich., and Boston, Mass.; Plymouth Antiquarian Society at Plymouth, Mass.; and in museums at Cleveland, Ohio, and Brooklyn, N.Y. The Fairfield Collection of the State Historical Society at Madison, Wis., is also famous.

Doll Festivals and Customs

For hundreds of years, the Japanese have paid the highest honor to their dolls. They hold a three-day Festival of Dolls on the third day of the third month of each year. Sometimes the celebration is called the Girls' Festival, because all Japanese girls celebrate their birthday at that time, even if it falls on some other day.

The festival dolls are not playthings. They are brought out only on this special day. During the year they are packed away carefully in the family treasure chest. Every family has these special dolls, which are passed on from parents to children. During the festival, five shelves are set up in the best room in the house. The dolls are arranged on these shelves. Richly dressed emperor and empress dolls are placed on the highest shelf, where none can look down on them. The other dolls are placed on the lower shelves in the order of their importance. The children's play dolls are not allowed on the shelves. But the children take care of the festival dolls, and entertain friends who come to visit them. Tea is served to the dolls, the family, and the guests. Japanese children cherish the dolls as living things, and look forward to this charming holiday.

Various peoples held their own beliefs about dolls. The Hopi Indians of the southwestern United States carve wooden dolls called *katcinas* or *kachinas* for use in their religious ceremonies. Each color and each design has its own meaning for the Hopi. After medicine men have used these spirit dolls, they give them to the children to play with (see INDIAN, AMERICAN [color picture, Pueblo Indians]).

In some parts of England, dolls take part in the harvest thanksgiving festivals. Each autumn the smallest ears of corn are bound up as a doll and hung in the farmer's house. There the doll stays until next harvest time. Then a new one is made and hung with great ceremony. The old doll is carefully burned.

In Belgium a special doll is given to each baby to help the child cut its teeth with less pain. This doll is dressed in white and has a tooth pinned to its dress. Nearly everyone believes that it brings good luck. In Africa, fishermen on the Congo River carry dolls which they believe will keep them from drowning. The Eskimos of the Far North carve dolls from bone to hang in their *kayaks* (canoes). They believe that these dolls keep the kayaks from turning over. In Korea, in the Far East, a straw doll is thought to bring good luck.

Making Dolls

Today, most of the world's dolls come from the United States. American manufacturers sell more than 40,000,000 dolls every year. Skilled craftsmen design new dolls, and often create complete wardrobes and elaborate accessories for them.

Manufacturers often use washable cloth to make dolls for very young children. Various types of plastics furnish the best material for most other dolls. In the first step, an artist makes a model in clay or wax. A metal mold is then formed around the model. Workmen pour liquid vinyl plastic into the molds and let it solidify. The plastic is soft and durable, and seems like real skin. The workmen usually cast the doll's body in one piece and its head in another. Then other workers put together a whole doll, attaching its head, arms, and legs to the body. Artists paint faces on the heads. As finishing touches, they add the doll's clothes, its eyes, and a nylon wig. The dolls are inspected to make sure they are perfect. Then they are tagged and packed, and they are ready for shipment.

NINA R. JORDAN

Related Articles in WORLD BOOK include:

Hobby	Katcina	String Figure
Japan (picture,	Puppet	Toy
On Girls' Day)		

Outline

I. Dolls of Early Days
   A. Good-Luck Dolls
   B. Paddle Dolls
   C. Doll-Size Figures
   D. Fashion Dolls
   E. Pantin Dolls

II. Dolls in America
   A. Indian Dolls
   B. Colonial Dolls
   C. Improvements in Dolls

III. Modern Dolls
   A. Europe
   B. United States

IV. Homemade Dolls
   A. Stocking Dolls
   B. Rag Dolls
   C. Two-in-One Dolls
   D. Cork Dolls
   E. Making the Doll's Clothes

V. Dollhouses

VI. Doll Collections
   A. Famous Collectors
   B. Noted Collections

VII. Doll Festivals and Customs

VIII. Making Dolls

Questions

Why did Roman girls take their dolls to the altar of Diana?

Why did the paddle dolls of the Egyptians have no legs?

Why were English "fashion dolls" sent to India?

What were dolls called in the colonial days of America?

What is the name of the oldest doll in America? How old is she?

Why did early American dolls have tiny feet?

What children made dolls that could be seen to grow older? Of what were they made?

When was the *ma-ma* doll invented?

What famous queen of England had a large collection of dolls?

Why do the Eskimos carry dolls in their kayaks?

**A $100,000 Bill,** above, passes only between the Treasury Department and the Federal Reserve Banks. The dollar sign ($) is thought to come from the Spanish piece of eight (eight *reals*), left. The S in the sign is believed to be a broken 8, and the two bars are thought to represent the two Pillars of Hercules visible on the coin.

The First Silver Dollar was minted in 1794. It had an eagle on the back, *left,* and a liberty head and 15 stars on the front, *above.*

The "Peace Dollar" was issued from 1921 to 1935. It has the word *Peace* on the back, *left.* The coin has a liberty head on the front, *above.*
Chase Manhattan Bank Money Museum

DOLLAR is the name of several different coins used in various countries. The name comes from the old German word *thal,* meaning *valley.* This name was adopted because the first coins of this type were made in 1519 in the valley of St. Joachim in Bohemia. These coins were called *Joachimsthaler,* then merely *thaler,* which in English became *dollar.* The dollars of the United States and Canada are silver coins equal to 100 cents.

The dollar became the basic unit of money in the United States through the Coinage Act of 1792. It was copied after the Spanish dollar then being widely circulated in America. The dollar became the basic unit in Canada in 1858. United States paper dollars were printed as early as 1775. The first United States silver dollars were coined in 1794, and nearly 900,000,000 were made from that time to 1935, when the Treasury stopped minting them. Silver dollars circulated mainly in the West, Southwest, and Northwest. People in the East objected to their weight and demanded paper dollars. The silver dollar weighed 416 grains at first, but its weight was changed to $412\frac{1}{2}$ grains in 1837 by special legislation of Congress.

From 1873 to 1885, a special dollar weighing 420 grains was issued. This was called the *trade dollar* and was intended to help American trade in the Orient, where the Mexican dollar was being used. At various times the United States government issued gold pieces with values of $1, $2.50, $3, $5, $10, and $20. The one-dollar soon went out of use because it was so small. Coinage of gold ceased in the United States and all gold coins were taken out of circulation in 1933.

A form of the dollar is found in Mexico, where it is known as the *peso.* Another form, called the *yuan,* has been used in China. The British government issued a coin called the *Hong Kong dollar,* for use in Hong Kong. Many other countries issue silver coins of about the same size and weight as the dollar. These coins have other names, but they are often called "dollars."

The origin of the dollar sign is not certain. Several theories explain it, the main one being that the S in the sign is a broken 8. That figure was on the old Spanish pieces of eight, meaning 8 *reals.* The two bars appeared as the Pillars of Hercules on pieces of eight minted by the Spaniards in Mexico City as early as 1732. Some people believe the dollar sign is a monogram of U.S., standing for United States, with the "S" superimposed on the "U."   LEWIS M. REAGAN

Chase Manhattan Bank Money Museum
Canada's Silver Dollar honors Queen Elizabeth II on its front, *left,* and voyageurs of the fur trade on its back, *right.*

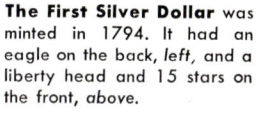

DOLLAR DIPLOMACY

DOLLAR DIPLOMACY seeks to extend a nation's business interests in other countries by any means except war. The term was first applied to United States policy in the Caribbean and other areas during President William Howard Taft's administration. The period from 1909 to 1913 is generally considered to be the era of dollar diplomacy. See also TAFT, WILLIAM HOWARD (Foreign Affairs).

DOLLARFISH. See BUTTERFISH.

DOLLFUSS, *DAWL foos*, **ENGELBERT** (1892-1934), became Chancellor of Austria in 1932, at a time of political and economic trouble. He adjourned Austria's parliament in 1933, and then ruled the country as a dictator.

Although less than 5 feet tall, he was a forceful leader. Nazi revolutionaries assassinated him on July 25, 1934, because he tried to prevent Adolf Hitler from taking over Austria.

Dollfuss was born of peasant parents near Vienna, and was graduated from the University of Vienna. He served in World War I.   GABRIEL A. ALMOND

See also AUSTRIA (The Republic of Austria).

DOLLHOUSE. See DOLL (Dollhouses).

DOLMEN. See MEGALITHIC MONUMENTS.

DOLOMITE, *DAHL oh mite*, is a mineral composed of carbonates of calcium and magnesium. Dolomite is moderately soft, and is colored milky-white, brownish, or pink. Impurities in it sometimes give the mineral other colors. Geologists call crystals of the purest varieties *pearl spar*. The crystals have curved surfaces with a pearly luster.

Some dolomite is so much like calcite that a chemical test must be made to tell them apart. When the mineral dolomite is in large masses, it forms the kind of rock also called dolomite.

There are great mountain ranges of dolomite in Europe. In the United States, dolomite is found in New England, in the Appalachian Mountains, and in the Mississippi Valley.

Many limestones, and some of the finest statuary marbles, are made up of dolomite. Builders use compact varieties of the stone. The British chose this stone for building the Houses of Parliament in London. In steelmaking, dolomite can be treated and used to line Bessemer furnaces. The mineral is also used in the manufacture of Epsom salts.   A. PABST

See also CALCITE; DOLOMITES; LIMESTONE; MARBLE.

DOLOMITES, or DOLOMITE ALPS, are a part of the Alps mountain system in northeastern Italy and in the Austrian Tyrol. They were named for the French geologist Déodat Dolomieu, who discovered the magnesium-calcium rock called *dolomite* in these mountains (see DOLOMITE).

The Dolomite area covers about 200 square miles. The highest peak of the Dolomites is Marmolada (10,965 feet). Because of the minerals in them, some of the mountainsides are streaked with blue-black and yellow splotches, and others are a brilliant red. On the southern slope of the Dolomites lies the town of Pieve di Cadore. It is supposed to be the birthplace of Titian, a famous painter of the Renaissance.   SHEPARD B. CLOUGH

See also ITALY (color map).

DOLORES MISSION. See SAN FRANCISCO (History).

DOLPHIN

Flip Schulke, Black Star

DOLPHIN, *DAHL fin*, is a small whalelike animal whose snout forms a "beak." The dolphin is often confused with the porpoise, which has no beak. There are two chief kinds of dolphins: (1) bottle-nosed dolphins and (2) common dolphins.

The Bottle-Nosed Dolphin is a star performer in many aquariums. Almost all the "porpoises" that delight audiences with their tricks are really bottle-nosed dolphins. This dolphin can be trained to leap high into the air to grab a fish from its keeper's hand. It also can be taught to jump through a hoop and to fetch a thrown ball or stick.

Many scientists believe the bottle-nosed dolphin is one of the most intelligent animals. Some think its intelligence ranks between that of the dog and of the chimpanzee, the most intelligent animal. Others believe the dolphin would outrank even the chimpanzee if both animals could be given the same intelligence test.

Research has shown that dolphins communicate with each other by making various sounds. These

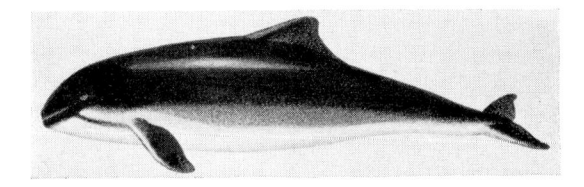

Dolphins Are Often Confused with Porpoises. The animals in water shows are often identified as porpoises, but they are really dolphins. The *common* porpoise, *above*, has a blunt snout. The *bottle-nosed* dolphin, *below*, has a beak-like snout.

Illustrated by Tom Dolan for WORLD BOOK

sounds include whistles, clicks, and barks. Bottle-nosed dolphins also have shown an ability to imitate some sounds of human speech. The U.S. National Aeronautics and Space Administration has sponsored a study of the dolphin's method of communication.

Dolphins also have a built-in sonar system. They use it to stay clear of enemies and underwater objects. Experiments have shown that bottle-nosed dolphins seem to hear the echoes of their own sounds when these noises are reflected by objects in the water. The U.S. Navy has supported research into how the dolphin's sonar system works.

The bottle-nosed dolphin is found in coastal waters. It grows up to 12 feet long and weighs as much as 800 pounds, but most are smaller. Its beak is about 3 inches long, and it has from 80 to 88 teeth. This dolphin has a grayish color, and its back is darker than its underside. In the early days, men captured bottle-nosed dolphins with nets in Cape Hatteras, off the coast of North Carolina. They used the oil from the animal's head for lubrication, and oil from the blubber for cooking. The meat was dried for use as human food.

The Common Dolphin is found in warm ocean waters. It grows to a length of 6 feet and weighs up to 150 pounds. Its beak is about 6 inches long, and it has from 80 to 100 teeth. This dolphin has a black back and a white underside, and prominent gray and brown stripes on its sides.

Sailors and passengers often see large *schools* (groups) of common dolphins leaping around ships in apparent joy. For hundreds of years, many seamen have regarded these dolphins as a sign that their voyage will be smooth and happy. For this reason, sailors frequently refuse to kill the dolphin, even though its meat is delicious. The meat was a welcome treat on the long whaling voyages of the early days.

The common dolphin appeared in ancient Greek and

Flip Schulke, Black Star

Dolphins Can "Talk" and scientists are conducting tests to learn more about the sounds they make. A scientist coaxes the dolphin into a small plastic tank, *above*. Then he records its sounds through a small microphone inserted in its blowhole, *below*.

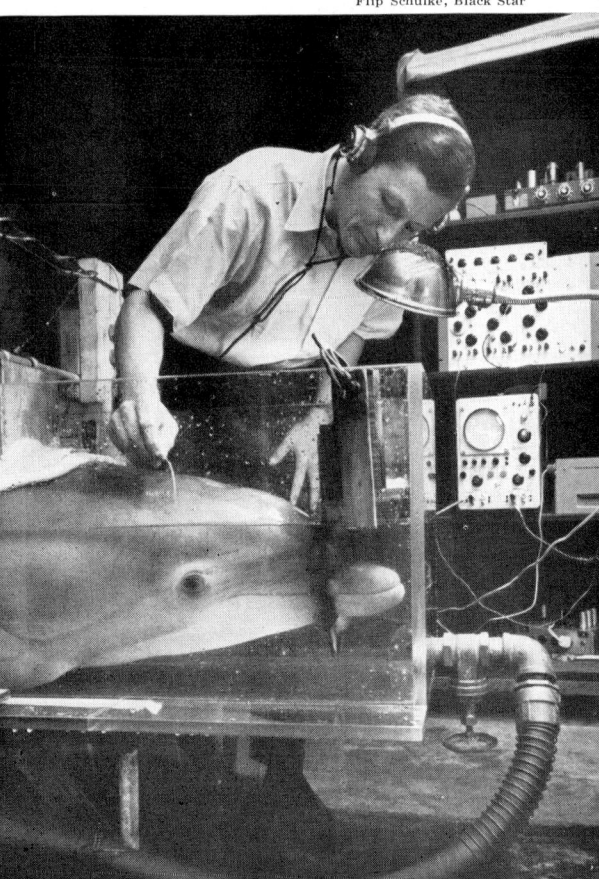

Flip Schulke, Black Star

Bottle-Nosed Dolphins Are Talented Entertainers. They are highly intelligent, and can learn to perform many tricks. For example, they can be taught to snatch food from a trainer's hand, *left;* leap through a hoop, *above;* and play basketball, *below.*

Roman mythology. The Greeks considered it sacred to the god Apollo.

Scientific Classification. Dolphins, porpoises, and toothed whales make up the suborder *Odontoceti.* Dolphins belong to the family *Delphinidae.* The bottle-nosed dolphin is genus *Tursiops,* species *I. truncatus.* The common dolphin is genus *Delphinus,* species *D. delphis.* RAMOND M. GILMORE

See also PORPOISE; WHALE.

DOLPHIN, DORADO, or CORYPHENE, is a large game fish that lives in warm salt waters. The largest dolphins are 6 feet long and weigh 75 to 100 pounds. They live in all tropical ocean waters. The dolphin's long body tapers toward a V-shaped tail. It is one of the fastest swimmers among fishes. Sometimes it chases flying fishes at sea, catching them for food. The dolphin is good to eat. It is blue and silver gray and sometimes changes into many colors when first removed from the sea.

Scientific Classification. The dolphin is a member of the family *Coryphaenidae.* It is genus *Coryphaena,* species *C. hippurus.* LEONARD P. SCHULTZ

See also FISHING (table, Game-Fishing).

DOMAGK, *DOH mahk,* **GERHARD** (1895-   ), a German physician, discovered the first of the sulfa drugs, the drug *prontosil.* He is best known for his work on a group of chemicals that included prontosil, a powerful destroyer of streptococcic bacteria. Domagk won the 1939 Nobel prize for this discovery. Domagk's early publications dealt chiefly with the search for a cancer cure. He has also worked on drugs for tuberculosis, and in 1952 described the drug *isonicotinic acid hydrazide* (INH), used in the treatment of tuberculosis. Domagk was born in Lagow, Germany. K. L. KAUFMAN

See also SULFA DRUGS (Development of Sulfa Drugs).

DOME is a kind of roof shaped like a bowl turned upside down. The word comes from the Latin *doma*, meaning *roof* or *house*, which in turn came from the Greek word *dōma*, meaning *housetop*. The ancient Assyrians, Persians, and Romans used domes on their buildings. But until the A.D. 500's, builders placed most domes on round or equal-sided buildings. The church of Saint Sophia in Constantinople (now Istanbul) was the first large rectangular building to be covered by a dome. It has a 107-foot dome. Later Byzantine and Russian churches usually had domes.

Most Arabian tombs and mosques are roofed with a dome. Builders in India copied the Arabs. An especially beautiful dome tops the Taj Mahal at Agra, India. The largest masonry dome now in existence is that on the Pantheon at Rome. It measures 142 feet in diameter and 142 feet in height. One of the largest domes in the world covers the Pittsburgh Auditorium. It is made up of stainless steel panels that slide open or closed. It measures 415 feet in diameter and 136 feet high at the center. The United Nations General Assembly Building in New York City has a stationary stainless-steel dome. Other noteworthy domes are those on Saint Peter's in Rome, Saint Paul's Cathedral in London, the Hôtel des Invalides in Paris, the Capitol in Washington, D.C., and the cathedral in Florence, Italy. KENNETH J. CONANT

See also CUPOLA; PANTHEON; SAINT SOPHIA; TAJ MAHAL.

FAMOUS DOMES

The Capitol in Washington, D.C. — Ewing Galloway

St. Peter's Church in Vatican City, Rome — Keystone

The Pantheon in Rome — Keystone

St. Sophia's Church in Istanbul, Turkey — Bosshard, Black Star

The Taj Mahal in Agra, India — Sawders

DOMEI

DOMEI. See KYODO.

DOMESDAY BOOK, or **DOOMSDAY BOOK,** was the first official record of the property owners living in England and the amount of land they owned. The information was collected and published at the command of William of Normandy. He ordered the territory to be taken from the nobility and large landowners and divided among his followers. William wanted to know how much land he owned, how the rest was divided, and how the land was peopled. The survey was ordered in 1085 and completed in 1086.

The country was divided into districts. Each district supplied census takers who knew the territory. The count of people and the survey of land covered all the territory William controlled. No survey was held in either London or Winchester, and the king's authority did not include Northumberland, Cumberland, Durham, or Westmorland. Information in Domesday Book was considered final and authoritative. Exact copies of the original Domesday Book were published in 1861 and 1865.

See also NORMAN CONQUEST.

The Domesday Book and Chest. The first official census of the English people and their possessions is recorded in two large volumes. One has 760 pages, the other, 900. The strongbox is the chest in which the two volumes were kept.

DOMESTIC ANIMAL. See ANIMAL (Domestic Animals).

DOMESTIC ART, or **DOMESTIC SCIENCE.** See HOMEMAKING.

DOMESTIC RELATIONS COURT. See COURT OF DOMESTIC RELATIONS.

DOMESTIC SYSTEM is an industrial arrangement in which a person works at home for an employer. The employer sells the product the person makes. It was in use as early as the 1200's, especially in such fields as clothing and weaving. See INDUSTRIAL REVOLUTION (The First Phase of the Industrial Revolution).

DOMINANT. See HARMONICS.

DOMINIC, SAINT, is a saint of the Roman Catholic Church. He founded the Order of Preachers, also called the *Dominican Order*. He was born at Calaroga in Old Castile about 1170, the son of Felix Guzman and Joanna of Aza. From 1184 to 1194 he studied at the University of Palencia. He became a canon of Osma, where he remained for some years. Later he entered the struggle against the Albigenses. He wanted to establish a new religious order for the purpose of preaching against heresy (see HERESY). After some difficulties, he finally got permission to do so from Pope Honorius III in 1216. When Dominic died in 1221, the Dominican Order he founded had spread over Europe. He was canonized in 1234. His feast day is August 3.   FULTON J. SHEEN

See also ALBIGENSES; DOMINICAN.

DOMINICA. See WINDWARD ISLANDS.

DOMINICAN, *doh MIHN ih kun*, is a member of an order of friars. It was founded in 1215 by Saint Dominic, to oppose the teachings of the Albigenses. The first house was established in France. In 1216, under the rule of Saint Augustine, the order received the approval of Pope Honorius III and the right to preach. The members are also known as the *Preaching Friars*. The order took definite shape in 1220. It soon became a power in the great universities of the day, as well as a preaching order. To these universities it contributed many learned men, among them Albertus Magnus and Thomas Aquinas. Four Dominicans became popes. Fra Angelico and Fra Bartolommeo, both Dominicans, were distinguished painters.

The members take the usual vows of obedience, poverty, and chastity, and lead very austere lives. Many features of monastic life, such as fasting and penitential exercises, are combined with their preaching ministry.

Saint Dominic also established an order of nuns in 1206. From the beginning it served as a shelter for the women of districts overrun by heresy, and later as a medium for the education of children.   FULTON J. SHEEN

See also DOMINIC, SAINT; FRIAR.

A Dominican Friar of the Roman Catholic Church wears a hooded white robe. The robe dates back to olden times when unbleached white muslin was the least expensive cloth.

Karmen-Winger

DOMINICAN COLLEGE OF SAN RAFAEL is a college for women located at San Rafael, Calif. It is controlled by the Roman Catholic Church, and offers work leading to the bachelor's and master's degrees. The school was founded at Monterey, Calif., in 1850, and first granted degrees in 1922. For enrollment, see UNIVERSITIES (table).

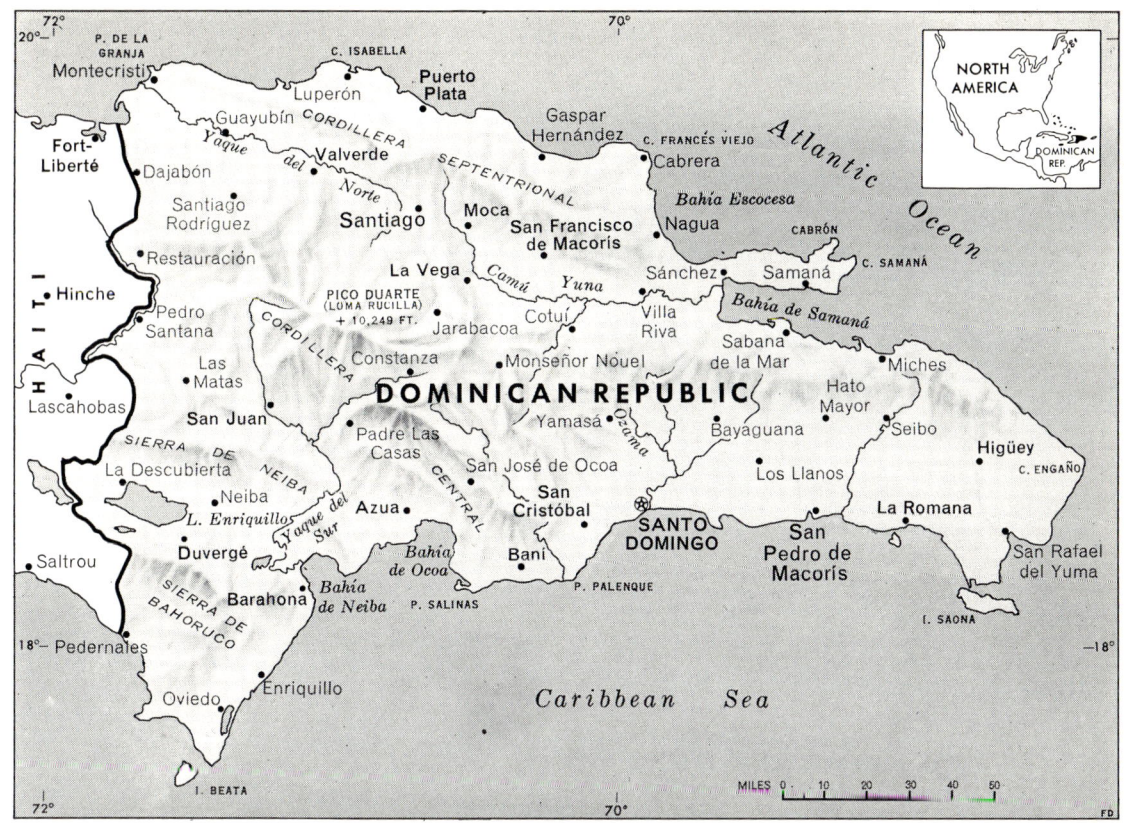

by Rand McNally for WORLD BOOK

DOMINICAN REPUBLIC is the country that makes up the eastern two thirds of the island of Hispaniola, in the West Indies. The country of Haiti is on the western end of the island. The name of the Dominican Republic in Spanish, the official language, is REPÚBLICA DOMINICANA. Santo Domingo is the capital and largest city.

The Dominican Republic is about the same size as New Hampshire and Vermont put together, but it has over three times as many people. Most Dominicans make their living from agriculture. Sugar cane is the chief crop and is the basis for most manufacturing.

Christopher Columbus discovered Hispaniola in 1492. He is said to be buried in the Cathedral of Santo Domingo in the nation's capital. Bartholomew Columbus, a brother of Christopher, founded Santo Domingo in 1496. The city is the oldest founded by Europeans in the Western Hemisphere. The Republic also has the oldest hospital in the Western Hemisphere, San Nicolas de Bari, founded in 1503 in Santo Domingo.

The Land and Its Resources

Location, Size, and Surface Features. The Dominican Republic is about 575 miles southeast of Miami, Fla. The *map* shows that it borders the Atlantic Ocean, the Caribbean Sea, and Haiti. The Dominican Republic covers 18,704 square miles. Four mountain ranges run east and west through the country. The Cordillera Septentrional is in the north. The Cordillera Central runs through the center of the country. The highest mountain in the West Indies, 10,249-foot Pico Duarte, is in this range. The Sierra de Neiba and Sierra de Bahoruco ranges lie in the southwest.

Rich valleys lie between the ranges. The largest lowland is the Cibao in the northern part of the country. Its eastern section is called the *Vega Real* (Royal Plain).

FACTS IN BRIEF

Type of Government: Republic.
Capital: Santo Domingo.
Divisions: 22 provinces and one district.
Head of State: President (4-year term).
Congress: Senate, 23 members (5-year terms); Chamber of Deputies, 52 members (5-year terms).
Area: 18,704 square miles. *Greatest distance:* (east-west) 225 miles; (north-south) 160 miles. *Coastline,* 1,017 miles.
Elevation: *Highest,* Pico Duarte, 10,249 feet above sea level. *Lowest,* Lago (Lake) de Enriquillo, 150 feet below sea level.
Population: 3,350,000. *Density,* 179 persons per sq. mi. *Distribution,* rural, 80 per cent; urban, 20 per cent.
Chief Products: *Agriculture,* bananas, cacao, coffee, rice, sugar cane, tobacco. *Mineral,* copper, gold, iron, bauxite, platinum, rock salt, silver. *Manufacturing and Processing,* baskets, cement, cigarettes, glassware, leather goods, peanut oil, pottery, rum, soap, sugar products, textiles.
Flag: A large white cross divides the flag into quarters which are alternately red and blue. The Dominican coat of arms is centered on the cross. See FLAG (color picture, Flags of the Americas).
National Holiday: Independence Day, February 27.
National Anthem: "Himno Nacional" ("National Hymn").
Money: *Basic unit,* peso. One hundred centavos equal one peso. For the value of the peso in dollars, see MONEY (table, Values).

The World's Largest Sugar Mill. The Río Haina Central, completed in 1952, can produce 15,000 tons of raw sugar each day.

The University of Santo Domingo in Santo Domingo is the oldest university in the Western Hemisphere. It was founded in 1538 under the name of Santo Tomás de Aquino.

The most important rivers are the Yaque del Norte, Yaque del Sur, Yuna, and Ozama. Enriquillo, a 200-square-mile lake in the southwest, is the largest in the country. It is 150 feet below sea level.

Climate. The Dominican Republic lies in the tropics. It has a warm climate, especially along the coasts, but is cooled by trade winds which blow in from the sea. The rainy season lasts from May to November.

Natural Resources. The rich soil of the valleys is the most important natural resource of the Republic. Many of the mountain slopes are covered with forests of such trees as the mahogany, satinwood, and cedar. The country has deposits of such minerals as gold, silver, platinum, iron, copper, bauxite, and rock salt.

The People and Their Work

The People. Most Dominicans are of Spanish and Negro ancestry. Many of the upper classes are white. The Arawak Indians once lived in the area, but they died out from disease and overwork after the Spaniards arrived in 1492. The Spaniards brought in other Indians, as well as African Negro slaves, to work their plantations. No European settlers except Spaniards were allowed in the country until the late 1700's. Refugees from Central Europe, mostly Jews, were admitted in 1940. They settled at Sosúa, a farm colony near Puerto Plata, and prospered so much that other Europeans were allowed to enter the country to live.

Way of Life. Most Dominicans live on farms or in small towns. They keep their cities and the countryside very clean. Dress in the cities is much like that in the United States. In the country, the men usually wear blue denim work clothes and the women, cotton dresses.

The people are hospitable and industrious. They have gay dispositions, are fond of music, and enjoy dancing the *merengue*, the national dance. Water sports and cockfights are popular. Much of the food is like that of Spain. *Arroz con pollo*, made of rice and chicken, is popular.

Cities. Santo Domingo (pop. 367,053), the capital, is the only city with more than 100,000 people. Santiago de los Caballeros has 83,523 people. The other cities have less than 30,000. These cities include San Francisco de Macorís (pop. 26,000), La Romana (pop. 24,058), San Pedro de Macorís (pop. 22,935), San Juan (pop. 20,449), Barahona (pop. 20,398), La Vega (pop. 19,884), Puerto Plata (pop. 19,073), and Valverde (pop. 17,885). See PUERTO PLATA; SANTIAGO DE LOS CABALLEROS; SANTO DOMINGO.

Agriculture. About four out of five Dominicans earn their living from agriculture. Important crops include sugar cane, cacao, coffee, tobacco, bananas, oranges, and rice. Cattle, hogs, goats, and chickens are raised. Some farmers have their own small farms. Others work on larger plantations. Still others live in one of the farm colonies that the government is developing for small farming.

Manufactures. The main industry of the country is preparing sugar for export. Many of the *centrales*, or sugar mills, are owned by United States interests. Other manufactured products include soap, textiles, glassware, leather goods, baskets, pottery, cement, rum, cigars, cigarettes, peanut oil, and furniture.

Trade. Sugar accounts for about half of the country's exports. Other exports include cocoa beans, coffee, molasses, bananas, meat, eggs, poultry, tobacco, and bauxite. The Republic imports textiles, clothing, processed foods, machinery, and fuel oil. Most trade is with the United States and Great Britain.

Transportation and Communication. The Republic has about 152 miles of public railroads, and 1,100 miles of private railroads belonging to the plantations. The Republic has about 3,000 miles of roads. Bus and air lines connect the main cities. Shipping is carried on along the coasts and on some rivers. The country has two television stations and over 40 radio stations.

Social and Cultural Achievements

Education is free, and the law requires all children to attend school. But many children go to school only a few years. Since the 1930's, the government has built many schools and trained many new teachers. A campaign against illiteracy began in 1941, and now about 73 of every 100 persons can read and write.

Religion. Roman Catholicism is the official religion of the Republic. But other faiths also are allowed.

The Arts of the Republic include the making of

DOMINICAN REPUBLIC

The Capitol of the Dominican Republic is built of pink marble, and was completed in 1947. It stands in Santo Domingo.

pottery, hammocks, baskets, and tortoise-shell articles. The popular music of the country comes from both Spanish and Negro sources. Many old churches contain religious paintings of colonial days.

Government

National Government. The head of state is a president. He is elected every four years by direct popular vote. One senator is elected from each province. One deputy is elected for each 60,000 people. All citizens over 18 years of age may vote in national elections. There are two major political parties, the Dominican Revolutionary and National Civic Union parties.

Local Government. Each province has a governor who is appointed by the president. Each commune is governed by a council which is elected by popular vote.

History

Colonial Years. Columbus discovered Hispaniola in 1492 and claimed it for Spain. The Spaniards called their colony Santo Domingo. In the 1600's, French colonists settled on the western part of the island, in the region later known as Haiti. Spain gave this part of the island to France in 1697 by the Treaty of Ryswick. In 1795, France received the eastern part of Hispaniola from Spain by the Treaty of Basel. The Dominicans revolted against the French in 1808 and 1809 and

---
RED-LETTER DATES IN THE DOMINICAN REPUBLIC
1492 Columbus discovered Hispaniola for Spain.
1496 First permanent European settlement in the Western Hemisphere, Nueva Isabela, was founded.
1795 France received the colony from Spain by the Treaty of Basel.
1808-1809 Dominicans revolted against France and returned to Spanish rule.
1821 Dominicans declared their country free of Spain.
1822 Haitians invaded and captured the country.
1844 Dominicans freed the country from Haiti.
1861 The Dominicans asked Spain to rule them again.
1865 Dominicans revolted and again became free.
1916-1924 United States Marines occupied the country.
1941 Dominican Republic entered World War II on the side of the Allies.
1947 Dominican Republic adopted a new constitution.
1961 Dictator Trujillo was assassinated.
1962 Juan Bosch was elected president of the Republic.

---

again placed the country under Spanish administration.

First and Second Periods of Independence. The Dominicans revolted in 1821, and declared their country free from Spain. In 1822, the Haitians invaded and captured the country. They held it until 1844, when the Dominicans revolted against them. Juan Pablo Duarte, Francisco del Rodario Sánchez, and Ramón Matías Mella led this revolt. The country was named the Dominican Republic in 1844. Leading Dominicans felt they needed protection from Haiti, and in 1861 they asked Spain to govern their country again. Spain ruled until 1865, when the people once more revolted.

Third Period of Independence. In the late 1860's President Buenaventura Baez offered to turn over the Republic to the United States. But the U.S. Senate refused. In the early 1900's, the Republic could not repay money borrowed from several European countries. Some of the countries wanted to occupy the Republic to get back their money. To prevent this, the United States began collecting customs duties in the Republic in 1905, and repaid the foreign loans in shares.

U.S. Marines occupied the Republic in 1916 because of internal political trouble. U.S. martial law continued until a new constitution was adopted in 1924.

The Trujillo Dictatorship started in 1930 when a military revolt ousted President Horacio Vasquez. Vasquez had been elected in 1924. In 1930, Rafael Leonidas Trujillo Molina became president, and ruled as dictator for the next 31 years.

Trujillo allowed very little freedom. Many who opposed him were killed or imprisoned. Other Latin American countries criticized his rule. But Trujillo did rebuild the capital city, and he built some new hospitals and housing projects. In 1941, the U.S. ended the collection of Dominican customs.

In 1959, the Organization of American States (OAS) condemned all dictatorships. In February, 1960, Venezuela asked the OAS to investigate charges that mass arrests by the Trujillo regime violated human rights. In August, 1960, the OAS denounced Trujillo for organizing a plot to assassinate President Romulo Betancourt of Venezuela. OAS member nations limited trade with the Republic and broke diplomatic relations.

Trujillo's Rule Ends. In May, 1961, Trujillo was murdered by assassins. His family and former aides were finally forced to leave the country late in 1961. A seven-man council, led by Rafael Bonnelly, was appointed to run the country until new elections could be held. The OAS members then lifted trade restrictions and resumed diplomatic relations with the Republic. In January, 1962, Bonnelly succeeded Joaquin Balaguer as president. In December, 1962, in the first free election in over 30 years, Dominicans elected Juan Bosch of the Dominican Revolutionary party president. Bosch planned an extensive program of land reform, with increased housing aid, rural loans, and technical assistance. He encouraged foreign investment in the Republic.

OTIS P. STARKEY

Related Articles in WORLD BOOK include:
Chocolate (table)	Santiago de los Caballeros
Haiti	Santo Domingo
Nueva Isabela	Trujillo Molina, Rafael L.
Puerto Plata	West Indies

DOMINION

DOMINION, *doh MIN yun,* is a self-governing country associated with Great Britain in the British Commonwealth of Nations. A dominion owes allegiance to the British Crown. Otherwise it is independent, with its own constitution, cabinet, parliament, and military forces. Dominions in the Commonwealth include Australia, Ceylon, and New Zealand. Canada became the first dominion in 1867, but dropped the title in 1949. The Union of South Africa became a dominion in 1910, but left the Commonwealth in 1961. ROBERT G. NEUMANN

DOMINION DAY is one of Canada's most important national holidays. It is often popularly called *Canada Day*. It is celebrated on July 1 of each year to honor the day the provinces of Canada were united in one government called the Dominion of Canada. On July 1, 1867, the Dominion of Canada was created by the terms of the British North America Act.

Dominion Day is a time for patriotic programs and activities. The national flag flies from every public building and schoolhouse. Dominion Day in New Zealand is a legal holiday observed annually on the fourth Monday in September. ELIZABETH HOUGH SECHRIST

DOMINION OBSERVATORY is the official government observatory of Canada. It is located in Ottawa, and is used to study earth tremors, to measure changes of the earth's surface, and for work in time service. It was founded in 1902.

The Dominion Astrophysical Observatory, in Victoria, British Columbia, has a large 72-inch reflecting telescope. This observatory determined the rate of rotation of the Milky Way. It has also specialized in observing double stars. It was founded in 1913. OTTO STRUVE

DOMINO. See MASK.

DOMINOES, *DAHM uh nohz,* is a game of chance and skill, played by two or more persons. Small, flat, oblong pieces of bone, wood, or ivory are used. A regular set consists of 28 dominoes. A line divides one side, or *face,* of each domino into two sections. Each section of 21 of the 28 dominoes is marked with from one to six dots. Both sections on one domino are blank, and six have one blank section and one with dots.

The players first place all the pieces face down and mix them well. Then each chooses a certain number, usually seven if there are two playing, or five if there are three or four. The player with the highest double number among his dominoes usually plays first. Suppose it is the 4-4. The player at the left plays next by matching any domino with four dots in one section to the 4-4 domino. For example, the matching domino may be the 4-6. The following player may then match a section with six dots to the 4-6 domino, or a section with four dots to the 4-4 domino. The sections can be matched by placing the dominoes end to end or end to side, but no section can be matched more than once. The game continues in this way, dot number being matched to dot number.

If a player cannot match from the dominoes he has chosen, he draws from the pile that remains until he finds a domino that will match. After the pile is all used, a player who cannot match must miss his turn, or *pass*. The one who first plays off all his dominoes wins the game. But sometimes dominoes are left that cannot be matched, and the game is said to be *blocked*. Then, in such a case, the player with the lowest number of dots wins. LILLIAN FRANKEL

Dominoes is played by matching pieces of bone, wood, or ivory. The players can add pieces only when they have the same number as that shown on the open end of a played domino.

DOMITIAN, *doh MISH ih un* (A.D. 51-96), was a cruel Roman emperor. His 15-year rule was a reign of terror and ended in his assassination. Jews, Christians, and members of his own family were his victims.

DON COSSACKS. See COSSACKS, DON.

DON GIOVANNI. See OPERA (Don Giovanni).

DON JUAN, *dahn JOO un,* or, in Spanish, *dohn HWAHN,* was the romantic hero of a legend that probably originated in Spain. The legend first took shape in a play by Tirso de Molina in 1630. The Don Juan story spread to other countries and inspired many writers and musicians, including Gluck, Molière, Byron, and Shaw. Mozart's opera *Don Giovanni* made the story popular throughout Europe.

In Tirso de Molina's play, Don Juan is a handsome, dashing, reckless member of the noble Tenorio family. He tries to carry off the daughter of the governor of Seville. The governor challenges him to a duel, and Don Juan kills the governor. Don Juan visits the tomb and jokingly invites the statue of his victim to dinner. To his horror, the "stone guest" appears at the feast. The statue returns the invitation, and Don Juan feels compelled to accept. In the graveyard, the statue takes his hand and the flames of hell seize Don Juan. ARTHUR M. SELVI

DON QUIXOTE, *KWIK soht,* or, in Spanish, *kee HO tay,* is the hero of a satirical novel *Don Quixote* by the great Spanish writer Cervantes. It was published in 1605 (see CERVANTES SAAVEDRA, MIGUEL DE).

Don Quixote is a simple-minded country gentleman who has read so many books of chivalry that he imagines himself a knight. He sets out to reform the world. He mistakes windmills for giants and flocks of sheep for

Don Quixote and Sancho Begin Their Amusing Travels.
Culver

252

armies. Sancho Panza, an ignorant country fellow, is his squire. Panza thinks only about eating and sleeping. Don Quixote thinks about ideals. Popular sayings that have come from *Don Quixote* include "Murder will out" and "A bird in the hand is worth two in the bush." The term *quixotic* has come to mean something idealistic but impractical.   GEORGE ROBERT CARLSEN

DON RIVER is an important waterway in the southern part of Russia. The Don rises from a small lake near Tula. It flows south for 1,220 miles and empties into the Sea of Azov. Large ships can sail on the Don for about 800 miles. At one point, the Don flows only 37 miles from the Volga River. The rivers are connected by a canal at this point. The northern part of the Don River flows through wooded, swampy land. But most of the river course is through rich farm and timber lands. The river carries large shipments of lumber, grain, and cattle. Many fishing villages lie along the Don, because its waters have valuable fish, especially sturgeon. The city of Rostov is near the mouth of the Don. The chief branch is the Donets.   THEODORE SHABAD

DONATELLO, DAHN uh TELL oh (1386?-1466), was one of the greatest sculptors of the early Italian Renaissance. He developed an extraordinary relief sculpture that had never been seen before. He used forceful rhythms and grace to give each statue individuality. He completed his *St. George* statue in Florence, Italy, in 1408. It was his first masterpiece. When Michelangelo saw the statue, it seemed so lifelike that he exclaimed, "March!" His *Singing Gallery* for the Florence cathedral is probably his most popular creation. This work showed how a sculptured border, or frieze, could be made part of a cathedral and still have great vitality and interest. Donatello's statue of the Venetian warrior Gattamelata on horseback is considered his best work. His statue *David* is in the National Gallery in Washington, D.C.

Donatello's Saint George was his first masterpiece.

Donatello was born in Florence. He was first apprenticed to a painter, then to the sculptor Ghiberti. He started work as a goldsmith and later turned to monumental sculpture. He studied classic sculpture in Rome, and then returned to Florence. He continued his metalwork and made many beautiful bronze statuettes, medals, and plaquettes.   MARVIN C. ROSS

See also SCULPTURE (Italy).

DONATI'S COMET. See COMET (Famous Comets).

DONELSON, JOHN. See TENNESSEE (Famous Tennesseans).

DONETSK, *dawn YEHTSK* (pop. 749,000; met. area, 1,600,000; alt. 500 ft.), is the largest city in the Donets River Basin of Russia. It lies in the Ukrainian Soviet Socialist Republic, about 80 miles northwest of Rostov

DONKEY

(see RUSSIA [color map]). Donetsk is in the center of the rich Donets coal fields. The coal is used in the huge iron and steel mills that make Donetsk one of the most important Russian industrial cities. Machinery and food products are also produced there.

The city was founded in the 1870's under the name Yuzovka. After the Russian Revolution, its name was changed to Stalin. In 1935, it became Stalino. The name was changed to Donetsk in 1961 as part of Russian Premier Nikita Khrushchev's drive to down grade Josef Stalin.   THEODORE SHABAD

DONIZETTI, DAHN ih ZET ih, **GAETANO** (1797-1848), an Italian composer, wrote nearly 70 operas. His comic operas, *Don Pasquale* and *L'Elisir d'Amore*, still delight both performers and audiences. His serious opera, *Lucia di Lammermoor*, with its "Mad Scene" and "Sextet," has been performed many times. He also composed *Anna Bolena*, *Lucrezia Borgia*, *La Fille du Régiment*, and *La Favorite*. Donizetti's style stands between the brilliance of Gioacchino Rossini and the more dramatic style of Giuseppe Verdi. He depended upon the vocal agility of his singers for effect.

Donizetti was born at Bergamo. He studied there and at Bologna Liceo Filarmonico.   THEODORE M. FINNEY

See also OPERA (Some of the Famous Operas [Daughter of the Regiment; Lucia di Lammermoor]).

DONJON. See CASTLE.

DONKEY, or **BURRO**, is the name of several animals which are relatives of horses, but are smaller and sturdier. Donkeys have huge ears. The wild ass of Abys-

J. C. Allen and Son

The Donkey, one of the first animals to be tamed by man, makes a gentle pet. Many donkeys, or burros, are exported from Mexico.

sinia and northern Africa is the ancestor of the common domestic donkey. This wild ass looks like a zebra with no stripes. It stands about 4 feet high at the shoulders. Its coat of hair is gray, with a darker line along its back. This intelligent animal can run swiftly.

Thousands of years ago men tamed the African wild ass and raised it for their own use. The domestic donkey is most common in southern Asia, southern Europe, and northern Africa. There are several varieties of the domestic donkey. People use light, speedy donkeys for riding. Those of a larger, heavier breed draw carts or carry loads on their backs. The hardy donkeys do not

253

DONN-BYRNE, BRIAN OSWALD

require as much or as good food as horses do. But they become stubborn and dull if badly treated. Female donkeys, or jennies, give good milk. In northern Africa, they were once kept in large herds for this purpose. The young donkey is called a *colt*. If a male donkey, or jack, is mated with a mare, the young animal that is born is a *mule* (see MULE). A cross between a female donkey and a stallion, or a male horse, is called a *hinny* (see HINNY). The small donkeys called *burros* are often used as pack animals, because they are sure-footed. Other kinds of wild asses are found in the dry plains of Asia. They include the *onager* and the *kiang* (see ONAGER).

Scientific Classification. Donkey belongs to the family *Equidae*. The domestic donkey and the African wild ass are genus *Equus*, species *asinus*.   VICTOR H. CAHALANE.

DONN-BYRNE, *dahn-BURN,* **BRIAN OSWALD** (1889-1928), was an Irish novelist. His best-known work, *Messer Marco Polo,* appeared in 1921. Byrne was born in Brooklyn, N.Y., and grew up in County Antrim, Ireland. He was a student at University College, Dublin, and later studied in Paris and Leipzig. He was a cowboy in South America for a time. His works include *Stories Without Women, Blind Raftery, Hangman's House,* and *Brother Saul.* He wrote his books under the name of Donn Byrne.   JOSEPH E. BAKER.

DONNE, *DUN,* **JOHN** (1571?-1631), was an English poet and clergyman. He disliked the sweet, pretty love poems of the time. He developed a new "metaphysical" style of poetry using *conceits,* or fantastic comparisons, and *paradoxes,* or contradictions. An example of a conceit is the poem in which he says it is easier to catch a falling star than to find a beautiful and true woman. One of his paradoxes is: *we die in order to live.* When he was older, Donne wrote fine religious poetry and preached some of the best sermons in the history of the English language.

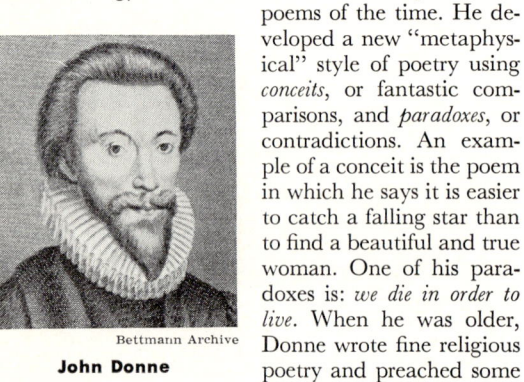

Bettmann Archive
John Donne

His early poems, both love poems and satires, were not published until after his death. They were passed around by his friends in handwritten copies. Hardly anyone read them 50 years after his death. But a group of young poets, led by T. S. Eliot, used Donne's poems as models for their own poems after 1910.

One of his *Devotions* contains the line ". . . send not to know for whom the bell tolls: it tolls for thee." Ernest Hemingway used part of the phrase as the title of his novel, *For Whom the Bell Tolls.*

Donne was born in London of a Roman Catholic family. He went to Oxford University, but Catholics could not receive degrees from Oxford then. He studied law from 1591 to 1594, then went on two military expeditions against the Spanish in 1596 and 1597. He became secretary to Sir Thomas Egerton in 1598.

He married Egerton's niece, Ann More, against her father's will three years later. The father had Donne imprisoned. He could not break up the marriage, but he ruined Donne's career. Donne wrote, "John Donne, Ann Donne, Undone." For several years the Donnes lived off the charity of friends. Donne had drifted away from Catholicism in the 1590's, and he wrote pamphlets against the Catholics in 1610 and 1611. King James I advised Donne to become a priest in the Church of England. He was ordained in 1615. He became Dean of St. Paul's, the principal church in London, in 1621 and became a famous preacher.   ARNOLD WILLIAMS.

DONNER PASS is one of the most important passes through the Sierra Nevada Mountains in California. It lies 7,089 feet above sea level. The first transcontinental railroad, completed in 1869, used the pass. U.S. Highway 40 also follows the route. The pass was named for George Donner, leader of a party of emigrants who wintered there in 1846.   JOHN W. REITH.

"DON'T GIVE UP THE SHIP." See LAWRENCE, JAMES.

DONUS became pope of the Roman Catholic Church in 676, following Adeodatus II, and served until 678. During his reign, he restored and decorated churches in Rome. He also forced the archbishop of Ravenna to recognize the superior authority of the papacy. Donus was born in Rome.

By an error, it was supposed that there was a later pope called Donus II. His date of election was given as 974. There never was such a pope. A medieval chronicler took the title *Domnus Papa,* meaning *the Lord Pope,* to be the personal name of someone different from Benedict VII, who actually was elected to the papacy in 974.   GUSTAVE WEIGEL and FULTON J. SHEEN.

DOODLEBUG. See ANT LION.

DOOLEY, THOMAS ANTHONY, III (1927-1961), an American physician, became famous in the 1950's as "the jungle doctor of Laos." He helped found MEDICO (Medical International Cooperation Organization) in 1957. Through it, he established two hospitals in Laos, and one each in Vietnam, Cambodia, and Malaya. He helped finance MEDICO with funds from lecture tours and books he wrote.

Dooley's first book, *Deliver Us from Evil,* (1956), described his experiences as a U.S. Navy doctor in Vietnam in 1954. There, he helped refugees fleeing from communist North Vietnam. He left the navy in 1956 and started his medical work in Laos. At the age of 34, he died of cancer. Dooley was born in St. Louis, Mo.   L. T. COGGESHALL.

DOOLITTLE, JAMES HAROLD (1896-   ), a noted American flier, led the first bombing raid on Tokyo in World War II. He led 16 B-25 twin-engine bombers, normally land-based planes, from the deck of the aircraft carrier U.S.S. *Hornet* in the surprise attack on Tokyo in April, 1942. Congress awarded him the Medal of Honor for this daring raid.

U.S. Army
James H. Doolittle

He rose to the rank of lieutenant general during World War II. He commanded the 12th Air Force in the North African invasion in 1942, and later the 15th Air Force in the Mediterranean area. He became commander of the 8th Air Force which bombed western Europe from British bases. He also commanded the 8th Air Force on Okinawa after Germany surrendered.

Doolittle was born in Alameda, Calif., and was graduated from the University of California. He studied aeronautical engineering at the Massachusetts Institute of Technology (MIT) and became an Army aviator. He gained fame as a stunt flyer. He joined the Shell Petroleum Corp. in 1930, and became a vice-president after World War II. Doolittle served as chairman of the National Advisory Committee for Aeronautics from 1956 to 1958. WESLEY FRANK CRAVEN

DOOM, or **DOUM, PALM** grows in Arabia, Upper Egypt, and Central Africa. Each branch of the doom palm ends in a tuft of deeply lobed, fan-shaped leaves. The doom bears an irregularly oval fruit about the size of an apple. It has a red outer skin covering a thick, spongy, and rather sweet substance which tastes like gingerbread. Because of this the palm has often been called the *gingerbread tree*. Large quantities of these fruits have been found in the tombs of the Egyptian pharaohs.

Scientific Classification. Doom palm is a member of the family *Palmae*. It belongs to genus *Hyphaene*, species *thebaica*. IVAN MURRAY JOHNSTON

DOOMSDAY BOOK. See DOMESDAY BOOK.

DOON, RIVER, is a stream in Ayr County of southern Scotland which was made famous by the poetry of Robert Burns. The River Doon rises in the Kells Range and flows northwest to empty into the Firth of Clyde near the town of Ayr. The cottage where Burns was born is two miles from Ayr. Also nearby is the bridge Burns made famous as the "Auld Brig o' Doon" in the poem "Tam o' Shanter." FRANCIS H. HERRICK

DOOR is an opening through which people enter and leave a room or building. The word also means the movable frame used to open and close such an opening. This frame may be hung on hinges. It may slide back and forth in a groove, turn on a pivot like a vertical axle, or fold on itself like an accordion. There are doors that are divided into two parts, so that the upper half can be opened while the lower half stays closed. This is a popular type in European cottages. The top section is opened to allow the people to see out while the bottom section remains closed to prevent the barnyard animals from coming into the house, or to keep in small children.

The revolving door, divided into four panels, turns on a central axle. It is an American invention dating to about 1880. It enables a great many people to go in or out of a building quickly and still keeps the door opening closed off. There are over 20,000 revolving doors in use in the United States.

Doors have sometimes been made of rare woods ornamented with carvings and precious metals. The Bible tells us that workmen made the doors of King Solomon's temple of olive wood and gold. Church doors are often made of or sheathed with bronze, on which beautiful designs and figures are placed. A fine example of this is the set of bronze doors made in the 1400's by Lorenzo Ghiberti for the Baptistery at Florence, Italy. The doors of the church of St. Michael at Hildesheim, Germany (1015), are another striking example of beautiful designs in bronze. KENNETH J. CONANT

DOORBELL. See ELECTRIC BELL.
DOORMAT is a weed. See KNOTGRASS.
DOORSTEP OF A CONTINENT. See NOVA SCOTIA.

Keystone
The White House Door, Washington, D.C., is the main entrance to the President's home on Pennsylvania Avenue. Every President since John Adams has passed through these portals.

The Baptistery Doors in Florence, Italy, were fashioned by Lorenzo Ghiberti in the 1400's. Years later, Michelangelo said "They are worthy to be the gates of Paradise."

Alinari

255

DOPPLER EFFECT

DOPPLER EFFECT is the apparent change in frequency of sound, light, or radio waves caused by motion. For example, the *pitch* (frequency) of a train whistle seems to become higher as the train approaches and becomes lower after it passes. The actual pitch of the whistle remains constant. Astronomers study the speed of a star by measuring the slight apparent change in the frequency of its light waves due to motion. Christian Doppler (1803-1853), a German physicist, first described the effect in 1842. RAWSON BENNETT

See also PITCH; RADAR (Other Radars); RELATIVITY (General Relativity Theory); SOUND (Pitch).

DORADO. See DOLPHIN, DORADO, or CORYPHENE.
DORCHESTER, BARON. See CARLETON, SIR GUY.
DORDOGNE RIVER. See GARONNE RIVER.
DORÉ, *daw* RAY, **GUSTAVE** (1832-1883), a French painter and sculptor, illustrated a large number of literary masterpieces. These include the Bible, the works of Rabelais and Balzac, Dante's *Divine Comedy*, LaFontaine's *Fables*, Tennyson's *Idylls of the King*, Cervantes' *Don Quixote*, Coleridge's "The Rime of the Ancient Mariner" and Poe's "The Raven." His style is dramatic and imaginative, but sometimes repetitious.

Doré was born PAUL GUSTAVE DORÉ in Strasbourg, Alsace-Lorraine. As a boy, he showed a remarkable talent for drawing. His work was in great demand

From *The Terrible Gustave Doré* by Lehmann-Haupt.
© 1943 by Marchbanks Press

Gustave Doré illustrated the fairy tales of Charles Perrault. This heavily detailed scene shows Tom Thumb entering the forest.

while he was still quite young. His fame outside of France rests chiefly on his illustrations. NORMAN RICE

For reproductions of Doré's works, see CAIN; CHARON; DANTE ALIGHIERI; EDEN; MOSES; PETER, SAINT.

DORIAN, *DO rih un.* The people known as the Dorians were the last and most warlike of three Hellenic groups that invaded Greece in prehistoric times. Their invasion began about 1150 B.C., and they quickly overran most of the Peloponnesus, Crete, and Rhodes. They drove out or destroyed most of the Achaeans and other earlier inhabitants, and put an end to Mycenaean civilization.

In historic times, the descendants of the Dorians retained much of their skill in warfare, but often developed a very conservative way of life. They spoke a peculiar dialect called *Doric*. The best-known Greeks of Dorian descent were the Spartans. Corinth, Argos, and Rhodes were Dorian cities. The Dorians are supposed to have taken their name from Dorus, the son of Hellen, who was the legendary ancestor of all Greek peoples. Many historians think they probably introduced iron into ancient Greece. JOHN H. KENT

See also ACHAEAN; CORINTH; GREECE, ANCIENT (History); SPARTA.

DORIC, *DAHR ik,* is the simplest of the three types of Greek columns. See COLUMN (The Greek Orders).
DORION, SIR ANTOINE AIMÉ. See QUEBEC (Famous Quebecers).
DORIS was a Greek goddess. See NEREID.
DORMER. See ARCHITECTURE (Architectural Terms).
DORMOUSE, *DAWR mous,* is a small rodent that looks somewhat like a squirrel (see RODENT). The dormouse lives in the warm parts of the British Isles, Europe, Asia, and Africa.

The dormouse is an attractive animal with fine, silky fur. It has a large head with a pointed nose and large eyes. Its ears are small like those of a mouse. The dormouse searches for its food at night. It sits up on its hind legs and holds its food between its two front paws. Its food consists of acorns, berries, hazelnuts, and grain.

The dormouse sleeps all through the winter. It curls up in its neat nest which it makes in bushes. It awakens now and then during the winter to eat some of its stored food. Lewis Carroll made the Dormouse a humorous character in his *Alice in Wonderland*.

Scientific Classification. The dormouse belongs to the family *Muscardinidae*. It is genus *Muscardinus*, species *avellanarius*. STANLEY P. YOUNG

The Dormouse Sleeps Through Most of the Winter.
U.&U.

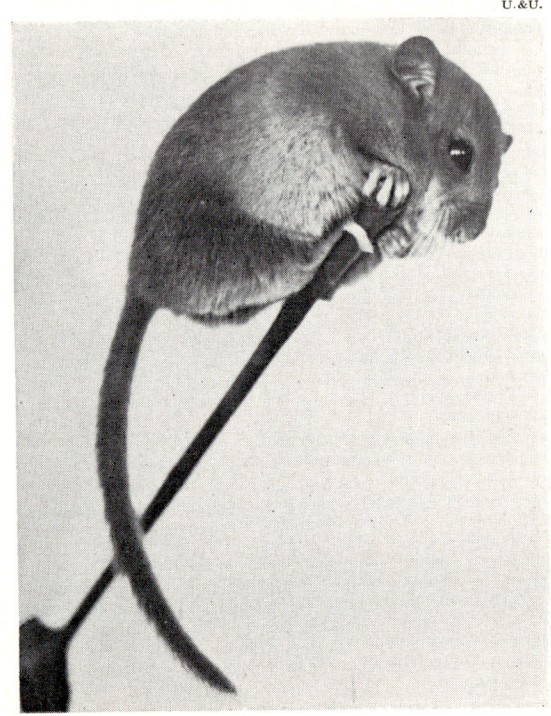

DÖRPFELD, WILHELM. See Troy (The Troy of Archaeology).

DORR, THOMAS WILSON. See Rhode Island (Famous Rhode Islanders); Dorr's Rebellion.

DORR'S REBELLION. Before 1843, factory workers and city dwellers in Rhode Island were not generally allowed to vote. This was because Rhode Island was still operating under its old charter of 1663, which restricted voting to landholders or their eldest sons. This deprived more than half of the state's adult males of the right to vote.

Thomas Dorr, a member of the state legislature from 1833 to 1837, voiced the discontent of the people with this arrangement. Dorr became head of a party which sought to grant the vote to all men of legal age. In October, 1841, the agitators held a convention and drafted a constitution. About the same time, the state government, realizing that affairs were drifting toward revolution, called a convention and drafted a constitution almost as liberal. This constitution was submitted to the people and voted down. In a separate election, Dorr's reform constitution received a decisive majority, but the government declared that it had been illegally adopted. Dorr's party then held its own election and chose Dorr to be governor, while Samuel W. King was elected governor at the regular state election. Dorr and his followers tried to sustain their government, but the rebellion was put down by state troops. Dorr was convicted of treason and sentenced to life imprisonment, but was released after one year.

Partly as a result of Dorr's Rebellion, Rhode Island obtained a new constitution in 1843. It gave native-born citizens the right to vote if they paid taxes of $1 a year or served in the militia. RAY ALLEN BILLINGTON

DORSEY, "TOMMY," THOMAS FRANCIS, JR. See Popular Music (Famous Popular Musicians).

DOSHISHA UNIVERSITY. See Japan (Education).

DORTMUND, *DAWRT moont* (pop. 641,500; alt. 249 ft.), is a major German industrial city. An iron, steel, and heavy machinery center, Dortmund stands in the heart of Germany's famous coal-bearing Ruhr district. The city is linked with the North Sea by the Dortmund-Ems Canal. Dortmund was founded in the 800's and became one of the cities of the Hanseatic League. It grew rapidly after 1870. During World War II, Dortmund was heavily bombed. Since then it has recovered rapidly, and is again famous for its brewing industry and its Westfalenhalle, one of the largest sports arenas in western Europe. For Dortmund's location, see Germany (color map). JAMES K. POLLOCK

DOS PASSOS, *dus PAS us,* **JOHN RODERIGO** (1896-), an American novelist, journalist, and traveler, became famous with his novel *Manhattan Transfer* in 1925. This was followed by a trilogy *U.S.A.* (1937), made up of *The 42nd Parallel, 1919,* and *The Big Money. U.S.A.* studies the United States' social development in the first quarter of the 1900's. It is an example of the social consciousness in Dos Passos' works.

Dos Passos was born in Chicago, and was graduated from Harvard University. He drove an ambulance in France during World War I, and traveled widely after the war. During World War II, he reported on the battle front and the home front. His books *Journeys Between Wars* (1938), *The Ground We Stand On* (1941), and *State of the Nation* (1944), are made up of these experiences.

Houghton Mifflin
John Dos Passos

Culver
Fyodor Dostoevsky

One of his writing devices is "the camera eye," in which he gives a sweeping panorama of American life by a series of impressionistic passages—fragments of headlines, popular songs, and advertisements. He also wrote *Three Soldiers* (1921), *Orient Express* (1927), *Adventures of a Young Man* (1939), *Number One* (1943), *The Grand Design* (1949), *Most Likely to Succeed* (1954), *The Great Days* (1958), and *Midcentury* (1961). JOHN O. EIDSON

DOSTOEVSKY, *DAHS tuh YEF skih,* **FYODOR MIKHAILOVICH** (1821-1881), must be regarded as one of the two or three greatest novelists Russia has produced. He is widely read today throughout the world.

Dostoevsky's novels are essentially novels of ideas embodied in his great characters. His characters are intensely individual, vital, and complex. They are usually caught up in tremendous dramatic situations as they struggle between good and evil in an effort to achieve salvation through suffering.

Dostoevsky was born in Moscow. By the time he had finished his education, he had already decided to make literature his career. His first story, *Poor Folk* (1846), won the enthusiastic praise of the critics because it added something new to Russian literature at that time—a deep psychological study of poor, unhappy people. Throughout his life, he wrote about the poor and unhappy, the insulted and injured, and the strange, abnormal people who defied conventional society.

While still a young man, Dostoevsky was arrested for taking part in a political conspiracy, and was sentenced to death. When he was on the scaffold waiting for his execution, the czar's courier brought a reprieve. Dostoevsky, instead, was sent to prison for four years to work at hard labor in Siberia. After serving four more years of punishment as a common soldier, he was permitted to return to St. Petersburg (now Leningrad) to resume his literary career. In his *Memoirs from the House of the Dead* (1861-1862), he told in brilliantly realistic detail of his prison life.

Years of bitter, poverty-stricken existence followed for Dostoevsky. He published periodicals, and always had to write against time to keep his creditors from sending him to a debtors' prison. After his *Memoirs from Underground* (1864), an extraordinary psychological study of a spiritual and intellectual misfit, he once again won popularity with his famous novel, *Crime and Punishment* (1866). This tells the story of a student who commits murder to fulfill a theory that would enable him to become one of the strong men of the earth.

DOTY, JAMES DUANE

Despite his success, Dostoevsky remained poor, largely because he was generous and could not take care of his money. He went abroad, and wrote two great novels, *The Idiot* (1868) and *The Possessed* (1871-1872). He later returned to Russia, and completed his last, and, in many respects, his greatest novel, *The Brothers Karamazov* (1880).   ERNEST J. SIMMONS

See also BROTHERS KARAMAZOV.

DOTY, JAMES DUANE. See WISCONSIN (Famous Wisconsinites).

DOUAY, or **DOUAI, BIBLE.** See BIBLE (The Vulgate and the Douai).

DOUBLE BASS. See BASS (musical instrument).

DOUBLE-ENTRY BOOKKEEPING. See BOOKKEEPING.

DOUBLE INDEMNITY. See INSURANCE (Insurance Terms).

DOUBLE STAR is a pair of stars which revolve around a center of gravity between them. Double stars are also called *binaries*. The term *binary star* was probably used for the first time by Sir William Herschel in 1802. There are three kinds of double stars, visual, spectroscopic, and eclipsing.

Many times double stars are so close together that even the largest telescope shows them as a single star. Sometimes two stars appear close together only because they are in nearly the same direction in space. One such star may be much closer to us than the other. Astronomers call such cases "optical pairs."

Most double stars appear as one to the unaided eye. If they can be seen as two stars, or if a telescope reveals them as two stars, they are called *visual doubles* or *visual binaries*. Mizar, the next to the last star in the handle of the Big Dipper, is the first visual binary ever discovered. John Baptist Riccioli discovered it in 1650. The smaller partner of Mizar is Alcor.

Mizar and Alcor have been shown to be *spectroscopic binaries*. So what may appear as a single star in the handle of the Big Dipper turns out to be four stars: a visual binary, each star of which is a spectroscopic binary.

Astronomers show the existence of spectroscopic binaries by an instrument called the *spectroscope*. At regular intervals, the lines in the spectra of such double stars appear alternately single and double so that we know two stars are present, revolving around each other.

Sometimes spectroscopic binaries revolve in such a way that one star comes between us and its companion star at regular intervals. The star in front eclipses the one behind. The light we see becomes less for a short period. Such double stars are called *eclipsing binaries*, and are discovered by their regular variations in degree of brightness. An example of an eclipsing binary is the star Algol.

CHARLES ANTHONY FEDERER, JR.

See also ALGOL; SPECTROSCOPE.

DOUBLEDAY, ABNER (1819-1893), an American army officer, is generally credited with inventing the

Natl. Museum of Baseball
Abner Doubleday

game of baseball in 1839. While a schoolboy at Cooperstown, N.Y., he organized the loosely-played game of town ball into the present game of baseball. Doubleday set the bases 60 feet from each other, and limited the teams to 11 players each. He also assigned defensive positions to the players, and conceived the idea of allowing putouts to be made by a fielder covering the base or tagging the runner. Because of him, the Baseball Hall of Fame is located at Cooperstown. The field there is named Doubleday Field.

Doubleday was born at Ballston Spa, N.Y. He was graduated from the United States Military Academy, and served in the Mexican War. He became a major general during the Civil War, and fought heroically at the Battle of Gettysburg. He was buried in Arlington National Cemetery in Arlington, Va.   ED FITZGERALD

See also BASEBALL (History).

DOUBLET, in clothing, see CLOTHING (Renaissance); in jewelry, see GEM (Imitation and Artificial Gems).

DOUBLOON is an old Spanish and Spanish-American gold coin. The name comes from the Latin *duplus*, meaning *double*. The doubloon was equal to four *pistoles*

Chase Manhattan Bank Money Museum

The Spanish Doubloon shows the face of Charles IV, King of Spain. The other side bears his royal coat of arms. This gold coin was circulated in the American colonies during 1790.

(sixteen silver dollars). It was also called *doblón de a ocho*, meaning *doubloon of eight*, because it was worth eight gold escudos. Its weight was about 27 grams. The coin is no longer in use.

DOUBTING THOMAS. See THOMAS, SAINT.

DOUGHNUT is a round, fried cake with a hole in the center. Dutch settlers brought the fried cake, or *olykoeck*, to colonial America. In 1847, Captain Hanson Gregory, a sea captain, invented the hole in the doughnut. He cut holes in the dough before frying to make the cakes more digestible. A bronze plaque marks Gregory's birthplace in Camden township (now Rockport), Me.

DOUGHTY, *DOW*tih, **CHARLES MONTAGU** (1843-1926), was an English author and traveler. He traveled in western and southern Europe, Egypt, the Middle East, and India, collecting inscriptions and writing on geology. He wrote *Travels in Arabia Deserta*, a vivid picture of Arabia in the 1870's. He also wrote two epic poems, *The Dawn in Britain* and *The Titans*, and a philosophic autobiography, *Mansoul*. He was born in Suffolk, England, and was graduated from Cambridge University. He wrote in the Elizabethan style.   WALTER WRIGHT

DOUGLAS. See MAN, ISLE OF.

DOUGLAS, DONALD WILLS (1892-   ), an American aircraft manufacturer, organized the Douglas Company in 1922. It became the Douglas Aircraft Corpora-

258

tion in 1928. He designed the army planes that made the first flight around the world in 1924. His firm has made widely used commercial airliners, such as the twin-engined DC-3. He was born in Brooklyn, N.Y. See also AIRPLANE (During World War I); AVIATION (Red Letter Dates in Aviation). V. E. CANGELOSI and R. E. WESTMEYER

DOUGLAS, SIR JAMES. See BRITISH COLUMBIA (Famous British Columbians).

DOUGLAS, SIR JOHN SHOLTO. See QUEENSBERRY, MARQUIS OF.

DOUGLAS, LEWIS WILLIAMS (1894-), an American diplomat and administrator, was the United States ambassador to Great Britain from 1947 to 1950 under President Harry S Truman. Douglas served three terms as a Democratic U.S. Representative from Arizona from 1926 until he became Director of the Budget under President Franklin D. Roosevelt in 1933. Douglas resigned in 1934 when he disagreed with New Deal policies. He was born in Bisbee, Ariz., and was graduated from Amherst College. HARVEY WISH

DOUGLAS, LLOYD CASSEL (1877-1951), a Lutheran minister, wrote the best-selling novels *Magnificent Obsession* (1929), *The Robe* (1942), and *The Big Fisherman* (1948). He also wrote *Forgive Us Our Trespasses* (1932), *Green Light* (1935), and *Invitation to Live* (1940). His autobiography, *A Time to Remember*, was published in 1951. As a novelist, his chief interest was always to inspire religious teaching, but, to his surprise, his books achieved great popularity.

Douglas was born in Columbia City, Ind. He was graduated from Wittenberg College. He began to preach in Indiana in 1903, and at 31 became pastor of a church in Washington, D.C. Three years later, he became Director of Religious Work at the University of Illinois. Later he served as a pastor in Ann Arbor, Mich.; Akron, Ohio; and Los Angeles, Calif. BERNARD DUFFEY

DOUGLAS, PAUL HOWARD. See ILLINOIS (Famous Illinoisans).

DOUGLAS, STEPHEN ARNOLD (1813-1861), was a popular and skillful American orator and political leader just before the Civil War. He became especially well known for his debates with Abraham Lincoln on the question of slavery. These debates ranked as noteworthy events in American history. See LINCOLN, ABRAHAM (Debates with Douglas).

Douglas was born on a farm near Brandon, Vt. Politics interested him and he wanted to become a lawyer. When he was 20, he went to Illinois. He was admitted to the bar at Jacksonville, Ill. Douglas, a Democrat, was elected prosecuting attorney for his district in 1835. The next year he was elected to the state legislature. He was judge of the Supreme Court of Illinois from 1841 to 1843. He was elected to the United States House of Representatives in 1843, and became a member of the United States Senate in 1847.

Douglas was a short man, with a large head and broad shoulders. Because of his appearance, he received

Brown Bros.
Stephen A. Douglas

DOUGLAS AIRCRAFT COMPANY

the nickname "The Little Giant." He won respect in the Senate for his ability, energy, sincerity and fearlessness, and became chairman of the Senate committee on territories.

The slavery controversy was the great issue of that period. As each territory applied for admission to the Union, a storm of debate arose in Congress as to whether the new state should be free or slaveholding. Douglas would not own slaves himself, but he was not opposed to slavery and did not believe that the Union should be sacrificed for it. He thought that the problem could be settled by peaceable means. He warmly favored westward expansion, but believed that the people of the territories should decide for themselves whether they wanted slavery. He called this principle *squatter sovereignty* (see SQUATTER SOVEREIGNTY). Douglas' committee reported the famous Kansas-Nebraska Bill in 1854. It included the principle of squatter sovereignty (see KANSAS-NEBRASKA ACT). Douglas' brilliant leadership was responsible for the passage of this much disputed bill.

When Douglas ran for re-election to the Senate in 1858, his Republican opponent was Abraham Lincoln, a man then almost unknown outside Illinois. During the campaign, the two men held a series of public meetings in which they debated the problem of slavery and its extension (see DEBATE [picture]). These meetings attracted the attention of the entire country.

Douglas argued that the people must have the right to control slavery. Lincoln said that a nation half-slave and half-free could not exist. Douglas won his re-election to the Senate, but some of his speeches in the debates displeased Southern Democrats. He was nominated for President by Northern Democrats in 1860, but the South refused to support him. The Democratic party split its votes among three candidates. Douglas received only 12 electoral votes. The Republican candidate, Abraham Lincoln, won the election.

Douglas offered his services to President Lincoln when the Civil War broke out. At Lincoln's request, he started on a tour of the border states to arouse enthusiasm for the Union cause. But two months after the fall of Fort Sumter, he died. He was buried in a small park at the foot of Thirty-Sixth Street in Chicago. JEANNETTE C. NOLAN

See also COMPROMISE OF 1850.

DOUGLAS, WILLIAM ORVILLE (1898-), is an associate justice of the Supreme Court of the United States. He gained renown not only because of his work as a member of the Supreme Court, but also because of his wide travels and his books on vital problems in America's national and international life.

Douglas, a Democrat, became an associate justice in 1939. On the Supreme Court, he strongly supported government regulation of business. He traveled widely, especially in Asia, and reported his findings in such books as *Of Men and Mountains* (1950), *Strange Lands and Friendly People* (1951), and *An Almanac of Liberty* (1954).

Douglas was born at Maine, Minn., and was graduated from Whitman College. He received his law degree from Columbia University. Douglas served as chairman of the Securities and Exchange Commission from 1937 to 1939. H. G. REUSCHLEIN

DOUGLAS AIRCRAFT COMPANY. See AIRPLANE (Leading Airplane Companies).

DOUGLAS FIR

DOUGLAS FIR is one of the largest and most valuable timber trees in the world. This softwood, or cone-bearing tree, produces more lumber than any other single tree in North America, and perhaps in the world. It is common in the western United States and Canada, both in the Pacific Coast region and the Rocky Mountains. This beautiful evergreen tree grows more than 250 feet tall and 12 feet thick through the trunk. Its flat needles are about an inch long. The egg-shaped cones have odd, three-pointed *bracts,* or leaflike structures. The Douglas fir is the state tree of Oregon.

Scientific Classification. Douglas fir belongs to the pine family, *Pinaceae.* It is genus *Pseudotsuga,* species *menziesii.* ELBERT L. LITTLE, JR.

See also CONE-BEARING TREES; PINE; SPRUCE; TREE (picture, Evergreen Trees).

Rutherford Platt

The Douglas Fir Tree, common in the Pacific Northwest, grows about 250 feet tall. Its egg-shaped cone, *below left,* has rounded scales. Its rough, uneven bark, *below right,* is colored deep red.

DOUGLASS, FREDERICK (1817?-1895), was a Negro orator, writer, and a leader of the antislavery movement in the United States. During the Civil War he organized two Negro regiments in Massachusetts. He visited President Abraham Lincoln several times, and discussed the problems of slavery with him. After the war, he served as United States marshal and recorder of deeds for the District of Columbia. He was U.S. minister to Haiti from 1889 to 1891.

The story of his life, from his birth as a slave at Tuckahoe, Md., to his escape to Massachusetts in 1838, is told in his autobiography, *Narrative of the Life of Frederick Douglass.* Douglass became one of the speakers for the Massachusetts Anti-Slavery society in 1841. Later he lectured for two years in the British Isles. Upon his return to the United States in 1847, he bought his freedom and founded the *North Star,* an Abolitionist paper. RICHARD N. CURRENT

DOUKHOBORS. See DUKHOBORS.
DOUM PALM. See DOOM PALM.
DOURO, *DOH roo,* or **DUERO,** *DWAY roh,* **RIVER** rises in the central plateau of Spain and flows west through Portugal to empty into the Atlantic Ocean. The Douro is 485 miles long and drains an area of about 37,000 square miles. Pôrto, the chief seaport of Portugal, is located about three miles from the mouth of the river. Large vessels cannot travel on the Douro because of its rapids. In Spain, the river is called the Duero; in Portugal, the Douro. WALTER C. LANGSAM

DOVE is a bird closely related to the pigeon. One of the best-known kinds, the *mourning dove,* lives in North America from southern Canada to Panama and from Maine to California. It gets its name from the soft, sad cooing call of the male. The mourning dove is sometimes wrongly termed a *turtledove* (see TURTLEDOVE).

The mourning dove is about one foot long. Its body is olive-brown with bluish-gray wings. It feeds on grains and on grass and weed seeds. The mourning dove is a devoted mate, but a careless housekeeper. It builds a flimsy nest which is usually made of a few sticks placed loosely together. The dove sometimes builds its nest on top of another bird's deserted nest.

The dove is a symbol of peace. The Bible says Noah sent doves to find out if the waters had gone down.

Scientific Classification. The dove belongs to the family *Columbidae.* The mourning dove is genus *Zenaidura,* species *macroura.* GEORGE J. WALLACE

See also BIRD (color picture, Birds of Other Lands [Pink-Necked Fruit Dove]); MOURNING DOVE; PIGEON.

DOVE PLANT is a tropical American orchid (see ORCHID). It grows in Central America. It has 3 to 5 large leaves growing at the top of the swollen base of the plant, called the *pseudo-bulb.* The leaves are about 36 inches long and 6 inches wide. The flowers are white with a purple-spotted lip, and they appear from August to October.

Scientific Classification. The dove plant belongs to the family *Orchidaceae.* It is a member of genus *Peristeria,* species *elata.* DONALD WYMAN

DOVEKIE. See AUK.
DOVER, Del. (pop. 7,250; alt. 55 ft.), is the state capital, and commercial center of a rich farm area. Dover is on the St. Jones River, about 45 miles south of Wilmington. The main industries include canning, and the manufacture of latex products. Delaware State College and Wesley College are in the city. Dover was founded in 1717 and became the capital of Delaware in 1777. It was incorporated as a town in 1829 and as a city in 1929. It has a council-manager government. On July 1, 1776, Caesar Rodney, a planter living near Dover, rode horseback to Philadelphia, where he cast a vote for the adoption of the Declaration of Independence. He broke a tie between the Delaware delegates to the Continental Congress. JOHN A. MUNROE

See also DELAWARE (Interesting Places to Visit [State House]; color map); RODNEY, CAESAR.

DOVER (pop. 35,248; alt. 195 ft.) is a British town located on the Strait of Dover about 65 miles southeast of London. It is the chief port for travel between England and France. On clear days, persons 22 miles away in Calais, France, can see the white chalk cliffs of Dover. The remains of Dover castle overlook the town from one of the chalk hills 320 feet above the water.

260

During World War II, German guns and planes shelled and bombed Dover heavily. For location, see GREAT BRITAIN (color map). FRANCIS H. HERRICK

DOVER, STRAIT OF, is a narrow channel which connects the North Sea with the English Channel and separates England and France at their closest points. The Strait of Dover is only about 21 miles wide and is very shallow, with an average depth of less than 100 feet. Chalk cliffs rise high on either side of the Strait. The cliffs on the English side inspired Alice Duer Miller's narrative poem of British heroism in World War II, *The White Cliffs*. The ports of Dover, England, and Calais, France, are located opposite each other on the Strait. A number of engineers have proposed digging a tunnel under the Channel.

Many athletes have set records by swimming the Channel, usually from Calais to Dover (see ENGLISH CHANNEL [Swimming the Channel]). FRANCIS H. HERRICK

See also GREAT BRITAIN (picture, The White Cliffs of Dover).

Location Map of the City and Strait of Dover

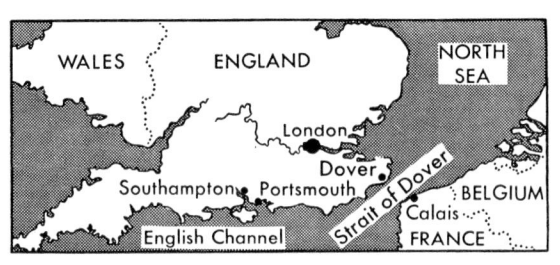

DOW, HERBERT HENRY (1866-1930), was an early leader in the American chemical industry. In 1897, he founded the Dow Chemical Company, which has achieved a prominent place in the industry. Through research, which Dow emphasized, the company has manufactured a variety of products. It mass-produced industrial chemicals; led in developing carbon tetrachloride; introduced a cheap phenol, or carbolic acid; and developed uses for bromine extracted from sea water (see BROMINE; CARBON TETRACHLORIDE).Ced. Dow was born in Belleville, Ont., Canada. J. R. CRAF

DOW, NEAL. See MAINE (Famous Maine Men).

DOW CHEMICAL COMPANY. See DOW, HERBERT HENRY; CHEMICAL INDUSTRY (10 Leading U.S. Chemical Companies).

DOW JONES INDEX is a list of stock-market averages prepared daily. It shows whether stock prices go up or down. The index lists separate averages for industrials, railroads, and utilities, as well as a combined average for all stocks. Averages are found by dividing the sum of closing stock prices in each group by a *constant divisor*, or fixed number.

DOWER is the life interest which a wife has in the real property of her husband after his death. At common law, a woman's dower right to a portion of her husband's property existed from the time of marriage but was incomplete until his death. Generally, a widow may not be deprived of her dower by the terms of her husband's will. She may *elect* to disregard what her husband has given her in his will, and take instead her legal interest in his estate. The laws regulating the interest which a widow has in her husband's estate vary in different states of the United States. The dower at common law was a life interest in one third of the real property. This is still true in many states, but others have given the wife outright ownership of a portion of her husband's assets. At common law, a surviving husband has an interest in his wife's estate, called an *estate by curtesy*. It has been modified by law in most states. JOHN W. WADE

DOWIE, JOHN ALEXANDER (1847-1907), founded a sect that stressed divine healing. He formed the Christian Catholic Apostolic Church in Zion in 1896 at Chicago. In 1901, he founded Zion City, Ill., north of Chicago, as the home for his church. Dowie banned doctors, drugstores, liquor, tobacco, dancing, and card playing from Zion. In 1906, he was deposed for unwise use of funds.

Dowie was born on May 25, 1847, in Edinburgh, Scotland. He went to Australia in 1860, and became a Congregational minister in 1870. After preaching in Alma and Sydney, he built a large independent tabernacle in Adelaide in 1882. He went to San Francisco in 1888 and to Chicago in 1890. EARLE E. CAIRNS

DOWLAND, JOHN (1562-1626), was an Irish composer of church, instrumental, and secular vocal music. He attained his greatest fame, however, by his excellent lute playing. His works include *Lachrymae, or Seven Teares*, and four books of *Ayres*.

Dowland was probably born in London. He traveled widely, and studied European music. He became a lute player to King Christian of Denmark and to Charles I of England. He was a leader in composition during the Elizabethan period, and did more to advance the art-song form than any other early composer. WARREN S. FREEMAN

DOWMETAL. See ALLOY (Alloys for Strength).

DOWN EAST. See MAINE.

DOWNEY, Calif. (pop. 82,505; alt. 120 ft.), is an industrial and residential city in the southeastern part of the Los Angeles metropolitan area. The city has more than 180 manufacturing and processing plants. The leading industries produce aircraft, missiles, and electronic equipment. The city was incorporated in 1956. Between 1950 and 1960, its population grew from about 30,000 to more than 80,000. Downey has a council-manager government. For location, see CALIFORNIA (color map). GEORGE SHAFTEL

DOWNING, *DOW ning*, **ANDREW JACKSON** (1815-1852), was considered the first great American landscape gardener. He helped produce a distinct American type of landscape architecture. He wrote many books that influenced his students and successors. He designed the grounds for many Long Island estates in the middle 1800's, and began the landscaping for the Capitol, White House, and Smithsonian Institution in 1851. He died before it was completed. Downing was born in Newburgh, N.Y. ROBERT E. EVERLY

DOWNING STREET. See LONDON (Trafalgar Square and Whitehall).

DOWNSTATE MEDICAL CENTER is a coeducational state-controlled college in Brooklyn, N.Y. It offers M.D. degrees and courses leading to Ph.D. degrees. It was founded in 1950. For enrollment, see UNIVERSITIES AND COLLEGES (table).

DOWNY MILDEW. See BORDEAUX MIXTURE.

DOWRY. See MARRIAGE (Marriage Customs).

Sir Arthur Conan Doyle, above, wrote many stories about Sherlock Holmes that later were made into movies. *The Hound of the Baskervilles* starred Basil Rathbone, *near right,* as Holmes, and Nigel Bruce, *far right,* as Dr. Watson.

Brown Bros.; 20th Century-Fox

DOYLE, SIR ARTHUR CONAN (1859-1930), a British novelist, created the famous character, Sherlock Holmes. This amazing amateur detective moved through exciting adventures in *A Study in Scarlet, The Adventures of Sherlock Holmes,* and *The Hound of the Baskervilles.* These stories show the author's humor, insight, and sense of the dramatic. Doyle's detective stories have been popular in plays, motion pictures, radio, and television.

Doyle was born in Edinburgh, Scotland, and was graduated from the University of Edinburgh. He practiced medicine on whaling and merchant ships and at Southsea, England. He wrote historical romances, and published *A Study in Scarlet* in 1887. This started his success as a detective-story writer.

Doyle quit practicing medicine in 1891 to give all his time to writing, but, during the Boer War, became the senior physician at a field hospital. He published a military history, *The Great Boer War,* and a book defending England's policy in South Africa. King Edward VII knighted him in 1902 for distinguished services to his country. WALTER WRIGHT

See also HOLMES, SHERLOCK.

D'OYLY CARTE, RICHARD. See CARTE, RICHARD D'OYLY.

DOZEN. See WEIGHTS AND MEASURES (Counting Measure).

DP. See DISPLACED PERSON; REFUGEE.

DRACHMA, *DRACK muh,* is a copper-nickel coin that is the monetary unit of Greece. It is divided into 100 *lepta.* The drachma was formerly made of silver.

Drachma Is a Coin Used in Greece.
Chase Manhattan Bank Money Museum

It was a standard coin of ancient Greece, and one drachma equaled six *obols.* Two drachmas equaled a *stater;* 100 drachmas, one *mina;* and 6,000 drachmas, one *talent.* For the value of the drachma, see MONEY (table, Values of Monetary Units). LEWIS M. REAGAN

DRACO, *DRAY koh,* or **DRACON,** *DRAY kohn,* was an Athenian legislator. He is credited with being the first man to introduce written law to Athens. He drew up a code of criminal law for Athens in 621 B.C., in order to halt feuds, civil disorder, and tyranny.

His code was severe, and made death the penalty even for small thefts. But it did distinguish between voluntary and involuntary homicide. Solon, a famous Greek lawmaker, later altered many of Draco's laws, and many of them are no longer remembered. His law of homicide was in force a long time. DANIEL J. DYKSTRA

DRACO, *DRAY koh,* the Dragon, is a constellation near Polaris, or the North Star. Four stars make up its head. The tail of Draco winds around the Big and Little dippers. See also ASTRONOMY (color picture, Constellations of the Northern Sky).

DRAFT is a written order drawn by one person, directing a second person to pay a definite amount of money to a third person at a stated time. If desired, the draft may be drawn payable to the person who draws it. A draft is the same as a *bill of exchange,* except that the term *draft* usually means a transfer of money between persons in the same country. A draft drawn on a bank is a *check.* Checks differ primarily from trade drafts in that checks originate with the buyer, but drafts originate with the seller.

A draft may read *pay at sight* or *on demand.* Then a debtor must either pay the amount of the draft at once or reject it. If the draft is payable within sixty days, he may *accept* it, in which case he agrees to pay it within the period set. He indicates his acceptance by writing the word *accepted* above his signature on the face of the draft. After he accepts a draft, he becomes legally responsible for its amount. It is then in effect a *note.*

Sellers frequently use drafts to transact business when they do not wish to assume the credit risk of open book accounts. When the seller ships goods to the buyer, the seller also draws a draft payable to himself for the

How a Draft Can Discharge Two Debts at Once. In this typical example, the Spurlock Company of Chicago owes $400 to William Brownell of Montreal. At the same time, E. J. Smith, also of Montreal, owes $400 or more to the Spurlock Company. Instead of paying Brownell directly with its own funds, the Spurlock Company sends him a draft in the form shown. When Brownell presents the draft to Smith, the latter pays Brownell $400. In this way, the Chicago company's debt to Brownell is canceled at the same time that $400 of Smith's debt to the Spurlock Company is canceled.

amount involved. Then his bank forwards the draft with the bills of lading to a second bank in the same city as the buyer. The second bank is directed to present the draft to the buyer and to obtain either his acceptance or payment. After the buyer accepts or pays, the second bank gives him the bills of lading.   ROBERT W. MERRY

See also BILL OF EXCHANGE; EXCHANGE; NEGOTIABLE PAPER; NOTE; TRADE ACCEPTANCE.

DRAFT, MILITARY, is a system of selecting men to serve in the armed forces. A citizen has an obligation to help defend his country. The government has the power to require him to serve. It enrolls men for military service, then, by a draft system, selects those qualified for active duty. The draft allows a country to obtain its most able-bodied men for this service. It also provides a fair system of choosing men. In wartime or in a national emergency, the country may also draft people for civilian work. Women may be drafted for duty in such wartime activities as civil defense and the home guard.

Draft Laws

Canada has used a draft only in wartime. But most other countries draft young men even in peacetime. Usually, men between 18 and 50 must register for the draft. Men 18 to 20 are drafted to serve one or two years. Then they become members of the reserves.

In the United States, each male citizen between $18\frac{1}{2}$ and 26 is liable for two years of active duty, two years in the Ready Reserve, and two years in the Standby Reserve. Men in the Ready Reserve must attend both weekly drills and a 15-day training session each year.

A boy between the ages of 17 and $18\frac{1}{2}$ may volunteer for six months' active service, then spend $4\frac{1}{2}$ years in the Ready Reserve and three years in the Standby Reserve. If he volunteers after the age of $18\frac{1}{2}$, he spends six months in active service, but must then serve $5\frac{1}{2}$ years in the Ready Reserve and two years in the Standby Reserve of the United States.

History

In Early Days, every able-bodied man made up a local army or defense force. Men in ancient Greece had to serve in the militia (see MILITIA). The ancient Egyptians and Romans used professional armies. In time of war, the militias supported these armies. By the 1000's in Europe, most rulers hired *mercenaries*, who served solely for pay, to fight their wars.

The Saxon rulers of early England formed the *fyrd*, a local defense force made up of men between the ages of 16 and 60. In 1261, Switzerland set up its first militia system. Beginning in the 1600's, countries began to find it more and more difficult to raise standing armies of volunteers because of the terrible living conditions in these armies. King Gustavus Adolphus of Sweden set a precedent then by conscripting men for his armies to fight the wars of the early 1600's.

The colonists brought the militia idea to America. Each colony required its men to serve in the militia when necessary. It usually required all white men between the ages of 16 and 50 or 60 to enroll in the militia. Persons who refused could be punished.

The Rise of Conscription. France was the first country to adopt the modern military draft system. In 1688, it drafted men for temporary service according to lots drawn in each parish. Drafted men did not fight in battles, and were not combined with the professional armies. The parishes showed favoritism in picking men for service. They also allowed men many ways to get out of service.

In 1792, the French government adopted conscription on a national scale. It made every able-bodied man liable for military duty. It gave each commune, or district, the power to select which men would serve. The following year, the government limited service to able-bodied men between the ages of 18 and 25. The French Constitution of 1798 included the principle of military conscription. It required military service of men between the ages of 20 and 25. The draft provided Napoleon Bonaparte with a large number of soldiers for his many conquests. France abolished the draft in 1814, but revived it in 1818.

Prussia used conscription to get around restrictions on the size of its army after 1807. Napoleon had forced Prussia to limit its army to 42,000 men. But the Prus-

263

Drawing the First Military Draft Number is a solemn occasion. Secretary of War Newton D. Baker, *blindfolded, above*, drew the first draft number of World War I in 1917. President Franklin D. Roosevelt, *left, below*, watched as Secretary of the Navy Frank Knox drew one of the first numbers of World War II. The United States drafted 2,810,296 men for military service in World War I and more than 10,000,000 men in World War II.

United Press Int.
Keystone

sian Army under the leadership of General Gerhard von Scharnhorst called up small groups of drafted men for short periods of intensive training. After the men had been trained, they were placed in the reserves. A new group then took their place. In 1814, the Prussian government adopted conscription permanently.

In the Civil War, the United States government first adopted the military draft system. On Mar. 3, 1863, Congress gave President Abraham Lincoln the power to draft men between the ages of 20 and 45. It exempted seven classes of men on the grounds that they were needed in their work or in supporting their families. Drafted men could avoid service by providing a substitute, or paying the government about $300 to hire one. The government also paid bounties to men enlisting in the Union Army. As a result, many men enlisted instead of waiting to be drafted. During the Civil War, 255,000 men were drafted. But, of this number, 204,000 men furnished substitutes or paid sums to hire them.

The Confederacy passed a conscription law on Apr. 16, 1862. It required three years of military service from all white men between 18 and 35, except those legally exempted. Later, it changed the age limits to 17 and 50. It also conscripted slaves in 1865.

After the 1870's, many countries adopted peacetime conscription. In 1873, Japan began drafting men. Between 1870 and 1914, Great Britain was the only major European nation that did not take up conscription.

Selective Service. During World War I, Canada and Great Britain first adopted the draft. The United States passed a selective service law on May 18, 1917, to raise armies for the war. Under this act, 24,234,021 men were registered. The government inducted 2,810,296 men. The first American peacetime draft act became law on Sept. 16, 1940. The Selective Service System administered the law (see SELECTIVE SERVICE SYSTEM). More than 6,000 draft boards decided who would serve in the armed forces. On Dec. 13, 1941, Congress extended each drafted person's term of service to six months after the end of World War II. All countries with armed forces in the war used the draft system. The United States drafted more than 10,000,000 men between the ages of 18 and 37. It stopped the draft in 1947. Maj. Gen. Lewis Blaine Hershey served as its director.

Congress passed a new Selective Service Act in 1948. After the Korean War broke out in 1950, the President received powers to order all members of the reserves to active duty. The Universal Military Training and Service Act, passed in June, 1951, required male citizens between 18 and 26 to register. KENNETH H. McGILL

See also ARMY (Conscription); WORLD WAR I (The United States Enters the War); WORLD WAR II (Expanding the Armed Forces).

DRAFTSMAN. See MECHANICAL DRAWING.
DRAG. See AERODYNAMICS (Drag).
DRAG, a means of transportation. See TRAVOIS.
DRAGLINE. See BUILDING AND WRECKING MACHINES.
DRAGO, *DRAH goh,* **LUIS MARÍA** (1859-1921), an Argentine statesman and jurist, supported the principle that became known as the *Drago Doctrine*. He was Minister of Foreign Affairs in 1902, when Great Britain, Germany, and Italy aroused Latin America by blockading Venezuelan ports. Drago argued that no European power could use public debt as an excuse for armed intervention or occupation of American territory. The Hague Conference of 1907 accepted his doctrine.

Drago was born in Buenos Aires. He studied law, and became a judge of both the civil and criminal courts. Great Britain and the United States asked him to arbitrate the Atlantic fisheries dispute in 1909 and 1910. The Carnegie Endowment of International Peace invited him to visit the United States. It described Drago as the "most eminent exponent of intellectual culture in South America." DONALD E. WORCESTER

DRAGON, *DRAG un,* was the name given to the most terrible monsters of the ancient world. Dragons did not really exist, but most people believed in them. They were huge fire-breathing serpents with wings like those of a great bat, and they could swallow ships and men at one gulp. Maps of early times represent unknown parts of the world as being the homes of these mythical creatures. The dragons of legend are strangely like actual creatures that have lived in the past. They are much like the great reptiles which inhabited the earth long before man is supposed to have appeared on earth.

Dragons were generally evil and destructive. Every country had them in its mythology. In Greece dragons were slain by Hercules, Apollo, and Perseus. Sigurd, Siegfried, and Beowulf killed them in Norse, German, and early English legend.

The dragon was a symbol of sin in early Christian times. Saint Michael and Saint George both had to fight these beasts, according to legend. The dragon represents evil in the book of Revelation in the Bible. But the Chinese took the dragon as a kingly emblem and thought of it as a god. PADRAIC COLUM

See also GEORGE, SAINT; MICHAEL, SAINT.

The Dragon of Selena was killed by the lance of Saint George. An early Christian legend claims that George rescued the king's daughter from the jaws of the vicious monster.
Brown Bros.

DRAGON OF KOMODO is the largest lizard living today. It also belongs to the most ancient group of lizards still alive. It lives only on some small islands of Indonesia, including Komodo. It has a long tail, and is covered with small dull-colored scales. The skin is rough. When the lizard opens its wide red mouth, it shows rows of teeth like the edge of a saw.

It has keen sight and smell and hunts other animals. Dragons of Komodo dig caves with their strong claws, and hide in them at night. They hunt during the day.

Scientific Classification. Dragon of Komodo is a member of the family *Varanidae*. It is genus *Varanus*, species *V. komodoensis*. CLIFFORD H. POPE

See also MONITOR.

American Museum of Natural History
The Dragon of Komodo is an Indonesian lizard that may grow to a length of 10 feet and weigh 250 pounds. It can tear off the hind legs of a boar and swallow bones and all.

DRAGONFLY is a beautiful water insect. It has four large, fragile wings which look like fine gauze. The wings shimmer and gleam in the sunlight when the insect flies. The dragonfly's long slender body is colored either green, blue, or brown. Large compound eyes, which look like beads, cover most of the head. The dragonfly can see motionless objects almost 6 feet away, and moving objects two or three times that distance. The insect has six legs covered with spines. It can use its legs to perch on a limb, but it cannot walk. As it flies through the air, it holds its legs together to form a basket in which to capture insects. The dragonfly grasps its prey with its legs or jaws, and eats it while flying. Dragonflies have been known to fly 50 to 60 miles an

Ralph Buchsbaum
A Living Dragonfly Clings to a Stem. The large eyes of this insect are able to see moving objects 18 feet away. They help the dragonfly to find its food, which is made up principally of small flies and mosquitoes.

DRAHTHAAR

hour. They fly so swiftly that they usually escape from birds or other animals. Some extinct species of dragonflies had wingspreads of 2½ feet.

The dragonfly mates while in flight. The female often drops her eggs from the air into the water, or inside the stem of water plants. The *nymph*, or young dragonfly, hatches from the egg in 5 to 15 days. It looks ugly, with its thick body, big head and mouth, and no wings. It has a folding lower lip which is half as long as its body. The lip has jawlike hooks at the end and can move out like an arm to catch victims. The nymph breathes by means of gills.

The dragonfly nymph remains in the water for 1 to 5 years. It eats water insects and other small water animals. Some large dragonfly nymphs feed on young fish. While developing into an adult dragonfly, the nymph *molts*, or sheds its skin, 12 or more times. After the last time, it crawls out of the water to the top of a reed or a rock as a fully formed dragonfly, which breathes air and can fly.

People often call dragonflies *devil's-darning-needles*. They are also known as *snake doctors*, *snake feeders*, *horse stingers*, and *mule killers*. They help man by feeding on harmful insects such as flies and mosquitoes. It has been said that humans would be unable to live on some Pacific islands if dragonflies were not present to keep down the number of mosquitoes. *Damsel flies* look like dragonflies, but they have more slender bodies. The small, graceful damsel flies have narrow, transparent wings.

Scientific Classification. Dragonflies and damsel flies belong to the class *Insecta*. They make up the order *Odonata*.
E. GORTON LINSLEY

See also ANIMAL (color picture, Leading Groups in the Animal Kingdom).

DRAHTHAAR. See GERMAN WIREHAIRED POINTER.

DRAINAGE. In all soil there is a point not far below the surface where it is soaked, or *saturated*, with water. This point is called the *water table*. In clay soil, the moisture often rises about 4 feet above the water table by capillary action, in the same way that ink will "climb" in a piece of blotting paper. In sand, moisture rises about 2 feet above the water table.

To provide ideal growing conditions for farm crops, the water table should be at least 4 feet or more below the surface. This is because plant roots stop growing when they reach the water table. If the water table is low, the roots of normally long-rooted plants will grow to be long enough to obtain their full share of nourishment from the soil above the water table.

By natural drainage, excess water above the water table seeps downward into the soil, is taken up by plants, or passes off by evaporation. In many areas, however, rain falls more rapidly than it can drain off naturally. In these areas, artificial drainage is needed to lower the water table.

Methods of Artificial Drainage. There are two chief methods of artificial drainage, the open-surface ditch and the underground drain. The *underground drain*, usually built of hollow tile, is the more useful and convenient method. The *open-surface ditch* takes up land which could be farmed and also prevents the free movement of men, animals, and machines in working the land. These ditches often fill with weeds and make good breeding places for mosquitoes.

Tile Drains are built to suit the particular kind of soil to be drained, the surface of the land, and the amount of water to be carried by the drain pipes. The main drain usually follows low places in the land where rain water runs off naturally. Branch drains enter the main drain from 2½ to 5 feet below the surface at angles of less than a right angle. Drains can be 30 feet apart in wet clay, or up to 150 feet apart in sandy soil. Drains laid near the surface should be closer together than deeper ones. The hollow tiles used in these drainage systems vary from 4 to 12 inches in diameter. The tiles are laid with their ends close together, but the ends are not sealed. This loose connection allows water to enter the drain but keeps out dirt. Branch drains should slope slightly downward toward the main drain. Two branch drains should not enter the main drain opposite each other. If the mouth of the main drain empties into a stream, it must be above the average high level of the water in the stream. It is important to select drain tile that is strong and durable. *Breathers*, or air vents, often run from the surface of the ground to the tile drain. They allow trapped air to escape and in this way improve the flow of water.

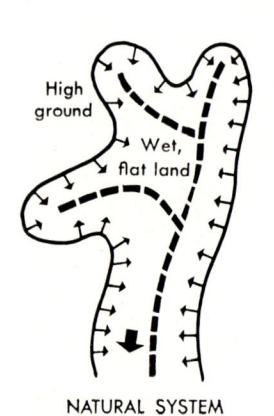

HOW TILES ARE USED FOR DRAINAGE

NATURAL SYSTEM   GRIDIRON SYSTEM   HERRINGBONE SYSTEM   INTERCEPTING SYSTEM

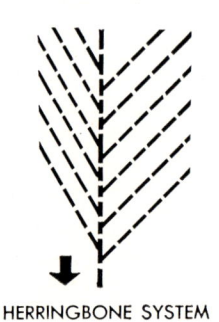

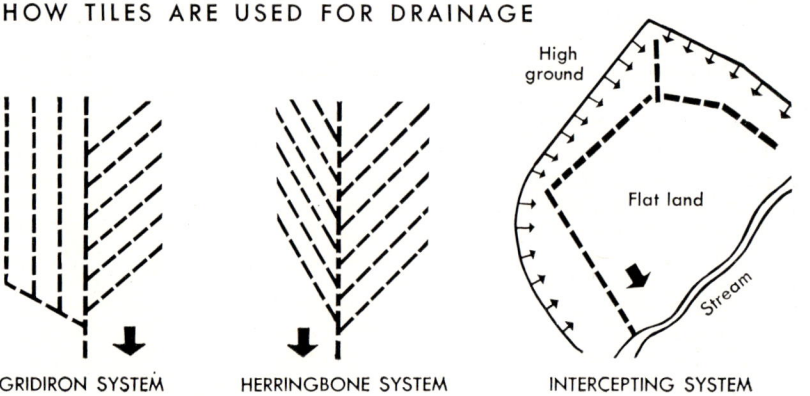

Drainage Tile Systems are designed to lower the water table in wet land and increase crop yields. Workmen bury the tiles in the pattern best suited to the terrain. The water enters the tiles through spaces left between them and flows in the direction indicated by the arrows. Main drainage lines usually follow low places in the land where rain water runs off naturally.

Effects of Drainage. Artificial drainage has created some of the best farming soil in the world by reclaiming lands that were standing under water. Some outstanding examples of usefully drained land are the lands back of the Holland dikes, the marshy *fen* lands of eastern England, the Po Valley of Italy, the Nile River Delta, and the Yazoo Delta of the Mississippi.

Artificial drainage has not only made land useful for growing crops, but also has given man new lands on which he can live in health and comfort. Before they were drained, large areas in the midwestern part of the United States were too damp for good health during much of the year. The draining of swamps in many parts of the world has destroyed the breeding places of disease-carrying mosquitoes.

Drainage creates problems as well as solving them. The drainage system must be kept in good repair or it may wash out and create gullies, thus ruining good farm land. Artificial-drainage systems which carry off the water too fast may increase erosion.   GLENN K. RULE

See also CAPILLARITY; EROSION.

DRAISINE. See BICYCLE (History).

DRAKE is the male duck. See DUCK.

DRAKE, EDWIN LAURENTINE. See PETROLEUM (The Birth of the Oil Industry; picture, Drake's Well).

DRAKE, SIR FRANCIS (c.1540-1596), was the first Englishman to sail around the world. He was the most famous of the Elizabethan sea captains. He made daring raids against Spanish sea power all over the world, and helped establish English control of the seas. Queen Elizabeth I permitted and even encouraged Drake's lawless attacks on Spanish shipping. She shared in the returns from the booty he seized. For all practical purposes, he was as much a pirate as any leader that ever flew the skull-and-crossbones flag. Such procedure was standard in those days.

Sir Francis Drake
Brown Bros.

Drake was born in Devonshire. He was attracted by adventure and showed early signs of leadership and inspiration amounting to genius, both based on deep religious sentiment. He served his apprenticeship on a small ship off the coast of England. His career was advanced by a distant relative, the famous British admiral, Sir John Hawkins, who probably secured a position for the young Drake in Capt. John Lovell's expedition of 1566 (see HAWKINS, SIR JOHN).

Drake became captain of a small ship, the *Judith*, at the age of 22. Then he began his raids against Spanish shipping, especially in the West Indies and the Caribbean. His object was to capture the Spanish galleons sailing from Nombre de Dios in Panama. These held silver that had been carried across the mountains by mules from Peruvian mines. On one occasion in 1572, he sailed with two ships and 73 men, and with his small force attacked Nombre de Dios. He looted the town and ambushed a treasure convoy. After this exploit the Spaniards called him "the Dragon."

In 1577, he sailed from Plymouth with five ships and

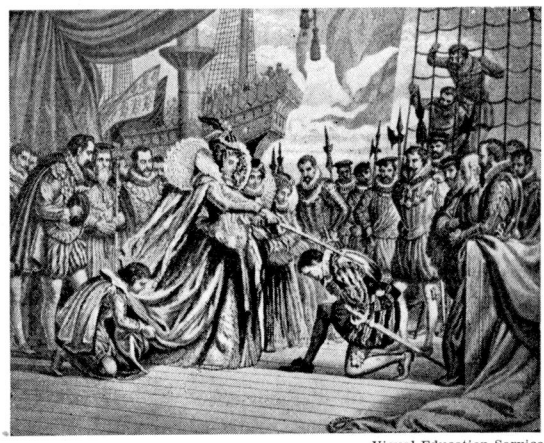

Visual Education Service

Queen Elizabeth I knighted Francis Drake aboard the *Golden Hind*, when Drake returned from his history-making three-year voyage around the world.

164 men on his most famous voyage. It took him around the world in three years. For a long time historians have wondered about the purposes of this voyage. Recent historical evidence has indicated that the objectives were more than mere exploration or plundering Spanish ports in South America. The secret instructions given to him indicate that he was to annex territories to promote English trade in the Pacific Ocean.

Drake sailed through the Strait of Magellan, but a storm blew him eastward, and he discovered Cape Horn. He then sailed up the west coast of South America, past Mexico, to California. He landed there and erected a brass plaque claiming the land, which he called *New Albion*, for England. In 1936, this famous "Plate of Brass" was discovered near San Quentin Bay, north of San Francisco. It was given many tests, and is regarded as authentic evidence of Drake's visit to California in 1579. It is now at the University of California.

Drake then sailed west across the Pacific, rounded the Cape of Good Hope, and reached England on Nov. 3, 1580. He was knighted by Queen Elizabeth I. Timber from his ship, the *Golden Hind*, was made into a chair that is kept at Oxford University. Drake later led other expeditions against Spain, and served as vice-admiral in the Battle of the Spanish Armada (see ARMADA). He died on January 28, 1596.   JAMES G. ALLEN

See also EXPLORATION AND DISCOVERY (map, Leading Voyages).

DRAKE, FRIEDRICH. See SCULPTURE (Germany).

DRAKE UNIVERSITY is a privately supported coeducational school in Des Moines, Iowa. The university has colleges of business administration, education, fine arts, journalism, law, liberal arts, and pharmacy. It also has a graduate division, a divinity school, and a University College program of evening and extension study for adults at centers throughout Iowa. Drake was founded in 1881. It is the home of the Drake Relays, an annual intercollegiate track and field meet. Its athletic teams are called the Bulldogs. The school colors are blue and white. For enrollment, see UNIVERSITIES AND COLLEGES (table).   H. G. HARMON

DRAKE WELL MEMORIAL PARK. See PENNSYLVANIA (Interesting Places to Visit).

DRAM. See APOTHECARIES' WEIGHT.

DRAMA

Drama Brings History to Life, as in This Production of *Mary of Scotland* Starring Helen Hayes.

DRAMA. There are few arts closer to the people than the drama. It is a form of expression which depends largely upon communication from a playwright to an audience through the medium of actors. Drama generally takes the form of a theater performance. But it can as easily be transferred to the motion-picture screen, to the radio through broadcasting, to a home television screen, or to the printed page.

A drama is a story told in such a way that it must be acted out by living players to obtain its full effect. The word *drama* comes from the Greek and means *to do* or *act*. The drama has mirrored the life, customs, manners, and general living habits of the people ever since its dim beginnings on the banks of the Nile in ancient Egypt about six thousand years ago. It is the most sophisticated and the most simple way of recording human endeavor. Its purpose is both to entertain and to instruct. The drama was brought into existence by the priests and poets of the ancient world as one of the first literary forms. Since its beginnings, it has had an important social function and influence. Man's morals, customs, and thought have been changed in content as well as reflected by the religious, social, and human implications of the drama.

Love of "play acting" seems to be a part of basic human nature. One of the most popular games children have is that of playing games something like "keeping house" or "Mrs. Smith and Mrs. Jones." Primitive peoples have chosen the drama as one of the most effective ways to tell a story or to express a poetic idea which has both beauty and heroism. This took form in dance and speech, and appeared as an art form with the ancient Greeks and Egyptians, as well as with the American Indians, the peoples of the South Sea islands, and the peoples of Asia. Drama exists today among aborigines of Australia and tribes of Central Africa.

Early drama drew upon the religious feelings of all peoples. It found its tongue in the chanting of the priests and warriors. It reflected the religions of various countries as they found the power of drama in teaching moral and religious principles. Gradually this art form developed into what we call the *play*.

The Plot and Structure of the Drama

The early plays of both the Egyptians and the Greeks were in elongated one-act form. A *chorus* interpreted the action for the audience. The number of words used was fairly small, and the *business*, or stage action, was long. The speeches were in turn explanatory, preachy, or advisory in tone. The chorus recited the reactions of the people to their betters, who were either their gods or their heroes. The form of the drama changed through the centuries. The chorus lost its importance until in the 1700's it appeared only in the prologue and epilogue of plays. It has disappeared almost entirely in drama today. Speeches have gradually changed from the classical long ones to the short and conversational dialogue which began with Shakespeare.

Classical drama was portrayed in continuous action. The playwrights of the Renaissance misunderstood the old Greek plays. They believed that a play should be broken up into five or more acts. In the 1800's, this number was reduced to four and then to three. The stage today frequently uses the two-act or play-in-scenes form, which is close to classical drama.

Kinds of Drama

Tragedy was the earliest form of drama. It showed the gods, the heroes, and men's relation to gods, in a series of unhappy events, usually ending in disaster. It can be as severe as a Greek drama of Aeschylus, in which the Fates pursue the main character to his eventual doom. It can be as classic and scholarly as a tragedy of Racine, or as loose in structure as Eugene O'Neill, Maxwell Anderson, or Sean O'Casey may care to make it.

Comedy is a play which reflects life and humanity

either humorously or seriously, but which ends without disaster or death. It may be what is called *high comedy*, which has fine characterization and witty dialogue. Or it may be *low comedy*, which uses absurd situations, "horse play," and characters from low life.

Farce is a kind of comedy which draws its humor from impossible situations and ridiculous characters.

Satire developed early, along with tragedy and comedy. It may be a happy or bitter comment on life.

The Development of Drama in the West

The Greek Theater was closely related to the earlier theater that developed in Egypt, as the writings of the historian Herodotus show. Greek theater began in the 500's B.C. with the first dramatist, Thespis. Our word for an actor, *thespian*, comes from his name. Three great dramatists, Aeschylus, Sophocles, and Euripides, dominated Greek drama. Many of their plays have been lost, but the remaining works, stories of Greek gods and heroes, are among the greatest of all dramatic writings. All-male casts presented the plays in magnificent outdoor theaters. The actors wore masks that expressed grief, horror, merriment, and other emotions. The masks helped spectators in the farthest parts of the theater to understand clearly what was going on in the action on the stage. These dramas had strong religious, social, and artistic impact for the people in such cities as Athens, Corinth, and Thebes. They clearly show the moral, social, political, and artistic levels reached by the citizens of the first democracies. Aristophanes, a comic writer, is usually called the greatest dramatic satirist of all time. He wrote about the life of his times, and Greek audiences greeted his works with delight. In his comedies, called *old comedy*, he used the chorus and dance, two elements of Greek tragedy. Menander (343-291 B.C.) introduced *new comedy*. It was purely dramatic in form, and the dramatist paid less attention to topics or events of the time.

The Roman Theater took its inspiration from the Greek theater which it imitated. Its dramas were never as great as those of the Greeks. The best Roman plays were comic, and Plautus was the best Roman writer of comedies. He frankly borrowed from Menander and the New Comedy of Greece. But he brought a robustness and a comic inventiveness which keep his plays alive today. He developed such stock characters as the cowardly bragging soldier, the blustering old man (usually the father), the scheming servant, and others. They were continued in the *commedia dell' arte*, which was popular in Europe as late as 1880. It can still be seen in the pantomimes and Punch-and-Judy shows presented for children in England (see PANTOMIME; PUNCH AND JUDY). Terence was Plautus's younger and more literary rival, but his comedies are less playable and less readable today. The Roman theater had few tragedies. Most serious plays were written to be read, or to be declaimed as a monologue at a party. Seneca was the most important Roman writer of tragedies. Many writers in the early Renaissance imitated his dull and lifeless style.

The Medieval Theater developed slowly. Wandering players, jugglers, and musicians kept theatrical traditions alive. Most of the people could neither read nor write. The Church used drama to teach them stories from the Old Testament, from the life of Christ, and

DRAMA

from the lives of saints. These dramas were called *miracle*, *mystery*, and *nativity* plays. They began as early as the 1000's, and developed chiefly in England, France, Germany, Italy, and Spain. At first, actors performed before the altar and in the nave of the church. Later, they played on the church steps and in the churchyard. Our terms *upstage* and *downstage* come from the fact that the actors moved up and down the church steps.

These early plays became widely popular, and were magnificently staged in the streets of the town. Various guilds took over the work and expense for the plays. Each guild put on the play most fitting to it. For example, shipbuilders put on the story of Noah's ark, watercarriers dramatized the Flood, and goldsmiths presented the story of the Three Wise Men and their gifts. Four towns in England, Chester, Coventry, Wakefield, and York, developed long *cycles* of these mystery plays. These cycles reveal to us much of the life in England during the Middle Ages. Later, in the 1400's and 1500's, *morality* plays developed. In them, each character represented a virtue to admire or a vice to avoid, such as Charity or Envy.

The English Theater developed out of the cycles of miracle plays. But the early English playwrights were strongly influenced by the classical revival of the Renaissance. The first true English comedy, *Ralph Roister Doister*, was written in 1533 for a school performance. Many stock characters of Roman comedy appear in these early English plays, and even in Shakespeare. This greatest of all dramatists created out of his own originality and lyric fire two of the most magnificent

Actors in an Ancient Greek Drama, from a painting by J. L. Gérôme. Actors wore masks to express various emotions. They also wore laced sandals with thick soles to make them look taller.

Bettmann Archive

DRAMA

characters in all drama — Hamlet and Lear. His historical plays, such as *Henry V* and *King Richard III*, are still popular.

Christopher Marlowe (1564-1593) established the style of writing in blank verse, or unrhymed iambic pentameter (five feet). His *Doctor Faustus* and *Tamburlaine* indicate that he might have equalled Shakespeare had he not been killed at so early an age. Ben Jonson (1573?-1637) excelled in comedy. He was also largely responsible for the introduction of the *masque*, a pastoral drama with dances and music, elaborately costumed and staged. This theatrical form came from Italy and France. It made important the designing of scenery, at which Inigo Jones was best known in England. Francis Beaumont and John Fletcher, Philip Massinger, John Ford, and John Webster were other great Elizabethan writers.

The Puritans closed the theaters in 1642. During the Civil War, the public was kept from theatrical entertainment until the restoration of the Stuart kings in 1660. The new theater brought in a group of brilliant and witty writers who created a comedy of manners known as *Restoration comedy*. Congreve (1670-1729), Etherege (about 1634-1691), and Wycherley (1640-1716) were the three great writers of the time. There was a stale period after Farquhar (1678-1707), in which appeared only sentimental comedy and such efforts to reach the middle-class level as George Lillo's *The London Merchant* (1731). There were no great English dramatists until Richard Brinsley Sheridan (1751-1816) came on the scene with his delightful comedies, *The Rivals* (1775) and *The School for Scandal* (1777).

The Continental Theater. The great contemporary of Shakespeare on the continent of Europe was Lope de Vega Carpio (1562-1635) in Spain. His style was less grand and more popular, and his comedies had a lively quality. He wrote a tremendous number of plays. Some 300 out of 1,800 survive. He dominated the drama of Spain, along with Calderón de la Barca (1600-1681), for two hundred years. There appeared at the same time in France the *neoclassicists* who followed the traditions of the classic Greek drama. Pierre Corneille (1606-1684) with *Le Cid* and Jean Baptiste Racine (1639-1699) with *Phèdre* dominated serious drama. But it was the creator of comedies, farces, and masques, Jean Baptiste Poquelin, known as Molière (1622-1673), who influenced the development of French drama in the generations to follow. His influence was also noticeable in the English Restoration comedies.

In Germany, the drama of the Middle Ages flowed into the main stream of the Renaissance through the writings of Hans Sachs (1494-1576). The first important playwright after Sachs was Gotthold Ephraim Lessing (1729-1781). He was perhaps not a great dramatist, but he reflected the spirit of the Age of Reason in his *Minna von Barnhelm* and *Nathan the Wise*, which the whole world respects for its plea for tolerance in religious matters.

The Romantic Revolt

The first rumblings of the opposition to the classic drama were heard in Germany. Johann Wolfgang von Goethe (1749-1832) was his country's greatest writer. His poetry won him wide acceptance among those who know his language. But his plays are sometimes difficult to translate satisfactorily, and his influence has been strongest inside Austria and Germany. Goethe was to his own people what Molière was to France, and Shakespeare to English-speaking countries. *Götz von Berlichingen* (1773), *Egmont* (1788), and *Faust* (1774-1805) are his greatest plays. Friedrich Schiller (1759-1805) worked at about the same time. His romantic plays won wider acceptance outside Germany than did Goethe's, and many consider him his country's greatest dramatist. *The Robbers*, *Don Carlos*, *Wallenstein*, *Wilhelm Tell*, and *Maria Stuart* are his best-known dramas.

In France, the great romanticist was Victor Hugo (1802-1885). His international fame as a novelist has obscured his considerable ability as a playwright. But, almost singlehanded, he was responsible for freeing the French theater from its neoclassic bonds. He widened the choice of subject matter and championed the revolutionary in thought and deed. *Ruy Blas* dealt the deathblow to the classic tradition of French drama.

The Rise of Realism

Most of contemporary drama stems from the Norwegian, Henrik Ibsen, who developed the first important social drama. In writing plays, he placed great emphasis on dramatic realism and on a natural approach to both character and subject matter. One of his most notable plays is *A Doll's House*. When its heroine Nora rushed out of her home banging the door, its slam was heard in every theater in the world. In Russia, Gogol and Chekhov; in France, Becque and Porto-Riche; in Germany, Hauptmann; in England, Robertson, Jones, and Shaw; in America, Howard, Herne, and Belasco— all heard and were inspired to write with an understanding of the social conscience of man.

The Oriental Drama

The drama of the East developed without outside influence. The Oriental drama at times since the 1700's has had a slight influence on the Western stage. But the West has never affected it. Chinese, Japanese, and other Oriental plays are often acted on bare, unornamented stages. The audience has to imagine the scenery, but the costumes are colorful and of extremely rich materials. It is necessary to know the meaning of a complicated set of signs if the audience is to understand the plays. A raised umbrella stands for a storm. An actor shows that he is mounting a horse by carrying a whip and lifting his left foot. One man with a banner stands for a thousand soldiers.

Music and dancing are used constantly in Oriental drama. Men's faces are painted to indicate the nature of their characters. Devils have green faces, and angels have gold. Most female characters are still played by men. Mei Lan-Fang (1894-1944) was the most celebrated of modern female impersonators. He toured widely in the United States and Europe.

The subject matter of the plays is usually drawn from old legends and stories. Drama in China dates back to 2000 B.C. *Hoei-Lan-Kin (The Circle of Chalk)* and *P'i P'a Chi (Lute Song)* are two of the best Chinese dramas. *Lute Song* was played in English on Broadway in 1946.

Korean drama dates from A.D. 900, and Japanese drama from about 1300. *Nō* (literary) and *Kabuki* (popu-

A Drama of East and West, John Patrick's *The Teahouse of the August Moon* tells how a U.S. Army officer tries to teach democracy to the people of a small village on Okinawa.

A Drama of Social Justice, Maxwell Anderson's *Winterset* tells the story of a son who tries to prove that his father was unjustly convicted and executed for a murder he did not commit.

DRAMA

lar) plays are the important types in Japan. Their staging is similar to the Chinese plays. One of the leading dramatists was Monzaemon Chikamatsu (1653-1724?). His best-known work is the romantic *Fair Ladies at a Game of Poem-Cards*. The modern Japanese theater includes classical dramas of both types, Western plays, and musical comedies. Other Oriental countries have a drama similar to China, Japan, and Korea. Hindu drama is highly poetic and literary. It is more closely related to Western drama than to that of the Orient.

Drama in the 1900's

The Irish Revival. A group of Irish poets and playwrights established the Irish National Theatre in Dublin in 1902. Within a few years, this promising theater group developed into the Abbey Theatre. During the years that followed, the Abbey Theatre produced plays by William Butler Yeats, Lady Gregory, John Millington Synge, and Lord Dunsany. Theirs was a poetic drama that brought the beautiful lilt and rich phrasing of the Gaelic language to English drama.

Later playwrights to come out of this literary movement are the Belfast-born St. John Ervine (1883-   ) and Sean O'Casey (1880-   ). Ervine's best-known plays are *Mixed Marriage*, *Jane Clegg*, and *John Ferguson*. O'Casey is a poet and realist who wrote of Ireland in the political turmoil of the Sinn Fein movement. He is best represented by *Juno and the Paycock*, *The Plough and the Stars*, and the symbolic *Within the Gates*. Many Irish plays have been presented in the United States by the Dublin group known as the Abbey Players.

In England. George Bernard Shaw was Irish born, but after the 1890's he came to dominate English drama. He was the great rebel of world drama. His unconventional and witty comedies helped bring about social and moral reforms. But his greatest works had deep religious values. *Saint Joan*, *Man and Superman*, and *Candida* won both critical and popular acclaim. Shaw outlived Oscar Wilde, whose comedies, such as *The Importance of Being Earnest* and *Lady Windermere's Fan*, influenced many later comic writers.

The distinguished novelist-playwright John Galsworthy (1867-1933) followed Shaw as a leader in the English theater. His *Justice*, which dealt with the law, and *Strife*, which bore on labor relations, are two of his most notable plays. There was a renewed interest in drama after World War I. It took about eight years to bring about a true dramatic picture of the war days. *Journey's End* by Robert C. Sherriff has been accepted as the most vivid and dramatic portrayal of the war. Most plays of the 1920's dealt with postwar morals. Noel Coward (1899-   ) is the best-known playwright of this period. His *Hay Fever*, *Private Lives*, *Tonight at 8:30* (nine one-act plays), and *Cavalcade* have been the most successful. Another important playwright was John van Druten (1901-1957), whose *Young Woodley* won him wide fame. He later transferred his nationality and his subject matter to the United States. *The Voice of the Turtle* and *I Remember Mama* are typical of his American plays. Sir James M. Barrie (1860-1937) put wry whimsey into his *Peter Pan* and *What Every Woman Knows*. J. B. Priestley (1894-   ) began as a writer of melodramas, but later studied philosophical problems. Christopher Fry (1907-   ) added a quality of imaginative poetry to such plays as *The Lady's Not for Burning*. Thomas Stearns Eliot (1888-   ) also wrote poetic dramas such as *The Cocktail Party* and *The Confidential Clerk*.

A group of playwrights called the *angry young men* won fame after World War II. Members of this group often used their plays to show their discontent with society. The group includes John Osborne (1929-   ), who wrote *Look Back in Anger* and *The Entertainer;* Arnold Wesker (1932-   ), author of *Roots;* and Harold Pinter (1930-   ), who wrote *The Caretaker*.

Continental Development and Influence. The Moscow Art Theater was established in 1898 under the direction of Vladimir Nemirovich-Danchenko (1858-1943) and Constantin Stanislavski (1863-1938). These two men invented a new method of acting. It set a high standard in the theater which the whole world has worked to imitate. The Moscow theater encouraged the great Russian dramatists Anton Chekhov (1860-1904) and Maxim Gorki (1868-1936). Perhaps Chekhov's best-known play is *The Cherry Orchard*, a delicate study of the decay of the Russian aristocracy. Gorki is famous for *The Lower Depths*, *Yegor Bulychev*, and other plays.

Gerhart Hauptmann (1862-1946) outranks any other German dramatist. His social plays, notably *The Weavers*, had great influence. Otto Brahm (1856-1912) and Max Reinhardt (1873-1943) were better known for their new devices in staging than for the quality of their plays. Franz Werfel (1890-1945), novelist and dramatist, influenced the modern theater with his *Goat Song*. Austria's Arthur Schnitzler (1862-1931) wrote wise and witty comedies, and Karel Čapek (1890-1938) of Czechoslovakia startled the world with *R.U.R.* In Italy the chief dramatist was Luigi Pirandello (1867-1936). His *Six Characters in Search of an Author* and *As You Desire Me* won world-wide fame. France was the home of the Belgian-born Maurice Maeterlinck (1862-1949), best known for *The Blue Bird*. The French stage has also seen plays by Sacha Guitry (1885-1957) and Jules Romains (1885-   ). Jean Anouilh (1910-   ), Paul Claudel (1868-1955), Jean Giraudoux (1882-1944), and Jean-Paul Sartre (1905-   ) wrote poetic dramas of great power. They won some popularity in the United States during the 1950's. The Romanian-born playwright Eugene Ionesco (1912-   ) won wide recognition for many of his plays, including *Rhinoceros*.

The Little Theater Movement offers the best proof of growing interest in the drama. The Irish National Theatre inspired amateur and young professional actors in all parts of Great Britain and the United States. Repertoire theaters sprang up in Birmingham, Manchester, and other English cities, and little theaters blossomed throughout the United States. Pioneers in the movement were Maurice Browne in Chicago, Gilmor Brown in Pasadena, Calif., and Frederic McConnell in Cleveland. In some communities, professional directors work with amateur actors as part of a community enterprise. Many actors who later won fame on Broadway and in Hollywood received their first experience and training in little theaters. Summer theaters are an outgrowth of the little theater movement. Both professional and amateur actors play at summer resorts or in tents, old barns, and theaters in-the-round.

Drama in the Schools. George Pierce Baker (1866-1935) established playwriting and the theater arts at

A High-School Production of *Pride and Prejudice* Was Dramatized from Jane Austen's Novel.

Harvard and at Yale. He made them proper college and university subjects for academic credit. Men like Frederick Koch (1877-1944) of the Carolina Players, E. C. Mabie of the University of Iowa, and Glenn Hughes of the University of Washington followed successfully in Baker's footsteps. The schools of Yale, Iowa, North Carolina, Western Reserve, Syracuse, Texas, Smith, Oklahoma, Vassar, and Washington are outstanding for their departments of drama. Plays are written as well as acted in the school dramatic departments. Some college plays have become professional successes, such as the 1945 Broadway hit *Dark of the Moon*.

Motion Pictures, Radio, and Television have drawn some of the audience away from legitimate theaters because they offer free or inexpensive entertainment. But the smaller, more dedicated audiences have often demanded better plays, raising the standards of drama. Many persons prefer legitimate theater to television and motion picture plays. They enjoy seeing stage celebrities in person. The theater has had a deep influence on the entertainment industry. Hollywood has adapted many plays into motion pictures, and stage actors and playwrights often work in motion pictures, radio, and television.

Drama in the United States

American drama can probably be said to begin with Thomas Godfrey's *The Prince of Parthia* (1765) in Philadelphia. The first notable American dramatist was William Dunlap (1766-1839), who was also a manager, painter, and historian of the theater.

Fashion (1845) by Anna Cora Mowatt was a pioneer in the American drama. The drama was firmly established by the Irish-born playwright and actor-manager Dion Boucicault (1820?-1890), Bronson Howard (1842-1908), James A. Herne (1839-1901) with *Shore Acres*, Clyde Fitch (1865-1909) with *The City*, and William Vaughan Moody (1869-1910) with *The Great Divide*.

Eugene O'Neill (1888-1953) was first successful with the Provincetown Players, an experimental producing organization. His *The Emperor Jones, Anna Christie, Desire Under the Elms, Strange Interlude*, and *Mourning Becomes Electra* made theatrical history.

Elmer Rice (1892-   ) was a social dramatist. *Street Scene* was his most popular play. Many American playwrights have had successful plays. Some of the best known are Robert E. Sherwood (1896-1955), with *Abe Lincoln in Illinois;* Marc Connelly (1890-   ), with *The Green Pastures;* Paul Green (1894-   ), with *In Abraham's Bosom;* George Kelly (1887-   ), with *The Show-Off;* and George S. Kaufman (1889-1961). Kaufman worked with many other playwrights such as Connelly, Moss Hart, and Edna Ferber to write such plays as *Dulcy, The Man Who Came to Dinner*, and *The Royal Family*. *Life with Father*, by Howard Lindsay (1889-   ) and Russel Crouse (1893-   ), set a record when it played on Broadway for more than seven years in the 1940's. Other well-known American playwrights are S. N. Behrman (1893-   ), with *The Second Man;* Maxwell Anderson (1888-1959), with *Winterset;* Philip Barry (1896-1949), with *Hotel Universe;* Sidney Kingsley (1906-   ), with *The Patriots;* Lillian Hellman (1905-   ), with *The Little Foxes;* William Saroyan (1908-   ), with *The Time of Your Life;* Tennessee Williams (1911-   ), with *The Glass Menagerie* and *A Streetcar Named Desire;* and Arthur Miller (1915-   ), with *Death of a Salesman* and *All My Sons*.

Outstanding playwrights who have gained fame since World War II include Edward Albee (1928-   ), with *The Zoo Story* and *Who's Afraid of Virginia Woolf?;* and Jack Richardson (1935-   ), with *The Prodigal* and *Gallows Humor*.

GEORGE FREEDLEY

DRAMA

Related Articles. See THEATER with its list of Related Articles. See also literature articles, such as AMERICAN LITERATURE; FRENCH LITERATURE. Other related articles in WORLD BOOK include:

AMERICAN PLAYWRIGHTS

Ade, George
Anderson, Maxwell
Barry, Philip
Belasco, David
Cohan, George M.
Connelly, Marc
Crothers, Rachel
Crouse, Russell
Custis, George W. P.
Davis, Owen
Ferber, Edna
Fitch, Clyde
Gillette, William H.
Glaspell, Susan
Green, Paul E.
Hammerstein (Oscar II)
Hart, Moss
Hecht, Ben
Hellman, Lillian
Herne, James A.
Howard, Sidney
Hughes, Rupert
Inge, William
Kaufman, George S.
Kelly, George
Kingsley, Sidney
Lindsay, Howard
Logan, Joshua
Luce, Clare Boothe
McCullers, Carson
Miller, Arthur
Moody, William Vaughan
Oboler, Arch
Odets, Clifford
O'Neill, Eugene G.
Payne, John H.
Poole, Ernest
Rice, Elmer
Rinehart, Mary R.
Saroyan, William
Serling, Rod
Shaw, Irwin
Sherwood, Robert E.
Tarkington, Booth
Van Druten, John
Wilder, Thornton N.
Williams, Tennessee

BRITISH PLAYWRIGHTS

Barrie, Sir James M.
Beaumont, Francis
Chapman, George
Collins, Wilkie
Congreve, William
Coward, Noel
Drinkwater, John
Dryden, John
Eliot, T. S.
Fletcher, John
Fry, Christopher
Galsworthy, John
Gilbert, Sir William S.
Goldsmith, Oliver
Granville-Barker, Harley
Jerome, Jerome K.
Jonson, Ben
Kyd, Thomas
Marlowe, Christopher
Maugham, William Somerset
Milne, Alan A.
Pinero, Sir Arthur W.
Priestly, John B.
Reade, Charles
Sabatini, Rafael
Shakespeare, William
Shaw, George Bernard
Sheridan, Richard B.
Webster, John
Wilde, Oscar
Williams, Emlyn
Zangwill, Israel

FRENCH PLAYWRIGHTS

Anouilh, Jean
Beaumarchais, Pierre A. C. de
Brieux, Eugène
Camus, Albert
Claudel, Paul
Cocteau, Jean
Corneille, Pierre
Dumas (family)
Gide, André
Giraudoux, Jean
Guitry, Sacha
Hugo, Victor
Lesage, Alain R.
Mauriac, François
Mérimée, Prosper
Molière
Musset, Alfred de
Racine, Jean B.
Romains, Jules
Rostand, Edmond
Sardou, Victorien
Sartre, Jean-Paul
Scribe, Augustine E.
Voltaire

GERMAN PLAYWRIGHTS

Barlach, Ernst H.
Goethe, Johann W. von
Hauptmann, Gerhart
Lessing, Gotthold E.
Schiller, Johann C. F. von
Sudermann, Hermann

IRISH PLAYWRIGHTS

Boucicault, Dion
Colum, Padraic
Dunsany, Lord
Gregory, Lady Augusta
O'Casey, Sean
Synge, John M.
Yeats, William B.

ITALIAN PLAYWRIGHTS

Alfieri, Vittorio
D'Annunzio, Gabriele
Pirandello, Luigi

RUSSIAN PLAYWRIGHTS

Chekhov, Anton P.
Gogol, Nikolai V.
Pushkin, Alexander S.

SCANDINAVIAN PLAYWRIGHTS

Björnson, Björnstjerne
Ibsen, Henrik
Lagerkvist, Pär F.
Strindberg, August

SPANISH PLAYWRIGHTS

Benavente y Martínez, Jacinto
Calderón de la Barca, Pedro
Echegaray y Eizaguirre, José
García Lorca, Federico
Vega, Lope de

ANCIENT GREEK AND ROMAN PLAYWRIGHTS

Aeschylus
Aristophanes
Euripides
Plautus, Titus M.
Seneca, Lucius A.
Sophocles
Terence

OTHER PLAYWRIGHTS

Bhavabhuti
Čapek, Karel
Maeterlinck, Maurice
Molnár, Ferenc
Stringer, Arthur J. A.
Werfel, Franz

UNCLASSIFIED

Burlesque
Comedy
Epilogue
Melodrama
Miracle Play
Morality Play
Musical Comedy
Mystery Play
Opera
Prologue
Shadow Play
Tragedy

Outline

I. The Plot and Structure of the Drama
II. Kinds of Drama
III. The Development of Drama in the West
  A. The Greek Theater
  B. The Roman Theater
  C. The Medieval Theater
  D. The English Theater
  E. The Continental Theater
IV. The Romantic Revolt
V. The Rise of Realism
VI. The Oriental Drama
VII. Drama in the 1900's
  A. The Irish Revival
  B. In England
  C. Continental Development
  D. The Little Theater Movement
  E. Drama in the Schools
  F. Motion Pictures, Radio, and Television
VIII. Drama in the United States

Questions

What is tragedy? Comedy? Farce?
What were the achievements of Aeschylus? Christopher Marlowe? Goethe?
How did Ibsen's *A Doll's House* influence later drama?
What was the Abbey Theatre?
What dramatists are called the *angry young men?* What are some of their plays?
Who was the first notable American dramatist?
Name the American dramatist whose plays made theatrical history.
Who is called "the greatest of all dramatists?" What are some of his plays?
Who wrote *The Importance of Being Earnest? The Confidential Clerk? Six Characters in Search of an Author? Death of a Salesman?*
Who were the French *neoclassicists?* When did they write?
What was the first true English comedy? When was it written?
Who was Germany's greatest writer?

DRAMAMINE is the G. D. Searle Company's trademark for a drug used to prevent motion sickness, and to control nausea and vomiting in certain illnesses. Dramamine, or *dimenhydrinate*, is one of the antihistaminic drugs. It acts as a mild sedative to reduce the activity of the central nervous system. Large doses may cause drowsiness. BENJAMIN F. MILLER

See also ANTIHISTAMINE; SEASICKNESS.

DRAMATIST. See DRAMA with its list of Related Articles.

DRAPER, DOROTHY (1889-   ), an American interior decorator, designed many hotel interiors, including the Hampshire House in New York City; the Greenbrier in White Sulphur Springs, W.Va.; and the Quintandinha at Petrópolis, Brazil. The Hampshire House interior designs, finished in 1933, represented the largest decorating contract ever awarded a woman.

In her decorating, Mrs. Draper used enlarged fabric patterns, furnishings, and ornaments; vivid colors; and contrasting textures, patterns, periods, and qualities. A cabbage rose on chintz virtually became her trademark. She also designed fabrics, wallpapers, lamps, and furniture. She was born in New York City. WILLIAM PAHLMANN

DRAUGHTS. See CHECKERS.

DRAVIDIAN. See INDIA (The People).

DRAWBRIDGE. See BRIDGE (Movable Bridges); CASTLE.

DRAWEE, and **DRAWER.** See BILL OF EXCHANGE.

DRAWING is the act by which an artist notes what he sees or feels. A drawing is the graphic result. It may be a finished work of art, or it may be a preparatory sketch for a work to be completed in another medium. For example, many painters first make drawings and layouts of their subjects. Sculptors often draw sketches to record structural details or characteristic movements.

There are many ways to draw, and each individual drawing has its own particular character. Some kinds of drawings are meant to look exactly like the objects they picture. Mechanical drawing gives precise sizes and details, so that the object can be made or copied (see MECHANICAL DRAWING). But other kinds of drawings are not meant to show just what the object looks like. Many drawings interpret the object or idea as it appears to the artist. Drawings are not photographs. They are made with a different technique for a different reason.

What to Draw. A beginner will find it best to start with simple subjects, such as a chair, an apple, a bookcase, or a tree. It is best for him to record what he sees as exactly as he can. Later, when his technique is better, he can experiment. He must learn by repeated efforts to see his subject clearly and to record carefully what he sees.

Techniques. One of the first things an artist learns to do is to compose his drawing, arranging the objects so that they form a pleasing design. He may use one or more of the elements of design (see DESIGN). The artist uses certain techniques, or effects, to achieve his ends. The most important techniques include perspective, solidity, and exaggeration.

The artist will use the principles of *perspective* to show depth in his drawing. The surface he is using is flat, so he must use tricks to get the effects of length, width, and depth. He uses the laws of perspective to do so. He may draw objects in the distance smaller than objects close at hand, in *foreshortening*. In some cases, he may

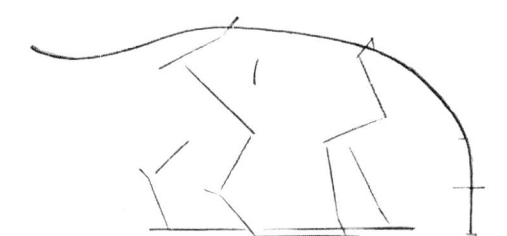

DRAWING

1. Main Proportions Shown by Curves and Angles

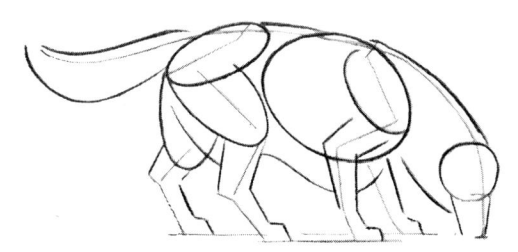

2. Main Masses of the Body Are Added to the Sketch

3. Masses Are Rounded Out by Means of Shading

4. Details of Structure, Texture, and Color Complete the Drawing

The Stages in Making a Drawing. By following the steps shown, the artist can create a drawing which is lifelike and has the proper proportions. This method is helpful either for a single figure or for a complete composition.

eliminate the middle distance and show only the foreground, and then much smaller objects far away. He may use slanting lines that seem to lead to a horizon. For example, he may draw two railroad tracks, which normally are parallel, wider in the foreground of the picture and narrower at the back. When the viewer looks at them, he sees that they *converge* (run together) at the horizon line. The artist may also exaggerate certain lines in his subject to get the result. He may emphasize lines on the "far" sides of his objects, and lighten lines

275

DRAWING

on the "near" sides. See PERSPECTIVE.

The artist may want to show *solidity*, or space composition. He may do so by using shadowing. He will use a heavily accented line on the light side. Or he may draw several lines close together, from light to dark, to give shadow and depth. Or he may smudge the lines into dark areas.

The artist uses *exaggeration* to achieve several effects. If he drew the moon exactly as it looks, it would often seem far too small in his landscapes. He might discover this by making a preliminary sketch. In his finished work, he would exaggerate by increasing the size until it seemed right. Botticelli, in *Primavera*, used flowing lines to show the movement of bodies blown by wind (see PAINTING [color picture]). He achieved a continuous line in his painting by exaggerating the length of the arms and legs of his subjects. He only suggested ankles and wrists, because they would interrupt the flowing line if he drew them as they really exist. Because he knew body structure, useful knowledge for any artist, he sensed that slight exaggeration would achieve his desired effect.

The cartoonist also uses exaggeration. He picks out the prominent features of an individual, such as a large nose or small eyes, and exaggerates them to achieve a comic effect in his cartoon or caricature. A great cartoonist will use this effect to bring out whatever qualities he wishes to emphasize. See CARICATURE; CARTOON; COMICS.

Drawing Materials. Pencil and paper are the most common drawing materials, although the pencil did not become popular until the 1800's. One of the oldest drawing media is ink. The ancient Chinese drew with a brush and ink, and many artists still do (see JAPANESE PRINT). The quill pen became popular in the Middle Ages. Pen and ink are more difficult to use than pencil. The best kind of ink to use is black *India ink*. Today, most cartoons and many other kinds of drawing are done in this medium. Some artists draw with colored inks, or with colored pencils used dry or dipped in water.

Chalk and charcoal are other ancient drawing materials that are still popular. Both are soft and can be rubbed to show mass. But they may smear. The artist can prevent this by spraying the drawing with a "fixative" after completing it. Drawings can also be made with crayons and pastels. Sometimes artists use an opaque or transparent wash to provide shading after the lines have been drawn with pen or pencil. An *opaque wash* consists of a mixture of lampblack, Chinese white, and water. A *transparent wash* is made of lampblack and water. See CHARCOAL; CRAYON; INK.

Uses of Drawing. Drawing is of basic importance to professional artists, cartoonists, painters, and sculptors. Drawing also plays a major part in industry. Engineers and draftsmen rely on drawing in designing everything from tiny machine parts to big factories (see BLUEPRINT).

Drawings are important in the basic planning stages of such fields as dress designing and interior decoration. The designer makes a preliminary sketch in order to get a rough idea of the finished product (see DRESSMAKING). Drawing also extends into other professions. We use pictures today to make and sell products and to develop and spread ideas. For example, the advertisements we see in magazines, on billboards, or on television are a combination of words and pictures. In advertising, the finished product began as an idea which became concrete through a sketch on an artist's drawing board. Artists who work in all these different fields are called commercial artists. See COMMERCIAL ART.

Illustrations for THE WORLD BOOK ENCYCLOPEDIA involve making preliminary sketches before completing the final work. Artists must also make *layouts*, or plans, of the finished pages. Such drawings serve to plan and place illustrations and text.

Illustrators in the field of science use drawings to show objects that cannot be photographed, such as prehistoric animals, or to clarify complicated structures, such as organs of the human body (see HEART [color pictures]).

Drawing is a useful tool for children in school. School subjects such as geometry and homemaking employ drawing of some kind. This helps the student understand better the principles and practices of the subjects involved.

WILLIAM MILLIKEN

Related Articles in WORLD BOOK include:

Blueprint	Charcoal	Ink
Camera Lucida	Comics	Mechanical Drawing
Camera Obscura	Crayon	Painting
Caricature	Design	Silhouette
Cartoon		

DRAWING, MECHANICAL. See BLUEPRINT; MECHANICAL DRAWING.

DREADNOUGHT, or **DREADNAUGHT,** is a type of battleship first launched by the British Navy in 1906. It carried batteries of big guns in turrets, and had heavy armor plate. Shipbuilders later developed the more powerful *superdreadnought*. See also WARSHIP.

DREAM is an experience a person lives through during sleep. Although dream experiences are imaginary, they seem very real. Some experiences are pleasant. Others are annoying, or even frightening.

Many persons say that they seldom dream, because they do not remember their dreams. The memory span of a dream experience is very short. Unless the dreamer is awakened, either by some external event or by the emotional excitement of the dream itself, he will not recall having dreamed when he gets up in the morning.

Scientists observe dreams in two ways. They connect wires from an amplifying and recording device, called the *electroencephalograph* to the head of the sleeper (see ELECTROENCEPHALOGRAPH). This instrument registers "brain waves," the tiny changes in the electrical potential of the resting brain. A certain pattern of these "brain waves" is a sign of dreaming.

Scientists also observe the sleeper's eyes. When a person dreams, he "watches" the action with his eyes. These eye movements can be seen through closed eyelids and also recorded automatically on moving paper tape.

As a result of these observations, scientists have found that everyone dreams four to six times a night. Each dream lasts between 15 and 20 minutes. Scientists also have found that dreams need not be started by outside happenings. However, such things as loud noises may affect the course of a dream. Sometimes they even become a part of the dream in some distorted form that a person cannot recognize.

NATHANIEL KLEITMAN

See also NIGHTMARE.

DREBBEL, CORNELIUS VAN. See Submarine (Development of the Submarine).

DRED SCOTT DECISION. Dred Scott was the slave of an army surgeon, Dr. John Emerson of Missouri. In 1834, Dr. Emerson took Scott to the free state of Illinois and then to that part of Wisconsin territory which later became the state of Minnesota, a region where slavery was forbidden by the Missouri Compromise. In 1838, Scott was taken back to Missouri, a slave state. Scott's master then moved from Missouri, leaving Scott behind. He was hired out, and later sold to John F. A. Sanford.

Meanwhile, Scott had been told by interested persons that his residence in a free state and territory made him a free man. He sued for his freedom in 1846, and the state circuit court gave a verdict in his favor. But the state supreme court reversed the decision. The case was then transferred to the federal courts, and eventually reached the Supreme Court of the United States. The name "Dred Scott Decision" refers to this court's decision.

The actual verdict of the Supreme Court was simply that it had no jurisdiction in the Dred Scott case. The court decided that Scott was still a slave. According to ample precedent, his return without protest to Missouri took care of that. As a slave, he was a citizen neither of Missouri nor of the United States, and therefore could not sue in the federal court. The court might well have stopped at this. But seven of the nine justices were Democrats. They seized the chance to record the opinion that the Missouri Compromise was unconstitutional and that slavery could not be excluded from the territories. The two Republicans held that this part of the decision was merely the opinion of a majority of the justices on a matter that was not before the court (in legal language, *obiter dictum*), and that it therefore had no legal force. The announcement of the 7 to 2 decision by Chief Justice Roger B. Taney on Mar. 6, 1857, aroused a violent public reaction. The Dred Scott Decision increased the tension between the North and the South. It was one of the important factors leading to the Civil War.   RAY ALLEN BILLINGTON

See also Taney, Roger Brooke.

DREDGING

DREDGING, *DREHJ ing*, is the work of clearing out the bottom of rivers, harbors, and other bodies of water so that ships can use them. The machines which do the work are called *dredges*. They work somewhat as a *power shovel* does on land (see Building and Wrecking Machines). Dredges usually are run by steam or diesel engines.

The *dipper dredge* has a large scoop shovel, or *dipper*, shaped like a box which hangs on a chain from a long steel beam. The steel beam, or *derrick*, is attached to a strong mast which can swing the beam and dipper in a wide semicircle. The chain can be wound and unwound to raise and lower the dipper, and the derrick also can be raised and lowered.

When the dredging begins, the dipper is lowered to the bottom of the river or harbor. The derrick arm is swung in a semicircle to drag the dipper across the bottom so that it scoops up dirt and mud. Then the dipper is raised above the water and swung above a barge nearby. The bottom of the dipper has a door which is pulled open by a long cord to dump the dirt into the barge. Then the dipper is lowered again to dig more mud.

The first steam dredge was used in England in 1796. It had a long endless chain with several buckets hanging from the chain. One end of the chain was lowered to the bottom. Then the endless chain was revolved until one of the buckets caught in the mud and was filled. The chain was revolved again and the bucket was raised while other buckets were lowered on the chain to dig. Barges were placed alongside the dredge so the buckets could be emptied.

The *hydraulic dredge* is the most efficient machine for moving large quantities of beach or river sand. The sand and water are sucked up through a suction pipe to a pump. A smaller discharge pipe leads from the pump to a barge or to a disposal area. Earth deposited by this process for dams, dikes, or building sites is called *hydraulic fill*.   R. G. HENNES

See also Gold (The Dredge; picture, Methods).

Great Lakes Dredge and Dock Co.

Dredging requires huge pieces of equipment. This 1,000-horsepower dredging unit has a 150-foot hull and a 240-foot steel and aluminum boom. The clamshell bucket that swings from the boom can scoop up from 6 to 12 cubic yards of material at a time from the bottom of a river or harbor. The operator runs the diesel-electric unit from a cab high above the hull's front end.

DREISER, THEODORE

Theodore Dreiser
G. P. Putnam's Sons

DREISER, *DRY sur,* **THEODORE** (1871-1945), was an American realistic novelist whose works have had a significant influence on contemporary writers. He regarded most earlier American writers as being evasive. He insisted on an author's right to interpret life frankly. His early books drew severe criticism. *An American Tragedy* was banned in Boston.

Dreiser revolted from his father's rigid Roman Catholicism and was influenced by such philosophers as Herbert Spencer. He saw man as an animal driven by lust and greed—his two main themes. His main belief was that only the strong survive in the ruthless struggle for existence. He said he got this main image of life by watching a lobster kill a squid in an aquarium in a store window.

Dreiser's early work as a newspaper reporter, especially in night police courts, gave him insight into many unusual areas of experience. He tried to document them in great detail. *An American Tragedy,* published in 1925, ranks as his best novel. He based it on newspaper reports of an actual murder and the trial. It later became a successful motion picture called *A Place in the Sun.*

He also wrote *Jennie Gerhardt; Sister Carrie;* his "trilogy of desire," *The Financier, The Titan,* and *The Genius; Tragic America; America Is Worth Saving; Cadenced and Declaimed; Dreiser Looks at Russia; Chains; Dawn; Thoreau;* and several autobiographical works.

Dreiser used an uneven and often bungling style to portray uncertain and indecisive characters. Perhaps his most appealing quality is his immense compassion for those caught in the tormenting conflict between their natural impulses and the laws and conventions of the community.

Dreiser was born in Terre Haute, Ind., the twelfth of thirteen children. He grew up in extreme poverty, which later influenced his writing. Dreiser attended Indiana University for one year, and then worked for eight years on newspapers in Chicago, St. Louis, Pittsburgh, and Cleveland. He served as editor in chief of *The Delineator* and *The Designer* from 1907 to 1910. One of Dreiser's brothers, Paul Dresser, wrote several popular songs. Dreiser wrote the lyrics for one of the most popular of them, "On the Banks of the Wabash." He died in Hollywood, Calif. HARRY H. CLARK

DRENNAN, WILLIAM. See EMERALD ISLE.

DRESDEN, *DREHZ dun* (pop. 493,600; metropolitan area, 700,000; alt. 375 ft.), lies on both sides of a broad curve of the Elbe River, in East Germany. For its location, see GERMANY (color map). It is a city of parks and gardens, and a center of the arts. Thousands of visitors travel to Dresden to see its churches and lovely buildings, and to admire its collections of paintings and sculpture. It was founded in the 1200's, and was the capital of the kingdom of Saxony (see SAXONY).

Dresden is a manufacturing and trading city. Porcelain and pottery factories use the *kaolin,* or porcelain clay, which lies in heavy deposits around the city. The city has given its name to the thin, delicate Dresden china, which has been made chiefly in factories at Meissen, 14 miles outside of Dresden (see DRESDEN CHINA). Other products include chemicals, cotton and woolen materials, pianos, beet sugar, and machinery.

Students from Germany and many other countries attend Dresden's schools. The schools include the Academy of Medicine and Surgery, the Royal Music School, the Technical High School, private and public elementary schools, and art institutes.

Dresden's museums and theaters are well known to students of art, history, and the drama. The Museum of Zwinger has housed such famous paintings as Raphael's *Sistine Madonna,* Correggio's *Holy Night,* Titian's *The Tribute Money,* Rubens' *The Boar Hunt,* Cranach's *Adam and Eve,* and an altarpiece by Jan van Eyck. During World War II, the Germans hid their art treasures in underground caves and mines so that bombs would not damage them. The Russians seized many of the paintings in 1945 when Dresden was captured. They returned about 750 of them to Dresden in 1956, in time for the city's 750th anniversary.

Dresden was the scene of street fighting and unrest after World War I. During World War II, bombs and artillery fire damaged Dresden, but the city was one of the last German strongholds to surrender.

The city of Dresden is now the capital of the district of Dresden, a division of Communist-controlled East Germany. JAMES K. POLLOCK

DRESDEN CHINA is a delicate white glazed porcelain decorated in relief, bright color, and gold. It was first produced in Meissen, Germany. But it was named after Dresden, where Johann Friedrich Böttger discovered the secret of porcelain-making in 1709. Böttger found that, by using a white clay called *kaolin*, he could produce porcelain like that made in China and Japan. See KAOLIN; PORCELAIN.

Augustus the Strong, Elector of Saxony and King of Poland, had ordered Böttger, an alchemist, to try to change lead into gold. But Böttger's discovery of porcelain led the king to establish a factory at Meissen, near Dresden. He put Böttger in charge.

Böttger perfected his porcelain, and developed a glaze and various methods of decoration. From 1719 to 1870, the Meissen factory flourished, in spite of wars and changes in management, artists, and workmen. During that period, the factory enjoyed the patronage of kings. Its products won great popularity in Europe and elsewhere. Large and elaborately decorated porcelains commissioned by Augustus the Strong and Frederick the Great are preserved as national treasures in Dresden and Meissen museums. Also on display are figurines, vases, urns, plates, bowls, and candelabra, all of Dresden china. Examples of such porcelain can also be found in museums and private collections in most European countries, in the United States, and in many other parts of the world. PAUL BOGATAY

See also BÖTTGER, JOHANN FRIEDRICH.

DRESS. See CLOTHING.

DRESSER, PAUL. See INDIANA (Famous Hoosiers).

Clyde Brown

René von Schleinitz

A Dresden Clock of fine Meissen porcelain serves a useful purpose, but its chief value lies in its beautiful detail.

Sight-Seers in Dresden, Germany, take an excursion boat cruise on the Elbe River. The Elbe flows through the center of the city, dividing New Town (Neustadt) from Old Town (Altstadt).

A Ram, of Meissen porcelain, is an excellent example of Dresden ware. Meissen artisans made many such figures.
Victoria and Albert Museum

279

DRESSMAKING

DRESSMAKING has regained popularity in recent years. But it was much more common 50 years ago, before the ready-to-wear industry developed. Many women and girls still prefer to make their clothes. To some, designing and making clothes is a means of creative expression. Others may sew for reasons of economy. Still others sew because they are unable to find ready-made garments that fit as well as clothing they make for themselves. Others prefer to make their own clothes because they feel that ready-to-wear garments have too little individuality.

Garment Design. In order to design her own clothes successfully, a girl must understand the principles of art and their application to the human figure. She must understand body structure, and be able to interpret and select lines that emphasize good features and conceal imperfections. She must learn to modify an extreme fashion so that the proportions and lines of the design are becoming to her. In selecting a commercial pattern, or in creating her own pattern, she must learn to use the principles of design as guides, rather than as rigid laws.

Four elements of art are basic in costume selection or pattern designing. They are line, form and space, color, and fabric texture. Unity of line, proportion and scale, and appropriate use of color and texture all contribute to a harmonious costume. A girl can make her clothing attractive if she uses materials appropriate to the garments. But she should make sure that the dress will be appropriate for its intended use in her wardrobe.

The shape of a garment design is often called its *silhouette* or *background area*. There are only three basic silhouettes: the *tubular*, or straight, the *bouffant*, or bell-shaped, and the *bustle*. These shapes may vary, depending on how much the lines are exaggerated or minimized. The silhouette indicates whether or not the garment is in style with the prevailing fashion.

A good silhouette should be related to body structure, and should have emphasis at points of juncture, such as the shoulder, elbow, wrist, natural waistline, and knee. It should also provide a proper background for individual shapes or details. The background spacing for a pocket or ornament is as important as the shape of the pocket itself.

In any garment, the total areas are made up of parts that must have individuality in themselves, but at the same time be in good relationship to each other. Four ways of achieving this relationship are proportion, scale, rhythm, and emphasis.

Proportion is the division of the total area into pleasing space relationships. Proportions of two to three or of three to five are usually considered pleasing. This principle may be applied to a decorative border design, or to the relationship of the length of a suit jacket to the length of a skirt.

Scale deals with the size relationships separate areas have to each other, as well as to the wearer. The size of the design in a printed fabric is one of the factors in scale.

Rhythm is the use of repeated design elements, as in the flowing lines of the classical Greek drapery or the vertical lines of a pleated skirt.

Emphasis is the selection of a major design factor. Minor points of interest should always support one main point. But there should not be so much emphasis that competition of interest results.

Color can either contribute to or detract from a costume's effectiveness. To use color successfully, a girl should judge its degree of brightness or intensity, its relative lightness or darkness, and the size of the area

STEPS IN MAKING A DRESS

Choose Fabric and Pattern carefully. Salespeople can help you select the most suitable material. The pattern tells you how much of it to buy.

Cut the Cloth, first pinning the pattern to it as directed. Cut notches and mark perforations where indicated.

Fit the Pattern to a dressmaker's dummy, or to yourself, after pinning it together. Adjust the pattern by taking tucks or adding inserts.

Baste the Pieces Together with very large stitches, using a contrasting thread. Fit each section as you go along to be sure that it is correctly basted.

where the color will appear. She can use a strong color successfully if she does not use too much of it. Otherwise, it may seem too strong. There is no simple formula that can guarantee correct or becoming use of color. Individual color and figure-type charts are merely guides, not rules.

Fabric. A girl should select the fabric and pattern in relation to each other. She can create highly individual clothing if she chooses a fabric that emphasizes the pattern and a pattern that emphasizes the fabric. She should learn to judge the *hand* of a fabric, or the way it drapes. In some patterns, knowing the hand of the fabric is as important as knowing the structure of the design.

Fabrics vary greatly as to the degree of skill required in cutting, sewing, pressing, and handling. Extremely smooth, slippery fabrics or heavy, bulky fabrics are difficult to handle. Soft fabrics that drape easily, such as crepe, lend themselves to fullness, gathering, or draping. Crisp fabrics, such as taffeta, are better for a bouffant effect. A firm fabric is better for the structural details of a suit.

If the garment is one that will require frequent laundering, it is important to know whether or not the fabric is preshrunk and colorfast. Fiber content alone is no longer the major factor in how well a garment can be washed or dry-cleaned. Finishes applied to fabrics frequently alter their characteristic behavior. Many fabrics are made from blends of two or more fibers. The fabrics gain improved characteristics because, through blending, each fiber may supplement the least desirable characteristics of the other. There are countless types of fabrics on the market, and fabric selection has become increasingly complex. Fabrics should have labels that provide information on colorfastness, resistance to creasing or wear, shrinkage, stretching, and recommended method of care.

Construction. The girl who sews will find many commercial patterns available. Certain ones may fit better than others, and require less adjustment. She should be sure to choose the correct pattern size. She will find dressmaking more enjoyable if her pattern does not go too far beyond her skill and experience in sewing. Cutting charts and step-by-step directions will prove helpful in making the garment.

Authorities often disagree on specific methods for construction processes. Some feel that simpler speed methods, such as basting with a sewing machine, are as good as traditional "custom" methods. The "custom" method is frequently slower, but it often produces a better appearance and fit. Both methods may produce satisfactory results. But the method that is most effective for one person is not necessarily the best method for another.

Methods in altering patterns and techniques of fitting are also controversial, but any one of a number of different methods may bring satisfying results.

Whether a girl uses a commercial pattern or drapes the fabric over a form, she must use and understand several basic factors. She must know which way the grain of her fabric runs. If she does not, the grain may spoil the appearance and fit of the finished garment. She must also make sure that the structural seam lines go in the proper directions, so they will not be subject to unnecessary strains, and so the fabric will lie smooth at the seams.

HAZEL B. STRAHAN

See also CLOTHING; FASHION; SEWING; SEWING MACHINE; TEXTILE.

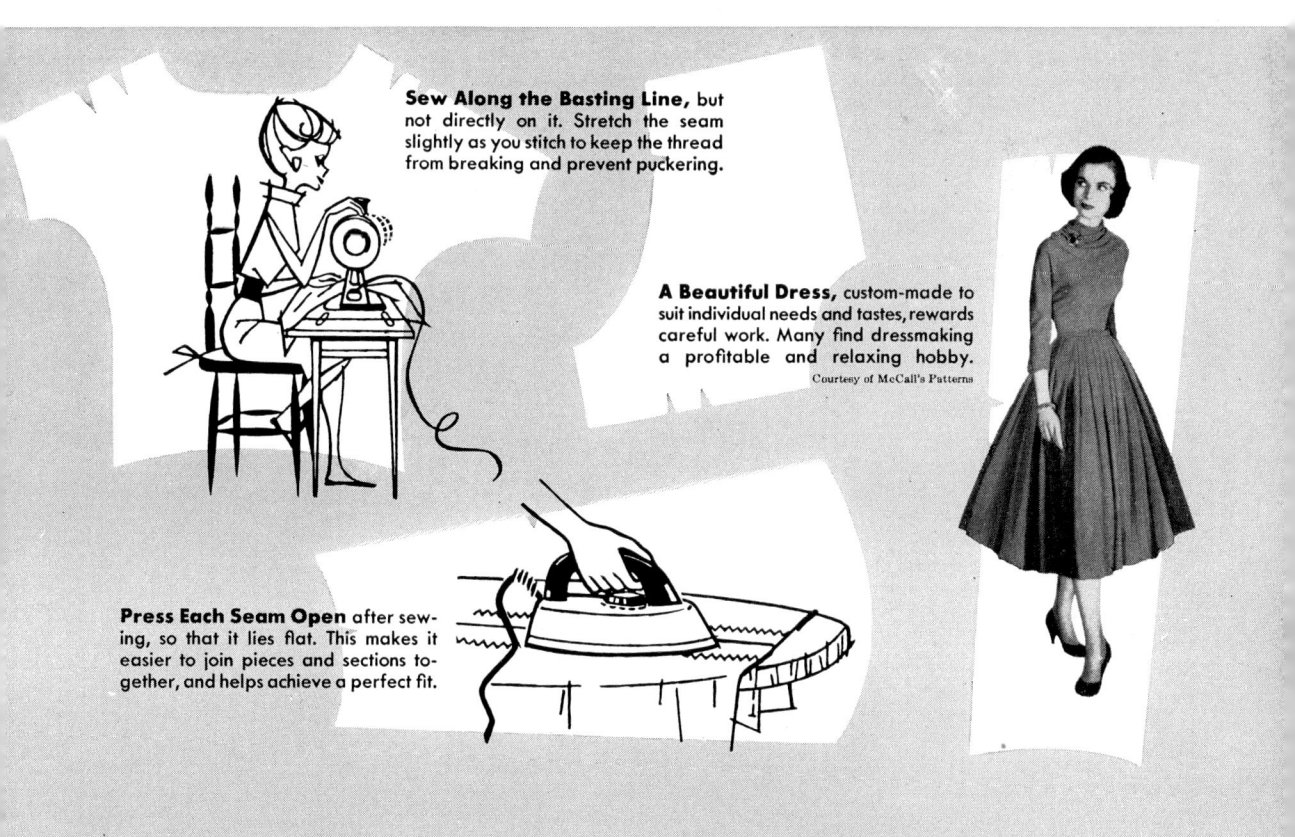

Sew Along the Basting Line, but not directly on it. Stretch the seam slightly as you stitch to keep the thread from breaking and prevent puckering.

A Beautiful Dress, custom-made to suit individual needs and tastes, rewards careful work. Many find dressmaking a profitable and relaxing hobby.
Courtesy of McCall's Patterns

Press Each Seam Open after sewing, so that it lies flat. This makes it easier to join pieces and sections together, and helps achieve a perfect fit.

DREW, CHARLES RICHARD

DREW, CHARLES RICHARD (1904-1950), a Negro surgeon, became known for research on blood preservation and for the organization of blood banks. He directed the blood plasma project for Great Britain in 1940 and then the American Red Cross blood program in New York City. He received the Spingarn medal in 1944 for his work. Drew served as professor and head of the Howard University surgery department and as chief surgeon at Freedman's Hospital, Washington, D.C., from 1941 until his death. He was born in Washington, D.C. HENRY H. FERTIG

DREW, JOHN (1853-1927), an American actor, became noted for his outstanding light-comedy roles. He was leading man opposite Ada Rehan in Augustin Daly's company and later joined Charles Frohman's company where he starred many times with Maude Adams. Drew played over 100 leading roles during more than 50 years on the stage. These included roles in *Rosemary*, *A Marriage of Convenience*, *Richard Carvel*, and *The Masked Ball*.

Drew was born in Philadelphia, Pa., the son of the Irish actor, John Drew, Sr., and the actress Louisa Lane Drew. He made his debut in his mother's theater in Philadelphia in 1873. He was the uncle of Ethel, John, and Lionel Barrymore, all of whom later won fame on the stage. WILLIAM VAN LENNEP

United Press Int.
John Drew

See also BARRYMORE; SHAKESPEARE, WILLIAM (picture).

DREW UNIVERSITY is a coeducational school at Madison, N.J. It is associated with the Methodist Church, and has a college of liberal arts, a theological seminary, and a graduate school. It was founded in 1867, but operated only as a theological school until the college was founded in 1928. For enrollment, see UNIVERSITIES AND COLLEGES (table).

DREXEL, ANTHONY JOSEPH (1826-1893), was an American financier and philanthropist. In 1847, he became a partner in Drexel and Company, a Philadelphia banking firm founded by his father, Francis Martin Drexel (1792-1863). He became head of the firm in 1863. He and J. P. Morgan established the international bank of Drexel, Morgan & Company in 1871. Drexel was born in Philadelphia. He was a co-owner of the Philadelphia *Public Ledger*. JOHN B. MCFERRIN

DREXEL INSTITUTE OF TECHNOLOGY is a privately endowed coeducational college at Philadelphia, Pa. It offers daytime courses in its colleges of engineering, business administration, and home economics. There is also a graduate school of library science. The evening college offers courses in architecture, engineering, and industrial administration. The Institute features the work-study plan in its day colleges. This plan combines classwork with on-the-job training. It is compulsory for courses in engineering. The college was founded in 1891 by Anthony J. Drexel. For enrollment, see UNIVERSITIES (table). See also DREXEL, ANTHONY J. ALLEN T. BONNELL

DREYFUS, *DRAY fus,* **ALFRED** (1859-1935), was a Jewish French army officer who became the center of a bitter quarrel as a result of political injustice. He was arrested on Oct. 15, 1894, on suspicion of spying for Germany. In December, a military court found him guilty. It suspended him from the army and sentenced him to life imprisonment on Devil's Island.

Throughout the trial, Dreyfus maintained that he was innocent. In 1896, a member of the French general staff, Georges Picquart, found documents that convinced him of Dreyfus' innocence. But his superiors ordered him to drop the matter. Many noted persons worked to get Dreyfus a new trial. Émile Zola wrote *J'Accuse*, demanding justice (see ZOLA, ÉMILE).

He received a second trial in 1899, but it was a mockery, because feeling against Jews was so bitter in the army. Many officials felt that the case was closed and that the army's honor was at stake. Testimony favorable to Dreyfus was barred, and the court again found him guilty. He was sentenced to 10 years' imprisonment, but President Émile Loubet pardoned him after he had been confined for only a few days.

Champions of justice, not only in France but throughout the world, protested the unfair trial. Finally, in 1906, the case was reviewed by the highest court in France, and Dreyfus was declared innocent.

Culver
Alfred Dreyfus

He became a major in the French army, and was enrolled in the Legion of Honor. At the outbreak of World War I, he commanded one of the forts defending Paris. He was born in Mulhouse, Alsace. ANDRÉ MAUROIS

DRIED FRUITS. See DATE AND DATE PALM; FIG; PRUNE; RAISIN.

DRIFT. See GEOLOGY (Some Terms Used in Geology).

DRIFT INDICATOR. See AIRCRAFT INSTRUMENTS.

DRIFT MINE. See COAL (Mining Methods).

DRILL is a strong cotton fabric with a diagonal weave, resembling denim (see DENIM). Drill may be used unbleached, although it is often bleached or dyed. Lightweight drill is used for blouses, suits, and play suits. *Khaki drill* is made into uniforms. *Boat-sail drill* is unbleached and is used for pocket linings as well as boat sails.

DRILL, or SEEDER, is a tractor-drawn machine used for planting seeds for farm crops. It has a narrow box, called a *hopper*, usually from 8 to 14 feet in length. It is mounted between two wheels connected by an axle. The seed to be planted is placed in the hopper, which has revolving *metering* devices at the bottom. The metering devices are spaced 6 to 8 inches apart, and are geared to the axle. These devices move the seed from the hopper to a row of tubes suspended beneath it. The seed drops through the tubes to shallow furrows made by hoe or disk openers. Wheels or short lengths of chain then push soil back into the furrow.

Grain drills are sometimes equipped with an additional hopper for spreading fertilizer. They are also manufactured with smaller hoppers for sowing grass, clover, and alfalfa seed. ROY BAINER

DRILLING TOOLS are used to make round holes in metal, rock, wood, plastic, or other materials.

Metal Drills are among the most useful tools used in machine shops and factories. They are usually made of specially hardened carbon or high-speed steel. Twist drills are the most commonly-used metal drills. Some twist drills have straight cutting edges separated by *flutes*, or grooves. However, most twist drills have spiraling cutting edges and flutes. The flutes carry chips out of the hole being drilled.

Twist drills can be used in hand-operated drills, in motor-driven hand drills, or in drilling machines or *drill presses*. The ordinary drill press has a platform similar to that on a butcher's scale. One or several drills are mounted above the platform. The operator pulls a lever to lower the drills to the metal placed on the platform. Some drill presses run automatically. They need an attendant only to supply material (see SOUND [picture, Ultrasound]).

Twist drills come in sizes based on the diameter of the holes they drill. The sizes are usually given in numbers, fractions, or letters. The numbers range from No. 80 (.0135 inch) up to No. 1 (.228 inch). The fractions increase by 64ths of an inch from $\frac{1}{64}$ to 2 inches. Fractions are also used for sizes up to $3\frac{1}{2}$ inches. Letters ranging from A (.234 inch) to Z (.413 inch) are used for sizes not covered by numbers or fractions.

Wood Drills are usually called *bits*. They resemble metal drills and can also be mounted on drill presses. Carpenters use bits chiefly to drill holes $\frac{3}{8}$ inch in diameter or less. Larger holes are drilled with special tools called *augers*. See BIT.

Reamers are drilling tools used to enlarge holes, and to give them a smooth finish. Reamers may have straight or spiral cutting edges like those on drills. *Solid reamers* come in various sizes to fit the hole being enlarged or finished. *Expansion* or *adjustable* reamers can be adjusted to fit the hole.

Rock Drills are usually run by compressed air that drives a chisel-shaped drill point. Some rock drills, such as those used to drill oil wells, have cutting edges like those on twist drills (see PETROLEUM [Drilling an Oil Well]; PNEUMATIC TOOL).   FRED H. COLVIN

DROMEDARY

DRINKWATER, JOHN (1882-1937), was an English playwright, poet, and biographer. He became known in the United States for his chronicle plays *Abraham Lincoln* and *Robert E. Lee*. His play *Bird in Hand*, was also produced in the United States. He wrote his most popular biography, *Pilgrim of Eternity*, about Lord Byron. In addition to writing plays, he also produced and acted, especially with the Birmingham (England) Repertory Theater. Drinkwater was born in Essex. He attended Oxford High School.   LEO HUGHES

DRIVE, in psychology. See AMBITION.

DRIVE-IN THEATER is an outdoor motion-picture theater. People watch the program while sitting in their automobiles. Some people call these theaters *ozoners*. The drive-in has a huge screen. Drivers park their cars on ramps facing the screen, and each car receives an in-car speaker. There are over 5,000 drive-in theaters in the United States and Canada. See also MOTION PICTURE (picture, Movie Theaters Old and New).

DRIVE SHAFT. See AUTOMOBILE (Parts; color diagram, How Your Car Runs).

DRIVER, WILLIAM. See TENNESSEE (Famous Tennesseans).

DRIVER EDUCATION. See AUTOMOBILE DRIVING (Driver Education).

DRIVING, AUTOMOBILE. See AUTOMOBILE DRIVING.

DROMEDARY, *DRAHM ee DAIR ih*, is a swift, slightly built camel used for travel in parts of India, Arabia, and Africa. It sometimes grows to be 7 feet tall. The dromedary has only one hump. It can live on small amounts of food and water and requires only short periods of rest.

The dromedary travels at the rate of about 9 miles an hour for many hours, and can cover 600 miles in five days. It moves with a swinging trot, much like the gait of a pacing horse and less jolting than an ordinary camel. The dromedary produces rich milk. Its hair is used for making cloth. No true wild dromedaries exist.

Scientific Classification. The dromedary belongs to the family *Camelidae*. It is a member of the genus *Camelus*, and is species *dromedarius*.   VICTOR H. CAHALANE

See also ANIMAL (color picture, Africa); CAMEL.

DRILLING TOOLS

Black & Decker Mfg. Co.

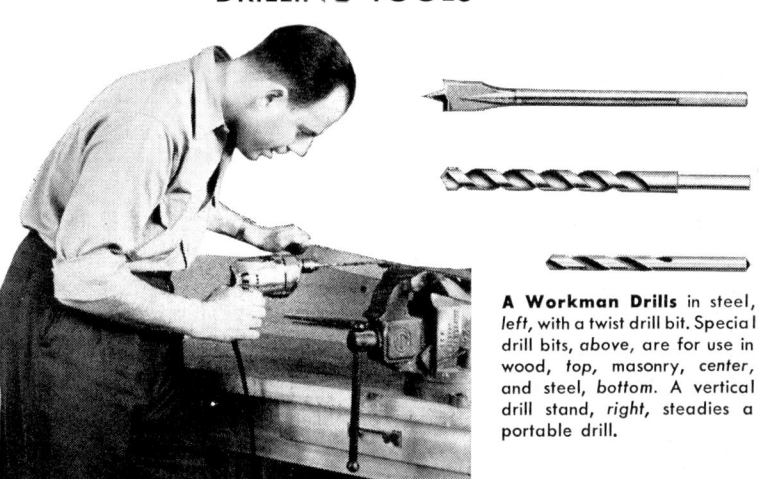

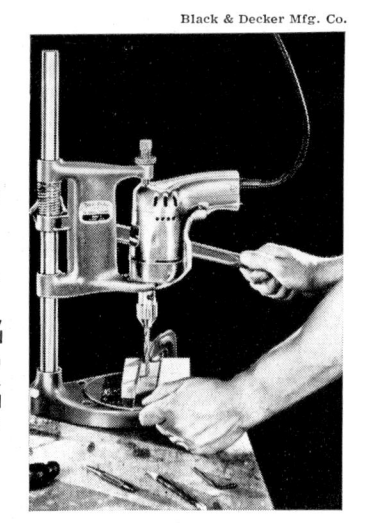

A Workman Drills in steel, left, with a twist drill bit. Special drill bits, above, are for use in wood, top, masonry, center, and steel, bottom. A vertical drill stand, right, steadies a portable drill.

DRONE. See BEE (Drones; picture).

DROP HAMMER. See FORGING.

DROPSIE COLLEGE is a private postgraduate school for men and women in Philadelphia, Pa. It has a college of Hebrew and cognate learning, a school of education, and an institute for Israel and Middle East studies. It grants M.A., Ph.D., and Ed.D. degrees. Dropsie College was founded in 1907. For enrollment, see UNIVERSITIES AND COLLEGES (table).

DROPSY is a condition in which a watery fluid gathers in the body cavities or tissues. It is sometimes called *edema* and occurs in diseases such as Bright's disease, cirrhosis of the liver, anemia, and some forms of heart disease. Disorders in the circulation of the blood cause dropsy.

Dropsy may occur generally in almost all parts of the body, or it may be local, or present in one part of the body. General dropsy is called *anasarca*. Dropsy is most common in the abdomen, chest, brain, kidneys, legs, feet, and around the eyes. It can be recognized by the small cavity that lingers when the swollen part is pressed. Dropsy should be treated by a physician. JOHN B. MIALE

DROUGHT, *drowt,* or **DROUTH,** *drowth,* is a condition which results when the average rainfall for a fertile area drops to less than 85 per cent of the normal amount for a long period of time. In areas which are not irrigated, the lack of rain causes farm crops to wither and die. Higher than normal temperatures usually accompany periods of drought. They add to the crop damage. Forest fires start easily during droughts. Millions of acres of valuable timberland have been burned during these dry periods. The soil of a drought area becomes dry and crumbles. Often the rich topsoil is blown away by the hot, dry winds (see DUST STORM). Streams, ponds, and wells often dry up during a drought, and animals suffer and may even die because of the lack of water.

Weather observers cannot predict with certainty just when a drought will occur. But they know that these drier-than-normal periods tend to alternate with wetter-than-normal periods in an irregular cycle. Droughts of the past can be read in the rings made by trees as they add a new layer of wood each year. In wet periods, the year's layer is thick, while in periods of drought, the ring is very thin.

The southwestern states of the United States suffered one of the worst droughts in their history from 1931 to 1938. The drought affected the entire country. Few food crops could be grown. Food became scarce, and prices went up throughout the nation. Hundreds of families in the Dust Bowl region had to be moved to farms in other areas with the help of the federal government (see DUST BOWL). In 1944, drought brought great damage to almost all Latin America. The drought moved to Australia and then to Europe, where it continued throughout the summer of 1945. From 1950 to 1954 in the United States, the South and Southwest suffered a severe drought. Hundreds of cattle ranchers had to ship their cattle to other regions because pasture lands had no grass. The federal government again conducted an emergency drought-relief program. It offered farmers emergency credit and seed grains at low prices during the program. EDNA S. STONE

DROWNING is death caused by suffocation in water or other liquid. A person who cannot swim can keep from drowning by floating upon the surface of the water. Floating is accomplished by rolling over on the back and extending the body in a relaxed position. Failure to float is usually the result of fear, which causes the body to stiffen and sink. A person becomes unconscious almost immediately after sinking. But death does not follow at once, for the heart continues to beat for several minutes. The popular belief that a person must come to the surface three times before finally sinking is false. He may not rise at all, depending upon circumstances, especially upon the position of his arms during his struggles. If they are held above the head, the body sinks deeper into the water. If they are held down at the sides, the body will probably rise to the surface.

Methods of Rescue. A drowning person should be rescued from a boat or with a life buoy whenever possible. This lessens the danger to the rescuer.

Rescue by Swimming. Approach the victim from the rear. Grasp his hair or coat collar, and swim vigorously with the free hand and both legs. The side stroke should provide sufficient power to move two people through the water. If the victim cannot be approached from the rear and starts to sink, grasp one of his hands and lie back in the water. Give a strong kick or two with the legs at the same time to keep from going under. A sharp pull with the right hand on that of the victim will turn him over on his back. Then the rescuer can swim with him and keep his head above water, using one of the following rescue methods:

In the *head carry* the rescuer swims on his back and holds the victim's head with both hands, at arms' length, in a floating position. In the *cross-chest carry* the rescuer holds the victim against his upper hip in a back-floating position, while swimming on his side. This position close to the rescuer means greater security. It is an excellent carry for panic-stricken victims.

Applying First Aid. Breathing, or respiration, should be restored as soon as the drowning person has been rescued. A person may apply artificial respiration himself or use such means as an inhalator. The person administering the artificial respiration must not give up easily. People have been saved after as many as eight hours. The person to person methods of applying artificial respiration include mouth-to-mouth, chest pressure-arm lift, or back pressure-arm lift. See ARTIFICIAL RESPIRATION; FIRST AID (picture, How to Give Artificial Respiration).

These methods can also be supplemented by the use of an instrument called an *inhalator* (see RESUSCITATOR). The inhalator consists of a face mask, a breathing bag, and two tanks, one for the oxygen, and the other for the mixture of oxygen and carbon dioxide. Fire departments or public-utility companies can usually supply inhalators. But only a trained person should use one.

Drowning as a Form of Punishment. Drowning was a common form of punishment in most European countries from ancient times until the early 1600's. A condemned man sometimes received a choice of death by drowning or by hanging, or "by ditch or by gallows." He usually chose drowning, since that was considered more honorable. In 1611, a man was drowned in Scotland for stealing a lamb. BENJAMIN F. MILLER

DRUG is a substance used to treat illness, to protect against disease, or to promote better health. The term *drug* includes all those things which are often called *medicines*. The word *drug* comes from the Dutch *droog*, which means *dry*. The name probably came into use because most early drugs were made from dried plants.

The Importance of Drugs

Modern drugs have made our lives today longer and healthier than ever before in history. A person born in the early 1900's could expect, on the average, to live less than fifty years. But a baby born today can expect to live almost seventy years. This great increase in the average person's length of life has resulted to a large extent from the discovery and use of more and better drugs.

The life-saving importance of drugs can be seen by looking at what has happened to such common diseases as pneumonia and meningitis. Before the sulfa drugs came into common use in the 1940's, about 33 out of every 100 people who became ill with pneumonia died of the disease. The death rate from meningitis was even higher. With the use of sulfa drugs and penicillin, the deaths from both these diseases have been cut to five or less out of 100 illnesses.

Modern drugs save the American people billions of dollars each year from loss of time from work because of illnesses. Drugs mean much less suffering and pain, and many fewer complications from illnesses that weaken the body and sometimes cause invalidism. Modern anesthetics and methods of administering them make it possible for surgeons to perform operations that were impossible only a few years ago. Other drugs, such as vitamins, amino acids, carbohydrates, plasma, and various substances taken from human blood, help surgeons to perform long and complicated operations that could not be made without drugs.

Invalidism and early death from the failure of body organs to act normally can be prevented by the use of such drugs as liver extract for anemia and insulin for diabetes. Gold salts, ACTH, and cortisone have made it possible for persons crippled with arthritis and similar diseases to recover enough to lead active lives. Such a simple drug as aspirin has relieved millions of persons from headaches and other aches and pains. Common antiseptics that kill germs have saved millions of lives and have prevented the loss of as many arms and legs from infection.

Dangers in Drugs

If you take drugs, it is important that you do so only under a doctor's direction. This is because a particular drug is useful only under certain conditions. A doctor first tries to find what is wrong with you before he decides what drugs, if any, you should use. If you take the wrong drug, severe injury to the body, and even death, can be the result. Also, and just as important, exactly the right amount of the correct drug must be used. The right amount depends upon many things, including your physical condition. Almost any drug can be poisonous if you take too much. Sometimes, drugs cause unexpected and harmful effects even when correctly used. Some persons are *allergic*, or unusually sensitive, to certain drugs. Sulfa drugs and penicillin, for example, cause rashes, digestive disturbances, and other uncomfortable reactions in some persons.

Hundreds of New Compounds are tested in drug company research laboratories for every successful new drug that is found. — Abbott Laboratories

Dangers in Self-Medication. There are many dangers in *self-medication*, or taking drugs without the advice of a doctor. One danger is that the wrong drug may be used unintentionally by someone who imagines that he has the same illness as a friend or relative who received the drug from a doctor. This has often happened with the sulfa drugs, for example. Some persons who have used such drugs without the advice of a doctor have caused permanent damage to their kidneys and other parts of their bodies. Others have died.

Another danger of self-medication is that it is sometimes possible to take just enough of a drug to stop the symptoms without affecting the disease itself. This may make it impossible for even a doctor to diagnose the disease correctly. This, too, can result in death. A person might treat himself for a cold when he has pneumonia. To do this is to flirt with death. Sometimes a person gives himself doses that are too small to overcome the disease. This has often happened with penicillin and other antibiotics. In such instances, the germs that cause the disease may develop the ability to resist the drug. In time, they become so resistant that even huge doses of the drug are ineffective.

Some persons become so accustomed to the effects of certain drugs that they think they cannot do without them. See DRUG HABIT.

Control Over Drugs. Certain laws have been passed to cut down the dangers associated with the use of drugs, and to protect people against careless or unscrupulous manufacturers. The Federal Food, Drug, and Cosmetic Act was passed in 1938 and became effective in 1940.

DRUG

It applies to all drugs produced in one state and shipped to other states. This act is an attempt to make sure that new drugs are properly tested before they are sold, and to ensure full and truthful labeling of drugs. The Federal Food and Drug Administration serves as a watchdog for this and other acts. In 1962, Congress passed a law tightening controls over new drugs. It provides that the sale of a drug may be stopped immediately if the drug is believed dangerous.

Another agency set up to help protect the public is the Federal Trade Commission, which tries to make sure drug advertising is truthful (see FEDERAL TRADE COMMISSION). The Division of Biologics Standards in the National Institutes of Health regulates biological products (serums, vaccines, hormones) just as the Food and Drug Administration watches over other drugs. Many states also have drug laws which provide for close supervision over the manufacture and distribution of drugs inside the state. The activities of the Council on Pharmacy and Chemistry of the American Medical Association are better known to physicians than to most other persons. This body examines new drugs to test their safety, usefulness, and claims made for them.

Certain drugs can be sold by a druggist only when a doctor's prescription is presented. This procedure is intended for the protection of the public and is enforced under a provision of the Federal Food, Drug, and Cosmetic Act. Many states and cities have laws making it impossible to obtain some drugs without a doctor's prescription. See PURE FOOD AND DRUG LAWS.

What Are Drugs Made From?

Drugs are made from various plants, animals, and minerals. Chemists also make drugs in their laboratories.

Drugs from Plants. The medicinal use of plants probably was discovered by accident. In very early days, primitive man used plants for food and in connection with religious festivals. As he tried different plants, undoubtedly he found that some of them produced definite reactions in his body. Digitalis, for example, is a drug that is found in the leaves of the purple foxglove plant. A small amount of this drug causes the heart to beat more powerfully. People used dried leaves of the purple foxglove to treat heart diseases long before scientists isolated the plant's digitalis.

Many drugs obtained from plants are used in medicine today. Some of the more important plant drugs include digitalis, quinine, benzoin, colchicine, ergot, opium, morphine, cocaine, belladonna, atropine, caffeine, and ephedrine. In recent years scientists have discovered an entire new group of "wonder drugs" called *antibiotics*, which are found in various molds and bacteria.

Drugs from Animals. The scientific use of drugs from animal parts is rather recent. Animal drugs became important when scientists discovered that some diseases are caused when glands in the human body do not function properly. Scientists found they could use chemicals produced by glands in living animals to make up for the lack of functioning of the same glands in the human body. Insulin, obtained from the pancreas of cattle and hogs, is used in treating diabetes. Extracts of animal thyroid glands and pituitary glands are other examples. These extracts take the place of the same *hormones* (body regulators) in human beings whose glands are not functioning correctly. The *serum* (liquid portion of the blood of animals) is used in fighting diseases such as diphtheria and tetanus. Animals also are used in producing vaccines.

Drugs from Minerals. Many minerals have common and important uses as drugs. Compounds of mercury and silver are used as antiseptics. Calcium, phosphorus, iron, and other minerals are given to provide essential materials for building sound bones and other body structures. Arsenic and antimony are used in the war against parasitic diseases.

Synthetic Drugs. Perhaps the greatest advances of modern medicine have rested upon the development of

Abbott Laboratories
Tablet-Making Machine, or rotary compressor, stamps 40,000 to 50,000 tablets an hour in a drug-manufacturing plant.

drugs in scientific laboratories. Some important synthetic drugs have been discovered by analyzing drugs taken from plants and animals. The chemist studies such drugs and then learns how to make them directly in the laboratory. In this way, scientists save the time and expense of extracting and purifying natural drugs.

A chief advantage of synthetic drugs over natural drugs is that the chemists can make slight changes in the chemical structure of the drug, so that the manufactured product is often better than the natural product.

The *sulfonamides* (sulfa drugs) are among the important drugs which have been developed in the laboratory. These drugs, which have saved millions of lives from pneumonia and other diseases in recent years, are totally different from any drugs found in nature. Vitamins, enzymes, hormones, and a wide variety of other important drugs are now being made in giant drug-manufacturing plants.

Types of Drugs

The following is a list of the most important types of drugs in terms of uses. Each type is listed by the name physicians ordinarily use for it. This technical name is followed by a brief description, and by a few examples.

Anesthetic, general (produces loss of consciousness): ether, nitrous oxide, cyclopropane, chloroform.

Anesthetic, local (produces loss of sensation locally): cocaine, Novocain, Stovaine.

Antacid (counteracts acid condition of stomach): sodium bicarbonate, magnesium hydroxide.

Antiarthritic (counteracts arthritis or its symptoms): cortisone, ACTH, cinchophen.

Antibiotic (prevents the growth of disease germs): penicillin, chloromycetin, terramycin, streptomycin.

Antihistaminic (used to treat asthma and symptoms of respiratory infections): Antistine, Benadryl, Histadyl, Pyribenzamine.

Antipyretic (fever reducer): acetanilide, acetphenetidin, acetylsalicylic acid (aspirin).

Antiseptic (kills disease germs or prevents their growth): iodine, alcohol, Mercurochrome.

Astringent (contracts tissues and lessens flow of fluids): alum, tannic acid.

Circulatory depressant (depresses heart action): glyceryl trinitrate, aconite, veratrine.

Circulatory stimulant (stimulates heart): digitalis, digitoxin, caffeine, Adrenalin, ammonia, cocaine.

Counterirritant (relieves deep-seated inflammations): cantharides, capsicum, chloroform, turpentine.

Demulcent (soothes irritation): gelatin, glycerol.

Depressant (acts on the nervous system to slow action of the body): alcohol, tranquilizers, soporifics.

Diuretic (promotes the secretion of urine): caffeine, hexamethylenetetramine, theobromine, theophylline.

Emetic (causes vomiting): apomorphine, ipecac, mustard, potassium antimony tartrate (tartar emetic).

Enzyme (substance produced normally by the body and which causes chemical changes, such as digestion, to take place): pepsin, pancreatin.

Expectorant (loosens up mucus and congested fluids from respiratory tract): ammonium chloride, ammonium anisate, eucalyptus, terebene.

Hormone (chemical, normally produced by the body, that travels in the blood and affects other organs or tissues): ACTH, Adrenalin, cortisone, insulin, thyroxin.

Laxative, cathartic, purgative (causes bowel movement): castor oil, croton oil, cascara.

Mydriatic (dilates eye pupil): belladonna, atropine.

Myotic (contracts eye pupil): eserine, pilocarpine.

Narcotic (sleep inducer): codeine, heroin, morphine.

Soporific, hypnotic (sleep producer): barbital and barbituric acid compounds, phenobarbital.

Tranquilizing agent (depresses central nervous system; sedative action): chlorpromazine, hydroxyzine, meprobamate, mepazine, reserpine.

Vaccine (substance containing living or dead disease germs): smallpox vaccine, Salk vaccine for polio.

The Discovery and Manufacture of Drugs

A new drug may be developed by long research in a laboratory or, rarely, it may be discovered by accident.

DRUG

Following the development or discovery of a new drug, there is a period in which it is tested in test tubes in the laboratory, on animals, and finally on a small number of persons who volunteer for the work. This testing determines the proper doses, the harmful properties, if any, and the diseases or symptoms for which the drug is actually useful. Then, if the drug seems to be useful, a drug manufacturer works out the problems of production. After these problems are overcome, a complete factory is built to permit mass production of the drug. Usually, several years are required from the time a new drug is proposed until it becomes available for use.

Penicillin offers an excellent example of how rapidly modern drug manufacturers can expand to meet the need for more drugs. In the first five months after the first factory started production, 400,000,000 units were produced. Five months later, 9,000,000,000 units were being produced monthly. A year later, monthly production had soared to 200,000,000,000 units. Today, billions of units of penicillin are produced each day.

Penicillin is obtained from a mold, as are most antibiotics. Thousands of molds from different parts of the world have been tested, but only a few have been found worth while for developing drugs. This is a painstaking and expensive method of searching for new drugs, but there is no short cut, except as occasional discoveries are made by accident. Even the synthetically produced drugs are subject to the same tedious, time-consuming searching. Only a very few of the sulfa drugs are used in medicine, but thousands have been made and tested—only to be discarded as worthless or harmful.

Mass production lowers drug prices. The cost of penicillin (in its simplest form) was originally $20 for 100,000 units. But mass production has brought the price down to just a few cents for 100,000 units. The cost of one vitamin has been brought down from $300 a gram to only 20 cents.

Huge quantities of drugs are needed to meet modern demands. For example, about 18,000,000 pounds of aspirin and more than 3,800,000 pounds of sulfa drugs are manufactured in the United States every year. Each year, drugstores fill more than 600,000,000 prescriptions for drugs. Many hundreds of thousands of additional drugs are sold without prescriptions.

Milestones of Discovery

1471 First Known Text on Drugs was published. It was called the *Antidotarium*, and was written by Nicholas, an Italian who lived in Salerno.

1796 First Vaccine. Edward Jenner successfully performed the first vaccination against smallpox.

1846 First Anesthetic. William Morton, an American, proved the value of ether as an anesthetic. It was first used in operations as early as 1842 by another American, Crawford Long.

1898 First Hormone Drug. Epinephrine, or Adrenalin, used in asthma and other illnesses, was extracted from the adrenal glands.

1910 First Successful Chemotherapeutic Drug. Paul Ehrlich, a German, discovered Salvarsan, the 606th arsenic compound he prepared in the laboratory in his search for a drug to combat syphilis.

1922 Insulin, a hormone produced by glands in the pancreas, was discovered by two Canadians, F. G. Banting and C. H. Best. Insulin has saved the lives of countless sufferers from diabetes.

1928 First Antibiotic, penicillin, was discovered by Alexander Fleming, a British bacteriologist.

1932 First Medical Value of Sulfa Drugs was discovered by Gerhard Domagk, a German. (The first sulfa drug, sulfanilamide, was discovered in 1908 by P. Gelmo, a German chemist.)

1949 Radioactive Isotopes were combined with established drugs, supplied to hospitals.

1955 Atomic Energy was first used to sterilize a drug product. In this process a stream of electrons is fired into a package after it has been sealed.

History of Drugs

For thousands of years, drugs have been used to help sick persons. Men have found ancient Assyrian clay tablets which list many drugs used in early times, from the fruit, leaves, flowers, bark, and roots of plants.

The first use of animal parts as drugs probably arose from a magical belief about diseases. People in ancient Babylonia believed various gods, demons, and magical forces controlled their lives. The god *Marduk* was supposed to be the one who healed diseases. Ancient records show that the physicians of the time often prayed to Marduk and conducted strange rites so that he would remove the demon believed to cause the illness. Parts and organs of animals were used as drugs. If a person was suffering from tuberculosis or some other disease of the chest, he was given an animal's healthy lung, or a small model of a lung, made of clay.

Scientific use of drugs was not made until the last half of the 1800's. Our understanding of drugs and their use has increased greatly as the science of chemistry has developed and our knowledge of how to conduct careful scientific experiments has increased.

The Drug Industry

More than 90,000 of the more than 100,000 pharmacists, or druggists, in the United States work in drugstores. About 3,400 work in hospitals, and a small number work for the federal and state governments in agencies that enforce laws regulating food and drugs. Drug manufacturers employ about 7,800 pharmacists. They also have many chemists, chemical engineers, physicians, bacteriologists, and other workers who do drug research.

Drug manufacturers produce two kinds of drugs: (1) *ethical drugs*, those that can be obtained only with a doctor's prescription; and (2) *proprietary drugs*, those that can be bought without a prescription. Sales of ethical drugs account for about two-thirds of the industry's income. In the 1950's, more than 250 drug companies competed with each other in the ethical drug field alone. They produced more than 300 new drugs annually that the Food and Drug Administration approved.

People in the United States spend more than $1,500,-000,000 annually to have prescriptions filled. They also use great amounts of proprietary drugs. For example, druggists sell millions of pounds of aspirin each year. The development of many remarkable new drugs, including the sulfas, penicillin, tranquilizers, antibiotics, and antihistamines caused the sales of drug companies to increase more than seven times during the 1940's and 1950's. The leading drug manufacturers include Abbott Laboratories, North Chicago, Ill.; American Cyanamid Co., Lederle Laboratories Division, Pearl River, N.Y.; American Home Products Corp., New York, N.Y.; Charles Pfizer and Co. Inc., Brooklyn, N.Y.; Eli Lilly and Co., Indianapolis, Ind.; E. R. Squibb and Sons, New York, N.Y.; Merck and Co., Inc., Philadelphia, Pa.; Parke, Davis and Co., Detroit, Mich.; and the Upjohn Co., Kalamazoo, Mich. AUSTIN EDWARD SMITH

Abbott Laboratories

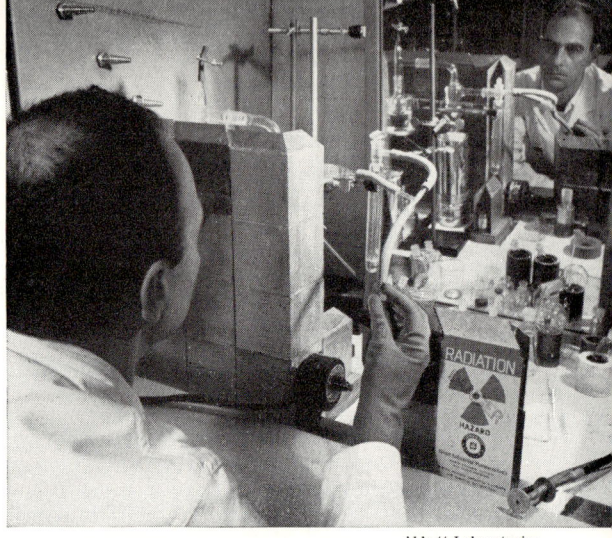

In a Radioactive Drug Laboratory, a researcher adjusts equipment by looking into a mirror, while he is protected from harmful radiation by a thick wall of lead.

Related Articles in WORLD BOOK include:

DRUGS FROM ANIMALS

A.C.S.	Animal (Drugs	Insulin
ACTH	from Animals)	Pancreatin
Adrenalin	Cortisone	Serum
	Halibut-Liver Oil	

DRUGS FROM MINERALS

Argyrol	Ichthyol	Mercury
Arsenic	Iodine	Petrolatum
Arsenical	Iodoform	Salts
Bromide	Iron	Seidlitz Powders
Calomel	Magnesia	Smelling Salts
Epsom Salt	Mercurochrome	Tartar Emetic

DRUGS FROM PLANTS

Aconite	Castor Oil	Ipecac
Aloe	Chloromycetin	Jimson Weed
Arnica	Cinchona	Kola Nut
Asafetida	Coca	Myrrh
Aureomycin	Colchicum	Nux Vomica
Balm	Creosote	Penicillin
Balsam	Cubeb	Psyllium
Balsam of Peru	Curare	Quinine
Belladonna	Digitalis	Sarsaparilla
Benzoin	Ephedrine	Scopolamine
Caffeine	Eucalyptus	Squill
Camphor	Gramicidin	Terramycin
Cascara Sagrada	Horehound	Thymol

DRUGS USED TO RELIEVE PAIN

Acetanilide	Codeine	Nitrous Oxide
Aspirin	Ether	Novocain
Atophan	Laudanum	Opium
Chloroform	Menthol	Paregoric
Cocaine	Morphine	Salicin

UNCLASSIFIED

Analgesic	Depressant	Opiate
Anesthesia	Diuretic	Patent Medicine
Antibiotic	Dramamine	Pharmacology
Antihistamine	Emetic	Pharmacopeia
Antiseptic	Germicide	Pharmacy
Antitoxin	Laxative	Prescription
Astringent	Medicine	Sedative
Chemotherapy	Narcotic	Sulfa Drugs

DRUG HABIT. Some people have a craving for drugs, such as opium, morphine, heroin, cocaine, or the habit-forming drugs in many sleeping tablets. These people are called *drug addicts*. The Federal Bureau of Narcotics has estimated that there are about 60,000 drug addicts in the United States.

A person who takes a habit-forming drug, such as morphine, during a long illness may develop a craving for it. Opium, a common drug in the Orient, deadens pain and brings on sleep. But if anyone takes it for more than a few days, the drug itself causes distress. Then he requires more opium to stop the distress. Unless someone prevents his taking opium, the addict may die. He needs more and more of the drug as long as he takes it, and will neglect his diet and his normal way of life.

This type of drug habit is *physiological*, because it is caused by bodily reactions that the addict cannot control. Drug addicts can often be cured of the physical need for drugs by decreasing the amount of drug given them each day, and through other treatments to remove body poisons. But many addicts are never really cured, since they like to feel "doped." They may feel unable to face life's problems. Treatment can cure them of the physical need for drugs. But it cannot always cure them of the need to escape problems by drugging themselves. Addicts in the United States sometimes smoke "reefers," or cigarettes made of marijuana leaves (hashish). Marijuana is a common weed in many parts of the country, but widespread efforts have been made to kill it.

Drugs that may cause addiction include morphine and its derivatives, heroin, codeine and its derivatives, Demerol, methadone, the bromides, the barbiturates, chloral hydrate, marijuana, and cocaine. Addicts are treated in sanitariums, some of which the federal government supports. National and international sale of habit-forming drugs is strictly regulated. A federal law passed in 1956 provides severe penalties for drug addicts and persons who sell drugs illegally. The World Health Organization and the United Nations Economic and Social Council study drug addiction and international trade in drugs. A. K. REYNOLDS

See also NARCOTIC; KEELEY, LESLIE; NARCOTICS, BUREAU OF.

DRUGGIST. See DRUG (The Drug Industry); PHARMACY.

DRUGSTORE BEETLE. See DEATHWATCH.

DRUID, *DROO ihd*, was a member of a priestly cult among ancient Celts in France, England, and Ireland. These priests worshiped some gods similar to those of the Greeks and Romans, but under different names. In forests and caves they gave instructions, foretold events, and administered justice.

People know little about Druid rites, because the priests handed down their doctrines by word of mouth, and swore their members to secrecy. The Druids held as sacred the hours of midnight and noon, the oak tree, and the mistletoe (see MISTLETOE). They forecast events by interpreting the flight of birds and the markings on the liver and other entrails of sacrificed animals. The folklore of early Ireland depicts Druids as offering human sacrifice. Some scholars think they used the structure at Stonehenge as a place of worship (see STONEHENGE). A group whose members call themselves Druids meet now at Stonehenge every year during the summer solstice. They conduct rites which they believe are like those of the ancient Druids.

The Druids urged their people to fight the Romans when Julius Caesar invaded Gaul and Britain. The Roman general Julius Agricola destroyed them in England in A.D. 78, but they were active in Ireland until the 400's, when Christianity displaced them. WILSON D. WALLIS

The Druids were the teachers and priests of ancient Britain, Gaul, and Ireland. They considered the hours of noon and midnight sacred and performed their rites in the light of the full moon.

DRUM is a musical instrument that is played by *percussion*, or striking sharply. It is made of an open cylinder or a kettle, with a skin called a *drumhead* stretched tightly across the opening. If it has an open cylinder, it has two drumheads. If it is built on a kettle, it has only one. When the drumhead is rapped sharply, it vibrates and produces a sound. This sound is *resonated* (increased) by the drum shell. Drumheads are usually made of stretched parchment or calfskin.

The drum is man's oldest musical instrument. It serves as a means of expressing his instinctive love of rhythm. It has also been used as a method of communication. It may be used as a center of ceremonial dances, as a call to battle, or as a requiem for the dead. Much of the force and vitality of popular music today would be lost without the constant rhythmic accent of the drums.

Most drums do not produce definite musical notes. They are said to have *indefinite pitch*. A *bass drum* is made of wood, with metal tension rods holding the drumheads in place. The rods can be tightened to increase resonance. The drummer uses a *beater* covered with felt or sheep's wool. A *snare drum* measures 14 or 15 inches across and from 5 to 10 inches deep. It is built like a bass drum, except that it has *snares*, or

289

The Bass Drum booms a deep, full tone. Drummers use it in bands and in symphony orchestras. It is the largest of all drums.

The Timpani, or Kettledrums, are the only drums that can be tuned to a definite pitch. They are used in symphony orchestras.

strings of catgut or wire, across the under side. They vibrate against the drumhead, giving the drum its penetrating tone. The drummer uses two wooden sticks in alternate double strokes. A *field drum* resembles the snare drum, but is larger and deeper in proportion to its diameter. It is used chiefly in military and marching bands and in drum and bugle corps.

The *timpani*, or *kettledrums*, are the only drums that can be tuned to a definite pitch. They are hollow halves of globes with single drumheads. The globes are usually made of brass or copper. The drumheads are usually of calfskin. The player tunes timpani by adjusting screws that hold the head in place. This changes the tension and pitch. Some have pedals for rapid changes in tone. Timpani are usually used in pairs. The player makes single strokes with two padded sticks. Tone is affected by the kind of stick. Timpani may be muted by small pieces of cloth.   CHARLES B. RIGHTER

See also MUSIC (Percussion Instruments, picture Percussion Parade); ORCHESTRA; SOUND (Musical Sounds).

The Snare Drum, *left,* provides rhythm in orchestras. The field drum, *right,* a larger snare drum, is played in marching bands.

Bongo Drums, *top,* are used in folk and popular music.

Conga Drums, *right,* are used in Latin American music.

DRUMFISH is the name given to two large fishes of North America. One lives in the fresh-waters of the Great Lakes and in large Mississippi Valley rivers. The other lives in the sea off the Atlantic and Gulf coasts.

The drumfish gets its name from the drumming sound it makes. It has teeth in its throat (*pharyngeal teeth*)

Hugh Davis

The Fresh-Water Drumfish, also called a *sheepshead,* has been known to weigh over 50 pounds and reach a length of 4 feet.

set in a thick, broad, triangular bone. The echo of its throat teeth on its air bladder makes a booming noise. The drumfish uses these teeth to crush the shellfish it eats. It usually weighs about 3 pounds, but some weigh 50 pounds. Some salt-water drumfish weigh over 100 pounds.

Scientific Classification. Drumfish belong to the family *Sciaenidae*. The fresh-water drumfish is genus *Aplodinotus*, species *A. grunniens*. The common salt-water fish is *Pogonias cromis*. LEONARD P. SCHULTZ

DRUMLIN. See GLACIER (Structure).

DRUMMOND, HENRY (1851-1897), a Scottish evangelist and author, became known for his books *Natural Law in the Spiritual World* and *The Ascent of Man*. He attempted to connect the theory of evolution with Christian belief. The religious movement he started spread through England, America, and Australia. He was born at Stirling, Scotland.

DRUMMOND, WILLIAM HENRY. See QUEBEC (Famous Quebecers).

DRUMMOND LIGHT. See OXYGEN.

DRUPE is a fleshy fruit containing a single seed, surrounded by a hard covering or *stone*. The pulp is not naturally divided into segments like the pulp of an orange. The whole drupe is usually covered with a thin skin. Common fruits which are drupes include the olive, plum, cherry, and peach. See also FRUIT (pictures, Nature Designs the Fruits). CLARENCE J. HYLANDER

DRURY, ALLEN (1918-), an American editor and writer, won the Pulitzer prize in 1960 for his novel *Advise and Consent*. The book, about Washington politics, was made into a motion picture. In 1962, Drury wrote a sequel *A Shade of Difference*. His editorials for the *Tulare* (Calif.) *Bee* won him the Sigma Delta Chi Editorial Award for 1941. Drury later reported national politics for the *Washington Evening Star* and *The New York Times*. He was born in Houston, Tex.

DRURY COLLEGE is a coeducational school at Springfield, Mo. It is a private, independently controlled liberal arts college, founded by the Congregational Church. Drury was founded in 1873. For enrollment, see UNIVERSITIES AND COLLEGES (table).

DRURY LANE THEATRE. See GARRICK, DAVID.

DRUSES, *DROOZ uz*, are an Arabic-speaking people of mixed origin, numbering about 200,000. About half of the Druses live in the Hauran districts of Syria, while most of the rest live in Lebanon. There are about 20,000 Druses in Israel who were recognized in 1957 as a separate religious colony. A few thousand Druses have emigrated to the United States and Canada. Their religion combines Christianity and Islam. Their principal settlement is in the Jabel Hauran mountain district of Syria, southeast of Damascus.

Hakim, sixth Fatimite caliph of Egypt, proclaimed himself the incarnation of God in the A.D. 1000's. When he was killed in a revolt, his confessor, Darazi, fled to the Syrian mountains, preaching the same religion. The name Druse is probably a corruption of Darazi (or Durusi). The religion is secret, and information about it is conflicting. The Druses believe in one God. According to *The Druse Catechism*, there have been 10 incarnations of God. The last was Caliph Hakim. The Druses await his second coming. VERNON R. DORJAHN

DRY CELL. See BATTERY (electric).

DRY CLEANING is a way of removing stains and dirt from cloth, by using little or no water. Actually, dry cleaning is not "dry," because *solvents*, or liquids, are used to remove the dirt.

Steps in Dry Cleaning. When you send a suit or other garment to the cleaner, several processes take place before the clothing comes back spic and span. First, a worker places tags on the clothing to show whose it is. Then an inspector examines the garment and places it with others of the same color and type of fabric. An employee called a *pre-spotter* removes stains that might be *set* (made permanent) by the cleaning process. Then the garment goes into a washer containing a movable drum filled with cleaning fluid. This liquid may be perchloroethylene or a highly refined petroleum solvent. Special soaps may also be used.

Next, the garment goes into a type of centrifuge called an *extractor*, which whirls the solvent from the clothing. A machine called a *tumbler* completes the drying by blowing warm air through the garment. This process helps to remove any odor left by the solvent. In some plants, the washing and drying are done in a single machine, called a *washer-extractor*. Some garments made of delicate material are cleaned by hand.

After drying, the garment goes to a highly skilled worker called a *spotter*. He uses chemicals, water, and a steam gun to remove any remaining stains. The chemical used depends on what substance has soiled the clothing. It is helpful if the customer tells the cleaner what caused the stain on the garment.

After spotting, the clothing goes to the *presser*. He uses a steam iron to smooth out the wrinkles and restore the shape of the garment. The dry cleaner may have a tailor to do minor repair work.

The Dry-Cleaning Industry is one of the largest in the United States. About 30,000 dry-cleaning plants operate in the country. In addition, there are about 37,000 shops that only do pressing, after sending clothing out to a wholesale dry-cleaning plant. Many laundries offer dry-cleaning service (see LAUNDRY). In the 1960's, coin-operated, self-service dry-cleaning shops became widespread. The dry cleaning industry employs more than 250,000 persons, and its income totals about $1,600,000,000 a year.

SOME COMMON STAINS AND HOW TO REMOVE THEM

Stains should be removed quickly. As a stain dries, it becomes harder to treat. Work on the reverse side of the fabric and place a pad or towel under the spot to absorb excess cleaning solvents. Some solvents can be dangerous. For example, carbon tetrachloride should be used only in a well-ventilated room because its fumes are harmful. Other solvents are inflammable.

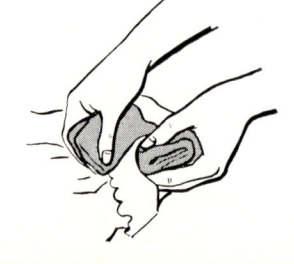

PROTEIN STAINS	Blood Chocolate Egg Ice Cream Milk Gravy	Treat these stains by sponging them with lukewarm water. You can also first sponge the spot with a dry-cleaning solvent. Allow the solvent to evaporate, then sponge the spot with cool water. If the stain has dried, sponge the spot with lukewarm water and a mild detergent or shampoo.
OIL AND GREASE STAINS	Bacon Grease Butter Car Grease Lipstick Margarine Salad Dressing	You can treat these stains in several ways. Place an absorbent towel under the spot. Then pour or pat carbon tetrachloride on the spot. You can also sprinkle the stain with an absorbent powder such as starch or talcum. Brush the powder off and repeat the process. Lubricate greasy stains on washable materials with a liquid detergent before washing.
PAINT STAINS	Finger-Nail Polish Oil-Based Paint Rubber-Based Paint Enamel Shellac Varnish	First scrape or wipe off as much of the stain as possible. Lubricate paint stains on unwashable materials with mineral oil. Then soak the spot in a solvent. Use carbon tetrachloride, turpentine, or kerosene for oil- and rubber-based paints, enamel, shellac, and varnish. Use nail-polish remover for lacquer and nail polish. Acetone-based nail-polish remover dissolves synthetic fibers such as acetate, Arnel, and Verel.
COLORED STAINS	Coffee Soft Drinks Fruits Candy Ink Grass	Treat these stains by sponging the spot with a mild liquid detergent. Then rinse the spot and apply white vinegar. If the stain remains, it may be necessary to bleach the spot.
WAX STAINS	Crayons Floor Wax Shoe Polish Candle Wax Paraffin Wax Beeswax	First scrape away as much of the wax as possible. For beeswax, paraffin wax, or candle wax, place the stained area between two pieces of blotting paper and melt the wax with a warm iron. The paper absorbs the wax. Use carbon tetrachloride on floor-wax, crayon, or shoe-polish spots.

Dry-Cleaning Plants have steam "puff irons" to finish parts of garments difficult to press. The steam removes wrinkles. The worker steps on a pedal to shoot puffs of steam from the iron.
National Institute of Dry Cleaning

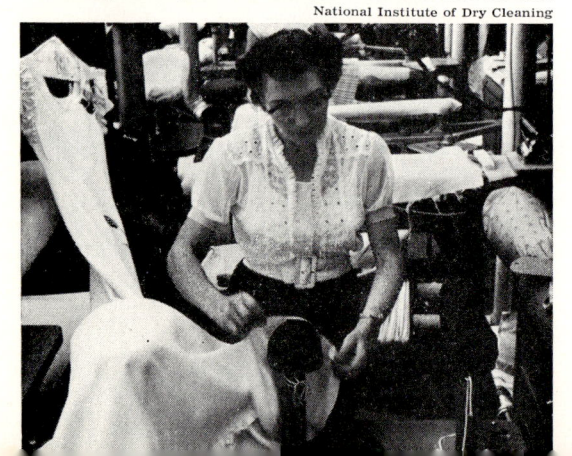

History. The possibilities of dry cleaning were discovered in France in the mid-1800's. According to one story, a maid spilled turpentine on a tablecloth. After the turpentine dried, the maid found that it had removed soiled spots from the cloth. In the United States, gasoline became popular for both commercial and home dry cleaning. But because gasoline catches fire easily, there were many accidents. Chemists developed safer and more effective synthetic cleaning solvents. But even now, persons removing spots at home should take great care. They should use a cleaning fluid that will not catch fire, explode easily, or spread poisonous fumes that might cause illness.   GEORGE P. FULTON

See also CLEANING FLUID.

DRY DOCK is a dock in which a vessel can lie out of the water while repairs are being made below its water line (see DOCK). The two chief kinds of dry docks are graving docks and floating docks.

Graving Docks are used chiefly to repair large ships in shipyards. *Graving* was a term used in the days of wooden ships to mean cleaning a vessel's bottom and coating it with tar. A graving dock looks like a huge, concrete bathtub sunk into the ground. One end of the dock opens onto a harbor, river, or other waterway. When a ship enters the dock, shipyard workers place a huge floating or sliding *caisson*, or gate, against the open end. Pumps suck the water out and the vessel slowly sinks. Its *keel*, or bottom, comes to rest on wooden blocks placed on the floor of the dock. These blocks support the ship. *Spars*, or long pieces of wood wedged between the ship and the sides of the dock, also help support the vessel. When repairs are completed, workers flood the dock until the water reaches the same level as the water outside the gate. It is opened and the ship leaves.

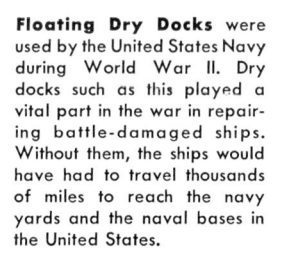

Floating Dry Docks were used by the United States Navy during World War II. Dry docks such as this played a vital part in the war in repairing battle-damaged ships. Without them, the ships would have had to travel thousands of miles to reach the navy yards and the naval bases in the United States.

U. S. Navy

Floating Docks can be self-propelled or towed from place to place. They are important in war to repair ships in forward battle areas. A floating dock looks like a shoebox with the top and ends removed. Some types are built in U-shaped sections that can be assembled to make one large dock. The *hull*, or bottom, and *wingwalls*, or sides, of a floating dock contain compartments. Water enters these compartments, making the dock sink low enough to allow a ship to enter. Pumps then suck the water out and the dock rises, lifting the ship out of the water. Wooden blocks and spars similar to those used on graving docks help support the vessel. When repairs are completed, the compartments are flooded again until the dock sinks enough to allow the ship to float. Such docks can raise an average-sized ship in from one to two hours.   WILLIAM W. ROBINSON

DRY FARMING is a method of farming without irrigation on land where little rain falls. Farmers use it in areas with a total of 8 to 20 inches of precipitation each year. Such a climate exists in many areas of the world.

DRY FARMING

In the United States, the dry-farming area extends north from western Texas to the Canadian border, and west from the Dakotas and western Kansas to the Rocky Mountains. Other dry-farming areas include the Great Basin country between the Rockies and the Cascade and Sierra Nevada ranges, and the Central Valley in California.

In dry farming, farmers plow their land so that the soil helps hold the rain and snow where it falls. Furrows run across, instead of up and down, the hillsides. This forms a series of troughs in the land, one above the other, that hold the rain. If hills are plowed up and down, the furrows provide troughs that allow the water to run off. Tilling the soil keeps out weeds that take moisture and plant food from the soil. Other factors that affect the dry-farming methods in an area include the kind of soil, the amount of moisture different crops need, the rate of evaporation of moisture, the intensity of rainfall, and the season at which the rain comes. After the land has produced a crop, the farmer allows it to lie *fallow*, or idle, the next summer. This enables the land to store up moisture.

The use of dry-farming methods has enabled farmers in the West to produce a large share of the nation's food. Early settlers in the West brought with them the seeds and farming methods used in moist areas. Crop failures occurred until the farmers learned that many of the crops and practices were not suited to the drier climate. Critical problems arose because the settlers plowed up grasslands not suited for crops in areas of limited rainfall. When immigrants from eastern Europe settled in the Great Plains, they brought with them varieties of hard wheat from the Black Sea region, which has a similar climate. Other cereal grains and sorghums were also grown. Then farmers developed new techniques and methods of farming more suited to the dry climate of the West.   A. D. LONGHOUSE

See also CONSERVATION (Soil Conservation).

DRY ICE

DRY ICE is the name for solid carbon dioxide (chemical formula, CO_2), used as a refrigerant. The name comes from the fact that solid carbon dioxide does not return to liquid form when it melts. It changes directly into a gas. Dry ice is much colder than ordinary ice and sometimes reaches a temperature as low as —80° C. Because of this low temperature, it will cause death if taken into the body. Dry ice can be used to ship perishable foods by parcel post, because it cannot melt and spoil the wrapping. Carloads of frozen fish packed with dry ice do not thaw during a five-day journey.

To make dry ice, the carbon-dioxide gas is compressed to a liquid and cooled. Some of the cold liquid is evaporated to make carbon-dioxide snow. Machines then compress the snow into blocks of solid dry ice. These are wrapped in paper and stored in an insulated chamber. In 1925, the Prest-Air Devices Company of Long Island City, N.Y., first manufactured dry ice commercially. GEORGE L. BUSH

DRY MEASURE. See WEIGHTS AND MEASURES.

DRY MILLING. See CORN (Milling).

DRY POINT. See ENGRAVING.

DRY TORTUGAS, tawr TOO guz, are a group of low coral islands, or *keys*, which lie about 60 miles west of Key West, Fla. Ponce de León discovered them in 1513, and called them the Tortugas (Spanish for turtles), because of the many turtles in the nearby waters. Spain ceded the Tortugas to the United States in 1819 along with Florida. Fort Jefferson was built on Garden Key in the Tortugas in 1846. The Tortugas became a federal bird reservation in 1908, and the government made Fort Jefferson a national monument in 1935. The Carnegie Institute maintains Tortugas Marine Laboratory on Loggerhead Key. KATHRYN ABBEY HANNA

DRYAD, *DRY ad*, or HAMADRYAD, *HAM uh DRY ad*, was a wood nymph in Greek mythology. The word *dryad* means *oak daughter*. The dryads lived in trees, and their lives were bound up with the lives of their trees. They died when their trees died. Often, however, they took human form and enjoyed dancing and frolicking with the gods. Both gods and men fell in love with them. Eurydice, the wife of Orpheus, was a dryad. See also EURYDICE; NYMPH; ORPHEUS. PHILIP W. HARSH

DRYDEN, JOHN (1631-1700), was an English poet, critic, and playwright. He dominated the literary life of England from 1660 to 1700, during the period known as the Restoration. Although many of his poems and plays declined in popularity a few decades after his death, his influence on English literature has been lasting and great. He put a clear stamp on the form and structure of the English language.

His Writings. He wrote poems to commemorate certain occasions. He wrote *Heroic Stanzas* (1658) in memory of Oliver Cromwell. But his loyalty to the Puritan side did not keep Dryden from celebrating the restoration to the English throne of Charles II in two poems, *Astraea Redux* (1660) and *Panegyric on the Coronation* (1661).

During the Restoration period, Dryden began to fulfill his literary ambitions. The mood of the time asked for heroic drama and for comic plays about court and town life. Dryden successfully judged this mood, and wrote several popular heroic plays, such as *The Indian Emperor* (1665) and the *Conquest of Granada* (1670). His best contribution to comedy was *Marriage-à-la-Mode* (1673). An intense interest in plays led Dryden to write *An Essay of Dramatic Poesy* (1668), which is now considered a major document in English criticism. By 1668, he had achieved such a reputation that Charles II appointed him poet laureate.

Other Works. Late in the 1670's, religious and political disputes shook England. From these disputes sprang the Whig and Tory parties. Naturally conservative, Dryden cast his lot with the Tories, and began a series of political satires on the Whigs. Two of the best of these satires are *Absalom and Achitophel* (1681) and *The Medal* (1682). Dryden contributed to the religious discussions of the time in *Religio Laici* (1682) and *The Hind and the Panther* (1687).

After the "Glorious Revolution" of 1688, which placed William and Mary on the English throne, Dryden lost his position of poet laureate. He did not favor the new rulers, nor did they favor him. To repair his poor financial position, he wrote poems and plays, and translated selections from earlier writers.

Dryden was born at the vicarage of Aldwinkle All Saints, in Northamptonshire, England. During his boyhood, his family sympathized with the Puritans. But he studied under a Royalist headmaster at Westminster School. From there, he went to Trinity College, Cambridge, and was graduated in 1654. GEORGE F. SENSABAUGH

See also ENGLISH LITERATURE (The Classical Age).

DRYING FOOD. See DEHYDRATION.

DUAL MONARCHY. See AUSTRIA-HUNGARY.

DUALISM. See METAPHYSICS (Doctrines).

DUANE, JAMES. See NEW YORK CITY (Famous New Yorkers).

DU BARRY, *dyoo BAH REE*, **MADAME** (1746-1793), MARIE JEANNE BÉCU, COUNTESS DU BARRY, was the beautiful country girl who became the mistress of King Louis XV of France (see LOUIS [XV]). She had little education. Instead, the beauty of this blue-eyed blonde and her pleasant manner were her greatest assets. She was not a meddlesome woman. But jealous rivals and the king's ministers hated her so much that she had to use her influence upon the king in self-defense. By the time Louis XV died of smallpox in 1774, she counted many friends at court.

She was born in Champagne, France. She first worked in a hat shop in Paris, but soon became the mistress of the Comte Jean du Barry. She met Louis in Du Barry's gambling rooms. She married William du

Brown Bros.
John Dryden

Brown Bros.
Madame du Barry

Barry, Jean's brother, to gain enough social rank to be presented at court. This was required before she could become Louis XV's official mistress. In 1793, the French republicans accused her of aiding enemies of the French state. She was dragged to the guillotine just five weeks after Marie Antoinette's execution.   RICHARD M. BRACE

DUBHE. See BIG AND LITTLE DIPPERS.

DUBINSKY, DAVID (1892-   ), an American labor leader, helped found the Congress of Industrial Organizations (CIO), and became president of the International Ladies' Garment Workers' Union (I.L.G.W.U.) in 1932. He became a vice-president of the American Federation of Labor-Congress of Industrial Organizations (AFL-CIO) in 1955. Dubinsky was born in Brest-Litovsk, Poland. He was arrested for union activity there and exiled to Siberia. He escaped and came to the United States in 1911.   JACK BARBASH

DUBLIN

DUBLIN (pop. 535,488; met. area 690,000; alt. 35 ft.), is the capital and largest city of the Republic of Ireland. It lies on the east coast, at the mouth of the Liffey River. See IRELAND (color map).

The city has spacious squares and broad thoroughfares. O'Connell Street, which is 150 feet wide, is one of the widest streets in Europe. Monuments of men famous in Irish history, and one of Lord Horatio Nelson of Great Britain, stand in the center of this street. Phoenix Park, covering 1,760 acres, is one of the world's largest city parks.

Dublin has many historic buildings. Dublin Castle was once the center of British rule. Leinster House, built in the 1700's, is the meeting place of the Dáil Éireann, the Irish House of Deputies. Dublin has

Irish Tourist Office

Dublin's O'Connell Street, *right,* is the city's main thoroughfare. The street, O'Connell Bridge, *foreground,* and the O'Connell Monument, *at the end of the bridge,* all honor Daniel O'Connell, an Irish patriot. The tall monument, *background,* is the Nelson Pillar.

DUBLIN, UNIVERSITY OF

a college of the National University, founded in 1854, and the University of Dublin, founded as Trinity College in 1591 by Queen Elizabeth I of England.

Trade and Manufacturing. Dublin serves as Ireland's chief port for trade with Great Britain, the country's biggest customer. Dublin's main products include biscuits, canned food, clothing, iron products, paper, processed tobacco, whisky, and *stout*, a dark, heavy beer.

History. Viking settlers established a town on the present site of Dublin in the 800's. The city was later named *Dublin*, from the Gaelic words *dubh*, meaning *dark*, and *linn*, meaning *pool*. This name refers to the dark waters of the Liffey River which the Vikings used as a harbor. Norman soldiers from England captured the city in 1170 and made it the capital of Ireland. They built Saint Patrick's Cathedral in 1190 and Dublin Castle about 1200. Dublin expanded greatly during the 1700's, when many of its present buildings, streets, and docks were built. In 1916, the city was the scene of the Easter Rebellion, which aroused the Irish to the final struggle that won their independence from Great Britain in 1921. T. W. FREEMAN

DUBLIN, UNIVERSITY OF, more generally known as Trinity College, Dublin, was founded in 1591 under a charter granted by Queen Elizabeth I. The financial support of this famous old Irish university came from funds and property given by James I. The university has faculties of arts and science, medicine, engineering, law, commerce, agriculture, divinity, music, and education. It has an average enrollment of 2,300. I. L. KANDEL

DU BOIS, *DYOO BWAH*, is the family name of an American artist and his son, a children's writer and illustrator.

Guy Pène du Bois (1884-1958) became well known for the witty and satirical style in his paintings. His works include *Bal des Quatre Arts* and *New Evidence*. He was born in Brooklyn, N.Y., and studied in New York and Paris.

William Pène du Bois (1916-   ), the son of Guy Pène du Bois, writes and illustrates children's books. He won the 1948 Newbery medal for his science fantasy, *The Twenty-One Balloons*. He also wrote *The Great Geppy*, *Peter Graves*, *The Three Policemen*, and *The Flying Locomotive*. He was born in Nutley, N.J., and was educated in France. JEAN THOMSON

DUBOIS, EUGÈNE (1858-1941), was a Dutch anatomist and physical anthropologist. While in Java in 1891-1892, he discovered the fossilized bones which he later named *Pithecanthropus erectus*, or *the apeman that walked erect* (see JAVA MAN). His discovery led to the theory of a single "missing link" in the chain of evolution joining apes and man. Later discoveries have led scientists to believe that Pithecanthropus is only one form among many in the evolution of mankind. DAVID B. STOUT

DU BOIS, *doo BOYCE*, **WILLIAM EDWARD BURGHARDT** (1868-   ), an American Negro sociologist and author, wrote many books about the Negro. He became a leader of the Negroes who favored a policy of working for complete equality. From 1910 to 1932, he edited *Crisis*, the official publication of the National Association for the Advancement of Colored People. Later, he served as the Association's director of special research. In 1943, he became the first Negro elected to the National Institute of Arts and Letters. He was born in Great Barrington, Mass. ARTHUR MIZENER

DUBONNET. See WINE (Types of Wine).

DUBOS, RENÉ. See GRAMICIDIN; TYROTHRICIN.

DUBUQUE, *duh BYUK*, Iowa (pop. 56,606; alt. 645 ft.), is a port located on the west bank of the Mississippi River opposite the boundary between Illinois and Wisconsin. For location, see IOWA (color map). Dubuque was named for Julien Dubuque, who began to mine lead here in 1788. Lead mining and fur trading have been replaced by lumber distributing and woodworking as the chief industries. The settlement of Dubuque began in 1833. A town government was organized in 1837. The city was governed under a special charter from 1841 until 1920, when the council-manager plan was adopted. WILLIAM J. PETERSEN

DUBUQUE, JULIEN (1762-1810), a French-Canadian adventurer, was the first white man to settle in Iowa. He began mining lead ore in 1788 along the Mississippi River south of the present city of Dubuque. He had a Spanish title to his claim and named it "The Mine of Spain." He earned the friendship of his Indian neighbors by learning their language and trading with them. They gave him the title "Little Night." The Indians gave him a chieftain's funeral when he died. Dubuque was born in Quebec province, Canada. THOMAS D. CLARK

DUBUQUE, UNIVERSITY OF, is a coeducational liberal arts and graduate theological school at Dubuque, Iowa. It was founded in 1852, and is one of the oldest Presbyterian institutions west of the Mississippi River. For enrollment, see UNIVERSITIES (table).

DUCAT, *DUCK ut*, is a coin first issued by Roger II of Sicily, Duke of Apulia, in the A.D. 1000's. It was called a ducat because it was issued by authority of a duchy. Later the coin was used in all southern European coun-

Chase Manhattan Bank Money Museum

Spanish Ducats like this one were used in the time of Ferdinand and Isabella. In the 1900's, ducats were common in Austria, Czechoslovakia, the East Indies, The Netherlands, and Yugoslavia.

tries, either in silver or in gold. The silver ones were worth between 75 cents and $1.10, and the gold ones, $1.46 to $2.32. In Shakespeare's *Merchant of Venice* Antonio's debt to Shylock was 3,000 Venetian ducats.

DUCCIO DI BUONINSEGNA, *DOO choh dee BWOHN een SEHN yah* (1250?-1319?), was the first great painter from Siena, Italy. He became noted for the graceful faces and the soft drapery of his figures. From 1308 to 1311, he painted *The Maestà*, the great altarpiece of the cathedral in Siena. It shows the Madonna enthroned, surrounded by many angels and saints, and is considered one of the masterpieces of Italian painting. Duccio also created miniature paintings for books. He was born in Siena. WOLFGANG LOTZ

Eliot Elisofon, *Life* © 1952 Time, Inc.

Nude Descending a Staircase, *right,* by Marcel Duchamp, was first shown in the United States at the Armory Show in New York City in 1913. This large exhibit of recent French paintings shocked the public. Duchamp's work was criticized because many persons did not realize he was showing motion by blending a series of movements into one picture. He developed the technique in painting long before it was perfected in photography. More than 40 years later, a photograph was taken showing Duchamp descending a staircase, *above.*

Courtesy of the Louise and Walter Arensberg Collection, Philadelphia Museum of Art

DUCHAMP, *dyoo shahn,* **MARCEL** (1887-), is a French painter. He first became noted about 1910, as a member of the cubist group of painters (see CUBISM). During and after World War I, he influenced the so-called Dada movement. This movement represented a pessimistic reaction against previously held ideas about the nature of art. Duchamp's best-known painting is *Nude Descending a Staircase.* It caused great excitement when it was shown in the New York Armory Show of 1913. Among his unusual ideas was that of showing what he called "ready-mades." One of these, a rack for empty wine bottles, was exhibited as a work of art. Duchamp was born in Blainville, France. He lived and worked in New York in his later years. JOSEPH C. SLOANE

DUCHESNE, ROSE PHILIPPINE. See MISSOURI (Famous Missourians).

DUCHESNE COLLEGE OF THE SACRED HEART is a Roman Catholic liberal arts college for women in Omaha, Nebr. It is directed by the Religious of the Sacred Heart. Duchesne was founded in 1881 as the Academy of the Sacred Heart. It assumed its present name in 1917 in honor of Mother Philippine Duchesne. Bachelors' degrees are granted. For enrollment, see UNIVERSITIES AND COLLEGES (table).

DUCHESS. See DUKE.

DUCIE ISLAND is an uninhabited coral island in the South Pacific. It is $2\frac{1}{2}$ square miles in area. It lies 325 miles east of Pitcairn Island in the eastern extremity of the Tuamotu Archipelago. The island was annexed by Great Britain in 1902. The inhabitants of British-owned Pitcairn Island claim rights to the control of Ducie Island. For location, see PACIFIC OCEAN (color map).

297

Wildlife Refuges along the major flyways provide feeding grounds for wild ducks in flights between the North and South. The bird shown in flight is a California murre.

U.S. Wildlife Service

DUCK is a web-footed bird that usually lives near the water. There are both domestic and wild ducks, and their flesh is very good to eat. Many wild ducks are highly prized as game birds. More than 40 different kinds of ducks live on the North American continent.

The Body of the Duck. Ducks have large heads and slender necks. Their necks are shorter than those of geese and swans, who are related to ducks. Ducks usually have broad, flat bills with tiny saw teeth around the edges. Their bills are useful in holding and straining food. The bodies of ducks are short and thick. They are covered with thick feathers. A layer of thick down lies beneath the feathers and close to the body. The feathers of many ducks are beautifully colored. All ducks keep their feathers well oiled by means of a large gland just above the tail. This gland gives off an oil which makes the duck's feathers waterproof. A duck will sink in the water if the oil is removed from its feathers.

It is hard for ducks to walk, because their legs are short and placed so far back. Ducks move clumsily. But the webfeet of the ducks make them swift swimmers. Some ducks are excellent divers. Their wings are strong, and wild ducks can fly fast and far. The male duck is called a *drake*, and the young, a *duckling*. The female duck has no special name.

Habits. Ducks eat insects, snails, frogs, and fish. They also feed on grains, grasses, and other kinds of plant life.

The mother ducks lay from six to perhaps sixteen eggs in a warm nest made of leaves, dry grass, and other materials. Sometimes two ducks lay eggs in the same nest. The nest is lined with down which the mother duck takes from her own breast. Nests are usually built on the ground near the water. Sometimes they are placed in a bushy field farther back. Some kinds of ducks may build their nests in hollow trees. The mother takes care of the family. For three or four weeks she remains almost constantly on the nest. The ducklings are covered with down when they break through their shell. The mother leads them to water as soon as they can travel. The ducklings cannot fly for six weeks or more after they are hatched. They must be carefully guarded by the mother.

When the ducklings are young, all the adult ducks shed many of their old, worn, and ragged feathers. The adult ducks cannot fly until strong, new feathers grow in.

The male ducks usually have more brilliant feathers than the females. When they shed their feathers in the summer, however, they become covered with an *eclipse* (dull) plumage. At this time they look more like the drab females.

Ducks often live together in large flocks. Some of them travel north in the spring, and south in the fall. Many of them are shot by hunters during the southward flight.

Wild Ducks. There are three main kinds of wild ducks. Diving ducks get their food below the surface of the water, often at great depths. River ducks feed in shallow water. Some ducks, including the mergansers, live on fish. Mergansers have very narrow bills.

Diving Ducks live both in the sea and in inland waters. Most of them breed in grassy sloughs and lakes. Unlike river ducks, they have a webbed hind toe. They often move about in large flocks and feed by day. Most diving ducks are not as good to eat as river ducks because they feed on animals that live in the water. This kind of food gives their flesh a disagreeable flavor. But the best-known diving duck, the *canvasback*, is considered excellent eating. Other important diving ducks include the *greater* and *lesser scaup ducks*. These ducks prefer to live in the salty or brackish water of bays or river mouths during the winter. Their feathers are colored in patches of black and white. The *bufflehead* is a small, handsome duck with black and white feathers. The male has green and purple feathers on the front and back of its head. The bufflehead is not good to eat. The *old squaw* is a large brown and white duck with a long tail. This duck, which lives on the seacoasts and in the Great Lakes, is not eaten. The *ring-necked ducks* have been almost killed off by hunters because of their delicious flesh. They are again increasing in numbers. Male ring-necked ducks have purplish-black and white bodies, bluish-purple heads, and a brown ring around their necks. The *redhead* was also famous for its meat, but it has now become quite rare. The male redhead has a gray and black body with a reddish brown head. The *goldeneye* is also good to eat. This duck has bright-yellow eyes and white cheek patches. The wings of the goldeneye give off a whistle as the bird flies. For this reason goldeneyes are often called *whistlers*. The *scoters* are common on the sea-

Aylesburys are the leading ducks raised for marketing in England. They weigh about 8 lbs.

Gray Calls are small and toylike. They are easy to raise, and usually are kept as pets.

Cayugas are native American ducks. They lay about 200 eggs a year.

coasts of Canada and the United States. The male scoters have blackish feathers with patches of yellow and red on their bills. The *harlequin* ducks are patched with gay plumage. They spend the summer in the far north near the Arctic Ocean.

River Ducks. The *mallard* is the most important of all wild ducks. It is an important game bird, and many of the tame ducks are descended from it. The other important river ducks, many of which are both common and important are the *teal*, the *pintail*, the *black duck*, *gadwall*, *baldpate*, *shoveler*, and *wood duck*. All these ducks are described in separate articles in THE WORLD BOOK ENCYCLOPEDIA. The last *Labrador* duck was killed in 1875. Too many sportsmen had hunted the Labrador for its eggs, its flesh, and its feathers.

Mergansers, or *sawbills*, eat almost nothing but fish. Their flesh is not considered good to eat because of its fishy flavor. See MERGANSER.

Domestic Ducks, except for the Muscovy duck, are all descended from the wild mallard. Nobody knows exactly when ducks were first tamed, but it must have been at least several thousand years ago. Tame or domestic ducks are divided into three kinds: (1) those bred for their meat, (2) those bred for their eggs, and (3) those bred for their fancy appearance. The most important meat ducks include the Pekin, Muscovy, Black Cayuga, Rouen, and Aylesbury. The *Pekin* originally came from China. It is a white bird of large size. The Pekin is the most important of all domestic ducks raised in the United States. Pekins carry their bodies at a slanting angle, with the front end higher than the tail. The *Aylesbury* is also a white duck, about the same size as the Pekin. It originally came from England. It carries its body almost parallel to the ground. The Aylesbury is not as hardy a breed as the Pekin. The *Rouen* duck looks like the wild mallard but it is much larger. Rouen drakes may weigh as much as eleven pounds. The *Black Cayuga* breed of all-black ducks was developed in the United States. It is not as popular as the Pekin. The *Muscovy* duck came from Brazil. There are white and colored varieties. The drake is larger than the female. The female does not quack.

The market for duck eggs in the United States is limited and not many egg-laying ducks are raised. The

A Pair of Young Ducks wait eagerly for a morsel of food. Ducklings make amusing pets, for they soon learn to follow boys and girls about, quacking loudly to be fed.

Indian runner, an erect, extremely slender duck, is among the most popular of the egg-laying ducks.

Ornamental ducks are grown by duck fanciers. The *gray call* duck is a miniature Rouen. *Mandarin* ducks are raised for their gay-colored feathers. *Wild wood* ducks have also been raised for their plumage. The *crested white* duck has a topknot of feathers on its head.

Duck Farming is carried on as a sideline on many farms in the United States. About 10,000,000 ducks are raised each year. Duck farming has been important as a principal activity of farmers on Long Island and in a few other places in the United States. Long Island

RAISING DUCKS

Duck Eggs are kept in incubator racks for 28 days.
Orlando, Three Lions

Newborn Ducks huddle beneath a light bulb to keep warm.
Orlando, Three Lions

Brooder Pens are the ducklings' home for five weeks.
J. C. Allen and Son

Ready for Market, below, these young Pekins, about 11 weeks old, weigh almost 6 pounds.
J. C. Allen and Son

Duck Eggs are collected and immediately put in incubators to repeat the hatching cycle.
Orlando, Three Lions

supplies the country with more than half of the ducks marketed each year. Most of these ducks are raised in a 15-square-mile area near the eastern tip of the Island. Many ducks from large commercial farms are sold when they are about 12 weeks old. They are called *green ducks*. Others are not sold until the fall. The care of ducks is much the same as that of chickens (see POULTRY). Duck raisers usually obtain the ducklings from a commercial hatchery, but they may be hatched by a duck or a hen. When hatched by a hen, their first swim is a nerve-racking experience for the foster mother.

Scientific Classification. Ducks belong to the family *Anatidae*. The mallard is genus *Anas*, species *platyrhyncos*. The Muscovy is *Cairina moschata*. The common teal is *Anas crecca*. JOSEPH J. HICKEY

Related Articles in WORLD BOOK include:

Bird (Migration Routes; Extinct Birds; color pictures, Wild Ducks and Geese)	Hunting
Baldpate	Mallard
Black Duck	Merganser
Canvasback	Pintail
Eider Duck	Poultry
Gadwall	Shoveler
Game (Game Laws)	Swan
Goose	Teal
	Widgeon
	Wood Duck

DUCK is a lightweight canvas usually made of linen or cotton in a plain weave. Duck is woven in many widths and weights. This stout, waterproof fabric is used for the aprons of cooks, waiters, and butchers; for the uniforms of dentists and surgeons; and for shower curtains, pressing cloths, and tennis shoes. The heaviest grades of duck are used to make machine aprons, machinery conveyer belts, boat sails, tarpaulins, tents, and mailbags. GRACE G. DENNY

See also CANVAS.

DUCK HAWK is the name given to the American variety of *peregrine falcon*, which is found throughout the world. It reportedly can reach speeds up to 175 miles per hour. See also FALCON AND FALCONRY.

DUCK MOUNTAIN PARK. See MANITOBA (National and Provincial Parks).

DUCKBILL. See PLATYPUS.

DUCKING STOOL was a form of punishment usually given to "witches and nagging women" in England and the American colonies from the 1600's to the early 1800's. The ducking stool was a chair fastened to the end of a long plank extended from the bank of a pond or stream. The victim of the punishment was tied to the chair and ducked into the water several times. See also COLONIAL LIFE IN AMERICA (picture, Punishing Wrongdoers). MARION F. LANSING

DUCKPINS. See BOWLING (Other Kinds of Bowling).

DUCKWEED is a tiny perennial water plant. It is the smallest flowering plant known. The duckweed floats on the surface of pools and ponds everywhere. It has no stems or true leaves. The plant consists of a flat green structure, or *frond*, with a single hairlike root underneath. The flowers and fruits are so small they can barely be seen by the naked eye. Duckweed is good food for ducks and large goldfish, and has a healthful laxative effect on some kinds of aquarium fish.

Scientific Classification. The duckweed belongs to the family *Lemnaceae*. It is genus *Lemna*. EARL L. CORE

See also PLANT (picture, Plant Oddities).

DUCTLESS GLAND

DUCTED FAN PRINCIPLE OF FLIGHT uses a propeller surrounded by a circular wing to power an aircraft. It was first used in the design of the *flying platform* developed by the U.S. Navy in 1955. The pilot stands on a grating over a hole in the center of the platform. Beneath him, two propellers spin in opposite directions. They suck air through the top of the hole and force it out the bottom. This lowers the air pressure above the curved *lip*, or edge, and creates a lifting force. The air also rushes up around the outside of the platform and pushes upward on the lip. The platform can take off and land vertically, hover over one spot, and move through the air in any direction.

A Flying Platform goes straight up or down, hovers, and flies in any direction. The pilot shifts his weight to change course.
Hiller Helicopters

DUCTILITY, *duck TIHL uh tih*, is that property of certain substances, especially metals, by which they can be drawn out into thin threads or wires without breaking. Ductility is an important property of metals in engineering. The common metals may be listed in the order of decreasing ductility as follows: gold, silver, platinum, iron, nickel, copper, aluminum, zinc, tin. Platinum may be drawn out into a thread about one twenty-thousandth part of an inch in thickness. To do this, the platinum must be covered with silver and both metals drawn out together. The silver is afterward dissolved in nitric acid, which leaves the platinum thread intact. Glass at high temperature is the most ductile of all materials. When sufficiently heated, glass may be drawn into threads so fine that a mile of the thread would weigh only one grain. See also WIRE. LOUIS MARICK

DUCTLESS GLAND. See GLAND.

Dude Ranches in the western United States are popular vacation resorts. They give vacationers the chance to live in the style of the Old West. This family stopped during an evening ride to eat by a campfire.

Northern Pacific Railway

DUDE, *dyood,* **RANCH** is a western-style ranch which receives paying guests who want a taste of life in the open. These guests are usually city dwellers who get little physical activity and contact with nature. Three brothers, Howard, Alden, and Willis Eaton, are believed to have established the West's first dude ranch near Sheridan, Wyo., in 1904.

Some dude ranches are regular cattle or sheep ranches that entertain a few guests as a sideline. But other ranches are devoted entirely to the business of entertaining guests, or *dudes.* Most of the dude ranches are in the "cow country" of Montana, Wyoming, Arizona, California, Nevada, Colorado, New Mexico, and Oregon. Guests at a dude ranch go on horseback rides along mountain trails, hunt, fish, and in some cases help with the livestock. The cost of a vacation on a dude ranch is sometimes as low as $30 a week, and sometimes much more expensive. H. B. MEEK

DUDEVANT, BARONESS. See SAND, GEORGE.

DUDLEY, EDWARD BISHOP. See NORTH CAROLINA (Famous North Carolinians).

DUDLEY, ROBERT. See LEICESTER, EARL OF.

DUDLEY, THOMAS (1576-1653), was a colonial governor of Massachusetts. Born in Northampton, England, he became steward to the powerful Earl of Lincoln, whose estates he managed. He sailed with John Winthrop on the *Arbella* in 1630 as deputy governor of the colony. He became governor four times, and served as deputy governor most of the other years until his death. Because he was a Puritan of the stern and harsh type, he often differed with the tolerant and kind Winthrop. He was a founder of First Church at Charlestown, Mass., of New Towne (now Cambridge, Mass.), and a promoter and overseer of Harvard College. BRADFORD SMITH

DUE PROCESS OF LAW, or simply *due process,* is the guarantee in the United States Constitution to every citizen that his life, liberty, or property will not be taken from him unfairly. It insures that he will be informed of any charge against him and will have a chance to present his side of the case. In more serious cases, such as a murder charge, due process requires that the accused have a trial by jury if he wishes. In less serious cases, such as a tax dispute, the hearing and defense may be before an administrative officer.

Due process of law is also called *due course of law* or *the law of the land.* The Fifth Amendment to the United States Constitution requires the federal government to give due process to everyone it governs. The Fourteenth Amendment makes the same requirement for every state government. ARTHUR E. SUTHERLAND

See also CIVIL RIGHTS; UNITED STATES CONSTITUTION (Amendments; Amendment V and Amendment XIV).

DUEL is a form of combat between two armed persons. It is conducted according to set rules or a code, and it is normally fought in the presence of witnesses. From early times through the 1800's, men of high rank settled personal quarrels with weapons. They generally used swords or pistols. Duels resulted from disputes over property, charges of cowardice, insults to family or personal honor, and cheating at cards or dice.

The duel probably originated in the custom of Germanic *judicial combat,* a method of administering justice. In judicial combat, the accused person challenged his accuser to a trial with weapons. The gods were supposed to give victory to the innocent man. Queen Elizabeth I of England was the first to abolish the duel as a form of justice. Later, all civilized countries abandoned the practice. But private duels are still fought in some parts of the world.

Some duels were more deadly than others. About 1800, French honor was satisfied by wounds, but the American dueling code at that time demanded death. The phrase *to give satisfaction* could mean either that blood must be drawn, or that one of the contestants must die. At other times it meant only that the challenged party had faced his enemy's fire.

The man challenged had his choice of weapons. The sword became the main dueling weapon in England and France. Duelists generally used pistols in America. Each duelist chose a friend who was called his *second,* and a surgeon usually attended. To avoid the police, the meeting usually took place in a forest clearing at daybreak. When duelists used pistols, they usually stood

302

back to back, and marched an agreed number of steps in opposite directions. Then one of the seconds dropped a handkerchief. The fighters turned quickly and fired.

Dueling was common in the United States up to about the middle 1800's. Many famous Americans fought duels. Aaron Burr killed Alexander Hamilton on July 11, 1804, in a pistol duel. Burr blamed Hamilton for his defeat in a New York election for governor of the state (see HAMILTON, ALEXANDER). General Andrew Jackson killed Charles Dickinson on May 30, 1806, in a pistol duel. Jackson challenged Dickinson because Dickinson denounced him in the press. The quarrel started in a dispute over a horse race. Commodore James Barron killed Commodore Stephen Decatur on Mar. 22, 1820, in a pistol duel. Barron claimed Decatur was persecuting him. Henry Clay fought John Randolph on Apr. 8, 1826, in a pistol duel, but neither was hurt. Clay challenged Randolph because Randolph made insulting remarks about him in the U.S. Senate (see RANDOLPH [John Randolph of Roanoke]).

Tennessee outlawed dueling in 1801, and the District of Columbia banned it in 1839. Several other states did so soon after that. Since then, one who kills an opponent in a duel can be tried for murder or manslaughter. Some German students still duel secretly with swords as a sport. They try only to inflict cheek wounds in duels with fellow members of the fencing fraternities in the German universities. HUGH M. COLE

DUERO RIVER. See DOURO RIVER.

DU FAY, *dyoo FAY,* **CHARLES FRANÇOIS** (1698-1739). The ancient Greeks discovered that a piece of amber, when rubbed with fur, could pick up bits of cotton. We say the amber has an *electric charge*. Over 2,300 years later, Du Fay, a French scientist, found that a charge of electricity can be put on *any* object. He also discovered that there are two opposite kinds of electricity, later called *positive* and *negative*.

Du Fay also studied phosphorescence, and double refraction, which occurs when a ray of light bends and breaks into two rays (see PHOSPHORESCENCE; REFRACTION).

Du Fay was born in Paris. He served in the army for a time, then devoted himself to science. He became a member of the French Academy of Sciences in 1733. He also served as superintendent of gardens for King Louis XV. IRA M. FREEMAN

DUFF, SIR LYMAN POORE (1865-1955), served for 37 years on the Supreme Court of Canada from 1906 to 1944. During the last 11 years, he was Chief Justice. He wrote many Supreme Court decisions. He considered the most important of these the ruling that decisions of the Canadian Parliament were not to be appealed to London. He was also a member of the British Columbia Supreme Court. King George V knighted him in 1934. He was born at Meaford, Ont. J. E. HODGETTS

DUFFERIN AND AVA, MARQUIS OF (1826-1902), FREDERICK TEMPLE BLACKWOOD, was a British diplomat and statesman. As Governor-General of Canada from 1872 to 1878, he helped strengthen the bonds between Canada and Great Britain. After leaving Canada, he served as ambassador extraordinary and minister plenipotentiary to Russia from 1879 to 1881, to Constantinople in 1881, and to Egypt in 1882. He served as viceroy of India from 1884 to 1888. He was born in Florence, Italy. LUCIEN BRAULT

DUISBURG

DUFY, *DYOO FEE,* **RAOUL** (1877-1953), was a member of the *Fauves,* a group of painters whose brilliant colors and freely handled forms shocked the conservatives of the Paris art world in the early 1900's. In addition to painting, Dufy also designed textiles and ceramics. His water colors, particularly, show the gaiety of color, economy of line, and simplified composition that brought him an international reputation. His water color, *Le Haras du Pin,* appears in color in the PAINTING article. JOSEPH C. SLOANE

DU GARD, ROGER MARTIN. See MARTIN DU GARD, ROGER.

DUGGAR, B. M. See AUREOMYCIN.

DUGONG, *DOO gahng,* is an unusual mammal of the Indian Ocean, the Red Sea, and the waters around Australia. Its head has a blunt, rounded snout, with a cleft and flexible, bristly upper lip. Its body is long and tapering like a whale's, and it has a forked tail. The paws or flippers have no nails. The dugong uses them

American Museum of Natural History
The Dugong lives mostly near the shore. Its edible flesh makes it valuable to commerce. The blubber oil of the Australian dugong can be used as a substitute for cod-liver oil.

only to swim and to push sea grass near its mouth. The dugong has a thick and smooth skin, bluish above and white underneath. The male can be recognized by its two long upper tusks and by the abruptly bent downward end of the upper jaw. A female produces only one offspring at a time. The stories about mermaids may have started when seamen saw this animal.

Scientific Classification. The dugong belongs to the order *Sirenia.* It is in the family *Dugongidae.* It is genus *Dugong,* species *D. dugon.* REMINGTON KELLOGG

See also SIRENIA.

DUGOUT. See BOATS AND BOATING (Unusual Boats).

DUGWAY is the central proving ground of the United States Army Chemical Corps. Tests are conducted there on chemical, biological, and radiological weapons. Dugway is 100 miles southwest of Salt Lake City, Utah.

DUIKERBOK. See ANTELOPE (picture).

DUISBURG, *DYOOS boork* (pop. 503,000; alt. 108 ft.), is a trading and manufacturing city in West Germany. It is the largest inland port of western Europe. The city is built on the point where the Ruhr River flows into the Rhine. It is a gateway to the factories and mineral deposits of the Ruhr Valley. Duisburg has long been important in German industrial life. The city's products include chemicals, furniture, silks and woolens, soap, and tobacco. JAMES K. POLLOCK

DUKAS, PAUL

DUKAS, DYOO KAH, **PAUL ABRAHAM** (1865-1935), a French composer, won recognition for his *The Sorcerer's Apprentice* (1897), an orchestral scherzo. His opera, *Ariadne and Bluebeard,* based upon Maurice Maeterlinck's play of the same name, is symphonic in form. It is second only to Debussy's *Pelléas et Mélisande* in importance among French operas of the 1900's. His last major work was a ballet, *The Peri* (1912). HALSEY STEVENS

DUKE is a European title. It comes from the Latin word *dux* (leader), and is the title next highest to *prince.* In England, there are few dukes outside the royal family, where the sons have the title of Royal Duke. The wife of a duke is a *duchess,* the oldest son is a *lord* with the rank of *marquis,* and younger sons and daughters are called *lords* and *ladies.* A duke is addressed as "Your Grace." In early days, a duke was a leader in battle, and sometimes a ruler as well. The first English duke was the Black Prince, oldest son of Edward III, who was made Duke of Cornwall in 1337.

Archduke was a title used by members of the royal family of Hapsburg from 1453 until the end of World War I. See also NOBILITY. MARION F. LANSING

DUKE, JAMES BUCHANAN (1856-1925), an American businessman and philanthropist, organized the American Tobacco Company in 1890. Duke University was named for him, and he established the Duke Endowment in 1924. He also gave funds to schools, hospitals, orphanages, and the Methodist Church. He was born near Durham, N.C. J. R. CRAF

See also AMERICAN TOBACCO COMPANY; DUKE ENDOWMENT; DUKE UNIVERSITY.

DUKE ENDOWMENT is a fund for education and charity established in 1924 by James Buchanan Duke, founder of the American Tobacco Company. Its purpose is "to make provision in some measure for the needs of mankind along physical, mental, and spiritual lines."

The original gift has been estimated at $40,000,000. Under the terms of the gift, $6,000,000 was used to build and equip Duke University. One portion of the income is used for maintaining the fund at a certain level. The rest goes to Duke University; to colleges, hospitals, and orphanages in North and South Carolina; and to rural Methodist churches and retired clergymen in North Carolina. The fund has offices at 30 Rockefeller Plaza, New York 20, N.Y. For assets, see FOUNDATIONS (table). *Critically reviewed by* THE DUKE ENDOWMENT

DUKE OF YORK ISLANDS. See BISMARCK ARCHIPELAGO.

DUKE UNIVERSITY is a private coeducational school at Durham, N.C. Its undergraduate divisions include Trinity College for men; the Women's College; the Engineering College; and the School of Nursing. Graduate training is offered in arts and sciences; divinity; law; medicine, and forestry.

The university library contains about 4,500,000 books and manuscripts. Duke Hospital is a noted teaching and training institution. The 7,200-acre Duke Forest serves as a laboratory for the School of Forestry. The marine laboratory near Beaufort, N.C., is used for training and research in marine biology and oceanography.

The school originated in 1838 as an academy. It became Union Institute in 1839, and was reorganized as Normal College in 1852 and as Trinity College in 1859. It is named after James B. Duke, a tobacco millionaire. His endowment in 1924 enabled the college to develop into a leading university. For enrollment, see UNIVERSITIES AND COLLEGES (table). ROBERT L. DICKENS

DUKHOBORS, *DYU koh bawrz,* is the name of a Christian sect in western Canada. It was founded by peasants in Russia about the middle of the 1700's. Their name means *spirit wrestlers.* They believe that "the voice within" each person is his guide. Therefore, there is no need for churches or for civil government. They refuse to give military service. Some refuse to pay taxes or permit their children to attend school.

In the 1800's, under Peter Verigin's leadership, the Dukhobors adopted many of the ideas of the Russian author Leo Tolstoy. In 1899, Tolstoy and others helped more than 7,000 Dukhobors emigrate to western Canada, where they established communal farms. The group still survives, but its communal life has largely died out because of indifference, land foreclosures, and the death of Verigin. In 1958, some Dukhobors sought permission to return to Russia. MATTHEW SPINKA

See also TOLSTOY, LEO (New Ideas).

DULCIMER, *DUL suh mur,* is an ancient musical instrument. It was probably invented in Persia or Arabia. It consists of a flat box with metal wires stretched across the top. These wires are attached to adjustable tuning pegs on one side of the instrument. The player strikes the strings with small wooden or cork-covered mallets. A keyboard was later substituted for the hammers to produce the *clavichord* (see CLAVICHORD). The piano developed from this instrument. CHARLES B. RIGHTER

DU LHUT. See DULUTH, SIEUR.

Arkansas Publicity & Parks Comm.

The Dulcimer is used by many gypsy bands in Central Europe. The player produces harsh tones by striking wires with wooden mallets.

DULLES, *DUL us,* **JOHN FOSTER** (1888-1959), an American lawyer and diplomat, enjoyed a long and distinguished career in helping formulate the foreign policies of the United States. He won international acclaim in 1951 as the chief author of the Japanese peace treaty. He also negotiated the Australian, New Zealand, Philippine, and Japanese security treaties in 1950 and 1951. In 1953, he became the 53rd Secretary of State of the United States, serving in the Cabinet of President Dwight D. Eisenhower.

Wide World
John Foster Dulles

Dulles was born in Washington, D.C. He was graduated from Princeton University, and received a law degree from George Washington University. His books include *War, Peace, and Change* (1939) and *War or Peace* (1950). Dulles helped form the UN, and later was a United States UN delegate. He served as a U.S. Senator from New York in 1949. F. JAY TAYLOR

DULUTH, *duh LOOTH,* Minn. (pop. 106,884), extends for 26 miles along the west end of Lake Superior. The city lies on Saint Louis Bay, 156 miles northeast of Saint Paul. For location, see MINNESOTA (color map). Duluth stands on a bluff which rises gradually from Lake Superior to a height of 600 to 800 feet. An electrical lift bridge, one of the fastest of its kind in the world, passes over the Duluth ship canal. The canal was cut through a sand bar called Minnesota Point in 1871. The bridge can rise to its full height of 138 feet in 55 seconds to allow ships to pass.

Industry and Commerce. Duluth is a natural shipping point for products of the Northwest. The harbor is a joint one with Superior, Wis. The volume of waterborne shipping at the Duluth-Superior harbor makes it one of the largest ports in the United States. Eight railroads carry goods to and from the port. Iron ore and grain are the principal exports, and coal is the chief import. Duluth has 37 commercial docks. A Duluth Port Authority was established in 1954 to plan and develop the port as a terminal of the Saint Lawrence Seaway. Duluth has over 20 grain elevators, as well as flour mills, three blast furnaces, a big steel plant, ironworks, machine shops, shipyards, and slaughterhouses. The city has airline and bus service.

Recreation and Cultural Life. Beautiful lakes nearby, a cool climate, and an excellent park and playground system make Duluth an attractive vacation center. It is the gateway to the scenic North Shore of Lake Superior and the great Superior National Forest. The Skyline Parkway along the heights of the city offers a picturesque view of Duluth and Lake Superior. The city has favorable conditions for summer and winter sports. The average summer temperature is 61°F., and temperatures from December through March average 15°F. Duluth's location in the Minnesota Arrowhead Country puts it close to excellent hunting and fishing territory. It is the home of the Duluth Branch of the University of Minnesota, and the College of St. Scholastica. Duluth also maintains its own symphony orchestra.

Government and History. Duluth is the county seat of Saint Louis County. The city has a council form of government (see CITY AND LOCAL GOVERNMENTS).

Duluth was named in honor of Daniel Greysolon, Sieur Duluth, a French trader who visited the site about 1679. In the 1700's, British traders replaced the French. Fond du Lac, now a suburb of Duluth, became the first permanent white settlement in the area after John Jacob Astor's American Fur Company started a trading post there in 1817. Settlers began to come to the Duluth area in the 1850's. Duluth became a city in 1870. It grew rapidly after 1880, when lumbering and iron-ore industries developed there. HAROLD T. HAGG

See also LAKE (picture, Lakeside Cities); MINNESOTA (color picture, Elevators at Duluth).

DULUTH, or **DU LHUT, SIEUR** (1636-1710), DANIEL GREYSOLON, was a French explorer for whom Duluth, Minn., was named. Duluth moved to Canada about 1674, and decided to explore the West. He set out for Lake Superior in 1678, but he had to make peace between the Chippewa and Sioux Indians before he could work in that area. He negotiated with the Sioux near the site of the city which now bears his name. He took possession of the area in the name of King Louis XIV. Duluth later explored near the headwaters of the Mississippi River. He was born in St. Germain-en-Laye, France. He was a cousin of Henri de Tonti, who was an explorer and companion of Robert Cavelier, Sieur de la Salle. WILLIAM P. BRANDON

Duluth Chamber of Commerce

Duluth, Minn., is the westernmost port on the Great Lakes. The 7-mile sand bar, *top center*, is called Minnesota Point. It runs from Duluth to Superior, Wis. Canals at each end of the sand bar allow ships to enter the harbor. Residents use the Aerial Lift Bridge, *left*, to cross the Duluth canal.

DUMA

DUMA, *DOO mah,* was a Russian parliament that existed between 1906 and 1917. It was called by Czar Nicholas II as a consequence of the Russian Revolution of 1905. The first Duma was elected indirectly by what was practically manhood suffrage. So widespread was the hatred of czarism that very few supporters of the government were elected. There were three leading parties. The moderately liberal Octobrists favored a political system on the model of that in Prussia. The liberal Constitutional Democrats (Cadets) looked to England as their political model. The radical Social Democrats wanted a republic along socialist lines.

The first Duma lasted only a few months. It was dissolved by the Czar on the ground that it did not "cooperate" with him. The second Duma, which met in 1907, was dissolved, after a stormy life of 104 days. The Czar then issued a new electoral law intended to elect a Duma which would yield to his wishes. Nearly all men could still vote, but the voters were divided into four classes. Each class elected a certain number of members to the electoral colleges that chose the members of the Duma. The propertied classes chose a great majority of the electors, so that the third Duma had a huge conservative majority. Only a few liberals and socialists were elected. At last the Czar had a Duma that was willing to "cooperate" with him.

Yet it was this "landowners' Duma" that helped to start the Russian Revolution of 1917 which overthrew Czarism. The terrible defeats inflicted on the Russians in World War I brought great discredit on the government. It was denounced as corrupt, inefficient, and traitorous. Discontent mounted high among all classes, and a revolutionary movement was soon in progress.

In March, 1917, demonstrations took place in Petrograd. Soldiers mutinied and joined the revolutionists. The Duma demanded that Nicholas abdicate, and voted to form a provisional government. On March 15, the Czar abdicated and a provisional government was formed. The government consisted of members of the moderate, liberal, and socialist parties headed by Prince Lvov and Pavel Milyukov. The Duma then ended along with the Romanov dynasty.   J. SALWYN SCHAPIRO

See also NICHOLAS (II) of Russia.

DUMAS, *du MAH,* was the family name of two French writers, father and son.

Alexandre Dumas, the Elder (1802-1870), novelist and dramatist, is considered one of the greatest French writers. He became one of the leaders of the Romantic movement in literature (see ROMANTICISM). He wrote thrilling historical novels of adventure. His book *Isabelle de Bavière* gave him the idea "to exalt history to the height of fiction." Thus he found the form of writing best suited to his talents and to the literary needs of his time. He did his best work between 1840 and 1853. This work included *The Count of Monte Cristo, The Three Musketeers, Twenty Years After,* and *The Viscount of Bragelonne.* Dumas' novels cover a large part of French history, including the 1700's and the French Revolution.

One of his contemporary critics accused him of running a "novel factory" because the list of his works was so large. Several hundred volumes bear his name, but he probably only sketched and revised the plots for many of them. His assistants wrote and did the necessary

Chicago Hist. Soc.
Alexandre Dumas the Elder

Chicago Hist. Soc.
Alexandre Dumas the Younger

research for his books. Dumas' "blood and thunder" plays were quite popular. One, *La Tour de Nesle,* ran for 800 consecutive performances at the time.

Dumas was born at Villers-Cotterêts, France, the son of a general in Napoleon's army. His name came from his grandmother, a Negro from Santo Domingo. As a youth, he loved hunting and the outdoor life. He went to Paris in 1823, and became a librarian-secretary to the Duke of Orléans, later King Louis Philippe. He studied and worked hard. He became friendly with the great writers, artists, and society people. Dumas traveled widely. He was extravagant by nature and died poor.

Alexandre Dumas, the Younger (1824-1895), son of the great novelist, first won fame in 1848 with his novel *La Dame aux Camélias.* It was translated into English as *Camille.* He dramatized this novel in 1849, and it provided the plot for Giuseppe Verdi's opera, *La Traviata.* His plays dealt with the problems arising from the business, political, and family life of his time. His best-known plays include *The Money Question, The Prodigal Father,* and *Monsieur Alphonse.* He was born in Paris and was educated by his father. He became a member of the French Academy in 1875, and critics in his own time considered him a greater writer than his father.   FRANCIS J. CROWLEY

DU MAURIER, *dyu MAW rih ay,* is the family name of two well-known English writers.

George Louis Palmella Busson du Maurier (1834-1896), a writer and illustrator, published his best-known novel, *Trilby,* in 1894. Trilby, the heroine, is an artist's model under the influence of a Hungarian musician. She becomes one of the greatest singers of her time by means of hypnotism. But when her teacher dies, she loses her powers. The novel became so popular that merchandise was named "Trilby," and "Trilby" parties were held.

His other novels, *Peter Ibbetson* and *The Martian,* are somewhat autobiographical, telling of Du Maurier's youth in Paris, London, and Antwerp.

Du Maurier was born in Paris, on Mar. 6, 1834. He studied to be a chemist, but turned to art at the age of 22. He illustrated books by such novelists as William Makepeace Thackeray, Thomas Hardy, George Meredith, and Henry James. He was famous for his graceful and satiric drawings for *Punch* from 1860 until his first novel, *Peter Ibbetson,* appeared in 1891.

Daphne du Maurier (1907-   ), LADY BROWNING, granddaughter of George du Maurier, wrote many successful novels, including *Rebecca, Jamaica Inn, Frenchman's Creek,* and *The Parasites.* Her works are lively, with

George du Maurier   **Daphne du Maurier**

a feeling for the dramatic. Her humorous story *The Du Mauriers* tells of her romantic, unconventional ancestors. Her works also include *Gerald, a Portrait*, a biography of her father; *The King's General; My Cousin Rachel; Kiss Me Again, Stranger;* and *The Scapegoat*. She was born in London, England.   WALTER WRIGHT

DUMBARTON OAKS was the name of an international conference held in August-October, 1944, at Dumbarton Oaks, an estate in Washington, D.C. The name was also given to the proposals agreed upon at the conference. Thirty-nine delegates from the United States, Great Britain, and Russia met to discuss plans for the creation of an international organization to be called the *United Nations*. After six weeks of discussion, the Russian representatives, as agreed in advance, left the conference, and delegates from Nationalist China replaced them.

The conference gave more attention to establishing ways to deal with "the maintenance of international peace and security" than it did to setting up agencies to handle economic and social problems. The delegates agreed that provision must be made for the peaceful settlement of international disputes and for the power to enforce the organization's decisions. The main achievement of the conference was the planning of a Security Council as the executive branch of the UN. Most of the provisions of the Dumbarton Oaks Proposals were put into the UN charter.   NORMAN D. PALMER

See also SAN FRANCISCO CONFERENCE; UNITED NATIONS (The Dumbarton Oaks Conference).

DUMBBELL or **BAR BELL** is a wooden or iron weight used for physical exercise. It consists of two balls or discs connected by a bar, which is used as a handle. When the handle is short, it is grasped with one hand,

Dumbbells Are Used in Weight-Lifting Exercises by persons interested in physical exercise and muscle development.
Wide World

DUNBAR CAVE

and called a *dumbbell*. When the handle is long, it can be grasped with two hands and is called a *bar bell*. Dumbbells and bar bells may be made heavier by attaching more balls and discs. The size of the balls and discs varies, depending on their weight.

Today, when machines do most physical work, many people keep their bodies strong through exercise with dumbbells and bar bells. For weight lifters who enter competition, there are set systems of exercise, and competition. Weight lifting has long been an Olympic Games sport.   T. K. CURETON, JR.

See also WEIGHT LIFTING.

DUN & BRADSTREET, INC. is a firm which furnishes businessmen with information about the financial standing of their customers. The firm publishes the famous *Dun and Bradstreet Reference Book*, which goes to its 80,000 subscribers. This book gives the names of about 2,900,000 companies and individuals in the United States and Canada, with the credit rating of each. There is a detailed, regularly revised report on file for each name. Dun & Bradstreet has thousands of reporters stationed in different parts of the country to gather this information. Correspondents in every business community forward information to the company. Its listing of business failures is among the most dependable of economic statistics.

The origins of the present Dun & Bradstreet, Inc., go back to 1841 when it was organized as The Mercantile Agency by Lewis Tappan. Abraham Lincoln, a friend of Tappan, served for a time as a Dun & Bradstreet correspondent. The firm now has 142 branch offices in the U.S. and Canada and offices and correspondents throughout the world. It publishes *Dun's Review* and *The Million Dollar Dictionary*.   DUN & BRADSTREET

DUNANT, *du NAHNG,* **JEAN HENRI** (1828-1910), a Swiss banker, was the founder of the International Red Cross. As a young businessman, he accidentally saw the battle of Solferino in 1859. He was shocked at the lack of care given the wounded. His book, *Recollections of Solferino* (1862), influenced the rulers of Europe tremendously, and in 1863 the Permanent International Committee was organized in Geneva. The next year, delegates of 16 countries agreed to the Geneva Convention for the treatment of wounded and prisoners (see GENEVA CONVENTIONS). The United States ratified this agreement in 1882.

Dunant himself went bankrupt and for 15 years his whereabouts was unknown. He was found in 1890, living in an almshouse, and in 1901 shared the first Nobel peace prize. He was born in Geneva.   ALAN KEITH-LUCAS

See also RED CROSS.

DUNBAR, BATTLES OF. See SCOTLAND (History).

DUNBAR, PAUL LAURENCE (1872-1906), was the first American Negro poet to express in distinguished verse the feelings of the Negroes. His dialect poems best represent his delicate art. His sense of humor found expression through his simple, warm language. Collections of his poems include *Majors and Minors* (1895), *Lyrics of Lowly Life* (1896), *Lyrics of the Hearthside* (1899), and *Joggin' Erlong* (1906). He was born in Dayton, Ohio, the son of parents who had been slaves.   PETER VIERECK

DUNBAR CAVE. See TENNESSEE (Interesting Places to Visit).

DUNBARTON COLLEGE

DUNBARTON COLLEGE OF HOLY CROSS is a liberal arts school for women at Washington, D.C. It is conducted by Sisters of the Holy Cross from Notre Dame, Ind. Students work toward a B.A. degree. The school was founded in 1935. For enrollment, see UNIVERSITIES AND COLLEGES (table).

DUNCAN, ISADORA (1878-1927), was an American dancer who played an important part in developing the dance as a creative, living art. She disliked the formal classical ballet, and based her own dances on free, natural movement. She danced in bare feet and wore a Greek tunic, using music by great masters such as Beethoven and Gluck. Her books include *My Life* and *The Art of the Dance*, a group of essays. She was born in San Francisco, Calif. She danced in Europe and the United States and established several schools, but none of them endured. She died in an automobile accident in France. Her influence has survived in the present-day American dance. See also DANCING (Modern Dance). LILLIAN MOORE

Brown Bros.
Isadora Duncan

DUNCAN I, *DUNG kun* (? -1040), succeeded his grandfather, Malcolm II, as king of Scotland in 1034. William Shakespeare's play *Macbeth* portrays the events in his life in a distorted manner (see MACBETH). A series of unsuccessful efforts to expand his kingdom marked Duncan's reign. He also failed to rule all Scotland. Macbeth of Moray, who had a claim to the throne by right of his wife, killed Duncan in a battle near Elgin. Macbeth reigned until 1057. ROBERT S. HOYT

DUNDEE, *dun DEE* (pop. 182,959; alt. 90 ft.), is a Scottish seaport, 60 miles north of Edinburgh, on the Firth of Tay (see GREAT BRITAIN [color map]).

World-famous candy and marmalade come from Dundee. Industries produce ships, metal castings, textile machinery, electric appliances, and linen. Dundee is the center of the British jute trade. An iron railroad bridge more than 2 miles long crosses the Firth of Tay at Dundee. WILLIAM A. HANCE

DUNE is a hill or mound of sand drifted by the wind. Dunes are common in all sandy regions. Many are found along coasts, near large bodies of water, and in deserts. A very large dune may grow to be 500 or 600 feet high. Most of them, however, are much lower. A traveling dune may move across the face of the desert as it loses sand on one side and gains it on the other. Some dunes make sounds as the grains of sand move across each other. They are called singing dunes. Dunes State Park in Indiana, at the southern end of Lake Michigan, has unusual dunes (see INDIANA [State Parks, Forests, and Memorials]). Other noted dune areas are the eastern shore of Lake Michigan, Cape Cod in Massachusetts, and along the Gulf of California. ELDRED D. WILSON

See also DEATH VALLEY (picture); DESERT; MICHIGAN (Interesting Places to Visit).

The Sleeping Bear Dunes Lie along the Shore of Lake Michigan on the Leelanau Peninsula of Michigan.
Michigan Tourist Council

DUNFERMLINE, *dun FURM lin* (pop. 47,159; alt. 335 ft.), is a textile center in the Central Lowlands of Scotland. It lies near the Firth of Forth, about 13 miles northwest of Edinburgh. The Gaelic word *Dunfermline* means *fort on the crooked linn (ravine).* For location, see GREAT BRITAIN (color map).

Linen, silk, and rayon fabrics are produced in the mills of Dunfermline, and its factories manufacture textile machinery. Other industries include metal foundries and food-processing plants. Dunfermline was an important center of trade as early as the 1000's. It was a favorite residence of early Scottish kings. Robert Bruce and other kings are buried there. The city became prosperous after linen damask weaving was introduced in 1718. Andrew Carnegie, the wealthy American steel manufacturer, was born in Dunfermline. He established the Carnegie Dunfermline Trust in 1903 to improve the community. WILLIAM A. HANCE

DUNG BEETLE. See TUMBLEBUG.

DUNIWAY, ABIGAIL JANE SCOTT. See OREGON (Famous Oregonians).

DUNKER. See BRETHREN, CHURCH OF THE.

DUNKERQUE, *DUN kurk* (pop. 23,894; met. area, 110,000; alt. 40 ft.), is a seaport on the northern coast of France. For location, see FRANCE (color map). Dunkerque means *the church among the dunes.* Other spellings of the name are *Dunkirk* or *Dunquerque.* The beaches here are wide and sandy, and long bridges connect the harbor to the town.

The harbor and town of Dunkerque were greatly damaged early in World War II, when German forces attacked retreating Allied troops. The British Expeditionary Force and other Allied soldiers withdrew into Dunkerque when the Belgian army surrendered. Dunkerque made a natural spot for defense because it was cut off from the country by canals at the sides and back of the town, and by the sea at its front. German forces surrounded Dunkerque, and German ships lay out in the English Channel. A fleet of almost 1,000 British and French ships carried nearly 350,000 Allied soldiers from Dunkerque to England. All kinds of vessels took part in the rescue, including destroyers, gunboats, minesweepers, yachts, cruisers, and rowboats. The withdrawal began late in May and ended on June 4, 1940. It has been called one of the best-ordered military movements in history. ROBERT E. DICKINSON

DUNLAP, WILLIAM. See DRAMA (Drama in the United States).

DUNLOP, JOHN BOYD (1840-1921), a Scottish veterinarian, developed the *pneumatic* (air-filled) *tire.* He made the first ones to replace solid rubber tires on his son's tricycle so it would ride more comfortably. Dunlop's tire was tested and patented in Great Britain in 1888 and in the United States in 1890. But he decided to continue his work as a veterinarian, and sold his tire patent and small company in 1896. Dunlop had no further connection with the Dunlop Tire and Rubber Corporation. SMITH HEMPSTONE OLIVER

DUNNE, FINLEY PETER (1867-1936), an American newspaperman and humorist, created the saloonkeeper-philosopher, Mr. Dooley. Dooley's biting criticism of the Spanish-American War and its results made Dunne famous. He began his Mr. Dooley series with *Mr. Dooley in Peace and in War.* He was born in Chicago, and worked for several newspapers there. EDWARD WAGENKNECHT

DUNNING, JOHN RAY (1907-), an American physicist, did research work important in developing the atomic bomb. He produced high-energy particles for changing atoms of one kind into atoms of another kind, by using a cyclotron (see CYCLOTRON). With the cooperation of Alfred O. Nier, who separated small quantities of U-235 and U-238 from uranium, Dunning, E. T. Booth, and A. V. Grosse proved that slowly moving neutrons can cause U-235, but not U-238, to *fission* (split) (see URANIUM [Fission]). Dunning also found that the neutron had magnetic properties.

Dunning pioneered in research on the discharge of neutrons from uranium fission. During World War II, he directed research in isotope separation which was put into large scale use at Oak Ridge, Tenn.

Dunning was born on Sept. 24, 1907, in Shelby, Neb., and was graduated from Nebraska Wesleyan University. He received his Ph.D. degree at Columbia University. Dunning became assistant professor of physics at Columbia in 1935, and Dean of Engineering there in 1946. RALPH E. LAPP

Columbia University
John Ray Dunning

DUNS SCOTUS, *dunz SKO tus,* **JOHN** (1265?-1308), was a Roman Catholic divine and one of the great thinkers of the Middle Ages. His birthplace is unknown. He entered the Franciscan order, studied at Oxford, and in 1301 became professor of theology there. He maintained the doctrine of the Immaculate Conception against the contrary opinion of Thomas Aquinas, a noted Dominican scholar. He is sometimes known by the title *Doctor Subtilis (Subtle Doctor).* His writings, which are only now being critically edited, combine full orthodoxy with a striking independence of thought. He wrote commentaries on the Bible and Aristotle, and also an *Opus Oxoniense (Oxford Work).* FULTON J. SHEEN

DUNSANY, LORD (1878-1957), EDWARD JOHN MORETON DRAX PLUNKETT, an Irish writer, became famous for his strange, imaginative plays, stories, and poems. His play, *The Glittering Gate,* deals with burglars breaking open the gates of heaven. He also wrote *The Book of Wonder, Fifty Poems,* the novel *Guerrilla,* his autobiography, *Patches of Sun-Light,* and the plays *The Gods of the Mountain* and *A Night at an Inn.* He was the 18th Baron Dunsany. He was born in London, England, and attended Eton and Sandhurst. JOSEPH E. BAKER

DUNSTAN, SAINT (925?-988), was a Roman Catholic archbishop and statesman. He was born and educated at Glastonbury, England, and later became abbot of the monastery there. Dunstan acted as adviser during the reigns of kings Edmund and Edred. Many wise religious and social reforms were begun under his direction, and he also aided in the conquest of the Danes.

He publicly criticized King Edwy, successor to King Edred. For this he was deprived of his offices and banished. But he returned to England in 957, and was made bishop of London the following year. In 960 he was

DUODECIMAL

elected archbishop of Canterbury. King Edgar, who followed Edwy, approved of Dunstan's reforms and gave him every assistance. Dunstan retired to Canterbury in 978 after the death of Edgar, and remained there until his death. He was considered a great scholar and statesman who worked for the unity and religious betterment of England. His feast day is May 19.   FULTON J. SHEEN

DUODECIMAL, DOO *oh DES uh mul,* is the name given to a system of numbers based on 12. The Romans, to whom the number 12 was sacred, used the duodecimal system in dividing the foot and pound into twelfths and the year into months. The words *inch* and *ounce* come from the Latin word *uncia,* which means *twelfth.* The system used by merchants in counting by the dozen and by the gross (12 dozen or 144) is a duodecimal system. The word *dozen* comes from *duodecim,* the Latin word for *twelve.* Some writers argue that a duodecimal system could be used more easily than the decimal system (see DECIMAL NUMBER SYSTEM).   HOWARD F. FEHR

DUODENUM. See ALIMENTARY CANAL; STOMACH.

DUPLICATOR is any machine that makes copies of writing, typing, or illustrations. Printing may be considered a form of duplicating. But the term *duplicator* is usually applied to a small, relatively simple unit of equipment that can produce a few hundred or a few thousand copies quickly and economically.

Stencil Duplicator. In 1876, Thomas A. Edison patented a stencil duplicator called *Autographic printing.* Albert Blake Dick invented the mimeograph in 1884. It is the most widely used duplicator. The chief part of the machine is an ink-filled cylinder about a foot long and a foot across. An ink pad covers the cylinder. The operator places a stencil, a strong, wax-covered sheet, over the ink pad. Typing, writing, or drawing on the stencil pushes aside the wax coating. Ink flows through openings in the cylinder onto the ink pad. A roller in the machine presses paper against the stencil. This squeezes the ink from the pad through the impressions on the stencil and onto the paper.

Spirit Duplicator uses a master sheet to produce the image. The operator types, writes, or draws on a master sheet backed up by a second sheet of paper coated with a dye-impregnated, waxy substance. Typing or writing pressure transfers a small amount of the coating to the back of the master sheet in reverse. In the machine, an alcohol-base fluid dissolves a portion of the dye in the image and transfers it to the copy paper in the form of the original typing or writing.

Azograph Duplicator is similar to the spirit duplicator. But the dye color is produced by a reaction between chemicals in the image on the master sheet and those in the moistening fluid. Copy forms only after contact with the fluid in the machine. Typists can handle the sheet easily without staining their hands.

Offset Duplicator operates on the same principle used in offset printing (see OFFSET; PRINTING [Offset Printing]). A grease-base image is put on a master sheet by writing, drawing, typing, or printing. The machine applies water and a grease-base ink to the master sheet. The ink sticks only to the grease-base image. The inked image is transferred from the master sheet to a rubber blanket. A roller presses paper against the rubber blanket, printing the image.

Frank Fenner

The Offset Duplicating Machine makes it simple and easy to turn out many copies of letters, drawings, and other forms, quickly and without the expense of regular printing.

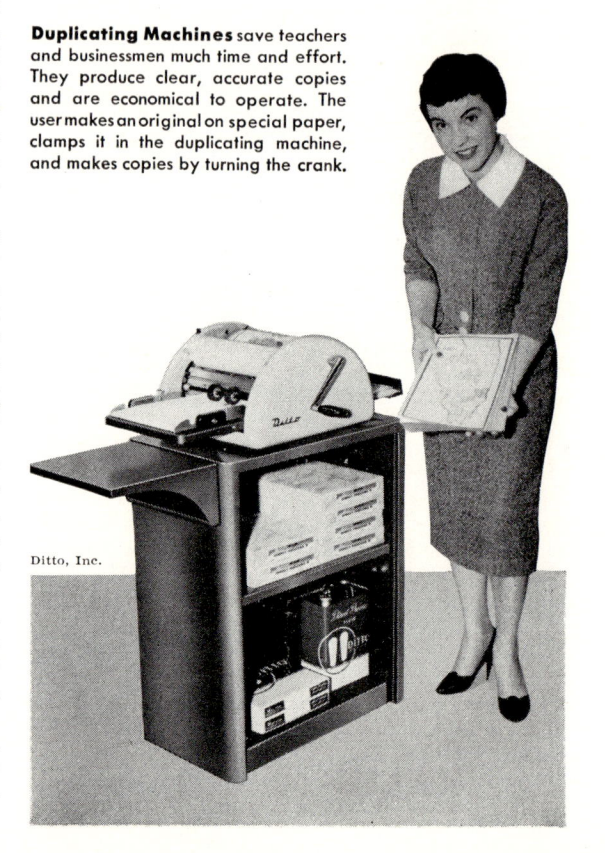

Duplicating Machines save teachers and businessmen much time and effort. They produce clear, accurate copies and are economical to operate. The user makes an original on special paper, clamps it in the duplicating machine, and makes copies by turning the crank.

Ditto, Inc.

Multigraph uses movable type that prints through an inked ribbon. It produces letters or other documents that look like typewritten copies. Pieces of metal with letters and other symbols on them are set into grooves on a cylinder. A sheet of paper is placed under the cylinder. The paper presses against an inked ribbon covering the type. This produces an image on the paper.

Other Duplicators. The *Addressograph* uses metal plates stamped with names and addresses to address envelopes. The plates print through an inked ribbon (see ADDRESSOGRAPH). Signature machines duplicate handwriting. One such device, the *Telautograph*, reproduces handwriting in one room at the moment it is written in another (see TELAUTOGRAPH). The *Flexowriter* uses punched tape to reproduce a typewritten letter that is an exact copy of the original. Other duplicators use the principles of photography to produce copies (see PHOTOGRAPHIC COPYING). C. M. DICK, JR.

See also EDISON, THOMAS A. (picture, Mimeograph Machine); HECTOGRAPH; OZALID PROCESS.

DU PONT COMPANY, officially the E. I. DU PONT DE NEMOURS & COMPANY, is the largest manufacturer of chemical products in the world. The company has 76 plants in the United States. It also has branches in Canada and other countries. These plants make cellophane, electrochemicals, explosives, paints, photographic film, plastics, dyes, and other synthetic organic chemicals. They also make insecticides and fungicides, synthetic textile fibers such as nylon and Dacron, and many other products. Headquarters and executive offices of the Du Pont Company are in Wilmington, Del.

Éleuthère Irénée du Pont, a student of the famous French chemist Antoine Lavoisier, founded the company in 1802. At first the company made only black gunpowder, but in 1880 it began the production of high explosives. In 1890, Du Pont started producing a smokeless explosive based on nitrocellulose. It then became interested in the many useful applications of cellulose (see CELLULOSE). The company began manufacturing lacquers, adhesives, finishes, and plastics. Since the early 1900's, Du Pont has rapidly enlarged its list of products, and today makes about 1,800.

During World War II, Du Pont designed, built, and operated the $350,000,000 Hanford Engineer Works near Richland, Wash., for the manufacture of plutonium (see PLUTONIUM). In 1956, Du Pont, in agreement with the Atomic Energy Commission, undertook the study and development of atomic reactors to generate electric power. Other developments since the war include Orlon fiber, Dacron fiber, and an industrial plastic called Teflon. The company makes annual grants of more than $1,000,000 to about 140 universities and colleges in the United States. Critically reviewed by the DU PONT COMPANY

See also CHEMICAL INDUSTRY (table); DELAWARE (color pictures; color map, Historic Delaware); DU PONT DE NEMOURS; MANUFACTURING (table).

DU PONT DE NEMOURS is the name of a famous Delaware family that established the great chemical firm of E. I. du Pont de Nemours & Company. Several members have also been active in public affairs.

Pierre Samuel du Pont de Nemours (1739-1817) was a French economist and statesman who came to the United States in 1800. He studied medicine, but turned to economic affairs as a result of national pressures in France. He was a close associate of many well-known French economists of his time, and became a noted author in economics.

Du Pont was caught in the conflicts following the French Revolution, and fled to the United States. President Thomas Jefferson recognized his ability, and asked him to prepare a plan for national education. After affairs quieted in France, Du Pont went back to his home country. He was born on Dec. 14, 1739, in Paris.

DU PONT DE NEMOURS

Du Pont
Pierre du Pont

Éleuthère Irénée du Pont (1771-1834), the son of Pierre Samuel du Pont, founded the powder works that formed the beginning of the present-day Du Pont Company. He was born in Paris, and ran his father's printing plant until the French Revolution. He fled from France to the United States with his father and older brother and their families. On his arrival, Du Pont saw the need for a powder plant in the new republic. He negotiated with Thomas Jefferson and others to establish it. In 1802, Du Pont chose a site on the banks of the Brandywine River four miles from Wilmington, Del., and founded the powder works.

Samuel Francis du Pont (1803-1865), grandson of Pierre Samuel du Pont, served as a rear admiral in the Union Navy during the Civil War. He commanded the South Atlantic Blockading Squadron, and led an unsuccessful attack on Charleston, S.C. He was born at Bergen Point, N.J.

Henry Algernon du Pont (1838-1926), grandson of Éleuthère Irénée du Pont, served as an army officer for 14 years. He was graduated at the head of his class from the United States Military Academy. Du Pont served as a Republican United States senator from Delaware from 1906 to 1917, and was chairman of the Senate Military Committee from 1911 to 1913. He was born near Wilmington, Del.

Thomas Coleman du Pont (1863-1930), great-grandson of Éleuthère Irénée du Pont, made a fortune at an early age in the coal and iron business. He served as president of the Du Pont Company from 1902 to 1915. It was under his leadership that the wide business interests of the family were combined under the present corporate charter of the E. I. du Pont de Nemours Powder Company. Du Pont was active in politics both on the state and national level. He represented Delaware as a Republican in the United States Senate from 1921 to 1928. He was born in Louisville, Ky.

Pierre Samuel du Pont (1870-1954), great-grandson of Éleuthère Irénée du Pont, served as president of the Du Pont Company from 1915 to 1919 and as chairman of the board from 1919 to 1940. He gave money for schools, hospitals, and other public purposes. He was a member of the Delaware State Board of Education from 1919 to 1921. Pierre Samuel du Pont was born in Wilmington, Del. W. H. BAUGHN

See also DELAWARE (color picture, Du Pont Powder Mill); DU PONT COMPANY.

DUQUESNE UNIVERSITY

DUQUESNE UNIVERSITY is a coeducational Roman Catholic school at Pittsburgh, Pa. It is conducted and controlled by the Congregation of the Holy Ghost. Courses are offered in the arts and sciences, business administration, education, law, music, nursing, and pharmacy. It also has a graduate school. Duquesne was founded in 1878 by the Fathers of the Congregation of the Holy Ghost. In 1911 the school became Duquesne University. For enrollment, see UNIVERSITIES AND COLLEGES (table). HENRY J. MCANULTY

DUR SHARRUKIN. See ASSYRIA (Art).

DURA MATER. See BRAIN (Brain Membranes).

DURALUMIN, *dyoo RAL yoo min*, is an alloy of aluminum with copper, manganese, and magnesium. It is used in the manufacture of aircraft, and such automobile parts as engines, rims, and wheels. Duralumin is strong but light. Its *tensile* strength, or the pull it can stand without tearing apart, is 55,000 pounds per square inch. Its specific gravity of 2.75 means it is $2\frac{3}{4}$ times as heavy as water. These qualities make it one of the most important aluminum alloys. GEORGE L. BUSH

DURANGO, *doo RANG goh* (pop. 754,220), is a state of northwestern Mexico. For location, see MEXICO (color map). It has an area of 47,691 square miles. Mountains of the Sierra Madre Occidental Range cover western Durango (see SIERRA MADRE). Silver, lead, copper, and iron are mined there. The eastern part of the state is largely a dry plain where ranchers raise cattle. Irrigation has aided farming in the Nazas River valley. The city of Durango is the capital. Durango became a state in 1823. CHARLES C. CUMBERLAND

DURANT, WILLIAM CRAPO (1861-1947), an American manufacturer, became known as the "godfather of the automobile industry." He outlined the principles of mass production, low costs, wide distribution, and increased profits. Durant organized the General Motors Corporation in 1908 and Chevrolet Motor Company in 1915. But he lost control of both in 1920. He organized Durant Motors, Inc., in 1921, and later became a manufacturer of rayon. He was born in Boston, Mass., and grew up in Flint, Mich. R. E. WESTMEYER

DURANT, "WILL," WILLIAM JAMES (1885-   ), historian, philosopher, and educator, first won recognition in 1926 for his popular history, *The Story of Philosophy*. He began his major historical series, *The Story of Civilization*, in 1935. Volumes in the series include *Our Oriental Heritage*, *The Life of Greece*, *Caesar and Christ*, *The Age of Faith*, *The Renaissance*, *The Reformation*, and *The Age of Reason Begins* (written with his wife, Ariel). His other books include *On the Meaning of Life* and *Philosophy and the Social Problem*.

Durant presents a lively picture of the physical, mental, and spiritual developments of each period. His books are generally considered well documented, and written in an interesting style.

Durant was born in North Adams, Mass., and was graduated from St. Peter's College in Jersey City, N.J. He taught at Columbia University and the University of California, and was director of the Labor Temple School in New York from 1914 to 1927. EDWIN H. CADY

DURANTE, *dyu RANT ih*, **"JIMMY," JAMES** (1893-   ), is an American entertainer. He was born in New York City, and began his career playing piano. His

Wide World
Will Durant

A. D. Cushman & Assoc.
"Jimmy" Durante

talent for singing comedy songs and clowning won him fame in vaudeville, the theater, motion pictures, radio, and television. He made his large nose the object of many jokes and became known as "the Schnozzle." In 1951, he received a Peabody award for outstanding television entertainment. The same year, his biography, *Schnozzola; The Story of Jimmy Durante*, written by Gene Fowler, was published. BOSLEY CROWTHER

DURANTY, *doo RAN tih*, **WALTER** (1884-1957), was a *New York Times* correspondent from 1913 to 1941. He also wrote novels, history, and books about his newspaper experiences. He covered the French Army in World War I, and was the *Times* Moscow correspondent from 1921 to 1934. A series of articles on Russia earned him a Pulitzer prize in 1932. He was born in Liverpool, England. JOHN E. DREWRY

DURBAN, *DUR ban* (pop. 553,900; met. area 655,400; alt. 25 ft.), is the chief eastern seaport in South Africa. It is the largest city of Natal Province (see NATAL). For location, see SOUTH AFRICA (color map).

Durban is a trading and industrial center and the most important resort city of South Africa. The city's public buildings face Victoria Embankment, a fine highway along Bay Beach. The jewelry, fruit, and herb stalls of the Indian Market attract many tourists. Durban was founded in 1834 and was named for Sir Benjamin d'Urban, who was then governor of neighboring Cape Colony. HIBBERD V. B. KLINE, JR.

DURBAR, *DUR bahr*, a Persian word which means *audience hall*, is a name given to government meetings and receptions in India. At a durbar, the leaders of India meet to discuss affairs of state. Great or famous visitors from foreign countries are greeted "in durbar" by the governors, rulers, and princes of India.

DÜRER, *DYOO rer*, **ALBRECHT** (1471-1528), a German painter, engraver, and designer, was one of the foremost artists of his country during the Renaissance. He was perhaps the most original creative German artist, and he influenced generations of artists in northern Europe. He learned much from the Italian painters, and combined their discoveries with the tradition of his homeland. Dürer combined a love of the ancient world with a deep Christian spirit.

His works include the engraving, *Knight, Death, and the Devil;* a woodcut series, *The Smaller Passion;* and the self-portrait in the Prado in Madrid. Two of his most notable paintings are *Martyrdom of the Ten Thousand* and *Adoration of the Magi*. One of his portraits, *Hieronymus Holzschuher*, appears in color in the PAINTING article.

Albrecht Dürer (self-portrait)
Bettmann Archive

As an engraver, Dürer developed the methods of Martin Schongauer, and combined them with the lessons of Andrea Mantegna to bring that art to its highest perfection in his century (see MANTEGNA, ANDREA; SCHONGAUER, MARTIN). He probably drew the designs for his woodcuts in the blocks, then carved away the wood to create wood engravings. They were widely copied, even in Italy. His woodcuts are energetic, inventive, exuberant, sometimes grim, and sometimes grotesque.

Dürer was born in Nuremberg, where he probably learned how to engrave from his father, a goldsmith. For three years, he was apprenticed to Michel Wohlgemuth (1434-1519). At 19, he may have visited Italy.

After 1505, Dürer lived in Venice. From his contact with the Venetian painters, Dürer learned to simplify and strengthen his work. He learned further refinements from Flemish painters during a visit to The Netherlands. He returned to Nuremberg after 1512, and became the favorite painter of Emperor Maximilian I. He achieved his greatest works there. He was admired by Raphael and Erasmus. S. W. HAYTER

See also BOOKPLATE; ENGRAVING; RELIGION (color picture, Praying Hands); WOODCUT (picture).

Knight, Death, and the Devil is one of the magnificent engravings of Albrecht Dürer. The fine details in both the figures and the background show Dürer's meticulous craftsmanship.
Allen Memorial Art Museum, Oberlin College, Oberlin, Ohio

DURHAM, *DUR um* (pop. 20,484; alt. 335 ft.), is an ancient fortress town in northeastern England. It stands on a hill that is almost surrounded by the River Wear. Its cathedral is a fine example of Norman architecture. The University of Durham is nearby.

DURHAM, N.C. (pop. 78,302; alt. 405 ft.), is a tobacco-manufacturing and textile center in the northeastern Piedmont Region of the state. Famous brands of cigarettes and smoking tobacco are manufactured in Durham. Factories in the city also make machinery and cotton goods. Durham is the home of Duke University and North Carolina College.

Durham was settled in the 1850's. In 1865, General Joseph E. Johnston surrendered his Confederate army to Union General William T. Sherman at the Bennett Place, just west of the city. Durham has a council-manager form of government. HUGH T. LEFLER

DURHAM, *DUR um*, **EARL OF** (1792-1840), JOHN GEORGE LAMBTON, an English statesman, became one of the great radical Whig political leaders of his day. His *Report on the Affairs of British North America* became a constitutional document of far-reaching importance. It was responsible for the union of Upper and Lower Canada, and became the basis of British colonial policy. It marked the peak of his short career as a diplomat. See CANADA, HISTORY OF (Struggle for Responsible Government).

Lambton became a member of the House of Commons in 1813, and advocated parliamentary reform. He became Lord Privy Seal in 1830, under his father-in-law, Earl Grey.

Earl of Durham

He was one of the four men chosen to draft the Reform Bill in 1832. He resigned as Lord Privy Seal in 1833, and received the title of the Earl of Durham.

Durham served as ambassador to Russia in 1836. He went to Canada in 1838 to settle matters after the rebellion of 1837 (see REBELLION OF 1837-1838). A special act of the British Parliament granted him special powers as high commissioner to Canada. He resigned this post in great anger in 1838 because the government would not support his highhanded policy toward the rebels. He returned to England in 1839, in failing health, and submitted his famous report. He lived only long enough to see the union of Canada become a reality. He was born in London, England. JAMES L. GODFREY

DURRA. See SORGHUM.

DURYEA is the family name of two brothers who were automobile pioneers. **Charles E.** (1861-1938) and **J. Frank** (1869-   ) built the first successful gasoline-powered automobile in America. Their one-cylinder model made a trial run in 1893 in Springfield, Mass. It is now on exhibition in the Smithsonian Institution in Washington, D.C. A second model of the Duryea car won the $2,000 first prize in the Chicago-Evanston, Ill., Thanksgiving Day race in 1895. This was the first gasoline-automobile race in the United States.

DUSE, ELEONORA

The brothers organized the Duryea Motor Wagon Company in 1895, and produced 13 cars in 1896. In 1898, Frank Duryea joined the Stevens Arms Company. There, he designed the four- and six-cylinder Stevens-Duryea automobiles. Charles was born in Canton, Ill., and Frank was born in Washburn, Ill. They were pioneers in their field. SMITH HEMPSTONE OLIVER

DUSE, *DOO zay,* **ELEONORA** (1859-1924), an Italian dramatic actress, has been called "the greatest actress of her time." She seemed to live her parts instead of act them. Critics praised her for her natural and sincere acting. Although a shy person, she felt at home on the stage.

Gabriele d'Annunzio wrote some of his best plays for her, including *La Gioconda* and *Francesca da Rimini* (see D'ANNUNZIO, GABRIELE). He also fell in love with her, and wrote a book, *The Flame* (1900), based on their love story. She went into retirement for almost 20 years because of this book. She was one of the first important actresses to act in Henrik Ibsen's plays, *Hedda Gabler* and *The Lady from the Sea.* She also acted in *Camille, Magda,* and *Cavalleria Rusticana.*

Bettmann Archive
Eleonora Duse

Miss Duse was born on a train while her actor parents were traveling from Venice to Vigevano, in Italy. She appeared with their company at the age of 4 as Cosette in Victor Hugo's *Les Misérables.* At 14, she played Juliet in *Romeo and Juliet.* She made several successful tours in Europe, South America, Canada, and the United States. She died in Pittsburgh, Pa., during her third United States tour, on April 21, 1924. RICHARD MOODY

DUSHANBE, *doo SHAHN beh* (pop. 248,500; alt. 2,600 ft.), is the capital of the Tadzhik Soviet Socialist Republic of Russia. The city is an important transportation and industrial center. The Tadzhik State University opened in Dushanbe in 1948. In 1929, the government changed the city's name to Stalinabad in honor of Joseph Stalin. During the "de-Stalinization" campaign in 1961, the government renamed the city Dushanbe.

DÜSSELDORF, *DYOOS ul dawrf* (pop. 702,600; met. area 1,020,000; alt. 118 ft.), is the capital of the state of North Rhine-Westphalia, in West Germany. It stands in the Ruhr Valley where the Düssel River flows into the Rhine. For location, see GERMANY (color map).

Düsseldorf acts as the business and financial center of the great Ruhr industries. Products include chemicals, iron and steel, machinery, railroad equipment, and textiles. Railroads and air lines connect the city with all the important cities in western Europe. Düsseldorf is a center of German learning. The university, which includes the Academy for Practical Medicine and an art school, was founded in 1767. The poet Heinrich Heine was born in Düsseldorf. At various times, Johannes Brahms, Robert Schumann, and Johann Wolfgang Goethe lived here. The city received its first charter in 1288. Bombers severely damaged the city during World War II. Düsseldorf rebuilt after the war, and became a center of drama, film making, and fashions. Düsseldorf has a fine art center. JAMES K. POLLOCK

DUST is made up of small fragments of all kinds of solid matter. The fragments must be small enough to be carried in the air. To be of true dust size, a particle must be smaller than $\frac{1}{1000}$ of a millimeter. Coarser dust may come as large as $\frac{5}{1000}$ of a millimeter. In the dust you could collect from your window sill you would find bits of mineral matter, soot (carbon), ash, and cinders; tiny shreds of animal and plant tissue such as spores, pollen grains, shreds of wood, and bits of wool, cotton, and hair.

By far the greatest part of all ordinary dust in the atmosphere is mineral matter picked up by the wind. It comes from dry places like the faces of rocks, bare soil, and crumbling rock ledges. It also comes from mud flats and plowed fields. In parts of the southwestern United States, the plants that cover the soil have been destroyed by too much grazing and farming and too little rain. The wind blows away the topsoil, and great storms spread dust eastward, sometimes as far as New England.

Volcanic Dust. A special kind of dust comes from volcanoes. Their explosions blow solid lava to powder and spray liquid lava into the air to form tiny drops and shreds of glass. In the past volcanoes spread large amounts of this dust over the earth's surface. When Katmai volcano in Alaska erupted in 1912, it sent so much dust into the air that some was carried as far as Seattle, Wash., 1,600 miles away.

Dust Deposits. True dust is easily picked up again and again by the wind or washed into streams. It is too light to form deposits on the ground. But coarser dust settles readily. Two kinds of dust deposits lie like a blanket over hills and valleys. The first is the volcanic dust. The second is ordinary mineral dust blown from bare mud flats. Such flats lay in front of the great ice sheets that covered North America and Europe during the ice age. The rich soil called *loess* that is found in Europe, Asia, and North America is made of such dust from the ice age (see LOESS). Both volcanic and mineral dust make very fertile soil that is free from stones.

Importance to Man. Some dust particles help form rain and snow. Condensing water vapor settles on the tiny dust particles to form water droplets. These droplets may unite with others to form rain or snow (see RAIN).

Dust causes haze which is hard to see through. It also keeps many of the sun's rays from reaching the earth.

In some quarries, mines, and factories there are large amounts of mineral dust in the air all the time. This dust may settle in workmen's lungs, and cause the disease known as *silicosis* (see SILICOSIS). Modern factories protect their workers with dust removers or masks. Dust also serves as a carrier for disease bacteria which are found in sputum and other materials. There is less danger if these materials are well exposed to the sunshine and air. The spore stages of some disease bacteria can be considered dust particles themselves. The same is true of certain mold spores and the pollens which produce hay fever, asthma, and other different allergies.

The study of dust is useful to the police. They sometimes find much information about the person who has lived in a room by examining the dust that has settled there. The dust that collects in clothing is also valuable evidence in criminal cases. ERNEST E. WAHLSTROM

See also DUST BOWL; DUST STORM.

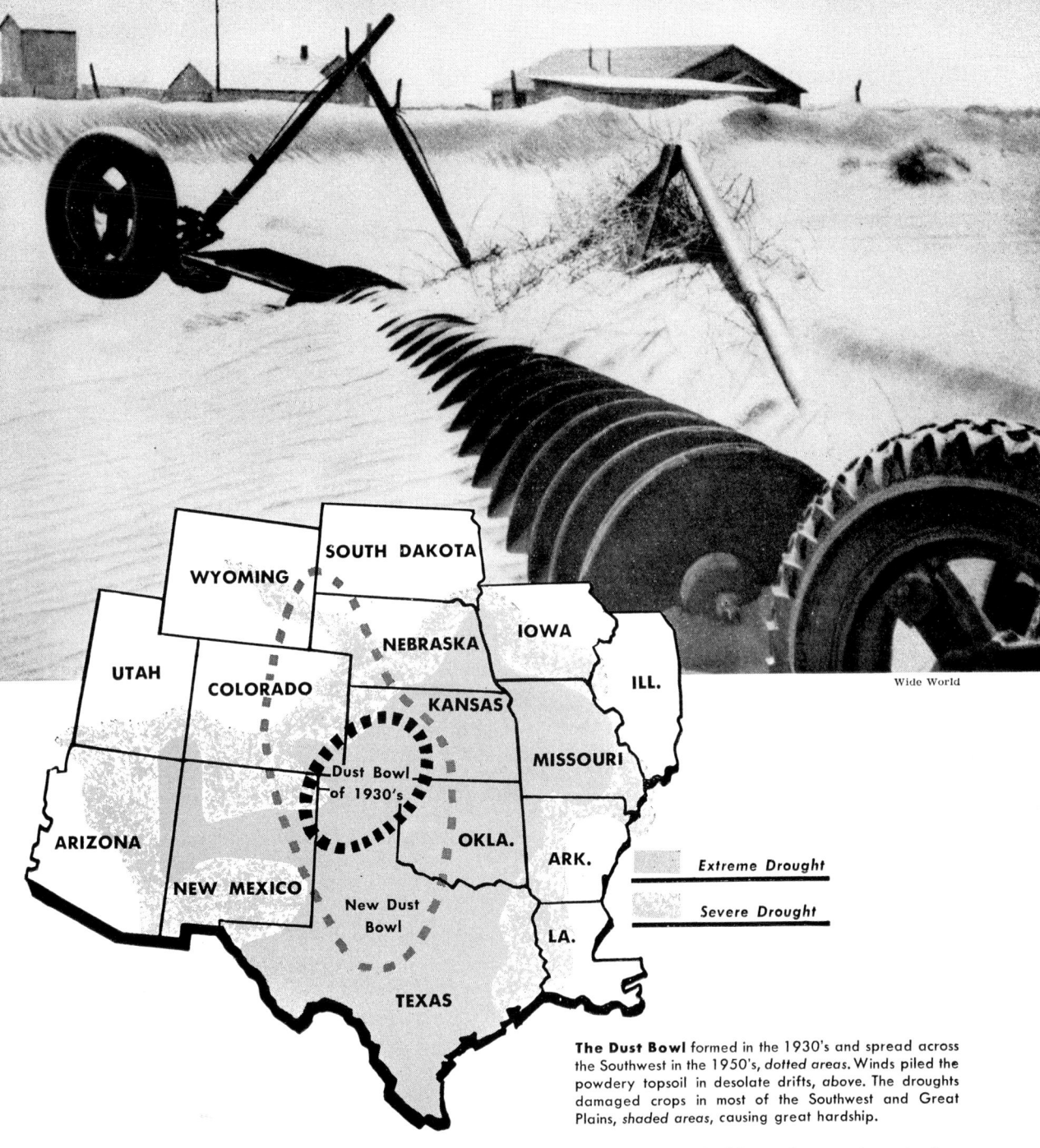

The Dust Bowl formed in the 1930's and spread across the Southwest in the 1950's, *dotted areas*. Winds piled the powdery topsoil in desolate drifts, *above*. The droughts damaged crops in most of the Southwest and Great Plains, *shaded areas*, causing great hardship.

DUST BOWL was a name at one time applied to a part of the Great Plains region of the southwestern United States. Much of the soil there had been damaged by wind and rain, and many severe dust storms occurred. The soil in this area was subjected to water and wind damage because the protective cover of vegetation was impaired or destroyed through poor farming practices and the grazing of too many animals. The area covered some 50,000,000 acres and included parts of Texas, New Mexico, Colorado, Kansas, and Oklahoma. Dust storms, however, have occurred in many other parts of the Great Plains, where the soil lacked sufficient vegetative cover to resist attacks by the wind. The Dust Bowl extended eastward from the Rocky Mountains to an irregular line where rainfall averaged only 20 inches a year.

Rainfall has often been scanty and scattered in this region. Rain may fall in large amounts at one point, while an area nearby remains dry. There may be a sprinkle of rain or a downpour. When rain does fall, it is usually accompanied by strong winds. Prevailing winds blow at rates from 8 miles an hour at the edge of the Great Plains to 16 miles an hour in this region and the eastern Dakotas. The temperature rises or falls rapidly. Wheat and sorghum grains are widely grown here and in other parts of the Great Plains. When contour cultivation is practiced, the yields frequently have

315

DUST EXPLOSION

been good even in years of scanty rainfall. The natural vegetation of the area is short grass, such as buffalo grass and grama. They furnish good grazing for animals, and also help to keep the soil from washing or blowing away.

The first farmers in the Dust Bowl were settlers who came west after the Civil War and took up homesteads. These farms were often successful in wet years. But nearly all the homesteads were too small to provide even a meager living for a family during periods of dry weather or drought.

Much of the Dust Bowl was sown in wheat during World War I, to meet the great demand for this grain. The wheat, as then grown, did not adequately protect the ground from winds, and the soil began to drift.

The most severe dust storms began in the Dust Bowl in the early 1930's, but many local storms occurred before that where the soil became exposed to the wind.

In 1934, great curtains of dust were carried clear across the continent to the Atlantic Coast and far out into the Gulf of Mexico. During such a storm, it was impossible to see for more than a few feet, and some persons in the area wore masks to protect throat and lungs. Farmhouses were sometimes nearly hidden behind drifts of dust. Many farm families left the region. *The Grapes of Wrath*, by John Steinbeck, is a story of some of these families on their migration to California. This novel also described the many hardships the farmers faced in the Dust Bowl. See STEINBECK, JOHN E.

In the late 1930's and early 1940's, a fair amount of rain fell in the Dust Bowl and farmers were able to harvest good crops of grain. There were very few dust storms. However, in the 1950's, below-average rainfall and high winds again caused the soil to begin blowing away. GLENN K. RULE

See also DROUGHT; DUST; DUST STORM.

DUST EXPLOSION takes place when a mixture of air and dust particles catches fire. Such explosions occur around threshing machines, flour mills, grain elevators, starch plants, cotton gins, coffee-roasting plants, aluminum factories, paper mills, and coal mines. They are a danger wherever particles that will burn collect in the air, and there is a source of heat nearby. Many materials that do not burn well in large pieces will burn easily and explode, when in the form of dust. Most metals, for example, act in this way. The flame or spark that sets off the explosion may come from matches, torches, static electricity caused by friction, incorrect or worn electric wiring, broken electric-light bulbs, and other sources. Eight hundred grain-dust explosions were reported in the northwestern states in one five-year period. Then the United States Bureau of Chemistry made a study of their causes and prevention. They recommended:

(1) Installing fans to remove the dust in machines
(2) Keeping fire extinguishers for emergencies
(3) Placing ground wires in threshers to remove the danger of electric charges

To prevent great damage from explosions in factories, the Bureau advised that buildings for dangerous operations be constructed separate from others. If the dust particles are free to pass from one building to another, a small explosion in one place may carry through the entire plant. RALPH G. OWENS

See also COMBUSTION.

DUST STORM is a wind which moves across a region picking up loose soil and carrying it many miles. This movement of soil which may rob farm land of its rich topsoil is sometimes called *wind erosion*. During a dust storm the air is usually very hot and dry. Sometimes the dust clouds are so thick it is impossible to see through them. Dust storms usually occur during a period of drought (see DROUGHT).

Dust storms are known to have occurred in the ancient world, for records have been found which describe clouds of volcanic ash which were carried for long distances by winds, and violent sand storms in the deserts. In 1902, dust clouds arose over Algeria, and were carried about 1,100 miles to the British Isles. Storms which carry off fertile soil have occurred in recent years. In the southwestern United States, dust storms caused serious damage during the early 1930's. Quantities of soil were picked up by winds and carried for great distances. Much rich farm land was destroyed in this way.

Dust storms are most likely to occur in regions where there is little rainfall, and where the natural grasses and the farm crops are not deeply rooted in the soil. Areas where the soil is blown away are harmed, but the areas where the soil is deposited are improved. Geologists believe that the lower Mississippi Valley was made more fertile by soil from dust storms. EDNA S. STONE

See also DUST BOWL; SHELTER BELT.

DUSTIN MONUMENT, HANNAH. See NEW HAMPSHIRE (Interesting Places to Visit).

DUTCH. See NETHERLANDS.

DUTCH AUCTION is a type of public sale which originated in The Netherlands. In a Dutch auction, property is offered to the public at a price beyond its value. Then gradually the auctioneer lowers the price until someone buys the property. The opposite procedure is followed in a regular auction. See AUCTION.

DUTCH EAST INDIA COMPANY was given a charter and Far Eastern trading privileges by the government of The Netherlands in 1602. This was to strengthen and protect Dutch trade in the East, and to prevent competition between Dutch companies. The headquarters of the company was at Batavia (now Djakarta), Java. Much of the trading was done in pepper and spices. The company was dissolved in 1798, and the Dutch government took over its property. J. SALWYN SCHAPIRO

DUTCH EAST INDIES. See INDONESIA.

DUTCH ELM DISEASE is a severe disease of the elm tree. It is caused by a fungus carried by the European

Ewing Galloway

A Greatly Enlarged Photograph shows the tiny American bark beetle. This insect is one of the two kinds of beetles which spread Dutch elm disease from tree to tree.

bark beetle and the smaller American bark beetle. The disease can cause the death of a tree in four weeks.

Dutch elm disease usually begins with a wilting of the younger leaves in the upper part of the tree. Later, the lower branches become infected. In about midsummer, all but a few of the leaves at the branch tips turn yellow, curl, and drop off. When diseased twigs or branches are cut, long brown streaks can be seen in the wood just beneath the bark.

Government agencies try to control Dutch elm disease by cutting and burning diseased trees. They also use DDT to prevent its spread (see DDT).

Dutch elm disease is so called because the Dutch first observed it in Holland in 1919. It became known in America in 1930, and was limited to an area close to New York City. The disease has now spread as far west as Denver, Colo., and as far north as Milwaukee, Wis. It afflicts many trees. THEODORE W. BRETZ

DUTCH GUIANA. See SURINAM.

DUTCH HARBOR, Alaska, was the site of a United States naval air base during World War II. Planes flying from that base formed part of the continental air defense of the United States. The base was deactivated after the war. Dutch Harbor was one of several Alaskan towns bombed by the Japanese in 1942. The town lies on Dutch Harbor, a natural bay on the eastern side of Amaknak Island in Unalaska Bay. For location, see ALASKA (color map).

According to tradition, the harbor received its name because a Dutch ship was the first to enter the bay, sometime in the early 1700's. LYMAN E. ALLEN

DUTCH LANGUAGE. See NETHERLANDS (The People).

DUTCH OVEN is a covered metal cooking pot used to cook on top of a stove or over hot coals. Modern Dutch ovens are usually made of aluminum. American pioneers used a cast-iron Dutch oven with a rimmed lid. The pot was set on hot coals, and coals were also placed on the lid. Brick ovens in fireplaces and chimneys are sometimes called Dutch ovens.

DUTCH REFORMED CHURCH. See REFORMED CHURCHES IN AMERICA.

DUTCH TREAT. See NETHERLANDS (Wars with England and France).

DUTCH UNCLE. See NETHERLANDS (Wars with England and France).

DUTCH WEST INDIA COMPANY was formed by Dutch merchants and chartered by the government of The Netherlands in 1621. The company was given trading and colonizing privileges for a period of 24 years in North America, the West Indies, and Africa. The colony of New Netherlands, which later became the state of New York, was founded by the Dutch West India Company. Its headquarters were at New Amsterdam (now New York City). J. SALWYN SCHAPIRO

DUTCH WEST INDIES. See NETHERLANDS ANTILLES.

DUTCHMAN'S-BREECHES, also called *white heart*, is a small delicate plant with flattened, heart-shaped flowers. This perennial grows in the rich soil of shady woods from Nova Scotia to Georgia and west to Nebraska. It is also found in Washington and Oregon. The plant has lacy, fernlike leaves, pale bluish-green in color. The stems are brittle and contain a watery sap. The stem grows from an underground tuber (see TUBER).

Dutchman's-breeches gets its name from the shape of its flowers. Each leafless flower stalk has four to ten

J. Horace McFarland

A Dutchman's-Breeches plant has a white blossom shaped like a tiny pair of Dutch pantaloons. The delicate blossoms are poisonous and have killed cattle which have eaten them.

nodding fragrant flowers that look like baggy trousers hanging upside down. The flowers are waxy white or pinkish-white with yellow tips.

Scientific Classification. Dutchman's-breeches is a member of the family *Fumariaceae*. It is genus *Dicentra*, species *Cucullaria*. ROBERT W. HOSHAW

DUTY, in economics. See CUSTOMS DUTIES; TARIFF.

DUVAL, WILLIAM P. See FLORIDA (Famous Floridians).

DUVENECK, *DOO veh neck*, **FRANK** (1848-1919), an American artist and teacher, influenced American art through his teaching. He taught his students good craftsmanship and brushwork. His best painting, *The Whistling Boy*, is in the Cincinnati Museum of Art. It shows his own mastery of brushwork. Duveneck studied in Munich, Germany. He opened a studio there in 1878 and taught young Americans. He also taught at the Cincinnati Art Academy from 1888 until his death. He was born in Covington, Ky. EDWIN L. FULWIDER

DUVETYN, *DOO vuh teen*, is a soft cloth with a fine, velvety surface like suede. The name *duvetyn* comes from the French word *duvet*, meaning *down*. The fabric was first made in Paris of soft woolen yarns.

DU VIGNEAUD, *dyu VEEN yoh*, **VINCENT** (1901-), an American biochemist, received the 1955 Nobel prize in chemistry for synthesizing the compound *oxytocin*, a hormone of the posterior pituitary gland. Such hormones aid in childbirth and act as regulators for such vital organs as the kidneys. Du Vigneaud was born in Chicago. He directed the synthesis of penicillin G at Cornell University Medical College, and established the structure of *biotin*, a member of the vitamin B complex group. See also BIOTIN. HERBERT S. RHINESMITH

DUVOISIN, *dyoo vwah ZAN*, **ROGER ANTOINE** (1904-), is an American artist and illustrator. He won the 1948 Caldecott medal for his illustrations in *White Snow, Bright Snow*, a children's book by Alvin Tresselt. He wrote and illustrated his first children's book, *A Little Boy Was Drawing*, for his son in 1932. He also wrote *And There Was America* and *Christmas Whale*. He illustrated many books by Tresselt and other authors, including Louise Fatio's *Happy Lion*. He was born in Geneva, Switzerland, but became a United States citizen in 1938. The West German government awarded him its 1956 prize for children's books. RUTH HILL VIGUERS

DVINA RIVER

DVINA RIVER, *dvee NAH,* is the name of two rivers in Russia. One, called the Western Dvina or Daugava, rises west of Moscow, and flows into the Gulf of Riga at Riga, Latvia. It is 633 miles long.

Another river, the Northern Dvina, is an important waterway in northwestern Russia. The Northern Dvina, formed by the Sukhona and Vychegda rivers, is 455 miles long. It flows northwest and empties into the White Sea at the port of Archangel. Steamboats travel on the Northern Dvina for its entire length. The Northern Dvina is connected to the Neva and Volga rivers by the Northern Dvina Canal. For location of the two rivers, see RUSSIA (color map). THEODORE SHABAD

DVOŘÁK, *DVAWR zhahk,* **ANTONÍN** (1841-1904), was a Czech composer, teacher, and violinist. He introduced the concerto form into Czech music. His works reflect the folk music of his own country and of American Indians and Negroes.

His musical career was influenced by the spirit of Bohemian nationalism. He turned for inspiration from German romantic melody and harmony to the folk songs and dances of his own people. He assured his success as a composer with a patriotic cantata, *The Heirs of the White Mountains.* His *Slavonic Dances* and *Rhapsodies* also became highly popular. He charmed audiences with his use of fiery folk rhythms and lyrical melodies.

Dvořák wrote nine symphonies, but the order became confused, and the last five he wrote are numbered as though they were his first five. Dvořák's songs won great popularity. Some of the best known are the 10 *Biblical Songs* and the seven *Gypsy Songs,* including the famous "Songs My Mother Taught Me."

Antonín Dvořák *Culver*

He was born near Prague. He became a violin prodigy, studying with the village schoolmaster. He attended an organ school in Prague from 1857 to 1859. The Czech composer, Bedřich Smetana, established the National Theater in Prague in 1862, and Dvořák became a viola player in the orchestra there. Later, he became a professor of composition at the Prague Conservatory. He was appointed director of the conservatory in 1901, a post he held until his death.

From 1892 until 1895, Dvořák served as the director of the National Conservatory in New York City. A pleasant part of his American experience was a summer spent in Spillville, Iowa, where many Czechs lived. He showed his deep interest in American folk music with the *Symphony in E minor: From the New World.* In this work he expresses the spirit of Negro spirituals. Dvořák's love of American Indian melodies appeared in his *American Quartet in F major* and *Quintet in E-flat major.*

Dvořák made nine trips to England, where he was very popular. He gave many concerts and composed several masterpieces there, including the exciting *Carnival Overture.* JOYCE MICHELL

See also IOWA (Interesting Places to Visit).

Brooklyn Botanic Garden
Dwarf Trees can be produced by placing seedlings in small containers and pruning the roots as they grow. Dwarf trees, such as this 50-year-old Japanese white pine, may be less than one foot tall.

DWARF is an unusually small adult human being, animal, or plant. A dwarf may have normal proportions or may be deformed. Dwarfs occur in nature both as occasional abnormal individuals and as entire races, such as the African Pygmies, the Shetland ponies, and the various kinds of dwarf trees (see PYGMY).

Human Dwarfs have been known throughout history. Norse mythology pictures them as ugly but powerful creatures called the *Nibelungs* (see NIBELUNGENLIED). During the Middle Ages in Europe, dwarfs often served as court jesters.

There are three different kinds of human dwarfs. These are (1) the pituitary, (2) the cretin, and (3) the achondroplastic, or chondrodystrophic.

The pituitary dwarf results from failure of the pituitary gland to function normally (see PITUITARY GLAND). Pituitary dwarfs usually look like smaller copies of normal people. They are usually normal mentally. Dwarfs with normal body proportions are often called *midgets.* The most famous midget was a pituitary dwarf named Charles S. Stratton, often called "General Tom Thumb" (see STRATTON, CHARLES S.).

Cretinism occurs when a child's thyroid gland does not produce enough of its hormone for normal growth. If untreated, cretins become misshapen and mentally deficient. Cretinism can be corrected by thyroid feeding begun when the victim is very young. See CRETINISM.

The achondroplastic, or *chondrodystrophic, dwarf* may result from some abnormality of the endocrine glands (see GLAND). This type of dwarf has short legs, a large head, and normal-sized body and arms. This is the dwarf described in Norse mythology. Achondroplasia can be inherited.

Dwarf Animals occur naturally, or may be developed by breeding. Among the naturally occurring dwarf animals are ponies, the dik-dik (a tiny African antelope),

318

A Dwarf Cow, center, is smaller than a normal cow, rear. The dwarf's normal-sized calf, foreground, carries dwarf genes. If mated with another carrier of dwarf genes, the calf's offspring may also be dwarfs.

H. Allan, Winnipeg *Tribune*

the downy woodpecker, and some kinds of tiny ants. Dwarf animals produced by selective breeding include the "toy" breeds of dogs, the Ancon sheep, and dwarf pigs. See CATTLE (Dwarf Cattle); DIK-DIK; TOY DOG.

Dwarf Plants also may occur naturally, or they may be developed by breeding or by artificial treatment. Dwarf plants may occur in nature as a result of mutation (see MUTATION). Poor soil or lack of food and water may also cause dwarfism in plants. Plant breeders have developed many kinds of dwarf plants. Dwarf fruit trees, for example, can grow in a small yard. Dwarf varieties of marigolds, dahlias, zinnias, and other flowers have been developed. Dwarf trees only a few inches high are artificially produced in the *bonsai* gardens of Japan (see BONSAI; TREE [Bonsai]). GAIRDNER B. MOMENT

DWELLING. See HOUSE; HOUSING; SHELTER.

DWIGHT, JOHN (1637?-1703), an English potter, won fame for creating "Fulham figurines," a group of portrait busts and figurines in salt-glazed stoneware. The figurines and others like them are collected in the British Museum and the Victoria and Albert Museum. Dwight may have been born in Oxfordshire. He founded the Fulham Pottery at Fulham, Middlesex, in 1671.

DYAK, *DIE ak.* The brown-skinned people known as Dyaks live along the seacoast of Borneo and in some inner parts of the island. They are about 5 feet in height, a little shorter than their neighbors, the Malays. As a rule the Dyaks are more gay and cheerful than the Malays. Dyaks have broad faces, light-brown to brown skin, dark eyes, and prominent cheekbones. Their hair is long and straight, and they tie it in a knot at the back of the head. Their mouths are generally reddened and ill-shaped, and their teeth are black, for both men and women are in the habit of chewing betel nuts (see BETEL).

The Dyaks' bamboo houses are built on poles, with the floors 6 to 10 feet above the ground. The length of the houses depends on the number of families living in them. They may be from 30 to 1,000 feet long. Each family farms its own land. Rice is the chief crop. The leading industries are boatbuilding and weaving.

The Dyaks used to be head-hunters. Men cut off and preserved the heads of their enemies as proof of their courage. They were often displayed at feasts and dances. It is said that many Dyak women would refuse to marry a man until he had captured a head. A chief who had not taken a head could not marry. WILTON MARION KROGMAN

See also RACES OF MAN (picture, Australia).

A Dyak Woman of Borneo spins the clothes for her family on this crude wheel. She wears a metal corselet around the upper part of her body. Her necklace is made of betel nuts.

Visual Education Service

DYER, MARY (? -1660), a colonist from England, became a martyr to the Quaker faith. With her husband, William, she arrived in Massachusetts about 1635. Because of religious intolerance, they later moved to Rhode Island. In 1650 she returned to England, and joined the Society of Friends, or Quakers. Seven years later, she came back to America. She was arrested repeatedly for "bearing witness to her faith." Finally, in Boston, she was charged with sedition, convicted, and hanged. IAN C. C. GRAHAM

DYES AND DYEING. For many thousands of years man has improved the appearance of fabrics, leather, paper, and other materials by dyeing them different colors. Beautifully colored garments and fabrics have been found in the pyramids of Egypt and in the burial tombs of the Incas of Peru. As early as 1000 B.C., the city of Tyre was noted for its purple dye. This dye was made from the glands of certain shellfish found in the Mediterranean Sea. It became known as royal purple because only the wealthy could afford it. The oldest dye known to mankind is indigo. One garment discovered in Thebes had been dyed with indigo about 3000 B.C.

Natural Dyes, those made from plants and animals, were the earliest used by man. They include indigo, cochineal, madder, and the purple dye from the Mediterranean shellfish. Dyes made from natural materials such as butternut, hickory, and various roots and berries were used by pioneer women in the United States.

319

SOURCES OF DYES

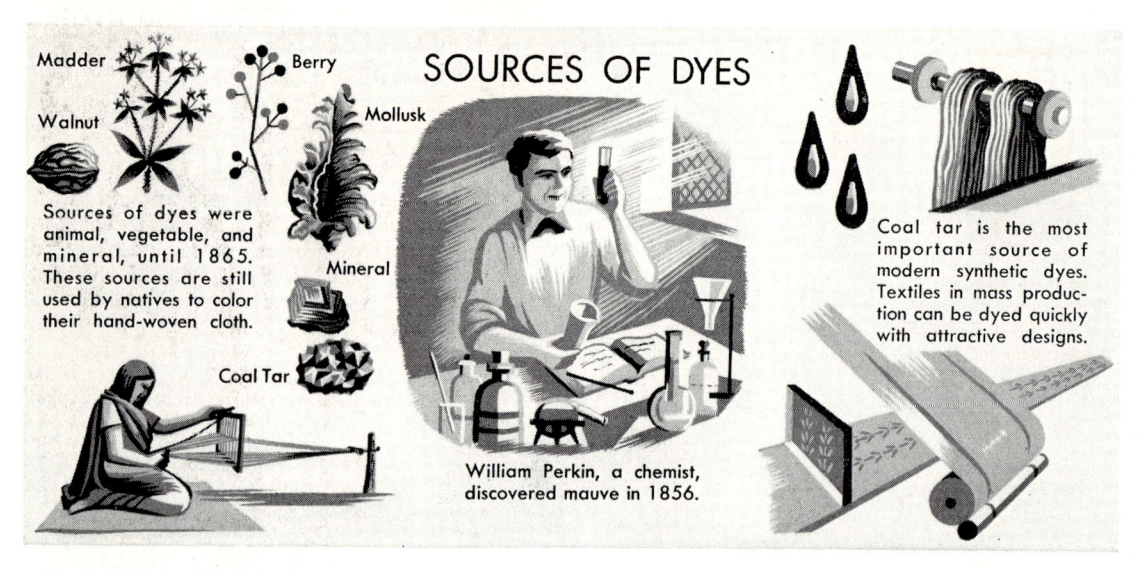

Sources of dyes were animal, vegetable, and mineral, until 1865. These sources are still used by natives to color their hand-woven cloth.

Coal tar is the most important source of modern synthetic dyes. Textiles in mass production can be dyed quickly with attractive designs.

William Perkin, a chemist, discovered mauve in 1856.

Mineral Dyes. Man also learned to make dyes from various minerals of the earth. He discovered that dyes made from certain minerals were "fast," or more permanent than the plant or animal dyes. Other minerals used with vegetable dyes produced brighter colors. Various kinds of rocks were pounded to a powder and used for dyes. Certain black muds and also water containing minerals such as sulfur were used.

Today both the natural and mineral dyes have been almost entirely replaced by synthetic dyes. Synthetic dyes can be produced more cheaply than other dyes, and in a far greater variety of colors. They are generally much faster and of more uniform composition.

Synthetic Dyes are made from coal-tar substances such as benzene, naphthalene, and anthracene. The first synthetic dye was discovered by the English chemist, William H. Perkin, in 1856. He accidentally produced aniline purple, or mauve, while trying to make quinine from aniline. Later other similar dyestuffs were made from chemicals, and a new era began in the textile-coloring industry. The greatest development took place in Europe, where most of the world's dyes were made until the beginning of World War I. When the United States could no longer obtain dyes from abroad, the American chemical industry started to manufacture dyes. Today, more than 1,000 different types of dyes are produced. There are complete ranges of colors for dyeing cotton, wool, silk, and rayon, nylon, and other synthetics as well as paper, leather, printing ink, carbon paper, and many other materials. About 95 per cent of the dyes used in the United States are manufactured here. Large quantities are also exported.

Processes. Dyeing is generally a complex procedure, done on soundly established chemical principles. The method followed depends upon the type of material, the type of color being applied, the nature of the equipment used, and the form of the textile to be dyed. Dyes can be applied to the raw material before it is spun into yarn, to the yarn after it has been spun, or to the material after it has been woven.

Principal Groups of Dyes classified on the basis of application are:

Acetate—for acetate rayon and nylon.
Acid—for wool, silk, and nylon.
Basic—for viscose-process rayon, cotton, and silk.
Chrome—for wool.
Developed or Diazo—for rayon, cotton, and silk.
Direct—for rayon, cotton, and silk.
Ice or Azoic—for cotton and rayon.
Sulfur—for cotton and rayon.
Vat—for cotton, rayon, linen, and,
   to some extent, wool.

Fabrics of animal origin, such as wool and silk, may require one type of dye, while the vegetable product, cotton, must be colored with another type. Some dyestuff produces a fully developed color upon textile material, and is called a *direct dye*. Other dyestuffs require the assistance of certain other substances in order to produce a fully developed color. Furthermore, a certain dyestuff may produce a direct color when applied to one type of fabric but may require assisting substances when used for some other fabric. Therefore, many types of dyes have developed. They vary widely in composition and fastness. Every dye has a definite use and should be selected according to the use for which the fabric was designed. Vat dyes are the most durable coloring agents, and produce the fastest shades obtainable for certain fibers.

ANSCO G. BRUINIER, JR.

Related Articles in WORLD BOOK include:

Aniline	Chromium	Henna	Mordant
Batik	Coal Tar	Indigo	Prussian Blue
Buckthorn	Cobalt	Lake (dye)	Stain
Carmine	Cochineal	Logwood	Tie Dyeing
Catechu	Color	Madder	Turmeric

DYNAMICS, *die NAM iks*, is the branch of physics which studies the laws of force and motion. The name dynamics comes from a Greek word meaning *power*. Forces cause a moving object to change its motion. Therefore, when we study forces, we examine moving objects whose velocity is being increased or decreased, or which are made to move in a different direction. We find that, in certain ways, all forces act in the same manner. We then say that they are subject to the same *laws*. Dynamics has to discover and also to clearly state these laws in order for us to use them.

In music, dynamics indicates the degree of loudness or softness of a tone. Some dynamics terms include *piano* (soft), *forte* (loud), *fortissimo* (very loud), *crescendo* (gradually louder), and *diminuendo* (gradually softer). See Music (Notation).

Psychologists use the term *group dynamics* to mean the study of how people work together in a group (see GROUP DYNAMICS). ROBERT F. PATON

See also FORCE; KINEMATICS; MECHANICS; MOTION; STATICS.

DYNAMITE, *DIE nuh mite*, is the world's most valuable industrial explosive. It is used to blast out dam sites, canal beds, and the foundations for large buildings. Mines, quarries, and dredging and construction projects in the United States use more than 2,500,000 pounds of dynamite every day.

Nitroglycerin is the principal explosive used in dynamite. It is mixed with other relatively inert materials, some explosive and some nonexplosive, to make an explosive charge. This charge is safe to handle until a *detonating cap* sets it off.

Dynamite may be packed in waxed paper cylinders called *cartridges*. These cartridges vary from $\frac{7}{8}$-inch to 8 inches in diameter, and range in length from 4 to 30 inches. There are nearly 200 kinds of dynamite, each of which is suited to some particular type of blasting.

The first dynamite was produced in 1867 by Alfred Nobel, Swedish chemist and donor of the five Nobel prizes. Nobel discovered that *kieselguhr*, a chalky earth, would absorb about three times its own weight of nitroglycerin. This mixture was much less sensitive to shock than pure nitroglycerin. It could be packed into paper tubes and inserted into drilled holes to make blasting more efficient.

Nobel improved his original formula by first substituting wood pulp and sawdust for kieselguhr. He added potassium nitrate to furnish oxygen for the explosion. The present-day *straight dynamites* are made from the same ingredients, except that sodium nitrate has replaced the more expensive potassium nitrate. Straight dynamites are used chiefly for certain types of earth blasting. Other kinds of dynamite are less dangerous to handle, and are more economical. But the straight dynamites still serve as the standard for determining the strength of all modern dynamites.

In 1875, Nobel patented a dynamite called *blasting gelatin*. This was a plastic, rubberlike explosive made by adding 7 to 10 per cent of nitrocotton to nitroglycerin. This dynamite had the property of keeping its full blasting efficiency under water. Later, Nobel added wood pulp and sodium nitrate to a new formula for blasting gelatin, producing the type of dynamite now sold as *straight gelatin*.

Ammonium nitrate is the major ingredient in most dynamite today. This type of dynamite is manufactured in the form of *ammonia dynamite* and *ammonia gelatin*. These are just as strong as the straight types, but are less dangerous to handle and cheaper to manufacture. Dynamite can now be handled with great safety. Special materials are now added to the nitroglycerin in dynamite to prevent it from freezing.

From 1900 to 1910, American explosives manufacturers, with the assistance of the U.S. Bureau of Mines, developed *permissible dynamites*. Low nitroglycerin and high ammonium-nitrate contents characterize these dynamites. They were designed to increase the safety of coal mining, and replaced black powder, which had been used as a mine explosive. The flame of a black-powder explosion has a tendency to ignite coal gas and coal dust. This had been the cause of many mine disasters. JULIUS ROTH

Dynamite blows a column of smoke and dirt skyward, above, as it makes a test hole for oil-well drillers. It is set off from a safe distance by the worker, right. He presses a handle to turn a generator that sends a detonating electric current through a wire to the charge.

Sun Oil Company; DuPont

Related Articles in WORLD BOOK include:

Blasting	Forcite	Nobel, Alfred
Cellulose	Fuse	Bernhard
Explosive	Nitroglycerin	TNT

321

DYNAMO

DYNAMO. See ELECTRIC GENERATOR.

DYNAMOTOR, *DIE nuh MOH ter*, is an electric machine that can be used as both a motor and a generator. It can change a direct current from high to lower voltage, or from low to higher voltage. Transformers usually handle only alternating current. The dynamotor might be called a direct-current transformer. Its armature has two windings, and each winding can be used as either a motor winding or a generator winding. Dynamotors are used to change low voltage into higher voltage to start a motor. They may also divide a high voltage into small voltages in devices which are used to control speeds. RAYMOND F. YATES

See also ELECTRIC GENERATOR.

DYNE, *dine*, is a unit of the metric system which is used to measure force. A dyne is defined as the force which, acting upon one gram of matter, will give it an acceleration of one centimeter per second for every second the force acts. The dyne is the scientific, or absolute, unit in the centimeter-gram-second (C.G.S.) system of units, and corresponds to the *poundal* in the English system (see FOOT-POUND). An *erg* of work is the work done by a force of one dyne acting through a distance of one centimeter. For large measurements it is customary to use the *megadyne*, which is equal to 1,000,000 dynes. E. G. STRAUS

DYNEL, *DIE nul*, is a warm, strong, light-weight synthetic fiber (see FIBER [Synthetic Fibers]). It can be spun on the same machines as cotton, wool, or silk. Manufacturers use dynel, alone or in combination with other fabrics, to make clothing, blankets, draperies, and industrial products. Dynel fabrics launder easily and dry quickly. They resist moths, fungi, and mildew.

D'YOUVILLE COLLEGE is a liberal arts school for women in Buffalo, N.Y. It is controlled by the Grey Nuns of the Sacred Heart, but its student body is not limited to Roman Catholics. The school grants the bachelor's degree. It was founded in 1908. For enrollment, see UNIVERSITIES AND COLLEGES (table).

DYSENTERY, *DIHS un TER ih*, is a severe disease which affects the colon. There is inflammation of the colon with painful diarrhea. Blood and mucus are passed in the stool. In some cases there may be fever and delirium. The two most common kinds of dysentery are *amebic* dysentery and *bacillary* dysentery.

Amebic Dysentery is caused by a one-celled animal called an *ameba* (see AMEBA). It results in severe inflammation of the colon, bloody diarrhea, and sometimes formation of abscesses in the liver or brain. The disease is spread by taking the tiny amebas into the mouth on food and objects. Fresh vegetables and fruits which have been handled and those which have been grown in soil fertilized with human feces may be infected. The organism at this time is in a resting, or dormant, stage called the *cyst*. As it enters the intestinal tract, however, it becomes very active, growing and reproducing itself. The organism causes the formation of holes, or ulcers, in the bowel and liver.

Amebic dysentery is most common in warm and tropical countries. It may break out in cooler climates, however. A very severe epidemic of amebic dysentery occurred, for example, in Chicago in 1933.

Amebic dysentery can be prevented by cleanliness and sanitation, careful examination of food handlers, and purification of water and sewage. A person living in a region in which there is much amebic dysentery must be especially cautious about everything that is handled or eaten. Amebic dysentery can sometimes be cured by the drugs emetine and stovarsol.

Bacillary Dysentery is caused by bacteria. It occurs in all countries and climates, and is especially common during the summer. The disease occurs frequently in institutions and camps.

The symptoms of bacillary dysentery include severe, bloody diarrhea; abdominal cramps; fever; and loss of appetite. The disease is spread by eating contaminated foods. It can be prevented by cleanliness, sanitation, and the purification of water and food supplies. Treatment of bacillary dysentery includes complete bed rest, a liquid diet, and the use of sulfadiazine, one of the sulfa drugs. E. CLINTON TEXTER

DYSPEPSIA, *dis PEP shuh*, is a term which is loosely used to refer to a disorder in digestion. Dyspepsia usually has such symptoms as pain in the upper abdomen, heartburn, belching, fullness and heaviness in the stomach region, and spitting up food or sour-tasting liquid. Dyspepsia may be caused by ulcers of the stomach or duodenum, hyperacidity, cancer of the stomach, gallstones, infection of the gall bladder, colitis, constipation, adhesions, chronic appendicitis, and worry and nervousness. It can be treated only by treating the disorder which is causing it. In many cases, proper diet is part of the treatment. HYMAN S. RUBINSTEIN

DYSPROSIUM, *dihs PROH shih um* (chemical symbol, Dy), is one of the rare-earth metals. Its atomic number is 66, and its atomic weight is 162.50. The name comes from the Greek word *dysprositos*, meaning *hard to get*. French scientist Paul Émile Lecoq de Boisbaudran discovered dysprosium in 1886. It is found associated with erbium, holmium, and other rare earths in the minerals gadolinite, euxenite, xenotime, and others. Dysprosium is best separated from the other rare earths by ion-exchange processes (see IONIZATION). At low temperatures, dysprosium is strongly attracted by a magnet. See also RARE EARTH. FRANK H. SPEDDING

DYSTROPHY, MUSCULAR. See MUSCULAR DYSTROPHY.

DZHUGASHVILI, IOSIF. See STALIN, JOSEPH.